LIVY

BOOKS XXXIV–XXXVII

A COMMENTARY ON
LIVY

BOOKS XXXIV–XXXVII

BY

JOHN BRISCOE

Senior Lecturer in Greek and Latin,
University of Manchester

OXFORD
AT THE CLARENDON PRESS
1981

Oxford University Press, Walton Street, Oxford OX2 6DP

OXFORD LONDON GLASGOW
NEW YORK TORONTO MELBOURNE WELLINGTON
KUALA LUMPUR SINGAPORE JAKARTA HONG KONG TOKYO
DELHI BOMBAY CALCUTTA MADRAS KARACHI
NAIROBI DAR ES SALAAM CAPE TOWN

Published in the United States by
Oxford University Press, New York

British Library Cataloguing in Publication Data

Briscoe, John
    A commentary on Livy, books XXXIV–XXXVII
    1. Livy. Ab urbe condita. Books 34–37
    I. Title
    II. Livy. Ab urbe condita. Books 34–37
    937'.04   PA6459   80–41210

    ISBN 0–19–814455–5

Printed in Great Britain
Latimer Trend & Company Ltd
Plymouth

TO
CELIA AND IVAN

PREFACE

THE present volume follows the format of my commentary on books xxxi–xxxiii. There is, however, rather more linguistic and textual discussion, for which two separate factors are responsible. Firstly, there is no reliable critical edition of the second half of the fourth decade: I had therefore to make my own collation of the principal manuscripts for books xxxvi and xxxvii and have also checked McDonald's reports for books xxxiv and xxxv. As a result I have learned a good deal more about the evidence for the text of the fourth decade. Secondly, during the writing of this book I have enjoyed the company of Dr. J. N. Adams and Professor H. D. Jocelyn as colleagues in Manchester. I have learned a lot of Latin from them and have become far more aware of linguistic and stylistic issues. I fear, though, that they will still find much in the book that they will label as 'subjective criticism' and will, oddly, ascribe this to the continuing influence of my first University.

In the preface to the previous volume I felt obliged to apologize for the second-hand nature of my comments on Greek topography. On this occasion I have been able to visit most of the sites in Greece and Turkey mentioned by Livy and though there are few places where I can claim to have added to previous discussions, I hope that I am now writing with a proper appreciation of the terrain over which the campaigns described in these books took place.

I am once again most grateful to Professor R. G. M. Nisbet for giving me his opinion on a large number of textual and linguistic points. I must also thank Mr. W. C. Brice for helping me with the maps and Dr. P. S. Derow, Professor W. G. Forrest, Dr. E. B. French, Dr. A. H. Jackson, Dr. R. J. Ling, Dr. M. J. Price, and Mr. N. G. Wilson for advice on various matters. Professor A. E. Astin very kindly allowed me to see the proofs of his *Cato the Censor* in advance of publication and Professor F. W. Walbank did the same for his commentary on books xx and xxi of Polybius.

The collation of the manuscripts and my travels in Greece and Turkey were made possible by two generous grants from the British Academy and I have received a number of smaller grants from the University of Manchester, one of which enabled me to visit the archives of the *Thesaurus Linguae Latinae* in Munich. I am grateful to the authorities of the British Library, the Bodleian Library, the Bibliothèque Nationale, Paris, the Biblioteca Apostolica Vaticana, the Biblioteca Medicea–Laurenziana, and the Real Biblioteca de San Lorenzo de El Escorial for allowing me to collate their manuscripts, and I owe a particular debt to Dr. B. Schemmel of the Staatsbibliothek, Bamberg, for his great helpfulness on my two visits to Bamberg and for answering a number of subsequent queries. Professor Jocelyn kindly offered to read the proofs, and his diligence has eliminated a number of errors that would otherwise have gone unnoticed.

Typing of the final copy of the book began in March 1979 and I have been able to do no more than add references to works which came to my notice between then and November 1979. Some references to works available to me after the latter date will be found in the addenda.

J. B.

Manchester
August, 1980

CONTENTS

CONTENTS

ABBREVIATIONS

Th is is a list of modern works referred to in an abbreviated form. It is not a bibliography. Abbreviations of periodicals are those used in *L' Année Philologique*. The numbers in brackets following the names of individual Romans are those of the articles on the persons concerned in *RE*. My commentary on books xxxi–xxxiii is referred to as 'vol. i'.

Accame, *Espansione romana*	S. Accame, *L'espansione romana in Grecia* (Naples, 1961).
Afzelius	A. Afzelius, *Die römische Kriegsmacht* (Copenhagen, 1944).
ANRW	*Aufstieg und Niedergang der römischen Welt* (Berlin–New York, 1972–).
Ashby, *Campagna*	T. Ashby, *The Roman Campagna in Classical Times* (London, 1927; republished London, 1970).
Astin, *Cato*	A. E. Astin, *Cato the Censor* (Oxford, 1978).
Aymard, *Assemblées*	A. Aymard, *Les Assemblées de la confédération achaienne* (Bordeaux–Paris, 1938).
Aymard, *ÉHA*	A. Aymard, *Études d'histoire ancienne* (Paris, 1967).
Aymard, *PR*	A. Aymard, *Les Premiers Rapports de Rome et de la confédération achaienne* (Bordeaux–Paris, 1938).
Badian, *FC*	E. Badian, *Foreign Clientelae, 264–70 B.C.* (Oxford, 1958).
Badian, *Publicans and Sinners*	E. Badian, *Publicans and Sinners* (Oxford, 1972).
Badian, *Studies*	E. Badian, *Studies in Greek and Roman History* (Oxford, 1964).
Bakhuizen	S. C. Bakhuizen, *Salganeus and the Fortifications on its Mountains* (Groningen, 1970).
Bar-Kochva	B. Bar-Kochva, *The Seleucid Army, Organization and Tactics in the Great Campaigns* (Cambridge, 1976).
Bean, *Aegean Turkey*	G. E. Bean, *Aegean Turkey, an Archaeological Guide* (London, 1966).
Bean, *Lycian Turkey*	G. E. Bean, *Lycian Turkey, an Archaeological Guide* (London, 1978).
Bean, *Turkey beyond the Maeander*	G. E. Bean, *Turkey beyond the Maeander, an Archaeological Guide* (London, 1971).
Bean, *Turkey's Southern Shore*	G. E. Bean, *Turkey's Southern Shore, an Archaeological Guide* (London, 1968).

Bengtson, ii   H. Bengtson, *Die Strategie in der hellenistischen Zeit*, ii (Munich, 1944).

Béquignon   Y. Béquignon, *La Vallée du Spercheios des origines au ive siècle, études d'archéologie et de topographie* (Paris, 1937).

Bikerman, *Institutions*   E. Bikerman, *Institutions des Séleucides* (Paris, 1938).

Bleicken   J. Bleicken, *Das Volkstribunat der klassischen Republik* (Munich, 1955).

Bömer   F. Bömer, *P. Ouidius Naso, Die Fasten* (Heidelberg, 1957–8).

Bornecque   H. Bornecque, *Tite–Live* (Paris, 1933).

Bredehorn   U. Bredehorn, *Senatsakten in der republikanischen Annalistik* (Marburg, 1968).

Brueggmann   H. Brueggmann, *Komposition und Entwicklungstendenzen der Bücher 31–35 des Titus Livius* (Kiel, 1955).

Brunt   P. A. Brunt, *Italian Manpower, 225 B.C.–A.D. 14* (Oxford, 1971).

Cabanes   P. Cabanes, *L' Épire de la mort de Pyrrhos à la conquête romaine (272–167)* (Paris, 1976).

CAH   *Cambridge Ancient History*

Casson   L. Casson, *Ships and Seamanship in the Ancient World* (Princeton, N.J., 1971).

Chausserie-Laprée   J. P. Chausserie-Laprée, *L'Expression narrative chez les historiens latins* (Paris, 1969).

CIL   *Corpus Inscriptionum Latinarum*

Cook, *Troad*   J. M. Cook, *The Troad, an Archaeological and Topographical Study* (Oxford, 1973).

Cook, *Zeus*   A. B. Cook, *Zeus* (Cambridge, 1914–40).

Crawford, *RRC*   M. H. Crawford, *Roman Republican Coinage* (Cambridge, 1974).

Dahlheim   W. Dahlheim, *Struktur und Entwicklung des römischen Völkerrechts im dritten und zweiten Jahrhundert v. Chr.* (Munich, 1968).

Deininger   J. Deininger, *Der politische Widerstand gegen Rom in Griechenland, 217–86 v. Chr.* (Berlin–New York, 1971).

De Regibus   L. De Regibus, *Tito Livio, ab urbe condita, liber xxxvii* (Turin, 1928).

De Sanctis   G. De Sanctis, *Storia dei romani* (Turin–Florence, 1907–64).

Drakenborch   A. Drakenborch, *T. Liuii Patauini historiarum ab urbe condita libri qui supersunt omnes*, iv–v (Amsterdam–Leiden, 1741–3).

Ducrey	P. Ducrey, *Le Traitement des prisonniers de guerre dans la Grèce antique* (Paris, 1968).
Economic Survey	*An Economic Survey of Ancient Rome*, ed. T. Frank (Baltimore, Md., 1933–40).
Ernout–Meillet	A. Ernout and A. Meillet, *Dictionnaire étymologique de la langue latine* (4th edn., Paris, 1967).
Errington	R. M. Errington, *Philopoemen* (Oxford, 1969).
FGH	*Die Fragmente der griechischen Historiker*, ed. F. Jacoby (Berlin–Leiden, 1923–).
FIRA, i	*Fontes Iuris Romani Anteiustiniani*, i, ed. S. Riccobono (2nd edn., Florence, 1941).
Flacelière	R. Flacelière, *Les Aitoliens à Delphes* (Paris, 1937).
Flurl	W. Flurl, *Deditio in Fidem* (Munich, 1969).
Fraccaro, *Opuscula*	P. Fraccaro, *Opuscula* (Pavia, 1956–7).
Fraenkel, *Horace*	E. Fraenkel, *Horace* (Oxford, 1957).
Fraser, *Ptolemaic Alexandria*	P. M. Fraser, *Ptolemaic Alexandria* (Oxford, 1972).
Fraser and Bean, *RPI*	P. M. Fraser and G. E. Bean, *The Rhodian Peraea and Islands* (London, 1954).
Götzfried	K. T. Götzfried, *Annalen der römischen Provinzen beider Spanien von der ersten Besetzung durch die Römer bis zum letzten grossen Freiheitskampf, 218–154* (Erlangen, 1907).
Goodyear	F. R. D. Goodyear, *The Annals of Tacitus, books 1–6*, i (Cambridge, 1972).
Hammond, *Epirus*	N. G. L. Hammond, *Epirus* (Oxford, 1967).
Handford	S. A. Handford, *The Latin Subjunctive, its Usage and Development from Plautus to Tacitus* (London, 1947).
Hansen, *Attalids*	E. V. Hansen, *The Attalids of Pergamon* (2nd edn., Ithaca, N.Y., 1971).
Harris	W. V. Harris, *War and Imperialism in Republican Rome, 327–70 B.C.* (Oxford, 1979).
Hellmann	F. Hellmann, *Livius–Interpretationen* (Berlin, 1939).
Heuss, *Stadt u. Herrscher*	A. Heuss, *Stadt und Herrscher des Hellenismus* (*Klio*, Bhft. xxxix, Leipzig, 1937).
Heuss, *VG*	A. Heuss, *Die völkerrechtlichen Grundlagen der römischen Aussenpolitik in republikanischer Zeit* (*Klio*, Bhft. xxxi, Leipzig, 1933).
Historical Commentary on Thucydides	A. W. Gomme, A. Andrewes, K. J. Dover, *A Historical Commentary on Thucydides* (Oxford, 1945–).
Hoch	H. Hoch, *Die Darstellung der politischen Sendung Roms bei Livius* (Berlin–Schöneberg, 1951).

Holleaux, *Études*	M. Holleaux, *Études d' épigraphie et d' histoire grecques* (Paris, 1938–68).
Holleaux, *Rome*	M. Holleaux, *Rome, la Grèce et les monarchies hellénistiques au iiie siècle avant J.-C.* (Paris, 1920).
Hopp	J. Hopp, *Untersuchungen zur Geschichte der letzten Attaliden* (Munich, 1977).
HRR	*Historicorum Romanorum Reliquiae*, ed. H. Peter (Leipzig: vol. i, 2nd edn., 1914, vol. ii, 1906).
H–S	J. B. Hofmann and A. Szantyr, *Lateinische Syntax und Stilistik* (Munich, 1965).
IC	*Inscriptiones Creticae*, ed. M. Guarducci (Rome, 1935–50).
IDelos	*Inscriptions de Délos* (Paris, 1926–37).
IG	*Inscriptiones Graecae*
I.I.	*Inscriptiones Italiae*
ILLRP	*Inscriptiones Latinae liberae rei publicae*, ed. A. Degrassi (Florence: vol. i, 2nd edn., 1965, vol. ii, 1963).
ILS	*Inscriptiones Latinae Selectae*, ed. H. Dessau (Berlin, 1892–1916).
ISE	*Iscrizioni storiche ellenistiche*, ed. L. Moretti (Florence, 1967–76).
IvP	*Die Inschriften von Pergamon*, ed. M. Fränkel (Berlin, 1890–95).
Kahrstedt	U. Kahrstedt, *Die Annalistik von Livius, B. XXXI–XLV* (Berlin, 1913).
Kajanto	I. Kajanto, *God and Fate in Livy* (Turku, 1957).
Kienast	D. Kienast, *Cato der Zensor* (Heidelberg, 1954).
Klotz, *Livius*	A. Klotz, *Livius und seine Vorgänger* (Stuttgart, 1940; republished Amsterdam, 1964).
Koestermann	E. Koestermann, *C. Sallustius Crispus, Bellum Iugurthinum* (Heidelberg, 1971).
KP	*Der kleine Pauly* (Stuttgart, 1964–75).
Krauss	F. B. Krauss, *An Interpretation of the Omens, Portents, and Prodigies recorded by Livy, Tacitus, and Suetonius* (Philadelphia, Pa., 1930).
Kromayer	J. Kromayer and G. Veith, *Antike Schlachtfelder in Griechenland* (Berlin, 1903–31).
Kromayer–Veith	J. Kromayer and G. Veith, *Heerwesen und Kriegführung der Griechen und Römer* (Munich, 1928).
K–St	R. Kühner and C. Stegmann, *Ausführliche Grammatik der lateinischen Sprache* (3rd edn., revised by A. Thierfelder, Leverkusen, 1955).
Kühnast	*Die Hauptpunkte der Livianischen Syntax* (Berlin, 1872).

Larsen, *Greek Federal States*	J. A. O. Larsen, *Greek Federal States* (Oxford, 1868).
Larsen, *Representative Government*	J. A. O. Larsen, *Representative Government in Greek and Roman Antiquity* (Berkeley–Los Angeles, Cal., 1955).
Latte, *RRG*	K. Latte, *Römische Religionsgeschichte* (Munich, 1960).
Launey	M. Launey, *Recherches sur les armées hellénistiques* (Paris, 1949–50).
Lauterbach	A. Lauterbach, *Untersuchungen zur Geschichte der Unterwerfung von Oberitalien durch die Römer* (Breslau, 1905).
Le Bonniec	H. Le Bonniec, *Le Culte de Cérès a Rome des origines à la fin de la République* (Paris, 1958).
Le Gall	J. Le Gall, *Le Tibre, fleuve de Rome, dans l' antiquité* (Paris, 1953).
Lehmann	G. A. Lehmann, *Untersuchungen zur historischen Glaubwürdigkeit des Polybios* (Münster, 1967).
Löfstedt, *Syntactica*	E. Löfstedt, *Syntactica* (Lund: vol. i, 2nd edn., 1942, vol. ii, 1933).
L–S	C. T. Lewis and C. Short, *A Latin Dictionary* (Oxford, 1879).
Luce	T. J. Luce, *Livy, the Composition of his History* (Princeton, N.J., 1977).
Luterbacher	F. Luterbacher, *Der Prodigienglaube und Prodigienstil der Römer* (2nd edn., Burgdorf, 1904).
McDonald	A. H. McDonald, *Titi Liui ab urbe condita tomus v, libri xxxi–xxxv* (Oxford, 1965).
McShane	R. B. McShane, *The Foreign Policy of the Attalids of Pergamum* (Urbana, Ill., 1964).
Madvig, *Emendationes*	J. N. Madvig, *Emendationes Liuianae* (2nd edn., Copenhagen, 1877).
Magie	D. Magie, *Roman Rule in Asia Minor* (Princeton, N.J., 1950).
Marouzeau, *L'Ordre des mots*	J. Marouzeau, *L'Ordre des mots dans la phrase latine* (Paris, 1922–49)
Marquardt, *StV*	J. Marquardt, *Römische Staatsverwaltung* (2nd edn., Leipzig, 1881–5).
Meltzer–Kahrstedt	O. Meltzer and U. Kahrstedt. *Geschichte der Karthager* (Berlin, 1879–1913).
Merguet	H. Merguet, *Lexikon zu den Reden des Cicero* (Iena, 1877–84).
Merten	M.-L. Merten, *Fides Romana bei Livius* (Frankfurt, 1965).

Mommsen, *RF*	Th. Mommsen, *Römische Forschungen* (Berlin, 1864–79).
Mommsen, *StR*	Th. Mommsen, *Römisches Staatsrecht* (Leipzig: vols. i–ii, 3rd edn., 1887, vol. iii, 1887–8).
MRR	T. R. S. Broughton, *The Magistrates of the Roman Republic* (New York, 1951–60).
M. Müller	W. Weissenborn and M. Müller, *T. Liui ab urbe condita libri, pars iv, libri xxxi–xxxviii* (Leipzig, 1887–90).
Münzer, *RA*	F. Münzer, *Römische Adelsparteien und Adelsfamilien* (Stuttgart, 1920).
Nash	E. Nash, *Pictorial Dictionary of Ancient Rome* (London, 1961–2).
Naylor	H. D. Naylor, *More Latin and English Idiom, an Object-Lesson from Livy xxxiv, 1–8* (Cambridge, 1915).
Neue–Wagener	F. Neue and C. Wagener, *Formenlehre der lateinischen Sprache* (3rd edn., Leipzig, 1892–1905).
Niese	B. Niese, *Geschichte der griechischen und makedonischen Staaten seit der Schlacht bei Chaeronea* (Gotha, 1893–1903).
Nisbet, *in Pisonem*	R. G. M. Nisbet, *M. Tulli Ciceronis in L. Calpurnium Pisonem oratio* (Oxford, 1961).
Nisbet and Hubbard, i	R. G. M. Nisbet and M. Hubbard, *A Commentary on Horace: Odes book i* (Oxford, 1970).
Nissen, *IL*	H. Nissen, *Italische Landeskunde* (Berlin, 1883–1902).
Nissen, *KU*	H. Nissen, *Kritische Untersuchungen über die Quellen der vierten und fünften Dekade des Livius* (Berlin, 1863).
Ogilvie	R. M. Ogilvie, *A Commentary on Livy, books 1–5* (Oxford, 1965).
Ogilvie, *Phoenix*	R. M. Ogilvie, Review of McDonald, *Phoenix*, xx (1966), 343–7.
OGIS	*Orientis Graeci Inscriptiones Selectae*, ed. W. Dittenberger (Leipzig, 1903–5).
OLD	*Oxford Latin Dictionary* (Oxford, 1968–).
Oliva	P. Oliva, *Sparta and her Social Problems* (Amsterdam–Prague, 1971).
Olshausen	E. Olshausen, *Prosopographie der hellenistischen Königsgesandten, Teil i: von Triparadeisos bis Pydna* (Louvain, 1974).
Oost, *RPEA*	S. I. Oost, *Roman Policy in Epirus and Acarnania in the Age of the Roman Conquest of Greece* (Dallas, Tex., 1954).

*ORF*³	H. Malcovati, *Oratorum Romanorum Fragmenta* (3rd edn., Pavia, 1967).
Orth	W. Orth, *Königlicher Machtanspruch und städtische Freiheit* (Munich, 1977).
Otto	A. Otto, *Die Sprichwörter und sprichwörtlichen Redensarten der Römer* (Leipzig, 1890).
P–A	S. B. Platner and T. Ashby, *A Topographical Dictionary of Ancient Rome* (London, 1929).
Packard	D. W. Packard, *A Concordance to Livy* (Cambridge, Mass., 1968).
Paschkowski	I. Paschkowski, *Die Kunst der Reden in der 4. und 5. Dekade des Livius* (Kiel, 1966).
Pédech	P. Pédech, *La Méthode historique de Polybe* (Paris, 1964).
Petrocheilos	N. K. Petrocheilos, *Roman Attitudes to the Greeks* (Athens, 1974).
Pettersson	O. Pettersson, *Commentationes Liuianae* (Uppsala, 1930).
Petzold	K.-E. Petzold, *Die Eröffnung des zweiten römisch-makedonischen Krieges* (Berlin, 1940).
Petzold, *Studien*	K.-E. Petzold, *Studien zur Methode des Polybios und zu ihrer historischen Auswertung* (Munich, 1969).
Pianezzola	E. Pianezzola, *Traduzione e ideologia: Livio interprete di Polibio* (Bologna, 1969).
P–K	A. Philippson and E. Kirsten, *Die griechische Landschaften* (Frankfurt, 1950–9).
Preuss	S. Preuss, *De bimembris dissoluti apud scriptores Romanos usu sollemni* (Edenkoben, 1881).
Pritchett, i	W. K. Pritchett, *Studies in Ancient Greek Topography*, part i (Berkeley–Los Angeles, Cal., 1965).
RE	*Real-Encyclopädie der classischen Altertumswissenschaft.*
Rich	J. W. Rich, *Declaring War in the Roman Republic in the Period of Transmarine Expansion* (Brussels, 1976).
Riemann	O. Riemann, *Études sur la langue et la grammaire de Tite-Live* (Paris, 1884).
Roebuck	C. A. Roebuck, *A History of Messenia from 369 to 146 B.C.* (Chicago, 1941).
Sage	E. T. Sage, *Livy with an English Translation, ix–x, books xxxi–xxxiv, books xxxv–xxxviii* (Loeb Classical Library; Cambridge, Mass. and London, 1935).
Salmon, *Colonization*	E. T. Salmon, *Roman Colonization under the Republic* (London, 1969).

Salmon, *Samnium*	E. T. Salmon, *Samnium and the Samnites* (Cambridge, 1967).
Schlag	U. Schlag, *Regnum in Senatu* (Stuttgart, 1968).
Schleussner	B. Schleussner, *Die Legaten der römischen Republik* (Munich, 1978).
Schmitt, *Antiochos*	H. H. Schmitt, *Untersuchungen zur Geschichte Antiochos' des Grossen und seiner Zeit* (*Historia*, Einzelschriften vi, Wiesbaden, 1964).
Schmitt, *Rom und Rhodos*	H. H. Schmitt, *Rom und Rhodos* (Munich, 1957).
Schulten, *FHA*, iii	A. Schulten, *Fontes Hispaniae Antiquae*, iii (Barcelona, 1935).
Scullard, *Elephant*	H. H. Scullard, *The Elephant in the Greek and Roman World* (London, 1974).
Scullard, *RP*²	H. H. Scullard, *Roman Politics, 220–150 B.C.* (2nd edn., Oxford, 1973).
Scullard, *SA*	H. H. Scullard, *Scipio Africanus, Soldier and Politician* (London, 1970).
SEG	*Supplementum Epigraphicum Graecum.*
Seibert	J. Seibert, *Historische Beiträge zu den dynastischen Verbindungen in Hellenistischer Zeit* (*Historia*, Einzelschriften x, Wiesbaden, 1967).
Sherk	R. K. Sherk, *Roman Documents from the Greek East* (Baltimore, Md., 1969).
Sherwin-White, *RC*²	A. N. Sherwin-White, *The Roman Citizenship* (2nd edn., Oxford, 1973).
Shimron, *Late Sparta*	B. Shimron, *Late Sparta, the Spartan Revolution 243–146 B.C.* (Buffalo, N.Y., 1972).
Skard	E. Skard, *Sallust und seine Vorgänger* (Oslo, 1956).
Sommer	F. Sommer, *Handbuch der lateinischen Laut- und Förmenlehre* (Heidelberg, 1914).
Stählin, *HTh*	F. Stählin, *Das hellenische Thessalien* (Stuttgart, 1924).
Studies in Ancient Society	*Studies in Ancient Society*, ed. M. I. Finley (London, 1974).
StV, iii	H. H. Schmitt, *Die Staatsverträge des Altertums*, iii (Munich, 1969).
*Syll.*³	*Sylloge Inscriptionum Graecarum*, ed. W. Dittenberger (3rd edn., Leipzig, 1915–24).
Taübler	E. Taübler, *Imperium Romanum*, i (Leipzig, 1913).
Taylor, *RVA*	L. R. Taylor, *Roman Voting Assemblies* (Ann Arbor, Mich., 1966).
Texier	J. G. Texier, *Nabis* (Paris, 1975).

ABBREVIATIONS

Thiel	J. H. Thiel, *Studies on the History of Roman Seapower in Republican Times* (Amsterdam, 1946).
TLL	*Thesaurus Linguae Latinae* (with no reference following, indicates material derived from the archives of the *Thesaurus* in Munich).
Toynbee	A. J. Toynbee, *Hannibal's Legacy* (London, 1965).
Tränkle	H. Tränkle, *Livius und Polybios* (Basle, 1977).
Tränkle, *Cato*	H. Tränkle, *Cato in der vierten und fünften Dekade des Livius* (Akademie der Wissenschaften und der Literatur, Mainz, Abhandlungen der geistes– und sozialwissenschaftlichen Klasse, 1971, 4).
Tränkle, *Gnomon*	H. Tränkle, review of McDonald, *Gnomon* xxxix (1967), 365–80.
Tränkle, *WS*	H. Tränkle, 'Beobachtungen und Erwägungen zum Wandel der livianischen Sprache', *WS* lxxxi (1968), 103–52.
Ullmann, *Étude*	R. Ullmann, *Étude sur la style des discours de Tite-Live* (Oslo, 1929).
Ullmann, *Technique*	R. Ullmann, *La Technique des discours dans Salluste, Tite-Live et Tacite* (Oslo, 1927).
Versnel	H. S. Versnel, *Triumphus: an inquiry into the origin, development and meaning of the Roman triumph* (Leiden, 1970).
Volkmann	H. Volkmann, *Die Massenversklavungen der Einwohner eroberter Städte in der hellenistisch–römischen Zeit* (Akademie der Wissenschaften und der Literatur, Mainz, Abhandlungen der geistes– und sozialwissenschaftlichen Klasse, 1961, 3).
Walbank, *Aratos*	F. W. Walbank, *Aratos of Sicyon* (Cambridge, 1933).
Walbank, *Commentary*	F. W. Walbank, *A Historical Commentary on Polybius* (Oxford, 1957–79).
Walbank, *Livy*	F. W. Walbank, 'The Fourth and Fifth Decades', *Livy*, ed. T. A. Dorey (London, 1971).
Walbank, *Philip V*	F. W. Walbank, *Philip V of Macedon* (Cambridge, 1940).
Walbank, *Polybius*	F. W. Walbank, *Polybius* (Berkeley–Los Angeles, Cal.–London, 1972).
Walker, *Supplementary Annotations*	J. Walker, *Supplementary Annotations on Livy* (London, 1822).
Walsh, *CR*	P. G. Walsh, review of McDonald, *CR* n.s. xvii (1967), 53–6
Walsh, *Livy*	P. G. Walsh, *Livy, his Historical Aims and Methods* (Cambridge, 1961).

Walsh on xxi ...   P. G. Walsh, *T. Liui ab urbe condita liber xxi* (London, 1973).

Wege zu Livius   *Wege zu Livius*, ed. E. Burck (Darmstadt, 1967).

Wegner   M. Wegner, *Untersuchungen zu den lateinischen Begriffen Socius und Societas* (Göttingen, 1969).

Wehrli   C. Wehrli, *Antigone et Démétrios* (Geneva, 1969).

Weinstock   S. Weinstock, *Divus Julius* (Oxford, 1971).

Welles, *RC*   C. B. Welles, *Royal Correspondence in the Hellenistic Period* (New Haven, Conn., 1934).

Will, *HP*   E. Will, *Histoire politique du monde hellénistique* (Nancy, 1966–7).

Wiseman, *New Men*   T. P. Wiseman, *New Men in the Roman Senate, 139 B.C.–A.D. 14* (Oxford, 1971).

Wissowa, *RuK*²   G. Wissowa, *Religion und Kultus der Römer* (2nd edn., Munich, 1912).

Witte   K. Witte, 'Über die Form der Darstellung in Livius' Geschichtswerk', *RhM* lxv (1910), 270–305, 359–419.

W–M   W. Weissenborn and H. J. Müller, *Titi Liui ab urbe condita libri* (Berlin, 1880–1911: 'W–M' indicates a note in the latest edition in this series whether it is the original note of Weissenborn or a fresh contribution by Müller. 'Weissenborn' indicates a note in one of the earlier editions [1853–78]).

Wölfflin, *Ausgewählte Schriften*   E. Wölfflin, *Ausgewählte Schriften* (Leipzig, 1933).

Woodman   A. J. Woodman, *Velleius Paterculus: the Tiberian Narrative (2.94–131)* (Cambridge, 1977).

Wülker   L. Wülker, *Die geschichtliche Entwicklung des Prodigienwesens bei den Römern* (Leipzig, 1903).

Zimmerer   M. Zimmerer, *Qu. Claudius Quadrigarius* (Munich, 1937).

Zingerle   A. Zingerle, *T. Liui ab urbe condita libri, partes v, vi fasc. i* (Vienna–Prague–Leipzig, 1890–3).

INTRODUCTION[1]

I. SOURCES AND METHODS OF COMPOSITION[2]

THE following passages of books xxxiv–xxxvii correspond to surviving portions of Polybius:[3]

LIVY	POLYBIUS
xxxv. 45. 9–46. 1	xx. 1
xxxv. 50. 5	xx. 2
xxxvi. 5. 1–6. 3	xx. 3, 7. 3–5
xxxvi. 11. 1–4	xx. 8
xxxvi. 27–9	xx. 9–11. 8
xxxvi. 30. 4	xx. 11. 11
xxxvi. 33. 7	xx. 11. 12
xxxvi. 35. 11–13[4]	xxi. 3. 1–3
xxxvii. 1. 5–6[5]	xxi. 2. 3–6
xxxvii. 6. 4–7. 7	xxi. 4–5
xxxvii. 9. 1–4, 9	xxi. 6. 1–7
xxxvii. 11. 13	xxi. 7. 1–4
xxxvii. 12. 9	xxi. 7. 5–7
xxxvii. 18. 10—19	xxi. 8. 3, 10. 1–14
xxxvii. 20. 2	xxi. 9
xxxvii. 25. 4–26. 2	xxi. 11
xxxvii. 27. 5	xxi. 12
xxxvii. 33. 6–36. 9	xxi. 13. 10–15. 13
xxxvii. 44. 6, 45. 4–21	xxi. 16–17
xxxvii. 52–6	xxi. 18–24. 15

[1] In the first two sections of this introduction I shall not repeat the arguments set out in the introduction to vol. i. With regard to the speeches I have on this occasion considered Ullmann's analyses in the commentary. It may be useful, though, again to note the number of 'rhetorical features' observed by Ullmann, *Étude*, in relation to the length of each of the speeches he considers (cf. vol. i. 22: the numbers of lines are those of the Teubner edition). Cato (xxxiv. 2–4) 49: 145, Valerius (xxxiv. 5–7) 43: 162, Nabis (xxxiv. 31) 10:56, Flamininus (xxxiv. 32) 12:65, Hannibal (xxxvi. 7) 13: 72, Glabrio (xxxvi. 17) 9: 53, Scipio (xxxvii. 45) 4: 32, Eumenes (xxxvii. 53) 18: 97, Rhodians (xxxvii. 54) 17: 86. As in books xxxi–xxxiii these figures cause no surprise. For the politics of the period cf. *Latomus* xxxi (1972), 47 ff. and my forthcoming article in *ANRW*, ii. 30.

[2] See further the notes on the passages referred to.

[3] Tränkle, 30.

[4] Not listed by Tränkle.

[5] Rejected by Tränkle, 27–8 n. 10.

In addition the following sections of the narrative can confidently
be asserted to be essentially of Polybian origin: xxxiv. 22. 4—41
(campaign against Nabis), 48. 2–52. 1 (Flamininus' final activities
in Greece and return to Rome), 60–62 (events in Carthage), xxxv.
12–19 (events in Greece and Asia, 193 B.C.), 25–39, 42–51 (events in
Greece and Asia, 192 B.C.),[1] xxxvi. 5–35 (events in Greece, 191 B.C.),
41–45. 8 (events at sea and in Asia, 191 B.C.), xxxvii. 4. 6—7
(events in Greece, 190 B.C.), 8–45 (events in Asia, 190 B.C.), 60
(events in Crete and Thrace, 189 B.C.).

Annalistic additions to Polybian material occur at xxxiv. 41.
8–10, 61. 1, 62. 2–3, xxxvi. 21. 10–11, xxxvii. 52–6, and possibly at
xxxv. 19. L. makes use of Polybius for events at Rome at xxxiv. 43.
1–2, 57–9, xxxvi. 21. 6–8, xxxvii. 1. 1–6, 49, 52–6. In the last of
these passages it is clear that L. has used annalistic as well as Polybian material and he may have done so in the others.[2] As in books
xxxi–xxxiii[3] it is often impossible to ask precisely where the division
lies between Polybian and annalistic sections. Attention may be
drawn to the passages of transition at xxxiv. 22. 4–13, 52. 2 ff., xxxv.
12. 1, xxxvi. 21. 4 ff., xxxvi. 35. 11–13, xxxvii. 51. 8–52. 6.

Cases of misunderstanding of Polybius can be detected with varying degrees of probability at xxxiv. 28. 12, 35. 9, xxxv. 30. 6, 35. 18,
36. 8, 50. 9, xxxvi. 10. 11, 11. 7–8, 41. 3, xxxvii. 21. 4, 41. 3–4, 41.
6–7. At xxxiv. 51. 5 and xxxv. 38. 3 L. produces anachronistic
statements by heedlessly taking over present tenses from Polybius.

As far as the non-Polybian sections are concerned, there are
strong reasons for thinking that most of xxxiv. 8. 4—21 comes
directly from the elder Cato. Otherwise, the only certain attributions
that can be made are xxxiv. 10. 2 (and probably the whole chapter),
15. 9, 44. 5, xxxv. 2. 8, xxxvi. 19. 12, 36. 4, 38. 6, xxxvii. 48, 60. 6
to Valerius Antias, xxxv. 14. 5–12 to Claudius Quadrigarius, and
xxxiv. 44. 6–8 to Clodius Licinus. Sempronius Tuditanus appears
to be the ultimate source of xxxiv. 52. 2 ff. From xxxvi. 36. 4 it
follows that Antias is not the source of xxxiv. 54. 3.

[1] L. seems to have omitted part of Polybius' account of Asian events for 193/2,
describing, *inter alia*, the mission of Thoas to Antiochus (xxxv. 32. 2, xxxvi. 7. 12).
Cf. Nissen, *KU*, 167–8, Leuze, *Hermes* lviii (1923), 241.
[2] At both xxxvii. 1. 1–6 and 45. 7 both L. and Diodorus have material missing
in Polybius. It is usually assumed that Diodorus follows Polybius faithfully and
that the material in question must have been omitted by the excerptor of Polybius.
We should, though, consider the possibility that both Diodorus and L. have combined Polybius and an annalistic source. On balance I regard it as probable that
Polybius is the sole source of both Diodorus and L. at xxxiv. 43. 1–2, 59. 5, xxxvii. 1.
1–6: nor would scepticism be in place about xxxvii. 34. 6, a passage not concerned
with events in Rome (cf. also xxxiii. 39. 5–6 n.). At xxxvii. 45. 7 and 49. 1–7,
however, the question is more open. [3] Cf. vol. i, 10.

Doublets and variants which appear to derive from the use of different sources, without it being possible to identify those sources, occur at xxxiv. 48. 1, xxxv. 3, 21∼xxxv. 11, xxxv. 21. 7–22. 4, 24. 1–3∼xxxv. 40. 2–4. On the other hand there is no need to posit the use of different sources at xxxiv. 21. 8∼42. 1, xxxiv. 52. 4∼xxxv. 10. 5, xxxiv. 53. 1∼xxxv. 40. 6,[1] xxxiv. 53. 7∼xxxv. 41. 8,[2] xxxiv. 55. 1∼ xxxv. 40. 7 ff., xxxv. 7. 8∼22. 7–8, xxxv. 10. 12∼41. 10, xxxvi. 1. 9∼37. 6, xxxvi. 1. 9∼xxxvii. 2. 6, xxxvi. 2. 11∼xxxvii. 2.8, xxxvi. 21. 10–11∼39.1 ff., xxxvii. 3. 8∼46.4.

A probable case of the removal of an implication of Roman duplicity standing in Polybius occurs at xxxv. 14. 3.

2. LANGUAGE AND STYLE

(i) I suggested in volume i[3] that poetic and archaic usages in the fourth decade occurred particularly 'when L.'s attention was sufficiently engaged on a particular episode'. I list here the most striking poeticisms and archaisms which I have noticed in books xxxiv–xxxvii, including most of those mentioned by Tränkle (*WS*). I have, however, excluded usages which, though they may be highly stylized or poetic, do occur more than once in Cicero.[4] My concern is to draw attention to the incidence of L.'s departures from Ciceronian usage, not to attempt to define the stylistic level of different parts of L.'s work.[5]

accola: xxxvii. 53. 25. Before L., who uses it thirty-five times, it occurs only in Plautus and once in each of Cicero, Sallust, and Virgil (*TLL*, i. 328–9).

---

[1] Strangely claimed as a doublet by Kahrstedt, 42.

[2] Regarded as a doublet by Lauterbach, 84, Kahrstedt, 39, Walsh, *Livy*, 148, Walbank, *Livy*, 70 n. 89. Cf. xxxi. 20. 12 n.

[3] p. 13.

[4] Usages listed by Tränkle but excluded on these grounds are *capere* with an emotion as a subject (xxxv. 33. 11, xxxvi. 11. 3), *adfatim* (xxxiv. 26. 10, 37. 5), *ergo* as a preposition (xxxvii. 47. 4), *fando audire* (xxxv. 48. 5), *intempesta nocte* (xxxvii. 14. 3), *nimbus* = 'shower' (xxxvi. 18. 5, cf. xxxviii. 3. 3 n.), *sopire* (xxxv. 27. 6, xxxvi. 18. 8, 24. 3). Most of the matters discussed by Adams, *Antichthon* viii (1974), 54 ff. are similarly excluded. Nor do I list *inuius* (xxxvi. 18. 4), found in Sallust and Virgil, while *litora, oram legere, trepidi rerum,* and *uoluere fluctus,* found in Virgil, are included in my list of usages appearing for the first time in L. or his contemporaries. It may nevertheless be observed that most of the instances referred to in this note occur in the same contexts as those I do list, or in others (e.g. xxxvi. 18) which can be equally regarded as 'written up' (cf. pp. 7–8 n. 4).

[5] I have very much in mind Adams's warning (op. cit., 55) that it is virtually impossible to make a complete division between 'artificial' and 'non-artificial' elements in L.

aereus: xxxiv. 52. 4, xxxv. 36. 9. It occurs first in Varro, *Men.* 169, several times in Virgil, and three times in L. (*TLL*, i. 1059 ff.).

ambages: xxxiv. 59. 1. Not found in prose before L. It occurs eight times in the first decade and also at xliv. 27. 3 (*TLL*, i. 1833 ff., Tränkle, *WS*, 113).

animum adicere: xxxv. 38. 2, xxxvi. 8. 4. The phrase occurs in Plautus and Terence and not again before L. (*TLL*, i. 666. 56 ff.).

astu: occurs in early poetry and not again before the Augustan period (cf. xxxv. 14. 12 n.).

captus: xxxvi. 11. 1. *capere* of sexual emotions is poetic: cf. iv. 9. 4, xxxix. 9. 7, *TLL*, iii. 337. 75 ff.

carnis (as nominative of *caro*): cf. xxxvii. 3. 4 n.

celeber: xxxvii. 48. 1. In the sense of 'often repeated' *celeber* occurs in Accius, only here in L., Ovid, *Ars* ii. 705, *Pont.* i. 9. 25, and then in Curtius, the elder Pliny, and Tacitus (*TLL*, iii. 739).

consonare: xxxvi. 34. 5. Before L. *consonare* occurs only in Plautus, *Amph.* 228, Varro, *RR.* iii. 16. 30, Virgil, *A.* v. 149, viii. 305. The participle in an adjectival sense is not found before this passage (*TLL*, iv. 482).

consuetum: xxxvi. 7. 5. In the sense of 'the one they are used to' this is a verse usage, found in Sallust (*Iug.* 15. 5, 85. 7) and L. (also at iii. 20. 8, v. 23. 4, ix. 45. 15) (*TLL*, iv. 552. 24 ff.).

cupido: xxxiv. 4. 9. *cupido* is absent from prose before Sallust who prefers it to *cupiditas* by 20: 3. L.'s usage is 19: 59. (Tränkle, *WS*, 134).

ditare: xxxvii. 54. 13. In prose before L. occurs only at *ad Her.* iv. 66 (Tränkle, *WS*, 114).

dubiis: xxxvii. 16. 5. *dubius* meaning 'now going in one direction, now in another' is normally confined to poetry (*TLL*, v. 1. 2108. 47 ff., with no exact parallel to this passage).

expirare: xxxv. 35. 19, xxxvii. 53. 10. A poetic word for 'die', found once in Sallust (*H.* i, fr. 44) and 21 times in L. (*TLL*, v. 2. 1902–3).

exterrere: xxxvii. 24. 3. In Cicero and Caesar it occurs only in the passive. (On *terrere* and *exterrere* see Adams, op. cit., 57).

fidere: xxxv. 3. 4, 27. 15. Other than in the present participle *fidere* does not occur in prose before L., who uses it on 14 occasions (cf. Adams, *BICS* xx [1973], 137).

fluidus: xxxiv. 47. 5. A poetic word, not found in prose before L., and only here in L. (*TLL*, vi. 1. 952).

gracilis: xxxv. 11. 7. Not found in prose before L. (*TLL*, vi. 2. 2130).

impetrabilis: xxxvi. 33. 5. Before L. only in Plautus, and in him in an active sense (*TLL*, vii. 1. 597–8).

inclutus: xxxv. 47. 6. A poetic word, found in prose in the elder Cato, Sallust's histories, and 19 times in L. (Tränkle, *WS*, 115).

infrenare: xxxvii. 20. 4, 12. Found only in Ennius, Accius, and Cicero, *Pis.* 44 before these passages (*TLL*, vii. 1. 1489. At xxi. 44. 1 *infrenatos* means 'not bridled'.)

ingenium: xxxvii. 54. 21. Of natural qualities of lands and plants confined to poetry apart from Sallust, *Histories* and L. (Tränkle, *WS*, 124).

ingruere: xxxvii. 23. 2. Found once in Plautus and then in Virgil. It occurs seven times in the first decade and a further seven in the other extant books (Ogilvie, 675).

inhibere: xxxvi. 28. 5, xxxvii. 51. 4. In the sense of 'exercise' found only in Plautus, *Bacch.* 448, Cicero, *Phil.* xiii. 37, and eight times in L. (*TLL*, vii. 1. 1592. 11 ff.).

in rem esse: xxxv. 35. 13. Found in Plautus and Terence, Sisenna, once in Sallust, and seven times in L. (Tränkle, *WS*, 127).

intermori: xxxiv. 49. 1. The first occurrence of any part of the verb other than *intermortuus* since Cato, *Agr.* 161. 3 (*TLL*, vii. 1. 2230).

iter insistere: xxxvii. 7. 8. *insistere iter, viam,* etc. is found before L. only in Plautus, Pacuvius, Accius, and Lucretius (*TLL*, vii. 1. 1922. 43 ff.).

iuuenalis: xxxvii. 20. 5. Not found in prose before L. (*TLL*, vii. 2. 728).

iuuenta: xxxv. 42. 12, xxxvi. 17. 6. Not found in prose before L. (cf. Adams, loc. cit.).

mendicare: xxxv. 49. 11. Before L. found only in Plautus (*TLL*, viii. 706 ff.).

moliri: xxxvi. 24. 3. Meaning 'move' occurs in Accius and not again before L.: cf. xxxiii. 49. 7 (*TLL*, viii. 1361. 78 ff.). xxxvii. 11. 12, adduced by W–M, is not strictly parallel. *moliri* in a variety of senses is a favourite word of L.

non ab re esse: xxxv. 32. 6. *ab re* occurs only in Plautus before L. (also at viii. 11. 1) and not again before the elder Pliny (*TLL*, i. 24. 65 ff., H–S, 256. W–M's note is misleading). Except for Plautus, *Trin.* 239 the phrase is always negative.

obambulare: xxxvi. 34. 4. Found three times in Plautus and not again before Virgil (*G.* iii. 538) and L. (also at xxv. 39. 8, xxvii. 42. 12) (*TLL*, ix. 2. 35).

parce + infinitive: xxxiv. 32. 20. Otherwise a verse usage (K–St, i. 206, *TLL*: at xxv. 25. 6 L. uses *parce* with *ab* and ablative, a usage unique in Latin).

patrare: xxxv. 35. 15. Found in Plautus and Cato, thereafter almost exclusively confined to historiography (Tränkle, *WS*, 126). *patrare* does occur twice in Cicero, but as Tränkle (n. 110) says, both occurrences are determined by unusual reasons.

pauere: a poetic, perhaps colloquial word, not found in Cicero (apart from in verse at *Tusc.* ii. 23) and Caesar. It is used three times by Sallust and 26 by L., usually, as in these instances, as a present participle (L. uses *timere* 136 times, *metuere* 54, and *uereri* 37. Cf. P. C. Gernia, *L' uso di metuo, timeo, uereor, formido, paueo e dei termini correlati nel latino arcaico e classico* [Turin, 1970], 113 ff., 143 ff.).

paululus: xxxv. 11. 7. Apart from Cicero, *Sex. Rosc.* 115 *non paululum nescio quid, paululus* as an adjective occurs in Plautus, Terence, and Cato, and not again before L. (*TLL.* It is, of course, common as a noun and adverb. In the passage of Cicero, though grammatically an adjective, it is much closer in sense to *paululum* as a noun than to genuinely adjectival usages like the present passage).

pensi fuisse: xxxiv. 49. 7. *pensi esse* (*habere*) occurs previously only in Plautus and Sallust (Tränkle, *WS*, 126–7).

perplexus: xxxiv. 57. 6, xxxv. 14. 12, xxxvi. 5. 8, 12. 8, xxxvii. 54. 7. occurs in Plautus, Terence, and Lucretius, but not in prose before L. (*TLL*).

praedatorius: xxxiv. 36. 3. Before L. only in Plautus and Sallust (cf. n. ad loc.).

quassare: xxxvii. 31. 6. Used literally *quassare* occurs in Cato, *Agr.* 23. 3, 88. 1, but is otherwise confined to poetry (*TLL*: it is not used by Tacitus).

renidere: xxxv. 49. 7. Not used in prose before L. (*TLL*).

simulacrum pugnae: xxxv. 26. 2. Not used in prose before L. (Tränkle, *WS*, 128).

stolidus: xxxiv. 46. 8. Used by second-century poets, it occurs once in Cicero and not at all in Caesar (Tränkle, *WS*, 145).

subtexere: xxxvii. 48. 6. Not found in prose before Nepos and L. (*TLL*).

talis meaning 'the following': xxxv. 38. 2, xxxvi. 23. 7. Not found in prose before Nepos and L.

terriculis: xxxiv. 11. 7. Occurs in Accius and Afranius and not again before L. (also at v. 9. 7: Ogilvie, 646, Tränkle, *WS*, 121–2).

temperare irae: xxxvi. 35. 3. *temperare irae, linguae*, etc., occur in Plautus and not again before L. (though Cicero and Caesar use *mihi, tibi, sibi temperare:* K–St, i. 340, *TLL*).

uaniloquus, uaniloquentia: xxxiv. 24. 1, xxxv. 48. 2. Both occur in Plautus and not again before L. (Tränkle, *WS*, 122).

uectare: xxxiv. 3. 9, xxxv. 35. 11, 35. 15. Found at Cato, *Agr.* 10. 1, Varro, *RR* i. 19. 3 (derived from Cato), possibly at Plautus, *Merc.* 76, and four times in L. (*TLL*).

uoluere of cogitation: xxxv. 18. 6. A verse usage found in Sallust and L. (Tränkle, *WS*, 118). As Tränkle says, the whole phrase *ingentes iam diu iras in pectore uoluere* is remarkably poetic in tone.

I have referred in all to 65 instances. The majority of these occur in passages which L. can clearly be seen to have 'written up'. *cupido* and *uectare* occur in the debate on the repeal of the Lex Oppia, *terriculis*[1] in the speech of the Ilergetes at xxxiv. 11, *uaniloquus* in the account of the conference of the Greeks which discussed war against Nabis, *parce* + infinitive in the speech of Flamininus at xxxiv. 32, *praedatorius*[2] and *pauere* in the account of the climax of the war with Nabis, *stolidus* and *fluidus* in the account of the battles with the Boii at xxxiv. 46–7, *intermori* and *pensi fuisse* in the account of Flamininus' departure from Greece, *perplexus* and *ambages* in the account of the negotiations with the representatives of Antiochus, *gracilis* and *paululus* in the account of the battle with the Ligurians, *perplexus* and *astu* in the story of Scipio's meeting with Hannibal, *uoluere* in Alexander of Acarnania's emotional speech to Antiochus, *simulacrum belli* in the story of Philopoemen's disastrous attempt at naval warfare, *non ab re esse* in the account of the Aetolians' decision to call on Antiochus to come to Greece, *aereus*, *expirare*, *in rem esse*, *patrare*, and *uectare* in the story of the murder of Nabis, *talis* = 'the following' and *animum adicere* in the account of the Aetolian attack on Chalcis, *iuuenta* in the report of Thoas' speech dissuading Antiochus from giving Hannibal a fleet, *mendicare*, *renidere*, and *uaniloquentia* in the account of the meeting of the Achaean League, *consuetus* in Hannibal's speech to Antiochus, *animum adicere* in the account of the burial of the Cynoscephalae dead, *captus* in the story of Antiochus' Chalcidian nuptials, *iuuenta* in Glabrio's speech before the battle of Thermopylae, *talis* = 'the following' and *moliri* = 'move' in the account of the capture of Heraclea, *inhibere* = 'exercise' in the account of the negotiations between Glabrio and the Aetolians, *consonans*, *obambulare*, and *temperare irae* in the story of Flamininus at Naupactus, *iter insistere* in Africanus' speech to his brother, *infrenare* and *iuuenalis* in the account of the siege of Pergamum, *exterrere* and *ingruere* in the account of the battle of Side, *inhibere* = 'exercise' in the story of the conflict between Crassus and Fabius Pictor, *accola*[3], *ditare*, *expirare*, *ingenium* and *perplexus* in the speeches of Eumenes and the Rhodians.[4]

---

[1] The word may have occurred in Cato.

[2] Though the occurrence of *praedatorius* here is scarcely significant. There is nothing particularly remarkable about the word and its history can be regarded as coincidental.

[3] Again not significant, since L. also uses *accola* in passages of no great moment.

[4] It will, I think, be generally agreed that the episodes referred to can be described as 'written up' and that there is no circularity in the argument. In several of them we find the expressions which though poetic in tone I excluded from my list (p. 3 n. 4) and many contain items appearing in my list of words and

There are, however, a number of cases which do not, prima facie, fit the case I am arguing. (i) The passages in which *fidere* occurs are of no special moment. The evidence indicates, however, that L. used *fidere* and *confidere* interchangeably (Adams, *BICS* xx, 137) and L. was probably not conscious of *fidere* as a particularly poetic usage. Similar considerations apply to (ii) *pauere* at xxxv. 35. 5, xxxvii. 42. 7, 46. 7, and (iii) *perplexus* at xxxvi. 5. 8, 12. 8, used by L. as an alternative to *impedtius* (cf. xxxvii. 54. 7). (iv) *aereus* at xxxiv. 52. 4 occurs in the report of the triumph of Flamininus. Such reports are usually written in an unadorned, annalistic style (cf. vol. i, 16–17). But Flamininus' triumph was a most impressive and unusual occasion and L.'s choice of language was probably designed to add extra colour. The triumph report, moreover, forms a whole with the 'written up' account of Flamininus' departure from Greece (cf. xxxiv. 48. 2—52 n.). (v) *celeber* and *subtexere* come in L.'s report of Valerius Antias' story of the rumour of the capture of Scipio Africanus in Asia and such variants are usually reported in a fairly straightforward way. On this occasion, however, Antias' story is of the stuff of legend (*fabula*) and poetic language is therefore appropriate (one cannot exclude the possibility that Antias himself used *celeber*). (vi) *impetrabilis* occurs in the account of Philip's attack on Demetrias, which does not appear to be given any special emphasis by L. It does, however, form a link between the descriptions of Flamininus at the meeting of the Achaean League (xxxvi. 30–1) and at Naupactus (xxxi. 34–5), both of which are described by L. with special care. What is more, there are three other striking usages in close proximity to *impetrabilis*—*turbatio*, *a spe destituti*, and *inconditus*.[1] (vii) *quassare*. L. uses *quassare* on eight occasions, as against ten instances of *quatere*. There is no obvious difference in stylistic level between the two words, and since *quassare* occurs metaphorically in Cicero, its history is probably to be regarded as a coincidence. (viii) *carnis*. See xxxvii. 3. 4 n. for the factors determining L.'s usage.

I now turn to cases of words which do not appear in Latin at all before L., or which L. uses in a new sense. I include here cases

meanings first found in L. or his contemporaries (p. 9). One may also note in xxxiv. 46–7 the typical description of the emotions of the combatants and the postponement of *castra* (47. 7), in the negotiations with the ambassadors with Antiochus the use of *quin* with the present indicative to express heightened emotion (xxxiv. 59. 1) and *supersedere* with the infinitive found elsewhere only in Sisenna, in the account of the Aetolian attack on Chalcis *catena* in a very rare metaphorical sense (38. 10), in the description of Flamininus' dealings with the Aetolians a very unusual use of *fidem mouere*, talk of the human race as a whole, and description of the Aetolians as *lanistae*.

[1] Cf. nn. ad locc.

where the first occurrence is in a writer contemporary with L., even if it occurs in a work published before its first appearance in L.[1] *absistere* used absolutely xxxvi. 45. 3, *ad liquidum* xxxv. 8. 7, *agilitas* of ships xxxv. 26. 2, xxxvii. 30. 2, *ancorale* xxxvii. 30. 10, *aspretis* xxxv. 28. 9, *capessere oculis* xxxvii. 24. 6, *caput* = 'mouth' xxxvii. 18. 6, 37. 3, *cardo* = 'limit' xxxvii. 54. 23, *citato gradu* xxxv. 36. 1, *commendabilis* xxxvii. 7. 15, *concitor* xxxvii. 45. 17, *coniecti* = 'placed' xxxvi. 12. 4, *conuiuator* xxxv. 49. 6, *destinare* = 'mark out' xxxv. 20. 1, *a spe destitui* xxxvi. 33. 3, *distincte* xxxiv. 58. 1, *edicere pro contione* xxxvii. 4. 1, *exasperati* xxxvi. 29. 1, *exsequi* + indirect question xxxv. 28. 4, *foedera* = 'articles of a treaty' xxxvii. 56. 8, *frontalia* xxxvii. 40. 4, *hebetare* xxxvii. 41. 3, *inaequaliter* xxxvii. 53. 6, *inaestimabilis* xxxv. 14. 12, *incessere* xxxiv. 23. 4, xxxvii. 57. 15, *inexsuperabilis* xxxvi. 17. 3, *infabre* xxxvi. 40. 12, *insistere* + dative = 'devote oneself to' xxxvii. 60. 2, *insociabilis* xxxvii. 1. 4, *intercipere* = 'remove' xxxv. 36. 7, *interfari* xxxvi. 27. 3, 28. 4, *legiuncula* xxxv. 49. 10, *litora, oram legere* xxxv. 27. 6, xxxvi. 21. 5, xxxvii. 17. 8, *mirabundus* xxxvii. 10. 4, *nautici* xxxvii. 28. 5, *nubes* (of soldiers) xxxv. 49. 5, *nudare* = 'lay bare' xxxv. 32. 2, *obmoliri* xxxvii. 32. 7, *onerare* = 'increase the gravity of' xxxiv. 62. 5, *permissio* xxxvii. 7. 2, *perpacare* xxxvi. 21. 3, 42. 3, *praeflorare* xxxvii. 58. 8, *praegrauare* xxxv. 42. 14, *praetextus* (or *-um*) xxxvi. 6. 5, *principia rerum* = 'the beginning of the action' xxxvii. 37. 4, *reconciliator* xxxv. 45. 3, *seruus* (as an adjective, other than with *homo*) xxxvii. 54. 6, *soliferreis* xxxiv. 14. 11, *tenere* intransitive = 'continued' xxxvi. 43. 11, *trepidi rerum* xxxvi. 31. 4, *turbatio* xxxvi. 33. 2, *uelamenta* = ἱκετηρία xxxv. 34. 7, xxxvi. 20. 1, xxxvii. 28. 1, *uoluere fluctus* xxxvii. 13. 2, *uoti compos* xxxv. 18. 6.

The picture here differs from that derived from consideration of archaic and poetic usages. Some of these instances do occur in passages which I have already described as being 'written up' or in others which can be regarded as having been treated with special care (*soliferreum* in Cato's great battle near Emporiae, *ancorale, nautici,* and *uelamenta* in the account of the battle of Myonnesus, *obmoliri* in the story of the siege of Phocaea, *concitor* in Scipio's speech to the ambassadors of Antiochus, *incessere* in the account of the trial of Glabrio). But over half the instances do not fall into this category, and in the case of *ancorale, nautici, obequitare,* and *uelamenta* their presence in such passages is probably coincidental, as they also occur in passages which cannot be regarded as having been written with special care. For the rest, some are coinings or extensions of

[2] Cf. nn. ad locc. For some items omitted here see addenda.

usages to convey the concept which L. wanted to express,[1] in others he took over a usage invented by one of his contemporaries because it suited what he wanted to say, not in order to give a special tone to his narrative. In this he was following in a long tradition.[2]

One of L.'s greatest merits is to adapt his style to the matter with which he is dealing.[3] In these books we may note the curt military style at xxxiv. 16. 9, xxxv. 11. 7–8, 27. 13 ff., 35. 11 ff., xxxvi. 24. 5–6, xxxvii. 5. 6.[4] For straightforward military narrative L. can write almost like Caesar, as at xxxiv. 9. 11–12, 14. 1. When he wants to describe an atmosphere of intrigue and suspicion he writes almost as Tacitus was to do in similar circumstances (xxxv. 15). When he reports the attempt of Alexander of Acarnania to persuade Antiochus that Philip would revolt from Rome his language becomes deliberately epic (xxxv. 18. 6).[5] The repetitions in xxxiv. 8. 4—21 and the artless asyndeton at xxxvii. 48. 3 may be deliberate imitations of the style of his sources.[6] In military writing military jargon is appropriate (xxxv. 5. 9, 28. 8, xxxvi. 38. 3), in giving the terms of a peace treaty a legalistic style is employed (xxxiv. 35). We may note the way in which the construction of the period at xxxvii. 29. 4 appears to reflect the confusion of the situation and the affable manner of Flamininus is well reflected in the free-flowing style of the speech attributed to him at xxxv. 49.[7]

It is perhaps presumptuous for modern readers to attempt to criticize L. for his lapses from the highest standards,[8] but I would draw attention to the extremely obscure period at xxxv. 37. 4–5, the abrupt *uenerunt*, ending a string of verbs, at xxxv. 50. 9, the harsh constructions at xxxvii. 20. 11, 39. 13, and the oddity of *stationes . . . posuerunt castra* at xxxvii. 21. 1.

---

[1] *Caput, foedera,* and *permissio* are obviously the result of the influence of the language of Polybius and the same is probably true of *legiuncula.* See nn. ad locc. (cf. also xxxiv. 58. 1 n. on *distincte*).

[2] Cf. vol. i, 14.

[3] Vol. i, 17. The remark of Quintilian about the speeches (x. 1. 101) can properly be applied to L.'s work as a whole.

[4] Cf. xxxi. 23. 6—7 n.

[5] Cf. p. 6.

[6] Cf. p. 13 n. 3. On the question whether L. imitates Cato in the speech attributed to him at xxxiv. 2–4 cf. xxxiv. 1–8. 4 n. On *celeber* at xxxvii. 48. 1 see p. 8.

[7] See *conuiuator, nubes,* and *renidere* above. We also find in this speech *condimentis* in its literal sense not found between Plautus and this passage, and *ferina,* the only examples of which in prose before this passage are Sallust, *Iug.* 18. 1, 89. 7. I excluded the last two cases from my list of archaisms and poeticisms since language of the culinary register is not the sort of thing one meets with very often in extant Latin literature and the stylistic level of the words cannot therefore be assessed.

[8] Cf. vol. i, 17, though my remarks there about repetition are misplaced. See below p. 13.

(ii) I now turn to a number of aspects of L.'s writing which are important both in themselves and because textual decision often depends on awareness of L.'s practice, and MSS. evidence for it, as a whole.

(a) *Asyndeton*

Preuss demonstrated a hundred years ago the prevalence of two-membered asyndetical expressions in Latin.[1] He showed that many of them denoted concepts which naturally went in pairs and that they had become formulaic, though he was probably over-schematic in his attempt to separate the formulaic occurrences (*usus sollemnes*) from those which do not fall into this category. In books xxxiv–xxxvii examples unanimously attested by the MSS. are xxxiv. 3. 4 *accepistis iussistis*, 7. 4 *teritur absumitur*, 35. 7 *liberos coniuges*, xxxv. 21. 9 *nocte clam*, 34. 7 *insontem indemnatum*, 35. 7 *terras maria armis uiris*, 35. 16 *animos dextras*, xxxvi. 18. 1 *arma tela*, 38. 1 *nocte improuiso*, xxxvii. 53. 9 *terrestribus naualibus*. At xxxiv. 1. 6 *oppidis conciliabulis*, 5. 12 *uiros feminas*, 61. 5 *circulis conuiuiis*, xxxvi. 26. 2. *terrestribus naualibus* a -*que* in χ is missing in B. Despite the tendency of B to omit words in F[2] the parallels for *uiri feminae* and the unanimously attested *terrestribus naualibus* at xxxvii. 53. 9[3] make it more or less certain that B should be followed. I think the asyndeton may be right in what is clearly a formulaic phrase at xxxiv. 1. 6 but I would be far less confident about *circulis conuiuiis*: at xxxii. 20. 3 the MSS. have *conuiuiis et circulis*. At xxxv. 44. 5, where the MSS. have *armis, uiris, equisque* there is a good case for an *asyndeton trimembre*.

There are, of course, countless examples of colon and sentence asyndeton in L. Textual problems arise at xxxiv. 7. 3, xxxv. 14. 7, 16. 6, 23. 6, 29. 5, 34. 8, 36. 3, xxxvi. 2. 15, 22. 3, 43. 1, xxxvii. 2. 6, 13. 11, 23. 6, 26. 8, 49. 5, 50. 3. No general rule can be enunciated and the case for accepting an asyndeton varies greatly from passage to passage. Judgement is bound to be influenced, however, by awareness of the other passages where some or all of the MSS. omit connecting particles.

(b) *Variation of tenses*

L.'s fondness for the historic present and historic infinitive and for alternating tenses in narrative needs no illustration.[4] I merely draw

---

[1] *De bimembris dissoluti apud scriptores Romanos usu sollemni* (1881).   [2] See p. 17.

[3] See also xxxiii. 38. 10 n. Consular dates in the ablative absolute can also be classified as *asyndeta bimembria*: cf. Naylor, 31.

[4] Cf. Chausserie-Laprée, 369 ff., and, for the first decade, J. L. Catterall, *TAPhA* lxix (1938), 308 ff.

attention to a number of cases where the MSS. present different tenses, or, where unanimous, have been emended. xxxiv. 12. 5, 12. 7, 17. 4, 19. 2, 29. 7, 29. 13, 39. 8, 62. 6, 62. 16, xxxv. 15. 2, 48. 10, xxxvi. 10. 12, 15. 2, 20. 3, 21. 5, 32. 1, 33. 3, 35. 2, 42. 5, xxxvii. 10. 6, 20. 6, 20. 7, 20. 14, 21. 2, 27. 4, 32. 5, 45. 4, 46. 4, 47. 1, 60. 7.

(c) *Ellipse*

Ellipse of parts of *esse* is common in L. On many occasions, however, editors have felt the necessity for supplementation where the MSS. omit parts of *esse*. Goodyear[1] has suggested that when an ellipse presents 'grave ambiguity' (i.e. as to whether we are dealing with a participle or a main verb) it would not have been tolerated, and he would, on these grounds, favour supplementation at xxxi. 25. 5, xxxiv. 17. 6, and xxxvii. 36. 2. I fully endorse Goodyear's statement that a full investigation of ellipse in general would be necessary in order to reach firm conclusions. My own feeling, though, is that the accumulation of MSS. evidence should be taken as an indication that L. was willing to admit ellipse even in circumstances which may seem intolerable to us.

I list the cases in books xxxiv–xxxvii where some or all of the MSS. omit parts of *esse* or where my note makes some allusion to the question: xxxiv. 17. 6, 25. 8, 27. 6–8, 32. 7, 36. 7[2], 39. 4, xxxv. 5. 14, 12. 8, 15. 4, 15. 9, 35. 1, 41. 6, xxxvi. 2. 8, 6. 4, 12. 2, 14. 5, 15. 7, 22. 4, 35. 6, 35. 7, 39. 1, 45. 9, xxxvii. 15. 2, 24. 7, 36. 2, 37. 9, 39. 2, 42. 2, 53. 19, 55. 2, 55. 4, 55. 5.

Reference may be made to other categories of ellipse or possible ellipse. Of the subject: xxxvii. 25. 3, 40. 2, 42. 6. Of the object: xxxvi. 21. 7, 39. 1. Of verbs of saying: xxxiv. 27. 6–8, 32. 14, xxxv. 12. 15, 35. 2, xxxvii. 26. 12, 39. 1. Of verbs of moving: xxxiv. 26. 9, xxxvi. 7. 15, 11. 1. Of an apodosis: xxxv. 15. 3. Of *ut*: xxxvii. 39. 3, 50. 3. Of an accusative (with infinitive) xxxiv. 31. 5, xxxv. 46. 10, xxxvi. 7. 20, 28. 4, 31. 3, xxxvii. 6. 7, 50. 7.

Pettersson[3] argued that L. often omitted a connecting *is* or *hic* at the beginning of sentences and that emendations which added some part of these pronouns are mistaken. Of three cases in book xxxvii I think he is right about 45. 6, but find it difficult to accept his arguments on 17. 5 and 43. 1.

---

[1] Appendix 5.

[2] The passage is a salutary warning against over-enthusiastic acceptance of ellipses. The evidence of the Rome fragments (R) proves that *esse* is the transmitted reading. But contrast xxxv. 5. 14 where the fragments of F convict χ of an unnecessary addition.   [3] 41 ff.

(d) *Repetition*[1]

It has been widely recognized that repetition of a word or phrase in the same sentence did not offend Latin writers in the way it does a modern reader, and any emendation whose aim is merely to remove repetition should be viewed with the greatest suspicion. Some of L.'s repetitions are clearly deliberate and serve to make a particular point. For others it is harder to discern any particular reason and they must simply be accepted. I list repetitions in books xxxiv–xxxvii by these two categories.[2] Deliberate repetitions: xxxiv. 8. 5, 9. 11–12, 13. 9, 14. 8, 19. 11, 21. 4,[3] 32. 7, 35. 3, 50. 9, xxxv. 22. 6, 26. 9, 29. 8, 45. 5–7, 49. 4, 49. 11–12, xxxvii. 14. 7–15. 2, 58. 8. Non-deliberate repetition: xxxiv. 22. 7, 26. 5, xxxv. 20. 12, 33. 3–7, 35. 6–7, 44. 3–6, 45. 1–2, xxxvi. 9. 15, 13. 4, 14. 5, 15. 1, 23. 5, 33. 3, 34. 2, xxxvii. 6. 7, 10. 2, 14. 6–7, 23. 6, 25. 3–4, 51. 5, 54. 12, 56. 7.

(e) *Word-order*[4]

It is clear that L. is willing to countenance some startling departures from normal word-order. In some cases his purpose is to give particular emphasis to a certain word or phrase, in others his aim is far from obvious. A full investigation of L.'s word-order would be a major piece of research in itself. My purpose here is merely to illustrate L.'s practice by drawing attention to a number of passages in books xxxiv–xxxvii. I do not, of course, claim to have discovered every case of unusual word-order in these books.

In three passages the order does seem to serve a specific purpose. At xxxiv. 15. 2 *integri recentibus telis fatigatos adorti hostes* the aim is to emphasize the contrast between *integri* and *fatigatos*. At xxxv. 17. 7 *initium semper a paruis iniusta imperandi fieri* L. may have wanted to avoid putting *iniusta imperandi* in the unemphatic second position in the colon. At xxxv. 46. 11 *pacem eiusdem populi Romani beneficio et libertatem habeant* L. wants to emphasize *libertatem*, which is the keynote of the exchanges between the Aetolians and the Chalcidians.

---

[1] See Pettersson, 101 ff., Gries, *CPh* xlvi (1951), 36–7, R. G. Austin on *pro Caelio* 3. 16, Ogilvie, 38, 81–2, 279, 288, 306, 650, Woodman, *CQ* n.s. xxv (1975), 278 n. 3.

[2] For other passages where texual problems involve repetitions cf. xxxiv. 5. 9, 12. 6, xxxv. 5.11, xxxvii. 20. 6.

[3] 13. 9 apart, there is no specific purpose in these first six passages, but repetition is a feature of Cato's own style and L. may well have been deliberately reflecting that.

[4] For the basic principles of Latin word-order see Marouzeau, *L'Ordre des mots*, Adams, *IF* lxxxi (1976), 70 ff. On L.'s word-order a number of perceptive remarks are to be found in Naylor. See also Ogilvie, index iv, *s.u.* hyperbaton.

In the other passages I am unable to discern any external motive for the artificiality of the order. In three passages there is a deliberate 'interlacing' of two grammatical elements.[1] xxxiv. 41. 8–10 *castri aduersus Romana positis castra*, xxxvi. 6. 8 *quorum omnibus qui aderant uoluntas temptanda uidebatur*, xxxvi. 16. 10 *ad opem propinquis ferendam ciuitatibus suis*. Next three passages where a participle is widely separated from the part of *esse* with which it belongs: xxxv. 47. 1 *haec renuntiata regi ad naues ubi restiterat cum essent*,[2] xxxvi. 17. 4 *munitiones et locis opportunioribus tunc fuerunt et ualidiores impositae*, xxxvi. 19. 7 *quae temptata ... sine ullo haud parum audacis incepti fuerant*. Two of these passages come close together, but much more remarkable are four passages towards the end of book xxxv where some part of *rex* appears in an unexpected position: 42. 6 *hic idem ausus de Hannibale est mouere sententiam prope iam certam regis*,[3] 44. 1 *aegre a Phaenea praetore principibusque aliis introductus silentio facto dicere orsus rex*,[4] 46. 3 *itaque cum mille peditibus rex qui Demetriade secuti erant*, and 47. 2 *consultare cum Aetolis rex quid deinde fieret*. Gries observed that when L. employed an unusual word he often repeated it within a short distance.[5] It seems that the same applies to unusual word-order.

Hyperbaton of different kinds is, of course, common in Latin and no one would be particularly disturbed by xxxvii. 26. 3 *momentum in praesentia spei* or xxxvii. 46. 7 *huius triumphi minuit laetitiam*.[6] xxxvi. 6. 1 *causas in speciem irae*, where the genitive does not go with the noun nearest it, belongs to a pattern found elsewhere in ancient literature and used several times by L.[7] And xxxvii. 31. 2 *non enim tueri solum Lysimachiam a primo impetu Romanorum facile erat, sed obsidionem etiam tota hieme tolerare* belongs to a set of passages where *solum, modo,* or *tantum* appear in a position where instead of limiting the whole of a clause they strictly limit only one element of it.[8]

---

[1] See Goodyear's note on Tacitus, *A.* i. 10. 1, with a number of examples from other authors, Woodman, 119–20. For examples of chiastic order see xxxiv. 31. 7, xxxv. 23. 11, 49. 6, 51. 8, xxxvi. 22. 3, xxxvii. 54. 27.

[2] For less striking examples cf. xxiv. 33. 1, xxvii. 26. 5. xxi. 11. 13, xxxiii. 6. 2, adduced by W–M, are not parallel, since they involve only the postponement of *cum* (cf. W–M on xxi. 11. 13). I do not include xxxvi. 15. 7 here, as I do not think that *est* there is modal and the text is in any case doubtful. See n. ad loc.

[3] *de Hannibale* is anteposed for emphasis, but this would not itself affect the position of *regis*.

[4] Bχ, *rex dicere orsus* Mg.

[5] op. cit.

[6] Cf. xxx. 21. 1.

[7] Cf. xxxiii. 42. 10 n. Add xxvi. 21. 14 and perhaps xxix. 34. 7.

[8] See Pettersson, 20 ff. In this case there is the additional factor that it is the siege of Lysimachia itself that is in question. L. could equally well have written *illius urbis obsidionem* and there would then have been no illogicality at all.

xxxvii. 18. 7 *in Gallorum mercede conductis quattuor milibus* is probably to be explained by the fact that L. began as if he were going to write *in Gallis mercede conductis* and the addition of *quattuor milibus* made him change *Gallis* to *Gallorum*. The postponement of *naues* in xxxvi. 20. 6 *tres quae ex Asia profectae eundem portum tenuerunt naues*,[1] and of *pars* in xxxvi. 22. 8 *e regione sinus Maliaci quae aditum haud facilem pars habebat* are not so readily explained, and no less remarkable are xxxv. 37. 7 *duo milia peditum Thoas et ducentos equites*,[2] xxxvi. 10. 12 *in suos receperunt se fines*, the wide separation of *ut . . . primum* at xxxvi. 44. 4, and the hyperbaton of *ad Thermopylas* at xxxvii. 57. 10.

Finally, I list a number of passages where my note discusses word-order, or where the variations between the MSS. consist entirely of differences of word-order.[3] xxxiv. 9. 6, 21. 1, 32. 12, 62. 16, xxxv. 26. 5, 27. 16, 29. 2, 35. 7, 38. 8, 41. 1, 44. 1, 46. 11, 48. 7, 49. 9, 50. 11, xxxvi. 2. 2, 17. 9, 21. 3, 21. 10, 22. 5, 23. 8, 25. 3 (*bis*), 25. 7–8, 27. 8 (*bis*), 29. 1, 30. 4, 32. 3, 34. 2, 35. 5, 39. 7, 42. 7, 44. 8, 45. 5, xxxvii. 5. 4, 6. 2, 6. 3, 17. 10, 18. 8, 19. 1, 19. 2, 24. 1, 24. 2, 25. 4, 27. 9, 29. 9, 30. 1, 32. 9, 33. 3, 36. 1, 37. 8, 39. 5 (*bis*), 39. 12, 43. 3, 46. 7, 50. 2, 53. 8, 53. 25, 54. 8, 54. 14, 54. 19, 54. 23, 55. 5, 55. 6, 57. 14 (*bis*), 60. 7.

3. TEXT[4]

I have collated the seven principal manuscripts (B, AEP = ϕ, NVL = ψ, $\phi + \psi = \chi$) for books xxxiv–xxxvii.[5] Where books xxxvi–xxxvii are concerned I present the evidence only when my note discusses a textual matter, or, occasionally, when it seems desirable to be explicit. For the rest, I decided that it would be wrong to attempt to anticipate the forthcoming Oxford text of books xxxvi–xl. The lemmata for books xxxiv–xxxv give the

[1] This belongs to the class of instances of separation of a noun from its attribute, on which see W-M on *praef.* 5, Ogilvie, 162, and references there cited. In this case, though, I can see no reason for wanting to emphasize *tres*.

[2] It makes no difference whether or not we omit *et*: cf. n. ad loc. The position of *Thoas* is parallel to that of *rex* at xxxv. 46. 3, discussed above.

[3] By no means all of these passages are discussed in the commentary. In very many of the places where Bχ differ from Mg, or B from χ (with no evidence about Mg) on a matter of word-order, there is no way of deciding between them. (In books xxxvi–xxxvii, in such cases, I merely give the evidence and refer to the present list.) For further passages, omitted above, see addenda.

[4] For fuller discussion of several of the matters mentioned here see *BRL* lxii (1980), 311 ff.: the appendix to that article contains a list of additions and corrections to McDonald's apparatus to books xxxiv–xxxv.

[5] The sigla are those of McDonald.

reading of the Oxford text, those for books xxxvi–xxxvii those of the Teubner edition of Weissenborn and M. Müller (1890).[1] If the lemma is not followed by any indication of its source, it may be assumed that it is to be found either in the *codices deteriores*[2] or in one of the printed editions prior to the Mainz edition of 1518. Further information will be found in Drakenborch, W–M, and Zingerle.

I would draw attention to the following points:

(a) Where the MSS. of the ϕ and ψ groups are not unanimous, I have given the readings of the individual MSS., rather than use these sigla to denote agreement of any two of the manuscripts of each group.

(b) With regard to the readings of the lost Mainz and Speyer manuscripts (Mg, Sp), when a reading is given by Gelenius (in the Basle edition of 1535) and is not attested by Carbach (in the Mainz edition of 1518), I have listed the reading as 'Gel.' and indicated, whenever possible, exactly what Gelenius says about it. On several occasions Gelenius' implication that a reading stood in both Mg and Sp is shown to be impossible by the agreement of $B\chi$.[3]

(c) My study of A (BL Harl. 2493) has convinced me that Mc-Donald[4] is incorrect in his statement that most of the annotations in the fourth decade are by Petrarch, with only a few additions by Valla. In fact a substantial number of conjectures are in a hand which is neither that of Petrarch nor that used by Valla in the first and third decades. I refer to conjectures by Petrarch as A^2, those in the other hand as A^z.[5]

(d) When $B\psi$ agree against ϕ, I have on several occasions described the reading of ϕ as being an emendation by Landolfo di Colonna. In so doing, I have accepted the view of Billanovich[6] and McDonald[7] that Colonna was responsible for the apograph (ϕ) of the Chartres codex (χ), from which AEP were copied. Recent statements by Billanovich suggest that this account may be in need of revision, but pending the publication of Billanovich's introduction to the facsimile edition of A, I have deemed it best not to depart from the

---

[1] When the lemma includes a word or words enclosed in square brackets in the Teubner and is followed by '$B\chi$', I mean, of course, that the word or words in brackets stand in $B\chi$. In a number of cases I say 'MSS.' to indicate the reading standing in $B\chi$ with no indication of an alternative reading in Mg.

[2] See McDonald, xxv ff.

[3] For the relation of Sp to χ cf. McDonald, xxxiv–xxxvii.

[4] xxii.

[5] A^x denotes a passage where I cannot determine which of the two hands is involved.

[6] *JWI* xiv (1951), 151 ff.

[7] xxxiii–xxiv.

conventional view. Similarly, it can no longer be regarded as certain that ψ was another apograph of χ, independent of ϕ. It may be that it is ψ and χ, not ϕ and ψ that are twins.[1]

(e) In volume i[2] I suggested that in books xxxi–xxxiii there were a considerable number of passages where words or phrases in χ, omitted in B, should be regarded as interpolations. In books xxxiv–xxxvii I have noted 243 passages where words or phrases in χ are omitted in B: of these only 50 appear to me as probable or possible interpolations. There are also a number of places where words omitted in Bχ are attested only by Mg. In some of these, particularly in the first part of book xxxiv, there are strong reasons for regarding them as interpolations. The most striking is xxxiv. 16. 1–2, and if this is regarded as an interpolation, one is bound to look with more suspicion on such passages as xxxiv. 7. 2 and 16. 5 (though in both the latter cases the balance of probability, to my mind, is against seeing an interpolation). One must, of course, be aware of the danger of circular argument, and the only proper procedure is to judge each case on its merits. Nevertheless the case for seeing interpolations is cumulative.[3]

(f) In my note on xxxi. 3. 3 I stated that L. used both *proconsul* and *propraetor* as nouns. I have now examined all the passages in the fourth decade where modern texts print such usages and the evidence suggests that in most instances only the abbreviations *procos.* and *propr.* stood in F, to be transcribed as they stood in B and interpreted in various ways by Renaissance scribes. As far as the fourth decade is concerned, therefore, there are no valid grounds for attributing *proconsul* and *propraetor* to L. That is not to say, of course, that the evidence shows that he did not use these forms.

4. THE CALENDAR

Although the existence of severe dislocation of the Roman calendar in the first third of the second century B.C. has been well known since the beginning of modern historical research, there have been remarkably few attempts to work out the precise implications of this in terms of Julian[4] equivalents of Roman dates. Our basic knowledge depends on the dates of two eclipses given by L. From xxxvii. 4. 4 we know that 14 March 190 (Jul.) fell on 11 July in the Roman year 190/89 and from xliv. 37. 8 that 21 June 168 (Jul.) fell on 3

---

[1] Cf. *BRL* lxii, 318–19.

[2] 47–8.

[3] See especially the notes on the passages mentioned and on xxxiv. 15. 3, 16. 3.

[4] I follow the convention of referring to the extrapolated dates as Julian: they are in fact Gregorian.

September in the Roman year 168/7. In other words in 190 the calendar was about four months ahead of the Julian equivalent, in 168 about two and a half months. In the nineteenth and early twentieth century several writers made calculations about the number of omitted intercalations that could have produced such a situation, but more recently most historians have contented themselves with vague estimates of the amount the calendar was ahead at any given time, or have proclaimed that our evidence is insufficient to allow any attempt to draw up a table of precise equivalencies between Julian and pre-Julian dates.[1] In 1973, however, Marchetti and Derow, in two quite independent articles, brought a new and far more methodical approach to the subject: Marchetti was concerned with the period from 203 to the eclipse of 190, Derow to that between the two eclipses. In 1976 each published articles dealing with the period originally discussed by the other.[2] The present discussion is restricted to the earlier period.

The normal system of intercalation provided for intercalary months of alternately 22 and 23 days to be added every other year to the standard Roman year of 355 days—a total, that is, of 45 days in four years. The months were added after 23 or 24 February— in fact the intercalary month had 27 days and February lost either 4 or 5 days of its ordinary length.[3] Now if there had been regular intercalation between 203 and 190 the calendar would have been three and a half to four and a half months ahead throughout the period, and we would have to believe that dislocation had taken place during the Second Punic War. At first sight that is an attractive idea; the crisis of the invasion of Hannibal might well have led to the omission of intercalation, either through preoccupation with the war, or, to adapt a suggestion made by De Sanctis to support a different conclusion,[4] through a belief—perhaps a prophecy—that the war would last a fixed number of years which would only be lengthened by intercalation. Such a possibility, however, can be excluded. Not only does Livy's narrative of the later years of the war give no indication that the consuls were entering office in

---

[1] Cf. De Sanctis, iv. 1. 376–9, A. K. Michels, *The Calendar of the Roman Republic* (Princeton, 1967), 170. I must include myself in this category.

[2] P. Marchetti, *AC* xlii (1973), 473–96, *BCH* c (1976), 401–26, P. S. Derow, *Phoenix* xxvii (1973), 345–56, xxx (1976), 265–81. My table (p. 25) differs from those of Marchetti and Derow because I posit a 23-day intercalation in 191/0 and a 22-day intercalation in 189/8 (Derow assumes the reverse) and because they both misplace extrapolated leap years. The leap years in the period from 203 to 189 are 197, 193, and 189. Derow places leap years in 203, 199, 195, and 191, Marchetti in 200, 196, and 192.

[3] See Michels, op. cit., 160 ff.

[4] See pp. 24–6.

November or December of the preceding calendar year,[1] but for 203—the penultimate year of the war—more precise calculations are available.[2] Ovid[3] gives 22 June as the date of the defeat of Syphax by Massinissa, an event described by Livy in xxx. 11–12. The campaign which led to this event commenced at the beginning of the spring[4] and the chronological indications given by Polybius and L. make it manifestly impossible for the dislocation to have been of the same order as it was in 190.

We can, then, exclude the possibility that there had been regular intercalation between 203 and 190. In 191 the consul M'. Acilius Glabrio carried a *lex de intercalando*.[5] It is reasonable to assume that this was occasioned by realization of the extraordinary degree of dislocation that had been reached by that time. Since the consuls entered office on the Ides of March the first intercalation that can have taken place after the passage of the law would have been that after 23/24 February in the year 191/190. It would, I think, be virtually impossible to argue that there was not an intercalation at that time. Detailed argument in support of that view, and to ascertain whether that was the only intercalation in the period depends on consideration of the chronological implications of a number of passages.

We start with the events of 203 to which I have already referred. Marchetti, arguing partly from the specific time intervals given by Polybius, partly from general probability, arrives at the conclusion that the defeat of Syphax cannot come before the end of May. If there had been three intercalations in the period the defeat of Syphax on 22 June in the Roman calendar would have taken place on 29 April. One might disagree with some of the intervals proposed by Marchetti, but his conclusion that 29 April is far too early for the defeat of Syphax is inescapable. We are left, then, with the possibility that the number of intercalations was nought, one, or two.

Derow, however, holds that far more can be deduced from these events. He argues that the interval between the beginning and end of this campaign was 70 days, and, counting this from 15 March, that the Julian equivalents of 22 June involved in positing either one intercalation—or *a fortiori* no intercalations—produce dates which are far too late—15 June and 8 July respectively. I think, however,

---

[1] Derow (1976), 279 ff.

[2] I am here adapting the argument of Marchetti (1973), 478 ff. for a purpose slightly different from his own.

[3] *Fasti* vi. 769.

[4] Pol. xiv. 2. 1.

[5] Macrobius i. 13. 21.

that Derow is pushing the evidence too hard. The interval between τὰ μὲν τῆς ἐαρινῆς ὥρας ὑπέφαινεν ἤδη[1] and Scipio's firing of the Carthaginian and Numidian camps[2] cannot be precisely determined. Derow puts the latter at 15 March, but a date a month later could not be totally excluded. And his reduction of the interval between the arrival of Laelius and Massinissa in Numidia and the final battle to two weeks fails to convince. Marchetti was right to argue that the events of 203 cannot exclude anything other than three intercalations.

We come next to the events of the winter of 198/7—the conference of Nicaea between Philip V and Flamininus and the subsequent embassies to Rome, culminating in the rejection of Philip's terms and the prorogation of Flamininus' command.[3] Marchetti used these events to exclude the possibility that there were no intercalations in our period. For on that hypothesis the Ides of March, 197 would have fallen on 29 January 197. By working forward from the probable date of the conference of Nicaea Marchetti argued that the ambassadors of Philip and the Greek states must have arrived in Rome several weeks before this. It is generally agreed that the whole logic of Polybius' account of Flamininus' manœuvrings at this time depends on the discussion of peace and the assignation of provinces for the consuls of 197 taking place at very near the same time, and it would follow that the Ides of March, 197 cannot have fallen on 29 January.

Derow argues that a precise date for the debates cannot be reached by working forward from the beginning of winter, but nevertheless claims that a date of arrival at the end of January cannot be excluded. But here again Marchetti is on stronger ground. *hiems iam eo tempore erat*[4] is the beginning of L.'s adaptation of Polybius' account of the events of winter 198/7 and Derow's hypothesis that the sequence of events could have begun as late as the middle of December is, I think, impossible.[5] The beginning of Polybius' winter can be placed anywhere in the last third of October and the first third of November,[6] but it is most implausible to think that Flamininus' agreement to meet Philip[7] could be placed in the middle of December. L.'s account begins *capta Elatia* and that took place *aestate*.[8]

---

[1] Pol. xiv. 2. 1. [2] Pol. xiv. 4–5, L. xxx. 5–6.
[3] Pol. xviii. 1–12, L. xxxii. 32–7: cf. vol. i, 24 ff.
[4] xxxii. 32. 1.
[5] Marchetti and Derow do not disagree about the amount of time to be ascribed to the events.
[6] Cf. *Historia* xxvi (1977), 248–50.
[7] xxxii. 32. 6. [8] xxxii. 24, cf. 25. 12.

In fact, of course, Derow does not want to argue that the Ides of March 197 was on 29 January. What he does want to argue is that it was on 6 January, and that, since by his arguments from the events of 203, there were two intercalations on the period, the first of these had already taken place by 197. He reaches this conclusion by arguing backwards from the beginning of the campaign leading to the battle of Cynoscephalae in 197. His case is that since Philip and Flamininus began military preparations only at the very beginning of spring[1]—i.e. the beginning of March—, the envoys must have returned from Rome only a few days before this, in the second half of February; the two months' truce allowed for the negotiations[2] will thus have begun in the second half of December, and if the consuls had entered office as early as 15 December 198, as would be the case if there had been two intercalations between 197 and 190, the logic of Polybius' account would be broken. But, as Derow himself admits, the time allowed for the truce was very short, and it cannot be ruled out that it had expired before the return of the ambassadors. It would still be likely that no military moves were made before they returned.

I conclude that again Derow is attempting to be too precise; the only certain conclusions that can be drawn from the events of 203 and 198/7 are those drawn by Marchetti. We can exclude the possibilities that there were either three or no intercalations in our period. Whether there were one or two, and if two, whether the first was before or after 197 depends on further considerations.

There are in fact three reasons which lead me to think, with Marchetti, that there were two intercalations, and that the first of these was in 193/2.

(i) Zonaras,[3] summarizing Dio, reports a total eclipse of the sun just before the battle of Zama. There was in fact a partial eclipse on 19 October 202. The defeat of Vermina is recorded by L.[4] as having taken place on the first day of the *Saturnalia*—December 17. Marchetti calculates about 10 days as the interval between Zama and the defeat of Vermina. With two intercalations between 203 and 190 17 December 202/1 = 1 November 202 (Jul.), with only one intercalation 23 November 202. In other words, the interval between the Julian date of the eclipse and the Roman date for the defeat of Vermina accords better with the hypothesis of two intercalations rather than one. Objections can be raised—the

---

[1] xxxiii. 3. 1.

[2] Pol. xviii. 10. 4, L. xxxii. 36. 8.

[3] ix. 14. 7. This argument, the least impressive of the three, is taken directly from Marchetti (1973), 481 ff.

[4] xxx. 36. 8.

evidence comes from Zonaras alone and the eclipse was not in fact total. But if the notice is genuine and it is not a pure fluke that there was a small partial eclipse at the time mentioned by Zonaras, then we must agree that a date of 23 November for the defeat of Vermina would allow an improbably long interval between the battle of Zama and that event.

(ii) In 217 a *uer sacrum* had been vowed and it was performed in 195.[1] In 194 it was declared to have been incorrectly performed and was repeated with the provision (in McDonald's text) *uer sacrum uideri pecus quod natum esset inter kal. Martias et pridie kal. Maias P. Cornelio et Ti. Sempronio consulibus.*[2] *pridie kal.* is the reading of Mg, *id.* (expanded to *idus* in φL) of Bχ. Heurgon[3] argued that P. Licinius Crassus, the *pontifex maximus*, will have chosen the Kalends of March after consulting his archives on the performance of the *uer sacrum*, and that as the feast of Mars, that was the appropriate date. He may be right, but on the other hand the *uer sacrum* was vowed to Jupiter, not Mars,[4] and there is the additional problem that the Kalends of March fell in the consulship of Cato and Flaccus, not in that of Scipio and Sempronius Longus. Heurgon argues that the consular date would not have stood in the decree as it would have been obvious that the reference was to the current year, and implies that it was added by a historian writing after 153, who had forgotten that in 194 the consuls entered office on the Ides of March, not the Kalends of January. But while it may seem obvious that the reference is to animals already born and now to be slaughtered, not to those to be born in the coming March–May period (as is clear anyway from *natum esset*), and I can produce no parallel, a consular date seems to me perfectly natural in a *s.c.* of this kind, and in that case we should consider reading *id. Mart.* for *kal. Mart. id. Mai.* in F would then have arisen from a transposition of *id.* and *kal.*

Now the dates in the *s.c.* (continuing to read *kal. Mart.*) are equivalent to 31 October or 22 November 195, and to 1 or 23 January 194. Not very many animals would have been born in this period and the loss to farmers of fulfilling the vow would not have been great. We must now consider the connection of the *uer sacrum* with the dislocation of the calendar. First, though, we may wonder why Crassus first declared to the pontifical college that the performance in 195 had not been satisfactory. As Heurgon points out, the original vow in 217 had gone to most unusual lengths in stating that all sorts of contingencies and mistakes should not

---

[1] xxii. 9. 10–10. 6, xxxiii. 44. 1–2.
[2] xxxiv. 44. 3.
[3] *Trois études sur le Ver Sacrum* (Brussels, 1957), 45 ff.
[4] xxii. 10. 3.

constitute non-fulfilment of the vow, and most of the obvious loopholes which would have permitted a claim that the due rites had not been performed had been closed in advance.[1] Heurgon suggested that Cato, devoted to the prosperity of Italian agriculture and sympathizing with the losses that would be suffered, was less than whole-hearted in seeing that the terms of the vow were adhered to. Crassus' move, backed by the pontifical college, should probably be seen as aimed at discrediting Cato. On two other occasions in this period Crassus can be seen to have used his office for political reasons, and in all three the objects of his attack are people whom I would argue are opponents of the Scipios, while Crassus is a Scipionic supporter.[2]

Crassus, then, would appear to have scored a point against Cato and then secured the performance of the vow *rite* without causing further loss to farmers by choosing dates which were theoretically *uer* but which, because of the dislocation of the calendar, in fact correspond to winter months. Marchetti[3] appears to suggest that intercalation had been omitted since 203 with the deliberate aim of celebrating the *uer sacrum* at a time when it would cause minimum dislocation and yet still meet the requirements of the vow.[4] This is scarcely believable: what would be more readily believable is that the circumstances surrounding the repetition of the *uer sacrum* led to a greater realization of the degree of dislocation of the calendar and to an intercalation at the end of the following consular year.

(iii) Under the year 193 B.C. L. reports measures to deal with an increasing debt problem. *Socii* who had made loans to Roman citizens after the festival of the *Feralia quae proxime fuissent* were to declare those loans, and litigation about them was to take place *quibus debitor uellet legibus*.[5] The *Feralia* was a festival of the dead, held on 21 February. Is it the *Feralia* of 194/3, or that of 193/2 that is meant? The events appear to have been taking place near the end of 193/2, and if it is the *Feralia* of 194/3 that are in question the senate would have been making a retrospective decision covering a period of nearly a year, and that would seem very unfair to the creditors. Against this it might be argued that the time between the *Feralia* of 193/2 and the date of these decisions is too short for the large number of debts which the consequent declarations revealed.

---

[1] xxii. 10. 4–6.
[2] cf. xxxi. 9. 7, xxxvii. 51. 1–6 n. For the composition of the pontifical college see my forthcoming article in *ANRW*, ii. 30.
[3] (1973), 495–6.
[4] Cato and Flaccus may well have chosen dates corresponding to the actual spring. On the date of Cato's departure for Spain cf. pp. 65–6.
[5] xxxv. 7. 2–5: cf. nn. ad loc.

But it may be that it was precisely the amount of debt contracted in so short a period that caused alarm, and I am inclined to think that it is 193/2 that is meant.[1]

It has been argued by Michels[2] that when the *Fasti Triumphales* date a triumph by the *Quirinalia* (17 February) or the *Terminalia* (23 February) the year in question was intercalary. In 167/6 L. dates the triumph of L. Anicius to the *Quirinalia* and states a little later that the year was intercalary.[3] There is a similar date in the *Fasti* for 175/4 as well as five in the fourth and third centuries.[4] This may seem rather thin evidence, but, as Michels stresses, there are no other dates used in this way in the *Fasti*. The point of the procedure is that the *Quirinalia* and the *Terminalia* would be *a.d. viii* and *prid. kal. intercalarias* with an intercalation after 23 February (a 22-day intercalation) but *a.d. ix* and *a.d. iii kal. intercalarias* with an intercalation after 24 February (a 23-day intercalation). Of course, in a reference back to the date, it would be known when intercalation had taken place, and precise dates were available. But in, say, a contract dated after the Ides of February there might be uncertainty about the length of intercalation in a particular year, and hence dates were made by the fixed points of the festivals. An inscription from Capua dating to *a.d. x Terminalia*[5] suggests that the festivals were used to indicate dates other than the festivals themselves. I suspect, in fact, that because of the possible uncertainty, there was a general reluctance to date by the Kalends of the intercalary month.[6] In the case of the *Feralia* there is no such evidence for its use to date events between the Ides of February and the intercalary Kalends, but it is, I think, not unreasonable to use this passage of L. as supporting evidence for an intercalation in 193/2.

Of my three arguments none, taken alone, is compelling. Cumulatively, their force is greater.

I can offer no convincing explanation for the omission of intercalation. Marchetti's suggestion concerning the *uer sacrum* is improbable. De Sanctis[7] argued from Macrobius' statement[8] *uerum*

---

[1] If the *Feralia* had been later than the *s.c.* we should have expected *futura essent* (cf. Cic. *Fam.* viii. 8. 6): for *proxime fuissent* of a date prior to the *s.c.* cf. Pliny, *Epp.* viii. 6. 13.

If my argument does not commend itself, it would follow that the intercalation should be placed in 194/3. The argument from the *uer sacrum* would not be inconsistent with such a conclusion.

[2] Op. cit. (p. 18 n. 1), 171 ff.　　　　　　　　　　　　　　　　[3] xlv. 43. 1, 44. 3.

[4] *Fast. Triumph.* s.a. 361/0, 350/49, 322/1, 276/5, 273/2.

[5] *ILLRP* 719: for the context cf. M. W. Frederiksen, *Abhandlungen der Akademie der Wissenschaften in Göttingen, philologisch–historische Klasse* 3, xcvii (1976), 350 ff.

[6] The only example I can find of such a date is Cicero, *Quinct.* 79.

[7] iv. 1. 37.　　　　　　　　　　　　　　　　　　　　　　　　　　[8] i. 14. 1.

DATES OF THE IDES OF MARCH
203–188

	No Intercalations	1 Intercalation (191/0)	2 Intercalations (193/2, 191/0)	3 Intercalations (201/0, 197/6, 193/2)	2 Intercalations (203/2, 191/0)
203	30 March	7 March	13 Feb.	21 Jan.	12 Feb.
	203	203	203	203	203
202	20 March	25 Feb.	3 Feb.	11 Jan.	25 Feb.
	202	202	202	202	201
201	10 March	15 Feb.	24 Jan.	1 Jan.	15 Feb.
	201	201	201	201	201
200	28 Feb.	5 Feb.	14 Jan.	14 Jan.	5 Feb.
	200	200	200	200	200
199	18 Feb.	26 Jan.	4 Jan.	4 Jan.	26 Jan.
	199	199	199	199	199
198	8 Feb.	16 Jan.	25 Dec.	25 Dec.	16 Jan.
	198	198	199	199	198
197	29 Jan.	6 Jan.	15 Dec.	15 Dec.	6 Jan.
	197	197	198	198	197
196	18 Jan.	26 Dec.	4 Dec.	26 Dec.	26 Dec.
	196	197	197	197	197
195	8 Jan.	16 Dec.	24 Nov.	16 Dec.	16 Dec.
	195	196	196	196	195
194	29 Dec.	6 Dec.	14 Nov.	6 Dec.	6 Dec.
	195	195	195	195	195
193	19 Dec.	26 Nov.	4 Nov.	26 Nov.	26 Nov.
	194	194	194	194	194
192	8 Dec.	15 Nov.	15 Nov.	8 Dec.	15 Nov.
	193	193	193	193	193
191	28 Nov.	5 Nov.	5 Nov.	28 Nov.	5 Nov.
	192	192	192	192	192
190	18 November, 191				
189	8 November, 190				
188	19 November, 189				

fuit tempus cum propter superstitionem intercalatio omnis omissa est that there was a belief that the length of the Hannibalic war was fixed in years and that intercalation would add to the length of the war. But there is no evidence for such a belief and in any case, such a view scarcely explains why intercalation should be omitted after the end of the Hannibalic war. Nor is there much to be said for the view that intercalation was omitted in order not to have consuls entering office at the very beginning of the campaigning season.[1] That could much more easily have been achieved, as it was in 153, by altering the date of entry into office, and if it had been the intention, the situation was allowed to go too far.

5. CHRONOLOGY

It will be convenient to use the preceding discussion as a framework for determining the chronology of events from 195 to 190.[2]

Book xxxiv

The consuls of 195/4 entered office on 24 November 196. The debate on the repeal of the *Lex Oppia* cannot be dated: Cato did not go to Spain until late summer and his campaign continued into 194.[3] Flamininus' campaign against Nabis occupied the summer of 195 (22. 4—41). The consuls of 194/3 entered office (43. 1) on 14 November 195 (43. 1) and as we have seen the *uer sacrum* was performed between then and 1 January 194. The campaign of Sempronius in Gaul (46–7) took place at the height of summer (47. 5). In Greece, Flamininus had spent the winter of 195/4 on political arrangements (48. 2) and the meeting of the representatives of the Greek states at Corinth (48. 3—50) took place at the beginning of spring 194 (48. 3). He then spent some time in Thessaly (51) and his return to Rome and triumph will come at the end of summer.[4] The temple of Fortuna Primigenia was probably dedicated on 25 May 194/3 = 23 January 194, that of Veiovis on the island on 1 January 194/3 = 5 September 194, that of Iuno Sospita on 1 February 194/3 = 4 October 194, and that of Faunus on 13 February 194/3 = 16 October 194.[5] The *Megalesia* referred to in 54. 2 took place on 4 April 194/3 = 4 December 195. The consuls of 193/2 entered office on 4 November 194 (55. 1). The war in Liguria (56) cannot be securely dated.

---

[1] E. Cavaignac, *Klio* xiv (1915), 38–9, Derow (1973), 348 n. 12.

[2] For eastern events much of what follows is taken directly from Walbank, *Philip V*, 326 ff., where further references will be found. I have accepted the implications of L.'s chronological links in non-Polybian sections except where they can be shown to be false. I do not mean to imply complete confidence in their reliability (cf. *De Sanctis*, iv. 1. 390).

[3] Cf. pp. 65–6.

[4] Walbank, *Philip V*, 326.

[5] Cf. 53. 3–7, xxxi. 21. 12 nn.

Antiochus had invaded Thrace in 195 (25. 2) and perhaps again in 194.[1] He despatched Hegesianax and Menippus to Rome in the autumn of that year, and the debate in chs. 57–9 should also be placed in the autumn, since the Roman envoys sent in return arrived at the same time as Antiochus began his Pisidian campaign *principio ueris*.[2] The events at Carthage (60–2) belong to the summer–autumn of 194 with the consequent Roman embassy in the spring of 193.

Book xxxv

The events in Spain described in 1. 1–2 belong to 194, those in the rest of the chapter to 193;[3] the events in Gaul and Liguria in chs. 3–6 cannot be precisely dated but it is clear from 6. 1–7 that they continued until near the time of the consular elections for 192/1— i.e. September–October 193. The senatorial decisions on debt in ch. 7 date from the end of the year.[4] The dedication of the temple of Victoria (9. 6) took place on 1 August 193/2 = 12 April 193; but the events recorded in 9. 1–5 may belong to later in the year in which case *iisdem diebus* at 9. 6 is inaccurate.[5] The fighting in Liguria in ch. 11 is said to be *extremo anni*, perhaps in October 193.[6]

The Aetolian meeting referred to in 12. 3 is the *Panaetolica* of spring 193. But Dicaearchus' mission to Antiochus (12. 15–17) comes after the events in Asia described in chs. 14–19, since Alexander of Acarnania shows no knowledge of his mission.[7] Nabis' siege of Gytheum can be placed in autumn 193.[8] The decisions made by the senate at the beginning of the consular year 192/1 (ch. 20) belong to November 193. The return of the Roman ambassadors to Antiochus occurred about the same time (20. 14, 22. 1). The date of the departure of the consuls for the north (22.

---

[1] L. refers only to an expedition in 195 (xxxiv. 33. 12). Appian, *Syr.* 6. 21–3 relates an expedition which ends with Antiochus returning to Ephesus and sending Hegesianax and Menippus to Rome. Hence it is assumed (cf. Leuze, *Hermes* lviii [1923], 205 ff., Walbank, *Philip V*, 326) that there were two expeditions, conflated by Appian, with only the first mentioned by L. It is in fact just as likely that Appian has simply run together the expedition of 195 with the despatch of Menippus and Hegesianax in 194. The fact that Antiochus spent the winter of 194/3 at Raphia (xxxv. 13. 4) is consistent with either hypothesis.

[2] xxxv. 13. 6. Walbank, *Philip V*, 326 wrongly places the arrival of the Roman *legati* in late summer.

[3] Cf. xxxv. 1. 1 n.

[4] They follow decisions concerning the holding of the elections.

[5] Cf. xxxv. 9. 6 n.

[6] Though one can put little trust in L.'s account of this episode: cf. xxxv. 11 n.

[7] Cf. xxxv. 18. 4 n.

[8] I see no difficulty in letting the siege last through the winter: *contra* see Walbank, *Philip V*, 327.

3–4) and of the events in Spain in 22. 5–8 cannot be determined. The elections for 191/0 took place early (24. 1), though how early we cannot tell. Baebius will have crossed to Greece in autumn 192 (24. 7).[1] The events in Greece described in chs. 25–31 took place in the first few months of 192, preceding the *Panaetolica* of 192 (32. 7).[2] The events of chs. 34–9 will cover April–June 192. The senatorial decisions in ch. 41 belong to the end of the year— perhaps October 192. The dedication of the temple of Veiovis on the Capitol (41. 8) is probably March 7 192/1 = 28 October 192.[3] Antiochus crossed to Greece (ch. 43) in October 192, and the succeeding events occupy November and early December.

Book xxxvi

The war vote against Antiochus and subsequent decisions (chs. 1–3) will come in November–December 192. (The consuls entered office on 5 November 192.) The war vote is taken without knowledge of the Delium episode.[4] In Greece the events up to ch. 10 belong to December and January; at 6. 9 we are in the middle of winter.[5] We need not allow too much time for the alleged revels at Chalcis (ch. 11).[6] Glabrio left Rome on 3 May 191/0 = 27 December 192 and ordered his troops to marshal at Brindisi on 15 May 191/0 = 4 January 191. I follow those who place the battle of Thermopylae *c.* 24 April 191.[7] The siege of Heraclea then begins at the end of May and lasts 24 days (23. 6). Philip's siege of Lamia (24) is contemporary with the siege of Heraclea. The negotiations with the Aetolians (27–9) come in July and the siege of Naupactus (30. 6, 34. 2) in August and September. Flamininus' dealings with the Achaeans (31–2) and Philip's acquisition of Demetrias, Dolopia, Aperantia, and Perrhaebia (33) fall at the same time. The Epirote embassy to Glabrio (35. 8–10) follows the lifting of the siege of Naupactus.

If my emendation of 37. 1 is right, we can place the dedication of the temple of Magna Mater on 10 April 191/0 = 1 December 192; the campaigns of Minucius and Nasica in the north (38) cannot be precisely dated. The naval events leading to the battle of Corycus (41–5) can be dated by the synchronisms in 42. 3 (referring to the sieges of Heraclea and Lamia) and 43. 1 (referring

---

[1] Walbank, *Philip V*, 328. [2] Walbank, *Philip V*, 327.
[3] Cf. xxxi. 21. 12 n. [4] Cf. xxxvi. 3. 12 n.
[5] Cf. Pédech, 463. [6] Cf. xxxvi. 11. 1–4 n.
[7] See Walbank, *Philip V*, 329 ff., *Commentary*, iii. 732–3.

to the siege of Naupactus). The battle itself can be dated to September/October: soon after it winter was approaching (45. 8).[1]

Book xxxvii

The consuls of 190/89 entered office on 18 November 191. The reception of the Aetolian envoys (1. 1–6) and the subsequent decisions (1. 7—2) will have followed immediately. Scipio's army was ordered to marshal at Brindisi on 15 July 190/89 = 18 March 190. The naval commander L. Aemilius Regillus left at the same time. The events in Aetolia described in 4. 6–7. 7 will have taken place in April. The Roman army reached the Hellespont in October —the month of March, during which Africanus, as a *Salius*, could not move, began on 25 October 190. Of the naval and land events in Asia described in chs. 9–32 the defeat of the Rhodians at Panhormus comes in March/April (9. 5),[2] the battle of Side (22–24) in mid-summer (23. 2), the battle of Myonnesus (27–30)[3] will be in September (cf. the synchronism in 33. 1), the fall of Phocaea at the end of October (32. 14 n.). The battle of Magnesia itself took place in December 190.[4]

The date of the triumph of Glabrio (46. 2–6) cannot be determined. The statement at 47. 3 that the news of both the battle of Myonnesus and of Scipio's crossing into Asia arrived at Rome shortly before the consular elections cannot be accepted since the army did not cross until the end of the consular year.[5] The consuls of 189 entered office (48. 1) on 8 November 190: the Aetolian embassy, if the episode has not been misplaced by L. was received in the senate shortly after this (49).[6] The news of the battle of Magnesia (51. 8–9) will have arrived in January/February 189. The embassies from the East were received (52–6) in the summer.[7] The news of events in Liguria is said to have arrived at the same time (57.1). The censorial elections (57. 9–58. 2) are said to be contemporaneous with the return of Regillus: he triumphed on 1 February 189/8

---

[1] Walbank, *Philip V*, 331 placed it in September, since he then accepted Holleaux's view that Polybius' winter began with the autumn equinox: cf. *Historia* xxvi (1977), 248–50.

[2] At 16. 14 Livius' return to Greece is synchronized with the time the Scipios are in Thessaly—i.e. May.

[3] The use of xl. 52. 4 and Macr. i. 10. 10 to date the battle to 24 August (Leuze, *Hermes* lviii [1923], 283–7, following Mommsen) is quite illegitimate. The former passage does not mean that Regillus dedicated the temple on the anniversary of the battle.

[4] Walbank, *Philip V*, 332.

[5] Cf. n. ad loc.

[6] Cf. 49. 6 n.

[7] Pol. xxi. 18. 1.

(58. 4) = 16 September 189, and Lucius Scipio triumphed *mense intercalario pr. kal. Mart.* (59. 2) = 5 November 189. Labeo's activities in Crete (60) cannot be dated.

6. THE OUTBREAK OF THE SYRIAN WAR[1]

The events that led to the war with Antiochus do not present problems of the complexity that beset the study of the origins of the Second Macedonian War.[2] The war is, though, of enormous importance in Rome's progress towards complete domination of the Mediterranean world, and it may be useful to present my assessment of the motives of Rome and Antiochus and, in particular, to discuss some of the views put forward by Badian in an influential article published in 1959.[3]

It will be generally agreed that Antiochus was not aiming at conquest of Italy nor Rome at destruction of the Seleucid Empire.[4] The most plausible interpretation of Antiochus' aims involves accepting the professions he made at Lysimachia in 196, and through the mouths of his representatives at Rome and Ephesus in 194–3.[5] His purpose was to reconstitute the Empire as it had stood at the death of Seleucus I. That had been the purpose, and result, of his great Eastern expedition of 212 to 205.[6] In the West, it meant reasserting control of Asia Minor and Thrace, the latter having, in Antiochus' view, passed to Seleucus as a result of his victory over Lysimachus at the battle of Corupaedium. Antiochus could not, on this basis, have asserted a claim to control the Greek mainland. That is not to say, though, that he did not welcome any opportunity that arose to increase his influence outside his empire.[7]

The senate did not accept alleged rights derived from ancestral possessions:[8] for them it was the existing situation that counted. That is made abundantly clear by Flamininus to Hegesianax

[1] For bibliography cf. Will, *ANRW*, i. 1. 590 ff.; see also Harris, 219 ff. For an analysis of Polybius' picture of the causes of the war cf. Pédech, 166 ff. I forbear from discussing Schlag's view that the war was deliberately provoked by a group led by P. Sulpicius Galba: see my comments in *Latomus* xxxi (1972), 39.
[2] See vol. i, 36 ff.
[3] 'Rome and Antiochus the Great: a study in cold war', *CPh* liv (1959), 81 ff. = *Studies*, 112 ff.
[4] Though Petzold, 96 ff. comes near to the latter view.
[5] xxxiv. 57. 10, xxxv. 16. 2–6.
[6] Cf. Schmitt, *Antiochos*, 86 ff.
[7] Cf. my comments on the policies of the Antigonids in the third century in *Imperialism in the Ancient World* (ed. P. D. A. Garnsey and C. R. Whittaker, Cambridge, 1978), 145 ff.
[8] Cf. xxxiii. 40. 4–6 n.

(xxxiv. 58. 10) and by Sulpicius to Minnio (xxxv. 16. 8–13). The initial disagreement between Rome and Antiochus arose from a number of factors. The senate was aware that its claims to have fought Philip in order to defend Greek freedom would look hollow if they allowed Antiochus to destroy the freedom of the Asiatic Greeks. But more than that, there was a fear that Antiochus' crossings into Europe were indeed the precursor of an invasion of Greece. That was unacceptable for two reasons. Firstly, Roman *dignitas* was involved in the maintenance of the settlement that she had imposed on Greece: secondly, there was the fear of an invasion of Italy itself.[1] The invasions of Pyrrhus and Hannibal had left a lasting effect on Roman attitudes, and Romans, like Greeks, constantly overestimated the resources at the disposal of Eastern rulers.[2]

By the time of the conference of Rome in 194/3, the first of these factors had given way in importance to the other two. Flamininus' compromise offer—that, if Antiochus kept out of Europe, Rome would not bother about Asia,[3]—represented a willingness completely to abandon the Asiatic Greeks to Antiochus. It was on this issue that compromise was impossible. Antiochus would not renounce what he regarded as his ancestral rights in Thrace, and Rome would not tolerate his presence west of the Hellespont. Since neither would give way, conflict was in the end inevitable. That does not mean that either side was looking for a war. The senate was willing to try and get its way by negotiations since it was Rome that would have to act; Antiochus could allow his military preparations to proceed gradually. But in the last analysis Rome was ready to enforce her demands militarily, and Antiochus was not prepared to withdraw in face of threats of military intervention. It is for that reason that I cannot accept Badian's description of the period from 196 to 192 as 'cold war' and his view that both sides were eager to avoid war but war came about as the result of a series of accidents.

What is true is that on this analysis war might have been expected to come when Rome despaired of negotiations and responded to one of Antiochus' Thracian invasions with force. In fact Antiochus invaded Greece when he did, despite his lack of adequate forces, because he had been misled by Thoas about the degree of support for him in Greece.[4] He probably felt that if he did not intervene

[1] It would be wrong to rationalize the first reason as really amounting to fear that if the settlement of Greece were disturbed, a threat to Italy would follow. For similar factors at other times cf. *Imperialism in the Ancient World*, 150.

[2] Cf. xxxv. 32. 4 n.

[3] xxxiv. 58. 2–3 n.

[4] xxxv. 42. 5–6, 49. 4, xxxvi. 7. 12, 15. 2.

himself, Rome would herself use force to re-establish the position in Greece and would then be in a far stronger position to enforce her demands in respect of Thrace. It had not been his original intention to invade Greece; he might, as I have said, have expected Rome to make the first move. He could re-affirm his position by continuing his incursions into Thrace, and for that large forces were not necessary. But that does not mean that until his decision to invade Greece he had not been contemplating the use of force to resist Rome's demands.

To a considerable extent Badian's case depends on his interpretation of three passages in L. After the abortive negotiations at Ephesus L. describes the conference held by Antiochus and concludes *ex consilio ita discessum est ut bellum gereretur*.[1] Badian calls this 'patently absurd' because of the inadequacy of the king's forces when he did invade Greece.[2] But L. does not say that Antiochus decided to make war at once. What he means is that the *consilium* decided that Rome's demands could not be accepted, and that, in Antiochus' judgement, this meant that, sooner or later, war would come. Antiochus would continue his excursions across the Hellespont[3] and he finally agreed to create a diversion in Africa.[4] It was not to be on the scale that Hannibal wanted[5] but it was clearly an act of aggression. To say, as Badian does,[6] that such a move 'was intended to avoid war for the king himself rather than to bring it about' and that 'there was no reason to think that Antiochus' very limited participation in the venture would tempt the Romans into that attack on him which they had shown every sign of wanting to avoid' is to misconceive what the Roman response to such action would have been.

Secondly, the Roman ambassadors on their return from Ephesus reported *nihil quod satis maturam causam belli haberet nisi aduersus Lacedaemonium tyrannum*.[7] Badian says 'the Roman envoys sensibly reported that they had seen no preparations for war'.[8] What L. means is that there were not yet sufficient reasons for declaring war on Antiochus. Naturally the measures which the senate took immediately were 'purely defensive',[9] for Rome must not appear as an aggressor. To go to war simply on the grounds that Antiochus had again invaded Thrace would appear inadequate—even though he had now, if not earlier, captured Thracian states freed from

---

[1] xxxv. 19. 7.
[2] *Studies*, 129. Cf. Aymard, *RPh* 3ème série, xiv (1940), 94 n. 1.
[3] As he did in 192: cf. xxxv. 23. 10 n.
[4] xxxv. 42. 3 ff.   [5] Cf. xxxiv. 60. 5.   [6] *Studies*, 133.
[7] xxxv. 22. 2.   [8] *Studies*, 128.   [9] Ibid., 129.

Philip.[1] If Antiochus were to make, as he finally did, a pre-emptive strike into Greece, the senate's moral case would be immeasurably stronger. But it is wrong to regard the measures taken by the senate as insubstantial. The details given by L. are unacceptable.[2] But the force under Baebius was ready to contain the challenge if it came and large forces were being made ready for the spring: the elections were held early[3] so that the new consul could leave as soon as possible.

Thirdly, Badian says that the Aetolian decree inviting the Aetolians into Greece[4] 'merely called upon Antiochus to free Greece and arbitrate between the Aetolian League and Rome'.[5] This is indeed the interpretation that Phaeneas wanted to put on the decree[6] but the opposite view prevailed, and it was doubtless the first part of the decree that was used as the final lever to persuade Antiochus to come to Greece.[7] Of course, if Rome had agreed to Antiochus' demands on behalf of the Aetolians, war would have been avoided. But nobody could possibly imagine that she would do so, and thus the decree was tantamount to a declaration of war.[8]

7. ROMAN POLICY IN NORTHERN ITALY AND SPAIN

(a) *Northern Italy*[9]

Rome had completed her conquest south of a line between Rimini and Pisa by 272. Whether the senate would have immediately proceeded to extend Roman domination into Northern Italy and was prevented only by the First Punic War, and, if so, whether it regarded the peoples of Northern Italy as a threat to the security of the area already conquered or was motivated by a desire for expansion for its own sake are not questions that can profitably be entered into. What is clear is that the Gallic invasion of Roman territory in 225[10] was met by a deliberate and successful attempt to conquer the Po valley in the following years, culminating in the establishment, in 218, of colonies at Placentia and Cremona. The area was, of course, immediately lost to Hannibal. It would be hard to believe that after the battle of Zama the senate would have been

---

[1] Cf. xxxvii. 60. 7 n.   [2] See p. 37.   [3] xxxv. 24. 1 ff.
[4] xxxv. 33. 8.   [5] *Studies*, 131.   [6] xxxv. 45. 3.
[7] xxxv. 42. 5.
[8] I see no evidence for Badian's statement (*Studies*, 131) that Damocritus had promised Menippus not to declare war.
[9] The best discussion of these events is by Toynbee, ii. 260 ff. See also Lauterbach, *passim*, McDonald, *Antichthon* viii (1974), 44 ff., Harris, 210 ff., 225 ff.
[10] For the sources for events from 225 to 222 see *MRR*, i. 230 ff.

content to leave the area outside Roman control. If L. sometimes describes Roman actions as being motivated by Gallic attacks, we may justifiably refuse to believe him, at least as far as the beginning of the process goes.[1] Once the Gauls realized that it was again Rome's purpose to conquer their lands, they would naturally do their best to hit back.

In the period covered by books xxxiv–xxxvii L. records Roman conflicts with three peoples, Insubres, Boii, and Ligurians. The Insubres lived in the neighbourhood of Milan, the Boii between the Po and Bologna.[2] The Ligurians in question are those living in the area of the Apuan Alps between Genoa and Pisa: the Ligurians who lived on the riviera to the west of Genoa appear to have come to an agreement with Rome in 201.[3]

Despite the substantial victories over the Boii and the Insubres reported by L. under 196 (xxxiii. 36–7), neither people capitulated.[4] But no more is heard of the Insubres after L. Valerius Flaccus' victory over them in 194 (xxxiv. 46. 1).[5] Further conflicts with the Boii are recorded every year from 195 to 192 (195: xxxiv. 22. 1–3. 194: xxxiv. 46–48. 1. 193: xxxv. 4–5. 192: xxxv. 22. 4, 40. 3) and in 191 P. Scipio Nasica appears to have won a decisive victory leading to the final capitulation of the Boii. A substantial amount of land was confiscated from them and a colony settled at Bologna in 189 (xxxvi. 38. 5–7, xxxvii. 2. 5, 47. 1–2, 57. 7–8).

The Apuan Ligurians are first heard of in these years as launching a major and unexpected attack on Pisa in 193 (xxxiv. 56, xxxv. 3, 11). Q. Minucius Thermus, the consul of 193, remained in the area until 191 (xxxv. 20. 6, 21. 7–11, xxxvi. 38. 1–4, 40. 2) and in 190 misleadingly claimed that Ligurian resistance was at an end (xxxvii. 2. 5).

---

[1] e.g. xxxi. 2. 5. I cannot accept Schlag's view (40 ff.) that most Roman commanders in the 190s embarked on unprovoked raids merely to increase their own military glory and that Nasica's total defeat of the Boii in 191 represent a completely different policy. It is much more reasonable to think that Roman policy was to weaken the Boii by sporadic raids until the final blow could be delivered (cf. McDonald, op. cit., 50 ff.).

[2] Cf. xxxi. 2. 5, 10. 2 nn.

[3] xxxi. 2. 11. For possible hostility in 189 cf. xxxvii. 57. 1–2 n.

[4] I cannot follow McDonald's view that the defeat of 196 eradicated the southern Boii and that subsequent attacks were directed against the northern Boii. McDonald's view forces him to separate the foundation of Bononia from the land confiscated from the Boii at xxxvi. 39. 3. The *silua Litana*, moreover, is to be located near Bononia (xxxiv. 22. 1 n.).

[5] It is remarkable that the decisive victories over the Insubres and the Boii are reported extremely briefly while other less significant episodes are 'written up'. Cf. p. 7.

(b) *Spain*[1]

Uncertainty both about the precise extent of Roman control in Spain at the end of the Second Punic War and about the precise location of several of the places mentioned by L. makes it difficult to assess how far Roman commanders in the 190s were fighting outside the existing boundaries and seeking to extend the area subject to Rome. *A priori*, though, it is reasonable to think that Roman governors did not regard their provinces as having a fixed boundary with the hinterland and that the senate did not look with disfavour on attempts to extend the area of Roman domination.[2]

There is no need to doubt that the senate genuinely believed that a major rebellion had broken out in Spain in 197 and that at the beginning of the consular year 195/4 it held that the situation was serious enough to justify the sending of a consular army. The position may not in fact have been as serious as L. implies and Cato himself may well have exaggerated it in order to justify his own actions. He did not leave for Spain as early as was expected and news of a victory by Q. Minucius Thermus reduced fears in Rome.[3] It would be wrong to conclude, however, that most of the area north of the Ebro was not still in a state of rebellion when Cato arrived and that, as Schlag claims, all Cato did was to make a journey round Citerior and into previously unconquered territory, regulating affairs and amassing booty.[4] His operations against the Celtiberians (xxxiv. 19. 9–11) certainly involved operations outside the existing boundaries, though there is no reason to doubt that some Celtiberians had served as mercenaries in the army of the Turdetani (xxxiv. 19. 2–8).

In 194 there were further rebellions in Citerior[5] and in 193 P. Scipio Nasica attacked Lusitanians who had invaded Ulterior.[6] One may well wonder whether the attack did not in fact

---

[1] On events in Spain see Götzfried, 50 ff., Schulten, *FHA*, iii. 177 ff., *CAH*, viii, ch. 10, Badian, *FC*, 118 ff., Schlag, 22 ff., Astin, *Cato*, ch. iii, Harris, 209. Sumner's reassertion of his view that Spain was not divided into Citerior and Ulterior at this period (*CPh* lxxii [1977], 126–30) convinces me no more than his earlier argument (cf. vol. i. 345: Sumner's reference to that page [op. cit., 126 n. 3] is most puzzling).

[2] Schlag's attempt, however, to place virtually all the events recorded by L. outside the existing provinces, and to see the commanders of the period as motivated mainly by a desire for plunder, is extreme and in several instances depends on misinterpretation of the evidence.

[3] On events in 197 and 196 see xxxiii. 21. 6–9 n.

[4] Schlag, 34–6: Astin, loc. cit., gives a well-balanced account of Cato's campaign.

[5] xxxv. 1. 1 n.

[6] xxxv. 1. 5: Schlag, 37, has mistranslated the Latin and makes the Lusitanians attack Scipio who is transporting *ingens praeda*.

take place outside the province.[1] In the same year Flaminius'
conflict with the Oretani was clearly outside his province, though
conceivably inside Ulterior.[2] But the governor of Ulterior, M.
Fulvius Nobilior, was certainly going well outside the existing
province when he defeated the Vaccaei, the Vettones, and the
Celtiberians near Toledo. These peoples' homelands were in fact
a good way from Toledo—perhaps they were provoked by Fulvius'
invasion.[3] The same two governors remained in office in 192.
Flaminius' attack on Licabrum can again not be firmly placed
either inside or outside Citerior: indeed, if Schulten's identification
of Licabrum is correct, he is again fighting in Ulterior.[4] Fulvius
was inside his province when he captured Vescelia and Helo, but
his subsequent attack on the Oretani was certainly outside the existing boundaries.[5] L. has no report of events in Spain in 191.[6] In 190
Aemilius Paullus' conflict with the Bastetani can be inside Ulterior,
but his defeat of the Lusitanians in 189 is certainly outside the
province.[7]

8. ROMAN LEGIONS[8]

195–194. In 195 Cato and Flaccus had two legions each in Spain
and Gaul respectively. There were also two praetorian armies in
Spain and two legions remaining in Greece under Flamininus
(xxxiv. 43. 6–8). That would appear to make a total of eight legions.
In 194, however, L. reports that the armies of Cato and Flaccus
were to be disbanded and two *legiones urbanae* enrolled, producing
a total of eight legions. It would follow that there must in fact have
been ten legions in 195 and Afzelius thus assumed that the two
legiones urbanae raised in 196 (xxxiii. 25. 10) were sent to Gaul in
195 (in addition to the two legions assigned to Flaccus) and that
two of the Gallic legions of 196 went to Spain with Cato. This is,
however, unnecessary. Most of Cato's campaign in fact took place
in the consular year 194/3 (see pp. 65–6) and L. is therefore wrong
to say that his army was disbanded. We may, however, accept his

---

[1] Cf. Schulten, *CAH*, viii, 313.   [2] xxxv. 7. 7 n.   [3] xxxv. 7. 8 n.
[4] xxxv. 22. 5 n.   [5] xxxv. 22. 6–7 nn.   [6] Cf. xxxvii. 46. 7 n.
[7] xxxvii. 46. 7–8, 57. 5–6.

[8] The basis of study on these matters is Afzelius, ch. iii: cf. also Kahrstedt, ch. ii.
I do not here list the various allied contingents which accompanied the Roman
legions. Official legion numbers are given at xxxiv. 46. 12, xxxv. 5. 6, xxxvi. 3. 13,
from which it appears that the legions in Gaul continued to be numbered II and
IV, while those in Greece in 191 were I and III, as they had been under Flamininus
(cf. xxxiii. 22. 8 n.). *secundam* at xxxiv. 15. 3, however, cannot be taken as an official
number, since the events described belong to 194 (see above) and would therefore
conflict with xxxiv. 46. 12. It must mean merely 'the second of Cato's two legions'.

report of the total number of legions. It will follow that Cato's army comprised the *legiones urbanae* of 196.

193.[1] The *legiones urbanae* of 194 were sent to Liguria and two new *urbanae* enrolled (xxxiv. 56. 3–4). The consul L. Cornelius Merula had two legions with which to fight the Boii (xxxv. 5. 5 n.). The praetorian legions remained in Spain, producing once again a total of eight legions.

192–191. In 192 two legions were given to Cn. Domitius Ahenobarbus, and the two under Merula passed to L. Quinctius Flamininus. The legions in Liguria and Spain remained where they were. The two *urbanae* of 193 were given to M. Baebius, producing a total of ten legions (xxxv. 20. 4 ff.).[2]

L.'s statements on the troops that crossed to Greece for the war against Antiochus raise a number of problems.[3] At xxxv. 20. 11 Baebius is given two legions and at 24. 7 ordered to cross to Epirus *cum omnibus copiis*. At xxxv. 41. 4 L. Flamininus is ordered to raise a further 10,000 troops (4,000 citizens, 6,000 allies) for the war with Antiochus and at xxxvi. 1. 6–7 Glabrio is assigned the army that had crossed with Baebius, together with the supplementary troops raised by Flamininus. At xxxvi. 14. 1, in what is clearly a Polybian section, the MSS. say that Glabrio crossed *cum decem milibus peditum*. These statements cannot be accepted as they stand. It is clear from the narrative of xxxvi. 5–13 that no substantial Roman force was yet in Greece and Appian (*Syr.* 17. 71) gives the army that crossed with Glabrio as 20,000 infantry and 2,000 cavalry. There is, however, no need to reject the annalistic statements completely. The total of the Roman infantry assigned to Baebius and raised by Lucius Flamininus amounts to about 14,000. The army that crossed with Glabrio could well have been composed of those in Bruttium who did not cross with Baebius and the troops levied by Flamininus. The actual force that crossed with Baebius perhaps amounted to 4–5,000 in all. He detached 2,000 to Larisa under Ap. Claudius, so the total must have been somewhat larger than that[4]. It is wrong,

---

[1] There is no formal list of assignations for this year and deductions have to be made from the subsequent narrative.

[2] At xxxv. 20. 11–12, 21. 1 L. reverses the provinces of Atilius and Baebius. See the note on the former passage.

[3] On this matter see Kromayer, ii. 98 ff., 206, De Sanctis, iv. 1. 156 n. 75, Aymard, *PR*, 327 n. 14, Walbank, *Philip V*, 199 n. 6, Bredehorn, 157–9, Brunt, 657–8.

[4] App. *Syr.* 16. 68–9: cf. Kromayer, ii. 206. Walbank, *Philip V*, 199 regards Baebius' force as being only *c.* 2,000.

37

however, to amend xxxvi. 14. 1 to accord with Appian. L. may well have been trying to make his narrative consistent with the statements in xxxv. 41.[1]

In 191, then, there were two legions in Bruttium (xxxv. 41. 7, xxxvi. 2. 7), two in Liguria (cf. xxxvi. 38), two in Gaul (xxxvi. 1. 9), two in Spain (xxxvi. 2. 8–9), and two *urbanae* (xxxvi. 1. 9).

190. The legions of Glabrio passed to L. Scipio. Laelius had two new legions in Gaul. The two previous *urbanae* went to Apulia. The Ligurian legions passed to Scipio Nasica. One new legion was stationed in Etruria and the Spanish armies remained (xxxvii. 2. 2–11). L. also states (xxxvii. 2. 7) that A. Cornelius Mammula was, if L. Scipio so decided, to take his legions from Bruttium to Aetolia. He appears in Aetolia in the story of Valerius Antias reported at xxxvii. 48 and in the dispositions for 189 (xxxvii. 50. 4) it is assumed that his army is in fact there. It is clear, however, from Polybius xxi. 25. 9~L. xxxviii. 3. 9 that the army in fact crossed with M. Fulvius Nobilior in 189. It is, however, not necessary to reject the *s.c.* of xxxvii. 2. 7 since its execution was dependent on the wishes of L. Scipio. Once the truce had been arranged with the Aetolians, there was no need for it to cross immediately. L. or his source was unaware of this and assumed that when the senate made its dispositions for 189 the army was in fact in Aetolia.[2]

---

[1] It remains the case that the total number of troops under Baebius and levied by Flamininus amount to *c.* 35,400, well in excess of the actual number transported to Greece. As Brunt (658) suggests, however, it may be that it did not prove possible to levy all the troops authorized by the senate, or that Polybius gave 20,000 as the total of Glabrio's forces under the mistaken belief that the proportion of allied to Roman troops was still 1:1 (the 60,000 of Appian, *Syr.* 15. 65 is, of course, quite impossible).

[2] See Brunt, loc. cit., Walbank, *Commentary*, iii. 120.

BOOK XXXIV

195 B.C.

1–8. 3. *The Repeal of the Lex Oppia*

L. devotes a considerable amount of space—over an eighth of the whole book—to what might appear to be a comparatively minor question. Two principal problems arise.

(i) There can be no doubt that the speech of Cato is a free composition by L., and that he is not merely reworking the actual speech of Cato. Though we have fragments of a very large number of Cato's speeches, there is not a single fragment of a speech against the repeal of the *Lex Oppia*. The reverse side of the argument is that this is the only occasion (the purely conventional speech before battle at 13. 5–9 aside) that L. gives Cato a speech in *oratio recta*. Yet on three occasions he shows that he is aware of the existence of the original speech. At xxxviii. 54. 11 he refers to the speech *de pecunia regis Antiochi*; at xxxix. 42. 6–7 he mentions the extant *acerbae orationes* against those whom Cato punished during his censorship, the most severe of which was the one against L. Quinctius Flamininus; and at xlv. 25. 2–4 he says of the famous speech of Cato in 167, arguing against the proposal to declare war on Rhodes, *non inseram simulacrum uiri copiosi, quae dixerit referendo: ipsius oratio scripta exstat Originum quinto libro inclusa*. The position is clear: where Cato's speech was extant, L. could not include it. For either he would have to insert the actual speech of Cato, which would be plagiarism, or he would

39

have to invent one of his own, which L. (unlike Tacitus) felt would be absurd if the original were available. It was the same considerations—and not bias against Cicero—which prevented Sallust from including in his monograph on the Catilinarian conspiracy a version of Cicero's first Catilinarian oration. L., who wanted to put a speech into the mouth of Cato, had to find an occasion when there was no speech extant.

That conclusion, however, does not preclude the possibility that L., so adept at varying his style to fit the occasion (Quint. x. i. 101: cf. p. 10) has written a speech which deliberately copies the style of Cato. There is only one clear case of an archaism in the speech—the form *faxitis* at 4. 21, and since that occurs in a formula, and is used in similar contexts on nine occasions by L. (cf. n. ad loc.), it is of no special significance. There are two other cases (3. 5, 3. 9) where the manuscripts present a construction and a form (respectively) which are archaic. In the first of these emendation seems unwise, though the construction may be as much a colloquialism, or even an instance of anacoluthon, as a deliberate archaism. In the second, where the manuscripts are not unanimous, the supposed archaism may well be a simple corruption. (There is an inevitable element of circularity in the arguments here: those who want to believe there are archaisms will accept the readings, those who do not will dispute them.)

In a search for further Catonian elements Paschkowski (107 ff., 248 ff.) compared the speech of Cato with three other speeches in the fourth and fifth decades—that of Valerius here, and those of M. Servilius Geminus and L. Aemilius Paullus in xlv. 37–9, 41. He claims that idioms and constructions found in the works of Cato himself are far more prominent in the speech of Cato than in the other three speeches. Paschkowski's evidence must be considered on its merits, though it should be said that it would have been better if Paschkowski had analysed all the speeches in the fourth and fifth decades, and not merely chosen three as a control group.

There are six main items in Paschkowski's case:

(*a*) A demonstrative as antecedent to a *si* clause is found in Cato fr. 169M and 3. 5, but in none of the control group. This is irrelevant: the example in Cato is a true conditional, L. is using *si* in an indirect question. Cf. n. ad loc.

(*b*) In 3. 4, 3. 5, and 3. 6 there are instances of what Paschkowski calls 'umständliche und übergenaue Beziehungen', found in Cato but not in the control group. In themselves there is nothing particularly striking in these constructions: for the repeated *ut*, for example, W–M rightly compared xxii. 11. 4 (not even in a speech). What may be true is that the form of the sentences does serve to make Cato's point with particular clarity and emphasis, and that is a characteristic of the historical Cato.

(c) *ego*, in various phrases, is found seven times in Cato's speech. It occurs twice in Valerius, four times in Servilius, and not at all in Aemilius. There may be a point here. Cato was a forceful personality, given to stressing his own view, and L.'s usage could be deliberate. But if it is, it is more a general reflection of Cato's character than an imitation of a particularly striking element in his speeches. Speeches, moreover, are naturally likely to contain first (and second) person pronouns. Paschkowski refers to the fivefold anaphora of *numquam ego* in fr. 203M: but cf. e.g. Cic. *Pis.* 4–5. *ego* at 4. 21, moreover, follows a regular formula at the end of deliberative speeches: cf. n. ad loc.

(d) For the doubling of the temporal adverb in 3. 3 *extemplo simul* Paschkowski compares Cato frs. 29, 173M, and says there are no parallels in the control group. But *simul . . . extemplo* occurs at x. 35. 18, xxiii. 29. 14, xxiv. 38. 3, xxvi. 43. 4 (only the third example is in a speech). Cf. *TLL*, v. 2. 1967.

(e) Repetition of a verb in a different form (*polyptoton*), common in Cato, occurs nine times in Cato's speech, four times in Valerius, three times in Servilius, and not at all in Aemilius. This is not significant: for example, there are six repetitions in the speech of Sulpicius in xxxi. 7, and that speech is less than half the length of Cato's. It is found frequently in speeches in L. (cf. Ullmann, *Étude*, 78 ff.) and could not conceivably be meant by L. to be specifically Catonian. For *polyptoton* in the speeches in Tacitus cf. J. N. Adams, *BICS* xx (1973), 139 nn. 13–14.

(f) *nunc* to mean 'as it is' is found seven times in the works of Cato, three times in the speech of Cato, and once each in Valerius and Aemilius. I doubt very much if these figures are meaningful. The usage is so common that L. could not possibly think that its use three times in the speech would be noticed as an echo of Cato himself. (In any case, two of the examples, 2. 12 and 4. 18 can be taken as purely temporal usages. Nor do I see any grounds for Paschkowski's claim that the usage is colloquial.)

Thus, Paschkowski's case is very much less impressive than he claims. The speech of Cato in L. reads like a speech of L., and not at all like a speech of Cato. What L. may have done, however, is subtly to introduce a few phrases or idioms which are reminiscent of the historical Cato. This is quite possibly the case with the repeated use of the first person pronoun and, as we have seen, the constructions mentioned in (b) above help to produce a certain pungency which has the mark of the historical Cato. In addition Tränkle (*Cato*, 12 ff.) has drawn attention to four phrases which may originate from Cato himself—the details are discussed in the notes on 2. 13–3. 3, 3. 9, 4. 2, and 4. 3. It is noteworthy, however, that Cato's common use of *atque* before a consonant is absent from the speech, though not usually avoided by L. elsewhere.

(ii)   Why does L. choose this occasion to present a full-scale debate? Part of the answer has already been given. L. knew that Cato took part in the debate—Ennius, *Ann.* fr. 352V conceivably comes from Cato's speech—and there may even have been a speech attributed to him in one or more of the annalistic accounts: since no speech was extant, it was a good opportunity to compose a speech for Cato. More than that, though, 195 marked the first important stage in the long career of Cato (before his consulship L. mentions him only incidentally—xxix. 25. 10, xxxii. 7. 13, 8. 5, 27. 3) and the speech serves to characterize Cato. The attitudes of Cato are very typical of him: he is unbending, authoritarian, single-minded. L. admired Cato in certain ways, but has no real sympathy for his attitude. The speech of Valerius is a deliberate contrast. It is a mild, almost ironical speech and one is left with the impression—and I suspect this was L.'s intention—that Cato was not to be taken too seriously.

There is a temptation, given the subject under discussion, to see some connection with Augustus' social legislation. But it would be very rash to argue that L. was taking any particular attitude towards that legislation and there is certainly little to be said for the view of F. Hellmann (*NJAB* iii [1940], 85–6) that L. was seeking to make the point that laws could not alter human behaviour. And since Valerius appears the more attractive person, it is hard to accept Luce's view (252 ff.) that L. emphasized the subject because it illustrated the theme of the decline of Roman character caused by foreign influence.

Dio also seems to have invented speeches for the occasion: cf. Zon. ix. 17, Nissen, *KU*, 154.

On the section see E. Pais, *AAN* n.s. i (1910), 123 ff., Fraccaro, *Opuscula*, i. 115 ff., 177 ff., Ullmann, *Technique*, 6, M. Krüger, *NJAB* iii (1940), 65 ff., Hellmann, ibid., 81 ff., Skard, 89 ff., Scullard, *RP*, 257, Kienast, 21 ff. and nn., Paschkowski, 70 ff., 248 ff., J. P. V. D. Balsdon, *Roman Women* (London, 1962), 32 ff., Tränkle, *Cato*, 9–16, Schlag, 159, Astin, *Cato*, 25 ff.

It will be convenient to consider here the structures of the speeches of Cato and Valerius. In vol. i, 19 ff. I expressed reservations concerning the analyses proposed by Ullmann. In the present case it seems to me that Ullmann's attempt to divide the speeches to fit the requirements of rhetorical theory is particularly misleading.

Ullmann divides the speech of Cato as follows (*Technique*, 140–

141). (i) 2. 1–4 *prooemium*. (ii) 2. 5–4. 18 *tractatio*: (*a*) 2. 5–10 *honestum*; (*b*) 2. 11–3. 2 *tutum*; (*c*) 3. 3–9 *utile*; (*d*) 4. 1–11 *necessarium*; (*e*) 4. 12–18 *aequum*. (iii) 4. 19–21 *conclusio*. As usual, the main divisions of the speech are clear enough, though in fact 4. 19–20 are closely connected with what precedes, and I would regard only the formulaic ending at 4. 21 as the *conclusio*. But Ullmann's subdivisions of the *tractatio* are entirely artificial. The only sensible way of dividing the *tractatio* is by its arguments, not by attaching arbitrary labels (the point is forcibly made by Paschkowski, 100–1, n. 1: I differ in some respects from Paschkowski's own analysis). I suggest the following division. (*a*) 2. 5–3. 2 the behaviour of the women, the dangers inherent in it, and comparison with the past; (*b*) 3. 3–5 the law should serve the general interest; (*c*) 3. 6–9 the real motives of the women; (*d*) 4. 1–11 the dangers of the growth of *auaritia* and *luxuria* and comparison with the past; (*e*) 4. 12–20 what will happen if the law is repealed.

Ullmann divides Valerius' speech thus (*Technique*, 141–3). (i) 5. 1–3 *prooemium*. (ii) 5. 4–7. 10 *tractatio*: (*a*) 5. 4–6 *honestum*; (*b*) 5. 7–13 *tutum*; (*c*) 6. 1–6 *utile*; (*d*) 6. 7–18 *necessarium*; (*e*) 7. 1–10 *aequum*. (iii) 7. 11–15 *conclusio*. Again the division of the *tractatio* is totally misleading (cf. Paschkowski, 148 n. 1). The thematic divisions are (*a*) 5. 4–13 reply to Cato's claim that the women's actions are unprecedented; (*b*) 6. 1–18 reply to the argument that repeal of the *Lex Oppia* entails the invalidation of all laws. Valerius argues that it was passed for an emergency which no longer exists; (*c*) 7. 1–10 it is unfair to deprive women of their luxuries when others have theirs; (*d*) 7. 11–15 women do not constitute a danger to male authority. Ullmann has a certain case for labelling 7. 1–10 as *aequum* in that it contains moral rather than prudential arguments.

1. 1. bellorum magnorum . . . finitorum: for the homoioteleuton in -*orum* cf. xxiii. 15. 13, xxvi. 5. 9, Cic. *Mil.* 64, *Tusc.* iv. 53, K–St, ii. 596. *uixdum finitorum* refers only to the war with Philip: the plural is natural in a phrase of this sort, and reference to the Second Punic War is, as W–M say, out of place six years after the peace with Carthage. The *bella imminentia* are the wars with Antiochus (cf. xxxiii. 45. 1–5) and in Spain (cf. xxxiii. 21. 6–9 n.).

2. M. Fundanius: (3). Not otherwise known. He is not likely to be identical with M. Fundanius Fundulus, plebeian aedile in 213.

L. Valerius: (350). Probably L. Valerius Tappo, praetor in 192, with command prorogued in 191, and a *iiiuir* for the supplementation of Placentia and Cremona in 190, and the settlement of Bononia in 189. As a plebeian, he cannot be a close relative of the patrician Valerii, including the consul of the year, but could well be a descandant of a freedman of a Valerius, or of a person granted viritane enfranchisement on the proposal of a Valerius. In any case, it is worth noticing that we have two Valerii taking opposed views on the matter, since there can be little doubt that Flaccus supported Cato: cf. § 7 n.

ad plebem tulerunt: I see no reason for W–M's statement that the bill appears not to have been discussed in the senate before being put before the *concilium plebis*.

3. C. Oppius: (8). Oppius is known only as the author of the law under discussion. (The statement in *MRR*, i. 255 that he was possibly also the author of a law on the purchase of slaves for military purposes [cf. 6. 12] is no more than a guess.) There is no means of attaining certainty about his *praenomen*. Bχ have *M.*, Mg had *C. Cn.* in the *periocha* of the book is scarcely sufficient to tip the scales decisively in favour of *C.*

Q. Fabio Ti. Sempronio consulibus: the consuls of 215. Fabius is the great Q. Fabius Maximus, the Cunctator (116) and Sempronius is Ti. Sempronius Gracchus (51), great-uncle of the Gracchi. He had been curule aedile in 216 and *magister equitum* under the *dictator* M. Iunius Pera in the same year. After his second consulship in 213 his command was prorogued for 212, but he was killed in that year.

The date is clearly indicated in 6. 9 and 8.3, and the fact that L. said nothing of the law in his account of 215 does not mean that there is any uncertainty between 215 and 213, when Gracchus' colleague was Q. Fabius Maximus, the son of the Cunctator.

plus: the omission of *quam* is regular: cf. K–St, ii. 471–2.

semunciam: an *uncia* is a twelfth part, and hence a twelfth of a libral *as* (cf. Crawford, *RRC*, i. 6). In 210 the consul M. Valerius Laevinus urged the senators to contribute their possessions to the state, leaving, *inter alia*, *singulas uncias auri* for their wives and each daughter (xxvi. 36. 5). We must suppose that the provisions of the *Lex Oppia* had not been strictly enforced.

neu (uestimento): χ, *nec* B. *ne . . . nec . . . nec* occurs at ii. 32. 10 and *nec . . . neu* is the transmitted reading at xxviii. 43. 8. *nec . . . neue* (*neu*) is otherwise found only in verse (H–S, 517) but the evidence is just sufficient to make it possible that L. used it here. L. might have felt that the first two clauses went more closely with each other than with the third (cf. Shackleton Bailey on Cic. *Att.* xi. 25. 3).

uersicolori: as W–M say, both Cato and Valerius refer only to purple garments (3. 9, 7. 3) and the reference is probably to purple, not to multicoloured clothes. The word is used of cloth where the warp and the woof are of different colours (J. André, *Étude sur les* *termes de couleur dans la langue latine* [Paris, 1949], 231). Shackleton Bailey (*Propertiana* [Cambridge, 1956], 180) renders it 'of changing sheen'.

urbe oppidoue: the law evidently applied to the whole of the *ager Romanus* and *urbe* does not refer to Rome alone.

propius inde mille passus: for *propius* with the accusative of distance, always in legal or quasi-legal contexts, cf. xl. 44. 6, Cic. *Phil.* vi. 5, vii. 26, *legg.* ii. 61, K–St, ii. 471–2. In all these cases, however, the place to which the distance is reckoned is given in the accusative, and this appears to be the only example of *inde* or an ablative (Cic. *Att.* viii. 14. 1, cited by Naylor, 36, is not parallel).

4. M. et P. Iunii Bruti: Marcus (48) was plebeian aedile in 193, praetor in 191 (xxxv. 24. 6, xxxvi. 2. 6, 2. 15, 21. 6, 36. 4), and consul in 178, with command prorogued in 177. He was a member of the *xlegati* for the settlement of Apamea (xxxvii. 55. 7) and a *legatus* to Asia in 172 and 163. The other Brutus is almost certainly to be identified with the curule aedile of 192 and praetor of 190 (54) and since the MSS. at xxxv. 41. 9, xxxvi. 45. 9, and xxxvii. 2. 9 consistently give the *praenomen* of the latter as *P.*, we should follow Mg's *P.* here as against the *T.* offered by Bχ.

Capitolium: for meetings of the tribal assembly held on the Capitol cf. xxxiii. 25. 7 n. Although, of course, the speeches are delivered before the preliminary *contio* (cf. xxxi. 7. 2 n.) it is likely that the formal vote also took place on the Capitol.

5. imperio: for those who were in the *manus* of their husbands. In fact many marriages were 'free'—i.e. did not involve *manus*—by this time. Cf. P. E. Corbett, *The Roman Law of Marriage* (Oxford, 1930), 90 ff.

6. oppidis conciliabulisque: χ. B omits *-que*. In view of formular phrases like *oppedeis foreis conciliaboleis* (*FIRA*, i. 92. l. 31) it is possible that L. may have been led to use an *asyndeton bimembre* here. Cf. p. 11.

conciliabula are communities of Roman citizens lacking a full municipal organization: they were probably the centres of the rural tribes. Cf. Sherwin-White, *RC*[2], 74–5.

conueniebant: Mg. The pluperfect of Bχ is inappropriate to the series of imperfects.

7. et . . . -que et: the consuls and praetors are coupled together as the senior curule magistrates. W–M take the first *et* as 'also'— i.e. magistrates in addition to *priuati*. A tricolon *A Bque et C* is common enough in L. (cf. *TLL*, v. 2. 878. 55 ff.) but in this case the balance of the sentence is against such an interpretation.

utique: Cato takes the lead in the opposition, but the implication is that Valerius Flaccus is also opposed to the repeal. Cf. § 2 n.
habebant: 'continued to find'.

2. 1. in sua ... matre: 'in the case of'. Cf. xxxv. 28. 10 n.

2. impotentia muliebri: for the phrase cf. Goodyear, 124.
obteritur: 'ground down'. For L.'s use of the verb cf. Ogilvie, *YCS* xxiii (1973), 166.

sustinere non potuimus: χ. B omits *sustinere*, and this has led to a variety of emendations for *potuimus*, on the grounds that another verb was first corrupted to *potuimus*, and *sustinere* then added to complete the sense. But omission in B of a word found in χ is not in itself a cause for disquiet (cf. vol. i, 47–8) and when Madvig argues (*Emendationes*, 494) that Cato should be censuring what has caused the trouble, not the absence of what ought to have happened, he is making a distinction without a difference. McDonald's defence of χ's text (approved by Tränkle, *Gnomon*, 371) is convincing. *sustinere* meaning 'restrain' is entirely apposite. Cato is made to use a number of metaphors from horses (*obteritur et calcatur* here, *date frenos* in § 13): for *sustinere* of horses cf. Caes. *BG* iv. 33. 3.

3. equidem: Cato uses the first-person pronoun also at 2. 8 (*equidem*), 2. 4, 4. 11 (*atque ego*), 4. 3, 4. 5, 4. 21 *ego* (but at 4. 3 it is in an unemphatic position). Cf. p. 41.

fabulam ... sublatum esse: the legend of the women of Lemnos who murdered their husbands. In some versions the king Thoas escaped, saved by his daughter Hypsipyle. For details and evidence cf. L. Preller–C. Robert, *Griechische Mythologie*, ii. 3 (Berlin, 1921), 849 ff. There is not the slightest reason to think that the reference to the Lemnian story represents a genuine Catonian element in the speech (thus Nissen, *KU*, 154).

4. statuere apud animum meum: Tränkle, *Cato*, 11 n. 6 compares Cic. *II Verr.* 3. 95 *habuisti statutum cum animo*.

5. alterum ... alterum: chiastic; the people as a whole are concerned with the *res*, the magistrates with the *exemplum*, as Cato elaborates in what follows.

utrum ... existimatio: for *existimatio* introducing an indirect question cf. iv. 20. 8, xxiii. 47. 8, *TLL*, v. 2. 1513.

6. consternatio: for the use of the word in similar contexts cf. Goodyear, 274.

tribuni: not necessarily a reading of Sp, as claimed by Tränkle, *Gnomon*, 369. Gelenius merely says 'uocatiui sunt Fundani et Valeri, sicut sequenti uersu tribuni, non tribunis'.

7. feminas ... seditiones: dett. Bχ have *ad feminas concitandas*.
But, as McDonald rightly argues, the tribunes had not created a
seditio in order to stir up the women: it is the women who created
the *seditio*.

si ut plebis ... sunt: an odd statement, for the women are not
making, or threatening to make, a *secessio*. Nor is the historical Cato
likely to have shown disapproval of the steps by which the plebeians
gained political equality with the patricians during the struggle of
the orders. For the secessions of the *plebs* see ii. 31–3, iii. 50–4,
per. xi.

8. equidem: cf. § 3 n.
quod nisi: for the phrase at the beginning of a sentence cf. K–St,
ii. 322.

10. sui iuris: in the sense that lacking the franchise they had no
right to concern themselves in private with public affairs.

11. ne priuatam ... uirorum: a confused statement. The first
clause refers to women who were *sui iuris*—i.e. not under anyone's
potestas—but the second would appear to refer to women who were
subject to *potestas*. That, however, would be the case only with
fathers and, in the case of marriages with *manus*, husbands. A man
could never exercise *potestas* over his sisters. Women who were *sui
iuris* had to have a *tutor* throughout their life, and required his
sanction for certain classes of legal transaction. But the tutorship
became a formality, and the *tutor* lacked any real power of veto.
   Cf. H. F. Jolowicz and B. Nicholas, *Historical Introduction to the
Study of Roman Law* (3rd edn., Cambridge, 1972), 121, W. A. J.
Watson, *The Law of Persons in the Later Roman Republic* (Oxford,
1967), 110, Balsdon, *Roman Women*, 276, J. A. Crook, *Law and Life
of Rome* (London, 1967), 113–15.
   tutore auctore should be taken as 'a *tutor* as authority' and not as
an *asyndeton bimembre*: cf. Preuss, 82–3.
   prope: Mg, *quoque* Bχ. Many editors have accepted *quoque*, but
McDonald points out that in 3. 6 Cato is made to imply that the
women are not actually in the forum, and that this outweighs the
statement in § 2 *libertas nostra ... his quoque in foro obteritur et calcatur*.
To this it may be added that at 1. 5 L. portrays the women as blocking the roads leading to the forum, approaching the men as they
descend to the forum, but not themselves actually being in the forum.

12. quam (legem abrogandam): the MSS. have *alia* or *aliae*,
which make no sense. In view of iv. 4. 6 *quid est aliud quam exilium
intra eadem moenia, quam relegationem pati*, Harant's *quam* is probably

correct. On *quid est aliud* cf. Nisbet, *in Pisonem*, 109. (F. Walter's *coalitam legem* [*PhW* lx (1940), 350] is absurd.)

censent: the technical word for giving an opinion in the senate (cf. Mommsen, *StR*, iii. 988) but often used by L. for expressing a view in general. Hence there is probably no implication that the women are behaving as if they were senators.

13–3. 3. date frenos . . . superiores erunt: possibly a deliberate echo of the apophthegm of Cato mentioned by Plutarch, *Cato mai.* 8. 4 πάντες ἄνθρωποι τῶν γυναικῶν ἄρχουσιν, ἡμεῖς δὲ πάντων ἀνθρώπων, ἡμῶν δ᾽ αἱ γυναῖκες, as argued by Tränkle, *Cato*, 13–14.

14. nisi uos facietis: sc. *modum licentiae.*

3. 1. recensete omnia: χ. B's *recens et ea omnia* is effectively the same reading but for one letter, and Madvig's *recensete animo* (*Emendationes*, 494) is quite unnecessary.

per quaeque: Gel. ('repositum est'), A . B has *perquae* (*perq̄.*, an abbreviation for *quae* also used at xxxi. 46. 15. B's abbreviation for *-que* is *-q;*, and McDonald's suggestion that B's reading represents *-que* corrected to *quae* is mistaken), χ *perquamque*. It is unnecessary to add *eas*, as urged by C. Wulsch, *De praepositionis 'per' usu Liuiano* (Halle, 1880), 65–6 n. 54, as the slight zeugma involved in *licentia* being the syntactical object of *subiecerint* is perfectly easy. (xxiv. 24. 8, adduced by McDonald, is not parallel: it was, though, correctly adduced by Wulsch as a reply to Madvig's objection [*Emendationes*, 494–5] that *per quaeque* could not stand for *et per quae*.)

2. exaequari: Mg, *aequari* Bχ. It is difficult to make a decision here. *exaequare* occurs only four times in L. (Packard, ii. 463–4), while *aequare* is very common (Packard, i. 264–5) but the word itself is common enough (*TLL*, v. 2. 1141–3) and it would be wrong to argue for it as the *lectio difficilior*. McDonald points to *exaequationem* in 4. 14 and claims there is deliberate alliteration here. But there are only two cases of notable alliteration in Cato's speech (2. 4, 4. 13, Paschkowski, 115) and although alliteration is certainly common in Cato, we have seen that clear imitations of Cato's style in the speech are not extensive and certainly not sufficient to justify *exaequationem* here. Nor is it always possible to be certain when alliteration is deliberate (cf. in general Goodyear, appendix 3). It is just as easy to hold that Mg added *ex-* here because of *extorquere* and *extremum*.

3. extemplo simul: cf. p. 41. *extemplo* goes with the main verb, and it is better, with W–M, to punctuate with a comma after it. For *simul* alone with the indicative, found in Cato, but common first in L., cf. K–St, ii. 360.

4. accepistis ... iussistis: a variation on the formula *uelitis iubeatis* used in asking the people for their vote: cf. Preuss, 94–5.

5. prodest: MSS. *si* with the indicative is found in indirect questions in early Latin (cf. Riemann, 301, K–St, ii. 426, H–S, 543) and *si* in indirect questions is common in L., but always with the subjunctive (for *quaerere si* cf. xxix. 25. 8, xxxix. 50. 7, xl. 49. 6). Corruption from the subjunctive seems improbable and McDonald argues that L. has introduced a deliberate archaism. But the indicative in indirect questions remained in colloquial speech and occasionally as a colloquialism in literary Latin (cf. K–St, ii. 488 ff., H–S, 537–8) and the usage should perhaps be regarded more as a colloquialism than an archaism. (It cannot be excluded that we have to do with an anacoluthon, L. continuing as if he had begun *id satis est*.)

6. foro se et contione: *se* stands in the unemphatic position in the colon.

7. ut captiui ... earum: in 216, after the battle of Cannae: cf. xxii. 58–61. For *parentes, uiri, liberi, fratres* cf. xxii. 60. 1 *liberos, fratres, cognatos*.

piis precibus: cf. Ovid, *Met.* vi. 161 (C. Brakman, *Mnemosyne* n.s. lv [1927], 54).

8. at: an imaginary statement in defence of the women—'but, I suppose'.

matrem ... sunt: the Magna Mater was brought from Pessinus in 205 (xxix. 10. 4–11. 8, 14. 5–14: for the *matronae* receiving her xxix. 14. 10 ff.). On the episode cf. T. Köves, *Historia* xii (1963), 321 ff., and on further developments 54. 3, xxxvi. 36. 3–4 nn.

On the independent temple state of Pessinus cf. Magie, ii, 769–70. Most ancient authorities agree with L. that the Magna Mater came directly from Pessinus, but according to the versions of Varro, *LL* vi. 15 and Ovid, *Fasti* iv. 247 ff., she was given to the Roman ambassadors by Attalus and there is no mention of Pessinus. For details and discussion cf. Bömer, ii. 228 ff., Magie, ii, 769–70.

The *a* before *Pessinunte*, found in Mg, is omitted in Bχ. *a Pessinunte* occurs at xxix. 10. 5, but *Pessinunte* alone at xxxv. 10. 9. Decision is impossible.

honestum ... saltem: 'if they were to speak the truth'.

9. auro et purpura: Tränkle, *Cato*, 12, points out that the phrase occurs twice in Cato (frs. 224M, 113P), three times in this speech (cf. 4. 10, 4. 14), and only three times elsewhere in Latin. He plausibly suggests, therefore, that L. has deliberately used a phrase which has Catonian flavour. On *purpura* cf. 1. 3 n.

fulgamus: B, *fulgeamus* ψ, *fulgeam* φ. Seneca, *NQ* ii. 56 says that *fulgĕre* is an archaic verb, replaced by *fulgēre*. Like other verbs in *-o* replaced by ones in *-eo*, it is found in verse of many periods, but never in prose (cf. Neue–Wagener, iii. 268–9, A. Ernout, *Morphologie historique du Latin*² [Paris, 1927], 233–4). As in the case of *prodest* (§ 5) McDonald defends it as a deliberate archaism. The arguments for reading *fulgamus*, however, are considerably weaker than those in favour of *prodest*. We are not dealing with the unanimous reading of the tradition, and corruption from *fulgeamus* in B is extremely easy. Cf. Ogilvie, *Phoenix*, 346, Tränkle, *Gnomon*, 377–8.

carpentis ... diebus: on ordinary as well as on festival days. This would restore the situation as it existed before the *Lex Oppia*. Cf. v. 25. 9. Hence there is no conflict between this passage and 1. 3, as W–M think. The women still had the right to ride in chariots at festivals (*sacrorum publicorum causa* and *festis diebus* have the same reference). That there were in any case other restrictions on the use of carriages in the city, as W–M say, is irrelevant. There is no evidence for their being applied to women: cf. Mommsen, *StR*, i³. 393. (Becker, *Gallus*², iii. 12 seems to have thought that *profestus* meant a kind of *dies festus*.)

triumphantes: for the chariot of the *triumphator* cf. L. B. Warren, *JRS* lx (1970), 58.

et captis et ereptis: the omission of the second *et* in the OCT is a misprint.

uectemur: cf. p. 6.

4. 1. saepe ... audistis: slightly anachronistic, in so far as the famous attacks on private conspicuous consumption came in Cato's censorship in 184. But there is no reason to doubt that he made his views clear at the beginning of his political career. His attacks on Scipio (Plut. *Cato mai.* 3) may be apocryphal, but for his praetorship in Sardinia in 198 cf. xxxii. 27. 3–4 n. Cf. Fraccaro, *Opuscula*, i. 121–2, Astin, *Cato*, 13 ff., 93 ff.

2. diuersis ... luxuria: the phraseology is remarkably similar to Sallust, *Cat.* 5. 8 *corrupti ciuitatis mores, quos pessuma ac diuorsa inter se mala luxuria atque auaritia uexabant.* Tränkle (*Cato*, 14) considers the possibility that both Sallust and L. have used a Catonian phrase, but admits that it is equally possible that L. has simply been influenced by Sallust (cf. vol. i, 15). Cf. also *praef.* 11, Longinus, περὶ ὕψους 44. 6–7, Chrysippus, *SVF* iii. 102, F. Nagy, *AAntHung.* xvi (1968), 275–7. On L.'s view of Roman decline see Luce, 250 ff.

quae ... euerterunt: again the idea is present in Sallust: cf. *Cat.* 2. 3–6. But though the language reminds us of Sallust, Horace (e.g. *Odes* iii. 24), and L. himself in the *praefatio*, the motif of corruption of morals caused by private wealth is much older. It was doubtless a common theme in Hellenistic literature (cf. G. W. Williams, *Tradition and Originality in Roman Poetry* [Oxford, 1968], 608 ff.) and Fabius Pictor (fr. 20P) talked of the date of the introduction of πλοῦτος at Rome. Cato himself placed his animadversions on private conduct in the context of the decline of old virtue (cf. Astin, *Cato*, 100).

3. quo magis imperium crescit: Mg, undoubtedly correctly. Bχ have *imperiumque crescit*, which makes a very flat conclusion to the sentence.

Asiamque: manifestly anachronistic. A Roman army did not cross to Asia until 190. Kienast's claim (137 n. 13) that the Romans were already contemplating such a move would be irrelevant even if it were true.

omnibus ... gazas: Whether many *gazae regiae* had been captured in the war with Philip may be open to doubt. Asia is a stock example of luxurious living: W–M compare Cic. *ad. Q. fr.* i. 1. 19, Tac. *Agr.* 6. 2. For Greeks Lydia, Phrygia, and Persia epitomized wealth and luxury: cf. e.g., Nisbet and Hubbard, i, 110, 423–4 L. himself dated the increase of *luxuria* at Rome to the return of the army that had fought against Antiochus (xxxix. 6. 7). Sallust thought that *luxuria* did not arrive until the return of Sulla's army (*Cat.* 11. 5–6).

ne illae ... illas: the same idea as in Horace's famous *Graecia capta ferum uictorem cepit* (*Epp.* ii. 1. 156). That both were depending on Cato is again possible: cf. Tränkle, *Cato*, 14–15, with a valuable collection (15 n. 4) of similar plays on *uincere* and *capere*. There is, however, no evidence that Cato himself associated the growth of *luxuria* with Greek influence: cf. Astin, *Cato*, 173–4.

4. infesta ... inlata: the statues were taken by Marcellus after the capture of Syracuse in 212 (xxv. 40. 1–3, xxvi. 21. 8; cf. Pol. ix. 10 and the evidence cited in *MRR*, i. 273–4). Marcellus' conduct over the booty from Syracuse was the subject of criticism at the time. Cf. Münzer, *RE*, iii. 2748–9, Walbank, *Commentary*, ii. 134–5.

infesta ... signa ... illata is perhaps a play on *signa inferre* meaning 'advance the standards', as suggested by Naylor, 88. R. Chevallier and R. Girod, *Caesarodunum* v (1970), 288 see Cato as indicating that the gods will take vengeance for the removal of the statues.

Corinthi et Athenarum: for early Roman contacts with Athens cf. xxxi. 5. 8 n. Roman ambassadors had visited Corinth as well as Athens in 228, and Rome had been admitted to the Isthmian Games (Pol. ii. 12. 8). Zonaras viii. 19. 7 gives the name of the first Roman victor there. A number of Romans will have visited Corinth and Athens during the course of the Second Macedonian War.

antefixa fictilia: the cases are not really parallel. Even if the images of the gods on pediments of temples were still of terracotta, statues inside the temples were not always so. Cf. Pliny, *NH* xxxiv. 15, of the bronze statue in the temple of Ceres, providing an exception to the general rule expressed at xxxiv. 34 *lignea potius aut fictilia deorum simulacra in delubris dicata usque ad deuictam Asiam, unde luxuria.* I cannot follow von Puchstein's view (*RE*, i. 2348) that *antefixa* here refers to all the ornaments of a temple.

5. in suis . . . patiemur: i.e. and do not replace them with foreign gods.

6. patrum nostrorum memoria: inexact. Only a small number of the senate of 195 will have had fathers who remembered the events of the Pyrrhic War.

per legatum . . . temptauit: Cineas, a Thessalian, was a minister of Pyrrhus. The sources record two missions to Rome to negotiate peace, one after the battle of Heraclea in 280, the other after the battle of Asculum in 279. It has been much disputed whether one of these, and if so which, should be regarded as a doublet. See Olshausen, no. 185. Cineas' efforts to bribe the women of Rome are also mentioned by Plut. *Pyrr.* 18. 4, Val. Max. iv. 3. 14, Zon. viii. 4. 9.

7. nostris: L. All the other MSS. have *uestris*. At 7. 1 and 7. 9 *uestras* and *uestri* in the MSS. have also regularly been altered to *nostras* and *nostri*. Corruption of *noster* to *uester* is, of course, easy (though less so in an uncial manuscript), but the accumulation of evidence in the speeches of Cato and Valerius perhaps suggests that on all three occasions the paradosis is correct. As in 3. 4, the speaker is addressing the *contio* collectively without completely identifying himself with them.

sanciundi: Mg, *sanciendi* Bχ. The older gerundive in *-undus* occurs occasionally in the MSS. of L., and its occurrence here in Mg suggests that it is what L. wrote. It is particularly appropriate in legalistic phraseology. Cf. Neue–Wagener, iii. 337–8, Sommer, 616–18.

8. sic . . . leges: cf. Tac. *Ann.* xv. 20, Macr. iii. 17. 10, Otto, 192.

9. legem Liciniam . . . continuandi: the date of the law restricting the holding of *ager publicus* to a maximum of 500 *iugera* is disputed. L. clearly believed it to have been part of the Licinian–Sextian rogations passed in 367 (Varr.): see vi. 35. 4, x. 13. 14. The same view was taken by Varro, *RR* i. 2. 9, Vell. Pat. ii. 6. 3, Col. *RR* i. 3. 11, Pliny, *NH* xviii. 17, Val. Max. viii. 6. 3, Plut. *Cam.* 39. 5–6, Gell. xx. 1. 23, *de uir. ill.* 20. 3. Appian, however (*BC* i. 8. 33), places the law after the Hannibalic war. All that is certain is that the law existed before 167, when Cato made an oblique reference to it (fr. 167M). The most likely solution is that the original law does belong to the fourth century, but that it was reaffirmed, perhaps with the limit raised to 500 *iugera*, in the early second century. See Tibiletti, *Athenaeum* n.s. xxvi (1948), 191 ff., xxvii (1949), 12 ff., Gabba, *Commentary on Appian, BC* i, 20, Frederiksen, *Dialoghi di archeologia* iv–v (1970–1), 332, Astin, *Cato*, 241–2.

L.'s language reflects the agrarian conditions of the late republic. On the size of estates in the second century cf. Frederiksen, op. cit., 330 ff.

cupido: cf. p. 4.

legem Cinciam ... coeperat: probably passed in 204 by M. Cincius Alimentus (cf. 56. 1 n.). Tacitus (*Ann.* xi. 5, xiii. 42, xv. 20) regards the law as prohibiting payments in money or kind to advocates, but there is no reason to doubt that this was only part of its provisions. But Cato's description of the *plebs* as so completely beholden to the senators is doubtless highly exaggerated.

10. data et oblata ultro: *ultro* goes with both the participles. For the neuter plural following *aurum et purpura* cf. K–St, i. 32–3.

11. circumiret ... inuenisset: the pluperfect conveys the meaning 'if he were to be going round, he would (already) have found ...'.

causam ... rationem inire: 'discover the reason for'. Cf. Pliny, *NH* xxxvii. 26. *rationem inire* is common (though normally in the sense of 'devise a plan for') and *causam* is easily added to the phrase. See *TLL*, vii. 1. 1298.

12. ut ... sic: 'granted that ... yet'. Cf. K–St, ii. 251, H–S, 633–4.

ne in se conspiciatur: they fear the lack of adornment may be seen.

13. cum ... non habetis: 'at a moment when ...'.

14 ff. One is reminded of the arguments sometimes advanced in favour of school uniforms.

14. hanc ... illa locuples: cf. xxxiii. 13. 11 n.

exaequationem: apart from Vitruvius v. 12. 4, where it is used technically, the earliest occurrence of the word, and its only occurrence in Classical literature (cf. *TLL*, v. 2. 1140–1). One wonders

if L. coined it on the model of Catonian neologisms, or even found
it in the works of Cato himself.

habiturae ... uideantur: 'it may appear that they would have
possessed it, if it were lawful'. The standard tenses for an unfulfilled
present conditional in *oratio obliqua*.

15. pauperes ne: a comma is needed after *pauperes*.

16. ne: 'indeed'. Cf. K–St, i. 795 ff.

⟨**eas**⟩: I am not convinced that Lentz's supplement is necessary.
Cf. iii. 19. 7, 52. 7, Damsté, *Mnemosyne* n.s. xliii (1915), 163.

coeperit: I see no merit in Walsh's proposal (*CR*, 55) to read
ceperit (*ceperit* is, of course, what appears in the χ MSS. and *coeperit
quod oportet* is missing in B because the scribe's eye jumped from the
first *oportet* to the second). Walsh claims that *coeperit* is tautologous.
Even if this were true, it would not be wholly objectionable in this
speech. But in fact *coepi* is often used in a semi-tautologous way to
stress the inceptive nature of an action. Cf. H–S, 319.

17. datum ... uidebit: connected with what follows. There is no
implication of the gift being given as a prelude to adulterous
relations.

18. legem ... impetrant: cf. 1. 5. I am not sure that *rogant* is
used as a deliberate play on *legem rogare* 'to carry a law' (cf. 3. 5)
as W–M claim.

modum ... facere ... facies: taking up the language of 2. 13.

19. ⟨Quirites⟩: an old supplement. The sentence runs perfectly
well without it. The position is not at all parallel to § 15 where B
could not read *Quirites* in F, and, as was his custom in such cases,
left a space.

20. inritata ... emissa: the MSS. have *inritatae ... emissae*, but
the words go with *ipsis uinculis* and the latter cannot be part of the
sicut clause.

21. ego: for *ego* at the beginning of the last or penultimate sentence
of speeches cf. Walsh on xxi. 10. 13.

censeo: cf. 2. 12 n. *censeo* occurs at vi. 41. 12 and x. 8. 12 at the
end of speeches before a *contio*, but the fact that Cicero does not use
it in such speeches as *pro lege Manilia* and *de lege agraria* ii makes it
very likely that L.'s usage is incorrect.

faxitis: B, trivialized to *facitis* in χ. The only certainly archaic
usage in the speech (cf. 3. 5, 3. 9 nn.). It also occurs at vi. 35. 9,
41. 12, xxii. 10. 4, 10. 6 (*bis*), xxiii. 11. 2, xxix. 27. 3, xxxvi. 2. 5.
It is clearly used by L. in formulas of the present kind, and is not

meant to import a specially Catonian flavour. Cf. Neue–Wagener,
iii. 506 ff., Paschkowski, 109–10.

5. 1. tribuni ... cum ... tum: for the position of *cum* cf. Varro,
RR iii. 5. 18, H–S, 399: see also p. 14 n. 2 and addendum thereto.
For *cum ... tum* cf. Ogilvie, *YCS* xxiii (1973), 160.

priuati: private individuals could speak at a *contio* only at the
invitation of the presiding official: cf. G. W. Botsford, *The Roman
Assemblies* (New York, 1909), 146.

satis ... existimarem: as W–M rightly say, this indicates that
speeches had been made for the bill as well as against it.

2. clarissimus: Mg, *grauissimus* Bχ. McDonald claims that *clarissimus* is more appropriate to Cato as consul and Tränkle (*Gnomon*, 373
n. 5), supporting *clarissimus*, adduces Sallust, *Cat.* 51. 19 *diligentia claris-
simi uiri, consulis*. But *clarissimus* is not applied particularly to consuls
and it could be said that *grauissimus* goes better with *auctoritate*.
Other arguments, however, give strong support to *clarissimus*. Political speeches of this sort occur rarely in L., and his own usage is
not all that significant. Nevertheless, it is worth saying that *uir
grauissimus* (or *grauissimus uir*) never occurs in L. while *uir clarissimus*
is found at xxxviii. 54. 8, 59. 10 and *clarissimus uir* at viii. 32. 15.
More significant is Cicero's usage in his speeches. *uir clarissimus* and
clarissimus uir occupy nearly three columns in Merguet's lexicon
(i. 545–6) while *grauissimus uir* occurs only six times and *uir grauissimus* never.

longa ... paucis: in fact the speech of Valerius is longer than
that of Cato.

accurata: 'carefully composed'. *accuratus* is widely used as a
technical term in rhetoric: cf. xxxv. 31. 4, *TLL*, i. 342. 74 ff. This
meaning apart, the word is rare in Classical Latin (v. 37. 3 *dilectum
accuratiorem* is the only instance in L.).

necesse: Bχ, *necessum* Mg. The archaic form *necessum* occurs up
to Lucretius and in the archaizing Aulus Gellius (Neue–Wagener,
ii. 181–2). Gelenius has *necessum* 'uetus lectio' at xxxix. 5. 9, but there
is even less case here for an archaic form than in Cato's speech (cf.
3. 5, 3. 9 nn.).

3. plura uerba: 3. 3–6 and ch. 4 are about the merits of the bill
itself. Just over half Cato's speech is concerned with the behaviour
of the women.

4. magis ... insimularet: 'more by way of a verbal attack than
because he wanted to make any serious accusations'.

hoc: that the tribunes had been responsible for the *seditio* of the
women.

5. coetum ... seditionem ... secessionem: for *coetus* cf. 2. 4, for *seditio* 2. 7, 3. 8, for *secessio* 2. 7.

publico: φ's reading is *publicum*, not *cum* as McDonald's apparatus implies. In fact A has *publico*.

per bellum: balanced by *in pace*, and therefore probably 'during the war', not 'because of the war'.

6. conquirantur: probably subjunctive only because it stands in *oratio obliqua*, and not representing an original relative clause with the subjunctive, as W–M believe.

cum ... mitis: a nice depreciating touch. Of Cato's speech for the Rhodians in 167 L. says *plurimum causam eorum adiuuit M. Porcius Cato, qui, asper ingenio, tum lenem mitemque senatorem egit* (xlv. 25. 2). The evidence as a whole scarcely bears out Valerius' claim: see xxxix. 40. 10, Astin, *Cato*, 8 n. 18. For *ingenio mitis* cf. Vell. Pat. ii. 117. 2, Tac. *Ann.* vi. 15. 1 (Woodman, 190).

7. tuas ... reuoluam: the second clear anachronism in the debate (cf. 4. 3 n.). The ancient evidence states quite unequivocally that Cato began the *Origines* in his old age. See Nepos, *Cato* 3; cf. Cic. *Brut.* 89, *sen.* 38, Pliny, *NH* iii. 114 (= fr. 49P), Peter, *HRR*, i². cxxvii ff., Astin, *Cato*, 212.

reuoluam: 'unroll', with literal reference to the book rolls. The usage is not the same as Hor. *Epp.* ii. 1. 223, Quint xi. 2. 41, as the article in L–S suggests. The verb is future, not present subjunctive, as Sage takes it. Not only is this required by *aduersus te*, but the jussive subjunctive normally occupies the first position in its clause: cf. Marouzeau, *L'Ordre des mots dans la phrase latine*, ii (Paris, 1938), 52.

8. iam ... sedatum est: i. 13. Valerius does not, of course, mention that the *matronae* were the Sabine women themselves.

9. Coriolano ... auerterunt: for the story of Coriolanus cf. ii. 33. 3—40, Ogilvie, 314 ff.

For the inversion of *nomen* and *cognomen* cf. xxxiii. 30. 10 n., to which add references to W–M on iv. 14. 6, Syme, *Historia* vii (1958), 172 ff., Ogilvie, 570, Shackleton Bailey, *Cicero's Letters to Atticus*, i (Cambridge, 1965), 402–3, Goodyear, 148, Adams, *CQ* n.s. xxviii (1978), 165.

iam urbe ... nonne: Bχ have *aurum quo redempta urbs est nempe ...*, Mg had *quo redempta urbs est; nempe aurum ...* Madvig (*Emendationes*, 495–6) retained Mg's text, deleting *urbe* and putting a question mark after *est*. McDonald follows Duker in reading *nonne* and otherwise keeping the word-order of Bχ. His principal argument is that in the long series of questions *nonne* occurs three times

and we should not expect the sequence to be broken here. Tränkle
(*Gnomon*, 379) has two counter arguments. (*a*) The sentence as it
stands is impossible Latin: *urbs* in the relative clause would have to
be deleted and *redempta est* changed to *redimeretur* because the ransom-
ing of the city was a consequence of the women's action. I can see
nothing wrong with the simple relative and arguments based on
repetitions are always dangerous (cf. p. 13). (*b*) Given the series
of *nonnes* it is unlikely that *nonne* here would be corrupted into
nempe. There is some force in this, and given the fact that *quo . . .
nempe aurum* is the reading of Mg, there is a good deal to be said
for Madvig's text. With Madvig's test, of course, *quo* means 'by
whom', not 'how', as Sage takes it. For the omission of *ab* with a
person cf. H–S, 122.

   For the story cf. v. 50. 7, Ogilvie, 741.

10. proximo bello: the Second Punic War. In fact the Second
Macedonian War is now the most recent war. L. is using the phrase
employed in xxxi. 7. 3 (cf. n. ad loc.).
   cum pecunia . . . aerarium: in 214 (xxiv. 18. 14).
   cum di . . . accipiendam: cf. 3. 8 n.

11. nec mihi . . . satis est: hardly a convincing reply.
   For L.'s use of *purgare* with the accusative and infinitive to mean
'prove by way of defence' cf. xxiv. 47. 6, xli. 19. 5, xlii. 14. 3.

12. feminas: B, *feminasque* χ. For the asyndeton cf. xlv. 24. 11,
[Sall.] *Epp.* ii. 4. 2, Cic. *Clu.* 148, Pliny, *NH* xxxvii. 201, Sen. *dial.*
v. 2. 3, Preuss, 93. On this occasion it is more likely that χ added
-*que* to produce the more normal idiom than that B omitted it.

6. 1. id de quo agitur: as distinct from the behaviour of the
women. Cf. 5. 3.
   duplex . . . lata esset: the general argument in 3. 3–6, the
specific one in ch. 4. Cato had not in fact argued that no law should
be repealed, but that if a law were to be repealed only because it
adversely affected particular interests, all laws were liable to be
repealed.

2. pro legibus: with what follows (W–M), not 'a general appeal
on behalf of the laws', as Sage translates: *uisa* would be too emphatic
at the beginning of the colon.
   seuerissimis moribus: i.e. Cato's.

3. utraque re: the phrase is perfectly natural and Gelenius's
deletion of *re* to make *utraque* agree with an understood *ratione* is
unnecessary.

4–5. In fact the same arguments are valid for the repeal of both types of law. Valerius does not really reply to Cato's argument: cf. § 1 n. The argument smacks of the declamations of the Augustan period. For the sentiment cf. xlv. 32. 7 (Naylor, 144). For the indicatives in *oratio obliqua* in this sentence cf. 20. 2 n.

6. ut ... usui sunt: an almost Platonic argument by analogy.

secunda ... aduersa tempestate: Bχ. Mg had accusatives. Both constructions would be possible: for the accusative cf. 7. 3. (McDonald's quotation of xxxviii. 3. 11 is not relevant, and should, I suspect, read xxxviii. 22. 3).

7. ⟨num⟩quae uetus: McDonald's own conjecture. The MSS. read *quae* or *quia*. Madvig (*Emendationes*, 496–7) proposed *quam uetus? regia scilicet simul ...* But *quam uetus* is rather abrupt in the smooth style of Valerius' speech (the change to *scilicet* is not essential to Madvig's solution) and the same objection applies to McDonald's reading. Ogilvie (*Phoenix*, 347) suggests joining *numquae uetus* with what follows, as otherwise *regia ... abrogemus* is not obviously a question. (It is in any case necessary to punctuate with a colon after *scripta*: *verendum sit* cannot be taken with *sine qua*. Walsh's proposal [*CR*, 55] to accept *numquae uetus* but to make the following sentence into a statement rather than a question is quite impossible: the sentence would then have no syntax at all.) I am attracted by Damsté's suggestion (*Mnemosyne* xliii [1915] 163–4) of deleting *quae(quia) uetus* as a gloss.

8. regia lex: *leges regiae* are laws believed to date from the regal period, but in many cases they were probably merely very old laws for which no date or author was known. Cf., however, S. Tondo, *SDHI* xxxvii (1971), 1 ff., W. A. J. Watson, *JRS* lxii (1972), 100 ff.

ab decemuiris ... scripta: cf. iii. 33–42, Ogilvie, 451 ff.

9. Q. Fabio ... latam: cf. 1. 3 n.

10. ⟨uetus⟩: *aut ideo lata esset* requires a supplement. McDonald argues that Valerius is still considering the question whether the law is old or recent, and therefore accepts the *uetus* of A. Mayerhoefer, *Critika Studia Liuiana* (Bamberg, 1880), 44–6. But Valerius has already shown that the *Lex Oppia* is not an ancient law, and there is no doubt that the simplest solution is to omit *aut*, as proposed by H. Hill, *CR* xlv (1931), 127–8. Hill claimed that *aut* arose from *autem* below, but even if this is unlikely, as McDonald argues, that would not in itself be a strong argument against the emendation. In fact Hill's explanation of the corruption is probable enough. The scribe began by looking at *lata* below, but before realizing his mistake and stopping, he had already begun to write *autem* and he forgot to delete it.

indicabit: *indicauit* MSS., but the future is essential for the sense.

11. iam ... iam ... iam: cf. viii. 38. 12, xxxvii. 5. 3 with similar reference to an accumulation of problems. Contrast 29. 6 n.

Tarentum: in fact Tarentum did not fall until 212: cf. *MRR*, i. 270, Walbank, *Commentary*, ii. 5. The lists of defectors in xxii. 61. 11–12, Pol. iii. 118. 2–3 contain a number of anachronisms. For details cf. De Sanctis, iii. 2. 211 ff., 223 ff., 274, Walbank, *Commentary*, i. 448, ii. 29, 100, Salmon, *Samnium*, 299.

Arpos: Arpi, in Apulia, north of Foggia; it was known in Greek as Ἀργύριππα. Arpi supported Rome against the Samnites and Pyrrhus, but defected to Rome after Cannae (Pol. iii. 118. 3, App. *Hann.* 31. 130) and later had its land confiscated: cf. 45. 3. See Hülsen, *RE*, ii. 1217–18, J. Bradford, *Antiquity* xxxi (1957), 167–9.

Capuam: for its defection cf. xxiii. 2 ff., J. von Ungern-Sternberg, *Capua im zweiten Punischen Krieg* (Munich, 1975), 24 ff.

ad urbem Romam ... uidebatur: which he did not in fact do until 211: cf. xxxi. 31. 12 n.

defecerant socii: cf. § 11 n.

12. socios nauales: L. uses *socii nauales* to mean nothing more than 'sailors', even when they are clearly Roman citizens. The explanation of the term lies in the fact that most of Rome's navy came originally from the Greek *socii* in Southern Italy, and thus came to be used for sailors in general. When the word is applied to foreign navies there is no implication that the sailors were allies of the state concerned. My notes on xxxii. 36. 10, xxxiii. 38. 14 are misleading. See Mommsen, *StR*, iii. 659 n. 3, Thiel, 12, 77 n. 127, Toynbee, ii. 518 ff., A. Milan, *Critica Storica* x (1973), 193–221, Walsh on xxi. 49. 8.

serui ... emebantur: after Cannae (xxii. 57. 11). Delayed payment is not mentioned there, and is implicitly denied at xxii. 61. 2. The owners of those manumitted by Ti. Sempronius Gracchus in 214 offered to delay payment (xxiv. 18. 12). Cf. also Val. Max. vii. 6. 1.

13. in eandem ... erant: this occurred in 215 (xxiii. 48. 5 ff.) and, for religious matters, in 214 (xxiv. 18. 10–11). Cf. Badian, *Publicans and Sinners*, 16 ff.

seruos ... dabamus: in fact in 214, after the passing of the *Lex Oppia*. See xxiv. 11. 7–9.

14. aurum ... conferebamus: in fact in 210 (xxvi. 36).

uiduae ... deferebant: in 214: cf. 5. 10 n.

quo ne plus: B, A (but with a space between *ne* and *plus*), *quo ne quo plus* PE, *ne quo plus* LV, *ne plus quo* N, *ne plus* φmg. For the phrase cf. K–St, ii. 210.

quo ne plus . . . haberemus: again in 210, at the same time as the events just referred to: see xxvi. 36. 5–6. In fact gold and silver were defined by weight, objects (*facti*) apart. But the inconsistency is trivial.

haberemus—: I see no point in the dash, and would prefer a full stop.

15. Oppia lex: B, *lex Oppia* χ. Madvig (*Emendationes*, 497) may have been right to delete *Oppia*. For other possible cases of a gloss being inserted in the text at different places in different branches of the tradition cf. 49. 8, xxxvii. 11. 3 nn. (see also xxxi. 7. 3 n.). The search for glosses on the basis of such variations in word-order was much overdone by Conway and Walters (see their note on *praef.* 5). Cf. Ogilvie, *CR* n.s. xvii (1967), 305.

Cereris . . . iussit: in 216 (xxii. 56. 4). On the festival cf. Le Bonniec, 400 ff.

16. inopiam . . . scripsisse: J. F. Gronovius first drew attention to Hyperides fr. 28 (Kenyon): οὐκ ἐγὼ τὸ ψήφισμα ἔγραψα, ἡ δ’ ἐν Χαιρωνείᾳ μάχη. For other personified subjects in L. cf. xxxv. 19. 4 n.

17. pecunias . . . priuatis: cf. xxxi. 13 n. W–M say that the argument is irrelevant, because the money was intended as a loan. But Valerius’ point is that if the conditions were the same as when the *Lex Oppia* was passed, the money would not yet be repaid.

publica . . . locamus: referring to the delayed payments of § 13.

7. 1. omnes . . . sentient: part of the question, not ‘all will feel’ as Sage translates (he rightly takes *purpura . . . mortui* in §§ 2–3 as questions).

nostras: *uestras* Bχ. Cf. 4. 7 n. There is somewhat more case for the alteration here, with *liberi nostri* in § 2. But there is nothing objectionable about the transition from second to first person.

2. praetextati . . . utentur: cf. xxxiii. 42. 1 n.

magistratibus . . . municipiisque: cf. Hor. *Sat.* i. 5. 36, Petr. *Sat.* 71, Lex Col. Gen. 62, 66 (*FIRA*, i. 179, 181). As the late M. W. Frederiksen pointed out to me, Horace’s reference suggests that the practice was regarded as presumptuous at his time.

hic Romae . . . uicorum: Mg, om. Bχ. Dio lv. 8. 6–7 relates Augustus’ institution of the *uicorum magistri* in charge of the streets of Rome in 7 B.C., when they were allowed to wear ἐσθῆτι τῇ ἀρχικῇ.

But republican *uicorum magistri* are known (*ILS* 6075) and are probably to be identified with the *magistri collegiorum* mentioned by Asconius (p. 7C), who wore the *toga praetextata* when holding games (Cic. *Pis.* 8, 23, Asc. loc. cit.). L., however, seems to imagine the *magistri* as *praetextati* all the time. Weissenborn, following Marquardt, deleted the phrase as a gloss, and if I am right in regarding 16. 1–2 as an interpolation in Mg, it is tempting to see one here also. In this case, however, it is hard to see what could have given rise to such a gloss in late antiquity and the combination of the anachronism with the omission in Bχ must be regarded as a coincidence. Cf. Bleicken, *RE*, viiiA. 2480.

L. cannot, however, have been writing book xxxiv as late as 7 B.C. (cf. Hus, Budé edition of book xxxi, xvi–xvii) and we must assume that the words are an addition to an earlier draft.

3. id: χ, om. B. It is uncertain whether it was in Mg, and it may well be an addition in χ. Cf. Tränkle, *Gnomon*, 373 n. 2.

solum habeant [tantum] insigne: (χ has *habent*). *tantum*, as Madvig argued (*Emendationes*, 497–8), cannot mean 'so great a distinction' because Valerius is arguing that purple is a common badge of honour. It must mean 'only', and therefore reduplicates *solum*. The question, then, is whether *solum* or *tantum* should be deleted. In favour of deleting *solum* (thus Madvig) is the fact that it is far more likely to have been a gloss for *tantum* than vice versa. (There is nothing objectionable about the postpositive usage of *solum*: cf. v. 42. 3, Naylor, 173). It might be argued, however, that we should expect *uiui tantum habeant insigne*. See, though, vi. 16. 5 *unum defuisse tantum superbiae*. The word-order in our passage, moreover, may be motivated by a desire to mark a contrast between *uiui habeant* and *crementur mortui*.

cum . . . mortui: W–M compare Pol. vi. 53. 1 κομίζεται μετὰ τοῦ λοιποῦ κόσμου. Walbank (*Commentary*, i. 737) translates this 'with every kind of honour' but it does seem to mean 'with the rest of the adornment (sc. that they had in life)' and is rightly taken as a parallel to our passage. Cf. Mommsen, *StR*, i³. 441, Ogilvie, 725.

usu: B has *usui*, χ *usum*. The accusative of the thing prohibited is regular with *interdicere* (*TLL*, vii. 1. 2173) but L. uses only the ablative (Packard, ii. 1269) and the emendation is therefore inevitable. The dative is a later construction (*TLL*, vii. 1. 2175).

in uestem stragulam: 'a covering garment'. For the construction cf. 6. 6 n.

et equus: B omits *et*, perhaps correctly.

4. teritur absumitur: cf. p. 11.

iniustam quidem ... sed aliquam: for the *confessio* cf. Ull-mann, *Étude*, 65. Naylor, 177, points out that L. elsewhere uses *quidem ... sed(autem, uero)* = μὲν ... δέ, but there are no other ex-amples with an adjective.

in auro ... experti estis: one is reminded of President de Gaulle's eulogy of 'les privilèges d'or' (*The Times*, 28 Nov. 1967).

manupretium: an easy and obvious change for the *manui pretium* or *manus pretium* of the MSS. We are to imagine a small craftsman whose return to labour on making solid gold into golden objects is small. The proposal of J. F. Killeen (*RhM* cxi [1968], 96) to read *manus pressum*, with reference to the loss of gold through handling, has nothing to commend it.

intertrimenti: used of silver at xxxii. 2. 2, but with reference to debasement (cf. n. ad loc.).

sicut ... estis: with reference to the contributions mentioned in 5. 10, 6. 14.

5. nullam ... aiebat: 4. 12–16.

sociorum Latini nominis: cf. xxxi. 8. 7 n.

uident: Bχ, *uideant* Mg, perhaps rightly. The *cum* is not strictly temporal, and there is no other example of L. using *cum* and the indicative with words expressing emotion.

6. uehi ... imperium sit: presumably Latin and allied women were not prohibited from riding in carriages in Rome, while Roman women were so prohibited in allied states (cf. 1. 3). As W–M say, Valerius deliberately ignores the fact that the women could ride in litters.

7–10. Valerius' defence of the women's interest here is fairly scathing about women's ability (quite typically, of course).

7. muliercularum: the diminutive occurs elsewhere in L. only at xxvii. 15. 9. The word is usually used in a patronizing way. Cf. *TLL*, viii. 1575–6.

9. haec ... hunc: the standard attraction of the pronoun. Cf. K–St, i. 34–5.

nostri: *uestri* MSS. Cf. 4. 7 n.

11. scilicet: cf. xxxi. 29. 8 n.

12. et (ipsae): adversative 'and yet'. Cf. *TLL*, v. 2. 893.

13. Valerius argues that Cato's picture of women needing to be kept under control is completely wrong. The women are happy to accept the judgement of the men to whom they are subject, and the men should use their power with humanity.

14. seditionem ... secessionem: cf. 5. 5 n.

Sacrum montem ... Auentinum: for the different traditions on the site of the first two secessions cf. Ogilvie, 489. For the *mons Sacer*, a little to the north-east of the city cf. Ashby, *Campagna*, 84.

15. infirmitati: abstract for concrete. Cf. Riemann, 67, quoting Quint. ii. 2. 14 *infirmitas a robustioribus separanda est.*

8. 2. Brutorum: B Gel., *tribunorum* χ. An interesting example of a gloss replacing the word glossed. On the Bruti cf. 1. 4 n.

collegarum rogationi: Mg probably had *rogationi collegae* and Madvig (1863 edn., xxiv–v) considered the possibility that the other MSS. have a text which is a correction of a mistake by L. himself, who was thinking only of Valerius. This seems improbable, and Madvig dropped the idea in the *Emendationes* and the 1884 edition.

remissa ... est: tribunes did not press a veto against what was the clear wish of the people. Cf. xxxii. 7. 12 n., Badian, *ANRW*, i. 1. 699, and, for the withdrawal of a veto in the senate, xxxi. 20. 6 n., xxxii. 28. 8 n.

8. 4—21. *Events in Spain*

The detail of L.'s account of Cato's campaign, the ethnographical excursus on Emporiae, and the clear relation between L.'s words and the surviving fragments of Cato's speech *de consulatu suo* all make it certain that the ultimate source of L.'s narrative is Cato himself. The question in dispute is whether L. consulted Cato directly, or merely an annalist who had done so.

See in particular Unger, *Philologus* Suppbd. iii. 2 (1878), 63 ff., Fraccaro, *Opuscula*, i. 177 ff., Tränkle, *Cato*, 16 ff., Astin, *Cato*, 302 ff., Luce, 162 ff.

First, two general points. I have argued in the introduction to vol. i that there is no reason to doubt that L. had read second-century writers as well as annalists of the Sullan period. Secondly, there can be no serious doubt that L. has read some, at least, of the speeches of Cato himself. Otherwise he could not, at xxxix. 43. 1, have rebuked Valerius Antias for not reading Cato's speeches (cf. Tränkle, *Cato*, 7). These general considerations do not, of course, prove that L.'s account of Cato's campaign in Spain comes directly from Cato, but they do point in that direction, and since at one place (15. 9) L. quotes Cato personally, it is fair to argue that the burden of proof should be on those who wish to claim that L. did not use Cato directly.

The latter view has been largely based on the claim that L.'s account contains doublets or inconsistencies, and that this could not have occurred if L. had consulted Cato himself. Even this argument is not compelling, for if such confusions could have been made by Valerius Antias or Claudius Quadrigarius, there is no logical reason why L. should not have made the same error himself, conflating one, or more, annalistic accounts with the account of Cato. It might be urged against this possibility that L. would surely have been aware of Cato's superior authority. But L. was equally well aware of the superiority of Polybius as an authority on Greek affairs, yet could insert annalistic falsehoods into a Polybian narrative without acknowledging their provenance or doubting their truth (cf. vol. i, 7, Tränkle, 59 ff., 144 ff.). But if the alleged doublets or inconsistencies do not exist, the case for thinking that Cato is L.'s immediate source for most of the campaign is very much strengthened.

It is generally agreed that ch. 10 is non-Catonian in origin, and comes from Valerius Antias. Formally the mention of Antias refers only to the number of enemy dead, but it is likely that the whole chapter comes from him and that L., who is generally suspicious of such numbers in Antias (cf. vol. i, 11, 15. 9, xxxvi. 38. 7 nn.) is indicating doubt about the figure. The area in the vicinity of Cato's camp near Emporiae is described as *tuta ab hostibus*, which is not true before the battle described in chs. 14–15.

The alleged doublets have been fully discussed by Astin. I have nothing to add to his reply to the claim that ch. 21 is a doublet of the rebellions of the Bergistani mentioned in 16. 9–10. Nor is there any reason to hold that 11–13. 3 are a fuller description of events described more briefly in 9. 11–13 (Astin, 306–7, who, however, misrepresents the position of Unger and Fraccaro: they did not hold, as he states, that 13. 2–3 take up the narrative from 9. 12–13, with chs. 11 and 12 as an insertion). As to 17. 1–4, which interrupts references to the Bergistani in 16. 10 and 17. 5 and anticipates the account of the war against the Turduli in ch. 19, Astin is willing to see an annalistic provenance but holds that L. has made it consistent with his Catonian evidence. This seems unnecessary—there is no reason why Cato should not have referred to the events in the order in which they appear in L.

It remains to consider whether L. used Cato's *Origines* or his speech *de consulatu suo*, or both. There are a number of correspondences with the fragments of the speech, but none with the *Origines*. The latter fact, however, is of no significance, since only one fragment of Cato's account of 195 in the *Origines* survives (fr. 93P). It would be quite possible that Cato should have used similar language in the *Origines*, or even inserted his actual speech, as he did on other occasions (cf. Tränkle, *Cato*, 6). But even if neither of these possibilities is the case, I cannot share Tränkle's dismissal of the possibility that L. used both the *Origines* and the speech. The digression on Emporiae must come from the *Origines*—which in many ways reflected that ethnographical tradition which was so strong in Hellenistic historiography. L. could easily have combined material from different works of Cato.

I turn now to the chronology of Cato's campaign, which depends to a considerable extent on the meaning of *castra hiberna* in 13. 3. It will be convenient to begin from Astin's discussion (*Cato*, 308–10). He argues from the fact that Cato set out immediately after the debate on the *Lex Oppia* (8. 4) and Cato's references to the speed of his preparations (*ORF*[3], fr. 28) that Cato must have left Italy in April. The grain *in areis* (9. 12) will point to a date in June. Astin then places the battle near Emporiae in late summer, and thus holds that the whole of the campaign belongs to 195. This, he says, is confirmed by L.'s report (42. 1) that news of the successes of Cato in Spain and of Flamininus against Nabis arrived at Rome contemporaneously.

This chronology, however, has to accommodate L.'s statement at 13. 2 *ipse, cum iam id tempus anni appeteret quo geri res possent, castra hiberna tria milia passuum ab Emporiis posuit*, which must be derived from Cato, *ORF*[3], fr. 35 *sed ubi anni tempus uenit, castra hiberna* ... Astin follows those (e.g. De Sanctis, iv. 1. 388) who take *castra hiberna* to mean not a camp for winter, but as equivalent to *castra statiua*, 'a strongly built, more permanent camp'. There is, however, not a shred of evidence that *castra hiberna* can have this meaning, and I do not follow Astin's claim that L. makes it clear that he intends this sense by saying *cum iam id tempus anni appeteret quo geri res posset*. The latter is a difficulty on either interpretation of *castra hiberna*. On Astin's chronology we are in the summer, not at the beginning of the campaigning season. De Sanctis took the phrase to mean that it was now cool enough for serious operations, and thought of a date in September. I am unaware, however, of any evidence that Roman armies found it too hot to campaign in Spain in the summer.

I conclude that *castra hiberna* must be given its natural meaning, and that *cum iam . . . possent* must be regarded as a misunderstanding of what Cato said in fr. 35, or of something very similar to it. A consequence of this view is that the events described in chs. 13–21 in fact took place in 194. There is no difficulty in supposing that Cato arrived in Spain in late summer 195. Cato entered office on 24 November 196 (cf. p. 25). We know that surprise was expressed at his delay in going to Spain (xxxiii. 44. 4) and since delay during

the winter would not cause all that much surprise, this means that
he did not set out, as might have been expected, at the beginning of
spring 195. Time was taken up by the *uer sacrum* (xxxiii. 44. 1–2)
and by the debate on the repeal of the *Lex Oppia*. There is, then, no
obstacle to placing Cato's arrival in Spain in late summer. The
synchronism in 42. 1 can simply be rejected.

(W–M had already argued that the war against the Lacetani in
ch. 20 belonged to 194, on the grounds that it was the factual basis
for Plutarch's otherwise fantastic story [*Cato mai.* 11. 1–2] that
Scipio succeeded Cato in Spain and defeated the Lacetani: cf.
43. 7 n.)

For other sources on Cato's Spanish campaign cf. *MRR*, i. 339.
Ennius, *Ann.* 503V may refer to the campaign. See further p. 35.

8. 4. Lunae portum: Luna, modern Luni, lies on the south side of
the River Magra (ancient Makra), separated by a headland from
the Gulf of La Spezia. There has been considerable controversy,
however, as to whether *portus Lunae* lay near to Luna itself (the
remains are now some 2 km. from the sea) or in the Gulf of La
Spezia. The main reason for holding the latter view is that the Gulf
of La Spezia appears to correspond, and Luni itself not to do so, to
Strabo's statement (v. p. 222C) that the harbour is surrounded by
tall mountains, and to Pliny's description (*NH* iii. 50) of Luna as
oppidum . . . portu nobile. There is nothing particularly striking about
the beach near Luni now. But Strabo may not have visited the area
himself, and though Luni is not 'surrounded' by tall mountains, the
impressive range of the Apuan Alps to the east could easily lead to
exaggerated language. As to Pliny, it is quite possible that the harbour has silted up since antiquity, and that there was once a greater
recess. There are considerable difficulties in holding that *portus
Lunae* was in the Gulf of La Spezia. That gulf is separated from the
plain of the Magra by mountains, and access to the gulf would not
have been easy by land. And the distance from Luna makes it
rather odd that it should be called *portus Lunae*. In addition, the
gulf is a collection of separate bays: only one of these could actually
be *portus Lunae*, while Strabo's description, if applied to the gulf,
would have to refer to the whole gulf. In antiquity a gulf as large as
that of La Spezia was not regarded as an ideal harbour.

The most convincing discussion of the problem is by L. Banti,
Luni (Florence, 1937), 68–81, who gives references to earlier literature and from whom several of the above points are derived.

5. ab Luna: cf. xxxiii. 21. 1 n.
  edixit: χ, *dixit* B. *dixit* does not give the required sense and the

repetition after *edicto* is no argument against *edixit* (cf. p. 13). In § 6 χ again has *edixerat* against B's *dixerat* but in that case *dixerat* is quite possible and χ has probably been influenced by *edicto* ... *edixit* here.

*ORF*³, fr. 28 refers to the size of Cato's forces.

portum Pyrenaei: this is the only mention of *portus Pyrenaei*, and it is probably to be identified with *portus Veneris*, itself taken as the modern Port Vendres, just on the French side of the present Franco–Spanish border. Cf. J. Jannoray, *RE*, xxii. 411–18, R. Grosse, *RE*, xxiv. 12, Schulten, *FHA*, iii. 179, J. F. Hind, *RSA* ii (1972), 44–5 (who discusses the possibility that *Portus Veneris* is to be identified with Port Bou rather than Port Vendres).

*ORF*³, fr. 30 reads *ita nos fert uentus ad primorem Pyrenaeum, quo proicit in altum* (*primorem* is Mommsen's plausible emendation for the MSS.' *priorem*). That will be Cape Creus, the easternmost extremity of the Pyrenees, and will have been reached after the rendezvous at *portus Pyrenaei*.

6. sinumque Gallicum: the Gulf of Lyons, to the west of Marseille. *ORF*³, fr. 29 says ... *Massiliam praeterimus, inde omnem classem uentus auster lenis fert ... ultra angulum Gallicum ad Illiberim atque Ruscinonem deferimur* ... But *sinus Gallicus* and *angulus Gallicus* cannot possibly designate the same area. As Suetonius says (ap. Isid. *de natura rerum* xliv = p. 243 Reiferscheid) *sinus maiores recessus maris dicuntur, ut est Caspius, Arabicus, Indicus: minores autem anguli dicuntur, ut Paestanus, Amyclanus et ceteri similes.* Clearly the Gulf of Lyons could not be called an *angulus*. But it is equally hard to see what small recess would be given the epithet *Gallicus*. I suspect that *angulus* here may mean 'corner' and refer to the place where the coastline turns north–south from east–west. *angulus* is not found elsewhere in this sense in second-century Latin (*TLL*, ii. 58) but with a word of this sort, that is not decisive. One cannot dismiss the possibility that Cato was trying to bamboozle the audience with pseudo-geography. It is certainly hard to see how a *lenis auster* would be very helpful for reaching Illiberis and Ruscino.

Rhodam: Rhode, modern Rosas, was probably founded in the sixth or fifth century, either, like Emporiae, from Massilia, or perhaps directly from Emporiae. For the legend that it was a Rhodian foundation cf. Strabo iii. p. 160C, [Scymnus] 205–6. See Schulten, *RE*, iA. 954, A. Garcia y Bellido, *Hispania Graeca*, i (Barcelona, 1948), 166–7, Hind, *RSA* ii, 48 n. 24. The view of A. G. Woodhead, *The Greeks in the West* (London, 1962), 66–7 that Rhode was only an earlier name for Emporiae is disproved by the present passage.

7–9. 13. Emporiae, modern Ampurias, was founded from Massilia
c. 550. For the literary sources—among which the present passage
is the most important—cf. Hübner, *RE*, v. 2527–9, M. Almagro,
Las Fuentes Escritas Referentes a Ampurias (Barcelona, 1951), for later
literature Grosse, *RE*, Supp. ix. 34–6. See also Garcia y Bellido,
op. cit., 164 ff.

For a brief introduction cf. Almagro, *Ampurias: history of the city
and guide to the excavations* (Barcelona, 1956), P. MacKendrick, *The
Iberian stones speak* (New York, 1969), ch. 3, J. Boardman, *The Greeks
Overseas* (2nd edn., Harmondsworth, 1973), 211. For an argument
that *Pyrene* in Avienus, *Ora maritima*, 563 refers to Emporiae cf.
Hind, *RSA* ii, 39 ff.

The native inhabitants were the Indiketes (Strabo iii. p. 160C)
and their town may have been called Indike (cf. Steph. Byz. s.v.).
Emporiae had served as a Roman naval base in the Second Punic
war: cf. 16. 6 n., xxi. 60. 2, xxvi. 19. 11.

The name in Greek is normally Ἐμπόριον. The plural is used
because of the existence of two separate communities.

7. socios nauales: cf. 6. 12 n.

9. 1. iam: emphatic, rather than temporal, as it is taken by Hof-
man, *TLL*, vii. 1. 116.

Phocaea . . . Massilienses: cf. xxvi. 19. 11 *Emporiis urbe Graeca—
oriundi et ipsi a Phocaea sunt.* In fact Emporiae was a colony of Massilia
itself and perhaps originally subject to Massiliot control. Cf. Strabo
iii. p. 159C, [Scylax] 2, [Scymnus] 202 ff., F. Gschnitzer, *Abhängige
Orte im griechischen Altertum* (Munich, 1958), 25–6. Massilia was
founded from Phocaea *c.* 600. Cf. Ogilvie, 711–12. Relations between
Rome and Massilia began very early, perhaps as early as the sixth
century. Cf. Just. xliii. 3. 4, G. Nenci, *RSL* xxiv (1958), 24–97,
G. V. Sumner, *HSCP* lxxii (1967), 208 n. 10.

2. minus . . . patentem: for the omission of *quam* cf. 1. 3 n. The
Cyclopean walls, constructed in the third century, measure 200 m.
on the west and 130 m. on the south: cf. Almagro, *Ampurias, History
of the City,* 71, *Fuentes escritas,* 50 ff.

3. tertium . . . adscitis: this is the only evidence for Caesar's
action. Almagro, *Fuentes escritas,* 58 suggested that the Greeks of
Emporiae followed the Massiliots in opposition to Caesar and that
Caesar showed his favour to the native inhabitants by giving them
citizenship first. The sons of Pompey, Gnaeus and Sextus, were
defeated at the battle of Munda in 45. Gnaeus was killed but
Sextus escaped.

There is no reason to doubt that all the inhabitants of Emporiae were eventually enfranchised. Cf. Pliny, *NH* iii. 22, Sherwin-White, *RC*², 346–7. For other instances of towns consisting partly of Roman citizens, partly of native inhabitants see Sherwin-White, 355. On the physical changes made by Caesar see Almagro, *Fuentes escritas*, 52 ff., on the creation of a *municipium* cf. Brunt, 603–4, H. Galsterer, *Untersuchungen zum römischen Städtewesen auf der Iberischen Halbinsel* (Berlin, 1971), 26. (The inscription referred to by W–M is a forgery: cf. *CIL* ii. 427* and p. 615).

This is the only reference to the Dictator in the extant books.

4 ff. For similar caution by Massilia itself against its Ligurian neighbours cf. Momigliano, *Alien Wisdom* (Cambridge, 1975), 52.

4. miraretur: for the use of the imperfect rather than the pluperfect subjunctive cf. K–St, i. 179, Handford, 111.

fera ... obiectis: χ. B has scrambled *bellicosa gente* into *bellicos agenti esse*. The 1535 edition had *Hispanis, tam ferae et bellicosae genti obiectos*, and this was read without comment by Madvig and Weissenborn. But there is no clear evidence that this reading has MS. authority, and since the reading of Bχ makes excellent sense, it should be retained.

inter ualidiores: 'when one is surrounded by stronger people'. Sage's translation and note are absolute nonsense.

5. semper: Mg; om. Bχ, but it makes excellent sense, and it is unlikely to have been inserted as part of a gloss on *assiduus*.

6. moris ... legis: Mg. Bχ have the more expected order *moris aut legis causa*. The latter could be right, but it is perhaps more likely that L. wrote the unusual word-order, and it was altered in transmission.

9. Emporiae was thus doing what its name suggests was its original function. It was a trading post developed to take advantage of the possibilities of trade. A very large number of Greek colonies, of course, were of this type, though it was unusual for their primary market to be so close at hand. The Spanish ignorance of the sea applies only to those of this region. Cf. xxi. 7. 3, J. M. Blazquez, *Economia de la Hispania Romana* (Bilbao, 1978), 229.

exigere: 'export'. The verb is found with this meaning elsewhere only at Col. x. 317, though *exactus* means 'exporting' at [Quint.] *Decl.* 12. 19 (*TLL*, v. 2. 1452. 57 ff.).

mutui ... desiderium: a desire on both sides for the advantages which both would share.

10. erant ... fide: cf. § 1 n. Presumably Emporiae entered into relations with Rome at the same time as Massilia itself.

sicut ... pari: for the omission of *ita* after *sicut* cf. W–M's note on xxiv. 3. 13.

tum ... acceperunt: cf. *ORF*³, fr. 31 *mihi atque classi obuiam fiunt* (Astin, *Cato*, 302 n. 1).

11–12. id tempus ... tempus: for the repetition, perhaps a deliberate reflection of Cato's style, cf. p. 13. But the passage as a whole is in a deliberately straightforward military style. § 11 is almost Caesarian in structure.

omne ... consumpsit: cf. 13. 3 n.

forte: cf. xxxii. 39. 4 n.

tempus ... haberent: for such consecutive clauses cf. K–St, ii. 244 ff. For the chronology cf. pp. 65–6 and addendum thereto.

redemptoribus: for their functions in supplying the Roman army cf. Badian, *Publicans and Sinners*, 16 ff. The action is typical of Cato's attitude to *publicani* and desire to save expenditure. On Cato's clashes with the *publicani* in 184 cf. Badian, op. cit., 35 ff., Astin, *Cato*, 85 ff. J. S. Richardson, *JRS* lxvi (1976), 150 points out that Cato's action indicates that there was no regular procedure for the collection of a corn levy in Spain at this time.

bellum ... alet: as W–M say, the concept is not new. But it is very likely that the phrase itself is a genuine Catonian utterance.

10. *The return of M. Heluius.* For the source of this chapter see p. 64.

10. 1. eodem tempore: If I am right in thinking that the battle described in chs. 14–15 took place in 194 (see pp. 65–6) *quia tuta iam ab hostibus regio erat* in § 3 will have to be rejected, not used as a reason for placing this episode after the battle. Helvius' *ouatio* preceded Minucius' triumph (§ 6) and it would be very difficult to postpone the latter to 194.

M. Heluio: (4). Cf. xxxii. 27. 7 n.

decedenti ex: χ. B omits *ex*. L. often uses *decedere* with the ablative alone (Packard, i. 1143–4) and I suspect an addition in χ.

ulteriore ... Iliturgi: this Iliturgi is not the town in Ulterior (mod. Mengibar: cf. A. Blanco, *AEA* xxxiii [1960], 193 ff.) but is to be placed in Citerior, to the south of the Ebro (cf. Schulten, *Hermes* lxiii [1928], 288–301: *contra* J. Vallejo, *Emerita* xi [1943], 175–7). This is probably the explanation of the statement in § 5 that Helvius was fighting *in aliena prouincia*, though it could be that the *ouatio* was for action taken after the defeat of Sempronius Tuditanus in 197 (cf. xxxiii. 25. 9 n.: thus also J. M. Gazquez, *Pyrenae* x [1974], 173 ff.). *ceterum* in § 5 perhaps makes the latter more likely. McDonald's argument that the mention of the Celtiberians points to Iliturgi being in Ulterior depends on holding that the Turdetani in 17. 1–4 and ch. 19 are those of south-west Spain: cf. 17. 1 n.

The Celtiberians had originally supported Rome during the Second Punic War (xxii. 21. 7 ff., xxiv. 49. 7–8) but it was their desertion which led to the disaster to the Scipios in 211 (xxv. 33 ff.) and later some fought for Carthage (xxviii. 1. 4, 24. 4, xxx. 8. 6). For conflicts with them in 193 see xxxv. 7. 8.

B has *Liturgi* here and *Liturgi* in § 2, and *Iliturgi* is the reading of φ in § 2. *Iliturgi* occurs as a nominative in xxiii. 49. 5, xxviii. 19. 1. Cf. Neue–Wagener, i. 948–9. (Names of towns after *oppidum* in L. always stand in apposition.)

Ap. Claudio: (245). Cf. xxxii. 35. 6–7 n. For his appointment to Ulterior see xxxiii. 43. 5.

2. Valerius: Antias. Cf. xxxii. 6. 5 n. and above p. 64.

3. ouans: cf. xxxi. 20. 5 n. For Helvius' *ovatio* cf. *I.I.* xiii. 1. 552.

4. Tenney Frank (*Economic Survey*, i. 138: cf. Van Nostrand, ibid., iii. 128 ff.) held that the booty figures from Spain at this time included profits from the operation of the mines. This is extremely improbable. Cf. Brunt, *Second International Conference of Economic History* (Paris, 1965), i. 139, Badian, *Publicans and Sinners*, 32, J. S. Richardson, *JRS* lxvi (1976), 140 ff. See also 21. 7 n.

argentum Oscense is the Spanish *denarius* coinage, perhaps instituted in 197, as argued by Crawford, *NC* 7, ix (1969), 82–3. R. C. Knapp, *NC* 7, xvii (1977), 1–18 argues that payment of tribute to Rome was not the only reason for the institution of the coinage, as claimed by Crawford. Cf. also id., *Aspects of the Roman Experience in Iberia 206–100 B.C.* (Valladolid, 1977), 70 ff. Osca is modern Huseca, north of Ilerda (cf. Schulten, *RE*, xviii. 1. 1536) but the name is only a label, and Osca was not the only mint.

signati bigatorum: cf. xxxi. 49. 2 n., addendum thereto, and Crawford, *RRC*, ii. 630.

5. alieno ... prouincia: for the requirement to fight *suis auspiciis* cf. xxxi. 4. 1, 47. 4 nn. Helvius was *suis auspiciis* but it could be argued that he was not fighting in the province where he could legitimately operate them—whether he was claiming a triumph for fighting in Citerior in 197 or for his recent victory (cf. § 1 n.). *et*, therefore, is explicative (cf. *TLL*, v. 2. 873 ff.).

ceterum: cf. § 1 n.

successori Q. Minucio: in fact Minucius was the governor of Citerior (xxxiii. 26. 2). If not a simple mistake by L. or his source, this too may point to the action taken by Helvius in 197 (cf. § 1 n.). On Q. Minucius Thermus (65) cf. xxxii. 27. 8 n.

insequentem: B, *sequentem* χ. L. always uses *insequi*, not *sequi*, with *annus*. Cf. Ogilvie, 447.

6. ante . . . quam . . . triumpharet: L. uses the subjunctive with *antequam* and *postquam* to a considerably greater extent than earlier writers. Cf. K–St, ii. 366, H–S, 600–1. Kühnast's discussion (238 ff.) is unintelligible.

For Minucius' triumph cf. *I.I.* xiii. 1. 552–3.

11. 1. Ilergetum: the Ilergetes lived in the neighbourhood of Ilerda. Under their leaders Andobales and Mandonius they repeatedly defected from Rome during the Second Punic War, but were finally subjected in 205. Cf. Schulten, *RE*, ix. 999.

2. Bilistage: not otherwise known.

uenerunt . . . misisset: cf. Cato, *ORF*³, fr. 33.

uenerunt: *conuenerunt* MSS., which is clearly inappropriate, and the change has been universally accepted. (Rossbach, *WKlPh* xxxiv [1917], 1132 suggested that *con-* was the beginning of the name of Bilistages' son.)

praesidium Romanus misisset: L. An interesting case of corruption occurring early in transmission. B has *praesidium Romanis missis et*, χ *praesidium Romanis* (or *Romani*) *misisset* (or *misissent*). Mg's *praesidio Romanus miles esset* is clearly an attempt to make sense. The true reading is scarcely in doubt (cf. Tränkle, *Gnomon*, 374).

4. quam mox . . . expectet: 'was waiting to see how soon he would have to fight'. For other instances of *expectare quam mox* cf. iii. 37. 5 and passages quoted at *TLL*, v. 2. 1898. 52 ff.

7. potuisse: could have, at the beginning of the rebellion.

terriculis: cf. pp. 6–7.

8. Saguntini: for other references to Rome's dilatoriness in helping Saguntum cf. xxxi. 7. 3 n.

12. 1. sic: χ, om. B. It is rather odd as it stands, since we are not told explicitly of Cato's reaction to the speech of the Ilergetan envoys. W–M's parallels of xxx. 31. 10, xxxi. 32. 5, and xxxii. 37. 5 are not the same, since in those passages *sic* or *ita* summarizes what had gone before. If it was in all the MSS., I would be inclined to accept it, but as it is not found in B, it may well be an addition in χ. Weidner proposed *sicut* on the grounds that the Ilergetes had been given a reply in § 3: but L. is here talking of the second speech of the envoys. Cf. M. Müller, *Beiträge zur Kritik und Erklärung des Livius* (Stendal, 1866), 14.

4. uana . . . ueris: for the alliterative conjunction cf. xxxv. 40. 8 and the passages collected by Wölfflin, *Ausgewählte Schriften*, 277–8.

5. respondet: *respondit* MSS. In § 7 χ has *iubet*, B *iussit*. Given L.'s fondness for *uariatio* in tenses (cf. pp. 11–12) it is possible that the perfect is right in both places.

6. iubet . . . [iussit:] the repetition is obviously impossible and it is a question of which should be deleted. It is far more likely that *iussit* was added by a scribe who did not understand the construction of *expediri* than that *iubet* should have been added in the middle of the sentence. Perizonius's suggestion of deleting *iubet* and changing *iussit* to *iussisse*, with the infinitive still dependent on *respondet*, is far too cumbersome and involves two changes rather than one.

13. 2. cum . . . hiberna: see p. 65.
    quo . . . possent: a relative consecutive clause. At ix. 3. 12 L. uses the indicative in a similar sense. Cf. K–St, ii. 296, H–S, 559.
    ducebat: B, *educebat* χ, perhaps rightly: cf. xxxi. 34. 9 n.

3. Unless we have deliberate rearrangement by L., these events are not those described by Cato, *ORF*[3], fr. 35, as W–M say, since the latter preceded the pitching of the *castra hiberna*. The fragment could be connected with 9. 11 *omne id tempus exercendis militibus consumpsit*.

4. [satis] admodum: χ has *satis*, a clear case of a gloss by a scribe who thought that *admodum* meant 'to a sufficient extent'. Since this is obviously the case, it is not worth considering Duker's *satis ad hunc modum* or Madvig's *ubi ad hunc modum* (*Emendationes*, 498). But McDonald's statement 'neque modeste de Catone scriptum est' is scarcely a compelling argument.
    praefectosque: not *praefectos sociorum* only, as W–M say: cf. Schleussner, 111 n. 40.

5–10. A conventional speech before battle. It cannot be identified with the speech *Numantiae apud equites* (*ORF*[3], frs. 17–18). Cf. Fraccaro, *Opuscula*, i. 181 ff.

5. ostendendi: χ. *ostendere* B. The simple infinitive with nouns like *spes, timor, potestas* is mainly a verse construction (K–St, i. 743–4, H–S, 351). *spe posse* occurs at 24. 7, but it would be rash to introduce another example here on the authority of B alone. The double spondee, moreover, is the commonest clausula in L.'s later books: cf. H. Aili, *The Prose Rhythm of Sallust and Livy* (Stockholm, 1979), ch. 5.

6. conferetis manus: the emendation in the later MSS. is clearly right. A future is needed, and it well explains both the *confertis* of Bχ and the *conseretis* of Mg. (In itself *conseretis* is, of course, perfectly acceptable.)

7. ⟨in⟩ Hispania ... essent: the only way of taking the paradosis would be to understand *esset* with *Hispania Carthaginiensium*, but this is very harsh, and in any case it is the strength of the army, not the ownership of Spain that Cato is seeking to emphasize. The old insertion of *in*, with Madvig's deletion of *ibi* remains the neatest solution. There is not much to be said for Rossbach's suggestion of *ii* (= *duo*) for *ibi* (*WKlPh* xxxiv [1917], 1132–3) on the grounds that with *nullum ... duo ... tres* in what follows a number is required. In any case Hasdrubal was the only Carthaginian commander in Spain at the time of the Ebro treaty, and the plural is rhetorical.

addi ... finis: the Ebro treaty of 226. See Pol. ii. 13. 7. This is not the place for a discussion of the treaty for which see Walbank, *Commentary*, i. 168–72, with references to the ancient sources and modern literature: for subsequent literature see Errington, *Latomus* xxix (1970), 25 ff., Sumner, *Latomus* xxxi (1972), 475 ff., Th. Liebman-Frankfort, *RD* 1 (1972), 193 ff. *imperii sui*, of course, is anachronistic. Cf. Harris, 106 n. 2.

addi: Madvig's correction of the *addere* of the MSS. is clearly right. In the case of clauses of decrees, treaties, etc. it is L.'s practice to use the passive. Cf. vii. 41. 4, xxi. 19. 4, xxiv. 18. 9, xxvi. 24. 9, xxx. 38. 3, xxxi. 11. 17, 44. 7, xxxii. 25. 2, 36. 9, xxxviii. 38. 18, xl. 43. 2, xli. 14. 10. The force of the verb is that the Ebro treaty was regarded (by Rome anyway: cf. Walbank, *Commentary*, i. 170) as an additional clause to the treaty of Catulus, concluded in 241 to put an end to the First Punic War.

8. duo praetores: Ap. Claudius Nero and P. Manlius (xxxiii. 43. 5).

tres exercitus: for the praetorian armies cf. xxxiii. 43. 7–8.

decem ... annis: Scipio had driven the Carthaginians out of Spain in 206 (sources in *MRR*, i. 299) so that *prope* means 'about' not 'almost'.

citra Hiberum: Cato's point is that the Ebro treaty abandoned Spain south of the Ebro to Carthage: now it is that part of the province north of the Ebro that is being lost.

9. rebellantem ... bellantem: perhaps a deliberate echo of Cato's style: Cato was fond of achieving effect by repetitions of this sort. *rebellare* is common in L., but not found in authors before his time. *magis* goes with *rebellantem temere* as a whole.

10. corpora curanda: see to their bodily needs, with food and toilet, not to sleep, as Sage indicates.

14–15. *The battle near Emporiae.* On the site of the battle see Astin, *Cato,* 311–18.

14. 1. Cf. Cato, *ORF*³, fr. 36. L.'s sentence has a plain periodic structure, quite Caesarian in effect.

sentirent: for the absolute use of *sentire* cf. xxxii. 17. 8 n.

circumducit: this is the only instance in L. of *circumducere* used absolutely, though *ducere* is so used (cf. W–M ad loc.). Cf. Plaut. *Most.* 680 (*TLL,* iii. 1134).

2. ⟨et⟩ ipsi: L. is extremely fond of *et ipse* (Packard, ii. 324–7) and Duker's supplement, universally accepted since, is almost certainly right. For another probable case of *et* omitted before *ipse* cf. xliv. 6. 14.

3–4. Appian (*Ib.* 40. 162) adds the important detail that part of Cato's strategy involved sending the Roman ships back to Massilia. See further 16. 1–2 n. For possible motives for Cato's actions, other than morale-boosting, see Astin, *Cato,* 37–8.

3. ego sedulo . . . feci: W–M argue that this is a colloquialism, on the strength of occurrences of the phrase in Terence. *sedulo facere* is certainly common in Plautus and Terence, but it also occurs in Cicero, *Clu.* 58, where a colloquialism would be inappropriate (*fin.* iii. 16 could conceivably be colloquial). Nor are *sedulo facere* in xxxiii. 11. 10, xxxvi. 15. 4 plausibly regarded as colloquialisms. Moreover, L–S seem right to put the present passage in the category where *sedulo* means 'intentionally', not 'carefully'.

4. quod . . . tutissimum: for parallels see Woodman, 182. χ adds *est,* a clear example of unintelligent emendation. McDonald's *uix necessarium* is too weak: *idem tutissimum est* would totally destroy the pithiness of the utterance.

in uirtute . . . habere: Cato repeats, at the end of a very short speech, what he had said at the beginning. I have played with the idea that the words are a gloss.

6. induxit: Mg, *eduxit* Bχ. Both W–M and McDonald support Mg's reading by reference to 15. 1 *in pugnam inductis.* Walsh (*CR,* 55) objects that the meaning there is different. I fail to see the difference, or the relevance of the fact that Cato is on horseback. Both *educere* and *inducere* are widely used in military contexts (for *educere* cf. xxxii. 11. 3 n.). *educere* is the commoner, but not so much so that corruption to *inducere* could be excluded. But there is a strong case for *induxit*. *educere* has more the sense of 'lead out from a place (e.g. *castris*) to a battlefield'—it is commonly used with *in aciem*. But from there to the actual fighting 'lead out' is less appropriate than 'bring in'. *educere* is never used with *pugna* and *in pugnam inductis* is therefore more relevant than Walsh allows.

7. Cf. Cato, *ORF*³, fr. 37 *nostros pone uersus hosteis esse ab dextra parte*.

8. dextrae alae: cf. xxxi. 21. 7 n.

ut ... hostem: cf. Suet. *DJ* 62 *obsistens fugientibus retinensque singulos et contortis faucibus conuertens in hostem*.

uerteritque in hostem: Bχ. *et aduersos in hostem uerterit* Mg. Tränkle (*Gnomon*, 375 n. 1) defends Mg's reading—with *aduersos* changed to *auersos*—on the grounds that *auersus* is just the right word for soldiers fleeing from battle (see further *TLL*, ii. 1323). For the repetition of the root he compares v. 38. 3, xxxi. 37. 7, and for similar shortening of the text in F xxxiii. 18. 10, 34. 1. He presents a powerful case, and it is certainly difficult to see why *aduersos* should have been inserted as a gloss. One may note that immediately afterwards Bχ omit *ita*, clearly incorrectly.

11. soliferreis: Mg. (Bχ have *soliferis*, not *soliferris*, as McDonald implies). The word is found only here, in Gell. x. 25. 2, and Festus, pp. 372–3, 384–5L. *sollus* is an Oscan word for *totus* and we should probably read *solliferreis*. Festus says L. also used *sollicuria*. Cf. Conway, *Italic Dialects* (Cambridge, 1897), i. 219, Ernout–Meillet, *Dictionnaire étymologique de la langue Latine* (4th edn., Paris 1967), 633. The word may well have been used by Cato himself. Cf. p. 9.

phalaricisque: a javelin covered with pitch and set on fire, often propelled from a catapult. Cf. xxi. 8. 10 and Walsh ad loc. I cannot understand W–M's note with its reference to Pol. vi. 23. 5 and Tac. *H.* iv. 29.

caecis: 'whose source was unknown' (cf. 39. 6, Ovid, *Fasti* i. 62, Sil. It. ix. 105, *TLL*, iii. 46. 34–5), not 'ohne sicheres Ziel', as W–M say.

15. 1. subsidiariis: probably allies (W–M).

cohortibus: on the use of cohorts as the tactical unit in Spain cf. M. J. V. Bell, *Historia* xiv (1965), 404 ff., Astin, *Cato*, 30 n. 6, 39 n. 30.

2. integri ... hostes: on the word-order cf. p. 13.

3. secundam: cf. p. 36 n. 8.

reuehitur: Bχ, *equo reuehitur* Mg, a manifest gloss. For *reuehi* without *equo* cf. ii. 47. 6, viii. 7. 12. Ogilvie (*Phoenix*, 344) defends *equo* on the grounds that Mg also makes omissions at 16. 1–2 and 16. 5 and that *equo reuehi* occurs at vii. 41. 3. The latter is irrelevant, and as to the former we shall see that 16. 1–2 is very probably an interpolation in Mg. For another clear case of interpolation in Mg cf. § 5 *castra hostium*.

prae se ferri: MSS. It has been objected to on the grounds that Cato cannot have gone into battle at the head of his army with the standards in front of him. 'totum ridiculum est' proclaimed Madvig (*Emendationes*, 499), 'a sense of display or ostentation which would be absurd here' says Ogilvie (*Phoenix*, 347). But ostentation is precisely what Cato is indulging in: Weissenborn drew attention to προκινδυνεύων in Appian, *Ib.* 40. 165 and McDonald points out that in § 4 Cato must be in front of the legion. McDonald is right to keep the paradosis. (Seyffert, *NJPhP* lxxxiii [1861], 825 proposed *proferre*, not *proferri*, as Madvig and McDonald state.)

plenoque gradu: a quick march. Cf. W–M ad loc., *TLL*, vi. 2. 2144. 45 ff.

4. interequitans: B, absurdly altered to *inter equites* in χ. The word is found also at vi. 7. 3, xxxv. 5. 10. It does not occur before L., but it may be a military technical term, not a coining by L.

sparo: a small curved spear: cf. W–M ad loc. The word may have been used by Cato (cf. Tränkle, *Cato*, 18). Sage translates 'spear-shaft', which is no doubt true, but misleading.

5. pro uallo: cf. Cato, *ORF³*, fr. 38 *iam apud uallum nostri satis agebant.*

6. qua: it is unclear whether *qua* means 'where' (cf. K–St, ii. 284) or is to be taken with *ea parte*. L. would perhaps have regarded the question as an unreal one.

principes hastatosque: cf. xxxiii. 1. 2 n.

7. apposita: *opposita* MSS., but the dative is used after *opponere* only of the thing to which the object stands in opposition and *porta* is not in opposition to the *statio* (x. 43. 1 is not parallel: the object there is the attacking soldiers). *apposita* is in the 1518 Mainz edition and should not be ascribed to Doujat.

9. Valerius Antias: cf. p. 64, 10. 2 n.

detractator: B, *detractor* χ. Neither form occurs before L., but since he always uses *detractatio*, not *detractio*, it is virtually certain that he wrote *detractator*.

16. 1–2. A desperate problem. The passage is omitted in Bχ and preserved only in Mg. Weissenborn deleted it, but found no followers. A trenchant attack on its authenticity was launched by Tränkle, *Gnomon*, 374–5 n. 3. He has four main points. (*a*) The section is omitted in its entirety in Bχ, and it is therefore unlikely that its absence is due to a mechanical error in the course of transmission (as, for example, in § 5 where Bχ omit *uinoque et cibo curatos*: in that case the scribe's eye jumped from *appellatos* to *curatos*). (*b*) The text presents the impossible construction *ubi spem nisi in uirtute haberent. nisi* for *non nisi* is a Late Latin construction (cf. Löfstedt, *Coniectanea* [Uppsala–Stockholm, 1950], i. 29 ff.). (*c*) *putatur* at the beginning without an indication of the agent is very strange. McDonald's attempt to justify it by comparison with *laudant me* in Cato, *ORF³*, fr. 28 is irrelevant: ellipse of the subject when it is 'people in general' is common enough (cf. K–St, i. 5), but what is needed is a parallel for the passive. (*d*) Virtually the whole of the section repeats notions already found in the account of the battle.

To this it can be replied (cf. W–M and McDonald) that one detail, *procul nauibus*, is not in the main narrative, but since it is in Appian (cf. 14. 3 n.) it must derive from Cato himself, in which case its mention at this point must be due to L., not to an interpolator. But the interpolator could have read Cato (it is unlikely that he would have read Appian), or the statement could just be an inference from the narrative as a whole. The cumulative effect of Tränkle's argument is very strong, and I think he is right to hold that we have to do with the paraphrasing comments of a 'spätantike Schulmeister'.

3. suos: χ, *suis* B, *milites* Mg. Another example of a gloss in Mg.

4. Emporitanos Hispanos: cf. 9. 1–4.

5. uinoque et cibo curatos: Mg. Again missing in Bχ. After §§ 1–2 one is suspicious. Weissenborn commented that while *cibo curare* is used of soldiers before and after engagements, this is the only example of *uino et cibo curare*. But these are not soldiers, and for *uino curare* cf. Enn. *Ann.* 368V.

6. legati dedentium: 'ambassadors from peoples surrendering'.

Tarraconem: mod. Tarragona. It was first captured by Cn. Scipio in 218 (xxi. 61. 4) and was the main base for Roman operations in the Second Punic War. Emporiae was used only when Tarraco was in the hands of rebellious peoples. Cf. Alföldy, *RE*, Supp. xv. 570 ff. I see no evidence for W–M's claim that it had remained loyal to Rome.

7. socium ac Latini nominis: cf. xxxi. 8. 7 n.

uariis casibus ... reducebantur: of their own volition, but Cato would doubtless have insisted on this anyway. The nature of the *casus* is left obscure. Some had doubtless been arrested at the beginning of the rebellion, others may have been kidnapped by private individuals. How far the captives were themselves private individuals is not clear. (On private settlement in Spain cf. A. J. N. Wilson, *Emigration from Italy in the Republican Age of Rome* [Manchester, 1966], 22 ff.)

in Hispania: χ, om. B. It is not impossible that it is a gloss. Cf. 21. 8 n.

8. in Turdetaniam: cf. 17. 1 n.

deuios: used by L. of peoples only here, at 20. 2, and xxxviii. 45. 9. Otherwise the usage is rare: cf. *TLL*, v. 1. 867. Its occurrence twice within five chapters might be added to Gries's list (*CPh* xlvi [1951], 36 ff.) of unusual words or phrases which L. repeats within a short space.

9. Bergistanorum: thus the MSS. here. At 17. 5, 21. 6 they have *Bergustanorum* and at 21. 2 *Vergestanus*. They may be the same as the *Bargusii* of xxi. 19. 7, 23. 2, Pol. iii. 35. 2. If Bergium (21. 1) is modern Berga, they lie to the west of the Ilergetes. Bergium can scarcely be the Βεργίδιον, (or Βεργουσία) of Ptol. *Geog.* ii. 6. 67, as Hübner, *RE*, iii. 292 suggests, as this is a town of the Ilergetes, and if they were now in revolt, we would expect that to be made clear.

eos deducto: Bχ. *eo deducto* Mg, *eos educto* J. F. Gronovius. With *eos* we must understand *eo*, with *eo*, *eos*. *deducere* is widely used by L. in military contexts (cf. *TLL*, v. 1. 274–5: cf. xxxii. 11. 3 n.) and since it occurs in all the MSS., it is very unwise to change it. As for *eos* or *eo*, I can find no example in L. of *deducere* of an army being used without any indication of where they were being led from or to, while the omission of the object gives a curtness appropriate to the style of the narrative. Cf. §10 *defecerunt iterum subacti*.

10. uenia uictis: one wonders if the alliteration comes from Cato himself.

17. 1–4. Cf. p. 64.

1. P. Manlius: (31). Cf. xxxiii. 42. 1 n. For his appointment cf. xxxiii. 43. 5.

Q. Minucio: (65). Thermus. He will have only just left. For his triumph cf. 10. 5 n.

adiuncto ... exercitu: on Claudius cf. 10. 1 n. His army is *uetus* because it contains the legion previously held there by Q. Fabius Buteo (cf. xxxiii. 43. 7). Sage's translation 'also made up of veterans' is misleading.

in Turdetaniam: the location of these operations is a major problem. Are these the Turdetani of South-West Spain, or those in Citerior, near Saguntum? (Cf. xxxiii. 44. 4 n.: I cannot share the scepticism of Astin, *Cato*, 41 n. 32.) Two arguments are of particular importance. (*a*) If Helvius' battle in ch. 10 did not take place in Ulterior (cf. n. ad loc.), there is no other trace of trouble in Ulterior. (*b*) The clear implication of *ex ulteriore Hispania* is that Claudius' army leaves Ulterior to join Manlius, not vice versa. Manlius' appointment is clearly limited to Citerior (xxxiii. 43. 5), and if fighting were taking place in Ulterior, it would be very odd for the Roman forces not to be under the command of Claudius. Cf. Schlag, 33 n. 60.

Astin (loc. cit.) argues for the Ulterior Turdetani on the grounds (*a*) that Plutarch, *Apophth. Catonis* 24 (= *Mor.* 199C) refers to the Baetis in connection with the episode reported at 19. 3 ff. But since Plutarch elsewhere confuses the Baetis with the Ebro (cf. § 11 n.), that argument is of little weight: (*b*) that the rebellion of 197 occurred in this area (xxxiii. 21. 7–8) and the involvement of Claudius suggests that the fighting was in Ulterior. Argument (*b*) above is a reply to this. (It may be added that if the campaign is in Ulterior, Cato's march back to Segontia [19. 10] is enormous.)

2. imbelles: for such depreciative comments on barbarian peoples cf. 47. 5 n.

3. nullius ... certaminis: 'was more or less no contest'. L. is fond of this use of the genitive of *certamen* (cf. W–M's note and Packard, i. 743–4).
   haud dubiam: predicative.

4. Celtiberum: cf. 10. 1 n.
   Turduli: a mere variant for Turdetani, though the Turduli and Turdetani of Ulterior may originally have been separate. Cf. Pol. xxxiv. 9. 1–2, Strabo iii. p. 139C, Ptol. *Geog.* ii. 4. 5, Walbank, *Commentary*, iii. 602–3.
   alienisque armis: taking up *imbelles*.
   parabant: for a present followed by an imperfect in L. cf. Chausserie-Laprée, 388–90.

5. rebellione Bergistanorum: 16. 9–10.

6. passi: see p. 12.

genus: Mg, *gens* Bχ. Either is possible, but *gens* is much commoner, and corruption from *genus* the more likely.

8. ut ne: for *ut ne* in final clauses cf. K–St, ii. 209, H–S, 643. The only other occurrence in L. is xliii. 12. 4 (at xxi. 49. 8, referred to by W–M, *ut* is an emendation). It occurs in Old Latin, but is not an archaic usage, and is unlikely to be a deliberate archaism by L.

11. concilio: *consilio* MSS., perhaps rightly. Cf. 26. 4 n.

uno die: cf. Pol. xix. 1, from Plut. *Cato mai.* 10: Πολύβιος μέν γέ φησι τῶν ἐντὸς Βαίτιος ποταμοῦ πόλεων ἡμέρᾳ μιᾷ τὰ τείχη κελεύσαντος αὐτοῦ περιαιρεθῆναι· πάμπολλαι δ' ἦσαν αὗται γέμουσαι μαχίμων ἀνδρῶν (Plutarch, or possibly Polybius himself, confuses the Baetis with the Ebro). In the later sources this is connected with a stratagem by Cato, who writes letters to all the cities to arrive on the same day, ordering them to destroy their walls. Cf. App. *Ib.* 41, Front. *Strat.* i. 1. 1, Polyaenus viii. 17, Zon. ix. 17. 6, *uir. ill.* 47. 2. See Walbank, *Commentary*, iii. 63.

dicionem: MSS. Usually emended to *deditionem*, but McDonald is right to keep the transmitted reading. For L.'s use of *dicio* cf. Packard, i. 1229–30, and for *in dicionem accipere* xxxiii. 20. 5.

12. Segesticam: the form used by L. is quite uncertain. *Segesticam* is the closest to B's *acceptis egestioam* (B's tendency to transliterate nonsense makes his text a better guide than χ's *Segestiam*). I would not imagine that at this stage Cato is operating outside the provincial boundary, and it is thus unlikely that Segestica is modern Segeda, as suggested by P. Bosch Gimpera and P. A. Bleye, *Historia de España* (Madrid, 1935), ii. 84 n. 41.

grauem: 'important'. Cf. 49. 2, *TLL*, vi. 2. 2279, Hübner on Tac. *H.* ii. 61.

uineis et pluteis: on these protective devices for besiegers cf. Vegetius, *Mil.* iv. 15, Kromayer–Veith, 444. *plutei* were arched hurdles made from trellis-work covered with skins, *uineae* were made from brushwood, and also had a skin covering.

18. 1. primi: Cn. and P. Cornelius Scipio, consuls in 222 and 218 respectively. Gnaeus was there in 218 (xxi. 60. 1–2), Publius arrived in 217 (xxii. 22. 1, Pol. iii. 97. 1–2).

2. uelut: 'as it were', with the whole clause. L. is using the technical vocabulary of the *causa liberalis* (cf. in general Ogilvie, 476 ff.).

sustentaturi fuerint: 'they were not going to sustain it any longer'. There is a suppressed apodosis *nec sustinuissent*. Cf. xxxii. 25. 8 n.

3–5. For similar praise of generals see the passages collected by Woodman, 174: add Valerius Corvus (vii. 32. 12 ff., 33. 1) and the professions of Marius (Sall. *Iug.* 85. 34–5), brought together with the present passage by Koestermann on Sallust, loc. cit., Tac. *A.* xiv. 24. 2. For other evidence on Cato's practices in these matters see Astin, *Cato*, 36 n. 23.

5. ultimis: 'the least of the soldiers'. Cf. xxx. 30. 4 *in ultimis laudum.*
honorem: 'rank'.

19. 1. difficilius ... faciebant: cf. 17. 1–4.
consul: cf. Cato, *ORF*[3], frs. 40–1.

2. facere ... abire: Mg, *faciebant ... abibant* Bχ. Alteration from the historical infinitive is much more likely than the reverse process.

3–7. *Negotiations with the Celtiberi.* Cf. Plut. *Cato mai.* 10. 2, *Mor.* 199C, Front. *Str.* iv. 7. 35, Zon. ix. 17. 7, Astin, *Cato*, 44. *ORF*[3], fr. 42 refers to this episode.

4. et duplex: χ, om. *et* B, probably rightly. In the case of the other alternatives, the offer is followed by the terms attached to it as an apodosis, and *et* occurs only here. L. varies the constructions, using first an infinitive after *iubet*, then an accusative and infinitive, and finally an indirect command.

5. noxiae: Bχ, *noxae* Mg. Either form is possible: cf. xxxi. 13. 4 n.

8. communi: 'mutual', not 'gewöhnlich, regelmassig' as W–M suggest. For trading by soldiers cf. xxxiii. 29. 4 n.

10. Seguntiae: the town in question is almost certainly Segontia, modern Siguenza (Götzfried, 55 n. 2, Schulten, *Numantia* i (Munich, 1914), 133, M. Fernandez Galiano, *EClás.* xvii [1973], 291 ff.). What L. wrote, however, is uncertain. B has *Saguntiae*, χ *Secuntiae*. L. could have assimilated the name to the famous Saguntum (at xxvi. 20. 6 he appears to confuse the two) and I think it is possible that he wrote *Saguntiae*.
sarcinas impedimentaque: cf. xxxv. 28. 4 n.
eo ... ducere: his main army, not just the cohorts of § 9, as Astin, *Cato*, 44–5, claims.

11. Astin (loc. cit.) associates Front. *Str.* iii. 1. 2 with this episode and thinks that Cato did succeed in capturing Segontia.
praetoris: Bχ. *praetorianis* (Mg) is Post-classical. *praetoriis* is possible, but the repetition of *praetoris* is not objectionable (cf. p. 13) and there is little case for altering it.
ad Hiberum: probably to the part near Numantia, not to its mouth (though cf. Astin, *Cato*, 46). For the fragment of Cato's

speech to the cavalry at Numantia cf. *ORF*³, fr. 17. Harris' statement (209 n. 2) that Cato 'campaigned at Numantia' is misleading:
cf. Astin, *Cato*, 46.

20. The operations described in this chapter take place in an area
which has, apparently, already been pacified (cf. 16. 6, 17. 6 ff.).
But the events here are entirely different from those described in
chs. 16–17 and we must assume that these peoples had again
rebelled.

20. 1. Sedetani: cf. xxxi. 49. 7 n.: add G. Fatas Cabeza, *AEA* xliv
(1971), 111 ff., placing them near Zaragossa.

   Ausetani: at the foot of the Pyrenees, near the coast. Cf. Pliny,
NH iii. 22, Barbieri, *Athenaeum* n.s. xxi (1943), 116.

1–2. Suessetani. Lacetanos: different authors provide the names
of three tribes in this part of Spain, the Iacetani, the Lacetani, and
the Laeetani. Many have followed Hübner (*Hermes* i [1866], 337 f.)
in removing the Lacetani and changing all occurrences of that name
to one of the others. But though the change is easy, the name occurs
often and consistently enough for it to be likely that a separate tribe
is involved and Barbieri (*Athenaeum* n.s. xxi, 113–21) has shown that
the evidence is consistent with putting the Laeetani on the coast,
the Lacetani between them and the River Siris, and the Iacetani
to the west of the Siris. The Lacetani make perfectly good sense
here. (De Sanctis, iv. 1. 453 talks of the Laeetani, but makes no
specific comment on our passage. G. Fatas Cabeza, *AEA* xliv [1971],
109, is unaware of Barbieri's argument). If one takes this view, the
Suessetani, probably to be identified with the Cessetani, will be
located fairly near the coast to the north of the Ebro (Schulten,
RE, ivA. 588). Those who think the Iacetani are involved place the
Suessetani to the south-west of the Iacetani (Fatas Cabeza, op. cit.).

2. esset: *est* MSS. I am not convinced that Madvig's correction
(*Emendationes*, 500 n.), universally accepted since, is correct. For the
indicative in *oratio obliqua* in L. cf. 6. 4, xxxvi. 7. 5, 39. 10, xxxvii.
17. 6, 34. 6, 56. 2, 60. 6 nn., K–St, ii. 544–5. Madvig objected to
the perfect, but for *dum* with the perfect cf. K–St, ii. 376.

4. tantundem: 'so much'. The word occurs five times in L., the
first in book xxviii.
   habebant: cf. 9. 1.

6. persultassent: χ, *insultassent* B. Cf. xliv. 9. 7. There are no
parallels for such a literal use of *insultare*.

7. tulere: χ, *tulerunt* B. Decision is impossible. Forms in *-ere* are rarer in the later books (statistics in E. B. Lease, *AJPh* xxiv [1903], 408 ff.) and B may be right. But there are, according to Lease, fifteen occurrences of *-ere* in book xxxiv, enough to make speculation unprofitable.

21. Cf. p. 64.

21. 1. Bergium: doubtless the chief town of the Bergistani: see 16. 9 n.

castrum ducit: Mg, *ducit castrum* Bχ, but there would be no point in such a dislocation of the normal word-order.

praedonum: J. M. Gazquez, *Pyrenae* xi (1975), 99 ff. suggests that the *praedones* were in fact bands of migrating Celts.

7. This sentence would appear to refute by itself Tenney Frank's view that the Roman state operated the Spanish mines directly until 178: cf. 10. 4 n. For the method used to establish *uectigalia* cf. Richardson, *JRS* lxvi (1976), 139 ff., arguing that the mines were leased directly to individual contractors, not to the *societates publicanorum*. For the Spanish *denarius* coinage cf. 10. 4 n. Cato refers to the Spanish mines in fr. 93P.

locupletior ... prouincia: the wealth from the province. There is no implication, or probability, that the income from Spain was spent on bettering the life of the inhabitants. On the question of whether it was Cato who first properly organized the tribute in Spain cf. Badian, *FC*, 121, R. Bernhardt, *Historia* xxiv (1975), 421, Richardson, op. cit., 147–9.

8. in Hispania: Mg, om. Bχ, perhaps correctly. Cf. 16. 7 n.

22. 1–3. *Events in Italy*

22. 1. Boiorum: cf. xxxi. 2. 5 n.

manu: φ (*manum* B, *manus* ψ). Mg's *exercitu* is a manifest gloss.

Litanam siluam: for its probable position, to the north-east of Bologna, cf. A. Rubbiani, *Atti e memorie della reale deputazione di storia patria per le provincie di Romagna*, iii. 1 (1883), 118 ff., Brunt, 176 wrongly places it in the Apennines. L. elsewhere describes it as *uasta* (xxiii. 24. 6). A Roman army was defeated there in 216 (loc. cit.).

On the forests in the Po valley at this time cf. 48. 1, xxi. 25. 9, xxxiii. 37. 4, Toynbee, ii. 259–60, Brunt, 176 ff.

2. octo milia: probably exaggerated. Cf. Astin, *Cato*, 28 n. 3.

3. Placentiae et Cremonae: cf. xxxi. 10. 2 n.: on Cremona add G. Pontuoli, *CSDIR* i (1967–8), 163 ff.

22. 4—41. *Events in Greece*

22–24. *The Congress at Corinth*

On the congress cf. Aymard, *PR*, 203 ff.

Although the section as a whole is manifestly of Polybian origin, 22. 4–13 shows considerable signs of reworking by L. This occurs elsewhere in passages of transition (cf. p. 2). §§ 4–5, with their extreme praise of Flamininus, are unlikely to have appeared in this form in Polybius (cf. Tränkle, 163) and the description of Philip's wrongdoings reflects the language of xxxi. 1. 9–10. There is a clear reference to the alleged Macedonian contingent at Zama, and though it is possible that this reflects contemporary propaganda, it is unlikely that Polybius believed it to be true (cf. xxxi. 1. 10 n.). Aymard's claim (*PR*, 204) that Flamininus' speech contains nothing that did not appear in Polybius is quite unsubstantiated.

4. hic status rerum: for the phrase cf. xxiii. 34. 10, xxvii. 1. 1, Goodyear, 197.

Aetolis ... contigerant: for the rejection of Aetolian demands by the senate cf. xxxiii. 49. 8, for their discontent xxxiii. 11. 4 ff., 31. 1–3, 35. 9–12.

nec diu ... poterat: cf. xxxiii. 44. 7 *ingenio inquietam ... gentem.* For Polybius's hostile view of the Aetolians cf. Walbank, *Commentary*, i. 237, Petzold, *Studien*, 126, K. S. Sacks, *JHS* xcv (1975), 92, xxxv. 49. 2 n.

pacis ... bonis: cf. Tac. *A.* i. 4 *bona libertatis* (noted by Fletcher, *JRS* lxiii [1973], 295). For *bona pacis* cf. Woodman, 157.

5. temperantiam ... moderationem: cf. xxxiii. 33 and the similar language in Plutarch, *Flam.* 2. 5. See also xxxviii. 56. 11 (of Scipio) *laudes moderationis et temperantiae.* On L.'s use of *moderatio* see V. Vipelli Santangelo, *BStudLat.* vi (1976), 71 ff.

senatus consultum ... adfertur: in xxxiii. 45. 3–4 Flamininus is given discretion with regard to the war with Nabis, and it is clear that the former version is correct (cf. n. ad loc.). It has usually been thought that in this case an annalistic account is preferable to that of Polybius, but in view of the other indications of reworking in this chapter, I am now inclined to think that L. may not have reported Polybius correctly here.

7. bellum ... belli: L. will not have worried about the repetition, and *bellandi* is quite unnecessary.

10. Argos ... occupatos: cf. xxxii. 38–40.

11. in media Graecia: in the sense of being more or less half-way between Thessaly and the Peloponnese.

quo ... esse: for the accusative and infinitive in relative clauses in *oratio obliqua* cf. Riemann, 285 ff., K–St, ii. 545–6.

13. ne serpat ... mali: for Achaean fear of the export of revolution cf. *Studies in Ancient Society*, 61.

23. 1. percenseri: 'reviewed', by Flamininus. The usage has nothing to do with the senatorial formula *quid censes*, as W–M think.

2. [auxilium]: the word is intolerable here. The balance of the two clauses is clearly *imploratos ... opem, non rogatos ... auxilium.* Moreover, as Madvig pointed out (*Emendationes*, 501), *implorare* is not used with a double accusative (cf. *TLL*, vii. 1. 647. 75 ff.).

4. incessi: *incessere* is not found before the Augustan period. It occurs once in Virgil (*A.* xii. 596) in a literal sense, but is reasonably common in L. (cf. *TLL*, vii. 1. 889–90, Packard, ii. 1157—the form of the concordance makes it inevitable that forms of *incedere* and *incessere* are tabulated indiscriminately). See p. 9.

Alexander: Isius. Cf. xxxii. 33. 9 n.

princeps: cf. xxxi. 17. 11 n.

libertatis ... auctores: at the time of the Persian wars.

adsentationis propriae: as W–M say, *propria* goes rather oddly with *adsentatio*. It is, presumably, a brachylogy for 'flattery to secure their own interests'.

6. [est]: clearly inserted at an early stage of transmission by a scribe who failed to see the syntax of this extremely long period.

Philippi ... transfugas: for the position of Corinth in the negotiations of 198 cf. xxxii. 19. 4, 33. 8 nn. For its return to the Achaeans in the peace settlement of 196 cf. xxxiii. 31. 11, 34. 9: the Acrocorinth remained for the moment in Roman possession (xxxiii. 31. 11).

7. primos ... Philippi: with reference to the First Macedonian War, when the Aetolians allied with Rome, not to the Social War of 220–217.

semper ... Romanorum: the Aetolians did not accept the Roman view that the peace of 206 brought an end to Aetolia's alliance with Rome (cf. xxxi. 1. 8, xxxiii. 13. 9–12 nn.).

pactos ... Pharsalo: it is not clear whether there is any significance in the omission of Larisa Cremaste here. Cf. xxxiii. 34. 7 n. For the disputes about the towns see xxxiii. 13. 9–12 n.

8. Chalcidem et Demetriadem: cf. xxxiii. 31. 11. For their role in the negotiations with Philip cf. vol. i. 25–6.

9. Chalcisque: *Chalcis* Bχ. L., unlike Cicero, does not avoid the order A, B, *et* C, and the paradosis may well be correct. Cf. K–St, ii. 32, *TLL*, v. 2. 877. Madvig (*Emendationes*, 82 ff.) attempted to make L. conform to the Ciceronian rules, but his attitude does too much violence to the MSS. tradition. Cf. Ogilvie, 393.

Corinthus: here for the Acrocorinthus: cf. § 6 n.

10. postremo: in fact Flamininus was keen to evacuate Greece as soon as possible. Cf. vol. i, 34 ff., 43. 3–9 n.

24. 1. uaniloquentia: cf. p. 6. *uanitas* is constantly applied to the Aetolians. See xxxv. 47. 8, 49. 4, xxxvi. 15. 2, 17. 8, 29. 3.

Aristaenum: cf. xxxii. 19. 2 n.

praetorem Achaeorum: Aristaenus was *strategos* in 196/5, his second tenure of the office (cf. Errington, 251).

2. ne ... sirit ... ut: for *sinere ut* cf. G. B. A. Fletcher, *Annotations on Tacitus* (Brussels, 1964), 11–12, K–St, ii. 225, for the perfect subjunctive xxxi. 7. 8 n., for the form *sirit* Neue–Wagener, iii. 458.

Iuppiter ... Argi: Hera was worshipped at the famous Argive Heraeum, half-way between Argos and Mycenae (cf. Pease on Cic. *n.d.* i. 82). The reference is not to Hera Acraea (Paus. ii. 24. 1) as W–M suggest (and she, in any case, is nothing to do with the Iuno Acraea of xxxii. 23. 10). There was a temple of Zeus on the Larisa (Paus. ii. 24. 3) and there were also temples of Zeus Nemeios and Zeus Soter (Paus. ii. 20. 3, 6). For the many other Argive Zeuses cf. Cook, *Zeus*, ii. 1144.

3. mare ... nos: Aetolia had launched attacks on the Peloponnese in the third century. Cf. Walbank, *Philip V*, 24 ff.

in media Peloponneso: scarcely true of Argos. The exaggeration may be due to L. Cf. 22. 11 n.

3–4. linguam ... uiuunt: *linguam ... Graecorum* looks forward to *quam ulli barbari*, *speciem hominum* to *immanes beluae*. Polybius did not regard language as the distinguishing mark of barbarians. That view had already been challenged by Eratosthenes (Strabo, i, p. 66C) and the existence of states like Rome and Carthage made it difficult to maintain the Greek–Barbarian dichotomy. Barbarism became a matter of civilization, not language. Cf. xxxi. 29. 12–15 n., to which add references to T. J. Haarhoff, *The Stranger at the Gate*

(Oxford, 1948), 216 ff., Walbank, *HSCP* lxxvi (1972), 158 ff., H. C.
Baldry, *Entretiens Fondation Hardt* viii (1961), 191 ff., Fraser, *Ptolemaic
Alexandria*, i. 530–1, ii. 761 n. 87 (for earlier expressions of Era-
tosthenes' view), S. Perlman, *Historia* xxv (1976), 3 n. 8.

In 198 Philip V had suggested that the Aetolians were not really
Greeks. Cf. xxxii. 34. 4 n., Pol. xviii. 5. 8.

For *speciem hominum . . . immanes beluae* cf. xxix. 17. 11, Vell. ii.
117. 3, Curt. v. 5. 7 (passages collected by Woodman, 191), Cic.
de r.p. ii. 48.

pacata haec: χ, *pacata* B. *haec* to mean 'the situation in a state'
is common (cf. W–M on xxxi. 7. 12, Nisbet, *in Pisonem*, 76) and
Madvig's *pacatam* (sc. *Graeciam*) or Damsté's *pacatas* (with *res*) are
less satisfactory than χ's reading. χ was not a good enough Latinist
to have added *haec*.

6. opinione ea . . . esset: the one expressed by Aristaenus.

referre . . . placeret . . . nisi: as elsewhere the language of
senatorial procedure is used. Cf. xxxii. 20. 4, xxxiii. 12. 1 nn. The
nisi clause represents the ultimatum in an *indictio belli* (cf. xxxi. 8.
3–4 n.). Aymard (*PR*, 199 n. 9, 210, 214) noted that the Romans are
not mentioned as making any such formal *indictio belli* to Nabis, and
he thinks that this was because they did not want to be tied to any
such limited demand as the surrender of Argos when it came to
making peace, and was justified by the facts that Nabis had placed
himself outside the pale of legal requirements, and that Achaea and
Nabis were still formally at war. But Rome considerably altered her
demands to Philip between the ultimatum at Abydus and the conference of Antigonea (cf. xxxii. 10. 3 n.) and there is no reason why
the same should not have been done with Nabis. I think it possible,
therefore, that a formal *rerum repetitio* and *indictio belli* was in fact
made at some point.

7. pro uiribus suis: not implying any fixed levy: cf. Aymard,
PR, 212 n. 2.

quaeque: probably to be taken as a singular (*contra* W–M). The
plural of *quisque* is normally used only with neuter superlatives, or to
indicate a group or class. Cf. K–St, i. 646, ii. 636. For L.'s use of the
plural of *quisque* cf. Riemann, 184: xli. 25. 8 is the only example of
the plural with a noun, not referring to a class.

ad Aetolos: the Aetolians had, it seems, left the meeting before
the vote was taken (Aymard, *PR*, 210).

spe . . . posse: cf. 13. 5 n.

25–29. *The Attacks on Argos, Sparta, and Gytheum*

Cf. Zon. ix. 18. 1–3, Aymard, *PR*, 214 ff.

25. 1. Elatia: cf. xxxii. 18. 9 n. It was the Roman army's base in
the winters of 198/7 and 197/6 (xxxii. 39. 2, xxxiii. 27. 5) and presumably so again in 196/5.

2. Antiochi legatis: the ambassadors dispatched after the conference of Lysimachia: cf. xxxiii. 41. 5 n.

societate: De Sanctis's view (iv. 1. 125) that Antiochus was
offering help against Nabis is most improbable. Doubtless he was
simply raising the same questions as had been discussed at Lysimachia, and L.'s language should not be pressed. Cf. Aymard, *PR*,
213 n. 4.

nihil ... habere: Flamininus does not, of course, mean that if
the *x legati* had been present, the matter could have been settled
without reference to the senate. Cf. Schleussner, 38.

Romam eundum: it is not at all certain that they did: cf.
Holleaux, *Études*, v. 164–6.

3. ipse: in contrast to the military tribunes who had brought the
army from Elatia. The notice about the ambassadors from Antiochus
breaks into the narrative (cf. W–M) and was perhaps an addition by
L. after he had completed his account of the preparations for the
war with Nabis.

Cleonas: cf. xxxiii. 14. 7 n.

4. campum Argiuum: on the plain of Argos cf. P–K, iii. 1. 134 ff.

ferme: Mg, *fere* Bχ. On *fere* and *ferme* in L. cf. Goodyear, i. 241,
Adams, *Antichthon* viii (1974), 57. It should be observed, though,
that manuscript vagaries mean that statistics derived from Packard
on this kind of matter are not totally reliable.

5. Pythagoras: Ziegler's statement (*RE*, xxiv. 302) that
Pythagoras was an Argive depends on the acceptance of Wilhelm's
view that Nabis's wife Apega was in fact Apia, the daughter of the
Argive ex-tyrant Aristippus. Cf. Aymard, *PR*, 150 n. 60, 216 n. 12,
Walbank, *Commentary*, ii. 421, Texier, 18.

arces ... Argi: cf. xxxii. 25. 5 n. and addendum thereto.

aut ... aut: Mg. Bχ omit the first *aut*, perhaps correctly. Cf.
Walsh, *CR*, 54.

7. Damocles erat: for the *ecphrasis* idiom, introducing this episode,
cf. xxxiii. 28. 11 n., xxxv. 26. 5. Damocles is not otherwise known.

fidei: explained by the next sentence.

8. hortatusque ⟨est⟩: cf. p. 12.

potius quam . . . morerentur: cf. xxxiii. 13. 3 n. (*extorquere* occurs there also, though in a metaphorical sense).

9. qui . . . uellent: a Roman formula. Cf. Cic. *ap.* Asc. p. 75C, and Merguet iv. 383. For other instances in L. cf. iv. 38. 2, xxii. 50. 9, 53. 7.

12. ⟨alii⟩: McDonald's supplement, in preference to the usually accepted *multi*. I suspect, though, that the paradosis is correct. We should punctuate with a comma after *coniecti*, and take L. to indicate that those imprisoned escaped over the wall (thus also Damsté, *Mnemosyne* n.s. xliii [1915], 165).

26. 2. Cylarabim: the famous gymnasium to the south of the city: cf. Vollgraff, *BCH* xxxi (1907), 178–9, Pieske, *RE*, xi. 2451–2. According to Pausanias (ii. 18. 5, 22. 8) it was named after a legendary king of Argos, Cylarabes.

id est: for L.'s use of *id est* to explain a Greek term cf. xli. 20. 7 and, perhaps, ix. 19. 7 (Ogilvie *YCS* xxiii [1973], 163).

minus . . . passus: cf. 9. 2 n.

4. si: for *si* clauses depending on the concept of waiting to see understood from the context cf. K–St, ii. 425–6.

metu: perhaps they were in favour of Nabis' reforms (Aymard, *PR*, 216). Cf. 27. 3 n.

consilium: MSS., *concilium* J. F. Gronovius. Cf. 17. 11, xxxiii. 12. 1, xxxv. 32. 1 nn.

5. principum: cf. xxxi. 17. 11 n. There must have been contingents from Greek states other than Achaea, Thessaly, and Macedon, though only these three are specifically mentioned by L. Polybius xxiii. 5. 1–2 implies the presence of a Messenian contingent. Cf. Aymard, *PR*, 213 n. 4, 219 n. 25.

ordiendi bellum: Mg, *ordiendi belli* B (*ordinendi* or *ordinandi belli* χ). Most editors have accepted Gelenius's *ordiendum bellum* but McDonald defends Mg's reading, with the genitive depending on *sententia*. The construction is possible, although one would expect the gerundive, as in B, rather than the gerund (cf. Weissenborn's note in the 2nd edition of the commentary, repeated on p. 197 W–M). Yet there is no clear case of *sententia* with a genitive and in view of 33. 6 it seems best to follow Gelenius (cf. Ogilvie, *Phoenix*, 347).

6–8. On Flamininus' reasoning cf. Aymard, *PR*, 217 ff.

7. susceptum sit: for L.'s use of the primary subjunctive in historic sequence in *oratio obliqua* cf. K–St, ii. 194 ff., Conway, *Livy*, *book ii* (Cambridge, 1910), 187 ff., M. Andrewes, *CR*, n.s. i (1951), 143 ff., H–S, 552, Walsh on xxi. 10. 3.

8. maturi ... uiride: W–M argue that these are substantival neuters, and that *frumentum* is not to be understood, on the grounds that *frumentum* in the singular is used only of grain gathered in. The evidence fails to support that claim (cf. *TLL*, vi. 1. 1410).

9. Parthenio: part of the mountain range between the Argolid and Arcadia: cf. Ernst Meyer, *RE*, xviii. 2. 1887–90, P–K, iii. 1. 242.

praeter Tegeam: sc. *profectus* (Pettersson, 84). Cf. xxxvi. 7. 15 n.

Caryas: in the extreme north of Laconia, it had been free from Spartan control since *c.* 338. Cf. Loring, *JHS* xv (1895), 54 ff., von Geisau, *RE*, x. 2245–6, P–K, iii. 2. 474, Walbank, *Commentary*, ii. 172.

sociorum: cf. § 5 n.

10. a Philippo: it was, of course, Philip who had originally given Argos to Nabis (xxxii. 38–40). The Achaeans ignored their decree (xli. 23. 1, xlii. 6. 2) forbidding any Macedonian to set foot on Achaean soil: cf. Aymard, *PR*, 112 n. 4.

adfatim: the word occurs in Livius Andronicus and Plautus, then in Cicero (only of food apart from the letters to Atticus), twice in Sallust, and ten times in L. As a substantive with a genitive it occurs in Plautus and not again before L. (six instances). It is probably to be regarded as a colloquialism. Cf. *TLL*, i. 1172–4, Tränkle, *WS*, 123, who, however, omits the occurrences of *adfatim* of food in Livius and Cicero (*Tusc.* ii. 24, Cicero's own translation of Aeschylus, *n.d.* ii. 127).

11. Leucade: cf. xxxiii. 17. 6 n.

L. Quinctius: (43). Cf. xxxi. 4. 5, xxxii. 16. 2 nn.

tectae naues: cf. xxxi. 22. 8 n.

Eumenes: for Pergamum's part in the campaign cf. *Syll.*³ 595, Hansen, *Attalids*, 73.

12–14. The Spartan exiles bedevilled relations between Rome, Achaea, and Sparta in this period. Cf. *Studies in Ancient Society*, 63 ff., Errington, chs. viii–xi.

12. reciperandae: χ, *recipiendae* B. A clear case of *lectio difficilior*.

13. aliquot aetates: an exaggeration. Cleomenes did not begin his revolution until 227.

14. Cleomenes III, though a perfectly genuine Heraclid, is regarded by Polybius as a tyrant because he abolished the dual kingship. Cf. Walbank, *Commentary*, i. 245–6. Agesipolis, still a child, had succeeded to the Agiad throne on the death of Cleomenes in 219, and Lycurgus, though not in the direct line of descent, was appointed as Eurypontid king. Cf. Pol. iv. 35. 10–14, xxiii. 6. 1, Walbank, *Commentary*, i. 484, iii. 224. The present passage is the only evidence for the expulsion of Agesipolis by Lycurgus, and the date of the event is uncertain. Cf. Shimron, *Late Sparta*, 73, Oliva, 268 ff. (rightly rejecting the view that *qui ... fuit* refers to Lycurgus and that Cleomenes is not the king, but the uncle of Agesipolis, appointed as regent for him [Pol. iv. 35. 12]).

L. can here describe Lycurgus as a *tyrannus*, though at 32. 1 his son Pelops is, for Flamininus, a *rex iustus ac legitimus*.

27. 1. uere ... uires: Mg. Bχ have *esset uires suas hostiumque aestimanti*. It is unlikely that Mg should have invented *uere* but in that case its omission in F or its exemplar would be best explained by its being immediately followed by *uires*, and this consideration, I think, marginally outweighs the attraction of the more elegant word-order of Mg.

2. The figures here given appear to omit troops in Argos and garrisons in Perioecic towns. Cf. Oliva, 290 n. 3.

a Creta: cf. xxxi. 35. 1 n.

castellanis agrestibus: Helots, as is clear from § 9. L. clearly has no precise idea of the history of the Helots. Polybius would not have thought it necessary to explain them, and the note may well be L.'s addition from his own knowledge (cf. Shimron, *CPh* lxi [1966], 6 n. 25). In the Classical period Helots were not normally armed (cf. K. M. T. Chrimes, *Ancient Sparta* [Manchester, 1949], 382: for exceptions cf. Andrewes, *Historical Commentary on Thucydides*, iv. 35), but these clearly are. Hence Chrimes (*Ancient Sparta*, 37 ff.: cf. also W. S. Robins, *University of Birmingham Historical Journal* vi. 2 [1958], 93 ff.) argued that these are not real Helots, but *neodamodeis*, free but compelled to guard *castella*. She argued that Helots as such no longer existed by the time of Nabis. Yet there is no reason to doubt the continued existence of Helots well after this time (L.'s language in § 9 clearly indicates that he believed that they existed in his time). Chrimes believed that L.'s statements came from a Roman source who meant people of the same status as the *Hastensium seruei* referred to in *ILLRP* 514. There is, however, no reason to suppose that L.'s statements do not come from Polybius. But even if they did come from a Roman source, and a well-informed one, Chrimes's conclusion would not follow. *castellani* are simply rural inhabitants, not

defenders of strong points. Cf. *TLL*, iii. 524, Walbank, *CR* n.s. i
(1951), 99. Nor is it necessary to regard them as freed Helots, as is
done by Robins, op. cit., K.-W. Welwei, *Unfreie im antiken Kriegsdienst* i (Wiesbaden, 1974), 169–72, Texier, *DHA* i (1974), 189 ff.
(see also Oliva, 280 ff.) since there is no reason to think that all the
Helots were freed by Nabis (Shimron, *CPh* lxi, 1 ff.). For Nabis'
freeing of Helots cf. 31. 11, 31. 14, Pol. xvi. 13. 1.

3. fossa ... communiuit: at 38. 2 L. implies that walls had been
built only by the tyrants (i.e. from the time of Cleomenes III onwards). But other evidence points to the earliest fortifications being
built either at the time of the attack by Cassander in 315 (Just.
xiv. 5. 6) or of that by Demetrius Poliorcetes in 295 (Paus. vii. 8. 5):
Nabis extended the fortifications (Paus., loc. cit.), though they were
still not complete (37. 8, 38. 2). See A. J. B. Wace, *BSA* xii (1905–6),
284 ff., xiii (1906–7), 5 ff., Bölte, *RE*, iiiA. 1356, Shimron, *Late
Sparta*, 90–1 n. 30. For tiles from the walls with the name of Nabis
see *IG* v. 1. 885. Nabis may have completed the walls after the
present war: cf. Bölte, loc. cit., Aymard, *PR*, 297 n. 16.

    metu ... poterat: Polybius thought so, but he is not necessarily
to be believed. Cf. 26. 4 n.

4. Dromon ... uocat: Mg, om. Bχ, but the comment must come
from Polybius and is not the sort of thing that could have been added
in transmission. Since it is the *campus*, not the *copiae*, that are the
Dromos, Meursius proposed placing the parenthesis after *campum*, and
it could be argued in favour of this that the omission of the clause in
Bχ suggests that it stood in the margin at one point, to be omitted in
one branch of the tradition and inserted in the wrong place in the
other. W–M say that L. often postpones a parenthesis to the end of
the clause containing the word to be explained, but none of their
parallels involve possible ambiguity about which word is being
explained. Yet there is not really any ambiguity, since it would
never occur to anyone that *copiae* was being explained, and L. may
well have thought that *eductis in campum—Dromon ipsi uocant—omnibus
copiis, positis armis* . . . gave a less attractive clause balance and
preferred to split up the two ablative phrases by the parenthesis.

    On the *Dromos*, near the Eurotas, cf. Bölte, *RE*, iiiA. 1367–9.
Bölte argues that the *Dromos* described by Pausanias iii. 14. 6 is
different, as that lay within the city walls.

6–8. pauca praefatus ... tradidit: everything down to *emissurum*
is the content of the *praefatio*, in apposition to *pauca*, and there is no
real anacoluthon, as W–M claim. The passage thus gives no support
to the alleged anacoluthon at xxxiii. 12. 3–4 (cf. n. ad loc.) where

there is, in the transmitted text, no main verb. It would be possible, but not necessary, to take *praefatus* as an indicative, and allow the main part of the speech to begin with *et ipsorum*. For the main part of a speech in the accusative and infinitive after a verb of saying understood following *praefari* cf. iii. 45. 1, xxiii. 2. 6, for *praefari* with an accusative and infinitive, followed by *iubere*, cf. xxvii. 10. 5, xxxv. 25. 7.

7. esse: cf. 22. 11 n.

9. Ilotarum ... genus: cf. § 2 n. Nepos, *Paus.* 3. 6 is the only other reference to the Helots in Latin.

28. 1. satis iam: *satis iam* and *iam satis* are colloquial phrases and L. is the first writer to use them, as here, in a clearly non-colloquial way. Cf. Fraenkel, *Horace* (Oxford, 1957), 243, *TLL*, vii. 1. 117. 13 ff.

Sellasiam ... dicebatur: on the battle of Sellasia in 222 cf. Pol. ii. 65–9, Walbank, *Commentary*, i. 272 ff., on the site, ibid., 277 ff. Sellasia is about 12 km. north of Sparta, the Oenus is the modern Kelephina, joining the Eurotas a little north of Sparta. On Antigonus Doson cf. xxxii. 21. 25 n.

dimicasse dicebatur is a rather odd phrase, which cannot represent anything in Polybius. L. clearly knew little of the circumstances of the battle.

2. De Sanctis (iv. 1. 107 n. 220) took L. to mean that because the route was difficult, he made a detour and took an easier route, suggesting that he followed the valley of the Oenus. That, however, would have been even more difficult (cf. W. Loring, *JHS* xv [1895], 60). In fact *breui ... circuitu* goes only with *praemissis*. Flamininus took the normal route to Sparta, his advance party fortifying the difficult part of the route, and he then reached the easy final part of the journey. There is no implication in *lato ... limite* that Flamininus had been misinformed about the difficulties of the journey.

4. peditibus ... pedites: the *expediti* of § 3.

5. trepidantes: of the troops of Nabis, as before (§ 4) of the Romans. L. thus gives point to the change in the situation.

6. acie derecta: in properly ordered line. For *aciem de(di-)rigere* cf. *TLL*, v. i. 1235–6. Attempts to distinguish between the meaning of *derigere* and *dirigere*, going back to Isidorus (cf. e.g. Conway–Walters on ii. 49. 11), are not borne out by the evidence. See *TLL*, v. 1. 1231–2.

94

7. Menelai montis: Menelaus, together with Helen, was worshipped at the Menelaeum, in the hills to the south of Sparta, on the east of the Eurotas. Cf. Hdt. vi. 61. 3, Isoc. x. 63, Pol. v. 18. 3, 21. 1, 22. 3, 8, Paus. iii. 15. 3. For earlier excavations at the Menelaeum cf. A. J. B. Wace–M. S. Thompson–J. P. Droop, *BSA* xv (1908–9), 108 ff., xvi (1909–10), 4 ff., for recent ones *AR* xx (1973–4), 14–15, xxi (1974–5), 12–15, xxii (1975–6), 13–15, xxiv (1977–8), 31.

agmen cogebant: for *agmen cogere*, 'to bring up the rear of a column' cf. *TLL*, i. 1345–6.

8. intra murum: W–M wrongly say that this is an indication that the city walls extended east of the Eurotas. This is in any case ruled out by § 2 *sub ipsis prope fluentem moenibus,* and no trace of walls has been found on the east bank. Clearly Nabis' troops attacked across the river, which in summer would not have contained all that much water.

10. Ap. Claudius: (294). Pulcher. Cf. xxxiii. 29. 9 n., E. Rawson, *Historia* xxii (1973), 225, 229.

inopinatum: Bχ, *necopinatum* Mg. *necopinatus* was displaced by *inopinatus* in the first century A.D. and it is therefore quite likely that Mg preserves the correct reading. At i. 57. 7 and iii. 26. 5 *necopinatus* was altered to *necinopinatus*. The only certain occurrence of *inopinatus* in the first decade is at vi. 40. 3. In the later books, however, L. uses both forms. Cf. Ogilvie, 440–1, who is, however, misleading about the occurrences of *inopinatus* after the first decade.

11. infesta ac: M. Müller, 'deinde quae minus infida ac trepida: ubi haec uox interciderat' Gel., om. Bχ. Since *infida* makes no sense (it cannot mean that the troops of Nabis could not trust their flight, as suggested by Walker, *Supplementary Annotations*, 201), the best solution may be to keep the text of Bχ especially as Gelenius's words leave it far from clear what stood in Mg.

The Roman troops will have crossed the Eurotas in the course of their pursuit.

12. On Amyclae cf. Walbank, *Commentary*, i. 553 ff. It was probably captured and incorporated in the Spartan state in the eighth century. Cf. G. L. Huxley, *Early Sparta* (London, 1962), 24. It lay to the west of the Eurotas, but *castra mouit ad fluvium Eurotam* suggests that Flamininus' camp remained on the east bank. It is hard, however, to make sense of *inde . . . euastat* if he did not move his camp to the west of the river, and we must assume that L. has misunderstood Polybius. Cf. De Sanctis, iv. 1. 107 n. 220.

Taygeto: the great mountain range dividing Laconia from Messenia. Cf. P–K, iii. 2. 417 ff.

29. 1. L. Quinctius: cf. 26. 11 n.

metu aut ui: Strabo viii, p. 366C suggests that all the towns
came over voluntarily: cf. Aymard, *PR*, 220 n. 29. G. Gitti, *RAL* 6
xv (1939), 189 ff., supported by Shimron, *Late Sparta*, 88 n. 27,
argued that Strabo's notice refers not to this occasion, but to the
appeal of the Laconians to Augustus against the domination of
Eurycles: *contra* see G. W. Bowersock, *JRS* li (1961), 116 n. 38.

recepit: 'took', not 'recovered', for they had not been in Roman
or Achaean possession before. Cf. xxxiii. 18. 22 n.

2. Gytheum: the dockyard of Laconia. Cf. Philippson–Bölte, *RE*,
vii. 2102–4 (2102 on the form of the name), P–K, iii. 2. 463, Walbank, *Commentary*, i. 555. For a dedication to Flamininus at Gytheum,
clearly commemorating its capture from Sparta, see *Syll.*[3] 592.

3. incolarumque: probably metics, but it is conceivable that Polybius spoke of Spartiates acting as a garrison, and ordinary Laconian
inhabitants.

4. Eumenes: cf. 26. 11 n.

5. e tribus ... opera: cf. xxxii. 16. 10 *trium iunctarum classium
naues ... opera.*

6. iam ... iam: the anaphora of *iam*, indicating contemporaneous,
not successive events, conveys a sense of climax and excitement. For
its use in similar contexts cf. i. 29. 4, v. 18. 11, 21. 5, 49. 5, Caes.
BG vii. 59. 1. Cf. *TLL*, vii. 1. 117. 63 ff. The anaphora of *iam* at 6. 11
(with single words, not whole clauses) has a different effect. Cf. n.
ad loc. and addenda.

7. a portu: W–M's note, based on the assumption that the harbour
was far from the town, is quite mistaken. They were unaware that
the MSS. reading at Polybius v. 19. 6 is certainly wrong: cf. Walbank, *Commentary*, i. 556. It is unclear whether the allied forces had
to fight to enter the harbour, and were only now able to advance
from it, or whether advance from the harbour was delayed until a
breach had been made in the wall.

distenderent: Mg, *descenderent* B, *discenderent* ψ, *discederent* φ. The
slightly unusual word has been trivialized in transmission. *distendere*
occurs five times in L., and outside L. is found in a military context
only at Caes. *BC* iii. 92. 2 (*TLL*, v. 1. 1513. 53 ff.).

conabantur: Mg, *conantur* Bχ. The present may well be correct.
L. regularly uses historic sequence with the historic present: cf.
K–St, ii. 176.

8. Dexagoridas et Gorgopas: not otherwise known. For other Spartans called Gorgopas cf. Niese, *RE*, vii. 1657, A. S. Bradford, *A Prosopography of Lacedaemonians from the death of Alexander the Great, 323 B.C., to the Sack of Sparta by Alaric, A.D. 396* (Munich, 1977), 99.

10. erat ... superuenisset: cf. xxxii. 25. 8 n.

11–14. Part of this section survives in fragments of F. For details cf. H. Fischer, *SBAW* 1907, 106.

11. supercilio: 'the brow of the hill'. The word does not occur in this sense before *Bell. Afr.* 58. 1.

L. Quinctius ... terra marique: his forces, that is. Lucius himself could not direct operations by both land and sea.

13. pactus ... abducere ... liceret: cf. xxxii. 25. 9.

tradidit: *tradit* Bχ (and clearly also in F, though that adds nothing to the case) is quite possible. Cf. Chausserie-Laprée, 383 ff.

14. Pythagoras: cf. 25. 5 n.

Timocrati Pellenensi: cf. xxxii. 40. 10 n. He came from Laconian Pellana, not Pellene in Achaea. Cf. Ehrenberg, *RE*, viA. 1264–5. Walbank, *Commentary*, ii. 571 oddly says that Timocrates is known only from Polybius xviii. 17. 1.

duobus ... Argiuorum: soldiers, not hostages, as W–M say. Cf. Aymard, *PR*, 216–17 n. 17. There is no reason to think that they were compelled to join Pythagoras. See Aymard, loc. cit., Oliva, 291 n. 2.

30–35. *Negotiations with Nabis*

30. 2. esse ⟨et⟩ ... interclusum: the insertion of *et* is much simpler than supplying a verb with the *a mari ... interclusum* clause.

3. caduceatorem: cf. xxxi. 38. 9 n.

explorandum si: cf. 3. 5 n.

7. Sosila Rhodio: not otherwise known.

Achaeorum praetore: B and two MSS. of the ψ group have *Achaeo*, and it is therefore very unlikely that ϕ's *Achaeorum tribunis* possesses any authority (*tribunis* in V is to be regarded as a coincidence). Despite 24. 1 it is quite possible that on this occasion L. did write simply *Aristaeno Achaeo*.

On the reasons for the presence of Aristaenus, alone of the mainland allies, cf. Aymard, *PR*, 221–2.

descendit: from the *tumuli* to lower ground, not from their horses.

31. *The speech of Nabis.* It is quite likely that Polybius inserted

speeches by Nabis and Flamininus at this point and much of the
material may, therefore, be Polybian. But it would be surprising if
L. had not allowed himself a certain degree of freedom in his
presentation.

Ullmann (*Technique*, 143–4) analyses Nabis' speech thus. (i) §§ 1–
5 *prooemium*. (ii) §§ 6–16 *tractatio*: (*a*) §§ 6–10 Nabis' occupation of
Argos; (*b*) §§ 11–13 his title; (*c*) §§ 14–16 his freeing of slaves and
distribution of land. (iii) §§ 17–19 *conclusio*: (*a*) §§ 17–18 *amplificatio*—
he is faithful to his country's tradition; (*b*) § 19 *peroratio*. Ullmann
is right to abandon any attempt to divide the *tractatio* by *topoi*, and
the only correction I would make to his analysis is to include §§ 17–
18 as a final part of the *tractatio* rather than as part of the *conclusio*.
Ullmann also points out that the *prooemium* is an *insinuatio*. Nabis,
while ostensibly distinguishing the Romans from those well-known
treaty breakers, the Carthaginians, is in fact hinting that Rome has
broken her treaty with Sparta.

31. 1. permisso [ut]: sc. *utrumque facere*. The insertion of *ut* was
caused by misunderstanding of the construction.

2. perirem: χ, *repperirem* B. Rossbach's *deperirem* (*WKlPh* xxxiv
[1917], 1133) would completely destroy the rhetoric of the sentence.

3. Carthaginienses ... haberet: the charge that the Carthagi-
nians always broke their treaties goes back at least as far as the elder
Cato (fr. 84P). For references to *Punica fides* in Latin authors cf.
Walbank, *Commentary*, i. 412.

4. fidem socialem: 'loyalty to your allies'.

5. ⟨me⟩: omission by haplography is easy, but ellipse is possible
(cf. K–St, i. 700 ff.) and there is no need for Nabis to emphasize
that he is the subject of the infinitive.

uobiscum ... renouata: Nabis' claims here are challenged by
Flamininus at 32. 1, and if L. is reflecting Polybius at all closely, the
precise position must have been open to some doubt. An alliance had
been concluded with Sparta in 210, and despite Spartan inclusion in
the Aetolian peace with Philip in 206, they were also included in the
peace of Phoenice, and their treaty with Rome therefore continued
in existence (cf. xxxii. 39. 10 n., Walbank, *Commentary*, ii. 516–17:
contra Holleaux, *Rome*, 261 ff., Walbank, *Philip V*, 101 n. 3, 103 n. 6.
Dahlheim, 221 ff. unconvincingly denies that there ever was a *foedus*
between Rome and Sparta). There is no difficulty in believing that
Pelops, only a boy, was the titular king of Sparta at this time, and
that it is therefore to the original treaty that Flamininus is referring

in 32. 1. Nabis removed Pelops in 207 (Diod. xxvii. 1) and must therefore have been in charge when the Spartans were included as *adscripti* in the peace of Phoenice (xxix. 12. 14). It may be that at this time Rome had some communications with Nabis, which he could represent as personal recognition as a *socius et amicus*, but which Flamininus claimed were merely in virtue of the old treaty with Pelops. When Nabis and Flamininus reached agreement in 198, no new treaty was made, but Nabis must have been recognized as a *socius et amicus*.

Flamininus' language at 32. 1, however, appears to be deliberately misleading. *amicitia et societas nulla tecum sed cum Pelope* . . . does not imply a rejection of Nabis' statement that there was a *foedus* between Rome and Sparta (and at 32. 16 it is explicitly acknowledged). Flamininus is denying Nabis' claim to have a relationship with Rome *meo nomine priuatim* and he thus uses the words Nabis had used to assert such a relationship. Again, he does not explicitly deny that *amicitia* was renewed with Nabis in 198, but *facta est* concentrates attention on the origins of the relationship. Flamininus is misleadingly trying to imply that Rome had never given recognition to Nabis' rule.

It would not be surprising if Flamininus did indeed attempt to twist the argument in this way: for another example of his failure to reply to the actual points made in debate cf. xxxiii. 13. 9–12 n.

7. hoc tuear: 'defend my action'. For the usage cf. Cic. *Cat.* iii. 29, *Sest.* 38, *de or.* i. 48, 169, ii. 292, iii. 62 (*TLL*).

re an tempore: the argument from the *res* is that he was invited into Argos, and that it was at that time an ally of Philip, Rome's enemy. That from *tempus* is that the action took place before his *societas* with Rome, and that no complaint was made about it then.

ipsis . . . accepi: not true. Cf. xxxii. 38. 4–6.

accepi urbem: a deliberate chiastic repetition to emphasize the status of Argos, and it is wrong to delete *urbem*. Gelenius's 'dele urbem' would appear to indicate his own emendation, not a reading based on manuscript authority.

8. A strong point. When Flamininus accepted Nabis an ally, he implicitly acknowledged Nabis' control over Argos.

9–10. A repetition of the arguments of §§ 7–8.

11–19. Nabis deals with three charges: (i) his being labelled as a *tyrannus*, (ii) his enfranchisement of Helots, (iii) his redistribution of land. As to (i) there can be no doubt that Nabis had been recognized as king of Sparta by Rome in their earlier dealings, and was so regarded by the Spartans. Cf. xxxi. 25. 3 n., Walbank, *Commentary*, ii. 420, Oliva, 278. On the Helots cf. 27. 2 n. Nabis gave land to mercenaries as well as to Spartiates (Pol. xiii. 6. 3, Oliva, 280).

13. nomen imperii: 'the title by virtue of which I rule'.

inconstantiae: xxix. 37. 16 is the only other occurrence of the word in L.

16–18. Nabis' claim to have acted in a 'Lycurgan spirit' is very far-fetched. The Lycurgan system was based on suppression of the Helots and Messenians. And § 18 is an odd description of the Lycurgan constitution. The Gerousia had considerable powers *vis-à-vis* the assembly, and the equality was only of the Spartiates, not of all the inhabitants. Nabis (like Cleomenes) was in fact undoing some of the main elements in the Lycurgan arrangements. Lycurgus was believed to have made an assignation of land, giving each Spartiate his inalienable *kleros*, and on this aspect of his policy Nabis' claims are rather more respectable (on the *kleroi* cf. A. Andrewes, *Greek Tyrants* [London, 1956], 70–1, W. G. Forrest, *A History of Sparta, 950–192 B.C.* [London, 1968], 135 ff.).

Cf. in general Shimron, *Late Sparta*, 94 ff., but his suggestion that the *legum lator* in § 18 is a deliberately vague reference to Cleomenes, and is not Lycurgus, is ludicrous. Lycurgus was commonly referred to as ὁ νομοθέτης and cf. 32. 4.

17. exigere: 'inquire into'. The word first occurs in this sense in Varro, *LL* x. 11. Cf. *TLL*, v. 2. 1462–3, wrongly including Cael. *ap.* Cic. *fam.* viii. 6. 1.

nihil … singula: there may be an oblique reference to the fact that Sparta was often compared with Rome as an example of a mixed constitution. Cf. Pol. vi. 3. 8, 48–50, Cic. *r.p.* ii. 15, 24, 42–3, 50, 58, Walbank, *Commentary*, i. 641.

uos … uultis: a fair description of the Roman constitution.

18. fortunae … fore: all the MSS. have *ad* for *ac*, and it looks as if this was the cause of *fore* for *fortunae* in Bχ and *dignitates* in Mg and three MSS. of the χ group.

19. me ipse: *met ipse* F. Weissenborn's suggestion of *memet ipse* is attractive. L. often uses *semet* and *sibimet* (Packard, iv. 572, 653), and *mihimet* occurs (also with *ipse*) at xxii. 22. 14.

pro … breuitate: F., as one would expect, has *patrio sermone* ⟨*bre*⟩*uitatis*, not *patrio* ⟨*bre*⟩*uitatis*, as McDonald's apparatus may suggest: Madvig's emendation is clearly correct. Spartan brevity was well known from at least the fifth century: cf. Hdt. iii. 46,

E. Rawson, *The Spartan Tradition in European Thought* (Oxford, 1969),
19 ff.

32. *The speech of Flamininus.* Ullmann (*Technique*, 144–5) analyses
the speech thus. (i) §§ 1–19 *tractatio*: (*a*) §§ 1–5 there is no alliance
with Nabis, but with Pelops; Nabis is a tyrant, and Sparta must be
freed from him; (*b*) §§ 6–8 the fact that Argos took Philip's side is
not a reason for leaving her in Nabis' control; (*c*) §§ 9–12 the
accusations against Nabis are of murder, not just of social reform;
(*d*) §§ 13–19 he broke the treaty by allying with Philip and by
attacking Messene. (ii) § 20 *peroratio*. As with the speech of Nabis,
Ullmann rightly desists from trying to divide the *tractatio* into *topoi*:
Flamininus is replying to Nabis' presentation of his case. I would
further divide §§ 1–5 as the argument about Pelops is really distinct
from the claim that it is Rome's duty to free Sparta as well as Argos.

On the speech cf. Aymard, *PR*, 233 ff. As Aymard says, it is not
a very convincing reply to Nabis. Aymard thinks that Flamininus
makes no reference to the allied decision to go to war because he
does not want to restrict the settlement to Argos alone. But as we
have seen, the demand to Nabis made when war was declared could
be exceeded when fighting had started: cf. 24. 6 n. Some of the
more implausible of Flamininus' arguments may well be due to L.
rather than to Flamininus himself.

32. 1. Cf. 31. 5 n.

2. cuius ius ... usurparunt: it is hard to think that this represents very closely anything that stood in Polybius. L. seems to be
under the impression that Pelops was king before the first of the
'tyrants', Cleomenes III (who, as an undoubted Heraclid, had a
much better claim to be a *rex iustus ac legitimus* than Pelops, the son
of Lycurgus: cf. 26. 14 n.). L. also seems to imply that Nabis' rule
dated only from the period of the Second Macedonian War.

3. eos: Bχ, usually emended to *nos*. But for *is* as an antecedent to
first and second persons cf. vi. 18. 8, xxx. 30. 3, K–St, ii. 286, *TLL*,
vii. 2. 465. 75 ff. The case is not improved by McDonald's claim
that L. is writing about liberators in general.

tyranno ... in suos: a desperate crux. The text is the reading of
B. χ omits *fuit*, Mg may have omitted *quam*. B's text is not Latin.
As Madvig stated with consummate clarity (*Emendationes*, 503), a
comparative clause cannot possibly follow a superlative. McDonald's
attempt to argue that L. started by writing *quam saeuissimo* and then
decided to refer to earlier tyrants is quite insufficient: L. cannot
have left his sentence as it stands in B (I do not understand

McDonald's claim that *qui* means *si qui*). Madvig therefore deleted *quam*. But it is far from clear that *tyrannus saeuissimus qui umquam fuit* is Latin for 'the most savage tyrant who ever existed'. There are examples of an idiom where *tam* with a positive is followed by *quam qui* and a superlative (K–St, ii. 479–80), but it requires drastic surgery to produce this from the received text. I would not be certain that there is not extensive corruption, but any solution on such lines (e.g. that of H. J. Müller, printed in W–M) must remain very speculative. One simple solution would be to read *si* for *quam*.

4. Lacedaemon ... suas: again perhaps not Polybian, since Flamininus resisted Achaean demands for the removal of Nabis from Sparta itself. Cf. Aymard, *PR*, 224–5 n. 44, who considers the possibility that Flamininus was attempting to force Nabis to agree to peace by making him fear that otherwise he would lose control of Sparta.

quarum ... fecisti: 31. 16–18.

5. Iaso et Bargyliis: cf. xxxii. 33. 6–7 n.: for their freeing in 196 cf. xxxiii. 30. 3.

lumina: 'ornaments': a Ciceronian usage (see the passages collected by Pease on *n.d.* i. 79). Cf. i. 39. 3, with Ogilvie's note.

6. at enim ... senserunt: argued by Nabis in 31. 7, 9.

duorum ... trium: not what is stated in xxxii. 25.

7. nihil ... actum: cf. xxxii. 38. 6.

esse: *si in* B, *sit* χ, neither of which makes sense. The simplest solution may be to omit it altogether.

8. Thessalos ... Phocenses ... Locrenses: on Thessaly cf. xxxi. 24. 1 n., on Phocis xxxii. 18. 4 n., on Locris xxxii. 21. 7 n. For their freedom in 196 cf. xxxiii. 32. 5 n.

9. ad libertatem uocatorum: *ad* Bχ, *in* Mg. L. uses *uocare ad* more frequently than *uocare in* (cf. Packard, iv. 1264–7) but there is no obvious principle of choice between the two prepositions.

egentibus ... mediocria: Polybius will not have intended to represent this remark as a criticism of Flamininus. Nor will L. have seen anything odd in it, despite Augustan land-assignations (which were, in any case, made exclusively to veterans).

nec ipsa: L. is the first writer to use *nec ipse* for *ne ipse quidem*. Cf. K–St, i. 630 and xxxi. 22. 7 n. For the intensifying negatives cf. K–St, i. 827–8, H–S, 803 ff.

10. liberam contionem: L. regularly uses *contio* of Greek assemblies (cf. e.g. xxxiii. 2. 3, 20. 10, 28. 4, xxxvi. 12. 1) and *libera contio* means 'an assembly free to make its own decisions', not a meeting at which freedom of speech was allowed. In that sense Roman *contiones* were not free: cf. xxxii. 20. 1 n.

11. uetustiora: prior to the present year.

Pythagoras ... tuus: cf. 25. 5 n., for the slaughter 25. 11–12.
tu ipse: 27. 8–9.

12. agedum: apart from Cic. *Scaur.* fr. (m), L. is the first prose author to use *agedum* and the only one to use *agitedum*. Cf. *TLL*, i. 1405–6.

tuis te: put together for emphasis, and clearly preferable to χ's *in custodia te traditurum.*

13. ut iam ... haec: *confessio* (cf. xxxii. 21. 21 n.). For concessive *ut iam* cf. H–S, 647.

14. uos ... uiolaui: i.e. nothing in his actions at Argos or Sparta was contrary to his relationship with Rome.

nolo pluribus: for ellipse of the verb of saying with an ablative cf. Ter. *And.* 29, 114. It is, of course, common with *plura* and *multa* (cf. *TLL*, viii. 1613–14).

16. Messenen ... acceptam: Messene, unlike Elis and Sparta, was not listed as a possible ally in the Romano–Aetolian treaty of 212/11 (xxvi. 24. 9), but seems to have made an alliance by 210 (Pol. ix. 30. 6; Walbank's doubts [*Commentary*, ii. 169] are not justified).

quo et Lacedaemonem: we must presumably understand *accepimus*, since I can find no parallel for such an attraction of a word in the relative clause other than the relative pronoun or its antecedent. It is scarcely relevant that the accusative and infinitive occurs in such clauses in *oratio obliqua*. Perhaps we should read *Lacedaemon*.

socius ... cepisti: in 201. Cf. 35. 6, Pol. xvi. 13. 3, Plut. *Phil.* 12. 4–6, Paus. iv. 29. 10, viii. 50. 5, Aymard, *PR*, 41 ff., Walbank, *Commentary*, ii. 517, Errington, 79–80, Oliva, 283.

17. et cum Philippo ... pepigisti: the second of the two ways of breaking *societas*. For the events cf. xxxii. 38. 3.

18–19. For Nabis' connections with the Cretan pirates cf. Pol. xiii. 8. 2. The charges made here are uncheckable. In one respect they are very implausible. *Macedoniae ora* is vague, but it presumably includes the coast of Thessaly. Yet there is no evidence that the Roman army was at any time supplied from the Aegean coast, and since Philip's fleet was based at Demetrias, it is rather unlikely that they should even have tried. Cf. Aymard, *PR*, 140 n. 28, Thiel, 206 ff., Texier, 31.

Maleum . . . Maleae: cf. xxxi. 44. 1 n. This is the only instance of the name occurring in the genitive with *promunturium* and I see no way of determining what L. wrote.

20. parce . . . iactare: cf. p. 5.

populari: as a Roman *popularis* might speak, with particular reference to the last part of Nabis' speech.

33. 2. The tyrants who had voluntarily abdicated and joined the Achaean League. They include Iseas of Ceryneia, Lydiades of Megalopolis, Aristomachus of Argos, Xenon of Heraea, and Cleonymus of Phlius. Cf. Pol. ii. 41. 14, 44. 3–6, Walbank, *Aratos*, 27, 62–3, 70–1, *Commentary*, i. 238–9. The picture of them living out their old age in quiet retirement is misleading. Lydiades and Aristomachus served as Achaean *strategoi* and both met violent ends, Lydiades being killed in battle (Pol. ii. 51. 3), Aristomachus executed for treachery (Pol. ii. 59–60, Walbank, *Aratos*, 103). It may be that Aristaenus was hinting that if Nabis surrendered his tyranny, Sparta could join the Achaean League and Nabis could hope to play an active part in it. Cf. Aymard, *PR*, 225 and n. 49.

3. nox prope: 'night almost broke up the meeting', meaning that they stopped just before nightfall compelled them to do so, not that they nearly stopped but in fact continued.

cedere . . . deducere . . . redditurum: for the variation of tenses W–M rightly compare xxxii. 35. 9–11, Sall. *Iug.* 62. 3.

6. maximae partis: perhaps all the Greeks, certainly Aristaenus among them. Cf. Aymard, *PR*, 227.

8. exemplo . . . incitaturum: cf. 22. 13 n.

9 ff. In fact one of Flamininus' main motives was his desire to limit Achaean expansion and maintain a balance of power in the Peloponnese: cf. *Latomus* xxxi (1972), 33–4.

9. inclinatior: the metaphorical use of *inclinatus* is much favoured by L., but before him it is found only in Cic. *r.p.* ii. 47. Cf. *TLL*, vii. 1. 949.

10. Gytheum: ch. 29.

11. fuisse: i.e. at the time of the attack on Sparta described in ch. 28.

12. On P. Villius Tappulus (10) cf. xxxi. 4. 3 n., on his mission in 195 xxxiii. 44. 5 n. L.'s words do not themselves imply that Villius had been conducting fresh negotiations with Antiochus, but such a possibility cannot be excluded. At 57. 4 L. says that some of the *legati* of 196 had met Antiochus *aut in Asia aut Lysimachiae*, and at 59. 8 that P. Aelius Paetus and P. Sulpicius Galba had been at Lysimachia. Aelius and Sulpicius are not listed among those who met Antiochus at Lysimachia in 196 (xxxiii. 39. 2, Pol. xviii. 50. 1–2) and it has often been assumed therefore that a second meeting took place at Lysimachia in 195, and that it is to this that L. is referring here and at 59. 8. Holleaux, however (*Études*, v. 166 ff.), argued that either Sulpicius and Aelius were in fact at Lysimachia in 196, and Polybius simply omitted to mention them, or that the statement represents a mistake by Polybius. *in Asia* at 57. 4 is certainly mistaken, for none of the envoys had met Antiochus in Asia. Walbank (*Commentary*, ii. 621) thinks that *inde* here may indicate that Villius had met Antiochus himself, but there is no evidence for Aelius and Sulpicius being involved and Walbank rightly prefers to leave the question open. See also Leuze, *Hermes* lviii (1923), 214 ff. Aymard, *PR*, 213 n. 3 thinks Villius was sent to consult Philip and Eumenes about Nabis.

On Antiochus' expedition to Europe in 195 cf. p. 27 n. 1. There is not the slightest reason for regarding the section an an annalistic insertion, as claimed by Petzold, 105 ff.: cf. Tränkle, 62 n. 14.

infidam pacem: cf. xxxi. 1. 9–10 n.

14. illa ... esset: for similar charges in 198 and 197 cf. vol. i, 24 ff. Scullard says of the present instance (*RP²*, 115 n. 4) that the motif now 'wears a little thin by repetition'. But Flamininus will doubtless have known that Scipio was standing for the consulship of 194, and since there could be little hope of a further prorogation for him, he could well have wanted to deprive Scipio of a possible argument for keeping the Roman army in Greece. Cf. *Latomus* xxxi (1972), 31–2. Plutarch, *Flam.* 13. 2–3 wrongly connects Flamininus' attitude with his rivalry with Philopoemen: the two men had not yet met. Cf. Niese, ii. 661 n. 2. (See also Harris, 218–19.)

tacita ... cura: cf. xxii. 12. 5, E. Dutoit, *Mélanges Marouzeau* (Paris, 1948), 146.

34. 1. simulando: I do not understand what Aymard (*PR*, 228 n. 61) means by saying that L. was the first to declare that Flamininus' apparent acquiescence in the Greeks' demands was a feint.

2. bene uertat: a colloquial phrase found often in Plautus and Terence and much favoured by L. Cf. *TLL*, ii. 2121. 72 ff.

illud ... [ceterum]: *illud modo ne fallat* occurs only in Mg. Its omission in Bχ would certainly explain *ceterum*, which makes no sense after *illud modo ne fallat*, but could easily have been inserted to provide a connection when the clause was omitted. But in that case it is very strange that *ceterum* should also have stood in Mg (McDonald's doubts as to whether it did or not are not justified) and it is therefore possible, as Walker, Weissenborn, and Zingerle held, that it is *illud modo ne fallat* which should be deleted. It will have originated as an explanatory gloss on *ceterum*. Walker, *Supplementary Annotations*, 202, well remarked that *iam . . . oportet* is redundant after *illud modo ne fallat*, but not after *ceterum*.

4. machinationes: cf. xxxvii. 5. 6 n.

5. uestris ciuitatibus: all the allies, not just the Achaeans. Cf. Aymard, *PR*, 215 n. 10.

7. ⟨sua⟩ cui⟨us⟩que: *cuique* MSS. The dative cannot stand. For though *domestica mala cuique respicienda erant* would be perfectly natural, in this case the subject of *respicere* has already been expressed. But I am not sure that *sua* is necessary. Weissenborn adduced xlv. 38. 12, where *quisque* occurs with a noun which could take *suus*, but does not. (He also quoted iv. 58. 13, but that is not relevant, as *cuiusque* there refers to the object, not the subject of the sentence.)

7–8. segnitiam . . . priuato: doubtless this stood in Polybius, who took a pretty poor view of Greek morale at the time. Compare the inability of the Aetolians to raise troops to fight with Antiochus (xxxvi. 15. 4–5).

8. difficilem ad: cf. xxxii. 17. 8, xxxvii. 16. 8. *difficilis ad*, other than with a gerund, is not found before L. (*TLL*, v. 1. 1090. 45 ff.).

35. *The terms offered to Nabis.* On these terms see especially Aymard, *PR*, 229 ff., and on the reasons for Flamininus' attitude, ibid., 233–44.

35. 1. legatis: the Roman military *legati* (Aymard, *PR*, 229 n. 1).

2. Eumeni . . . Rhodiis: the absence of any mention of the Greek mainland allies, especially of the Achaeans, is puzzling. It may be better to see a simple omission by L. rather than to search for complex reasons. Cf. the inconclusive discussion in Aymard, *PR*, 230 n. 3.

[ex] auctoritate senatus: at 43. 2 the peace appears to be ratified by the senate alone, and the same version appears in Diodorus xxviii. 13. But even if the war had not been formally declared (cf. 24. 6 n.), it seems unlikely that the peace would not have been submitted to the assembly, as argued by Schleussner, 27 n. 64, 46 ff. The agreement of L. and Diodorus does not affect the argument, for even if both were following Polybius, the latter could well have been mistaken on a matter of this sort. (For the probability that at 43. 1–2

L. was using Polybius for events in Rome cf. p. 2 n. 2 and 43. 1–2 n.)

L., however, must mean that the *auctoritas* of the senate would give validity to the peace, not that the peace would be approved (sc. by the people) on the authority of the senate. *ex*, therefore, must be deleted.

3–11. The terms are expressed in a deliberately formal, legalistic style. The fourfold repetition of *dies* in § 3 is a particularly striking example of this. For such repetition of a noun in a relative clause in legal contexts cf. 55. 4, xxxv. 7. 3, *FIRA*, i. 104. ll. 4, 13, Adams, *IF* lxxxi (1976), 87. (There is a threefold repetition of *dies* in xxxi. 42. 7, but that is in simple narrative: cf. n. ad loc.)

3. qua die ... ea dies ... ex ea die ... decimum diem: see appendix.

    ceterisque oppidis: probably settlements near Argos, rather than the other towns of the Argolid. Cf. Aymard, *PR*, 185 n. 3. For Nabis' occupation of Mycenae cf. xxxii. 39. 6 n.

4. regium ... priuatum: for L.'s *uariatio* of *uel*, -*ue*, and *aut* cf. *TLL*, ii. 1571. 56 ff. The public slaves are those of the Argive state, the private ones those of Argive citizens. Madvig's suggestion (*Emendationes*, 504) that we should read *nisi regium* is quite unnecessary. Flamininus was probably seeking to compensate the Argives for slaves previously removed. Cf. Aymard, *PR*, 232 n. 17.

    si qua ... forent: Bχ have simply *si qua ante educta forent* (χ has *et* before *si*), Mg had *sine dolo malo si qua publice aut priuatim ante educta forent*, and Madvig originally (*Emendationes*, 1st edn., 404) proposed to accept Mg's text. He then saw that in that case *recte* was otiose, and suggested attaching *sine dolo malo* to the preceding sentence. It is far from clear, however, that this would make any sense. McDonald believes that Bχ correctly preserve the beginning of the sentence and suggests that F omitted a whole line standing in his exemplar, while Mg corrupted *si qua* to *sine* and then inserted the correct *si qua* as a supplement. Simple deletion of the words in Mg omitted in Bχ is certainly implausible. As Madvig saw, it is highly unlikely that a scribe would invent the legal phrase (*sine*) *dolo malo* (cf. *TLL*, v. 1. 1862. 38 ff.). Yet in McDonald's text *dolo malo* is not really appropriate, for Flamininus would then be saying that slaves removed from Argos during the ten-day period without malice aforethought are not to be returned. I suggest that *sine dolo malo* was written by L., and was glossed by *recte*. The gloss later replaced the correct reading, *dolo malo* being relegated to the margin, to reappear in the wrong place in one branch of the tradition and disappear altogether in the other. I think it is also possible that *publice aut priuatim* should be deleted. It must refer to actions of Spartans, not Argives, though *publicumue aut priuatum* in the previous sentence refers to Argive slaves.

One may note that Flamininus now appears willing to accept Nabis as a *rex*.

5. ciuitatibus . . . redderet: presumably merchant ships adapted for piratical activities, since it is hard to imagine that the perioecic cities had fleets of their own.

sedecim remis: the number of rowers in *lembi* varied from 16 to 50. See Casson, 126.

6. sociis: and presumably to Rome as well. Cf. Aymard, *PR*, 232 n. 14.

Messeniis: cf. 32. 16 n.

comparerent . . . cognossent: the second clause restricts the applicability of the first. Only possessions found and recognized are to be returned. The unspecific neuter presumably includes both slaves and non-personal possessions.

7. liberos coniuges: for the asyndeton cf. xxvi. 13. 13, Preuss, 92.

8. mercennariorum: 27. 2.

9. For Nabis' influence in Crete cf. xxxi. 35. 1 n., Errington, 34 ff. Whether Nabis physically possessed any Cretan cities, as L.'s words imply, is open to doubt. Cf. Shimron, *Late Sparta*, 91 n. 31 (though Errington does not talk of physical possession, as Shimron claims). L. may have misunderstood Polybius.

10. quasque . . . tradidissent: it is hard to think that any Spartan garrisons were left in cities which had themselves made a *deditio* to Rome (as W–M say *restituissent* refers to the future, but *tradidissent* must relate to what has already happened).

11. obsides . . . futura: for similar accusatives and infinitives after nouns cf. K–St, i. 696.

filium: Armenas. Cf. 52. 9 n. He was probably not the only son of Nabis alive at the time. Cf. xxxii. 38. 3, xxxv. 36. 8, Aymard, *PR*, 233 n. 21.

in praesenti: not unparalleled, as Ogilvie, *Phoenix*, 347, asserts, unless we emend all the passages adduced by W–M. But L. uses *in praesentia* very commonly (Packard, ii. 1111), and it is very likely that it is what he wrote here.

36–40. 4. *Renewal of fighting and conclusion of peace*

36. 2. reducendorum exulum: cf. 26. 12 n., Aymard, *PR*, 241–4.

maritimae ciuitates: on the meaning of the term cf. xxxv. 13. 2–3 n.

3. Maleo: cf. 32. 19 n., xxxi. 44. 1 n.

praedatoriis: Mg, om. Bχ. It is not strictly necessary for the sense, but *praedatorius* is an uncommon word (before L. only in Plaut. *Men.* 344, 442, Sall. *Iug.* 20. 7 [*TLL*] and in L. only here, xxix. 28. 5 and xl. 28. 7) and scarcely likely to have been added.

ad supplementum ... militum: a brachylogy meaning 'to supplement his army, and providing by far the best kind of soldiers'.

4. fama ferebant: cf. Ogilvie, 165.

uanis ... ingeniis: one wonders whether Polybius made quite so generalized a statement about Hellenistic courtiers. Cf. 37. 4 n.

5. qui ... indignabantur: with reference to the provisions of 35. 7.

tamquam: on L.'s use of *ut* and *tamquam* with the future participle cf. Tränkle, *WS*, 139–40, xxxi. 42. 5 n.

6. seruis ... obuersabatur: this must refer to former Argive and Messenian slaves (35. 4, 6) who had presumably been freed. It cannot refer to free Helots, since Flamininus made no attempt to reverse the provisions of Nabis' revolution in Laconia itself.

fuisset: subjunctive because the sentence is a virtual *oratio obliqua*.

6–39. 2. The uncial Vatican MS. (R) is extant for parts of this section.

7. nullum esse: Rχ, om. *esse* B. Without R one would have been tempted to delete *esse* (as W–M did).

tyrannis: MgR, *tyranno* Bχ. L. is talking of tyrants in general, not of Nabis alone at this point.

37. 1. circulos serentes: RBχ. *circulos serere* is a perfectly natural phrase, particularly as the original meaning of *serere* is to weave, and the verb is thus easily used of something circular in shape (cf. *serta* = garlands).

It is true that elsewhere *serere* is used by L. with *in circulis* and a direct object of what is said. If, however, we emend to *in circulis* and *haec* is the object of *serere*, *primo* will have to be taken with *serentes*, not with *fremere*. It is clear, though, that *primo* goes with the sentence as a whole, to be followed by *deinde*.

2. There is no conflict between this and 36. 4. Originally Nabis may have wanted to keep the terms secret, but there is no reason to think that this was anything more than a temporary move, and the leaks will not have caused him much embarrassment. Cf. Aymard, *PR*, 245 n. 3.

3. grauiora ... adfinxisset: for a similar case of exaggerating demands in order to secure their rejection cf. Diod. xvii. 39. 2 (of Alexander).

4. solet: sc. *dicere*. For other generalizations in Polybian sections of L. cf. 36. 4, xxiv. 25. 8–9, xxxv. 43. 1, 43. 9, 48. 2. For a Polybian comment on crowd psychology cf. Pol. xxxvii. 9 and for generalizations in L. Dutoit, *RÉL* xx (1942), 100, Gries, *Hommages Renard* (Brussels, 1969), 385 ff.

fortes fortunam adiuuare: an old Latin proverb, found also in viii. 29. 5; for other examples of this and for different forms of the same sentiment cf. Otto, 144, Stübler, 110, Kajanto, 90. W. den Boer, *Historiographia Antiqua* (Louvain, 1977), 202. The *schema etymologicum*, which clearly impressed Romans, could not occur in Greek, and the only passage in Greek where it is fortune, rather than simply the gods, who favours the brave is Sophocles, fr. 927 (Radt) οὐ τοῖς ἀθύμοις ἡ τύχη συλλαμβάνει (attributed to Menander by Apostolius xiii. 36a). The Greek conception of fickle fortune would perhaps, in any case, not seem the sort of thing that would give particular help to the brave.

5. Antiochum ... adiuturos: an empty hope (cf. Accame, 251: *contra* Klaffenbach, *IG* ix². 1. p. xxxvii). There is no reason to think that Flamininus used similar arguments to attempt to persuade the senate to grant him a further prorogation, as argued by Schlag, 97. Cf. *Latomus* xxxi (1972), 31–2.

adfatim: cf. 26. 10 n.

6. pacis mentio: 'any idea of peace'.

et Romanis: 'the Romans too'. B has the nonsensical *qui et*, but with R and χ in agreement, there is no case for either deletion or supplementation.

8. intermissa ... moenia: on the Spartan walls cf. 27. 3 n.

38. 1. accerserent: on the forms *accersere* and *arcessere* cf. *TLL*, ii. 448–9. It is impossible to say which L. himself used on any given occasion.

Sparta: the name occurs only here and at xxxix. 37. 3, with

Spartanus at 41. 7 and xxxviii. 17. 12. Elsewhere L. uses *Lacedaemon* and *Lacedaemonius*.

difficiliora: R, *difficilia* Bχ. 'Higher and difficult to approach' gives as good if not better sense, and in view of the general inaccuracy of R, I am inclined to keep Bχ's reading.

3. corona: a technical term for surrounding a town with a body of soldiers formed in a circle. Cf. xxxvii. 4. 10, 5. 5, *TLL*, iv. 986. 57 ff.

sociorumque: i.e. the Greek allies. The Italian *socii* are here included in the Roman figure, as would be expected in Polybius.

The Roman forces amounted to about 22,000 men in all (cf. xxxiii. 4. 6 n.) so the allies will have contributed *c*. 28,000 less the Roman naval strength.

5. quod roboris: i.e. the main part of his army.

parte ... una ... altera ... tertia: in view of the unanimity of the MSS. it seems unwise to emend to accusatives (thus Madvig, *Emendationes*, 505). It is easy enough to understand *exercitum* or *duces* with *adgredi*.

a Phoebeo ... a Dictynnaeo ... ab ... Heptagonias: all these places are between the Roman army and Sparta, and so in fact Flamininus is attacking towards them. *a* therefore has the meaning 'from the direction of': cf. xxxi. 24. 9 n.

The Phoebeum is a shrine to the south of Sparta, not far from the Menelaion: cf. Bölte, *RE*, xx. 323–6 (323 for the form of the name). The Dictynnaeum is a shrine of Dictynna, a Cretan goddess syncretized with Artemis: on its site cf. A. M. Woodward, *BSA* xv (1908–9), 85 n. 7. Heptagoniae will have been to the north-west of the Dictynnaeum: cf. Bölte, *RE*, viii. 367–8. It is uncertain exactly what it was. (R, miraculously, preserves the correct form here, while Bχ have gibberish.)

omnia ... sunt: L.'s words must mean that the Phoebeum, the Dictynnaeum, and Heptagoniae are unfortified spots, not that they are the places on the city wall line left unfortified, as W–M seem to think (the Phoebeum is explicitly said by Paus. iii. 14. 9 to be outside the city). But L. may have misunderstood Polybius, who perhaps said that Flamininus attacked towards the wall at the places where there was no fortification. The three places are thus on the line of march, but not themselves on the line of the wall.

For *autem* in parentheses cf. *TLL*, ii. 1592, 58 ff.

6. laboraret: MgR, *laborabat* Bχ. For the iterative use of the subjunctive cf. xxxv. 4. 2, 28. 2, Riemann, 294 ff., K–St, ii. 206–7, Walsh on xxi. 4. 4.

7. inops: B(corrected)χ. *inbos* R. As McDonald says, it is most improbable that L. used the archaic *impos*, as argued by Vattasso (the publisher of the fragments of R).

uix mentis compos: L. typically ascribes panic to an enemy commander. Cf. xxxi. 17. 10, 34. 5 nn.

39. 1. in angustiis: quite what places were narrow is left obscure.
ternaeque acies: 38. 5.

2. uani: they missed completely.

3. non modo ... conarentur: for *non modo ... sed ne ... quidem*, without a second negative in the first clause cf. K–St, ii. 61–4, H–S, 519. There is another instance in § 6. In the present case, though, K–St argue that since the common verb is in the first clause a second *non* should be inserted. There is, however, a considerable number of passages where the MSS. omit a second *non* when there is not a common verb in the second clause (iv. 21. 6, xxv. 26. 10, xxxii. 20. 7 in L.), all of which K–St want to emend, and it seems best to accept the construction as what L. wrote. *non modo non* does, however, occur at iv. 3. 10, xxxv. 46. 13.

ut is placed inside *ne ... quidem* because the latter goes with the clause as a whole.

emittere must be understood with *conarentur*. I do not see the difficulty felt by Walsh, *CR*, 55, who proposes *iacularentur*.

4. ex aduerso: i.e. by those in the situation just described.
sunt: χ, om. B, perhaps rightly.

5. progressos: inside the line of the walls.

6. caecos: cf. 14. 11 n.

7. angustiae: the narrative makes it clear that these are different from the *angustiae* of § 1.
tenuerunt: 'held up'. For the omission of the object cf. xxxiii. 3. 7 n.

8. superiora: higher ground inside the walls.
trepidans: cf. 38. 7 n.
circumspectabat: Mg, *circumspectat* Bχ, perhaps rightly.

9. Pythagoras: cf. 25. 5 n.
tunc: thus the MSS. There is no other example of *cum ... tunc* in L. The collocation is presented by the MSS. at Lucr. i. 127 ff., Cic. *off.* i. 123, Juv. 9. 118, all of which have been emended at some time or other. Cf. J. Svennung, *Untersuchungen zu Palladius* (Uppsala, 1935), 411 ff. In the circumstances I am inclined to read *tum* here. (viii. 32. 10, cited by McDonald, is not parallel.)

12. impetus: Rϕ, *impetum* Bψ (F clearly had *impetum*). *impetum* is what one would expect and, I do not understand what McDonald means by 'cf. 38. 6'.

40. 1. nunc proeliis . . . intersaepiendoque: R and χ have *inter-saepiendoque*, B omits the *-que*. It is thus certain that the tradition in late antiquity had *-que*. *operibus*, as often, are siege-engines, not works in general, and it is not clear that these could be used for 'sealing off'. But McDonald is wrong to argue that while the *proelia* and the *opera* were used on several occasions, the 'sealing off' took place once only. Walsh's comments (*CR*, 56) are largely irrelevant, because he does not realize that it is the omission or otherwise of *-que* that is at issue.

2. comminationibus: used by L. only here and at xxvi. 8. 3, and before him only by Cic. *de or.* iii. 206 (*TLL*, iii. 1885–6).

Pythagoran: the presence of the Greek form in R makes it almost certain that this is what L. wrote, on this occasion at least (cf. xxxv. 29. 12 n.).

suppliciter . . . genibus: no doubt a theatrical display by Pythagoras. For the ritual significance of touching the knee in acts of suppliance cf. J. P. A. Gould, *JHS* xciii (1973), 74 ff.

3–4. Pythagoras begins by offering a complete *deditio*, which is rejected, and agreement is reached on the terms previously laid down. It seems odd that Flamininus should have refused the *deditio*, which would have given Rome complete discretion, but it may be that he did not want to be involved in further negotiations, and thought it preferable to keep to what had previously been offered. His own claim (*uelut . . . proficeret*) that Nabis could not be trusted to perform whatever Rome decided cannot be the real reason. There is no reason to think that the terms resulting from acceptance of the *deditio* would be more favourable to Nabis than those already offered, as claimed by Larsen, *CPh* xxx (1935), 198.

4. indutiae: presumably for six months, as previously proposed (35. 2). Cf. Aymard, *PR*, 247.

40. 5—41. *Events at Argos and reactions of the Achaeans*

5. aliis [prope] super alios: as was first seen by P. R. Müller (*Philologus* xii [1857], 59), *prope* has no sense here, and must be deleted. It will have originated as a gloss on *tantum non* below. Cf. Madvig, *Emendationes*, 505–6.

6. Pythagoras . . . excesserat: 29. 14.
   Archippo: not otherwise known.
   Timocratem: cf. 29. 14 n.

7. ab Laecedaemone . . . ad classem: they had come inland for
the negotiations: cf. 30. 7.

41. 1. Nemeorum: the Nemean Games, founded in 573 under
Argive protection, were held biennially, in the first and third year
of each Olympiad. In 209 Philip had presided at the festival (xxvii.
30. 17 ff., Pol. x. 26. 1). They were now held at Argos itself (Aymard,
PR, 66 n. 85).

   die stata: see addenda. The regular date was in July (Schol.
Pind. *Nem.*, hyp. d, e, Hanell, *RE*, xvi. 2325). W–M's references to
winter Nemeans are to be disregarded: cf. Hanell, op. cit., 2327.

   praefecerunt: i.e., as Plutarch (*Flam.* 12. 5) states, Flamininus
was to be ἀγωνοθέτης.

2. Cf. 29. 14 n. Those taken by Nabis may also have been soldiers.
Cf. Aymard, *PR*, 216 n. 17. For troops taken by Nabis from Mycenae
to Sparta cf. *Syll.*[3] 594.

3. redierant . . . effugerant: 25. 12.
   ex longo interuallo: in fact only three years.
   testata . . . Argiuorum: presumably at Flamininus' instance.
Plutarch (*Flam.* 12. 5) makes this into a repetition of the proclamation of 196 and Florus i. 23. 14 conflates the two announcements.

4. serua . . . praebebant: cf. xxxiii. 44. 8 n.

6. regem: Agesipolis. Cf. 26. 14 n.

7. Elatiam: cf. 25. 1 n. Flamininus will have proceeded thence to
the discussions at Corinth related at 22. 4 ff.
   Spartanum: cf. 38. 2 n.

8–10. L. now reports a variant account found in his annalistic
sources. He does not name his source, and the story may have
occurred in more than one writer: or it could be that the annalists
themselves mentioned this version as a variant.

8. castris . . . castra: for the artifical word-order cf. p. 14. It is
interesting that L. should adopt it on an occasion when he might
be expected to reproduce his source more or less unaltered.

10. quattuordecim milia: B has *xxiiii* with the first *x* deleted, χ
quindecim. Which figure, if either, L. wrote must remain uncertain.

42. *Events in Rome*

42. 1. *Supplicationes*

The notice of the *supplicatio* for Cato has already been given in 21. 8. That does not prove that the two notices necessarily stem from different sources. L. may simply have forgotten that he has already mentioned Cato's *supplicatio*, or, indeed, been aware that he had mentioned it but wanted to emphasize the synchronism of the news of the two campaigns and the decisions to grant both Cato and Flamininus a *supplicatio*. The synchronism is in fact false: cf. p. 66.

42. 2–5. *Elections*

42. 2. fusos ... Boios: cf. 22. 1–3 nn.

3. P. Cornelium ... iterum: Scipio's first consulship had been in 205, and so, after the elapse of a *decennium*, he was now entitled to stand for a second consulship.

Ti. Sempronium Longum: (67). Cf. xxxi. 20. 5 n.

horum patres ... fuerant: P. Cornelius Scipio (330) and Ti. Sempronius Longus (66) in 218. The two consuls of 194 are to be regarded as political allies. Cf. *Latomus* xxxi (1972), 47.

4. The praetorian elections resulted in a virtual clean sweep for the Scipionic group. Four of the praetors can be regarded as Scipionic supporters: cf. *Latomus*, loc. cit.

P. Cornelius Scipio: (350). Nasica. Cf. xxxi. 49. 6 n.

Cn. Cornelii ... Blasio: Cn. Cornelius Merenda (265) may have been one of the *legati* for the settlement with Antiochus: cf. xxxvii. 55. 7 n. On Cn. Cornelius Blasio (74) cf. xxxi. 50. 11 n.

Cn. Domitius Ahenobarbus: (18). Cf. xxxiii. 42. 10 n.

Sex. Digitius: (2). A protégé of Scipio (cf. *Latomus*, loc. cit.). See further xxxv. 1. 1 n. He was a *legatus* under L. Scipio in 190 (xxxvii. 4. 2), an ambassador to Macedonia in 174–173, and a *legatus* to buy corn in Southern Italy in 172.

T. Iuuentius Thalna: (32). He is known otherwise only as a *legatus* on the same mission as Digitius in 172. Cf. also xxxiii. 22. 8 n.

42. 5–6. *Dispute about citizenship*

The correct interpretation of this passage was given by R. E. Smith in *JRS* xliv (1954), 18–20. The senate's decision involved no alteration to the existing situation by which Latins enrolled in Roman colonies became *ciues Romani*. The men from Ferentinum had merely put their names down and been placed on the list of colonists. They had then claimed, on that basis alone (*ob id*), that they were Roman citizens. The senate's decision made it clear that a Latin gained citizenship only when he actually took up residence in the colony.

On Ferentinum cf. xxxii. 2. 4 n., on the decision to send out the colonies in 197 xxxii. 29. 3–4 n., on its implementation in 194 45. 1–2. The passage shows that the *nomen Latinum* at this time was not restricted to Latin *coloniae* to the exclusion of the original Latin towns. See Sherwin-White, *JRS*, lxvi (1976), 227–8.

6. adscripti ... dederant: this cannot possibly mean that only a proportion of those who put their names down were enrolled, as considered (but rejected) by Smith, *JRS* xliv, 18 n. 10.

194 B.C.

43–48. 1. *Events in Rome and Italy*

43. 1–2. *Ratification of peace with Nabis*

Cf. 35. 2 n. The absence of reference to representatives of Flamininus also being present (mentioned by Diodorus xxviii. 13) is not significant, and not an indication that the annalists left them out, as argued by Nissen, *KU*, 160.

43. 2. aede Apollinis: on the temple of Apollo, north of the site later occupied by the theatre of Marcellus and outside the *pomerium*, cf. P-A, 15–16, Nash, i. 28. The envoys were received there because representatives of states with whom Rome was at war could not cross the *pomerium* (cf. Mommsen, *StR*, iii. 930, Täubler, 30 n. 2). The temple of Apollo was similarly used for debates on triumphs (xxxvii. 58. 3, xxxix. 4. 2: cf. xxxi. 47. 7 n.), or where the presence of a pro-magistrate, who could not enter the city without forfeiting his *imperium*, was required (Cic. *Q. fr.* ii. 3. 3, *fam.* viii. 4. 4, 8. 5–6, *Att.* xv. 3. 1). This passage appears to be the only evidence for its being used to receive foreign envoys. For the use of the temple of Bellona for such purposes cf. xxxvii. 49. 4 n.

43. 3–9. *Provinces and armies*

Scipio wanted to succeed Flamininus in Greece because he believed that a Roman military presence was the best deterrent against Antiochus. Flamininus, on the other hand, thought that it was vital to redeem Rome's promise of freedom for Greece, and held that a free and grateful Greece constituted the best defence against Antiochus. Cf. *Latomus* xxxi (1972), 47. In addition, though, Scipio may

well have resented Flamininus' growing reputation and welcomed
the chance to seek a counterbalancing command for himself.

3. frequens: a full house. Cf. xxxi. 49. 1 n.

4. iam ... transgressum: cf. 33. 12 n. In fact, of course, Antiochus had first crossed into Europe in 196 (cf. xxxiii. 38. 1 n.).

5. Aetoli: there is no evidence that they were yet in communication
with Antiochus.
   Hannibal: now with Antiochus (xxxiii. 49. 7).

7. P. Cornelio Hispania ulterior: in succession to Ap. Claudius
Nero. Plutarch's statement (*Cato mai.* 11. 1) that Scipio Africanus
succeeded Cato is doubtless the result of a confusion with Nasica.
Nepos (*Cato* 2. 2) says that Scipio wanted the Spanish command,
but this is probably a simple mistake, and it is unnecessary to combine Nepos with L., and think that Scipio tried for the Spanish
command after he had failed to be appointed to Greece (thus
Nissen, *KU*, 160, Aymard, *PR*, 256–7 n. 2). Cf. Scullard, *SA*, 283 nn.
157, 159 and p. 66 above.

9. duas ... octo omnino: cf. pp. 36–7.
   censuisset: Mg, *uoluisset* Bχ. A strange error in F or its archetype,
because *senatus censuit* is so common a phrase that one would not
have thought it would have been in need of an explanatory gloss,
which then replaced the true reading.

44. 1–3. *Repetition of the* uer sacrum

For the problems raised by this section see pp. 22–3.

44. 2. ludosque magnos: vowed at the same time as the *uer
sacrum* in 217 (xxii. 10. 7) and performed in 207 (xxvii. 33. 8).
Nissen (*KU*, 161) thinks that *qui una uoti essent* is a mistake by L.
and that they are in fact the *ludi* vowed by Sulpicius in 200, referred
to in § 6. But that *uer sacrum* and its associated *ludi* are to be regarded
as a second set, and are distinguished by L. as such. Presumably it
was simply decided to repeat the games of 207.

44. 4–5. *The Censorship*

4. Sex. Aelius Paetus: (105). Cf. xxxi. 50. 1 n.
   C. Cornelius Cethegus: (88). Cf. xxxi. 49. 7 n.
   On the political significance of the election cf. vol. i, 33 n. 2.
   ⟨**ii**⟩: the supplement, suggested by H. J. Müller (though not
printed in W–M) is scarcely necessary, as it is quite possible to allow
creati to be a genuine participle, not punctuating after *Cethegus*.

principem ... legerunt: cf. vol. i, loc. cit. The *princeps senatus* had to come from the patrician *gentes maiores*. His name appeared at the top of the list and he had the right to speak first, but the position conferred no power. Cf. O'Brien Moore, *RE*, Supp. vi. 699, J. Suolahti, *Arctos* vii (1972), 207 ff.

tres ... praeterierunt: prosopographers would still have liked to have their names. It is unclear whether the three were actually full members of the senate, and were removed, or ex-magistrates who would have expected to become full members at the census following their magistracy.

5. gratiam ... spectarant: L. here follows the version of Valerius Antias, as reported by Asconius, p. 69C: there is no mention of Scipio's part in the decision. 54. 3–8 is not formally inconsistent with the present passage, but it is attached to an account of the *Megalesia* and would thus appear to be akin to the versions that placed the innovation at the *Megalesia* (Cic. *ap.* Asc. p. 70C, *har. resp.* 24, Val. Max. ii. 4. 3). Its elaborate pro and con reflections on the issue make it highly probable that L. is there using a different source: Klotz's view (*Livius*, 78, 84) that both accounts come from Antias is highly implausible. In a third version the change was instituted by Scipio himself at the *ludi uotiui* (Asc. p. 70C).

On the issue cf. Schlag, *Historia* xvii (1968), 509–12 (implausibly arguing that L. has attempted to combine the evidence of the two passages from Cicero), Wiseman, *Phoenix* xxvii (1973), 195, J. von Ungern-Sternberg, *Chiron* v (1975), 157–63.

These arrangements applied only to the theatre: the extension to the *circus* came later: cf. Dio lv. 22. 4, lx. 7. 4, Mommsen, *StR*, iii. 519.20. At i. 35. 8 L. had attributed the provision of separate seats in the *circus* for both senators and *equites* to Servius Tullius: cf. Ogilvie ad loc.

aedilibus curulibus: the curule aediles were normally in charge of the *ludi Romani*: cf. Mommsen, *StR*, ii³. 518.

atrium Libertatis: it was probably to the east of the Forum, but the exact site is uncertain. It contained a number of censorial records. Cf. P–A, 56–7.

uilla publica: cf. xxxiii. 24. 5 n.

44. 6–8. *Pleminius*

6. uer sacrum ... facti: cf. § 2 n. The vow of games is mentioned at xxxi. 9. 6–10, but nothing has previously been said of the vow of a *uer sacrum*.

Romani: Mg, om. Bχ, clearly rightly. The specially vowed

games are never called *ludi Romani* by L. McDonald's comment
that they are different from the *ludi* of § 2 is irrelevant.

Ser. Sulpicius Galba: in fact Publius (64: cf. xxxi. 4. 4 n.). But,
as McDonald says, the mistake may be due to L. himself.

6–8. cum ... necatusque: L. here follows the version of Clodius
Licinus, which he had mentioned at xxix. 22. 10: cf. xxxi. 12. 2 n.
It is rash to assume from this, however, that the version of the change
in the seating arrangements in the theatre which connected it with
the *ludi uotiui* (see above) also stems from Licinus (thus apparently
Wiseman, op. cit.).

inferiorem demissus: the Tullianum, or lower part of the
Carcer, where executions took place. Cf. Sall. *Cat.* 55, P–A, 99–100,
Nash, i. 206–7. As Licinus' version is probably false, it is not worth
considering how the senate came to condemn Pleminius to death of
its own accord.

45. 1–5. *Colonies*

The first five colonies mentioned were authorized, and the *iiiuiri*
appointed, in 197: cf. xxxii. 29. 3–4 nn. The colonizing activity has
been seen as a move inspired by Scipio for maritime defence against
Antiochus (T. Frank, *Roman Imperialism* [New York, 1925], 170,
Scullard, *RP*², 118). But the five planned in 197 were decided on
before there was any real fear of an invasion by Antiochus, and
certainly before there was fear of a coalition between Carthage
and Antiochus. (Only Sipontum and Croton are on the east coast of
Italy, so the defence would in any case be more against Carthage
than against Antiochus.) Cf. Schlag, 48 n. 98, Harris, 221 n. 5. L.
mentions the figure of 300 colonists only for Puteoli, Volturnum,
and Liternum but the figure may well have applied to the others as
well. Cf. Toynbee, ii. 145, Salmon, *Colonization*, 98.

2. Ti. Sempronius Longus ... erat: as consul his participation
in the final settlement of the colonies can have been little more than
formal. For another consul holding office as a commissioner see
xxxi. 4. 3 n. The scepticism of G. V. Sumner, *AJPh* xcvi (1975),
321, is quite unjustified.

ager ... fuerat: this must mean that the land for the colonies
came from that confiscated from the Campanians, not that there
was division of Campanian land in addition to the colonies. But the
statement cannot apply to Buxentum, which was not in Campania,
and strictly speaking Salernum was in the land of the Picentini
(Strabo v. p. 251C). Cf. Philipp, *RE*, iA. 1869, Radke, *KP*, iv. 845.
For similar indications of previous ownership cf. § 5, xxxv. 40. 6,

xxxvii. 57. 8, P. McKendrick, *Athenaeum* n.s. xxxii (1954), 242 (but his description 'abstracts of title' is highly misleading).

3. Sipontum: at S. Maria di Siponto on the coast of Apulia to the south of Manfredonia. Cf. Philipp, *RE*, iiiA. 271–2 and on the site and remains Touring Club Italiano, *Puglia* (Milan, 1962), 136.

Sipontum prospered later as an important port despite the un- popularity of the colony at the present time (xxxix. 23. 3). Cf. Brunt, 368–9.

Arpinorum: B, *Arpanorum* χ. *Arpanus* is found as the ethnic in the elder Pliny and the *liber coloniarum* (Hülsen, *RE*, ii. 1217) but *Arpinus* occurs consistently in the MSS. of L. on all other nine occurrences of the name. On Arpi cf. 6. 11 n.

D. Iunius Brutus: (45). Not otherwise known.

M. Baebius Tamphilus: (44). He was praetor in 192 (xxxv. 10. 11, 20. 12–13, 23. 5, 24. 7) with command prorogued in 191 (xxxvi. 1. 7, 8. 6, 10. 10, 13. 1–9, 22. 8), a *legatus* to Greece in 185– 184, and consul in 181 with command prorogued in 180. It is pos- sible that he was tribune in this year, and author of the *plebiscitum* authorizing the colony. Cf. *FIRA*, i. 112. l. 43, *MRR*, i. 346 n. 3, H. B. Mattingly, *Latomus* xxx (1971), 290: *contra* J. Carcopino, *Autour des Gracques* (2nd edn., Paris, 1967), 260.

M. Helvius: (4). Cf. xxxii. 27. 7 n., where reference to the present office is omitted.

4. Tempsam ... expulerant: Tempsa, usually Τεμέση in Greek, perhaps to be located at the mouth of the Savuto on the west coast of Italy. Coinage suggests that it was an ally of Croton, and perhaps colonized from there. It is not known when it was captured by the Bruttians: cf. Philipp, *RE*, vA, 459–60, J. Bérard, *La Colonisation grecque de l'Italie méridionale et de la Sicile dans l'antiquité* (Paris, 1957), 147–8, Kahrstedt, *Historia* viii (1959), 188–9. On Bruttium cf. xxxi. 6. 2 n., for confiscation of its land at the end of the Second Punic War, Appian, *Hann.* 61. 252.

Crotonem ... habebant: the Crotoniate aristocrats had been evacuated to Locri in 215 and their land occupied by Bruttians, together, perhaps, with the poorer Crotoniates (xxiii. 30. 6–7, xxiv. 2–3, De Sanctis, iii. 2. 253). But if it had remained in Bruttian possession, the situation would have been the same as at Tempsa, and L. would have mentioned the two in the same sentence. That means that we should keep Bχ's *habebant* and not be attracted by Weissenborn's *habuerant*, based on *habuerunt* in Mg. The Greeks are probably the 3,000 Thurians settled at Croton shortly before Hannibal left Italy (App., *Hann.* 57. 241–2).

5. Cn. Octauius: (16). Cf. xxxi. 3. 2, 11. 18 nn.

L. Aemilius Paullus: (114). The great Paullus, brother-in-law of Scipio. This is his first appearance in history.

C. Laetorius: (2). Cf. xxxi. 21. 9 n.

L. Cornelius Merula: (270). Cf. xxxii. 7. 13 n.

Q. ⟨...⟩ C. Salonius: *Merulaq.* B, *Merula* χ, 'L. Cornelius Merula et C. Salonius archetypa' Gel. It seems safest to assume that the *nomen* of the third triumvir has been lost. C. Salonius may be identified with the *xuir* for viritane assignations in 173. The elder Cato's second wife was a Salonia, but as she was the daughter of one of his tenants, it is rather unlikely that she was related to our Salonius (cf. Wiseman, *New Men*, 54).

45. 6–8. *Prodigies*

Cf. xxxi. 12. 5–10 n.

6. foro et comitio: although often confused with the *forum*, the *comitium* was strictly to the north-east of the *forum* and, before 145, used for voting in the tribal assemblies. The formal distinction of the two is expected in the official style of prodigy lists. Cf. P–A, 134 ff., Taylor, *RVA*, 4, 41.

sanguinis guttae: presumably falling from the sky. For similar prodigies cf. Luterbacher, 23, Wülker, 11, Krauss, 58–60 (and 92–5 for other prodigies involving blood).

terra ... pluuit: for similar prodigies cf. Wülker, 11–12, Krauss, 57–8.

caput Volcani arsit: on the temple of Volcanus cf. xxxii. 29. 1 n. For similar prodigies cf. xxxiii. 26. 8 n.

7. Nare ... fluxisse: for similar prodigies cf. Wülker, 13, Krauss, 65–6. The Nar, modern Nera, joins the Tiber near Orte.

pueros ... natum: for such human *Missgeburten* cf. Luterbacher, 26–7, Wülker, 14, Krauss, 129–30. For other prodigies in Picenum cf. xxi. 62. 5, xxxv. 21. 3, xxxix. 22. 3, Obs. 3, 43, 45, Val. Max. i. 6. 5, Plut., *Marc.* 4. 2, Oros. iv. 13. 12, Zon. viii. 20. 4, Wülker, 99. The *ager Picenus* is *ager Romanus* distributed *uiritim* by the *Lex Flaminia* of 232 (sources in *MRR*, i. 225).

pontificum: for involvement of the *pontifices* with prodigies cf. Wülker, 30–1, Luterbacher, 35.

8. For meteorite prodigies cf. Luterbacher, 23, Wülker, 12, Krauss, 55–7. The *sacrificium nouemdiale* was the normal expiation. Cf. i. 31. 1–4, Luterbacher, 42 n. 82, Wülker, 40, Krauss, loc. cit.

Hadria was a colony founded in the 280s (*per.* xi) at modern Atri. Cf. Weiss, *RE*, vii. 2164–5.

46–48. 1. *Events in Gaul and triumph of Cato*

On the Gallic events cf. Schlag, 46 ff.

46. 1. Flaccus: Mg, omitted in Bχ, perhaps rightly. Cf. 42. 2.

proconsul: there was no official prorogation of his command, as the consuls were to command in the north, but he remained in control of the army until they arrived.

Mediolanium: Milan, the chief town of the Insubres. Cf. Ogilvie, 713. Bχ repeat *circa Mediolanium* after *transgressi erant*. It cannot be determined which occurrence should be deleted.

Dorulato: not otherwise known.

2. M. Porcius Cato ... triumphauit: cf. *I.I.* xiii. 1. 553. For other evidence see *MRR*, i. 344, Astin, *Cato*, 47 n. 51.

tulit ... quadringenta: cf. 10. 4 nn.

3. ex praeda: Mg, om. Bχ. It is not always included in such statements (cf. e.g. 52. 11, xxxiii. 23. 7) and (despite Bχ's omission of *pondo ... quadraginta* above) Mg may have inserted it.

in singulos ... equiti: different decisions about the proportions to be given to the different categories were taken by different commanders (cf. xxxiii. 23. 7 n.) and it is quite wrong to alter the text to make it accord with other passages. L.'s precise figures, probably based on official records, are to be preferred to Plutarch's rather vague statement (*Cato mai.* 10. 4) that Cato gave each of his soldiers a λίτρα ἀργυρίου (which would imply a considerably larger number of *asses* than 270: cf. Crawford, *RRC*, ii. 594). For comparison of the figures with others of this period cf. Astin, *Cato*, 53.

4–47. 8. L. has clearly 'written up' this passage. See p. 6 and n. 4. One can feel little confidence in the details of the engagement. Cf. Münzer, *RE*, iiA. 1434.

4. Boiorix: not otherwise known.

si ... intrasset: it is clear that it is Rome which is taking the initiative. Cf. Schlag, 47.

5. si uideretur ei: because one consul could not issue orders to his colleague. Cf. xxxi. 4. 2 n.

7. nihil aliud quam: for this phrase, with verb omitted, and virtually equalling 'only', cf. xxxvii. 21. 9, *TLL*, i. 1634. 35 ff. L. regularly uses *nihil aliud quam* where Cicero has *nihil aliud nisi*: cf. H–S, 595.

simul ab omni parte: B, *ab omni simul parte* χ. Cf. xxiii. 44. 3, xxxii. 24. 2.

8. stolidam: see p. 6.

9. principalibus portis: the *porta principalis dextra* and the *porta principalis sinistra*, at either end of the *uia principalis*.

12. Q. Victorius: (1). Not otherwise known, and the only recorded republican Victorius. Despite the uncertainty about the narrative as a whole, I am loth to regard this man as an invention. Cf. Gundel, *RE*, viiiA. 2085.

primi pili centurio: the senior centurion of the first maniple of *triarii*, more fully called *primus pilus prior*. Cf. Kromayer–Veith, 320–1, Walbank, *Commentary*, i. 707.

C. Atinius: perhaps the praetor of 188, though he could be C. Atinius Labeo, praetor in 190 (cf. xxxvi. 45. 9 n.)

quartae . . . secundae: cf. p. 36 n. 8. It is clear from § 9 that the two legions are at different ends of the *uia principalis*. Victorius and Atinius, therefore, are taking the same action in different places.

saepe: parallels are collected by W–M ad loc.: add Frontinus ii. 8. 1–4.

iniecerunt: Mg, *iecerunt* Bχ, perhaps rightly.

secundani: soldiers of the second legion.

47. 1. quarta . . . haerente: see note on *quartae . . . secundae* above.

2. portam quaestoriam: another name for the *porta decumana*: cf. Kromayer–Veith, 344.

L. Postumium . . . Tympano: (65). Not otherwise known. The *cognomen* is unique, and Münzer (*RE*, xxii. 949) suggested that it was adopted to distinguish him from an otherwise homonymous member of the *gens*, and that he was in fact a son of L. Postumius Albinus, the consul of 234 and 229. But he may equally well have been a plebeian (thus Mommsen, *RF*, i. 116).

M. Atinium et P. Sempronium: (5) and (11) respectively. Not otherwise known.

praefectos socium: cf. xxxi. 2. 6 n.

3. cohors extraordinaria: on the *extraordinarii*, an élite group of allied troops separate from the main *alae sociorum*, cf. Pol. vi. 26. 6–9, Liebenam, *RE*, vi. 1696 ff., Kromayer–Veith, 267, Walbank, *Commentary*, i. 709.

4. tria proelia: at the two *portae principales* and the *porta quaestoria*.

5. labor . . . sitis: cf. xxxiii. 36. 8 n., v. 48. 3, x. 28. 4, xxii. 2. 4, xxvii. 48. 16, xxxviii. 17. 7, W–M ad loc., Walsh on xxi. 25. 6, Luce, 276.

fluida: see p. 4. Cf. *fluere* at x. 28. 4, xxxviii. 17. 7.

7. quae: Gelenius 'uetus lectio'. *qui* in Bχ is a result of misunderstanding the construction.

48. 1. The variant reports on the activities of Scipio apparently represent all that was to be found in L.'s sources. There is not a major inconsistency because what one could describe as a ravaging expedition, another could regard as being nothing worthy of note (cf. Bredehorn, 83–4, McDonald, *Antichthon* viii [1974], 51, Harris, 258). Fraccaro, *Opuscula*, i. 212, argues that the latter version is clearly correct, on the grounds that some writers refused to believe that Scipio did nothing during his consulship. Toynbee, ii. 271 strangely holds that Scipio, disgruntled at not getting the command in Greece, refused to take the Gallic campaign seriously.

quod: a misprint for *quoad* (spotted by Walsh, *CR*, 56).

48. 2—52. *Events in Greece and return of Flamininus to Rome*

Cf. Diod. xxviii. 13.

The section is a good example of L.'s skill at joining together material from Polybius and his annalistic predecessors. 48. 2–52. 1 must clearly be from Polybius, but the latter would not have included the details of Flamininus' triumph. As in other cases (cf. p. 2) it is not possible to ask precisely where the Polybian passage ends and the annalistic one begins.

2. What Flamininus was in fact doing was restoring power to the upper classes. It is they who had been 'suppressed' by Philip's agents. Cf. 51. 4–7, *Studies in Ancient Society*, 62.

eodem hoc anno: Mg, om. *hoc* Bχ. *eodem hoc anno* occurs otherwise only at xxxv. 40. 5, but it is far more likely that the tradition behind Bχ should have omitted *hoc* to produce the common *eodem anno* (cf. Packard, ii. 93) than that Mg should have inserted a *hoc* which added nothing to the sense.

The section corresponds to Polybius' account of Ol. 146. 2 = 195/4 B.C.

Elatiae: cf. 41. 7 n.

iure dicundo: Mg, *iure dicendo* Bχ. The archaic form is regular in this phrase (cf. *TLL*, v. 1. 967. 26). At xxii. 35. 5 the Puteanus has *iuri dicundo* though at xlii. 28. 6 the Vienna MS. has *iure dicendo*. Here, of course, the phrase is an ablative (cf. xxxi. 13. 5 n.).

praefectorum: cf. xxxi. 23. 1 n.

3. omnium . . . legationes: not specified as the allies of Rome, but probably in fact only those who had gathered at Corinth the previous spring (22. 6: cf. Aymard, *PR*, 258 n. 5).

contionis ... circumfusas: in other words it was more of a public meeting to hear Flamininus than a conference, as in 195.

6. haerentem ... ciuitatis: cf. 41. 4, xxxiii. 44. 8 n.

49. 1. habitus animorum: 'state of mind'. *habitus* is used in this sense in Plaut. *Stich.* 59, Cic. *Arch.* 15, and often in L. Cf. *TLL*, vi. 3. 2483. 54 ff.

fieri potuisset: sc. the removal of Nabis from Sparta.

3. intermori: cf. p. 5.

possit: clearly the reading of the paradosis. Cf. 26. 7 n.

uindicta libertatis: 'the winning of their freedom'. Varro, *RR*, iii. 9. 19 is the first instance of *uindicta* in a metaphorical sense. It first means 'revenge' in Ovid, *Am.* i. 7. 63 (*TLL*).

4. in animo esse: but in fact the senate's decision not to prorogue Flamininus' command (though certainly in accordance with Flamininus' own wishes) left him no alternative.

5. Demetriadis ... Acrocorinthum: cf. xxxiii. 31. 11 n. *Acrocorinthum* is a certain correction for *ac Corinthum* in the MSS. Mg at 50. 8 and both B and the Mainz edition at xxxiii. 31. 11 have *agro Corinthio* for *Acrocorintho*.

7. pensi fuisse: cf. p. 6.

⟨ex⟩ **factis, non ex dictis:** I cannot understand Walsh's apparent proposal (*CR*, 54) that we should retain the MSS.' *factis, non ex dictis* as '*uariatio* in phraseology'. A phrase of this sort demands symmetry between its two members.

a quibus ... sit: χ, om. *a* B. *cauere* with the ablative or dative alone is common in Plautus and Terence but there is no example in Classical Latin. (Cic. *Att.* ii. 20. 1, quoted by *TLL*, iii. 633. 23 is not an instance, for the ablatives do not go with *cauere*: see Shackleton Bailey's translation. The apparent reference in *TLL* to Cic. *Att.* vi. 8. 8 is an error. The passage does not come from Cicero at all.)

8–10. It is possible that L. has elaborated Polybius here. The language reflects the political preoccupations of L.'s own time and *concordia* is a common motif in the early books. Flamininus' exhortation, of course, means that the mass of the people should accept the rule of the upper classes. Cf. *Studies in Ancient Society*, 62.

8. praecipitem et effrenatam: Bχ. Mg had *effrenatam et praecipitem* and this could (but, of course, need not) be an indication of a marginal gloss being inserted in the text at different places (cf. 6. 15 n.). F. Ritschl (*RhM* xviii [1863], 479–80) proposed deleting *nimiam* and the second *esse*, and taking *praecipitem et effrenatam* as the subject, co-ordinate to *temperatam*, while Madvig (*Emendationes*, 506 n.1) argued that *et effrenatam* should be deleted, as it did not make sense in the context. But *effrenatus et* (*atque*) *praeceps* is found at Cicero, *Cael.* 35, *Har. resp.* 2, and if *effrenatam* is taken to mean 'uncontrollable' there is no difficulty in its going with *aliis*. Tränkle, *Gnomon*, 377 n. 3 supports Madvig.

9. principes et ordines: the leading citizens and the different ranks of society, not 'the upper classes and the other ranks' as W–M take it.

10. insidiantibus: a substantival participle. Cf. Adams, *Glotta* li (1973), 128.

pars ... cedat: precisely what Thucydides said about opposing classes in the Peloponnesian War (iii. 82. 1).

50. 1–4. Almost certainly a considerable elaboration of Polybius. Cf. Tränkle, 138 n. 21.

2. in pectora ... demitterent: cf. iii. 52. 2, Sall. *Iug.* 11. 7, 102. 11, Koestermann, 60, Skard, 41.

3–7. On the return of the captives cf. Diod. xxviii. 13, Val. Max. v. 2. 6, Plut. *Flam.* 13. 6–8, *Mor.* 197B, Ducrey, 249.

3. intra duos menses: Diod. loc. cit. says 30 days.

6. argumentum sit: Mg, Priscian, *de figuris numerorum* 12 (*GL* iii. 409), *argumentum est* Bχ. The independent evidence of Mg and Priscian makes it extremely probable that L. wrote *sit*. As McDonald says, the subjunctive is particularly appropriate for the calculation that follows.

centum ... denarios: 1,200 × 500 *denarii* = 60,000 *denarii* = 100 talents, by the usual equivalence of 1 *denarius* = 1 drachma (there are 6,000 drachmae in a talent). Cf. Walbank, *Commentary*, i. 176, iii. 63.

7. adice: on L.'s use of the imaginary second person singular (usually in the potential subjunctive) cf. xxxi. 7. 11 n., K. Gilmartin, *TAPhA* cv (1975), 99 ff.

quot ... totam: Val. Max. loc. cit. says the total number was 2,000 but it is doubtful whether he had any independent evidence for this figure.

8. Acrocorintho: cf. 49. 5 n.

9. secutus prosequentibus: deliberate repetition to emphasize the scene.

seruatorem liberatoremque: σωτῆρα καὶ ἐλευθερωτήν. Flamininus had been addressed as σωτήρ at the proclamation of the Isthmus in 196 (Pol. xviii. 46. 12, omitted by L.). For other evidence for the appellation cf. Walbank, *Commentary*, ii. 613. This is the earliest evidence for the title of ἐλευθερωτής applied to a man and Weinstock, 143, regards it as 'anachronistic'—i.e. an addition by L. to what he found in Polybius. At xxxv. 17. 9 the Roman people is referred to as *liberator*.

Elatiam rediit: 48. 2.

10. Ap. Claudium legatum: cf. 28. 10 n.

Oricum: on Oricum, between Apollonia and Corcyra, cf. Hammond, *Epirus*, 127 ff. It had been an ally of Rome since 214 (xxiv. 40). Badian, *Studies*, 24, seems right in his argument that Oricum was not included in the Roman protectorate established after the First Illyrian War.

se ibi: B, *ibi se* χ, perhaps rightly, for (i) with B's order *se* is too emphatic (ii) L. very rarely uses *atque* before a consonant when the *atque* joins two clauses. See Novak, *WS* xv (1893), 248 ff., H. J. Müller, *JPhV* xxi (1895), 41–4.

11. L. Quinctio . . . legato: cf. xxxii. 16. 2 n.

51. 1. Oreo atque Eretria: unless this is an error, we must assume that garrisons were placed in Oreus and Eretria in 196, despite the senatorial decision of xxxiii. 34. 10 (my criticism of Schlag in the n. ad loc. failed to take account of the present passage).

conuentum . . . ciuitatium: Flamininus was thus, probably, re-establishing the Euboean League. Cf. Holleaux, *Études*, i. 58, Larsen, *Greek Federal States*, 405.

2. admonitos: Bχ. Mg's *commonitos* is equally possible.

in quo statu: cf. Ogilvie, 519.

4–6. For this reorganization of Thessaly on a timocratic basis cf. *Studies in Ancient Society*, 56, 62–3. It is uncertain whether or not Flamininus left a full assembly in Thessaly, or whether that too was from a restricted franchise. Aymard (*ÉHA*, 175) argued that he did leave a democratic assembly. One of his arguments, however, is derived from § 5, which he regards as referring to full assemblies down to L.'s own time. It is quite likely, however, that *ad nostram usque aetatem* represent words of Polybius heedlessly taken over by L. (for similar instances cf. xxxiii. 17. 6, xxxv. 38. 3 nn.). Aymard's only other argument is based on L.'s use of *multitudo* in reference to a Thessalian gathering at xlii. 38. 7.

There is no need to think that *ex omni conluuione ac confusione* refers exclusively to the new citizens admitted to Thessalian cities on Philip's instructions (cf. *Syll.*³ 543) as argued by Niese, ii. 666 n. 1.

*Syll.*³ 674 = Sherk, no. 9 (*c.* 140 B.C.) refers to νόμους τοὺς Θεσσαλῶν ... οὓς νόμους Τίτος Κοΐγκτιος ὕπατος ἀπὸ τῆς τῶν δέκα πρεσβευτῶν γνώμης ἔδωκεν. (ll. 50 ff.). Since the *x legati* left Greece in the winter of 196/5 (xxxiii. 44. 5 n.) we must either assume that this is an inaccurate formulation or that Flamininus had begun the process of the reorganization of Thessaly in 196.

6. cui ... expediebat: a clear-cut statement that Flamininus was giving power to the rich, whose interest it was that their riches should be conserved. Cf. Cic. *r.p.* ii. 40.

52. 1. percensuisset: 'made a review of'. I find it hard to believe that L. is here using *percensere* in the sense of 'travel through' (cf. Ovid, *Fast.* iii. 109, *Met.* ii. 335), as suggested in L–S and *OLD*.

Oricum: cf. 50. 10 n.

2. prae se acto: with *agmine rerum captarum* (W–M).

3. extra urbem: cf. xxxi. 47. 7 n.

edisserendas: χ, *disserendas* B. Corruption from the more unusual *edisserere* is far more likely, and in any case L.'s normal practice with *disserere* is to say *disserere de rebus gestis* (though *disserendas res* occurs at xli. 6. 4). For *edisserere* cf. xliv. 41. 4, xlv. 40. 9.

lubentibus: I do not understand W–M's statement that the usage differs from that in Cic. *r.p.* i. 14, *Att.* iv. 2. 5.

4. triduum: the first recorded case of a triumph lasting longer than one day. Paullus in 167 also had a three-day triumph (*I.I.* xiii. 1. 556).

aerea: see p. 4.

plura ... adempta: from his residences on the Greek mainland and Euboea, not from Macedon itself (cf. Niese, ii. 667 n. 1: *contra* De Sanctis, iv. 1. 112). How Flamininus came into possession of a Macedonian statue of Zeus Ourios (Cic. *II Verr.* 4. 129: cf. Cook, *Zeus*, iii. 142 ff.) is obscure.

transtulit: on L.'s use of *transferre*, *traducere*, and *transuehere* in triumph reports cf. J. E. Phillips, *CPh* lxix (1974), 54–5, arguing that the reference is to carrying across the *pomerium*.

secundo: B, *secundo die* χ, a clear case of an explanatory gloss being inserted into the text.

5. infecti ... septuaginta: Plutarch (*Flam.* 14) reports figures for

the booty in Flamininus' triumph on the authority of οἱ περὶ Τοῦ-
⟨δ⟩ιτανόν (Cichorius' τὸν Ἀντίαν, accepted by Klotz, *Livius*, 11 is
palaeographically much less plausible). This presumably means not
that Plutarch himself used the work of C. Sempronius Tuditanus,
consul in 129 (on his histories cf. Peter, *HRR*, i². cci ff., 143 ff.) but
that his immediate source referred to it. He does not include all
the items mentioned by L., and it is therefore unlikely that L. and
Plutarch were using the same immediate source. But in all other
cases, except for a trivial discrepancy in § 7 (cf. n. ad loc.) the figures
given by both L. and Plutarch agree and in this case the second part
of the figure is the same. It is thus very probable that L. and Plutarch
both derive from the same original figures, and that there is either a
corruption in L. from *xl* to *xv* or a reverse error which occurred
between Tuditanus and Plutarch (it cannot be an error in the transmission of Plutarch, as McDonald seems to suggest, since at no stage
would the figures have been expressed in Roman numerals). It is
scarcely possible to decide which is correct, and McDonald is right
to say that arguments from the normal proportion of silver to gold
are not compelling in this case, when there was clearly an unusually
large amount of gold in the booty. See addenda.

fabrefacta: *fabrefacere* is used by L. also at xxvi. 21. 8, xxxvii.
27. 5, but not, probably, before him. *fabre* and *facere* are separate
words at Plaut. *Men.* 132, *Stich.* 570 and *fabre facta* at *Cas.* 861 should
therefore probably also be taken as such. Cf. *TLL*, vi. 11–12.

6. The fullest discussion of this passage is by R. Thomsen, *Early
Roman Coinage* ii (Aarhuus, 1961), 139 ff., of which what follows
(like McDonald's long note) is little more than a summary. See
also Crawford, *RRC*, i. 28 n. 4, xxxvii. 46. 3, 58. 4, 59. 4 nn.

L. usually equates the drachma with the *denarius* (cf. 50. 6 n.)
and a tetradrachm might therefore be expected to contain four, not
three *denarii*. Hence *quattuor* has been proposed instead of *trium*.
But the fact that the evidence of the MSS. is supported by the
independent evidence of Priscian (*de figuris numerorum* 13 = *GL* iii.
409) makes it very probable that L. wrote *trium*. This was, in fact,
roughly the weight of the cistophori which replaced the tetradrachm
about 166 B.C. The comment was made by L.'s source in reference
to the circumstances of his own time. The figure and comment do
not appear in Plutarch and it is possible that they did not stand in
Tuditanus.

Atticorum: Macedonian tetradrachms of Attic weight, not
Athenian coins.

tetrachma: the contracted form (albeit corrupted in various
ways) occurs in the MSS. at xxxvii. 46. 3, 58. 4, 59. 4, xxxix. 7. 1

and since the MSS. here have *tetrachiam* it is a more probable reading than the full form preserved in Priscian.

7. quattuordecim: Plutarch has 13. It is impossible to determine which is correct.

Philippei: the word here indicates gold staters on the Attic standard, first minted by Philip II. Posthumous coins bearing the names of Philip and Alexander were struck by the Diadochi and imitated elsewhere in the third century and later (cf. Seltman, *RE*, xix. 2196–8, M. J. Price, *NC* 7, ix [1969], 9–10, M. Thompson, *AJA* lxxiv [1970], 347 ff., M. Thompson–O. Mørkholm–C. M. Kraay, *Inventory of Greek Coin Hoards* [New York, 1973], no. 866), but there is no need to think that Flamininus' booty contained only coins bearing the name Φιλίππου, whether in reference to Philip II or to Philip V (whose staters were much rarer: cf. H. Gaebler, *Die Antiken Münzen Nordgriechenlands* iii. 2 [Berlin, 1935], 189–90). For the staters of Antiochus III see E. T. Newell, *The Coinage of the Eastern Seleucid Mints* (New York, 1938), nos. 242, 384, 397, *The Coinage of the Western Seleucid Mints* (New York, 1941), nos. 1688–9.

I am much indebted to Dr. A. H. Jackson and Dr. M. J. Price for advice on this matter.

9. Demetrius: cf. xxxiii. 13. 14 n.

Armenes: cf. 35. 11 n. Armenas is the Spartan form of the name. In 190 he alone of the hostages was not released, and he died in Italy soon afterwards (Pol. xxi. 3. 4).

10. est inuectus: by the *porta triumphalis*, which was not, however, a gate in the city wall. Cf. Nisbet, *in Pisonem*, 117, Versnel, 132 ff.

ut: the *in* of BψA is unintelligible, and its omission in PE a clear case of emendation. *ut* gives the sense that is needed. Walsh's suggestion of ⟨*sic*⟩ *currum . . . ut* is implausible. *ut . . . deportato* explains *frequentes*, not *secuti*.

11. Cf. 46. 3, xxxiii. 23. 7 nn.

12. capitibus rasis: the statement of W–M and Sage that the shaved head was a sign of slavery is not borne out by the evidence. It is clear that slaves on gaining freedom both shaved their heads and, in most cases, put on the *pilleus*. Cf. xlv. 44. 19, Plaut. *Amph.* 462, Val. Max. v. 2. 5, Petr. 41. 1–4, J. Marquardt, *Das Privatleben der Römer* (2nd edn., Leipzig, 1886), 355, Walbank, *Commentary*, iii. 441. See also xxxiii. 23. 6 n.

53–4. *Events in Rome and Italy*

53. 1–2. *Colonies*

53. 1. Q. Aelius Tubero: (153). Presumably a tribune of 193, as the decisions were made *exitu anni* (*MRR*, i. 346 n. 5). He is not otherwise known.

ex senatus consulto: *sc.* in B and Gelenius 'ex s.c. uetus lectio' make the reading certain. For the procedure cf. xxxii. 7. 3 n.

in Bruttios: cf. 45. 4 n. For the foundation of the colony cf. xxxv. 40. 6.

Thurinum agrum: Thurii, the pan-Hellenic colony founded under Athenian auspices in 443 near the site of Sybaris. It had joined Hannibal in 212 (xxv. 15. 7 ff.). On the foundation of the colony cf. xxxv. 9. 7–8 nn.

2. in triennium: cf. xxxii. 29. 4 n.

Q. Naeuius: perhaps to be identified with the praetor of 184 (16).

M. Minucius Rufus: (53). Cf. xxxii. 27. 7 n.

M. Furius Crassipes: (56). He was praetor in 187 and again in 173. His identification with the *legatus* in Greece in 201 (xxx. 42. 5) or the military *legatus* in Gaul in 200 (xxxi. 21. 8) is uncertain. Cf. xxxi. 21. 8 n.

Furius is one of five examples of double praetorships in this period. The others are A. Atilius Serranus (54. 3 n.), P. Manlius (xxxiii. 42. 1 n.: but cf. Astin, *Cato*, 80), P. Aelius Tubero (xxxvii. 55. 7 n.), and C. Livius Salinator (xxxii. 16. 3 n.). In the first century re-entry to the senate following expulsion was often gained by a second praetorship (cf. C. Antonius and P. Cornelius Lentulus Sura, expelled in 70, Cic. *Clu.* 119 ff.) and this may well be the case with the first four. If so, they were all expelled in 184, since in 199, 194, and 189 no holders of curule offices were removed (xxxii. 7. 3, xxxiv. 44. 4, xxxviii. 28. 2). But only for Manlius is there any kind of specific evidence, and that not certain (cf. Astin, loc. cit.). The case of Livius Salinator is odd: perhaps he thought he would improve his chances for the consulship by holding a second praetorship. He held the office immediately after the expiry of the *decennium* provided for in the *Lex Genucia* (vii. 42. 2).

A. Manlius: Vulso (90). Cf. xxxv. 9. 7. He was perhaps praetor in 189, and was consul in 178 with command prorogued in 177.

Q. Aelius: the MSS. have P. Aemilius, but at xxxv. 9. 7 L. says *Q. Aelius Tubero, cuius lege deducebatur* (cf. xxxiii. 42. 1 n.).

L. Apustius: Fullo (5). Cf. xxxv. 9. 7, xxxi. 4. 7 n.

Cn. ... urbanus: cf. 43. 6. For a praetor presiding at such elections cf. xxxi. 4. 2 n.

in Capitolio: cf. xxxiii. 25. 7 n.

53. 3-7. *Dedication of temples*

3. Iunonis . . . bello: in fact of Iuno Sospita. Cf. xxxii. 30. 10 n. and addendum thereto. On Iuno Sospita see further J. R. Fears, *Historia* xxiv (1975), 595–6. The temple was probably dedicated on 1 February (*I.I.* xiii. 2. 405).

The *forum holitorium* was the vegetable market, between the Capitol and the area later (and now) occupied by the theatre of Marcellus. Cf. P-A, 225.

censor: 44. 4.

4. Cf. xxxi. 50. 2, xxxiii. 42. 10 nn. The temple was dedicated on 13 February (*I.I.* xiii. 2. 409).

5–6. This notice presents some complex problems. Firstly, there was no Sempronius Sophus in office during the Second Punic War, and the reference is clearly to P. Sempronius Tuditanus, who vowed a temple to *Fortuna primigenia* during his consulship in 204 (xxix. 36. 8). But he was censor in 209, and so cannot have let the contract for a temple he had not yet vowed. It is impossible to say how the confusion arose. A P. Sempronius Sophus was consul in 268 and censor in 252. He vowed a temple to Tellus in his consulate (Flor. i. 14. 2) and this may have helped the confusion along its way. R. Seguin (*Latomus* xxxiii [1974], 19) suggests that the contract for the temple was in fact let by Scipio as censor in 199. That may be so, but Seguin's attempt to use the incident as evidence for Scipio's particular interest in *fortuna* is very far-fetched.

The evidence concerning temples of Fortuna in Rome is involved. Vitruvius (iii. 2. 2) refers to *tres Fortunae* near the Porta Collina and the *Fasti* give dedication dates for three temples. The first, on 5 April, is mentioned in two *Fasti* and described as *Fort(una) publ(ica)* and *Fortuna publica citerior in colle* respectively (*I.I.* xiii. 2. 437). On 25 May four *Fasti* talk of *Fortuna publica populi Romani* (one omits *publica*) and only the *Fasti Venusini* of *Fortuna prim(igenia)* (*I.I.* xiii. 2. 461). On 13 November the *Fasti Aruales* refer to *Fortuna prim(igenia) in c . . .* (*I.I.* xiii. 2. 530).

The simplest conclusion to be drawn from this is that the three entries in the *Fasti* refer to Vitruvius' three temples, and that at least two of them were temples of *Fortuna primigenia*. Since five *Fasti* mention the temple dedicated on 25 May, that is likely to be the temple in question here, since this is clearly the first occasion on which *Fortuna primigenia*, the famous goddess of Praeneste, was given a home in Rome. For this view cf. P-A, 216–17, Otto, *RE*, vii. 27 ff., Bömer, ii. 336.

Latte, however (*RRG*, 178–9), argued that the entry for 13

November should be supplemented in C⟨apitolio⟩, to accord with
the statement of Plutarch (*Mor.* 322F) that there was a temple of
Fortuna primigenia on the Capitol. He holds that this was the only
temple of *Fortuna primigenia* in Rome and that the *Fasti Venusini*
are in error in describing the May 25 temple as being of *Fortuna
primigenia*. He thus implicitly rejects the evidence of the present
passage and holds that the third temple of Vitruvius is otherwise
unknown. Degrassi (*I.I.* xiii. 2. 461, 530) accepts Latte's arguments
in respect of the November entry, but rightly refuses to reject L.'s
evidence here. In support of the third temple being on the Capitol
he also adduces *ILS* 3696, an inscription of A.D. 136 from Praeneste
which begins

> *tu quae Tarpeio coleris uicina tonanti*
> *uotorum uindex semper, Fortuna, meorum . . .*

But since both this inscription and Plutarch are much later than
Vitruvius, and we must in any case reject Plutarch's statement that
the Capitoline temple was built by Servius Tullius, it remains
simplest to hold that the temple on the Capitol was built sometime
in the first century A.D. and to identify the 13 November temple
with one of the temples of Vitruvius.

It should be added that the fact that L. is mistaken about Sempronius cannot of itself justify rejecting what he has to say about the
site of the temple.

The temples were at the top of the Quirinal, near the junction
of Via Pieve and Via XX Settembre.

7. et . . . locata: cf. xxxi. 21. 12 n., to which add a reference to
L. A. Holland, *Janus and the Bridge* (Rome, 1961), 183–4.

    C. Seruilius: possibly C. Servilius Geminus (60). Cf. xxxi. 4. 3 n.

    haec . . . acta: the year's events do not in fact conclude at this
point, and since *acta* occurs only in Mg, it may be that the phrase
has been displaced, and belongs after *malunt* in 54. 8.

54. 1–2. *Elections*

54. 1. uenit: Mg, *rediit* Bχ. A surprising variant, and it is scarcely
possible to tell which is correct. McDonald's statement that *uenit* is
'potius ex usu' is false: cf. Packard, iv. 287–8.

    L. Cornelius Merula: (270). Cf. xxxii. 7. 13 n.

    Q. Minucius Thermus: (65). Cf. xxxii. 27. 8 n.

    Again two Scipionic supporters are elected. Cf. *Latomus* xxxi
(1972), 48.

2. Of the six praetors, Fulvius, Scribonius, and Flaminius were aediles in 196. L. does not list the aediles for 195 but L. Scipio's aedileship must belong to that year (*MRR*, 1. 340) and Münzer (*RE* viiiA. 126–7) argued that Valerius and Porcius were also aediles in 195.

L. Cornelius Scipio: (337). The brother of Africanus. He had been a *legatus* under his brother from 207 to 202. His *elogium* (*I.I.* xiii. 3. 15) says that he held the quaestorship and the curule aedileship. The date of the quaestorship is unknown, for the aedileship see above. He was a *legatus* under Glabrio in 191 (xxxvi. 21. 4–11 n.), and consul in 190 (xxxvi. 45. 9, xxxvii, *passim*).

M. Fuluius Nobilior: (91). Cf. xxxii. 7. 8, xxxiii. 42. 8 nn.

C. Scribonius: (8). Cf. xxxiii. 42. 10 n. It is interesting that on this occasion the *cognomen* is omitted.

M. Valerius Messalla: (252). L. in *MRR*, i. 347 is a misprint. He was consul in 188, an ambassador to Macedon in 174–173, and *xuir sacris faciundis* from 172 until his death.

L. Porcius Licinus: (23). Consul in 184, with command prorogued in 183. A scribe at an early stage of transmission, puzzled by the *cognomen*, created a seventh praetor, M. Licinius.

C. Flaminius: (3). Cf. xxxiii. 42. 8 n.

54. 3–8. *Games*

On the establishment of separate seats for senators cf. 44. 5 n.

3. This means that this was the first occasion on which plays were performed at the *Megalesia*, not that it was the first time plays were performed at any *ludi*, and the passage does not, therefore, belong to the tradition that rejected the view that plays were first performed in 240, as is claimed by A. E. Douglas, *M. Tulli Ciceronis Brutus* (Oxford, 1966), 64 (cf. xxxi. 12. 10 n.). At xxxvi. 36. 4 L. appears to report that Valerius Antias placed the first plays, and indeed the first *Megalesia*, in 191: cf. n. ad loc.

The *Megalesia*, or *ludi Megalenses*, were first performed in 204, in celebration of the placing of the Magna Mater in the temple of Victoria (xxix. 14. 14). This was on 4 April, and the temple of the Magna Mater was dedicated on 10 April 191 (xxxvi. 36. 3–4 n.). Later, therefore, the games lasted from 4 to 10 April. Cf. Habel, *RE*, Supp. v. 626 ff.

A. Atilius Serranus: (60). He was praetor in 192, propraetor in 191, praetor again in 173 (cf. 53. 2 n.), with command prorogued in 172. He finally reached the consulship in 170.

L. Scribonius Libo: (17). He was praetor in 192, and a *iiiuir* for the supplementation of Sipontum and Buxentum in 186.

4–7. aliis ... institutam: the language reflects the ideological debates of the late republic.

4. existimantibus: Bχ, *censentibus* Mg. Neither is an unusual word, and hardly likely to be glossed by the other. That *censentibus* was caused by *tributum*, as McDonald suggests, is not very probable, and I see no way of deciding what L. wrote.

5. concordiae ... esse: on the construction cf. Ogilvie, 437.

6. quingentesimum ... octauum: cf. xxxi. 1. 4 n.
   cauea: the portion of the theatre where the spectators sat. Cf. *TLL*, iii. 629. 30 ff.

7. consessorem: the only occurrence of the word in L. It is also used of one's neighbour at the theatre in Cic. *Att.* ii. 15. 2. *consessus* is regularly used of a theatre audience: cf. *TLL*, iv. 424. 71 ff.

8. adeo ... est: as so often in the ancient world, the 'popular' side appeals to tradition. Compare the claim by the Athenian radicals in 462 that they were proposing merely to restore the original powers of the Areopagus.
   malunt: people in general, not with reference to the *aliis* of § 5.

193 B.C.

55–59. *Events in Rome and Italy*

55. 1–4. *Earthquakes*

Despite the importance attached to earthquakes as prodigies (cf. Wülker, 18, Krauss, 49 ff.), one suspects that there is a degree of exaggeration in this picture of the state completely given over to sacrificing. We are not told whether the earthquakes caused any damage, and it is clear that it is earthquakes reported elsewhere in Italy, not ones experienced in Rome itself, that are involved.

On the style of L.'s account here cf. McDonald, *JRS* xlvii (1957), 157, contrasting it with the formal report of xxxv. 40. 7. (It is quite wrong to see the two passages as a doublet, as claimed by Nissen, *KU*, 174, Lauterbach, 84.)

55. 1. feriarum ... indictarum: i.e. *feriae conceptiuae* (Varr. *LL* vi. 26) or *imperatiuae* (Macr. i. 16. 6).

3. decemuiris ... iussis: cf. xxxi. 12. 9 n.

3–4. supplicatio ... puluinaria: cf. xxxi. 8. 2 n.

4. coronati: cf. xxxvi. 37. 5, xl. 37. 3.

ne quis ... nuntiaret: it seems that it was the effect of making the announcement, not the actual occurrence of the earthquake that mattered. Cf. in general Jocelyn, *Journal of Religious History* iv (1966), 102, J. W. H. G. Liebeschuetz, *Continuity and Change in Roman Religion* (Oxford, 1979), 24 ff.

  quo die ... eo die: cf. 35. 3–11 n.

55. 5–6. *Assignation of provinces*

56. *Northern Italy*

The danger on this occasion may well have been serious, despite the doubts of Toynbee, ii. 56.

56. 1. M. Cinci: identified by *MRR*, i. 349 and Münzer (*RE*, iii. 2557) with the tribune of 204 (6), but the identification is far from certain. If it is correct, he will be related to the historian L. Cincius Alimentus.

  Pisis: in 195 a praetor had a command *circa Pisas* (xxxiii. 43. 9 n.). What forces were under Cincius' control is uncertain.

2. conciliabula: here just 'villages' (cf. 1. 6 n.).

  uniuersae gentis: given the size of the army (§ 10, xxxv. 3. 1) probably all the Cisalpine Ligurians, not just the Apuani. Cf. Toynbee, ii. 277.

  Lunensem ... agrum: on Luna cf. 8. 4 n.

3. patrum: Mg, *senatus* Bχ. As in 54. 1 it is impossible to decide what L. wrote. Both *ex auctoritate patrum* and *ex auctoritate senatus* are widely used by L., and neither would seem in need of a gloss by the other.

4. legiones ... essent: 43. 9. It seems that originally no new legions were to be recruited in 193.

  Arretii: cf. xxxi. 21. 1 n.

5. sociis ... eorum: 'the allies, that is their magistrates and representatives'. On this limiting apposition, an archaic construction not found in Cicero or Caesar, cf. K–St, i. 250, H–S, 428–9.

6. pro ... iuniorum: each state was required to provide a given number of troops, according to their actual number of men of military age, instead of in the fixed proportion laid down in the *formula togatorum*. This represented a concession to the allies, who were suffering from depopulation. Cf. xxvii. 9, xxxix. 3. 4–5, xli. 8.

6–12, McDonald, *JRS* xxxiv (1944), 20, Toynbee, ii. 130 n. 2, Brunt, 548.

8. In 196 each praetor in Spain had one legion plus 4,000 infantry and 300 cavalry supplied by the allies (xxxiii. 26. 3). In 195 each praetor was given in addition 2,000 infantry and 200 cavalry (xxxiii. 43. 7–8). In 194, apparently, no changes were made (cf. 43. 8–9). It is clear from xxxv. 2. 3 ff. that *ueteres milites* refers only to the veterans among the troops in Spain, not to all those serving there. The strength of the Spanish armies was thus being considerably increased.

9. For appeals to tribunes in matters concerning the levy cf. xlii. 32. 7 ff., L. R. Taylor, *JRS* lii (1962), 21 ff.

    emerita stipendia: in L. *stipendia emerere* always means completion of the compulsory *stipendia*. Though normally not liable for military service, such persons could be called up in an emergency (cf. Brunt, 391).

10. Ti. Semproni: the consul of 194, still in the north.

    agrum Placentinum: cf. xxxi. 10. 2 n.

11. tumultum: cf. xxxi. 2. 5 n.

12. socii ... essent: i.e. had been dismissed in Italy, and had not returned to Rome.

57–59. *Negotiations with the ambassadors of Antiochus*

I have discussed the interpretation and political importance of this conference in *Latomus* xxxi (1972), 34–6. It is also mentioned by Diodorus xxviii. 15 and Appian, *Syr.* 6. The similarities between L. and Diodorus make it probable that Polybius is their common and immediate source (though cf. p. 2 n. 2). It is, however, unprofitable to use Diodorus and Appian to determine L.'s additions to Polybius, as is done by Brueggmann, 177 ff. The conference marks a sharp break with Flamininus' previous insistence on Greek freedom, and the beginnings of a *rapprochement* between him and the 'Fulvians'.

57. 1. postulauit ... confirmaret: the ratification *en bloc* of the *acta* of a returning commander was the normal procedure. In 61 Crassus and Lucullus filibustered the ratification of Pompey's *acta* by insisting on a clause by clause discussion (App. *BC* ii. 9, Dio xxxvii. 49. 4–5). In this case, of course, most of the decisions had in fact been taken by the senate itself.

    It was now that Philip was promised remission of tribute and the return of Demetrius if he remained loyal (Diod. loc. cit., Walbank, *Philip V*, 191: cf. xxxv. 31. 5, xxxvi. 35. 11–14, xxxvii. 7. 16 nn.).

senatus: φ, om. Bψ. An intelligent supplement by Landolfo di Colonna.

4. in Asia: cf. 33. 12 n. *apud regem* goes with both *in Asia* and *Lysimachiae*. Leuze's attempt to deny this (*Hermes* lviii [1923], 216 n. 3), and thus absolve L. (or Polybius) of the possibility of an error is unconvincing.

Lysimachiae: cf. xxxiii. 39–41 and nn.

5. responderet ... possent: it seems that Flamininus and the commissioners were given full authority to negotiate: 59. 4 ff. is merely a report to the full senate, not a request for ratification of what they had done.

6. Menippus et Hegesianax: Appian adds Lysias, but in view of other inaccuracies in his account, he is probably wrong. On Hegesianax cf. xxxiii. 34. 2–3, 39. 2 nn., Walbank, *Commentary*, ii. 615–16, Olshausen, no. 136. Menippus (Olshausen, no. 139) was a Macedonian (xxxvi. 11. 6) and may be the same man as the officer of Philip V active in the First Macedonian War (xxvii. 32. 10, xxviii. 5. 11, Pol. x. 42. 2: Walbank's index conflates them, presumably deliberately). For other activities of Menippus in this period see xxxv. 32, 50. 7, 51. 4, xxxvi. 10. 5, 11. 6. On the present occasion he was instrumental in obtaining *asylia* for Teus from the senate: see *Syll.*[3] 601.

perplexi: cf. pp. 6 ff.

societatem: cf. 25. 2.

7–9. This passage was fundamental to Holleaux's view that *amicitia* always involved a *foedus* (cf. *Rome*, 52–3). But Menippus' *tria genera foederum* are not three different types of treaty, but three different ways in which two states may come to make a treaty. (This was seen by Täubler, 3, though he still believed in *foedera amicitiae*.) In many cases, of course, a *foedus* made for other reasons established *amicitia* as one of its results (cf. Pol. i. 62. 8, iii. 22. 4, 24. 3, xxi. 43. 1) but there is no case of a *foedus* which simply created *amicitia*, and *foedus amicitiae* is not to be regarded as a term of Roman public law. See L. E. Matthaei, *CQ* i (1907), 182 ff., Heuss, *VG*, 12 ff., 53 ff., Dahlheim, 136 ff.: *contra* M. R. Cimma, *Reges socii et amici populi Romani* (Milan, 1976), 80 ff.

7. ubi ... essent: for a *foedus* following a *deditio* cf. xxxi. 31. 10 ff. n. But in many cases peace was imposed on the defeated party without the latter making a complete *deditio*. This had been the case with Carthage, Philip, and Nabis (cf. 40. 3–4 n.). The Aetolians in 191 were the first non-Italian people asked to make a *deditio* (xxxvi. 27. 8 ff., xxxvii. 1. 5, 49. 4).

8. repeti ... res: i.e. demands made at the beginning of a war (*rerum repetitio*) would be settled by consent.

ex ... antiqui: if this reflects what Menippus really said, it probably implies a repetition of Antiochus' claims to the land occupied by his ancestors, as he had argued at Lysimachia: cf. xxxiii. 40. 4–6 n., xxxv. 16. 5–6 (*in antiquum ius repetit*).

10. leges ei dicere: the demands made at Lysimachia.

quas ... uetent: the indirect questions depend on *leges*.

11. amico: Antiochus is already an *amicus*: cf. xxxii. 8. 13 n.

58. 1. distincte: the context, and particularly *ego quoque* in the following line, seems to require the meaning of 'by making distinctions'. Menippus had distinguished three ways of coming to make a treaty, Flamininus will offer two alternatives to Antiochus. This sense of *distincte*, however, does not occur in Classical Latin (*TLL*, v. 1. 1532. 18) and W–M therefore take it in its regular sense of 'clearly'. But there is no real contrast with *perplexe* in 57. 6, as they claim, and I am inclined to think that L. was intending to convey the idea of making distinctions. He may have been influenced by the language used by Polybius (cf. p. 10 n. 1), though I can think of no Greek word on which *distincte* would be a calque. Cf. p. 9.

extra quas ... nuntietis: a relative final clause.

2–3. If Antiochus will keep out of Europe, Rome will not bother herself about Asia. But if he insists on asserting his claims in Europe, Rome will liberate Asia as well. Despite the strict implication of the Latin, Flamininus does not mean that if Antiochus wants Europe, he will have to grant Rome's demands in Asia. Cf. *Latomus* xxxi (1972), 35 n. 4.

4. enimuero: strongly affirmative, not explicative. Cf. *TLL*, v. 2. 592. 9 ff.

5. Seleucus ... reliquerit: cf. xxxiii. 40. 4–6 n. As is clear from § 10 below, L. is using *proauus* in its literal sense of great-grandfather. In fact Seleucus I was the great-great-grandfather of Antiochus III. Polybius presumably did not identify the exact degree of ancestry. (Corradi, *RFIC* l [1922], 30–1 wrongly took *proauus* in § 10 to mean Antiochus I, and thus sought to draw a distinction between the attitudes of Antiochus I and Antiochus II towards the Greek cities. Cf. Magie, ii. 927–8, criticizing Corradi but still failing to see that L. does not mean Antiochus I by *proauus*. Orth, 162–3 sees that he means Seleucus I, but nevertheless claims that *proauus* here means 'forefather' in general.)

ab Thracibus ... aedificauerit: the parts recovered by arms and the deserted parts are clearly subdivisions of the lands occupied by the Thracians. L. cannot have meant that parts were occupied by the Thracians, parts deserted, as claimed by Pettersson, 10–11 (thus arguing in favour of Bφ's *partim possessa*). In fact part of Thrace was lost to Egypt during the Laodicean War: cf. xxxi. 16. 4–5 n. For Antiochus' rebuilding of Lysimachia cf. xxxiii. 38. 10 ff.

6. simile ... et: for the construction cf. K–St, ii. 6–7.

8. quandoquidem: used by L. only in speeches: cf. Adams, *BICS* xx (1973), 137.

principi ... populo: very much the language of the late republic and the Augustan period. For *princeps populus* cf. xxxv. 14. 9, Cic. *Planc.* 11.

11–13. The fine language hardly squares with the fact that Flamininus was offering to trade the freedom of the Asiatic Greeks for a guarantee by Antiochus to remain east of the Hellespont. One suspects elaboration by L., though the statements about early Greek colonization in § 13 look as if they come from Polybius.

11. patrocinium: for the Roman notion of acting as patron of the Greeks cf. in particular Badian, *FC*, 69 ff.

12. quae ... sint: Mg, omitted in Bχ, who, however, have *Graecas Asiae urbes*. It is highly unlikely that the poetic form *Graius* cf.) *OLD s.u.*) would have been used by a glossator, and Mg's text should therefore be accepted.

59. 1. honestiorem ... titulo: 'a more honourable case was put forward under the banner of freedom than under that of slavery'. *titulo* is an instrumental ablative: W–M take it as a dative, and apparently regard *causam* as going with *libertatis quam seruitutis*—'the cause of freedom was more honourably put forward as a banner than that of slavery'. *praetexi* does not imply doubt as to Rome's sincerity in her claims to be protecting Greek freedom, as claimed by Merten, 15. *seruitus* is not a pretext and *praetexi* is determined by the metaphorical use of *titulus*.

quin mittimus: for this colloquial use of *quin* and the indicative to express 'heightened emotion' cf. Ogilvie, 221, H–S, 676.

ambages: cf. p. 4.

P. Sulpicius ... natu: P. Sulpicius Galba (64), consul in 211 and 200: cf. xxxi. 4. 4 n. His date of birth is not known, but he was the senior consular among the ten commissioners.

3. supersedete: *supersedere* with the infinitive is first found in Sisenna fr. 108P, and not again before L. (also at iv. 7. 8, xxi. 40. 1, xxxiii. 35. 12). Cf. K–St, i. 669. (*TLL*). See pp. 7–8 n. 4.

5. nisi ... Europa: on the question of whether Flamininus in fact said this, or concealed his volte-face when making his report to the senate, cf. *Latomus* xxxi (1972), 35–6.

6–7. Menippus and Hegesianax seem to have been genuinely afraid that the impasse which they had reached would result in an immediate declaration of war, and this they, and Antiochus, clearly wanted to avoid (at this moment at least). Cf. Badian, *Studies*, 127 and pp. 30–3.

8. eosdem ... P. Aelium: cf. 33. 12 n.

60–62. *Activities of Hannibal and events in Carthage*

The detail of this account, like that of xxxiii. 45. 6–49. 7, together with the evident use of a Greek source at 61. 15, make it very likely that Polybius is the source of the section. But there are at least two annalistic additions (cf. 62. 2–3, 10 nn.), the statement in 61. 1 is unacceptable, and there may be extensive writing up by L., especially, one would suspect, in ch. 61. Cf. xxxiii. 45. 6–49. 7 n.(b), Nissen, *KU*, 164–5, Klotz, *Livius*, 11–12, Walsh, *JRS* lv (1965), 157 (who, however, misrepresents Klotz on the matter): *contra* Badian, *FC*, 295–6, Walbank, *Commentary*, iii. 490–1.

For other sources on the episode cf. Nepos, *Hann.* 8. 1 (totally muddled), App. *Syr.* 7–8, Just. xxxi. 3. 5–4. 3, Zon. ix. 18. 12.

60. 2–6. On Hannibal's plan see above all Passerini, *Athenaeum* n.s. xi (1933), 10 ff., who argues strongly for the authenticity of L.'s version of Hannibal's proposal. A fragment of Ennius (*Ann.* 381–3V) describes Hannibal dissuading Antiochus from going to war. Passerini plausibly suggests that Hannibal was not here arguing against war *tout court*, but against Antiochus' intention to restrict the war to Greece. If his own proposal was not accepted, he was in favour of not going to war at all.

2. Hannibal ... dictum est: xxxiii. 49. 7.

uolutanti ... bello: i.e. wondering whether or not to commit himself to a war with Rome, as in xxxiii. 49. 7 *fluctuantem adhuc animo incertumque de Romano bello*. As we have seen, Antiochus was certainly not contemplating an aggressive war with Rome at this time (cf. 59. 6–7 n.).

3. Italiam ... hosti: cf. Cato's dictum at 9. 12.

4. regem ... gentem: two of the three divisions commonly used in the Hellenistic world—rulers, peoples, and city-states. Cf. Walbank, *Commentary*, ii. 117, *HSCPh* lxxvi (1972), 147, *Polybius*, 56 n. 145 (my note on xxxiii. 34. 1–2 misses the point).

6. et (quod): adversative (cf. 7. 12 n.).

61. 1. in hanc ... regem: it is, in fact, most improbable that Antiochus at any stage committed himself to Hannibal's plan. Cf. Badian, *Studies*, 132.

1–2. litteras ... Aristonem: as W–M rightly say, the word-order emphasizes the contrast.

2. Tyrium: for Hannibal's reception at Tyre in 195 cf. xxxiii. 49. 5.

3. quibus ... esset: for the construction cf. xxxi. 13. 6 n., K–St, i. 764–5, Walsh on xxi. 27. 3.

4. Aristonem ... cognouerunt: for the construction cf. xxxi. 27. 5 n.

5. circulis conuiuiisque: cf. xxxii. 20. 3 n.

7. concoqui: *colloqui* MSS. Most editors read *coqui*, but McDonald prefers Tafel's *concoqui*. Ogilvie's objection (*Phoenix*, 347) that this metaphorical use of *concoquere* does not occur elsewhere in L., fails to take account of xl. 11. 2, where Mg has *concocta*, often emended to *cocta*. *concoqui* explains the paradosis well and I would follow McDonald.

10. Ariston: here and in § 14 Bχ have *Ariston*, Mg *Aristo*. L. normally has the nominative in *-o* for Greek names of this formation (cf. M. Müller ad loc.) but the balance of probability is that in this case L. was following Polybius and used the Greek termination.

11. Barcinae ... factionis: the supporters of the family of Hannibal. For *factio* similarly used of the opponents of the Barcids cf. xxxiii. 45. 6, 46. 4, R. Seager, *JRS* lxii (1972), 56.

12–13. mali ... euenturum: the Carthaginians are typically concerned for the freedom of their citizens to trade without let or hindrance. On Carthaginian trade cf. B. H. Warmington, *Carthage* (2nd edn., London, 1969), 134 ff.

14. Punico ingenio: on Punic cunning cf. Walbank, *Commentary*, i. 412, Otto, 291.

tertia uigilia: the night was divided into four *uigiliae* of three hours each (cf. Kromayer–Veith, 347).

15. sufetes: cf. xxxiii. 45. 6–49. 7 n. (c). In that passage L. refers to the sufete only as *praetor*.

seniores ... uocabant: L. is translating Polybius' γέροντες, which probably referred to the smaller council of 30, not the wider body of 300. Cf. xxxiii. 45. 6–49. 7 n. (c), Meltzer–Kahrstedt, ii. 37 ff.

16. publicato: 'made to apply to all', not 'made public knowledge'. In Cicero *publicare* has only its literal sense of 'make public property, confiscate'.

62. 1. infames: 'in bad repute' (sc. with Rome).

sensit: read by Gelenius as 'germana scriptura', omitted in Bχ, and replacing *senatui* in the 1518 Mainz edition. A verb has clearly fallen out in the extant manuscripts, and it may be that *sensit* stood in the margin of Mg, to be put in the text at different points by Carbach and Gelenius.

principibus: i.e. the pro-Barcid leaders.

2. locum ... ratus: cf. v. 16. 3.

2–3. The Emporia were in the gulf of Quabes (cf. xxix. 25. 12, 33. 9, Pol. iii. 23. 2, xxxi. 21. 1, Walbank, *Commentary*, i. 145). But the mention of Leptis is puzzling. Leptis Magna is well to the east of the lesser Syrtes, and is not the only town on the coast. On the other hand Leptis Minor lies to the north of Thapsus, and cannot possibly have formed part of the Emporia. It must be that the name Emporia was extended to include the coast up to Leptis, which acted as an administrative centre for the region. L. will have misunderstood Polybius. For a possible parallel case cf. Walsh on xxi. 39. 4, though there the error may be due to Coelius. Cf. S. Gsell, *Histoire ancienne de l'Afrique du Nord*, ii (Paris, 1920), 127–8, P. Romanelli, *Leptis Magna* (Rome, 1925), 6 ff., R. M. Haywood, *CPh* xxxvi (1941), 251 ff., J. M. Reynolds and J. B. Ward-Perkins, *The Inscriptions of Roman Tripolitania* (Rome–London, 1952), 76–7: *contra* T. Kotula, *Africana Bulletin* xx (1974), 52 ff.

Polybius xxxi. 21. 2 says that Massinissa's attacks on the cities of the Emporia region began οὐ πολλοῖς ἀνώτερον χρόνοις before 162/1, and it is inconceivable that Polybius could have intended to refer to 193 by such a phrase. It seems that the incursions at this time were relatively minor, and did not include attacks on the towns of the area. L. has presumably conflated an annalist with Polybius. Cf. on the matter Meltzer–Kahrstedt, iii. 590 ff., De Sanctis, iv. 3. 9 n. 22, Badian, *FC*, 295–6, G. Camps, *Libyca* viii (1960), 192–3, S. Rosetti, *PP* xv (1960), 336 ff., Walsh, *JRS* lv (1965), 157, Kotula, op. cit., 47 ff., Walbank, *Commentary*, iii. 489–91.

3. agri uberis: cf. xxix. 25. 12.

Lepcis: the inscriptions cited by McDonald confirm the spelling (cf. Romanelli, *RAL*, 5, xxxiii [1924], 253 ff.). The evidence of the MSS. is irrelevant, since they treat *-ci* and *-ti* as interchangeable. On Leptis see particularly Romanelli, *Leptis Magna*, M. Floriani Squarciapino, *Leptis Magna* (Basle, 1966).

singula . . . dedit: the tribute will come from the area of which Leptis was the administrative centre. Cf. De Sanctis, iii. 1. 33 n. 88, Romanelli, *Leptis Magna*, 8, Reynolds and Ward-Perkins, *The Inscriptions of Roman Tripolitania*, 76–7: *contra* Meltzer–Kahrstedt, iii. 134 ff., Walbank, *Commentary*, iii. 491.

4. dubiae . . . esset: by the effects of his attacks. A crucial clause in the treaty of 201 had decreed that places which had belonged to Massinissa's ancestors should be returned to him (Pol. xv. 18. 5). Cf. xxxiii. 47. 8 n., add Walbank, *Commentary*, ii. 469, F. Gschnitzer, *WS* lxxix (1966), 286 n. 24.

5. illa onerarent: 'increase the gravity of the charges'. For this use of *onerare*, not found before L., cf. v. 39. 13, xxxi. 15. 2, xxxviii. 56. 11, p. 9.

iure uectigalium: i.e. from the Emporia region.

6. iniecere: χ, *inicere* B, perhaps rightly.

7. ea: 'the following', taken up by *quod*.

crimen urgebat: 'gave stimulus to the accusation'.

8–9. iure . . . finisset: the Carthaginians ignore the clause about the ancestral possessions of Massinissa (§ 4 n.), and the representatives of the latter make no more than debating points about it (§§ 11 ff.).

10. Aphthirem . . . petisset: Polybius (xxxi. 21. 7) also refers to this incident, though without any mention of Cyrene, and describing it as χρόνοις οὐ πολλοῖς ἀνώτερον. Presumably this too took place later than 193. The text of Polybius guarantees the form of the name, though it is clear that L. Latinized the ending, and will have spelt the beginning *Apth-* (cf. xxxii. 33. 16 n.).

12. The legend was that the Carthaginians were given by the Numidians the amount of land that could be covered by an ox-hide, and, with Punic cunning, cut the hide into strips. *bursa* is a Phoenician word meaning citadel, but was taken to be the Greek βύρσα, a hide. Cf. Virgil, *Aen.* i. 365–8, with R. G. Austin's note, C. R. Whittaker, *Imperialism in the Ancient World* (ed. P. D. A. Garnsey and C. R. Whittaker, Cambridge, 1978), 59. (Petrarch wrote out the four lines of Virgil at the foot of the page in A.)

13. eum: the land in question.

ceperint: clearly preferable to B's *coeperint*, which without an infinitive scarcely makes sense. In the Renaissance MSS., of course, *coeperint* would have been spelt *ceperint*, so χ can scarcely be given the credit for the correct reading.

[eos]: the non-reflexive form is clearly intolerable here, and it is a matter of choice whether it should be deleted or replaced by *se*. Madvig (*Emendationes*, 508) is wrong to say that L. did not omit *se* with a perfect infinitive. Cf. Kühnast, 106 ff.

14. The Numidians waive their claims under the clause about ancestral possessions, and say 'the area has always been controlled by right of conquest: please leave the situation like that'.

interponerent . . . teneret: L. deliberately uses legal language. For *se interponere* in legal contexts cf. *TLL*, vii. 1. 2248. 68 ff.

16. C. Cornelius Cethegus: (88). Cf. xxxi. 49. 7 n.

M. Minucius Rufus: (53). Cf. xxxii. 27. 7 n.
The commissioners consist, unusually, entirely of Scipionic members. On Cethegus cf. vol. i, 33 n. 1, on Minucius xxxi. 4. 4 n.

omnia suspensa: *omnia impensa* B, *suspensa omnia* χ. In view of the other mistakes by B in this sentence (see McDonald's apparatus) χ's word-order may be correct. There seems little point in *omnia* occupying the emphatic position in the colon.

reliquere: *relinquere* MSS., perhaps correctly.

17–18. For a similar case of an apparently deliberate failure to settle a dispute cf. *Historia* xviii (1969), 54. At first sight one would not expect to find Scipio lending himself to such a manœuvre, and if Polybius is still L.'s source, the surprise will doubtless have been expressed by him. But (i) the issue may have been genuinely obscure (ii) as L. indicates, given the danger from Antiochus, it would indeed have been undesirable to alienate either Massinissa or Carthage at this juncture, and even Scipio may have been willing to act ambiguously in such circumstances.

BOOK XXXV

1–11. *Events in Spain, Rome, and Italy*

1. *War in Spain*

Cf. Front. *Str.* iv. 1. 15, Oros. iv. 20. 16.

1. 1. principio ... praetor: Digitius ([2]: cf. xxxiv. 42. 4 n.) was praetor in 194 and L. has not mentioned him since reporting his appointment to Citerior in xxxiv. 43. 7. *principio anni* would appear to mean the beginning of the campaigning season of 193, but *praetor* indicates that Digitius was still in his year of office. L. can use *praetor* for a propraetor—he does so in § 8 (cf. McDonald's note and xxxi. 49. 4 n.) but the fact that in §§ 4–5 he carefully distinguishes the praetorship and the propraetorship of Scipio Nasica makes it unlikely that he was using *praetor* loosely here. I suspect that L. wrote *principio anni* in relation to Digitius handing over his depleted army to his successor, and then anomalously described the battles that Digitius had fought in 194 in a co-ordinate, rather than a subordinate clause. (The section is clearly annalistic in origin, and *principio anni* cannot therefore refer to the beginning of Polybius' Olympiad year 194/3.)

2. dimidium ... quam quod: for *dimidium* treated as a comparative, and constructed with *quam* (not found before L.) cf. K–St, ii. 460, H–S, 593. For *quam quod* cf. xxxiv. 19. 4, xlv. 18. 7. For the neuter singular in relation to the preceding plural cf. xxi. 59. 8, xxxi. 8. 8 (where my note misses the point of Madvig's objection to *praesidio*), xxxi. 46. 12 n., xxxiii. 14. 3 (where I would now retain B's *quod ... fuerat*), xxxvi. 19. 11 n., xliii. 6. 3, xliv. 1. 1, Löfstedt, *Syntactica*, i. 2 n. 3. (I am not sure whether McDonald's reference to xliii. 6. 2 is in fact to 6. 3, or to *quod militum* at 6. 2: if the latter it is not parallel.) As McDonald indicates, the MSS. often write *quod* for *quot* (Bψ at xxxiv. 50. 7, xxxv. 28. 4, xxxvii. 58. 3, Bχ at xxxvi.

146

10. 11, 40. 4) and in cases when *quod* is a possibility, we cannot be sure whether *quod* or *quot* is the transmitted reading.

successori: C. Flaminius (xxxiv. 55. 6).

3. P. Cornelius Cn. f. Scipio: (350). Cf. xxxi. 49. 6 n.

trans Hiberum: perhaps, that is, in the Southern part of Citerior.

5. Lusitanos: in Western Spain. This is the first recorded Roman conflict with them (cf. Schulten, *CAH*, viii. 313).

ingenti . . . adgressus: cf. p. 35 n. 6.

8. ludos . . . uouit: *ludi uotiui*, but not *magni* (cf. xxxi. 9. 5–10 n.). For the sequel to this vow cf. xxxvi. 36. 1–2.

9. Lusitanus: for the singular cf. xxxi. 7. 12 n.

10. quingenti: Mg, *ducenti* Bχ. Decision is impossible.

11. Ilipa: on the town, the site of Scipio's final Spanish victory in 206, cf. Walbank, *Commentary*, ii. 296.

11–12. exposita est . . . facta est . . . data . . . refectum est: the threefold inclusion of the modal is somewhat unexpected, though cf. iii. 5. 14, Ogilvie, 403. B omits *est* after *refectum*, and if there is to be deletion, that one is perhaps a better candidate than the *est* after *facta*, deleted in the 1535 Basle edition and by Madvig.

For the exhibition of booty to enable owners to claim their property see Ogilvie, 414. Presumably the Lusitanians had looted Ilipa before the conflict with Nasica. On the general's complete authority over the disposal of booty cf. xxxvii. 57. 12 n.

refectum: 'realized'.

2. *Senatorial decisions on Spain*

2. 1. nondum . . . profectus: Flaminius probably entered office on 4 November 194 (Jul.) (cf. p. 25) and must have stayed in Rome a considerable time. The dislocation of the calendar had now reached so advanced a stage that a praetor would have to wait for the whole winter to pass before contemplating the journey to Spain.

C. Flaminius: (3). Cf. xxxiii. 42. 8 n.

haec: all the events of ch. 1, but Flaminius may have heard only of the events of 194. In any case, as governor-elect of Citerior, he would have been primarily concerned with affairs there.

2. amicosque: his political associates, who would help him try to obtain what he wanted from the senate.

3–4. For the assignment of troops to Flaminius cf. xxxiv. 56. 8.
He had been given 3,000 infantry and 100 cavalry from Roman
citizens, and 5,000 infantry and 200 cavalry from allied sources,
and ordered *ueteres dimittere milites* (on the meaning of which cf.
n. ad loc.). He is now asking for a *legio urbana* (for their enrolment
in 193 cf. xxxiv. 56. 4), which would contain at least 4,200 infantry
and 200 cavalry. This would give a total of 12,200 infantry and
500 cavalry. It is inconceivable that he was asking to keep fewer
troops than had originally been assigned to him, and the solution
must be that Flaminius' request is concerned only with Roman
citizens. He is proposing to construct a legion of 6,200 infantry out
of a total of at least 7,200. A legion of this size is attested only in
xxix. 24. 14, and that is doubted by Brunt, 673. Legions of 6,000
are first found in the Third Macedonian War. Cf. further literature
cited in xxxiii. 1. 2 n.

Flaminius clearly regarded the remnants of Digitius' army as
useless, and wanted no part of them.

6. seniores: for the representation of the conflict as one between
the younger and older senators cf. xxxi. 48. 2 n.

    ratum: 'confirmed'.

6–7. The omission of *aut praetores* and *scribi . . . milites* in Bχ indicates
unusual carelessness in F or one of its ancestors at this point.

7. tumultus . . . Italiam: cf. xxxi. 2. 5 n. For levies in the provinces when a *tumultus* is declared cf. Brunt, 392.

8. Valerius Antias: cf. xxxii. 6. 5 n. The mention of Antias here
is not an indication that the rest of the account does not come from
him. Rather these details were in Antias alone, and L. is somewhat
sceptical about their authenticity. For a similar case cf. p. 64.
Brunt, 218 n. 2 suggests that Antias is reflecting conditions of his
own time, when landless soldiers looked for land in the provinces
in which they had served.

    sacramento rogasse: cf. xxxii. 26. 11 n.

3–5. *Wars against Ligurians and Boii*

3. 1. segnius: W–M state that this is an adjective, not an adverb,
but it is perhaps a false question to ask which L. intended.

    Pisas: cf. xxxiii. 43. 5 n.

    quadraginta: *quadringentis* Bχ, but an army of 400,000 is clearly
impossible, and not even Antias would have invented a figure of
that size, as Walsh, *CR*, 56, argues. At xxxiv. 56. 2 they number
20,000 (cf. n. ad loc.) and in 181 again 40,000 (Plut. *Paull*. 6. 4:
cf. Brunt, 189).

2. Arretium: cf. xxxiv. 56. 4, xxxi. 21. 1 n.

quadrato agmine: on the *agmen quadratum*, consisting of three separate columns, cf. Kromayer–Veith, 351 ff., Walbank, *Commentary*, i. 723. Sage's translation 'in a hollow-square formation' is misleading.

trans fluuium: the Serchio, ancient Auser. It now runs into the sea north of Pisa, but in antiquity it joined the Arno near Pisa. Cf. Strabo, v. p. 222C, Nissen, *IL*, i. 306.

4. nouo ... conlecto: W–M object to this description on the grounds that the legions had in fact been levied in 194 (xxxiv. 56. 4). But they had merely been held in reserve in Rome, and had done no fighting. Certainly this army is no more heterophyte than any other, but L.'s point is that the *socii* and the new legions had only just met together at Arretium and were not yet used to each other.

fidere: cf. pp. 4, 8.

5–6. W–M say that L. began as if he were going to write three clauses beginning with *et*, and then changed the subject in the third clause to *praesidium*. But there is no such change. The first two clauses, with *Ligures* as their subject, are balanced by and co-ordinate with *et cum ... ageretur*.

6. quod: *quos* MSS., probably rightly. A plural with a collective noun is perfectly common. Cf. Walsh, *CR*, 56, although 'variety of destinations' is scarcely the point.

4. 1. constitisset: 'had come to a halt'. Cf. Walsh on xxi. 49. 1.

L. Cornelius Merula: (270). Cf. xxxii. 7. 13 n.

per: Mg. Bχ have *praeter* but xxxiii. 37. 6 makes it very probable that *per* is correct. Merula presumably advanced northwards from Rome to the area where his colleague was operating, and then crossed the Apennines towards Bologna.

2. exiret: cf. xxxiv. 38. 6 n.

3–4. Mutinam ... finibus suis: Mutina was an Etruscan city not yet under Boian control, though in the midst of land occupied by the Boii (cf. xxxix. 55. 7). Merula was not, therefore, really leaving Boian *fines* by marching towards Mutina.

3. agmine ... incauto: for the phrase cf. ix. 38. 3, Tac. *H.* iv. 60. 2.

4. finibus suis: χ, *suis finibus* B, *e finibus suis* Mg. *suis* in the emphatic position is clearly wrong, but Mg's *e* may well be correct. *excedere ex* is found at ii. 19. 5 and xxvi. 30. 11. At xxix. 19. 3 the Puteanus has *templo*, the Spirensian tradition *ex templo*, and at xxxvii. 52. 9 χ has *templo*, B *ex templo*. W–M (viii. 271) argue that *excedere* with the ablative alone is L.'s regular usage and that *ex* should be deleted in all four instances (they wrongly claim that there is manuscript authority for deletion at xxvi. 30. 11 as well as at xxix. 19. 3). The MSS. evidence as a whole indicates that on some occasions L. did write *excedere ex* and it is perverse to emend this evidence away. In both the present passage and xxxvii. 52. 9 it is more likely that *ex* was omitted in accordance with L.'s normal practice than that it was added in Mg and B respectively.

5. multa nocte: 'in the depth of the night'. For the usage cf. *TLL*, viii. 1608. 53 ff.

6. quantae ... et in quo: χ. B omits *et* and is very probably right to do so. For L.'s practice of combining two separate questions in an indirect question cf. ii. 21. 4, xxx. 42. 18, xxxvi. 2. 1 n., Ogilvie, 291, K–St, ii. 497, H–S, 459–60.

   triarios: on the *triarii*, the third line in the manipular army, cf. Walbank, *Commentary*, i. 702.

7. uera uinceret uirtus: deliberate alliteration. For *uera uirtus* cf. Woodman, 174.

5. 1. sinistra ... ala: the *alae sociorum* were infantrymen (cf. xxxi. 21. 7 n.) and *equitum* is a clear gloss.

   extraordinarii: cf. xxxiv. 47. 3 n.

   consulares legati: it is unusual for men of consular rank to serve as military *legati* in this period, and it is possible that they were appointed by the senate, like Sulpicius and Villius in 197 (xxxii. 28. 12) and Lucius Flamininus in 191 (xxxvi. 1. 8).

   At 8. 6 Sempronius is distinguished from Marcellus as possessing *imperium*, but this is probably so only because he had remained in the north after the end of his consulship and hence had not formally relinquished his *imperium*, not because he had had it specially conferred on him for 193.

   M. Marcellus: (222). M. Claudius Marcellus, consul in 196. Cf. xxxi. 50. 1 n.

   Ti. Sempronius: (67). Longus, consul in 194. Cf. xxxi. 20. 5 n.

2. in subsidiis: 'in reserve', a military phrase widely used by L. (Packard, iv. 795). *subsidium* was also a name for the *triarii* in the manipular army (Varro, *LL*, v. 89).

3. Q. et P. Minucios: their identity is uncertain. Münzer (*RE*, xv. 1943) tentatively identifies Quintus with the *legatus* of 174 (xli. 25. 7) and/or the praetor of 165 or 164, but this is quite speculative.

Münzer also suggests that Publius may be the great-grandfather of the Gaius and Publius Minucii who made the dedication at Verona recorded in *CIL* i². 2164, and that he lived in Northern Italy.

4. Longo: Walsh (*CR*, 56) proposes to delete this as a gloss. But if someone were going to add the *cognomen*, he would have done it in § 1, not here. The variation is attributable to L. himself.

5. legionem ... duabus: though no assignment of legions to Merula is mentioned in xxxiv. 56, it seems that he had two legions, probably formed out of the four legions in Gaul under the consuls of 194. See 20. 5, Afzelius, 37, p. 37.

6. secunda: the official number of the legion: see p. 36 n. 8.

7. minime ... Gallorum: cf. xxxiv. 47. 5 n.
corpora Gallorum: χ, *Gallorum corpora* B. The fact that it is the Gauls who are suffering is being emphasized, and one would therefore expect the possessive to precede.
incumbentes: *incumbere* in the sense of 'leaning on' is not found before Sallust (*Hist.* iii. fr. 40M) and Virgil (*Ecl.* 8. 16). Cf. *TLL*, vii. 1. 1072–3.

8. C. Liuium Salinatorem: (29). Cf. xxxii. 16. 3 n.
alariis ... equites: the one allied, the other citizen. On the proportion of allied to citizen cavalry in the armies of this period cf. Brunt, 683 ff.

9. procella equestris: apparently military jargon for a cavalry charge, though not found before L. Cf. x. 5. 7, xxix. 2. 11, xxx. 18. 4, xxxvii. 41. 10 (qualified, though, by *uelut*), Tac. *H.* iii. 53. 2.
dissipauit: a military word for a rout. Cf. *TLL*, v. 1. 1490. 54 ff.

10. hastilibus ... interequitantes: cf. xxxiv. 15. 4, where *interequitare* again occurs, with reference to Cato hitting those who ran in front of the ranks. Cf. n. ad loc.
alarii: elsewhere in L. *alarius* is an adjective (*TLL*, i. 1481). *alaris* is found at x. 41. 5.
patiebantur: from here to 6. 1 fragments of F survive. For details cf. Traube, *ABAW* xxxiv, 1 (1904), 37.

11. paululum adniterentur: Mg, *paulum niterentur* χ (*paululum niterentur* N). But Merula would not have asked his soldiers for 'a very little effort' and *paulum* should be retained. (Ogilvie, *Phoenix*, 344 describes *paululum* as 'grotesque in the context'.) See also xxxvi. 43. 13, xxxvii. 40. 7 nn.
turbatos: Bχ, *perturbatos* Mg. *perturbandos* occurs in § 8, *turbauit* in

§ 9. Either is possible: *perturbare* occurs 22 times in L. and there is no reason why he should not have used it twice in the same passage.

sissent: χ, *sinissent* B. For *sissent* cf. xxvii. 6. 8, xlv. 44. 18 (the other passages quoted by W–M are emendations, not MSS. readings).

uexillarios: 'standard bearers'. Elsewhere in L. only at viii. 8. 8.

13. sexaginta tria: Mg, *centum duo* Bχ. Decision is impossible.

14. incruenta uictoria: a common phrase in the historians, found first in Sallust, *Cat.* 61. 7. Cf. xxxvii. 16. 12, Hoch, 27 n. 22, *TLL*, vii. 1. 1059. 36 ff.

amissa: B. χ adds *sunt*. The surviving letters in F make it clear that F did not have *sunt* and χ is convicted of an unnecessary supplement.

M. Genucius . . . legionis: for similar notices cf. Harris, 40 n. 1.

M. Genucius: (7). Not otherwise known.

et Q . . . tribuni: the first *et* apart, B alone preserves the correct reading, corrupted in both Mg and χ. The two Marcii (21) cannot be further identified.

6–7. 1. *Reports from the north and senatorial decisions thereon*

2–4. This is, of course, the letter from Minucius. The dislocation of the calendar meant that the elections had to take place by October.

2. suae sortis: i.e. he had drawn by lot the duty of presiding over the elections: cf. 20. 2 (for 192). This was the normal procedure. J. Linderski, *Historia* xiv (1965), 423 ff. unconvincingly argues that after Sulla the *consul prior* (the consul elected top of the poll) automatically presided at the elections.

3. profligatum bellum: for the phrase cf. ix. 29. 1, 37. 1, xxi. 40. 11, xxxix. 38. 5, Cic. *fam.* xii. 30. 2.

4. etiam atque etiam: regularly used for strong entreaties (cf. xxxvi. 9. 7, 28. 2, *TLL*, v. 2. 930. 18 ff.).

interregnum: there had not been an *interregnum* since 216 (on Mommsen's view that there was one in 208 cf. J. Jahn, *Interregnum und Wahldiktatur* [Kallmunz, 1970], 135 ff.).

5. C. Scribonio: (8). The *praetor urbanus*. Cf. xxxiii. 42. 10 n., xxxiv. 55. 6, 57. 3.

6. ni is: BφL, *in is* NV, *uelle ut is* Mg. *uelle* is manifestly a supplement designed to make sense after *ni* had been corrupted to *ut* and Madvig was misguided to base an emendation on it.

8. M. Claudius: cf. 5. 1 n. Since Marcellus is certainly no friend of the Scipios and Merula can be regarded as Scipionic, the criticism causes no surprise.

9. fortunae populi Romani: for this concept cf. i. 52. 3, ii. 40. 13, v. 21. 15, vi. 30. 6 (again connected with errors by commanders), vii. 34. 6, xxvi. 41. 17, xxviii. 44. 7, xxxviii. 46. 4, xlv. 3. 6, Kajanto, 65 ff.

fuerit: cf. xxxiv. 26. 7 n.

10. fugientes: Damsté (*Mnemosyne* n.s. xliii [1915], 167) proposed to add *longius* because in 5. 12 the legions are allowed to pursue the Boii. But Marcellus' accusations are not borne out by L.'s narrative, and it is perverse to attempt to reconcile them.

7. 1. frequentiores ... dilata: for a similar decision cf. *per.* xiii, Balsdon, *JRS* xlvii (1957), 19.

7. 2–5. *Debt*

The increase in debt was caused by a number of factors, among them the desire for cash to buy land when it was at a low price (cf. xxxi. 13. 6 n.). The introduction of the *denarius* coinage *c.* 211 will also have caused a considerable increase in the money supply. The laws in question are those that restricted the amount of interest that could legally be charged. The last recorded (vii. 42. 1) is said to have forbidden usury altogether, but this cannot have been enforced for long even though the law itself may never have been repealed (cf. App. *BC* i. 54. 232, Tac. *A.* vi. 16). See Klingmüller, *RE*, vi. 2192 ff., Last, *CAH*, vii. 544 ff., Gabba on Appian, loc. cit., Astin, *Cato*, 322 ff. It is clear from L.'s narrative that the praetor in Rome was giving judgement in favour of *socii* who had lent money at rates higher than those laid down by law.

On the relevance of the passage for the state of the calendar see pp. 23–4. On the subsequent *Lex Iunia de Faeneratoribus* and Cato's opposition to it see Astin, *Cato*, 54–5, 319 ff.

2. ciuitas ... laborabat: doubtless exaggerated. Not all, or even a majority of the citizens, had contracted debts. Many were so poor that they would not have been able to raise a loan in the first place.

transcriberent: apparently a legal word for such a transaction, used several times in the *Digest* in this sense.

libero faenore: a freely chosen rate of interest.

3. Feralia ... fuissent: cf. pp. 23–4.

pecuniae ... diceretur: i.e. the debtor could choose whether to have his case heard by Roman laws in which case the creditor would have no hope of getting his higher rate of interest. There could, no doubt, be factors which could persuade a debtor not to adopt such a course—the prospect of future loans, threats of violence, and so forth.

ex ea die should be taken with *ius diceretur*, not with *pecuniae creditae.* On *post eam diem . . . ex ea die* see xxxiv. 35. 3–11 n. and appendix.

4. M. Sempronius: (95). Tuditanus, praetor in 189, with command prorogued in 188, consul in 185, and a *pontifex* from 183 until his death in 174. He should be listed as a tribune of 192, not 193, as in *MRR*, i. 348.

5. ut . . . esset: in other words, the possibility of the two parties agreeing to an action based on a higher rate of interest is now removed. It should be stressed that this provision applies only to loans made to Roman citizens, and is not so great an interference in allied affairs as has sometimes been thought. See W. V. Harris, *Historia* xxi (1972), 640 ff. The ally could, of course, still sue in his own city, but he would have no hope of getting the judgement enforced.

7. 6–8. *Spain*

Cf. Oros. iv. 20. 16, 19 and p. 36.

6. nequaquam . . . fama: as in 195 (cf. xxxiii. 21. 6–9 n.).

7. C. Flaminius: cf. 2. 1 n.

Illuciam: perhaps to be identified with Ilugo, north-east of Castulo (Schulten, *RE*, xiii. 2119, *FHA*, iii. 196, Götzfried, 62). It cannot be the same as Lyco at xxxvii. 46. 7, which was *in Bastetanis* (cf. Klotz, *Hermes* i [1915], 497–8).

The MSS. have *Inluciam*: many Spanish names begin in *Il-* (not *Ill-*) but what L. wrote cannot be determined. (McDonald's implication that non-assimilation of the prefix is B's regular practice is not universally true. At 3. 4, 7. 8, and 22. 8, for example, he has *coll-*.)

Oretanis: they lived to the north of the Sierra Morena, perhaps extending south as far as the sea (i.e. within the boundaries of Ulterior) and it was perhaps in this area that Flaminius was attacking. Their chief town was Oretum. Cf. Schulten, *RE*, xviii. 1. 1018–19, Walbank, *Commentary*, i. 362.

hibernacula: strictly the buildings in a winter camp, but it may here mean only *hiberna* (cf. *TLL*, vi. 3. 2684). There is no doubt that *hibernacula* is the correct explanation of the MSS. readings.

8. gestae res: cf. xxxvii. 8. 3 n.

M. Fuluio: (91). Nobilior. Cf. xxxiii. 42. 8 n.: for his appointment to Spain cf. xxxiv. 55. 6.

Toletum: modern Toledo. It was the chief town of the Carpetani.

Vaccaeis ... Celtiberis: on the Vaccaei, who lived on the middle Duero, see Schulten, *RE*, viiA. 2034 ff., on the Vettones, to the west of the Vaccaei, Schulten–Grosse, *RE*, viiiA. 1873–4, on the Celtiberi xxxiv. 10. 1 n.

8. *The return of Merula*

1. comitorum: read *comitiorum*.

    M. Claudio: cf. 5. 1 n.

3. questus ... cum: the only example of *queri cum* in L. It occurs several times in Cicero: cf. J. S. Reid on *Acad.* ii. 81.

    postulauit ... decernerent: for the omission of *ut*, wrongly added in Mg, cf. iii. 45. 10, xxi. 12. 5, xxii. 53. 12, xliii. 15. 5, K–St, ii. 229, H–S, 530.

4. prius ... fieret: as W–M remark, one would expect Merula's comments to have been made as part of his formal *relatio*. L.'s narrative, however, presupposes that the consul made his complaints in a general way, and had not yet made a *relatio*.

    Q. Metellus: (81). Cf. xxxi. 4. 3 n. For the political importance of Metellus' action cf. *Latomus* xxxi (1972), 46 n. 5, 48 n. 2.

    consulis: from here to § 9 fragments of F survive: for details cf. Traube, op. cit. (5. 10 n.), 38.

5. dilatam: 7. 1.

6. uerius: 'more proper'. Cf. xxxii. 33. 4 n.

    imperium habenti: cf. 5. 1 n.

7. uideri amotum: *uidere se admonitum* stood in F (as is clear from both the remains of F itself and the agreement of Bχ). McDonald argues that *esse* should not be read, on the grounds that *si* was imported from the following line, and altered to *se*. But corruption from *uideri esse* to *uidere se* is a much simpler explanation of F's text and this outweighs the argument of H. J. Müller (*JPhV* xxviii [1902], 11) that when *uideor* and *dicor* are used with the nominative and infinitive L. either omits *esse* or places it after the participle, with the exception of i. 51. 6.

    ⟨**si**⟩ **... arguere:** Bχ have *qui eque scripsisset praesens diceret arguere*. Carbach quotes *ne ea quae scripsisset* and *aut argueret* from Mg. McDonald is right to prefer supplementation of F's text by *si* to more complicated emendations of Mg's reading, which has all the signs of itself being an attempt to emend a text which the scribe could not understand.

ad liquidum: 'to produce clarity'. The phrase does not occur before L. and rarely after him (*TLL*, vii. 2. 1487. 46 ff.) though *liquido* means 'clearly' in Cicero (ibid., 1488. 23 ff.). Cf. p. 9.

9. M. et C. Titinii: (5, 20). Gaius is not otherwise known. Marcus is probably one of the two Titinii who were praetors in 178 (cf. *MRR*, i. 395, 397 n. 6).

9. 1–2. *The census*

1. censores ... Cethegus: cf. xxxiv. 44. 4–5 nn.

lustrum condidit: on the meaning of *lustrum condere* cf. Ogilvie, *JRS* li (1961), 31 ff.

2. censa ... IV: Bχ have *CXLIIIDCCIIII*, but this figure is completely out of line with others of this period, and must be increased. See in particular Brunt, 71–2, arguing that there may be deeper corruption than the mere omission of *C* at the beginning (Brunt is unaware that the insertion of *C* was proposed long before Beloch).

9. 2–5. *Prodigies*
Cf. xxxi. 12. 5–10 n.

2. aquae ... inundauit: floods of the Tiber were frequent in antiquity. See Fraenkel, *Horace*, 246 n. 4, Nisbet and Hubbard, i. 24–5. For the treating of floods as a prodigy cf. Wülker, 22, Krauss, 61 ff.

3. portam Flumentanam: a gate between the Capitol and the Tiber. Cf. Wiseman, *Historia* xxviii (1979), 32 ff., refuting the attempt of H. Lyngby to place it south-west of the Aventine. Wiseman observes that this passage and 21. 5 are the only examples of *circa* in relation to a city gate. But I cannot share his view that the preposition is 'unexpected' and to be explained by the fact that in the time of L. or his source the wall in the area of the *Porta Flumentana* had been demolished or was no longer visible.

ruinis: there is no case for Zingerle's *ruina*. See the examples at Packard, iv. 450.

porta Caelimontana: on the Caelian, at the junction of the Via Claudia and Via S. Stefano Rotondo. Cf. P–A, 405, Nisbet, *in Pisonem*, 117.

fulmine ... tactus: cf. xxxii. 1. 10 n.

4. Ariciae: modern Ariccia, in the Castelli. Aricia was one of the old centres of the Latin League. It was enfranchised in 338 (viii.

14. 3). For other prodigies at Aricia cf. xxii. 36. 7, xxiv. 44. 8, xxx. 38. 9, Obs. 18, 44, Wülker, 95.

Lanuuii: cf. xxxi. 12. 6 n.

lapidibus pluit: cf. xxxiv. 45. 8 n.

Capua: cf. xxxi. 29. 10–11, xxxii. 9. 2 nn.

uesparum: the only instance of a swarm of wasps being reported as a prodigy. Swarms of bees are often mentioned. Cf. Wülker, 16, Krauss, 115–16.

Martis aede: the position of the temple is not known. Cf. J. Heurgon, *Recherches sur l'histoire, la religion, et la civilisation de Capoue préromaine* (Paris, 1942), 297. The temple had been struck by lightning in 208 (xxvii. 23. 2).

5. decemuiri libros: cf. xxxi. 12. 9 n.

nouemdiale sacrum: cf. xxxiv. 45. 8 n.

supplicatio: for a *supplicatio* after prodigies cf. Wülker, 42 ff.

urbs lustrata: for *lustratio*, taking the sacrificial victims round the city, cf. S. P. C. Tromp, *De Romanorum Piaculis* (Lyons, 1921), 136 ff., Luterbacher, 41, Wülker, 39–40.

9. 6. *Temple dedication*

The shrine of Victoria Virgo was on the Cliuus Victoriae, on the west side of the Palatine, running to its north side. Cf. P–A, 126, 570. There is no previous mention of Cato's vow.

The dedication date of both the temple of Victoria and of this *aedicula* was 1 August (cf. Latte, *RRG*, 235, Degrassi, *I.I.* xiii. 2. 489). This means either that *iisdem diebus* is inaccurate, or that the events of 9. 1–6 in fact belong to an earlier period of the year. *Kal. Aug.* was 12 April (Jul.) and storms in March, if not plagues of wasps, would be quite credible.

For coins of the Porcii Catones commemorating the shrine cf. Crawford, *RRC*, nos. 343, 462, for the Roman interest in *Victoria*, Harris, 123 ff.

9. 7–8. *Colony at Thurii*

7. castrum Frentinum: the three men mentioned here are appointed at xxxiv. 53. 2 to found a colony at Thurii. *Castrum Frentinum* must be the name of an otherwise unknown fort at Thurii and emendation is wrong.

cuius ... deducebatur: cf. xxxiii. 42. 1 n.

pro copia agri: it is hard to know whether the phraseology is accidental (for *copia agri* cf. Cic. *inv.* ii. 115) or whether L. is alluding to the fact that the colony, for a time at least, was known as *Copia* (Strabo vi. p. 263C, Steph. Byz. s.u. Θούριοι, *A Catalogue of the Greek*

Coins in the British Museum, Italy (London, 1873), 303, ?*CIL* x. 125.
These references apart, however, the colony is always referred to as
Thurii. The archaeological evidence indicates that the colony occupied the site of the Greek city and P. Zancari-Montuoro (*RAL*, 8,
xxviii [1973], 601 ff.) argues that the original site at *Castrum Frentinum* was called Copia, but that the settlers soon took over the
original town of Thurii. The original site was abandoned and the
name disappeared. It is just possible that the references to *Copia* and
Cornucopia in Plautus, *Pseud.* (produced in 191), 671, 736, were meant
to recall the name of the colony. See also Tibiletti, *Athenaeum* n.s.
xxviii (1950), 198, Kahrstedt, *Historia* viii (1959), 186–7, Toynbee,
ii. 662, Brunt, 538.

8. Toynbee, ii. 235 ff. speculates that in thus restricting the allotments the commissioners were promoting their private interests.
The remaining land was left for 'capitalists' operating a trans-
humance system between the plains and the Sila (he similarly
explains the small allotments at Vibo [40. 6 n.]). Salmon (*Colonization*, 99–100) thinks it was impossible to find more colonists. There
is no record of any further colonization at Thurii (cf. Brunt, 281).
Allotments of 15 (as at Vibo: cf. 40. 6) or 20 *iugera* are considerably
larger than many subsistence farms in the second century: cf. M. W.
Frederiksen, *Dialoghi di Archeologia* iv–v (1970–1), 342 ff. (for some
figures for modern Italy cf. J. M. Frayn, *Subsistence Farming in Roman
Italy* [Fontwell–London, 1979], 91). For allotments of 3, 5, 6, and 10
iugera cf. xxxix. 44. 10, 55. 9, xl. 29. 1, xlii. 4. 4, M. I. Finley, *The
Ancient Economy* (London, 1973), 80–1, 194 n. 56. For the 50 *iugera* at
Bononia cf. xxxvii. 57. 8 n.

tricena: the MSS., in various ways, say 40. *equites* did not always
have double the infantry allocation (cf. xxxvii. 57. 8) but *tertia pars*
in the next sentence makes emendation to 30 essential.

10. 1–11. *Elections*

On the political interpretation of the consular elections cf. *Latomus*,
xxxi (1972), 48–9. I cannot accept the view of F. Cassola (*Labeo* vi
[1960], 112) that Scipio's support of Nasica was only 'formal'.

10. 2. P. Cornelius Cn. filius Scipio: (350). Nasica. Cf. xxxi.
49. 6 n. For the one-year gap between praetorship and prospective
consulship cf. xxxiii. 24. 1 n.

   qui . . . gestis: ch. 1.
   L. Quinctius Flamininus: (43). Cf. xxxi. 4. 5 n.

3. Cn. Manlius Vulso: (91). Cf. xxxiii. 25. 1 n.
   C. Laelius: (2). Cf. xxxii. 24. 2 n.

Cn. Domitius: (18). Ahenobarbus. Cf. xxxiii. 24. 1, 42. 10 nn.
C. Liuius Salinator: (29). Cf. xxxii. 16. 3 n.
M'. Acilius: (35). Glabrio. Cf. xxxi. 50. 5 n.

4. patricii ambo: thus the MSS., and not a misprint for *ambo patricii* as claimed by Walsh (*CR*, 56).
rei militaris gloria: cf. Harris, 33.

5. accendebant: cf. xxi. 59. 8 and Walsh ad loc.
fratres: as explained in § 8, Africanus was in fact the cousin of Nasica. For *frater* meaning 'cousin' cf. *TLL*, vi. 1. 1254. 82 ff.
et: cf. xxxiv. 7. 12 n. *sed* is quite unnecessary.
maior . . . inuidiam: cf. ii. 7. 8, Sall. *Iug.* 55. 3, Skard, 36.
eo anno: in fact in the previous one (xxxiv. 52. 4). It is quite unjustified to think that the two passages come from different sources (thus Nissen, *KU*, 59) or to place the triumph in 193 (Klotz, *Livius*, 84–5).

6. Scipio had been consul in 205, censor in 199, and consul for the second time in 194.

8. legato: cf. xxxii. 16. 2 n. Bχ have *collega*, presumably originating in a gloss on *particeps*, which then displaced *legato*.

9. The passage is witness to the political importance of the *gens* in this period, and at the same time a warning against exaggerating its importance in elections.
ducebat: literally of Africanus, metaphorically of the *praeiudicium senatus*.
quem . . . acciperet: cf. xxxiv. 3. 8 n.: on the selection of Nasica cf. xxix. 14. 8.
Pessinunte uenientem: cf. xxxiv. 3. 8 n. L. need not have been consistent in his usage and the MSS. tradition should be followed: *contra*, without argument, Ogilvie, *Phoenix*, 347.

10. pro . . . niteretur: for the phrase cf. Tac. *H.* i. 55. 4, *A.* i. 34. 1, Goodyear, 254.

11. L. Scribonius Libo: (17). Cf. xxxiv. 54. 3 n.
M. Fuluius Centumalus: (44). Not known apart from his praetorship, unless he is the tribune of 198 (xxxii. 7. 8).
A. Atilius Serranus: (60). Cf. xxxiv. 54. 3 n.
M. Baebius Tamphilus: (44). Cf. xxxiv. 45. 3 n.
L. Valerius Tappo: (350). Cf. xxxiv. 1. 2 n.
Q. Salonius Sarra: (not in *RE*). Not otherwise known, but probably related to the C. Salonius of xxxiv. 45. 5.

10. 11–12. *Aedilician activities*

L.'s language cannot be taken to indicate that the building operations were carried out by the aediles directly, and not contracted to *publicani*, as claimed by Toynbee, ii. 357. See Badian, *Publicans and Sinners*, 31.

aedilitas: curule, of course.

M. Aemilii Lepidi: (68). Cf. xxxi. 2. 3 n.
L. Aemilii Pauli: (114). Cf. xxxiv. 45. 5 n.

12. Cf. xxxi. 50. 2, xxxiii. 42. 10 nn.: add R. A. Bauman, *Latomus* xxxiii (1974), 245 ff.

clupea: χ, *clipea* B. For the spelling cf. *TLL*, iii. 1451. *clupeus* is the regular spelling in inscriptions.

Iouis aedis: the temple of Capitoline Jupiter. Cf. 41. 10 n.

porticum … adiecto: adding (at the end of the portico) a wharf. The *porta Trigemina* is a gate between the Aventine and the Tiber: cf. P–A, 418, H. Lyngby, *Beiträge zur Topographie des Forum-boarium-Gebietes in Rom* (Lund, 1954), 168 ff., *Eranos* lvii (1959), 62 ff., *ORom* vi (1968), 75 ff. The portico was rebuilt and the wharf paved in 174 (xli. 27. 8). For the probable remains of the *emporium* and portico see G. Gatti, *BCAR* lxii (1934), 123 ff., Le Gall, 100 ff., Nash, ii. 238, F. Coarelli, *Guida Archaeologica de Roma* (Verona, 1974), 306.

The Greek word *emporium* occurs in Enn. *Ann.* 628V, Plaut. *Amph.* 1012, Cic. *Att.* v. 2. 2. and is a plausible emendation at Varro, *RR* ii. 9. 6. L. is fond of it and uses it 15 times. The MSS. read *empurio* here, and *inpurium* or *enpurium* (*empurium* P, *emporium* L) at xxxvi. 21.5. B has *empurium* at xxxviii. 30. 7, and that spelling is also found in a fourth-century A.D. inscription (*CIL* ix. 10). Cf. *TLL*, v. 2. 533. 57 ff.

porta Fontinali … esset: neither the site of the *Porta Fontinalis* nor that of the *Ara Martis* are precisely known, but it is clear that the gate must have been between the Capitol and the Campus Martius. Cf. P–A, 328–9, 408.

11. *War with the Ligurians*

The account is continued from ch. 3, but this is a separate, highly 'written-up' episode, and it is very likely that it comes from a source other than that of chs. 3 and 21. Cf. p. 3, W–M ad loc., Nissen, *KU*, 166, Kahrstedt, 69, Zimmerer, 33, G. Mezzar-Zerbi, *RSC* vii (1959), 152 ff., Lauterbach, 86.

The episode is also described by Frontinus, *Str.* i. 5. 16 (clearly derived directly from L.) and Orosius iv. 20. 17.

11. 3. et: = *etiam.*

Caudinaeque cladis: the famous disaster of the Caudine Forks in 321 (Varr.), narrated by L. in ix. 1 ff. For a recent discussion of the authenticity of L.'s account cf. Salmon, *Samnium*, 225 ff.

memoria: the story of it, not, of course, their own memory.

4. Numidas: for Numidian cavalry in the Roman army in the second century cf. xxxi. 19. 3, xxxviii. 41. 12, xlii. 35. 6, 62. 2, 65. 12, xlv. 13. 13.

praefectus: clearly a Numidian.

pars . . . uicis: i.e. the area beyond the end of the pass.

6. spe . . . onerat: B, *per praemiorum onerum ad* (or *at*) χ. The correct reading was divined by Petrarch in the margin of P.

hostium: Mg, om. Bχ. It may well be a gloss in Mg. Cf. § 10 n.

obequitare: the word is not found before L. (*TLL*, ix. 2. 49–50). Cf. p. 9 and addenda.

7–8. nihil . . . currentium: the clipped sentence, without a main verb, is quite Tacitean. It extends far longer than i. 41. 1 and the passages there adduced by W–M.

7. paululi . . . graciles: cf. pp. 4, 6.

discinctus: cf. Virg. *A.* viii. 724 (Walker, *Supplementary Annotations*, 206).

8. equi sine frenis: the Numidian cavalry were famous for not using bridles. Cf. xxi. 44. 1, Virg. *A.* iv. 41, with Pease's note (but xxi. 9. 3, there adduced, is not relevant).

spectaculo: on L.'s description of various episodes as *spectacula* cf. I. Borzsak, *ACD* ix (1973), 57 ff. See also xxxvii. 24. 6.

9. pars maxima: limiting apposition. Cf. xxxiv. 56. 5 n.

10. adequitare: found in Caesar alone (*BG* i. 46. 1) before L. (*TLL*, i. 632–3).

saltum: i.e. the end of it.

regendi: genitive with *impotentes.*

per medias: Bχ, *inter medias* Mg. Either is possible. Frontinus has *per intermissas hostium stationes* and Oudendorp (in his edition of Frontinus [Leiden, 1731], 78), proposed reading *per intermissas* here. But despite many phrases taken from L., Frontinus is not quoting him verbatim and it is rash to emend L. on the basis of Frontinus. Moreover the posited process of corruption is very tortuous. We should have to believe that *missas* was corrupted to *medias*, and with two apparent alternative prepositions *per* was chosen in the tradition of F, *inter* in that of Mg.

hostium: χ, om. B. After § 9 it is quite clear whose *stationes* are involved, but in view of Frontinus' text (see above) it should be retained.

12. clamor trepidantium: the language is typical of L.'s vivid descriptions of critical points in battles. Cf. Ogilvie, 191.

13. sine imperio: without obeying any commands.

12–19. *Events in Greece and Asia*

12. *Aetolian appeal to Philip, Nabis, and Antiochus*

12. 1. As often, the transition from the annalistic to the Polybian section is due entirely to L. himself. Cf. p. 2.

Boi neque Hispani: it is odd that there is no mention of the Ligurians, after the detailed account in the preceding chapter. But to insert them by emendation is misguided. L. had probably already written this introduction to the Polybian section, and then inserted the Ligurian episode into his narrative.

inimice infesti: the combination of synonymous adjective and adverb is found in early Latin, but not elsewhere in Classical Latin. (Passages such as iii. 29. 3, vii. 33. 2, ix. 29. 3, adduced by Brakman, *Mnemosyne* n.s. lv [1927], 60 are not relevant.) The obvious solution is to read *inimici et infesti*, which is palaeographically simpler than *inimice infestique*, favoured by most editors.

2. spe ... uenturum: the Aetolians, of course, did not want Antiochus to control Greece. What they disliked was the arrangements made by Flamininus, and they wanted Antiochus to undo them.

3. concilium Naupactum: probably the *Panaetolica* of spring, 193 (cf. xxxi. 29. 1 n., Badian, *Studies*, 138, n. 84, Deininger, 69 n. 6).

4. Thoas praetor: Aetolian *strategos* in 194/3. He was also *strategos* in 203/2, 181/0, and 173/2. See further 32. 2 ff., 34. 5, 37. 4 ff., 42. 4 ff., 45. 2 ff., xxxvi. 15. 2, 26. 1 ff., xxxvii. 45. 17, and on his career as a whole Geyer, *RE*, viA. 300–1, Walbank, *Commentary*, iii. 110.

statumque: 'the position'.

quod ... fuissent: cf. 48. 12–13, xxxiii. 11, 11. 8 nn.

gentium ciuitatiumque: ἔθνη καὶ πόλεις. Cf. literature quoted at xxxiv. 60. 4 n.

5. censuit: cf. xxxiv. 2. 12 n.

suis quemque stimulis: inducements appropriate to the particular circumstances of each of the three.

6. Damocritus: of Calydon. He was *strategos* in 200/199 and 193/2. See further 33. 9–10, 35. 4, xxxvi. 24. 12, xxxvii. 3. 8, 46. 5. Cf. xxxi. 32. 1 n., Deininger, 69 n. 9.

Nicander: from Trichonium, *hipparchos* in this year (*Syll.*[3] 598D) and *strategos* in 190/89, 184/3, and 177/6. See further xxxvi. 29. 3 ff. and on his career as a whole Stählin, *RE*, xvii. 247–9, Walbank, *Commentary*, iii. 82.

Dicaearchus: *strategos* in 195/4. He was an ambassador to Rome in 198 (Pol. xviii. 10. 9). See further xxxvi. 28. 3.

7. ademptis ... ciuitatibus: cf. xxxiv. 35. 10.

eneruatam: cf. xxxviii. 34. 9.

inde ... habuisse: cf. xxxiv. 36. 3.

naualesque socios: cf. xxxiv. 6. 12 n.

8. [et]: when *et* ... *neque* occurs in Latin *et* is never the first word of the sentence (H–S, 517–18). It will have been inserted by dittography after *praetermisisset*.

[propter]: obviously an intrusion. It arose from a failure to see that *Gytheum* ... *Laconas* was the object of *existimaturos*. *existimare* is commonly found with a double accusative (*TLL*, v. 2. 1519. 55 ff.) while *propter* would require the far more difficult ellipse of an existential *esse*. Cf. Madvig, *Emendationes*, 510.

Gytheum: cf. xxxiv. 29. 2 n.

transmittant: cf. xxxiv. 26. 7 n.

9. per sociorum iniurias: by attacking the maritime towns that were now *socii* of Rome. *sociorum iniuriae* were, of course, a regular Roman pretext for war. Cf., e.g., xxxi. 6. 1.

10. orationis materia: Bχ. Mg had *orationi*. There are eighteen instances of *materia* with the genitive and twelve with the dative in L. (Packard, iii. 215–16). Decision is impossible.

11. regum ... gentis: cf. xxxi. 1. 7.

12–13. *neque ... suadere* refers to *incepto*, *qui ... posse* to *euentu*.

14. quam quot: cf. 1. 2 n. Here, of course, *quot* is the only possible reading.

15. uictoriam Aetolorum: cf. § 4 n.

aditum in Graeciam: the same claim as in xxxiii. 35. 11 (cf. n. ad loc.).

18. totum ... terrarum: exaggerated, since the Aetolians' activities did not include the whole of the οἰκουμένη. For different kinds of exaggeration involving *orbis terrarum* cf. 42. 12 n., xxxviii. 8. 4.

13. 1–3. *Nabis and the Laconian towns*

13. 1. et ... tamen: for adversative *et tamen* cf. xxxiii. 4. 2, *TLL*, v. 2. 904. 44 ff. Deletion of *et* is quite unjustified.

2–3. L. has given no precise indication of the status of the Laconian towns in his account of the peace settlement with Nabis (xxxiv. 35). It seems that the towns were placed under Achaean protection, but without being either full members of the Achaean League or dependent subjects of the Achaeans. See Aymard, *PR*, 251–5.

maritimorum Laconum seems to represent a quasi-official title, though they were not all actually on the sea (cf. Aymard, *PR*, 251).

13. 4—19. *Negotiations with, and decisions by Antiochus*

4. ea hieme ... data: in the winter of 194/3. Cf. literature quoted in xxxiii. 40. 3 n.

Raphiae: for the site cf. Walbank, *Commentary*, i. 610 (written, of course, before the 1967 war). It was the site of a major battle between Antiochus and Ptolemy IV in 217.

Phoenice: this is the regular Latin spelling, transliterated from the Greek.

filia: Cleopatra.

Antiochiam: cf. xxxiii. 19. 8 n.

Tauro monte: the great mountain range of southern Anatolia: cf. Magie, i. 259–60, xxxvii. 35. 10 n.

Ephesum: captured by Antiochus in autumn 197. Cf. xxxiii. 38. 1 n.

5. Antiocho filio: cf. xxxiii. 19. 9 n., Schmitt, *Antiochos*, 13 ff. He had been joint regent with his father since 210/9.

ad custodiam ... regni: probably supreme commander of the eastern satrapies, a function which could scarcely be exercised from Syria. See Schmitt, *Antiochos*, 15–18, arguing that *misso in Syriam* is a mistake either of L. or of Polybius himself.

Pisidas ... incolunt: Bχ have *Sicam* and B has *et* after *incolunt*. *Sidam* is the easiest explanation of the MSS. reading. It is, of course, on the coast, in Pamphylia, not Pisidia (see Bean, *Turkey's Southern Shore*, 78 ff.) but in v. 73. 3 Polybius refers to inland peoples being ὑπὲρ Σίδης and he probably did the same here. Pisidia had never been brought under Antiochus' control, though the coastal cities of Pamphylia had been subject to him since *c*. 216. See Schmitt, *Antiochos*, 279.

Sindam proposed by J. Gronovius is scarcely possible. It is in Cibyratis (cf. Magie, ii. 1157) and though not far from Pisidia, its mention cannot be explained in the same way as that of Side. Nor

is there much to be said for Rossbach's *et Oroanda* (*WKPh* xxxiv
[1917], 1134). L. refers to a town called Oranda or Oroanda at
xxxviii. 37. 11, probably mistakenly (cf. Ruge, *RE*, xviii. 1. 1132,
Walbank, *Commentary*, iii. 155), but it is hard to see how he could
have combined it with Side in a reference of this sort.

6. eo tempore ... est: cf. xxxiv. 59. 8. P. Aelius Paetus is also
appointed there, but he does not appear in the present section. Cf.
Holleaux, *Études*, v. 169 n. 2.

Elaeam: the harbour of Pergamum. Cf. Walbank, *Commentary*,
iii. 101, with literature there cited: add Bean, *Aegean Turkey*, 112–14.

regia: on the palaces of the Attalids see Hansen, *Attalids*, ch. vii.

7–10. There is no doubt that Eumenes did his best to bring about
the conflict between Rome and Antiochus, though in the end the
events that led to the outbreak of war were quite independent of
Pergamene influence. Eumenes' hopes are here described (and
doubtless were by Polybius) very much *ex euentu*.

14. 3–4. See Pol. iii. 11. 2: οἱ δὲ πρέσβεις ὁρῶντες τον Ἀντίοχον
προσέχοντα τοῖς Αἰτωλοῖς καὶ πρόθυμον ὄντα πολεμεῖν Ῥωμαίοις,
ἐθεράπευον τὸν Ἀννίβαν, σπουδάζοντες εἰς ὑποψίαν ἐμβαλεῖν πρὸς τὸν
Ἀντίοχον. ὃ καὶ συνέβη γενέσθαι. (In fact the Romans could not yet
have had any knowledge of Antiochus' attitude towards the
Aetolians. They had perhaps heard of the visit of his ambassadors
to Delphi on their way home from Rome [*Syll.*[3] 585].) Polybius
doubtless described the affair in the same way in book xix, and
L., or perhaps Claudius Quadrigarius, removed the imputation
of deliberate subterfuge by the Roman ambassadors. See Tränkle,
160–1.

5–12. The passage gives rise to two problems.
(*a*) *Source.* At xxv. 39. 12. L. says *auctor est Claudius, qui annales
Acilianos ex Graeco in Latinum sermonem uertit.* The two passages are
not to be taken as meaning that Claudius published a translation of
Acilius' history. L. need be indicating only that Claudius referred to
Acilius as his source, and in the former passage was giving a verbatim translation of what Acilius had written. There is no reason
to doubt that Claudius is Q. Claudius Quadrigarius: see Peter,
NJPhP cxxv (1882), 103–5, withdrawing the views he had expressed
in the first edition of *HRR*, p. cclxxxxvii ff. (cf. 2nd edn., p. ccxcii):
contra Zimmerer, 10 ff. Acilius is the C. Acilius who is known to have
acted as interpreter for the embassy of Athenian philosophers in 155
(Plut. *Cato mai.* 22. 5, cf. Macr. i. 5. 16) and whose history is probably referred to in *per.* liii. See Peter, *HRR*, i². cxxi ff., 49 ff.

(b) *Authenticity.* Holleaux (*Études*, v. 184 ff.) showed beyond all doubt that the story of Scipio's meeting with Hannibal did not stand in Polybius and cannot be accepted. He went on to argue, however, that Scipio did undertake a mission to the East in 193, and thas this is the germ of the story. His argument is based on a combination of Zonaras ix. 18. 12–13, who says that after his embassy to Africa (xxxiv. 62. 16–18) Scipio ἐντεῦθεν δ' εἰς τὴν Ἀσίαν διέβη, dedications of Scipio and his brother Lucius at Delos (*IDelos*, 442B, ll. 89–91, 102) in which they are described as στρατηγὸς ὕπατος and στρατηγός respectively, and the fact that in 189 Scipio is described as a πρόξενος of Delos (*IG* xi. 4. 712). Holleaux argued that Scipio would only have been described as a consul very soon after his consulship and that if he was a proxenos in 189, he must have been made one on a previous visit: it was he who actually delivered the dedication of Lucius. None of this is compelling. If στρατηγὸς ὕπατος can be used of a time when Scipio was no longer consul, it can be used of any such time and the proxeny can have been conferred without Scipio making a personal visit to Delos. As for Lucius, στρατηγός can be used to refer to consuls as well as praetors. Dio was probably only seeking to reconcile the account of Scipio's activities in Africa with the story of his meeting with Hannibal. Against Holleaux see Leuze, *Hermes* lviii (1923), 247 ff., Schlag, 133 ff. For other literature cf. Robert *ap.* Holleaux, *Études*, v. 184 n. 1. Scullard, *SA*, 285–6 n. 163 is still inclined to follow Holleaux.

7. parua manu innumerabiles: *innumerabiles*, of course, means that the size of each army was innumerable, not that there were an innumerable number of armies. It is true that Alexander was often considerably outnumbered, but the disparity is greatly exaggerated by the sources. On Alexander's army at the beginning of his campaigns cf. R. Lane Fox, *Alexander the Great* (London, 1973), 116.

quod⟨que⟩: *quod* MSS, perhaps rightly. Cf. Walsh, *CR*, 54.

ultimas oras: for the language cf. Nisbet and Hubbard on Horace, *Odes*, i. 35. 29–30.

quas uisere ... esset: Mg. Bχ omit these three words, but their appearance in the *periocha* guarantees their authenticity.

9. castra metari: cf. Plutarch, *Pyrr.* 16. 7, xxxi. 34. 8 n.

tam diu ... terra: not true of Southern Italy, where Pyrrhus found his main support. For *populi ... principis* cf. xxxiv. 58. 8 n.

12. perplexum: cf. pp. 6–7.

Punico astu: cf. xxxiv. 61. 14 n. *astu* occurs as an adverb in the early poets, but is not found again before the Augustan period, when it is used as a noun, and in cases other than the ablative. It occurs in L. also at xxvii. 20. 9, xxviii. 21. 10, xlii. 47. 5. Cf. *TLL*, ii. 983, Tränkle, *Die Sprachkunst des Properz und die Tradition der lateinischen Dichtersprache* (Wiesbaden, 1960), 38–9, *WS*, 123. Cf. pp. 4, 7.

e grege . . . imperatorum: for *grex* in the contemptuous sense of 'the common herd' cf. *TLL*, vi. 2. 2333. 31 ff.: *inaestimabilis* is used by Cicero, *fin.* iii. 20 as a translation of the philosophical term τὸ ἀναξίαν ἔχον. It occurs three times in L.; at xxix. 32. 1 it means 'enormous' and at xxxi. 34. 3 'uncertain'. It becomes common only in Christian writers, but the present passage and Palladius, *hist. mon.* i. 48 are the only instances of its being used of persons. Cf. *TLL*, vii. 1. 813–15. It is possible that the word was a neologism of Claudius Quadrigarius. See p. 9.

15. The events described in this chapter—a death suspected to be poisoning, the innuendo of sham grief, the king under the control of one of his advisers—would have appealed to Tacitus. The striking thing is that not only the content, but also the style of the chapter is remarkably Tacitean in effect. There are many elliptical expressions (cf. nn. on §§ 3, 4, and 9: this strengthens the case for omitting *fuit* in § 4). L., I imagine, felt that this sort of writing heightened the atmosphere of suspicion and intrigue. The same considerations occurred, on a far larger scale, to Tacitus.

There is no reason to doubt that the innuendos stood in Polybius, and equally little reason to believe them. Cf. Schmitt, *Antiochos*, 18–19.

15. 1. Apameam: in Phrygia, due east of Ephesus. It was founded by Antiochus I and named after his mother Apama (cf. 47. 5 n.). See Magie, i. 125–6, ii. 983–4, Walbank, *Commentary*, iii. 154. It was the site of the peace concluded with Rome in 188 (xxxviii. 37. 11, Pol. xxi. 42. 9). There was another Apamea on the Orontes (cf. *Fouilles d'Apamée de Syrie*, Brussels, 1969–).

2. eadem . . . fuerat: xxxiv. 57. 4—59. Appian (*Syr.* 12. 45) reports an offer by Antiochus to leave free Rhodes, Byzantium, Cyzicus, and all the other Asiatic Greeks except the Ionians and Aeolians. It cannot be totally excluded that such an offer was indeed made. Cf. Badian, *Studies*, 138 n. 78, H. H. Rawlings, *AJAH* i (1976), 20.

mors . . . regis: *Antiochi* is omitted by B, perhaps rightly. L. gave the name at 13. 5, and χ could easily have added it here.

Antiochus died in year 119 of the Seleucid era—i.e. before 5 April 192. A document of January 192 still dates by him, but it is an inescapable conclusion from L.'s narrative that this document is anachronistic and that Antiochus died in late summer, 193. This

193 B.C.

was convincingly demonstrated by Aymard in *RPh* 3ème série, xiv (1940), 89–109: cf. id., *REA* lvii (1955), 107–8 (= *ÉHA*, 268), A. J. Sachs and D. J. Wiseman, *Iraq* xvi (1954), 207.

in Syriam: cf. 13. 5 n.

diremit: *dirimit* MSS., perhaps rightly.

3. contigisset ... appareret: an ellipse of *et regem magnum futurum fuisse* (cf. xxxii. 25. 8 n.: W–M's 'unklar' is rather hard).

4. carior ... acceptiorque: cf. Koestermann, 258.

fuit: χ, om. B, perhaps rightly (see 15 n.).

patrem ... sustulisse: sc. *suspexerunt* from *suspectior*.

spadones: as W–M point out, Agrippina used the services of a eunuch to murder the Emperor Claudius (Tac. *A.* xii. 66. 2).

talium ... regibus: the general reflection probably stood in Polybius. xlii. 15. 3 is a closer parallel for *ministeriis* than xlii. 41. 4, quoted by McDonald.

5. Seleuco ... dedisset: cf. xxxiii. 40. 6 n.

quam ... sedem: the common attraction of the noun and adjective into the relative clause. Cf. K–St, ii. 309 ff.

6. alieno tempore: 'an unseasonable time'. Cf. *TLL*, i. 1578. 28 ff.

omisso ... bello: against the Pisidians (13. 5).

7. Minnione: one of the commanders at the battle of Magnesia (xxxvii. 41. 1). Cf. Treves, *RE*, Supp. vii. 457–8, Olshausen, no. 140.

princeps amicorum: i.e. one of the πρῶτοι φίλοι, probably the top of the three grades of φίλοι. I am not convinced that there was a further grade of πρῶτοι καὶ προτιμώμενοι φίλοι, as argued by Bikerman, *Institutions*, 41 ff.

8. ignarus ... externorum: cf. 26. 4 n.

Asia: here for Asia as a whole, not just Asia Minor. The reference is to the great *anabasis* of 212–205.

9. experto: for the ellipse of *esse* after *experiri* cf. xlii. 45. 4.

16. There may be an element of elaboration by L. in this pair of short speeches. As at Lysimachia, the Roman concept of rights by possession clashes with Antiochus' claim to inherited rights. Cf. xxxiii. 40. 4–6 n.

16. 2–4. The same arguments as are used by the Macedonian speaker in xxxi. 29. 6–11. Cf. vol. i, 343.

2. statuitis: *statuistis* MSS., perhaps rightly: 'you have laid down for Antiochus, but (all the time) you are doing something different'.

3. Zmyrnaei Lampsacenique: cf. xxxiii. 38. 3 n.

Neapolitani ... Tarentini: on Rhegium and Tarentum cf.
xxxi. 29. 10–11 n. Naples became a Roman ally in 326 (Varr.) and
remained loyal to Rome. It had a particularly favourable *foedus*
(viii. 26. 6, Cic. *Balb*. 21, Badian, *FC*, 27).

stipendium: only Tarentum paid *stipendium*, imposed after its
revolt in the Second Punic War. Cf. Wuilleumier, *Tarente* (xxxi.
29. 10–11 n.), 167. Kahrstedt, *Historia* viii (1959), 206 regards the
payment as rent for *ager publicus*.

4. Cf. xxxi. 29. 6–7 n.

5. Zmyrna, Lampsaco: MSS. Insertion of *et* is not necessary. A,
B, *Cque* is regular even in Cicero (cf. xxxiv. 23. 9 n., K–St, ii. 31).

6. et stipendiarias: Mg, Bχ omit *et*, and asyndeton is quite possible. I do not see that McDonald's comment 'sed etiam de belli
iure agitur' makes any difference to the argument. Without *et* it
would be better to punctuate with a comma after *factas*.

in antiquum ius: Gelenius 'lege'. B has *Antiochum*, χ *Antiochus*.
The mention of the name here is unnecessary, and the presence of
the accusative in B and of *ius antiquum* in similar contexts at xxxiii.
40. 6, xxxiv. 57. 8 make it virtually certain that Gelenius was right.

8. uno ... intermisso: not true of Tarentum. For *uno tenore*, 'un-
interruptedly', cf. Otto, 344, E. Dutoit, *MH* ii (1947), 45–7, Ogilvie,
348. It is clear from Cicero, *Orator* 21, *uno tenore, ut aiunt* that the
phrase was well established, though in fact that passage is the only
example of *tenor* before the Augustan period. On its use in L. and
elsewhere see Dutoit, op. cit.

9. mutauerint: one might expect the indicative, as the clause
summarizes what Sulpicius himself has been saying. But attraction
into the subjunctive is perfectly natural and we should be guided
here by manuscript authority.

10–11. Even straight after the battle of Corupaedium the Seleucids
claimed to treat the Greek cities as 'free'. But that freedom had
to be seen as a gift from the ruler, not as a right claimed by the city
itself. The precise history of many states in the third century cannot,
of course, be traced. Cf. xxxiii. 38. 6–7 n., Magie, i. 95, ii. 926 ff.,
Orth, *passim*.

10. mansisse: not a misprint for *permansisse* as claimed by Walsh,
CR, 56. The MSS. unanimously have *mansisse*.

11. quod: φ, *qui* B, *quin* ψ. *quod* is clearly an emendation by

Colonna, but it must be right. Weissenborn's *quia* is impossible. *quia* cannot stand for *quod* in a noun clause, and if it means 'because', the sentence has no syntax.

post tot saecula: exaggerated.

12. nobis nihil: χMg, *nihil nobis* B. The agreement of χ and Mg proves that *nobis nihil* is the transmitted reading, but in any case the unemphatic second position in the colon is more suited to *nobis* than *nihil*.

17. 1. quantumcumque ... ducebat: as L. has already said in 13. 8 (cf. 13. 7–10 n.).

2. postulationes: Bχ, *expostulationes* Mg. At xlii. 42. 9 *expostulatione* is required (though the Vienna MS. has *postulatione*) as the context requires 'protest' not 'demand'. Here there is an antithesis with *querelis* and this appears to require *postulationes* (thus Madvig, *Emendationes*, 511 n. 1). But in Cicero, *dom.* 13 and Tacitus, *A.* i. 13. 5 *expostulatio* clearly means 'loudly expressed demand' and it is not therefore possible to decide between the two alternatives here. See *TLL*, v. 2. 1776. Both L–S and OLD are misleading about the meaning of *expostulatio*.

disceptatione altercationem: *disceptatio* and *altercatio* are also contrasted at xxxviii. 32. 4. L. frequently uses *altercatio* in a general sense, a usage found before him only in Plautus. In Cicero it appears to be a technical term for a dispute either in a law court or in the senate. Cf. *TLL*, i. 1749–50.

3–4. ibi alius ... alius: most editors have followed Crévier in deleting the second *alius*. McDonald argues that *alius alio ferocius* is equivalent to *omnes*, which is then distributed by *alius* in § 4 and *alii* in § 7. He adduces ix. 45. 11 as a parallel, but that shows only that *alius ... alii* can be used for *alii ... alii* (*alius* is the transmitted reading there, but many editors have altered it to *alii*). I can see no parallel for *alius ... alii* distributing a subject also expressed by *alius*, and the sentence that results is incredibly obscure. Walsh (*CR*, 56) thinks the meaning is improved by putting a stop after *maior erat*. But this involves an ellipse of the verb of saying which would be very strange in a sentence of this type. Crévier should be followed.

4. maximo: perhaps with deliberate allusion to Antiochus' appellation Μέγας (on which cf. Schmitt, *Antiochos*, 92–5).

imponentium: to be taken with *postulatorum*, not with an understood *Romanorum*.

5. et patria Lacedaemone: Madvig, *et patriam Lacedaemonem* MSS.
Madvig's 'rule in his own land and in his land of Sparta' is tautologous and scarcely makes sense. The MSS. reading is sense, but
'rule in his land and his land of Sparta were left for him' is still unnecessarily pleonastic. I suspect the whole phrase should be deleted
as originating in a gloss on *patria sua*.

6. Antiocho: dative with *imperata facere*: cf. xxxviii. 43. 2.

7 ff. The domino theory. Similar arguments were used by Pericles
in urging the Athenian assembly to reject Spartan demands about
the Megarian decree in the winter of 432/1 (Thuc. i. 140. 5).

The Roman demands, of course, were much wider than Smyrna
and Lampsacus but these cities had resisted Antiochus and it could
have been argued that if he abandoned his claims to them Rome
would not push her other demands in respect of either Asia or
Europe. Bruegmann, 208 ff. wrongly sees the inconsistency as a
sign of invention by L.

7. initium . . . imperandi: the text should be retained in view of
L.'s fondness for unusual word-order. In this case it may have been
determined by his desire not to have *iniusta imperandi* in the unemphatic second position in the colon. Cf. p. 13.

aquam terramque: the standard tokens of submission demanded by the Persians. Cf. the passages cited in J. E. Powell, *A
Lexicon to Herodotus* (Cambridge, 1938), 67.

8. temptationem: before L. only in Cic. *Att.* x. 17. 2 (of the onset
of a disease) but used in the present sense also at iii. 38. 7, iv. 42. 4,
ix. 45. 6, xli. 23. 14.

et: MSS., rightly retained by McDonald. 'The Romans were
trying a ploy and (if it succeeded) the other states would join Rome.'

liberatorem: cf. xxxiv. 50. 9 n. For a similar appositional use of
liberator cf. i. 56. 8.

18. 1. Alexander Acarnan: see further xxxvi. 11. 6, 20. 5–6.

2. gradum amicitiae: cf. 15. 7 n.

3. tamquam: hypothetical. *tamquam* in § 2, however, is explanatory.

4. W–M claim that this is anachronistic, as Antiochus had already
received Dicaearchus. But Polybius will have related Dicaearchus'
mission in the *res Graeciae*, while the present passage comes from the
res Asiae. We cannot, therefore, assume that 12. 18 precedes the

incident reported here. Cf. Nissen, *KU*, 167, Leuze, *Hermes* lviii (1923), 244.

umbilicum Graeciae incolerent: the phrase recurs at xxxvii. 54. 21. On the legend that the ὀμφαλός, the stone in the innermost part of the sanctuary at Delphi, was the centre of the earth cf. Parke and Wormell, *The Delphic Oracle* (Oxford, 1956), i. 6 ff., Platnauer on Eur. *I.T.* 1256, H. V. Herrmann, *Omphalos* (Münster, Westf., 1959).

antesignanos: for this rare metaphorical use of *antesignani* cf. *TLL*, ii. 160. 83 ff. (where the reference to the present passage is wrongly given). The metaphor is continued in *cornibus* and *bellicum cani*.

6. nosse ... uoluere: deliberately epic language, with an epic simile. Cf. p. 6.

7. uoti ... compos: cf. xxxii. 30. 10. The phrase does not occur before the Augustan period. See C. O. Brink, *Horace on Poetry*, ii (Cambridge, 1971), 166–7.

8. distringendos: for *distringere* in military contexts cf. xliv. 35. 8, Cic. *leg. Man.* 9, Front. *Str.* i *praef.*, *TLL*, v. 1. 1550. 75 ff.

19. *The oath of Hannibal.* Polybius described Hannibal's explanation of his oath to Antiochus as part of his account of the origins of the Second Punic War in iii. 11. 1 ff., and it is referred to by L. at xxi. 1. 4. Whether Polybius gave another full account when he reached the present stage in his history, we do not, of course, know. The language here, however, shows only limited similarities to that of Polybius in book iii, and it is quite possible that L. has used annalistic sources as well as Polybius, or has himself been responsible for considerable elaboration. There is an inconsistency in the narrative in that it first seems that Hannibal speaks privately to Antiochus, not having been invited to the *consilium*, but 19. 7 seems to indicate that L. envisaged Hannibal's speech taking place before the end of the *consilium* (cf. also § 6 n.). Nepos, *Hann.* 2 is closer to Polybius, but the similarity of § 4 to Nepos, with nothing corresponding in Polybius, and the use of *cogitare* by both authors (§ 6 n.) may also point to common use of an annalistic source.

See Walbank, *Commentary*, i. 314–15, iii. 764–5, J.-A. de Foucault, *REL* xlvi (1968), 214–19, H. A. Gärtner, *Beobachtungen zu Bauelementen in der antiken Historiographie* (Wiesbaden, 1975), 10 ff.

But though the ultimate Polybian source for the episode is not in doubt, it cannot be regarded as certain that it was actually on this occasion that Hannibal related the story to Antiochus. It is certainly not the case that before the conversation between Hannibal and

Villius, Antiochus was ready to take Hannibal's advice, and then
stopped taking it, only to be persuaded by this story. Cf. xxxiv. 61.
1 n., Badian, *Studies*, 139 n. 92. Errington (*Latomus* xxix [1970],
26 ff.) argues unconvincingly that the story of the oath was invented
by Hannibal to impress Antiochus.

19. 1. conloquia cum Villio: 14. 2–4.

2. tempore apto: Mg, *a tempore* Bχ. Mg's reading is perfectly
acceptable, and it is misguided to emend it to explain the reading
of Bχ or to accord with *tempore dato* in Nepos, *Hann.* 2. 3. Polybius
(iii. 11. 3) says ἐγένετό τις καιρὸς ὡς ἐπὶ λόγον ἀχθῆναι τὴν ὑποικουρουμέ-
νην ἀτοπίαν ἐν αὐτοῖς.

3. Hamilcar: on Hamilcar's command in Spain (237–229) cf.
Pol. ii. 1. 5 ff.
   paruum admodum: Pol. iii. 11. 5 ἔτη μὲν ἔχειν ἐννέα.
   cum ... admotum: Pol. iii. 11. 5 θύοντος δ' αὐτοῦ τῷ Διὶ
παρεστάναι παρὰ τὸν βωμόν.
   nunquam ... Romani: Pol. iii. 11. 7 μηδέποτε ῾Ρωμαίοις
εὐνοήσειν. Cf. Walbank, *Commentary*, i. 315.

4. sub ... militaui: cf. Nepos, *Hann.* 2. 5 *id ego iusiurandum patri
datum usque ad hanc aetatem ita conseruaui.*
   sacramento: as if the oath were a regular military oath of
allegiance. The use of εὐνοήσειν in Polybius conveys the same idea,
for εὔνοια is a word regularly used in Greek military oaths of loyalty
(cf. *CR* n.s. xxi [1971], 263). L., though, is hardly likely to have
been aware of that.
   sex et triginta annos: from 237 to the battle of Zama in 202:
cf. xxx. 37. 9.
   hoc me ... hoc duce: for the personified subject cf. ii. 35. 1
(*ira*), 44. 12 (*spes*), ix. 19. 13 (*timor*), xxxiv. 6. 16 (*inopia*). For *dux*
of abstract nouns cf. *TLL*, v. 1. 2326. 41 ff.
   ueniam: Madvig's correction (*Emendationes*, 511) for *inueniam* in
the MSS. is clearly correct.

5. quibus tuorum: any of Antiochus' *amici*.

6. cogitabis: cf. Nepos, *Hann.* 2. 6.
   primos amicos: in the technical sense (cf. 15. 7 n.). Mg has
primos amicos hos and it is just possible that L. wrote *hos primos amicos*,
referring to those present at the *consilium*.
   si qua res ... quaerito: Polybius iii. 11. 9 has: ἐπὰν δὲ διαλύσεις
ἢ φιλίαν συντίθηται πρὸς αὐτούς, τότε μὴ προσδεῖσθαι διαβολῆς, ἀλλ'

ἀπιστεῖν κὰι φυλάττεσθαι· πᾶν γάρ τι πρᾶξαι κατ᾽ αὐτῶν ὃ δυνατὸς εἴη,
which is much stronger.

7. ex consilio ... gereretur: cf. p. 32.

192 B.C.

20–24. *Events in Rome, Italy, and Spain*

20–21. 1. *Provinces and armies*

On this occasion L. marks the transition to the new year only by
the phrase *consulibus ambobus* (§ 2). Cf. xxxviii. 42. 8 (*consulibus nouis*).

20. 1. destinabant: 'marked out'. L. is the first writer to use
destinare in this sense. Cf. viii. 8. 18, ix. 16. 19, 24. 14, xxxiii. 28. 5,
TLL, v. 1. 759. 60 ff. See p. 9.

2. ita ... praeesset: as was normal (cf. 6.2 n.). It is specified here
only because a special provision was made concerning the consul
who was not to conduct the elections.

3. si quo ... legiones: as there had been no declaration of war
the task of the consul had to be left undefined.

5. duae ... habuisset: cf. p. 37.
    L. Cornelius: (270). Merula. Cf. xxxii. 7. 13 n.

6. Q. Minucio: (65). Thermus. Cf. xxxii. 27. 8 n. For his army
cf. xxxiv. 56. 4–6.

7. quo senatus censuisset: the phrase is used also at 41. 3, xxvii.
22. 3, xlii. 28. 6, 31. 9, xlv. 17. 10 in reference to cases where the
senate wants to leave a province unspecified in case of an emergency.
The senate's assignment of *siluae callesque* to the consuls of 59 (Suet.
Iul. 19. 2) is to be similarly explained: cf. Balsdon, *JRS* xxix (1939),
180–3.
    Gallia ... habenda: for similar conjunctions of a noun with a
gerundive phrase cf. i. 20. 7, v. 17. 1, xxxvi. 11. 2, J. L. Catterall,
TAPhA lxix(1938), 313.

9. deinde plebei ... scito: it is not clear why it was thought
necessary to get the people's approval for this change. Perhaps the
senate, fearful of a repetition of the rejection of the war-vote against
Philip in 200, wanted to secure a wider participation in these
preliminary moves towards war with Antiochus.

10. Macedonia: standing or Northern Greece in general: cf. vol. i, 10 n. 4.

Bruttii: cf. xxxi. 6. 2 n. Here because of the fear of an invasion from the East, and to organize Roman forces for embarkation at Brundisium.

11. Flaminio Fuluioque: cf. xxxiv. 54. 2 n.

11–12. Atilio ... Baebius: both here and at 21. 1 the names have been interchanged. It is unlikely that both errors are due to transpositions in transmission and we must assume that they are the responsibility either of L. himself, or of his source, with L. failing to spot them (Walbank, *Philip V*, 194 is confused).

11. duae ... fuissent: xxxiv. 56. 4. On the real size of Baebius' force see p. 37.

milia peditum: Mg. Bχ omit *peditum*, perhaps rightly. Cf. § 5.

12. triginta naues: cf. 24. 8 n. The ships he took were in fact old ones, and there is therefore no conflict with the figures in 37. 3 and xxxvi. 42. 7. See Thiel, 259–60. The ships may never have actually been built: cf. Thiel, 265 ff.

naualibus ... nauales: L. feels no difficulty in the repetition of the word in a different sense (cf. p. 13). On *nauales socios* cf. xxxiv. 6. 12 n.

consulibus ... pedites: to serve as marines: cf. Thiel, 277.

13. Nabim ... Romani: cf. 13. 1–3.

14. ceterum: i.e. they were really to be ready in case Antiochus invaded Greece.

21. 1. Fuluio ... erat: 20. 8.

prouincia: a very clear instance of *prouincia* in its original sense of 'sphere of operations'.

centum quinqueremes pararent: prepare, not build. The decision is additional to that recorded in 20. 12. The fleets of both Atilius and Livius were composed of these old ships: see Thiel, 264–5.

21. 2–6. *Prodigies*

Cf. xxxi. 12. 5–10 n.

2. supplicatio: cf. 9. 5 n.

3. capram ... edidisse: for a multiple human birth as a prodigy see *Obs.* 14. Cf. D.H. iii. 22. 10, Pliny, *NH*. vii. 33, Wülker, 15. This is the only example of an animal birth being so treated.

ex Piceno: cf. xxxiv. 45. 7 n.

Arreti: cf. xxxi. 21. 1, xxxii. 9. 3 nn.

puerum . . . unimanum: for similar prodigies cf. xli. 21. 12, *Obs.* 52, xxxiv. 45. 7 n.

4. Amiterni: in the Sabine country, 10 km. north-west of L'Aquila. It was the birthplace of Sallust. It had been captured in 293 (x. 39. 2: Salmon, *Samnium,* 270 argues that this passage refers to an otherwise unknown Samnite Amiternum). On the date of its acquisition of full citizenship cf. Taylor, *Voting Districts of the Roman Republic* (Rome, 1960), 65–6. For other prodigies at Amiternum cf. xxi. 62. 5, xxiv. 44. 8, xxxvi. 37. 3, *Obs.* 20, 21, 27, 41, Wülker, 95.

terra pluuisse: cf. xxxiv. 45. 6 n.

Formiis . . . tacta: cf. xxxii. 1. 10 n.

consulis Cn. Domiti: B omits *consulis* and that word could be a gloss. But Madvig's suggestion (1884 edn., p. xvi) that the whole phrase is a gloss is most implausible: it occurs in both the *periocha* and in Val. Max. i. 6. 5 (cf. W. Heraeus, *JAW* lxxx [1894], 126–7).

bouem locutum: for speaking oxen cf. xxiv. 10. 10, xxvii. 11. 4, xxviii. 11. 4, xli. 21. 13, *Obs.* 15, 26, 27, Tac. *H.* i. 86. 1, for cows iii. 10. 6, xli. 13. 2, xliii. 13. 3, *Obs.* 43, 53, Val. Max. i. 6. 5, Pliny, *NH* viii. 183, Wülker, 19–20, Krauss, 120–1, Ogilvie, 415.

Roma caue tibi: two dactyls (though the second syllable of *caue* is sometimes shortened). Whether this increased the importance of the prodigy is not clear.

5. bouem . . . alique: for similar provisions cf. xli. 13. 3, xliii. 13. 3. Clearly the animals were not regarded as malign. Cf. Krauss, loc. cit.

Tiberis . . . euertit: cf. 9. 2–3 nn.

⟨anno⟩: the supplement is not necessary. Cf. iv. 23. 6 *tanto maiore quam proximo conatu.*

duos pontes: the *insula Tiberina* is often referred to as *inter duos pontes* (cf. Le Gall, 84–5, 267–8, 278, G. Lugli, *Fontes ad topographiam Romae,* ii [Rome, 1953], 136 and the reference here is to the bridges connecting the island to the two banks of the river, not just to two bridges. The word-order also points in that direction. If L. had merely been defining the number of bridges destroyed we might have expected *pontes duos* (cf. e.g. 41. 8) while in place-names containing a numeral the numeral regularly precedes: cf. Marouzeau, *L'Ordre des mots,* i. 190.

The bridges were later the Pontes Fabricius and Cestius, but at this date were still wooden bridges. Cf. P–A, 399–400, M. Besnier, *L'Île tibérine dans l'antiquité* (Paris, 1902), 91 ff., Le Gall, 205 ff.

6. uicum ... Capitolio: the Vicus Iugarius ran from the north of the area later occupied by the Basilica Iulia to the river, thus skirting the southern foot of the Capitol. Cf. P–A, 574–5.

21. 7–11. *Liguria*

Cf. ch. 11 n.

7. Q. Minucius: cf. 20. 6 n.

9. nocte clam: cf. xxii. 22. 15, 24. 6, xxvii. 45. 12, xxxi. 12. 1, Preuss, 57–8. Cf. also xxxvi. 39. 1 n. (*nocte improuiso*). See p. 11.

    uacua castra Romanus: B, *Romanus uacua castra* χ. L. is marking a contrast between *Ligures* and *Romanus* and the unemphatic position in the colon is therefore inappropriate for *Romanus*.

10. laxamenti: often used by L. to mean 'respite' in war. Before him it occurs in a literal sense of 'distance' in Cato, *agr.* 19. 2, and meaning 'indulgence' in Cic. *Clu.* 89. Trebonius *ap.* Cic. *fam.* xii. 16. 3 uses it to mean 'respite'. Cf. *TLL*, vii. 2. 1069.

22. 1–2. *Decisions on Antiochus and Nabis*

22. 1. ab regibus: their mission had been only to Antiochus (xxxiv. 59. 8 *ad regem*) but L. presumably includes Eumenes here.

2. nihil ... haberet: cf. p. 32.

    nisi ... tyrannum: the *legati* had not been instructed to visit the Peloponnese.

    et Achaei: 13. 3.

    Atilius: 20. 10. L. now has the name right (cf. 20. 11–12 n.).

    tuendos socios: B, *socios tuendos* χ. Decision is impossible.

22. 3–4. *Events in Gaul*

An inscription (*SEG* xv. 254) records the presence of a contingent of Achaean soldiers fighting with a Cn. Domitius against Γαλάται and it is very likely that the reference is to Domitius' campaign in this year. See L. Moretti, *RFIC* n.s. xciii (1965), 278 ff. If this is correct, it would precede the date for the formal alliance between Rome and Achaea argued for by Badian, *JRS* xlii (1952), 76–80, but that would not be fatal to Badian's argument.

3. quando: cf. xxxiii. 2. 9 n.

    Arimino: cf. xxxi. 10. 5 n.

4. ad mille: for the adverbial *ad* with numerals cf. K–St, i. 575.

22. 5–8. *Spain*

Götzfried, 63 ff., argues unconvincingly that the events recorded in
7. 8 should be placed between the capture of Noliba and Cusibi
and the capture of Toletum: cf. Klotz, *Hermes* 1 (1915), 499–500.
On the significance of the events here recorded see p. 36.

5. Licabrum: identified by Schulten, *FHA*, iii. 197 with Igabrum,
modern Cabra, south-east of Corduba, with the implication that
Flaminius is operating within the boundaries of Ulterior (cf. J. S.
Richardson, *JRS* lxvi [1976], 151). Schulten argues that 'kings' are
found only in Turdetania and on the eastern coast.

uineis: cf. xxxiv. 17. 12 n.

Corribilonem: not otherwise known.

6. duobus ... duo ... duo: as if to emphasize the coincidence.

Vesceliam Helonemque: Vescelia is perhaps Vesci, between
the River Baetis and the sea. Cf. Schulten, *FHA*, iii, 197, Schulten–
Grosse, *RE*, viiiA. 1693. Götzfried, 64–5, Schulten, *FHA*, loc. cit.,
place Helo near Ilipula Minor, on the basis of a coin found there.
Schlag, 38, for no clear reason, locates both Vescelia and Helo
north of the Baetis.

7. Oretanos: cf. 7. 7 n. There Flaminius is fighting them, attacking
from Citerior.

Noliba et Cusibi: not otherwise known.

ad Tagum: north-east from the Oretani.

Toletum: cf. 7. 8 n. I cannot see any difference in the attitude to
the town here and in that passage, as claimed by W–M.

Vettonum: cf. 7. 8 n.

23. *Further decisions on Antiochus*

2. etsi ... explorabantur, tamen: Mog. (only *explorabantur, tamen*
is specifically attested from Mg), *et* ... *expromebantur, et quod* B and,
with the omission of the second *et*, χ. Any emendation of Bχ's text
which retains *expromebantur* gives an impossible sense. It is not the
case that everything (sc. about Antiochus' intentions) was laid in the
open by the *legati*. (Rossbach [*WKlPh* xxxiv (1917), 1134] proposed
et quidam, not *et quidem*, as stated by McDonald.)

identidem: three at the most—196, 195 (cf. xxxiv. 33. 12 n.),
and the recent one.

4. Atilium ... Graeciam: 22. 2.

5. auctoritate: three of the *legati* are consulars.

tenendos: *tuendos* MSS., clearly influenced by *ad tuendos socios*
in 22. 2.

Cn. Octauium: (16). Cf. xxxi. 3. 2, 11. 18 nn.

Cn. Seruilium: (44). Caepio. Cf. xxxiii. 47. 7 n. Scullard (*RP*², 107 n. 1) wrongly regarded the appointment of Octavius and Servilius as evidence that they were among the *x legati* of 196: cf. Schleussner, 24 n. 147.

P. Villium: (10). Tappulus. Cf. xxxi. 4. 3 n.

M. Baebius ex Bruttiis: cf. 20. 10 n.

6. legiones ... traiceret: cf. p. 37.

inde: despite the clear omission of *ut* in the MSS. before *M. Fuluius*, the asyndeton here is appropriate for the formal, clipped style of *senatus consulta* (cf. xxii. 1. 17, xxxvi. 2. 15 n.).

M. Fuluius: (44). Centumalus. Cf. 10. 11 n.

classem ... oram: this fleet remained off Sicily until 188. Cf. xxxvi. 2. 11, xxxvii. 50. 9, xxxviii. 36. 2, Thiel, 261.

7. cum imperio ... duceret: a *legatus cum imperio*. Cf. xxxii. 16. 2 n., W. F. Jashemski, *The Origins and History of the Proconsular and Propraetorian Imperium to 27 B.C.* (Chicago, 1950), 40, Thiel, 279.

L. Oppius Salinator ... fuerat: (32, cf. 19). Cf. 24. 6, xxxii. 28. 3 nn. On the aedileship see Festus, p. 258L, *MRR*, i. 347.

8. L. Valerio collegae: (350). Tappo. Cf. xxxiv. 1. 2 n.

exercitum: consisting entirely of Latins and Italians. Cf. xxxi. 8. 8 n., xxxii. 8. 7.

tumultuariorum: cf. 2. 7 n.

qua ... Graeciam: the east coast of Sicily.

9. circumiacentibus insulis: presumably Malta, which was under the control of the governor of Sicily (cf. Weiss, *RE*, xv. 546), and the Lipari Islands to the north.

10. Attali, Eumenis fratris: the future Attalus II.

Antiochum ... transisse: cf. 35. 7. Holleaux at *CAH* viii. 206 (= *Études*, v. 395), implicitly withdrew the doubts about the expedition expressed at *Études*, v. 194 n. 1. Cf. Leuze, *Hermes* lviii (1923), 244 n. 2, Aymard, *RPh* 3ème série, xiv (1940), 101: *contra* Walbank, *Philip V*, 328, Petzold, 108. Even if the expedition is accepted, it remains true that at this point Antiochus was only invading Thrace, not preparing to move against the mainland.

11. For other gifts to Attalus by the senate cf. Hopp, 14 n. 51.

Eumeni ... Attalo: a somewhat surprising chiasmus.

aedes liberae ... lautia: on *locus et lautia* cf. xxxiii. 24. 5 n.: add S. Timpanaro, *RFIC* xcv (1967), 432 ff., Walbank, *Commentary*, iii. 111–2. *aedes liberae* is added also at xxx. 17. 14 and stands alone at xlii. 6. 11. *aedes liberae* would appear to indicate something more lavish than *locus*—a house 'with vacant possession' (not 'free of charge', as L–S and Sage appear to think). Strictly *locus* is super-fluous with *aedes liberae*, but *locus et lautia* had become a stereotyped phrase, and *locus* was thus retained even when *aedes liberae* was added.

duo, bina: Priscian (*de figuris numerorum* 25 = *GL* iii. 414) has *et bina equestria arma*, and we should perhaps read *duo et bina* (cf. H. J. Müller, *JPhV* xxxii [1907], 9).

24. *Elections and further decisions concerning Greece*

24. 1. alii atque alii: in fact only Attalus on top of the *rumores* mentioned in 23. 2. For *alius atque alius* of a series cf. *TLL*, i. 1640.

2. M. Fuluius praetor: the *praetor urbanus*. Cf. 20. 8, 21. 1, 23. 6.
ad consulem: L. Flamininus (20. 7).

3. For other indications of urgency in holding elections cf. R. Rilinger, *Der Einfluss des Wahlleiters bei den römischen Konsulwahlen von 360 bis 50 v.Chr.* (Munich, 1976), 78 n. 58.

4–5. There are two Scipionic candidates for the patrician place, Scipio Nasica and Africanus' brother Lucius (cf. *Latomus* xxxi [1972], 48). With war with Antiochus now expected, it is not surprising that Scipionic candidates are successful (for M'. Acilius Glabrio cf. vol. i, 31 n. 5). Although no list of plebeian candidates is given, it is unlikely that Glabrio was elected unopposed.

4. quod ... petierunt: the *ambitio* was caused by the fact that three powerful candidates were competing for the one patrician place. It cannot have been all that unusual for there to have been more than two patrician candidates.
P. Cornelius Cn. f. Scipio: (350). Nasica. Cf. xxxi. 49. 6 n.
qui ... tulerat: ch. 10.
L. Cornelius Scipio: (337). Cf. xxxiv. 54. 2 n.
Cn. Manlius Vulso: (91). Cf. xxxiii. 25. 1 n.
ut ... appareret: perhaps consecutive rather than final, as W–M take it.
M'. Acilius Glabrio: (35). Cf. xxxi. 50. 5 n.

6. praetores: all the praetors except Livius and Oppius may be regarded as Scipionic. For the Iunii cf. *Latomus* xxvii (1968), 151 and n. 2, Münzer, *RA*, 158 ff.: for Livius cf. Scullard, *RP²*, 88 n. 1.
L. Aemilius Paullus: (114). Cf. xxxiv. 45. 5 n.
M. Aemilius Lepidus: (68). Cf. xxxi. 2. 3 n.
M. Iunius Brutus: (48). Cf. xxxiv. 1. 4 n.

A. Cornelius Mammula: (258). Apart from this praetorship and its prorogation in 190 (xxxvii. 2. 7–8) nothing more is known of his career. The MSS. have *L.* here, *A.* at the other places where he is mentioned. For similar uncertainties in the case of the praetor of 217 (probably his father) cf. xxxiii. 44. 2 n.

C. Liuius: (29). Cf. xxxii. 16. 3 n. This is his second praetorship (cf. xxxiv. 53. 2 n.).

L. Oppius: (32, cf. 19). Cf. 23. 7 n.

Salinator: at xxix. 37. 4 L. says that the *cognomen* was given to the father of this Livius because he had raised the price of salt as censor. This is made extremely improbable by the fact that it was also carried by the Oppii and that the Livius who was *xuir sacris faciundis* at the time of the putative *ludi saeculares* of 236 was also called Salinator. Cf. Münzer, *RE*, xiii. 898, Kajanto, *The Latin Cognomina* (Helsinki, 1965), 322.

qui . . . duxerat: 23. 7.

7. dum: 'until'. Cf. *JRS* lxviii (1978), 228.

M. Baebius . . . continere: cf. 23. 6 and p. 37.

Epirum . . . Apolloniam: cf. xxxi. 18. 9 n.

8. quinqueremes . . . quinquaginta: an increase of the order given at 20. 12, not an addition to it. Cf. Thiel, 265.

25–39. *Events in Greece*

25–30. *War between the Achaean League and Sparta*

Other sources: Plut. *Phil.* 14–15. 3, *Flam.* 17. 2, Paus. viii. 50. 7–10, Just. xxxi. 3. 3–4, *Syll.*[3] 600. For discussion of the episode cf. F. Rühl, *NJPhP* cxxvii (1883), 33 ff., Aymard, *PR*, 301 ff., A. M. Castellani, *Pubblicazioni dell' Università cattolica del sacro cuore, contributi dell' istituto di filologia classica, sezione di storia antica*, i (Milan, 1963), 78–9, Lehmann, 235 ff., Errington, 95 ff., Deininger, 109 ff. The events begin in the spring of 192 (Aymard, *PR*, 301 n. 40).

1. L.'s transition to the Polybian section. Cf. p. 2.

2. Nabis . . . bellum: cf. 13. 1–3, 20. 13, 22. 2. To begin with, presumably, Nabis' siege of Gytheum (13. 3) had been somewhat half-hearted.

Gytheum: cf. xxxiv. 29. 2 n.

infestus: Bχ, *infensus* Mg. Either is possible. Cf. Koestermann, 190.

quod . . . praesidium: cf. 13. 3.

agros . . . uastabat: Aymard, *PR*, 302 n. 46 doubts whether Nabis was entirely the aggressor in these incidents.

3. legati: cf. 13. 3, 22. 2.

4. reditum legatorum: for the date (*c*. Feb. 192) cf. Aymard, *PR*, 301 n. 40.

Sicyonem concilium: a *syncletos*. Cf. xxxi. 25. 2 n., Aymard, *PR*, 305 n. 57, *Assemblées*, 313 n. 3, Larsen, *Representative Government*, 172.

ad T. Quinctium: for his dispatch cf. 23. 5. Exactly where he was at this time is uncertain. Cf. Aymard, *PR*, 305 n. 55.

5. The language suggests that Flamininus' letter arrived after the *syncletos* had begun its deliberations. Cf. Errington, 95 n. 3.

iniecerunt: Mg, *fecerunt* Bχ. There can be no doubt that L. wrote *iniecerunt* and this was corrupted to the flat *fecerunt*. L. commonly uses *inicere* with states of mind as an object. Cf. Packard, ii. 1212–14.

praetorem: Atilius.

6. principum . . . multitudo: the political leaders and the mass of those present at the meeting. There is no class division in the difference of attitude.

Philopoemenis: cf. xxxi. 25. 3 n. He was *strategos* for 193/2, having recently returned from Crete. Cf. Errington, 90 ff.

7. ne . . . diceret: the only evidence for this provision. Cf. G. Busolt–H. Swoboda, *Griechische Staatskunde*, ii (Munich, 1926), 1529.

9. Because Philopoemen had assured them of his determination to carry out a decision for war conscientiously and energetically.

11. praeterquam . . . placeret: indicating that for Philopoemen the fact that Flamininus counselled waiting was itself a factor that weighed with him. Plutarch (*Phil.* 14. 4) and Pausanias (viii. 50. 7) make Philopoemen far more confident. Cf. Aymard, *PR*, 306 n. 1.

12. praesidium: cf. § 2 n.

26. 1. comparauerat . . . classem: perhaps before the war started; Nabis was thus acting in defiance of the peace treaty of 195: cf. xxxiv. 35. 5, Aymard, *PR*, 297 n. 16, Texier, 95 n. 14.

tectas naues: cf. xxxi. 22. 8 n.

pristesque: clearly the right reading. Cf. xxxii. 32. 9 n.

tradita . . . Romanis: xxxiv. 35. 5.

2. agilitatem: before L. used only of persons, but by him only of ships, as in xxvi. 51. 6, xxxvii. 30. 2. Cf. *TLL*, i. 1325–6, p. 9.

simulacris . . . pugnae: cf. p. 6.

3. terrestrium ... aequabat: for Philopoemen's military reforms in 208/7 cf. Pol. xi. 8 ff., Errington, 63–4. For Polybius' praise of Philopoemen's military ability in the comparison with Aristaenus see Pol. xxiv. 11. 2.

4. Philopoemen's experience was almost wholly limited to the affairs of the Peloponnese.

Arcas ... homo: Polybius was doubtless alluding to Homer's description of the Arcadians in *Iliad* ii. 614: ἐπεὶ οὐ σφι θαλάσσια ἔργα μεμήλει. Cf. Paus. viii. 50. 7.

externorum ... ignarus: *externorum omnium ignarus* is used of Minnio at 15. 8.

nisi ... militauerat: for Philopoemen's activities in Crete (220–210, 200–194) see Errington, ch. iii.

5. nauis erat: *ecphrasis* idiom. Cf. xxxiii. 28. 11 n., xxxiv. 25. 7.

quadriremis: called a trireme by Paus. viii. 50. 7.

octaginta ante cum: *ante octaginta cum* Bχ, *octoginta antequam* Mg. Either order is possible (cf. Packard, i. 402) but it is perhaps more likely that the order implied by Mg is the correction than vice versa.

octaginta ... ueheret: MSS. Plutarch (*Phil.* 14. 5) says it was forty years earlier. Craterus was the half-brother of Antigonus Gonatas. He was succeeded in command of the Macedonian garrison at Corinth by his son Alexander, who revolted from Gonatas *c.* 252. Alexander's wife was called Nicaea (Plut. *Arat.* 17. 2), but it is not impossible that it was also the name of the wife of Craterus. Plutarch's date is out of the question, since Corinth was in Achaean hands from 243. But it is hard to see in what circumstances the Achaean League as it was in 272 could have captured a Macedonian ship. That was the year in which Gonatas re-established himself in Macedon, but it seems very improbable that the renascent Achaeans would have taken sides so openly at that time. I am tempted to read *sexaginta*. About 252 Aratus was opposed to Alexander (cf. *Imperialism in the Ancient World* [xxxiv. 62. 12 n.], 150) and it could be that a Macedonian ship was bringing Alexander's wife or mother to him at Corinth when it was intercepted.

There is no case for taking *octoginta* as a round number and associating the episode with the Chremonidean War, as was done by Beloch, *Griechische Geschichte*, iv². 2 (Berlin–Leipzig, 1927), 519: cf. H. Heinen, *Untersuchungen zur hellenistischen Geschichte des 3. Jahrhunderts v.Chr.* (Wiesbaden, 1972), 192–3. Aymard, *PR*, 306 n. 2 supports the supplement *filii*, proposed by W. Schorn, *Geschichte Griechenlands* (Bonn, 1833), 271 n. 1.

6. Aegio: it had joined the league in 275 (Pol. ii. 41. 13) and at this period was the only place where a *synodos* could meet (cf. xxxi. 25. 2 n.).

putrem: the only occurrence of the word in L. It is first found in Varro, *RR* i. 8. 4. Cicero used *putridus* but that does not occur in L. at all.

7. praetoria naue: a 'flagship'. For examples see Packard, iii. 1089.

Patrensis Tiso: *Piso* MSS., which is not a Greek name. No other Tiso is known either, and the actual name must remain uncertain. The word-order is unusual. It is hard to see any reason for L. wishing to emphasize *Patrensis* (for the normal word-order with an adjective derived from a proper name cf. Marouzeau, *L'Ordre des mots*, i. 16 ff.).

8. compagibus: the only occurrence of the word in L.

9. speculatoria: Mg, *piscatoria* Bχ. It is unbelievable that Philopoemen was in a fishing boat, and *speculatoria* must be right. For *naues speculatoriae* cf. xxii. 19. 5, xxx. 10. 6, xxxvi. 41. 7, 42. 8, 43. 2.

fugit: χ, *fuit* BMg. The latter may be right, though the repetition *fugerunt . . . fugit . . . fugae* is not an argument against *fugit*. Indeed, if *fugit* is right, the repetition could be a deliberate attempt to emphasize Philopoemen's plight. (The alliteration *fugae finem . . . fecit* could also be deliberate.)

Patras: Philopoemen, as McDonald says, returned to his starting-point, and it is quite wrong to emend to *Prasias* (Rühl, *NJPhP* ccxvii [1883], 36: for his followers see Aymard, *PR*, 306 n. 2. See also Errington, 103 n. 1).

10. offendisset: implied *oratio obliqua*.

27. 2. Pleias ... Leucis ... Acriis: Acriae is Kokkina, on the east side of the Laconian Gulf and Leucae may be the plain to the south-east of Mt. Korkoula, rather than the town (cf. Strabo viii. 363C, Pol. iv. 36. 5, v. 19. 8, A. J. B. Wace, *BSA* xiv [1907–8], 162–3). It is tempting to identify Pleiae, known otherwise only from *IG* v. 1. 602. 12, with the modern town of Molaoi, which certainly commands the plain. It does not, however, command Kokkina and since no ancient remains have been found at Molaoi, it seems that Pleiae should be placed on the higher slopes of Mt. Korkoula. See Bölte, *RE*, xxi, 189–91, Walbank, *Commentary*, i. 485, 555.

Pausanias (viii. 50. 8) wrongly places the camp of Nabis attacked by Philopoemen near Gytheum itself.

3. statiua: a stationary camp, as opposed to a marching camp.

4. modo: i.e. but were no protection against storms, etc., or, as it turned out, were very much exposed to the sort of attack which Philopoemen launched.

praeberet: Frob. 1. *praeberent* Bχ, perhaps rightly, with *casas* as the antecedent of *quae* (cf. Pettersson, 39).

5. stationem ... Argiui: the southernmost part of Argive territory, over the border from Pleiae.

fundis: 'slings'.

alio ... armaturae: cf. W–M's note.

6. litora legens: *legere* with *litus, oram,* etc. does not occur before the Augustan age. Cf. xxi. 51. 7, xxii. 20. 7, xxxiii. 41. 5, xxxvi. 21. 5, xxxvii. 17. 8, xliv. 10. 8, *TLL,* vii. 2. 1127. 50 ff., Tränkle, *WS,* 125, p. 9.

propinquum: the nearest, but not all that near. Cf. Bölte, *RE* xxi. 190.

propinquum ... propinquo: cf. p. 13 and addenda.

egressus: probably to be taken with *callibus,* and therefore meaning 'marching from the shore', not 'disembarking', as it is taken by W–M, Sage, and *TLL,* v. 2. 284. 54.

7. sentirent ... senserant: 'realized': cf. xxxii. 17. 8 n.

8. ex tam ancipiti: *tam* Bψ, *tamen* φ, *tamen ex tam* Mg. The adversative is inappropriate and for *anceps* meaning simply 'dangerous' cf. *TLL,* ii. 25. 32 ff.

9–10. Tripolim ... discessit: on his way back to federal territory, not on a further expedition after such a return, as argued by Rühl, *NJPhP* cxxvii (1883), 36, Niese, ii. 683. Cf. Aymard, *PR,* 307 n. 4.

The only town of the Tripolis known is Pellana (cf. xxxiv. 29. 14 n.). See Bölte, *RE,* iiiA. 1319, Walbank, *Commentary,* i. 534. Pol. iv. 81. 7 is the only other reference to the Tripolis: W–M's note is incorrect.

11. concilioque: a *syncletos.* There is a brachylogy in the clause, since the allies could not participate in the *syncletos* itself.

sociis ... Acarnanum: presumably the alliances made at the time of the formation of the symmachy are regarded as being still in existence. Cf. Oost, *RPEA,* 56: *contra* Aymard, *PR,* 310 n. 16, Hammond, *Epirus,* 622, Cabanes, 279–80.

12. et suorum: *essent testes suorum et* MSS. McDonald's text (first printed in the 1513 Paris edition) makes excellent sense, but *essent testes* is an extraordinary corruption or interpolation and McDonald's explanation of it as a gloss on *principes* far from convincing. I suspect that something originally stood in its place.

restituti animi: I can find no parallel for *animum restituere* (*TLL*) though L. uses *restituere* in a wide variety of contexts.

13. Caryas: cf. xxxiv. 26. 9 n.

expugnatum est: Mg, *expugnatum* Bχ, probably rightly. The ellipse would be appropriate for this quick-moving military narrative.

Barbosthenem: both name and precise location are uncertain. B has *Barbosthenes* here, χ *Barbasthenes*, while at 30. 9 all MSS. have *Barnosthenes*. Loring (*JHS* xv [1895], 65) identified it with the mountain between Vasara and Vresthena, and it is certainly tempting to see a connection with the latter name.

14. Pyrrhi . . . castra: for the possible location cf. Loring, *JHS* xv, 65. It is not the same as the Πύρρου χάραξ of Pol. v. 19. 4 (cf. Walbank, *Commentary*, i. 555). For *castra Pyrrhi* in Epirus cf. xxxii. 13. 1 n. See also Oberhummer, *RE*, iii. 1771.

15. angustias viae: for a possible identification of Philopoemen's route see Loring, *JHS* xv, 65.

cogebatur agmen: cf. xxxiv. 28. 7 n.

militibus: χ, *equitibus* B, a clear case of careless copying, influenced by *equitibus* above.

quibus . . . fideret: cf. pp. 4, 8.

16. inopinatae: Bχ, *inopinantem* Mg. The position of *eum* is very strange, and it is possible that we should read *inopinantem* and delete *eum*.

28. See also Plut. *Phil.* 4. 9.

28. 1. ad id . . . animum: Mg, *se ad id* Bχ. Palaeographically it is easier to think that *animum* was omitted, and *se* added to complete the sense, than vice versa. Both phrases are perfectly suitable (*TLL*, v. 2. 1368–70), though neither occurs elsewhere in L.

2. faceret . . . haberet: for the iterative subjunctives cf. xxxiv. 38. 6 n.

3. derecta acie: *directa* B, *recta* χ. 'A drawn-out line of battle' is far more appropriate than χ's 'a due and proper line of battle' as in xxxiv. 28. 11. For *derigere* and *dirigere* cf. xxxiv. 28. 6 n.

4. exsequebatur: 'investigate'. The use of the verb in conjunction with the gerund or participle of another verb of inquiring and

followed by an indirect question appears to be confined to L. Cf.
vi. 14. 13, ix. 3. 11, 16. 4, xxv. 29. 10, xli. 7. 7, *TLL*, v. 2. 1853. 41 ff.

impedimenta ... sarcinas: *sarcinae* is the luggage itself, *impedimenta* the animals, attendants, etc., though *impedimenta* is sometimes used in the sense of *sarcinae* (*TLL*, vii. 1. 530). For the combination of *impedimenta* and *sarcinae* cf. xxv. 13. 12, xxxiv. 19. 10, xxxviii. 40. 10.

reiceret: for this use of *reicere* in the sense of placing in a position away from danger cf. viii. 8. 8.

8. Cretenses auxiliares: cf. 26. 4 n., xxxiii. 14. 4.

Tarentinos ... equos: *Tarentini* refers to a particular type of cavalry and does not indicate that they actually came from Tarentum. See G. T. Griffith, *The Mercenaries of the Hellenistic World* (Cambridge, 1935), 246 ff., Launey, i. 601–4, Walbank, *Commentary*, i. 529. This is the only evidence for 'Tarentines' having two horses (cf. the Numidians at xxiii. 29. 5). It is hard to believe and L. has probably misunderstood Polybius (cf. Griffith, op. cit. 248–9, Launey, i. 604).

aquari: the verb occurs almost entirely in military contexts (*TLL*, ii. 380–1).

9. aspretis: 'rough ground'. Used five times by L. and otherwise only in Grat. *Cyn.* 241 (*TLL*, ii. 846).

inaequabili: 'not level'. Elsewhere in this sense only in Varro, *RR* i. 6. 6 (*TLL*, vii. 1. 809).

10. riuo: = *torrentem* in § 8.

qualia [in] ... solent: for *in* 'in the case of' cf. xxvii. 42. 3, xxxi. 44. 2 n., xxxiv. 2. 1 n., Caes. *BG* vi. 7. 9, Pettersson, 7. Deletion is unnecessary, and *tam* narrows the point of *qualia ... solent*.

29. 1. Telemnastus: *Letemnastus* MSS., but the form is guaranteed by Pol. xxix. 4. 8, xxxiii. 16. 16. He is probably to be identified with the ambassador of Perseus mentioned in the former passage. He came from Gortyn (Pol. xxxiii. 16. 1: for Philopoemen's connections with that city cf. Errington, ch. iii, especially 37–8). For a monument to him at Epidaurus cf. *IG* iv². 1. 244 = *ISE* 49. See Olshausen, no. 125, Walbank, *Commentary*, iii. 558–9.

equitibus ... praeerat: i.e. he was *hipparchos*, the second-in-command to the *strategos* (cf. Aymard, *PR*, 304 n. 52). This is the first mention of Lycortas, the father of Polybius. For his career cf. Stähelin, *RE*, xiii. 2386 ff.

2. Cretenses ... Tarentini: I completely agree with McDonald's statement that the chiastic word-order is perfectly acceptable (it does not even seem particularly harsh) and that Madvig's suggested deletion of *Cretenses* and *Tarentini* and M. Müller's proposal to put a colon after *Tarentini* are both unnecessary and undesirable.

3. tyranni: χ, om. B. Something is needed, but I wonder if a word had dropped out and *tyranni* represents an emendation in χ.

effuse: *effusi* MSS., but the double participle cannot be paralleled, and *effuse sequi* occurs on nine other occasions in L. (Packard, ii. 39).

conuallem: a valley enclosed on all sides.

plerique ... et ... et: the repetition of *et* makes the illogicality much more striking than that in *multi caesi captique* in § 7 (cf. 30. 11, v. 26. 8, xxxvi. 19. 8). *uolnerati et occisi* occurs at ii. 17. 3 and *caesi et capti* at Vell. Pat. ii. 46. 1. Perhaps the first *et* should be deleted.

5. For the balance of this sentence cf. W–M's note.

et in hostes: χ, *in hostes* B, perhaps rightly (thus W–M, Walsh, *CR*, 54).

6. ad castra: Mg, *in castra* Bχ. *in castra* is L.'s normal usage, and *compellere in castra* occurs on twelve occasions (Packard, ii. 1044 ff.): but *compellere ad castra* is found at iv. 19. 6, x. 19. 20, xxxvii. 42. 8.

7. confragosa ... iniqua: *quacumque ... processisset* limits *iniqua* ('uneven in all those places where he had made a rash advance').

confragosus is a very appropriate word to apply to the country to the north-east of Sparta.

8. et ex ... et ex: Frob. 2. *et ex ... et* Mog (only the initial *et ex* is cited from Mg), *ex ... et ex* B, *ex ... ex* χ. *et ex ... et ex* is obviously what L. wrote. The repetition is unusual but is clearly designed to achieve emphasis.

fortuna pugnae: 'the outcome of the battle'. Cf. Kajanto, 78.

coniectans: the verb occurs in the edict of the elder Tiberius Sempronius Gracchus quoted by Gell. vi. 19. 7 (if that is genuine), once in Terence (*Eun.* 543), once in Caesar (*BC* iii. 106. 1), and eight times in L. (*TLL*, iv. 312–13).

9. ipsis ... moenibus: of Sparta. Cf. xxxiv. 28. 2.

progredi: Mg, *procedere* Bχ. Either is possible, and the fact that Bχ wrongly have *processit* at 27. 13 does not prove that *progredi* is correct here, as McDonald appears to suggest.

10. simul et: Mg, *simul etiam* Bχ. The latter collocation does not occur in Latin (cf. *TLL*, v. 2. 940 ff.).

11. fidem ... fecit: cf. xxxiii. 31. 9 n.

12. Pythagoran: cf. xxxiv. 25. 5 n. The MSS. evidence does not really justify McDonald's printing of the Greek formation here: cf. xxxiv. 40. 2 n.

30. 4. et diripiunt: Mg, om. Bχ. Though the understanding of *castra* from the previous clause is certainly not impossible (cf. W–M) I wonder if the phrase was added in Mg. (McDonald's 'sed impetu scriptum est' is an odd comment.)

    expediri: 'get through safely'. The MSS. have *expedire* which should be retained. Cf. Pettersson, 154 n. 2, Ogilvie, 435.

6. aduersae cadentes: why they all fall facing the enemy is not explained. (I cannot think what McDonald means by 'cf. *strage*'.) L. may well have misunderstood Polybius.

9. duarum portarum itineribus: the roads leading to the two gates.

    Pharas: possibly to be identified with Veria, a little north-east of Vasara. Cf. Loring, *JHS* xv (1895), 66 n. 153.

    Barbosthenem: cf. 27. 13 n.

10. regione eorum: McDonald defends the MSS. text as meaning (apparently) 'in the area where the Achaeans were'. But *se tenuerunt* conveys the idea of 'keeping away from' and the word-order strongly suggests that *regione* is to be taken with *tenuerunt*. *e regione* is therefore necessary.

11. praegressi ea sunt: both Landolfo di Colonna and modern scholars emended to *praetergressi*. McDonald's defence of *praegressi* (with *ea* = *ea via*) depends on his interpretation of *regione eorum*, rejected in the previous note. *praegredi*, however, equals *praetergredi* in Tacitus, *A.* xiv. 23. 3, and *praeuehi* in the sense of *praeteruehi* occurs at Tacitus, *Agr.* 28. 2, *H.* v. 16. 3, *A.* ii. 6. 4, and it does seem possible to conclude that L. used *praegressi* here to mean *praetergressi*. See Ogilvie, *Phoenix*, 347, Dorey, *JRS* lvii (1967), 279–80.

12–13. domum ... etiam: this final section of the narrative conceals the fact that Flamininus intervened to negotiate a truce with Nabis, by which Nabis surrendered the Laconian towns which he had occupied. See in particular Aymard, *PR*, 309–15. The truce is mentioned by Plutarch, *Phil.* 15. 3 and Pausanias viii. 50. 10. This intervention was probably the immediate cause of ill will between Philopoemen and Flamininus, enhanced by the Achaeans honouring Philopoemen in a way that equalled the honours given earlier to Flamininus (cf., apart from the present passage, 47. 4, Plut. *Phil.* 15. 1–2, *Flam.* 13. 2–3, Just. xxxi. 3. 3–4). L.'s omission of the episode is better explained if Flamininus' intervention came when the Achaean army was still in the field, as argued by Aymard, than if it occurred after Philopoemen's return to federal territory, as claimed by Errington, 106 and n. 1.

31–33. *The embassy of Flamininus*

Cf. Plut. *Flam.* 15. 1–4.

31. 1. circuire: B, *circumire* χ, *circumiere* Mog. Madvig's argument (*Emendationes*, 512) that the historic infinitive cannot be used because the action here is one that took place only once is not true in regard to the general rule, and even if it were, it is not the case that the verb here refers to only one action.

ad Antiochum: the Aetolians have not yet, of course, taken any firm decision to invite Antiochus to invade Greece.

2. quia ... esse: because both Nabis and the Aetolians were trying to upset the settlement of Greece imposed by Flamininus in 196 and 195.

3. Athenas ... Chalcidem ... Thessaliam: all places which had been freed from the fact (or, in the case of Athens, the threat) of Macedonian control by Rome's action in the Second Macedonian War. The ambassadors may have been responsible for imposing a pro-Roman government at Chalcis: cf. 37. 4, Walbank, *Philip V*, 195.

flexere: Mg, *direxere* Bχ. For *iter flectere* cf. viii. 19. 13, xxi. 31. 9, xxii. 18. 7, xxiii. 2. 1, xxv. 22. 14, xxxii. 29. 6, xxxviii. 22. 1, xlii. 67. 7. There is no example of *iter de(di-)rigere* in L., and the only example of the collocation in Classical Latin is Plancus *ap.* Cic. *fam.* x. 11. 2 (*TLL*, v. 1. 1240. 82 ff.).

3–4. Thessalos ... Magnetum: for the separate Magnesian κοινόν cf. xxxiii. 34. 6, Pol. xviii. 47. 6, Walbank, *Commentary*, ii. 617, Larsen, *Greek Federal States*, 295.

4. accuratior: cf. xxxiv. 5. 2 n.

principum: 'leading men', as usual: cf. xxxi. 17. 11 n.

5. reddi ... remitti: these promises were made in 193 but had not yet been implemented. Cf. xxxiv. 57. 1 n. See further xxxvi. 35. 11–14, xxxvii. 7. 16 nn.

uana ... esse: accepted as true by Holleaux, *Études*, v. 393 = *CAH*, viii. 205, Deininger, 76. (Deininger's claim that his view is shared by Walbank and Badian is unjustified: they rightly suspend judgement.)

6. Eurylochus: not known before these events. For a précis of his career cf. Deininger, *RE*, Supp. xi. 669–71.

princeps: again just 'a leading man', not 'der erste Mann', as W–M say. His official position is not given until § 11.

7. ita disserendum: L. thus approves of Flamininus' equivocations I doubt if Polybius also did so.

in quo ... esset: because in the event of an invasion by Antiochus Philip's loyalty was essential.

8. cum ... praecipue: a classic statement of the Roman view of a *clientela* relationship established by the performance of a *beneficium*. Ingratitude is a major crime in Flamininus' eyes. Cf. § 14, 39. 7, 48. 12–13 n., xxxvi. 20. 4, 35. 5, Badian, *FC*, 78 ff.

9. praesidium: cf. xxxi. 24. 1 n.

regiam: for the site of the palace cf. Wehrli, 196 n. 19, correcting F. Stählin–E. Meyer–A. Heidner, *Pagasai und Demetrias* (Berlin–Leipzig, 1934), 96 ff. The use of Demetrias as a royal residence is also mentioned by Strabo ix. p. 436C.

dominus: 'master'. Augustus did not permit the use of this form of address. Cf. Suet. *Aug.* 53. 1, Sherwin-White, *The Letters of Pliny* (Oxford, 1966), 557.

10. uetere: Mg, *noto* Bχ. *uetere* is clearly needed to balance *nouo* and, as McDonald says, *noto* must arise from a gloss on *experto*, which then replaced *uetere*.

11. summum ... uocant: L.'s own explanatory comment. Polybius will simply have said ὁ Μαγνητάρχης.

12. inconsultius euectus: Polybian interpretation. It could have been quite deliberate.

nutum: cf. 32. 9. These are the only two places where L. uses *nutus* of Roman domination of other peoples.

13. uariantis: 'intermingling', i.e. different sections of the crowd, not shouting different things at different times, as W–M suggest. *uariare* is regularly used with a direct object of the thing mixed and χ's accusatives must be read. When *uariare* is found with the ablative (cf. xxii. 36. 1, xxxviii. 57. 8) the ablatives mean 'in respect of' and do not define the content of the disagreement.

adeo exarsit: cf. Tac. *A.* i. 74. 4, '*Laudatio Turiae*' (*ILS* 8393), ii. 50.

perfidi: the OCT inadvertently omits *animi* after this word (spotted by Walsh, *CR*, 56).

14. eleganter actam: 'in a seemly way'. For similar usages cf. Cic. *Planc.* 31, *sen.* 13 (*TLL*, v. 2. 335. 74 ff.). One wonders what word Polybius used.

32. 1. concilio: L, *consilio* BNVϕ. L's reading is, of course, an emendation and *consilium* is often used in the sense of *concilium*. But since all the MSS. have *concilium* not only at 31. 3 (to which McDonald refers) but also (admittedly of a different meeting) at §§ 3 and 5 below, it does seem unlikely that L. wrote *consilium* here.

inde protinus: Mg, *protinus* Bχ. L. uses both *inde protinus* and *protinus inde*, but the phrase is not so common that Mg is likely to have added *inde* when L. wrote only *protinus*.

2. nudabant: 'laid bare'. Cf. xxiii. 5. 2, xxiv. 27. 4, xxxiii. 21. 8, xxxiv. 24. 7, xxxix. 15. 4, xl. 24. 2, xlii. 63. 1. Apart from L. the earliest examples of *nudare* in this sense are Horace, *Sat.* ii. 5. 47 and Ovid, *Am.* 2. 5. 5 (*TLL*).

forte: for *forte* of precise coincidence cf. 37. 3, J. Champeaux, *REL* xlv (1967), 378.

Thoas: cf. 12. 4 n.

quem . . . Antiochum: not previously mentioned (cf. p. 2 n. 1). He probably left in the autumn of 193: cf. W–M, Badian, *Studies*, 138 n. 84, Deininger, 69.

Menippum: cf. xxxiv. 57. 6 n.

3. concilium: the *Panaetolica* of 192. See § 7, Aymard, *RPh* 3ème série, xiv (1940), 102, Larsen, *TAPA* lxxxiii (1952), 25, Deininger, 70.

4. The inhabitants of Greece and Italy were always prone to exaggerate the resources of the rulers of the East. They did not realize that the latter could not conceivably commit the whole of their forces to an invasion of Europe, and leave the rest of their empire denuded of troops. Cf. 48. 2 ff., xxxiii. 19. 9 n., p. 31.

ex India elephantos: cf. xxxvii. 39. 13, 40. 2 ff. nn. On the form of *elephantos* cf. xxxii. 27. 2 n.

emere Romanos: to be taken literally, not as 'could bribe the Romans'.

5. apparebat: i.e. to Flamininus. Hence *nam* in the following sentence.

6. spes: *res* MSS. For *spem abscidere* cf. 45. 6, iv. 10. 4, xxiv. 30. 12, xlv. 25. 9. *rem abscidere* occurs at iii. 10. 8, but in the sense of 'their resources had been destroyed' and *abscisa res* would scarcely make any sense here.

non ab re esse: cf. p. 5.

7. Athenienses ... Aetolis: for other Athenian interventions in the Romano–Aetolian War cf. xxxvii. 6. 4–7. 7 nn., xxxviii. 10. 4–6, Pol. xxi. 31. 5–16. For Athenian relations with Aetolia cf. *StV*, iii. no. 470, a treaty dated to between 277 and 266/5: cf. Heinen, 141. For the renewal of relations after 228 cf. Flacelière, 256, 331. It is doubtful whether a formal treaty between the two states still existed. Athens seems to have demonstrated its non-involvement in the Aetolian disaffection by withdrawing from Amphictyonic meetings at this time: cf. Flacelière, 352 ff.

et propter: Mg, *propter et* Bχ. W–M's note says all that is necessary.

8. renuntiauit legationem: cf. xxxi. 17. 4 n.

intromissus: also used of *legati* at xxxii. 37. 5.

integris ... Antiochum: Antiochus had in fact remained deliberately neutral during the Second Macedonian War. He could have intervened if he had so chosen.

9. nutum: cf. 31. 12 n.

11. libertate ... quae: 'a freedom which ...'. The relative clauses do not define *libertas*, as Sage's translation suggests.

13. consilia ... esse: cf. xxxi. 32. 2, also in relation to the Aetolians.

14. uerbis ... disceptarent: i.e. negotiate.

33. This chapter probably represents a considerable elaboration of what L. found in Polybius. See the notes on *iusta ac necessaria, generis humani, lanistis,* and *maiestatem*. The two unusual usages of *mouere* also serve to emphasize the occasion.

33. 1. multitudo ... principum: the words here do not necessarily imply a class division, but the class meaning (in relation to the same point) is apparent at 34. 3 (see n. ad loc.): cf. *Studies in Ancient Society*, 56–7.

3. moturum aliquid: 'would produce some change in the situation'. The meaning is not quite the same as in xxviii. 36. 5, xxxiii. 35. 6, adduced as parallels by W–M, where *mouere* has the sense of 'stir up trouble'. L. uses *mouere* and *motus* four times in twelve lines here (§ 4 *fides mota*, § 6 *magno motu, mouissent*) and two of these instances are unusual.

iusta ... necessaria: the usual justification for all Rome's wars. L. may have elaborated Polybius here.

4. a principio societatis: i.e. in 212/1.

fides mota: as the Romans claimed, by making peace with Philip in 206: cf. xxxi. 1. 8 n. There is no other instance where Rome could claim that the Aetolians had broken their treaty obligations.

fides mota must mean something like 'refrained from keeping faithfully to their treaty' but it is hard to find any parallels for *mouere* in this sense (*fidem mouere* in Ovid, *Fasti* iv. 204 has a completely different meaning). *mouere* of violation of religion looks promising (*TLL*, viii. 1541. 8 ff.) but all the examples of this have a much closer physical meaning.

iure ... ambigeretur: i.e. the cities of Phthiotic Achaea. Cf. xxxiii. 13. 9–12 n. For the final senatorial decision cf. xxxiii. 49. 8 n.

5. mittere legatos: which is what they had already done, and achieved no satisfaction.

6. lanistis Aetolis: an entirely Roman notion, and it is very hard to think that anything comparable stood in Polybius. *lanista* in this metaphorical sense occurs several times in Cicero (cf. *TLL*, vii. 2. 933).

generis humani: for *genus humanum* cf. Plaut. *Poen.* 1187, Enn. *Ann.* 317V, Lucr. v. 1156, Cic. *de or.* i. 60, iii. 113, *n.d.* ii. 79. The concept of the human race as a whole is absent from Polybius and again one wonders whether he expressed himself in quite these terms here.

7. uaticinatus: i.e. what he said should be avoided in fact happened.

8. concilio: *consilio* Bχ. Cf. 32. 1 n.

   quo ... Romanos: see p. 33.

9–10. De Sanctis (iv. 1. 137–8) rejects this story (also referred to by App. *Syr.* 21. 94 and Zon. ix. 19. 12) on the grounds that Flamininus was still received as a friend and the peace was not yet finally broken. But that is no reason for refusing to believe that Damocritus behaved in a particularly arrogant way, and the decree was, after all, a virtual declaration of war (cf. p. 33).

9. Damocritus praetor: cf. 12. 6 n. He was federal *strategos* for 193/2.

10. maiestatem: a Roman concept, again probably not in Polybius.

aliud: Gel. 'in neutro inuenitur', *primo aliud* Bχ. *primo* is pleonastic with *in praesentia* and probably arose as a gloss on it. *aliud*, moreover, needs to be in the emphatic first position, in contrast to *decretum responsumque*.

34. *Aetolian activities*

34. 1. inde ut ... nihil: *inde ut quaeque de Antiocho* B, *inde ut quaeque de Antiocho nihil* ψ, *inde ut quemque de Antiocho nihil* φ. There is no prospect of finding anything like a satisfactory remedy for what may well be a very deep corruption. McDonald's supplement involves the assumption that the Aetolians did not want to appear to be inactive. But the effect of not holding assemblies and delegating all business to the *apocleti* was precisely to keep their activity secret, and *ne* gives the opposite of the sense required (if one reads *ut* the clause may be consecutive rather than final). Nor is it easy to follow McDonald in taking *inde* in a temporal sense. With *Corinthum* preceding the usage would be ambiguous, giving the impression of having a spatial meaning.

2. apocletos: on the *apocleti*, a committee of the council of the Aetolian League, see Walbank, *Commentary*, i. 454 ff., iii. 64, Larsen, *Greek Federal States*, 200 ff. See further 45. 9 n.

sanctius: 'venerable'. Also used of the Carthaginian inner senate at xxx. 16. 3.

consilium: *concilium* MSS., but an advisory body is normally called *consilium* and the form could very easily have been influenced by *concilium* above.

3. Cf. 33. 1 n. Deininger, 72–3, denies any implication of class division here too, arguing that Polybius referred only to οἱ τὰ βέλτισθ' αἱρούμενοι—those who chose the right policy (in Polybius' eyes). This is perverse: there is no reason to doubt that Polybius did refer to a class division here, though that does not mean, of course, that there were not individual anti-Roman *principes* (cf. Deininger, 72 n. 34). Thoas himself is called a *princeps* at 32. 2. χ in fact reads *principes optimum quemque* which gives just the sense that Deininger wants. But (*a*) it is unusual for B to make an addition to what stood in F (*b*) apart from i. 7. 5 L.'s normal idiom is to use a noun in the genitive plural with *quisque* and a superlative.

4. cum rei ⟨tum⟩: M. Müller, *uno die* MSS., which makes no sense. L. cannot have meant to say that all the decisions were taken on one day, and the words in this position cannot refer to a plan to capture Chalcis, Demetrias, and Sparta all on the same day, even if it were likely that the Aetolians would have entertained such a proposition (cf. Madvig, *Emendationes*, 513). *quoque* demands some sort of contrast, and this is certainly given by Müller's emendation (for *cum ... tum ... quoque* cf. i. 22. 2). Solutions introducing an epithet after *consilium* fail to give the required contrast, but again the corruption may be deep and Müller's reading can be regarded as no more than hypothetical.

5. Alexamenus: Aetolian *strategos* in 197/6. Cf. Walbank, *Commentary*, ii. 608.

Diocles: the *hipparchos* (§ 9). Not known otherwise.

6. exul . . . dictum est: 31. 11–32. 1.

7. sordida ueste: cf. i. 10. 1, of the parents of the Sabine women. One might compare the senate's assumption of mourning before the exile of Cicero in 58.

uelamenta: the ἱκετηρία, or olive-branch carried by a suppliant. Cf. xxxvi. 20. 1, xxxvii. 28. 1. The word is not used in this sense before L. Cf. p. 9.

⟨**in**⟩ **contionem . . . accierunt:** Madvig. *contionem . . . adierunt* MSS. The posited corruption is extremely easy, and the correction can be regarded as virtually certain.

insontem indemnatum: for the alliterative asyndeton cf. xxvii. 43. 7 *improuisum inopinatum*, Preuss, 52.

8. Aetolico: cf. 46. 3 n.

et pro se: Mg, *pro se* Bχ. The asyndeton is quite possible, though Bχ do wrongly omit *ex* in § 10 below.

9. luce prima: χ, *prima luce* B. Both are possible (Packard, iii. 122, 1097–8) and there is no obvious way of deciding between them.

10. desilire . . . ex equis: Mg, om. *ex* Bχ. *desilire* with the ablative alone does not occur in prose before the younger Seneca (*TLL*, v. 1. 721. 80 ff.).

itineris maxime modo: 'more as if they were on a journey than anything else'.

12. domos: the original form of the accusative plural. *domus* was later introduced by analogy. *domos* is the form found in the overwhelming majority of cases in the MSS. of L. (cf. *TLL*, v. 1. 1953. 10).

35–37. 3. *The murder of Nabis and its aftermath*

Cf. Paus. viii. 50. 10. Nabis' death is also mentioned by Plut. *Phil.* 15. 3, Zon. ix. 19. 2. On the date of the episode cf. Aymard, *PR*, 315 n. 7.

The Aetolian motive for murdering Nabis was presumably the desire to commit Sparta to the war against Rome. Despite his actions against the Laconian towns Nabis has not yet committed

himself to a final breach of his peace with Rome. Cf. De Sanctis,
iv. 1. 138.

35. 1. A carefully balanced sentence, with *Lacedaemone* at the beginning, in emphatic contrast with Demetrias, followed by exactly
corresponding word-order. The sentence is even more effective if
we follow B in omitting *erat*.

2. spoliatum ... Romanis: the reference must be to recent events,
not to the terms of the peace of 195 (xxxiv. 35. 10). Probably the
towns, including Gytheum, were surrendered by the truce arranged
by Flamininus (30. 12–13 n., Aymard, *PR*, 312). Others believe
that they had previously been recaptured by Atilius and, perhaps,
Eumenes (thus Holleaux, *CAH*, viii. 204 = *Études* v. 392–3, Walbank, *Philip V*, 195, Thiel, 284, Hansen, *Attalids*, 73). On Atilius
cf. 37. 3 n., on Eumenes 39. 1 n. Errington's implication (104) that
the coastal towns remained in Nabis' possession ignores the present
passage.

    qui occupasset ... laturum: *oratio obliqua* reflecting the
thoughts of the Aetolians. There is no case for supplementation,
and I do not find it particularly harsh, as McDonald claims.

3. illis ... rebellasset: cf. 12. 6 ff.

4. Alexameno: cf. 34. 5 n.
    consilio ... est: the *apocleti* (34. 2 n.). Here φNV have *consilio*,
BL *concilio*.

5. pro eo ... tamquam: the phrase appears to be a combination
of *pro eo ... quod* and *tamquam*. It is not really parallel to *pro eo ac*,
sicut, etc., as W–M claim.

6. On Alexamenus' route, and the possibility that he came by sea,
cf. Aymard, *PR*, 244 n. 61, 316 and n. 8.

7. iam transisse: cf. 23. 10 n.
    transisse in Europam: Mg, *in Europam transisse* Bχ. Decision is
impossible.
    terras ... uiris: for the asyndeton *terras maria* cf. xli. 3. 1, xliv.
22. 8, Preuss, 35–6, for *armis uiris* xxviii. 37. 8, Preuss, 74. For the
three-membered asyndeton *arma, uiri, equi* cf. 44. 5 n. See p. 11.
    completurum: χ, *impleturum* B. Either is possible, and though B
could have been influenced by *impleuit* above, the repetition is far
from impossible.
    numerum iniri: 'be calculated'. Cf. *TLL*, vii. 1. 1298, 63 ff.

9. Nabidi quoque et ipsi: Bχ. *nam id quoque ipsi* Mg. Madvig

(*Emendationes*, 515 n. 1) wrongly asserted 'quoque et ipse non recte dicitur' (cf. McDonald's parallels). The corruption of *Nabidi* does not instil much confidence in the rest of Mg's reading, and Bχ's text makes excellent sense. Alexamenus' point is that Nabis too, like the Aetolians, must have his army ready for the arrival of Antiochus. (But I do not understand what McDonald means by '*quoque* de re, *et* ad personam'.)

simul: joining *acueret* and *exerceret*, not linking them both with what precedes.

10. iniucundum: the only occurrence of the word in L.

11 ff. As the story reaches its climax L. heightens the effect by a series of sentences in asyndeton.

11. media fere in acie: B^{1}χ, *in media fere acie* B. F clearly had *media . . . in* and Walsh (*CR*, 54) wrongly suggests that *in media* is the reading of 'the earlier manuscripts'.

uectabatur: cf. p. 6.

12. ante auxiliares: presumably mercenaries.

13. in rem esse: cf. p. 5.

14. recipiendi: MSS. There is no other instance in L. of *recipere* for *se recipere*, but *se* is omitted with other similar verbs (cf. the passages adduced by McDonald) and *recipere* for *se recipere* is found in Caesar. The case for keeping the MSS. reading is therefore convincing (cf. Madvig, *Emendationes*, 515 n. 1: *contra* Ogilvie, *Phoenix*, 347).

15. patrando: L^2, clearly correctly, *parando* Bχ. On *patrare* cf. p. 5.

16. agenda . . . audendaque: cf. xxii. 14. 14, 53. 7, xxv. 16. 19, 23. 15, Skard, 12.

animos dextras: for the asyndeton cf. xxii. 29. 11, Preuss, 87–8.

17. cepit: cf. 36. 2, xxxi. 2. 9 n.

18. ponere hastas: almost certainly the same misinterpretation of Polybius as in xxxiii. 8. 13. Cf. n. ad loc., Tränkle, 180.

19. exspirauit: cf. p. 4.

36. 1. citato gradu: as in viii. 6. 2, xxviii. 14. 17. It presumably has the same sense as *pleno gradu* (cf. xxxiv. 15. 3 n.). Apart from L. *citato gradu* occurs in prose only at Curt. iv. 16. 6 (*TLL*, iii. 1201. 71 ff.). Cf. p. 9.

regiam: there is no evidence for the position of the royal palace.

2. cepit: cf. 35. 17 n.

3. et: Mg, om. Bχ, perhaps correctly.

4–5. Typically Polybian criticism of mistakes in political action. Cf. Aymard, *PR*, 317.

4. si: Walsh's suggestion of *ni* (*CR*, 56) produces complete nonsense. 37. 2 clearly refers back to this sentence, even though Philopoemen makes his speech to the *multitudo*, while Alexamenus ought to have addressed the *principes*.

5. oportuit: 'as was right that it should happen'. Polybius may have said only 'as was to be expected'.

　fraude: 'by deception'. Supplementation is unnecessary.

6. dux … Aetoli: though Alexamenus was an Aetolian. Cf. Cic. *diu.* i. 121 *Dareus et Persae ab Alexandro et Macedonibus uincerentur*, K–St, ii. 25.

7. contemptus: of the Spartans for the Aetolians.

　animos … fecit: cf. xxxi. 18. 3–4 n.

　uideretur interceptam: 'removed just when it seemed to be being restored'. The sense is far clearer if a comma is placed after *uideretur*. *intercipere* in the sense of 'remove' is not found before L. (*TLL*, vii. 1. 2165. 65 ff.). Cf. p. 9.

8. Laconicus: not known as a Spartan name. Nissen (*KU*, 173) may well have been right in suggesting that L. has misunderstood a phrase in Polybius referring to 'a Spartan boy': *contra* Bradford, op. cit. (xxxiv. 29. 8 n.), 257.

　eductus: cf. i. 39. 6, xlii. 19. 4, and, if the normal emendation is accepted, xxiv. 4. 5. *educere* meaning 'educate' is common in all periods of Latin. See *TLL*, v. 2. 119. 80 ff.

9. Chalcioecon: *Chalcioten* MSS. For the temple see Walbank, *Commentary*, i. 469–70.

　Mineruae … templum: perhaps added by L. from his own knowledge or inquiries. On *aereum* cf. p. 4.

10. Megalen polin: cf. xxxii. 5. 4–5 n.

　magistratibus: the local magistrates of the cities, not federal authorities.

37. 1–3. On Philopoemen's action in bringing Sparta into membership of the Achaean League and the terms of its adherence see Aymard, *PR*, 318 ff., Errington, 109 ff. Plutarch (*Phil.* 15. 4–5) distinguishes between those who were unwilling to join the Achaeans and the ἄριστοι who were so willing. As Errington says, the latter cannot have been completely hostile to Nabis, or they would not have been able to continue to live in Sparta under his rule.

L. has no mention of the offer to Philopoemen of 120 talents, proceeds from the sale of Nabis' property, reported by Pol. xx. 12, Plut. *Phil.* 15. 6–12, Paus. viii. 51. 2: cf. Errington, 111 ff., Walbank, *Commentary*, iii. 2, 85 ff. (dating the incident to 191).

1. audita caede: perhaps not immediately. See Aymard, *PR* 318 n. 21.

3. On Atilius (60) cf. 20. 9 ff., 22. 2, xxxiv. 54. 3 n. He had probably only just arrived in Greek waters: cf. Errington, 94 ff., against the view of Aymard, *PR*, 309 ff., that he came earlier, but was instructed by Flamininus to hold his hand. For the view that he was responsible for the recapture of the Laconian coast towns cf. 35. 2 n. Zon. ix. 19. 2 says that he did nothing. Atilius' decision to stay at Gytheum may have been determined by his hearing of the death of Nabis: cf. Aymard, *PR*, 318 n. 22.

forte: cf. 32. 2 n.

quattuor et uiginti: at xxxvi. 42. 7 he has 25. One, no doubt, was temporarily out of commission. See Thiel, 259.

37. 4—38. *Aetolian attack on Chalcis*

On these events cf. Deininger, 80 ff.

4–5. See W–M's comments on the lack of clarity in this period.

4. Thoas: cf. 12. 4 n.

Euthymidam: in Chalcis he was doubtless called Euthymides, and he is probably to be identified with the man given a proxeny by the Aetolians *c.* 208/7 (*IG* ix. 1². 1. 31. 67 ff.). See Schmitt, *RE*, Supp. ix, 65. Deininger, 81 nn. 7–8. Deininger's inference from 38. 1 that Euthymides was a magistrate at the time of his banishment is not justified.

5. Herodorum: not otherwise known.

Cianum mercatorem: on Cius cf. vol. i, 36–7, xxxi. 1. 9–10, 31. 4 nn. It had been an ally of Aetolia before its capture by Philip in 202. It had remained in Prusias' possession after 196 (cf. Walbank, *Commentary*, ii. 611) and it seems likely that Herodorus was a permanent exile rather than a merchant engaged in regular trading with his homeland.

6. Salganea: on Salganeus, a little north of the Euripus, see the full discussion of Bakhuizen, especially 133–9 on the events of this year.

Thronium: cf. xxxii. 36. 3 n.

7. Thoas et: *et Thoas* MSS. Deletion of *et*, adopted by Madvig, has a lot to be said for it. But the position of *Thoas* remains striking (cf. p. 15).

Atalanten: an island in the bay of Opus. Cf. Oberhummer, *RE*, ii. 1889, P–K, i. 2. 353.

8. pedestres: but clearly including the *equites* of § 7.

Aulidi: on Aulis, to the south of the Euripus, see Bakhuizen, 152 ff.

9. ipse: Thoas, but the meaning is not at all clear.

maxime: H. J. Müller's suggestion that *maxime* should follow *quanta* is quite gratuitous.

38. 1. Micythio: the form of the name is guaranteed by *Syll.*[3] 585, no. 106, *IG* xii. 9. 904, which probably refers to the same man. But Appian, *Syr.* 12. 49 is not evidence for the form, as McDonald suggests, since it is an emendation there also (Appian's mention of him at that point is in fact an error). The name is also corrupted in the Vienna MS. at xliii. 7. 5. Cf. Stähelin, *RE*, xv. 1561 ff.

Xenoclides: *enoclides* B, *enochides* χ, but the true form, correctly preserved in χ at 51. 6, is not in doubt. He is not known apart from these events.

2. prodi et deseri: for the phrase cf. Ogilvie, *YCS* xxiii (1973), 160–1.

consilio . . . adiecerunt: 'directed their attention to the following plan'. Sage mistranslates 'they increased their courage by the following scheme'. On *animum adicere* and *talis* meaning 'the following' see pp. 4, 6.

3. Amarynthidis Dianae: Amarynthus is just to the east of Eretria, within its territory. The temple of Artemis there (Ἄρτεμις Ἀμαρυνθία or Ἀμερυσία) was famous. Cf. Hirschfeld, *RE*, i. 1742, L. R. Farnell, *Cults of the Greek States*, ii (Oxford, 1896), 468.

celebratur: almost certainly taken over from Polybius anachronistically, and not used because L. knew of a continuing celebration in his own day. For similar cases of careless repetition of a Polybian tense cf. xxxiii. 17. 6, xxxiv. 51. 4–6 nn.

5. graue: a misprint for *graues*.

6. respectus: *respectus* in the sense of 'consideration for' occurs only in Cicero, *Phil.* v. 49 before L., who uses it frequently (*TLL*).

expertas: φ, clearly by emendation: *expertos* Bψ. A *constructio ad sensum* (cf. x. 1. 3, K–St, i. 27) would hardly be possible here.

7. Salganea: Bakhuizen, 134–5, argues convincingly that the Chalcidians encamped in hills south-west of Salganeus, not at Salganeus itself, and suggests that Polybius wrote κατὰ Σαλγανέα. For the fortifications in these hills see Bakhuizen, 41 ff.

8. caduceator: cf. xxxi. 38. 9 n.
  suo: placed first for emphasis.

10. catena: this metaphorical use of *catena*, in reference to rule by another, is very rare, and in the two other instances in Classical Latin (*Pan. Mess.* 117, Sen. *apoc.* 12. 16) *colla* is included in the metaphor. Cf. *TLL*, iii. 606. 58 ff.

13. profectosque: a somewhat odd word to use of a retreat.

14. Atalante: cf. 37. 7 n.

39. *Further events at Demetrias*

1. quoque: Flamininus, like Euthymides and Herodorus, made a move as a result of hearing what had happened at Chalcis. W–M are being rather hard in remarking that the connection is 'locker und unklar'.

  Chalcidi⟨co⟩: a certain correction for the *Chalcide* of the MSS. To the passages mentioned by W–M add Val. Max. i. 8. 10 *Chalcidico freto*. On the Euripus cf. xxxi. 24. 7 n., and add a reference to Pease on Cic. *n.d.* iii. 24.

  Eumeni: the first mention of his presence. For discussion of the possibility that he was present in Greece earlier see Errington, 104 n. 2 (add a reference to Thiel, 284 n. 370). Cf. 35. 2 n.

4. Eunomo praetori: Eunomus held office for only the last four months of 193/2, Epidromus being the original *strategos* (Eus. *Chron.* i. 243 Schöne, Niese, ii. 689 n. 5).

  scripsit ... iuuentutem: as a *legatus* Flamininus had no authority to issue such instructions, nor did the Thessalians have any treaty obligations to mobilize their forces on Roman orders.

  ⟨Villium⟩: Frob. 2, om. Bχ. Eunomus cannot be the object of *praemisit*. It is hard to conceive why the earlier editors should have printed *Iulium*. On P. Villius Tappulus (10) cf. xxxi. 4. 3 n.

5. Thiel, 286, thinks a naval engagement took place at this point: cf. xxxvii. 34. 5 n.

6. Magnetarches Eurylochus: cf. 31. 11. He was presumably reinstated as Magnetarches on his return to Demetrias.

    libertate: the Aetolians claimed to be liberating the places they occupied: cf. 38. 9.

7. altercatio: cf. 17. 2 n.

    ingratos: the same accusation as had been made by Flamininus at 31. 14: cf. 31. 8 n.

    inrito incepto: a favourite phrase of L. (Packard, ii. 1231, 1331).

8. praetorem: Eunomus.

40–41. *Events in Rome and Italy*

40. 1. For the sentiment cf. xxxiii. 20. 13 n.

    de spatio: 'off my course'. Cf. Cic. *am.* 40.

40. 2–4. *Wars in the North*

This report is a manifest doublet of 21. 7–22. 4, 24. 1–3. There Lucius Flamininus is recalled to hold the elections after both consuls have fought the Boii, Flamininus having gone there *per Ligures.* The victory over the Ligurians reported here is there given to Q. Minucius Thermus, the consul of 193. L. has clearly used two different annalistic sources in the two passages. Cf. Kahrstedt, 69–70, Lauterbach, 68 ff., G. Mezzar-Zerbi, *RSC* vii (1959), 154–5, 158 ff. (though Lauterbach and Mezzar-Zerbi think that 21. 7–11 comes from the same source as the present passage). Klotz, *Livius,* 85–6, Zimmerer, 33–5 most unconvincingly deny that there is a doublet.

For the later accusation that Lucius Flamininus killed a Boian chieftain to please his boy-lover cf. xxxix. 42. 5 ff.; for other sources see Astin, *Cato,* 80 n. 6. Cf. Toynbee, ii. 622–4.

3. senatus . . . sese: as in 22. 4 *pauci cum praefectis, deinde uniuersus senatus.* The expression there is far more logical.

    sese: χ, *se* B. Decision is impossible: L. uses both *se* and *sese* in the final place of a sentence (cf. Packard, iv. 537, 619–20).

4. praeda: cf. 21. 11.

40. 5–6. *Colonization of Vibo*

On the site of Vibo cf. xxxi. 3. 3 n. For the decision to found the colony see xxxiv. 53. 2. Velleius (i. 14. 8) wrongly dates the colony to 237.

6. triumuiri ... Crassipes: on the *triumuiri* cf. xxxiv. 53. 2 n.

quina dena ... equitibus: cf. 9. 8 n. Brunt, 193, oddly says that the infantry allocation was 30 *iugera*, and at 295 this has become 20 (Brunt gives the correct figure at *Latomus* xxxiv [1975], 623).

equitibus: Mg, *equiti* Bχ, correctly. 9. 8 and xxxiii. 23. 9, adduced by McDonald, are not parallel, and elsewhere L. always uses the singular in this phrase. Cf. Packard, ii. 125.

Bruttiorum ... Graecis: cf. xxxiv. 45. 4 n.

40. 7–8. *Earthquakes and fires at Rome*

The usual prodigy list for 192 occurs at 21. 6, immediately before the report of events in the north. It is thus very probable that this report comes from the same source as that of the variant report of northern events in § 2–4. On the style of this report cf. xxxiv. 55. 1–4 n.

7. [in] triduum: as McDonald says, L. uses *in triduum* only for the decreeing of *supplicationes*, etc. For the evidence cf. Packard, ii. 1141.

8. uanus ... uera: cf. xxxiv. 12. 4 n.

41. 1–7. *Provinces and armies*

41. 1. magis et: Madvig, *magna* Bχ. The change to *magis* is unavoidable, but the case for adding *et* is not compelling.

bello Antiochi: Mg, *Antiochi bello* Bχ. Decision is difficult. The former is the normal order, but L. may have wanted to emphasize *Antiochi*.

2. Normally decisions about provinces are made at the beginning of the new consular year. Though the consuls were elected earlier than usual there is nothing surprising in the decisions not being made immediately after the elections, as W–M claim. In any case there is no way of evaluating the relative chronology of L.'s various annalistic sections, and the actual date of the elections is quite uncertain. Since the lots are not drawn until the beginning of the consular year 191 (xxxvi. 2) it is not clear how the present decision would make the magistrates *intentiores*.

3. quo ... censuisset: cf. 20. 7 n.

eam: *iam* MSS., which scarcely makes sense. Madvig's emendation (*Emendationes*, 515) is inevitable.

4. Cf. pp. 37–8.

socium Latini nominis: cf. xxxi. 8. 7 n.

6. decretum est: χ, *decretum* B, probably rightly. Cf. xxxvi. 2. 8 n.,
Packard, i. 1156.

duae: sc. *prouinciae*. Madvig (*Emendationes*, 515–16) proposed
duplex, but withdrew this in the 1884 edition. For the combination
of the urban and peregrine praetorships cf. xxxi. 6. 2 n.

urbanaque: χ, *urbana* B. *-que* is not necessary, but it is unlikely
that χ would have seen any reason for adding it.

41. 8. *Dedication of temples*

For the problems involved in this passage see the discussion in
xxxi. 21. 12 n.

41. 9–10. *Aedilician activities*

9. On the laws that were being breached cf. 7. 2–5 n. The accusations are not for breach of the regulation reported at 7. 5 (thus
W–M) since that would not involve a criminal case.

On the judicial activities of aediles cf. xxxi. 50. 2 n., add R. A.
Bauman, *Latomus* xxxiii (1974), 245 ff. The procedure was probably
a direct accusation before a *iudicium populi*, not a trial following
prouocatio, as W–M say. Cf. W. Kunkel, *ABAW* n.f. lvi (1962), 34.

M. Tuccio: (5). He was praetor in 190 (xxxvi. 45. 9, xxxvii. 2. 6)
with *imperium* prorogued in 189 and 188, and a *iiiuir* for the supplementation of Sipontum and Buxentum in 186. He is the only
member of his *gens* known to have held a republican magistracy or
entered the senate.

P. Iunio Bruto: (54). Cf. xxxiv. 1. 4 n.

10. quadrigae inauratae: for similar dedications cf. xxix. 38. 8,
xxxviii. 35. 4, Weinstock, 56.

in cella . . . aediculae: the *cella* of Jupiter was the central of the
three *cellae* of the great temple of the Capitoline Triad. It is called
an *aedicula* only because it is a subdivision of the temple as a whole.
At 10. 12 L. says merely in *fastigio Iovis aedis*.

clupea inaurata: cf. 10. 12. There is no reason why such dedications should not have been made in successive years, and there is no
case for seeing the two passages as a doublet, as claimed by Walsh,
Livy, 148, Walbank, *Livy*, 70 n. 89.

portam Trigeminam: cf. 10. 12 n.

inter lignarios: the quarter of the carpenters. This is the only
reference to it. For possible remains of the portico cf. Le Gall, 103.

42–51. *Events in Greece and Asia*

This account comes from Polybius' narrative for the Olympiad year 192/1, in book xx.

Cf. Diod. xxix. 1, App. *Syr.* 12–13, Zon. ix. 19. 4–5.

42. 1. intentis: taking up 41. 2 *intentiores*.

ne ... quidem: 'not either'. Cf. xxxiii. 44. 7 n.

2. Zmyrna ... Lampsacus: on Smyrna and Lampsacus cf. xxxiii. 38. 3 n. Alexandria Troas has not been mentioned before, and it is best to assume that it had been captured by Antiochus, but had now defected. See Schmitt, *Antiochos*, 284, and literature there cited: *contra* Walbank, *Commentary*, iii. 106. It had been founded (as Antigonia) by Antigonus Monophthalmus between 310 and 301 and renamed by Lysimachus after the battle of Ipsus. Cf. Magie. i. 69, ii. 875 n. 63, Walbank, *Commentary*, i. 606–7. Wehrli, 86–7. For Smyrna's dedication of a temple to *Roma* in 195 see Tac. *A.* iv. 56. 1.

3. apertae: as McDonald rightly says, there is no case for emending or deleting this word on the grounds that at xxxiv. 60. 5 Hannibal had asked for *naues tectae*. Antiochus had never accepted the proposals made then by Hannibal, and the fleet now prepared was a compromise. Cf. xxxiv. 61. 1 n., Passerini, *Athenaeum* n.s. xi (1933), 13 n. 2.

4. Thoante: for Thoas' second embassy to Asia in 192 see also App. *Syr.* 12. 46–7.

Demetriadem ... esse: which was, of course, true.

6. mouere sententiam: 'to shake his resolve'. Cf. Cic. *Att.* vii. 3. 6.

regis: cf. p. 14.

11. prope: χ, om. B. *prope* weakens the force of the clause, and were it not for the many omissions by B in this chapter, I would be tempted to delete it.

12. iuuenta: cf. pp. 5, 7.

orbis terrarum imperium: exaggerated, but it could have stood in Polybius. For such phrases cf. Momigliano, *JRS* xxxii (1942), 53 ff., Fraenkel, *Horace* 451 n. 4. For other exaggerations with *orbis terrarum* cf. 12. 18 n.

14. praegrauatura: *praegrauare* occurs in Horace, *Sat.* ii. 2. 78, *Epp.* ii. 1. 13, and four times in L. (*TLL*: cf. E. Wistrand, *Eranos* lxiii [1965], 45–6). See p. 9.

43. 1. The comment may well have stood in Polybius, though for a similar remark by L. cf. vi. 34. 7. See also Sallust, *Cat.* 7. 2, Skard, 10, Gries, *Hommages Renard* (Brussels, 1969), i. 390. Cf. xxxiv. 37. 4 n.

uirtutem . . . alienum: *alienum* is to be taken with both *uirtus* and *bonum*. The alteration of *et* to *ut* would imply that such people had no *uirtus* at all (see Drakenborch ad loc.).

3. Ilium . . . sacrificaret: as did Xerxes when invading Greece (Hdt. vii. 43. 2: cf. How and Wells ad loc.) and Alexander and L. Scipio on invading Asia (Diod. xvii. 17. 6 ff., Arr. i. 11. 7, Plut. *Alex.* 15. 7 [Alexander], xxxvii. 37. 3 [Scipio]). For Ilium's submission to Antiochus, probably in 197, cf. Schmitt, *Antiochos*, 290 ff.

4. Imbrum: probably still independent at this time. Cf. xxxiii. 30. 11 n.

Sciathum: cf. xxxi. 28. 6 n. It was perhaps now part of the Magnesian *koinon*.

Pteleum: cf. xxxi. 46. 13 n.

5. Polybius (iii. 7. 3) regarded Antiochus' arrival at Demetrias as the ἀρχή of the Syrian War.

6. Appian (*Syr.* 12. 48) says merely that Antiochus brought 10,000 troops, doubtless giving a round number. Bar-Kochva, 15–17, argues that these figures were in fact of those present at the battle of Thermopylae and that the original landing force must have been considerably larger, given losses during the winter and garrisons left in various places. (xxxvi. 5. 3, 14. 5, 21. 2, 33. 4–6): these would have been much larger than such reinforcements as arrived from Asia (xxxvi. 15. 3). Bar-Kochva has a case, but he spoils it by wrongly taking xxxvi. 15. 4 as referring to the Seleucid forces (cf. n. ad loc.).

7. concilio: an extraordinary meeting of the full assembly, clearly held at Lamia (§ 9). Cf. Larsen, *TAPhA* lxxxiii (1952), 26.

8. Phalara . . . processerat: by sea, of course. On the position of Phalara cf. Walbank, *Commentary*, iii. 82.

9. Lamiam: on Lamia cf. xxxii. 4. 3 n. It is in Malis, an area removed from the Aetolians in 189 (cf. Flacelière, 358). On the site cf. Béquignon, 263 ff., with references to earlier literature.

quibus . . . significatur: cf. xxxiv. 37. 4 n.

44. 1. aegre: as W–M explain, it was difficult to introduce him because of the pressure of the crowd. The sense is clearer without

the paragraph division at the end of ch. 43. *aegre* is placed first
for emphasis.

Phaenea: *strategos* for 192/1. Cf. xxxii. 32. 11 n.

introductus: Mg, *in* Bψ, *inde* φ. *introductus* makes perfect sense,
and it is wrong to suspect that it was only an emendation in Mg,
and look for some alternative.

rex: cf. p. 14.

2. minoribus ... opinione: L.'s normal word-order with a comparative and *spe*. Cf. Adams, *IF* lxxxi (1976), 86.

3. immaturo: 'untimely', being near the beginning of winter.

5. equis: Frob. 2, *equisque* Bχ. *arma, uiri, equi* occurs at xxiii. 24. 9,
xliv. 1. 6 and Cicero, *Phil.* viii. 21 (four-membered asyndeton *armis,
uiris, equis, commeatibus* is found at xxii. 39. 12: 35. 7, adduced by
McDonald, is two-membered). At xxiii. 15. 13 and xxvi. 5. 9 we
find *uirorum, equorum, armorumque* but L. may have written -*que* there
to avoid three successive words ending in -*orum*. The balance of
probability favours the deletion of -*que* here. Cf. p. 11, Preuss, 74–5.

6. impensae: in a completely different sense from that in § 3.

7. annona: for *annona* referring to the price of food other than
corn cf. *TLL*, ii. 112. 1 ff.

45. 2. Phaeneam: EL, *Phaenean* BAPNV. I would not rule out the
possibility that in this chapter L. did use the Greek form and that
most of the MSS. preserve it on this occasion.

3. Phaeneas was putting forward an interpretation of the Aetolian
decree at 33. 8, laying emphasis on *disceptandumque inter Aetolos et
Romanos*. Cf. p. 33.

reconciliatore: found only here and at Apuleius, *Apol.* 18
(*TLL*). It is perhaps a neologism by L. Cf. p. 9–10.

4. bellare necesse sit: Mg, *bellarent* Bχ. It is hard to say whether
we have to do with an expansion in Mg, perhaps worried by the
alternation of present and imperfect subjunctives (cf. xxxiv. 26. 7 n.),
or a trivialization in Bχ.

5. Thoas accuses Phaeneas of being a secret pro-Roman, certainly
unfairly. Cf. Deininger, 75 n. 52.

relanguescat: the only occurrence of the word in L., though
W-M's statement that it does not occur before him is incorrect. Cf.
Caes. *BG* ii. 15. 4, Cic. *Att.* xiii. 41. 1.

7. elanguescendum: taking up *relanguescat*.

9. imperatoremque: cf. App. *Syr.* 12. 46: αὐτοκράτορά τε στρατηγὸν Αἰτωλῶν Ἀντίοχον ἀποφαίνοντες. Appian, however, wrongly places the declaration in the negotiations before Antiochus' decision to invade. For the similar appointment of Attalus in 209 cf. xxvii. 29. 10, Heuss, *Stadt u. Herrscher*, 43.

triginta ... delegerunt: Pol. xx. 1: τριάκοντα τῶν ἀποκλήτων προεχειρίσαντο τοὺς συνεδρεύσοντας μετὰ τοῦ βασιλέως. The thirty are, then, a section of the *apocleti*, on whom cf. 34. 2 n.

46. 1. rex ... consultabat: Pol. xx. 1: ὁ δὲ συνῆγε τοὺς ἀποκλήτους καὶ διαβούλιον ἀνεδίδου περὶ τῶν ἐνεστώτων.

2. Chalcidem ... temptatam: 37. 4—38.

celeritate ... esse: and therefore an appropriate undertaking when Antiochus' forces were still small.

3. rex: cf. p. 14.

Aetoli: an adjective, as at xxxvii. 48. 6, contradicting the rule I wrongly enunciated at xxxiii. 28. 3 n.

Chaeroneam: the Aetolians met Antiochus' troops there, and proceeded to the coast. Both contingents then went by sea. Chaeronea was not, of course, on the sea, and L.'s manner of expression is by no means clear.

The MSS. have *Chaeroniam* here and *Charoneam* at xxxvi. 11. 5. At xlii. 43. 6 the Vienna MS. has *Ceronia*. What L. wrote must remain uncertain.

constratis nauibus: thus B, as well as χ. McDonald's apparatus is incorrect.

5. The Aetolian suggestion, is of course, quite specious. Antiochus had arrived with an armed force, and *amicitia* with him would be quite inconsistent with maintaining that with Rome.

9. Micythio: cf. 38. 1 n. and addendum ad loc.

10. se: χ, om. B, perhaps rightly. Cf. p. 12.

foedere iniquo: *foedus iniquum* is not a technical term of Roman public law, and this is, in fact, the only occurrence of the phrase in Classical Latin. Cf. Badian, *FC*, 25 ff., especially 26 n. 3.

adligata: the fact that *illigare* is used in similar contexts at xxxiii. 12. 13, xli. 24. 15 is no reason for doubting *adligata* here. There is, it is true, no other example of *adligare* with *foedus*, but the expression is perfectly natural, and Cicero (*Clu.* 148, *Rab. Post.* 18) uses the verb with *lex*.

11. pacem ... libertatem: the word-order emphasizes *libertatem*, the keyword of the exchanges.

12. id . . . abeant: 'the thing that would make them behave like friends would be for them to get out of Euboea'.

13. non modo non: cf. xxxiv. 39. 3 n.

The sentiment is in fact a clear expression of the restrictions that *amicitia* with Rome imposed on Chalcis' freedom of action. Cf. Deininger, 83.

47. 1. haec . . . essent: cf. p. 14.

neque . . . posset: cf. 46. 2. Once the diplomatic ploy had failed Antiochus' forces were too small to capture Chalcis by force.

2. uanum: Mg, *inane* χ, *in naue* B. For *uanum inceptum* cf. xxxvii. 27. 9, xliii. 1. 4, for *uanum euadere* xxv. 23. 8. L. does not use *inanis* of actions.

rex: cf. p. 14.

⟨**Boeotos**⟩: the sentence contains a list of the states approached, expanded in what follows. The supplement is therefore inevitable. For Roman relations with Boeotia cf. xxxiii. 1–2, 27. 5—29.

Amynandrum . . . Athamanum: cf. xxxi. 28. 1 n. He had been one of Rome's most loyal supporters in the Second Macedonian War.

3. Brachylli . . . fuerant: xxxiii. 27. 5—29 and nn. Both here and at xxxvi. 6. 1 the MSS. have *Brachylli* and it is thus very probable that L. did form the genitive in this way.

4. Cf. 30. 12–13 n.

infestum inuisumque: for the collocation cf. ii. 56. 5, iv. 53. 9, v. 8. 9, xxvi. 39. 15.

5–8. This episode is also reported by Appian, *Syr.* 13. 50–52. On the possibility that Polybius had an Athamanian source for these details cf. Walbank, *Polybius*, 76.

5. Apamam: the original Apama, the daughter of Spitamenes of Sogdiana, was the wife of Seleucus I (cf. Seibert, 46). It is odd that Alexander of Megalopolis should have chosen this name for his daughter, rather than a genuinely Macedonian female name. Tarn (*CQ* xxiii [1929], 138–41) therefore plausibly suggested that there was a legend that Apama was in fact a daughter of Alexander himself, a claim apparently also made by Antiochus of Commagene in the first century B.C. (cf. *OGIS* 398). The legends about Alexander had certainly grown widely by this time. The 'historical source' of the Alexander-romance is usually dated about 200 B.C.

The name of the lady was certainly *Apama*. Bχ have *Apamiam*

here and at xxxviii. 13. 5 B has *Aphama*, NV *Aphyama*, L *Amphya*,
and φ *Apamia*. I would not exclude the possibility that L. spelt the
name incorrectly on this occasion.

6. inclutam: the MSS. reading (φ's *indutam* is effectively the same
reading) is perfectly acceptable. L.'s point is that though, perhaps,
no one took Alexander's claims seriously in his own town, the
marriage made it worth while for Philip to follow Apama to Athamania. Certainly none of the proposed emendations makes any
better sense. On *inclutus* cf. p. 4 and addenda.

7. forte: 'who was, as it happened. . .'. Cf. J. Champeaux, *REL*
xlv (1967), 373–4.

quod . . . esset: the reasons for encouragement offered to Philip
by Antiochus and the Aetolians. The claim to descent from the
Argeads would outstrip the lesser pedigree of the Antigonids.

8. uanitas: cf. xxxiv. 24. 1 n.

48. 1. Aegii: cf. 26. 6 n.

concilium: a *syncletos*. Cf. Larsen, *Representative Government*, 172–3.
For the date (November 192) cf. Aymard, *PR*, 325.

2 ff. Cf. 32. 4 n.

2. ut . . . alunt: cf. xxxiv. 37. 4 n.

uaniloquus . . . compleuit: a bold expression meaning 'he
claimed in his speech that Antiochus' forces filled all lands and seas'.
There is no evidence for taking the phrase to be a proverbial way of
referring to bombastic speech. Cf. 49. 5. On *uaniloquus* cf. pp. 6–7.

3. Hellesponto . . . Europam: cf. xxi. 56. 9 with Walsh's note.

loricatos . . . cataphractos: cf. xxxi. 24. 4 n. L. explains the
term again at xxxvii. 40. 5. The *cataphracti* had mail breastplates.

auerso . . . figentes: the 'Parthian shot'. For other references to
it in Augustan literature cf. Nisbet and Hubbard, i. 241. There is
no doubt that Weissenborn's correction of the MSS.' *auersos re-
fugiente(s)* is correct, but I do not understand McDonald's explanation of *auersos*.

5. The Greeks knew of Antiochus' great eastern expedition of 212–
205 and the ambassador could expect them to be impressed. Cf.
Schmitt, *Antiochos*, 91.

fando auditis: cf. Tränkle, *WS*, 115.

Dahas: they lived near the Caspian Sea, and had fought in
Antiochus' army at Raphia in 217 (Pol. v. 97. 3). They were mer-

cenaries, not subjects of Antiochus. Cf. Launey, i. 586, Walbank, *Commentary*, i. 607–8, Schmitt, *Antiochos*, 64, Bar-Kochva, 49.

Medos: it is scarcely likely that the Achaeans had not heard of Medes, and since the name is missing in Flamininus' reply at 49. 8, I wonder whether it should not be deleted here, rather than added in the latter passage.

Elymaeosque et Cadusios: subject peoples, living to the south-west of the Caspian Sea. See Walbank, *Commentary*, i. 575–6, Schmitt, *Antiochos*, 54. For Elymaeans at Magnesia cf. xxxvii. 40. 9, 14.

6. Sidonios . . . Aradios: all these places had come into Antiochus' possession as a result of his victories in the Fifth Syrian War. On Arados, an island off the Phoenician coast, cf. Walbank, *Commentary*, i. 594.

Sidetas: cf. 13. 5 n. For Sidetans in Antiochus' fleet cf. xxxvii. 23. 3.

7. abundasse semper auro: χ, *abundasse auro semper* B. The normal word-order would be *auro semper abundasse. abundasse* is placed first for emphasis and L. may have then retained the order *auro semper* (W–M print *auro semper* and Walsh *CR*, 54 appears to agree).

For gold as a feature of the Persian Empire cf. H. D. Broadhead, *The Persae of Aeschylus* (Cambridge, 1960), 38–9.

altero . . . incluso: *rege* is easily understood from *regno*. I am not sure whether L. omitted it in order to make the ambassador almost deny that Philip was a king in the same class as Antiochus, as W–M appear to suggest.

8. socios atque amicos: the actual treaty between Rome and the League may have been made shortly after these events. Cf. Badian, *JRS* xlii (1952), 76 ff.

9. The same demand was made to the Achaeans by Philip in 198 (xxxii. 21. 5).

non interponant: *non* is used rather than *ne* because the intention is to negative the one word *interponant*, not the whole sentence. See Anderson's note on ix. 34. 15.

10. Archidamus: cf. xxxii. 4. 2 n.

petiit: *petit* χ, *peti* B. The present is quite possible.

12–13. Turning the tables against the Romans' arguments. Cf. 31. 8 n. For the Aetolian claims to have been responsible for the victory at Cynoscephalae cf. 12. 4 n. The charges in § 13 (also reported by Plutarch, *Comparison of Philopoemen and Flamininus* 2. 6) are new, and manifestly unfair. J. W. H. G. Liebeschuetz, *Continuity and*

Change in Roman Religion (Oxford, 1979), 4, cites the passage as an example of Greek inability to understand Roman attention to the details of religious ritual.

49. On the alternation of direct and indirect speech in this chapter cf. Lambert, 42–3.

49. 2. There is no reason to doubt that the sentiment is Polybian, even though Polybius' attitude to Aetolian behaviour in the 190s is less hostile than for third-century events (cf. K. S. Sacks, *JHS* xcv [1975], 92 ff., though I cannot accept the whole of his case). For a similar comment about Athens cf. xxxi. 44. 9 n. For the Roman view that Greeks in general were better at speaking than doing cf. Petrocheilos, 37.

4. inflasse . . . inflatos: deliberate emphatic repetition. Cf. p. 13.
uana: cf. § 11, xxxiv. 24. 1 n.

5. sectam . . . secuturos: cf. xxxvi. 1. 5, xlii. 31. 1 (both in declarations of war), viii. 19. 10, xxix. 27. 2, E. Dutoit, *Hommages Herrmann* (Brussels, 1960), 332. Before L. it occurs in Naevius, *Pun.* fr. 6, Catullus 63. 15 (*exsequi*), Lucretius v. 1115, and ten times in Cicero (*TLL*).
nubes: the only parallel for *nubes* of soldiers is Sil. xii. 168, though for Greek examples cf. Homer, *Il.* iv. 274, xvi. 66, Hdt. viii. 109. 2. Virgil writes of *nubes belli* (*A.* x. 809: cf. Hom. *Il.* xvii. 243) and the poets of the first century A.D. often talk of *nubes telorum* and *nubes belli* (Stat. *Silu.* v. 1. 132, Luc. ii. 262, iv. 488, Sil. v. 379, vii. 595, ix. 12, xii. 334, xvi. 650) (*TLL*).

6–7. The same story is put into Flamininus' mouth by Plutarch, *Flam.* 17. 7 (cf. *Mor.* 197C) and therefore probably stood in Polybius. Such a piece of informal story-telling is unique in L.'s speeches, and L. has deliberately expressed it in a free-running style, employing concepts and vocabulary not normally found in the historical register. Cf. p. 10 n. 7.

6. Chalcidensis hospitis: for Flamininus' relations with Chalcis cf. vol. i, 28 n. 1.
hominis . . . conuiuatoris: for the chiasmus cf. p. 14 n. 1. This passage apart, *conuiuator* is found, in Classical Latin, only in Hor. *Sat.* ii. 8. 73 and Sen. *Dial.* v. 37. 4 (*TLL*, iv. 881. 3 ff.).
solstitiali: in republican and Augustan Latin *solstitium* and *solstitialis* refer only to the summer solstice, *bruma* and *brumalis* to the winter solstice.

tam ... uenatio: cf. Pliny, *Epp.* v. 6. 8 *frequens ibi et uaria uenatio* (also without a verb).

7. non qua: this is certainly the simplest change from the *non quam* (*ut*) of the MSS.

renidens: cf. p. 6.

condimentis: in its literal sense not found between Plautus and this passage (*TLL*, iv. 142. 24 ff.). For a cook's use of seasonings cf. Plaut. *Pseud.* 810 ff., for skill at disguising the true nature of food Mart. xi. 31.

ferinae: Sall. *Iug.* 18. 1, 89. 7 are the only instances of *ferinus* in prose before this passage (*TLL*, vi. 1. 507).

8. inauditarum: taking up *uix fando auditis* in 48. 5.

Dahas ... Elymaeos: cf. 48. 5 nn.

haud ... genus: for Syrians as natural slaves cf. xxxvi. 17. 5, Cic. *prou. cons.* 10. I wonder if Flamininus really expressed himself in this way, or if Polybius reported him as doing so, especially as the peoples mentioned are not Syrians, and the 'Syrians' in the Seleucid army were in fact settlers of Macedonian descent (cf. Bar-Kochva, 227 n. 110). The sentiment is not found in the parallel passage of Plutarch, but that is not necessarily significant, as Plutarch is clearly being selective. The subjects of the Achaemenids were regularly referred to by the Greeks as δοῦλοι. For a similar sentiment to the present passage cf. Herodotus viii. 68γ: σοὶ δὲ ἐόντι ἀρίστῳ ἀνδρῶν πάντων κακοὶ δοῦλοί εἰσί, οἳ ἐν συμμάχων λόγῳ λέγονται εἶναι, ἐόντες Αἰγύπτιοί τε καὶ Κύπριοι καὶ Κίλικες καὶ Πάμφυλοι, τῶν ὄφελός ἐστι οὐδέν.

9. oculis uestris: χ, *uestris oculis* B, perhaps rightly, conveying the meaning 'I wish you too could see what is happening, as others can'.

10. uix ... instar: the contempt for Antiochus' small force is built up by *uix ... legiuncularum ... instar. legiuncula* is found only in this passage, and is a clear case of a neologism. L. wanted a diminutive and since he could not find one in the existing language, he coined it. Plutarch, *Flam.* 17. 8 refers to ὁπλάρια, found elsewhere only in inscriptions, and it is possible that this word stood in Polybius and led L. to look for a diminutive himself (cf. *TLL*, vii. 2. 1114. 80 ff.). Cf. p. 10 n. 1. Ten thousand soldiers in fact represent the size of two 'large' legions (cf. xxxiii. 1. 2 n.), so Flamininus' language is scarcely justified.

mendicantem ... admetiatur: cf. 44. 7. For *mendicare* cf. p. 5.

12. spectataeque: deliberate repetition, in a different sense from *spectatis* in § 11.

13. non interponi: 48. 9.

immo: postposition is rare, but W–M are wrong to say it is first found in L. after Plautus. It occurs also in Cicero, *II Verr.* 3. 25 (*TLL*, vii. 1. 479. 78 ff.). Cf. xxi. 40. 9, xxxviii. 43. 6, xxxix. 40. 7.

quippe ... eritis: the same argument as that of Aristaenus in xxxii. 21. 34.

50. 2. eosdem ... iudicarent: the terms of a normal offensive–defensive alliance. The phrase perhaps supports Badian's view (*JRS* xlii [1952], 76 ff.) that the actual Romano–Achaean treaty was signed soon after these events. Indeed the terms of the declaration can be seen as an acceptance by the League of what would be involved in a formal treaty. (It is not, however, a 'reason for the declaration of war', as Badian, op. cit., 78, says.)

Philopoemen actively supported the present decision (Pol. xxxix. 3. 8, cf. Aymard, *PR*, 326 n. 6).

4. For these events in Athens cf. Deininger, 89–90 (on Cato's subsequent visit to Athens 90 n. 6). The anti-Romans were, no doubt, organized by Euthymides of Chalcis, who had been living at Athens (37. 6, 38. 13).

enim: χ, *autem* B. The latter could be correct, L.'s point being that though there was a garrison at the Piraeus, Athens was not completely loyal.

spe ... multitudinem: the phrase reflects Polybius' usual hostility towards Athens. Cf. xxxi. 14. 6 n.

Leonte: a member of a leading Athenian family in the Hellenistic age. See further xxxviii. 10. 4 ff., Pol. xxi. 31. 6 ff., Deininger, *RE*, Supp. xi. 874–6, Walbank, *Commentary*, iii. 131.

Apollodorus: not otherwise known (cf. Deininger, 89 n. 2).

5. Boeoti ... esse: Pol. xx. 2: οἱ Βοιωτοὶ ἀπεκρίθησαν τοῖς πρεσβευταῖς διότι παραγενομένου τοῦ βασιλέως πρὸς αὐτούς, τότε βουλεύσονται περὶ τῶν περικαλουμένων.

6—51. For the following events cf. Appian, *Syr.* 12. 49, Diod. xxix. 1.

6. Eumenem: the Pergamene troops had in fact been dispatched at an earlier stage (39. 2) but it seems that their arrival had been delayed.

7. Menippum: cf. xxxiv. 57. 6 n.

Polyxenidan: a Rhodian who was Antiochus' admiral during the war. Cf. xxxvi. 8. 1, 41. 7 ff., xxxvii. 8. 3, 10–13, 26–30, Lenschau, *RE*, xxi. 1850–1, Walbank, *Commentary*, ii. 239.

8. Xenoclide: cf. 38. 1 n.

9. Romani milites: presumably from Atilius' fleet: cf. Thiel, 288.
Salganea: again the fortifications in the hills, not the town: cf. 38. 7 n., Bakhuizen, 136.

Hermaeum ... Euboeam: the shrine of Hermes is said by Thucydides (vii. 29. 3) to be 16 stades (i.e. about 3 km.) from Mycalessus, which is to be located near modern Ritsona (cf. Dover, *Historical Commentary on Thucydides*, iv. 409). The *transitus* is not therefore the crossing of the Euripus but the route from Thebes to the coast and the *fauces* of § 11 are not the water, but the pass between Mycalessus and the Euripus (though it is possible that L. thought he was talking about the Euripus: he will not have had much idea of the topography). See Bakhuizen, 137 ff., with a possible identification of the Hermaeum.
uenerunt: cf. p. 10.

10. Micythio: cf. 38. 1 n.

11. obsessas ab hostibus: χ, *ab hostibus obsessas* B. I see no way of making a decision.
omisso ... itinere: for the road cf. Bakhuizen, 148 n. 25.
Delium: cf. xxxi. 45. 6 n.
ut ... transmissurus: cf. xxxi. 42. 5 n.

51. 1. templum ... abest: cf. Thuc. iv. 76. 4: Δήλιον ... τὸ ἐν τῇ Ταναγραίᾳ πρὸς Εὔβοιαν τετραμμένον Ἀπόλλωνος ἱερόν.
minus ... milium: cf. xxxiv. 1. 3 n. χ's *inde milium* may well be correct: cf. Pettersson, 163, Packard, ii. 1177.

2–4. A rambling, far from clear period. *ubi* goes with the main verbs.

2. templa ... appellant: surely L.'s own explanation. It is highly unlikely that Polybius would have felt it necessary to explain what an ἄσυλον was, as W–M suggest.
nondum ... indicto: by Rome: for the Achaeans cf. 50. 2. But both sides were clearly involving themselves in military activities and Roman complaints are exaggerated (cf. Diod. xxix. 1, quoted by W–M).

4. palatos: cf. xxxi. 2. 9 n.
† **eos:** clearly a numeral stood here. *CCC* provides an easy explanation of *eos* but cannot, of course, be regarded as certain. Walsh's *eorum ccc* (*CR*, 56) places far too much emphasis on *eorum*.

6. Antiochus ... exercitu: from Lamia (50. 7). For his route cf. 50. 11 n.

nuper: ch. 46.

7. in Euripo castellum: on the hill immediately north of the Euripus bridge. See Bakhuizen, 128.

Romani milites: another detachment, not the remnants of the Delium force, as Thiel (288 n. 393) thinks.

8. Salganea ... castellum: cf. p. 14 n. 1.

praesidio: Bakhuizen (136) plausibly suggests that Polybius wrote φρούριον with reference to the fortress in the mountains (cf. id., 43 ff., 89 ff.). Whether L. too meant a fort and not just 'garrison' by *praesidio* is uncertain.

10. id ... caput: the Euripus as the key to Euboea, not just Chalcis, as W–M say. For *id* cf. xxxvi. 11. 9 n.

BOOK XXXVI

191 B.C.

1–4. *Events in Rome*

1–2. *Preparations for war and assignments of provinces*

1. 1. P. . . . Scipionem: (350). Cf. xxxi. 49. 6 n.

Cn. filium: Mg, om. Bχ. L. distinguishes him in this way at xxix. 14. 8, xxxi. 49. 6, xxxv. 1. 3, 10. 2, 24. 4, xliii. 2. 5. He distinguishes him with the cognomen *Nasica* at xxxix. 55. 6, 56. 7, xl. 34. 3. No distinction is made at xxxiii. 25. 1, xxxiv. 42. 4, xxviii. 35. 4 (at xxxvi. 36–40 and xxxvii. 2. 5 there is no possibility of ambiguity and the passages should not therefore be included in the last category). On balance it is probable that Mg is right here, but one can certainly not exclude the possibility that L. did not distinguish him here and that we have a gloss in Mg.

M'. Acilium Glabrionem: (35). Cf. xxxi. 50. 5 n.

For the names of the consuls as objects of the first sentence of the narrative of a new year cf. xxxix. 8. 1.

consules: Mg, om. Bχ, perhaps rightly. At xxxii. 8. 1, where *inito magistratu* again occurs, *consules* is read by χ but omitted in B. The Vienna MS. omits *consules* at xlii. 1. 1.

2. res . . . hostiis: as in 200. Cf. xxxi. 5. 3 n.

lectisternium . . . solet: for these semi-permanent *lectisternia* cf. xl. 59. 7, xlii. 30. 8. They are attested only in this period, and are presumably a later development of the original occasional *lectisternia*. But I see no justification for Latte's statement (*RRG*, 263) that they can have taken place only on the initiative of private individuals.

quod . . . eueniret: cf. xxxi. 5. 4 n.

bene atque feliciter: in all other occurrences of the formula in L. *bene ac feliciter* is found (Packard, i. 601) and though there are variations in other authors, there is no case of *atque* (*TLL*, vi. 1. 450). We should follow Modius in reading *ac* here.

3. perlitatum: 'a favourable omen was obtained'.

eo . . . ostendi: cf. xxxi. 5. 7 n.: *contra* see Harris, 122.

5. quique . . . essent: cf. xxxv. 49. 5 n. The formula at 2. 2 is rather more limited, but both are probably pseudo-formulas invented by L. or one of his predecessors and the difference is not to be regarded as having any significance.

6–7. praeter . . . traiecisset: cf. p. 37.

consul: 'as consul'.

imperassetue, ut: ϕ, *imperasset uelut* Bψ. For the repetition of *ut* cf. p. 40, 3. 13, 16. 10, xxxvii. 4. 1, 50. 3, Pettersson, 103, H–S, 808. *imperasset* refers to the allied troops.

8. sociis . . . numerum: i.e. the Greek allies, not extra Italian troops separately dispatched. The limitation was presumably made to prevent exorbitant demands being made on the Greeks, and is the first indication of such concern. I suspect the influence of the friends of Flamininus on this decision (Flamininus himself, of course, was still in Greece).

L. Quinctium . . . placuit: nothing more is heard of him.

9. duobus . . . habuisset: xxxv. 20. 4–5. Cf. p. 38.

urbanae legiones: i.e. no new *legiones urbanae* were to be raised.

2. 1. his . . . foret: *his ita in senatu ad id quae cuius prouincia foret* χ. B has the same with the omission of *quae*, and *quae cuius prouincia foret* is quoted from Mg. Koch's *incerto*, accepted by W–M and Zingerle, involves taking *ad id* as meaning 'up to this time', as in iii. 22. 8, ix. 15. 1. It is, however, natural to think that the indirect question following *id* defines *id* and Madvig's *haud* both avoids this difficulty and is palaeographically as simple, if not simpler. H. J. Müller (*JPhV* xx [1894], 102–3) and Damsté (*Mnemosyne* xliii [1915], 446) unconvincingly proposed deleting *ad id foret* as a gloss.

2. quod . . . eo tempore: *quod populus Romanus* BNVϕmg, *quod praetor* L, *quo tempore* ϕ. There is clearly no authority for *eo tempore* and it should be deleted.

duellum: Bχ, *bellum* Mg, clearly trivializing. The archaic form is used by both Cicero and L. only in formal archaizing contexts. Cf. Packard, i. 1334–5, Ogilvie, 134. It had been obsolete since Plautus, and was reintroduced into the poetic language by Horace. Cf. *TLL*, v. 1. 2181. 49 ff.

supplicationem: cf. xxxi. 8. 2 n.

ludos magnos: cf. xxxi. 9. 5–10 n. χ has *ludos magnos*, B *magnos ludos*. *magni ludi* occurs only at v. 31. 2 and (not of Roman games) xlv. 32. 9. *ludi magni*, with no MSS. variations, occurs on eleven occasions, and the balance of probability favours that order here.

3. P. . . . maximo: cf. xxxi. 9. 7 n.

nuncupauit: a technical term used of a consul or praetor making a vow when setting out for his province (Fest. p. 176L).

populus: H. J. Müller rightly added *Romanus*. Such an omission of *Romanus* in the direct quotation of a formula is without parallel and highly unlikely. (xxxi. 8. 2 is not a direct quotation, and in xxii. 10. 5, 6 *populus* alone follows *populus Romanus* at the beginning of the formula.)

4. dies . . . continuos: as W–M note, this is the first time that the length of votive *ludi* is specified in the vow.

de pecunia . . . decreuerit: i.e. *de incerta pecunia*. Cf. xxxi. 9. 7–10 nn.

5. quisquis . . . sunto: the reason for this clause was presumably to prevent any demands for an *instauratio*, which for a ten-day festival could prove very expensive. Cf. the provisions for the fulfilment of the vow of the *uer sacrum* in xxii. 10. 4–6. *quisquis magistratus* is to be taken as excluding magistrates without *imperium*. Cf. Mommsen, *StR*, i³. 244 n. 4. For a similar usage cf. Cic. *leg. Man.* 62.

6. praetores: on the praetors cf. xxxv. 24. 6 nn.

iurisdictio utraque: cf. xxxi. 6. 2 n.

7. noui . . . consule: two legions, 20,000 allied infantry, and 800 allied cavalry (xxxv. 41. 7). See further xxxvii. 2. 7–8 and p. 38.

8. M. Fuluio proconsule: cf. xxxii. 7. 8, xxxiii. 42. 8 nn., xxxv. 20. 11.

decretum est: Mg, om. *est* Bχ, probably rightly. Cf. xxxv. 41. 6 n.

duae . . . esset: for the proportion of allied to Roman troops in this period cf. Toynbee, ii. 128 ff., Brunt, appendix 26.

9. citeriorem: *ulteriorem* MSS. It is not impossible that L. himself made a careless slip.

10. L. Valerio: (350). Tappo. Cf. xxxiv. 1. 2 n.

exercitumque: cf. xxxv. 23. 8.

11. pro praetore . . . retinere: I do not understand W–M's statement that this did not amount to a prorogation of Tappo's *imperium*.

It is to be exercised in a narrower *prouincia*, but it is still *imperium pro praetore*.

Pachynum ... Tyndareum: Pachynus is the cape at the south-eastern tip of Sicily, while Tyndaris (see below) is on the north coast. The points specified do not therefore divide Sicily into two. Only the stretch of coast from Pachynus to Tyndaris comes under Tappo, while the whole of the rest of the island remains the *provincia* of Lepidus. As Lepidus is a praetor, Tappo cannot hold an *imperium* less than that of Lepidus, and if no restriction at all had been made on Lepidus' *prouincia*, there would have been the possibility of the clash of two *imperia aequa*.

The Greek form is always Τυνδαρίς. *Tyndareum* occurs also in the *Tabula Peutingeriana*. Cf. Ziegler, *RE*, viiA. 1776 ff. On Pachynus cf. id., *RE*, xviii. 1. 2074–7. (The MSS. have forms in Phacy-, Phaci-, and Pachi-, but there can be no doubt as to what L. wrote.) Nitsche's *ad Tyndareum* (*JPhV* xxxiii [1907], 11) may be right.

uiginti ... longis: cf. xxxv. 23. 6 n.

12. duas decumas: on the *decuma* cf. xxxi. 29. 7 n. This is the first recorded instance of a second *decuma*. For subsequent levies cf. xxxvii. 2. 12, 50. 9, xlii. 31. 8, Toynbee, ii. 217. It is not clear whether Rome paid for this second levy, as later provided for in the *Lex Terentia Cassia* of 73 (Cic. *II Verr*. 3. 163, 5. 52). If so, it is somewhat odd that payment is specified for African corn in 3. 1, but not here. (Scramuzza, *Economic Survey*, iii. 240, assumes that Rome paid for the corn.)

13. Sardinia: it seems that some Sardinian peoples paid a tithe, others a direct tax: cf. xli. 17. 2.

14. triginta: in fact he had fifty (42. 1, cf. App. *Syr*. 22. 101). The decision was probably altered subsequently. Cf. Thiel, 261.

Atilio: (60). A. Atilius Serranus. Cf. 12. 9, xxxv. 37. 3 n.

15. socios nauales: cf. xxxiv. 6. 12 n.

libertinos: for the use of freedmen as rowers cf. xl. 18. 7, xlii. 27. 3, 31. 7, Thiel, 12, 195 ff. There is no reason to think that they are marines rather than rowers, as held by S. Treggiari, *Roman Freedmen during the late Republic* (Oxford, 1969), 68, Sherwin-White, *RC*², 325.

et (in eam): Frob. 2, om. Bχ, *ut* Mg. The asyndeton may be correct. Cf. xxxv. 23. 6 n.

3. 1. *Dispatch of ambassadors to Africa*

3. 1. in Africam ... Numidiam: as W–M say, *in Africam* must go with *in Numidiam* as well as with *Carthaginienses*. The MSS. omit *et*, but it is hard to envisage any alternative which would remove the difficulty. I have considered deleting *in Africam.*

pro quo ... Romanus: neither Carthage nor Massinissa had any treaty obligation to provide corn.

3. 2–3. *Prohibitions on movements of senators and magistrates*

3. quibusque ... liceret: this refers to persons of consular, praetorian, or curule aedilician standing who had not been members of the senate at the previous census. They are allowed to sit in the senate and vote, but they must await the next *lectio senatus* before becoming full members. Cf. Gell. iii. 18. 6–7, Rich, 130–1, Nicolet, *JRS* lxvi (1976), 25, Schleussner, 217. Walbank, *JRS* xxvii (1937), 196, is misleading.

minores magistratus: cf. xxxii. 26. 17 n. They should strictly include the curule aediles, but these are already covered by the first clause. The other *minores magistratus* could speak in the senate in their year of office. Cf. Mommsen, *StR*, iii. 943.

ne quis ... abessent: the first recorded instance of such a prohibition. For a subsequent occasion see xliii. 11. 4–5.

eo: MSS. *eo die* has no reference. We should adopt Fügner's *eodem.*

3. 4–6. Coloniae maritimae

It seems that the citizen colonies founded between the Latin and Hannibalic Wars, all of which were on the sea, were called *coloniae maritimae*, and their citizens were normally dispensed from military service. Some of them had unsuccessfully protested at being forced to serve in the army in 207 (xxvii. 38. 4). The lists in the two passages comprise ten names in all, and no case can be made for the existence of a *colonia maritima* which does not appear in either list. There is no need to assume that either of the lists is incomplete—some of the ten may not have asserted what they claimed as their rights on one occasion or the other. The colonies not mentioned on this occasion are Alsium and Sena. The colonies settled in 194 (cf. xxxii. 29. 3–4, xxxiv. 45. 1–5 nn.) were probably not granted the formal *uacatio* possessed by the other colonies. Cf. Salmon, *Athenaeum* n.s. xli (1963), 13 ff., *Colonization*, ch. iv, but his statement at *Colonization*, 98 that 'the Roman authorities ruled that henceforth no citizen colonist, not even those in the old *coloniae maritimae*, should any longer be exempt from service in the regular armed forces' goes well beyond what L. says in the present passage. Thiel, 276–7, strangely argues that the passage shows that the colonists were normally liable for naval service. Cf. Badian, *FC*, 292.

4. comparanda ... classe: BNV, *comparando ... classem* AP, *comparando ... classe* E, *comparanda ... classem* L. *comparanda ... classe* is clearly the transmitted reading, and no further consideration need be given to J. F. Gronovius's proposal to regard *classe(m)* as a gloss and take *comparando* absolutely.

5. ad senatum reiecti: the tribunes pass the matter to the senate without committing themselves. Cf. xxvii. 8. 3, xl. 29. 12, Bleicken, 85.

6. Ostia: for the original settlement in the regal period cf. R. Meiggs, *Ostia* (2nd edn., Oxford, 1973), 16 ff.: *contra* Toynbee, i. 387 ff. The precise date of the establishment of a colony is uncertain. Cf. Salmon, op. cit., 16–17.

 Fregenae: cf. xxxii. 29. 1 n., Salmon, op. cit., 25.

 Castrum Nouum: probably *Castrum nouum* in Etruria, south of Civitavecchia. See *per.* xi, Vell. i. 14. 8, Salmon, op. cit., 20 ff., *Colonization*, 180 n. 119.

 Pyrgi: the port of Caere. The date of the colony is not known. Cf. Salmon, op. cit., 23–4. *Colonization*, 79.

 Tarracina: Volscian Anxur, founded in 329 (viii. 21. 11). cf. Ogilvie, 622, Salmon, op. cit., 17–18.

 Minturnae et Sinuessa: founded together in 295 (x. 21. 8. Vell. i. 14. 6). On the site of Sinuessa cf. xxxi. 12. 7 n. Minturnae is a little to the north of Sinuessa, on the other side of Monte Massico, Cf. J. Johnson, *Excavations at Minturnae*, i (Philadelphia, 1935), Salmon, op. cit., 18, B. W. Frier, *Historia* xviii (1969), 510–12, Brunt, 543. See further 37. 3 n.

 certarunt: *certarent* B, *certauerunt* χ. On L.'s use of the contracted forms of the third person plural of the perfect cf. E. M. Lease, *CR* xviii (1904), 30–1. *certarunt* is attested at xxi. 1. 3.

3. 7–12. *Consultation of the* fetiales

Of the three questions addressed to the *fetiales* the first is the same as that put in 200 (xxxi. 8. 3) and receives the same reply. The third question appears to concern both Antiochus and the Aetolians, since the reply of the *fetiales* in § 10 precedes their reply concerning the Aetolians alone. B's omission of *eis* in § 8 (*eis* φ, *eius* L, *enim* NV) may therefore well be correct.

7. nuntiari: Kreyssig, *nuntiaret* B, *nuntiare* χ. The absolute use of *nuntiare* is quite possible (cf. Cic. *Sex. Rosc.* 19, 96, 98, *Verr.* i. 21, *II Verr.* 5. 93, *Mil.* 65, *Pis.* 45, *Phil.* ii. 84) but in view of xxxi. 8. 3 and *nuntiaretur* below *nuntiari* is almost certainly right.

10. cum ... censuissent: none of the negotiations with Antiochus or the Aetolians could be regarded as a technical *rerum repetitio*.

11. Demetriadem ... occupassent: xxxv. 34. 5–12.

12. Chalcidem ... issent: for the attempts to capture Chalcis cf. xxxv. 37. 4–38, 46, for its surrender to Antiochus xxxv. 50–1.

News of the Delium episode had not yet reached Rome: cf. p. 28.

3. 13–14. *The departure of Glabrio*

13. quos ... imperasset: cf. 1. 6–7 nn.

quos ... oporteret: i.e. excluding the troops recruited for service in Bruttium (xxxv. 41. 7).

primae et tertiae: cf. p. 36 n. 8.

ut (ii omnes): cf. 1. 7 n.

13–14. idibus Maiis ... nonas Maias: in fact 4 January 191 and 27 December 192 (cf. p. 25). See further 36. 3–4 n.

4. *Embassies from Philip, Ptolemy, Massinissa, and Carthage*

1–4. De Sanctis (iv. 1. 128 n. 42) rejected the report of the Egyptian offer, like that in 190 (xxxvii. 3. 9–11), on the grounds that the chief Egyptian aim was the recovery of Koile Syria, and they would not have subordinated this to the interests of Rome. But there is no evidence for Egyptian activity over Koile Syria at this time, and no inherent improbability either in the offer or the senate's response. Ptolemy, of course, was in no real position to assist Rome, and the senate would have been aware of that. That would not preclude the diplomatic niceties being observed.

Walbank (*Philip V*, 200) and Gruen (*CSCA* vi [1973], 131) reject the offer from Philip and the senate's response (which they wrongly describe as a refusal of the offer). Gruen argues that Philip did not in fact commit himself until the events described in 8. 3–6. But there is no reason why the embassy from Philip should not have been dispatched after the events there described (cf. 5. 1–6. 5 n., p. 28). *sub idem tempus*, of course, need not be taken strictly.

1. Philippo ... pollicente: Mg, *pollicentes* Bχ. If Mg's reading is accepted here, he should also be followed in omitting *etiam* in the following sentence, since *etiam* would indicate that Ptolemy's gifts of gold and silver were additional to offers made by both kings. If *etiam* is retained Bχ's *pollicentes* is necessary.

[Aegypti rege]: L. adds the explanation at xxxi. 2. 3, xxxii. 33. 4, xxxv. 13. 4, xlv. 44. 14, and despite the inconcinnity after *duobus regibus*, I am inclined to think that it should be retained here.

5 ff. For other offers of grain from Carthage and Massinissa cf. xxxi. 19. 1–4, xxxii. 27. 2, xliii. 6. 11–14, Toynbee, ii. 187.

5. modium ... milia: M. Müller. *modium U* B, *modium* ANV, *modium mille* PELA², *modia* (? *mille*) Mg. An offer of only a thousand *modii* is obviously impossible and there is no alternative to reading *milia* and assuming a numeral has been lost.

7. [suorum]: deletion is inevitable. Walter's *seorsum* (*PhW* lx [1940], 350) is far too emphatic.

stipendium ... daturos: on the indemnity laid down in the treaty of 201 cf. xxxii. 2. 1 n. It is a reasonable assumption that the Carthaginians hoped to tie themselves less closely to Rome by paying the whole amount in one sum, and in particular to secure the return of their hostages. Equally the senate's refusal of the offer (§ 9) was, in part at least, motivated by a desire to prevent such a situation.

8. legati: sc. *polliciti*. It would be preferable to punctuate with a colon after *petere sese* in § 6.

uiginti: χ, *xxx* B. Decision is impossible.

9. No reply is made to Massinissa's offer of troops.

si pretium acciperent: the offer of payment to Massinissa cannot be used to argue that he did not have a treaty with Rome, as is done by Dahlheim, 232: cf. M. R. Cimma, *Reges socii et amici populi Romani* (Milan, 1976), 50.

de classe ... deberent: by the terms of the peace treaty Carthage was to surrender all but ten triremes (xxx. 37. 3, Pol. xv. 18. 3). The senate viewed with alarm Carthage's proposal to build a new fleet. There is no mention in the peace terms of an obligation to provide ships. Six Carthaginian ships appear at 42. 2, but the language there (cf. also App. *Syr.* 22. 101) appears to distinguish them from the ships provided by states with treaty obligations, and I would prefer to think that the senate eventually agreed to accept this number rather than hold (with Thiel, 269) that there was a treaty obligation to provide six ships. Perhaps what the senate actually said was 'if you had a treaty obligation to provide ships, we would accept them: since you have not, we will not accept them'.

5–35. 10. *Events in Greece*

5. 1–6. 5. *Negotiations of Antiochus with Greek states*

L. now reports events in Greece in the winter of 192/1. The initial events belong to November–December 192, earlier than some of the events just described (cf. 3. 13–14, 4. 1–4 nn.). Chapter 5 is obviously derived from Polybius xx. 3, but it contains a number of ascriptions of motive which are not present in Polybius. Nissen (*KU*, 13) argues that these are political judgements that have all the marks of Polybian origin, and that we must therefore conclude that there has been considerable abbreviation by the excerptor of Polybius. The remarks do indeed interpret the situation correctly, but it is not necessary to believe that L. was incapable of intelligent comment, and his interest in motivation could easily have led him to add them to what he regarded as an over-austere narrative in Polybius. On the other hand *partim* . . . *legatis* in § 1, is a statement of fact, hardly likely to have been invented by L. Cf. Tränkle, 110 n. 29, who regards §§ 1 and 3 as containing additions by L., §§ 6 and 7 as of Polybian origin. See also Oost, *RPEA*, 59, Walbank, *Commentary*, iii. 65.

5. 1. Chalcide ... uenerunt: Pol. xx. 3. 1: Ἀντιόχου διατρίβοντος ἐν τῇ Χαλκίδι καὶ τοῦ χειμῶνος καταρχομένου παρεγένοντο πρὸς αὐτὸν πρεσβευταὶ παρὰ μὲν τοῦ τῶν Ἠπειρωτῶν ἔθνους οἱ περὶ Χάροπα, παρὰ δὲ τῆς τῶν Ἠλείων πόλεως οἱ περὶ Καλλίστρατον. As often L. omits the names of foreign ambassadors: cf. vol. i, 19 n. 5, 27. 1–2, xxxvii. 6. 4, 19. 1, 25. 9, 45. 4, 55. 1 nn.

On Charops' policy cf. Cabanes, 280–1, who, however, wrongly sees *communi gentis consensu* as a change from Polybius' παρὰ μὲν τοῦ τῶν Ἠπειρωτῶν ἔθνους imported from another source.

Chalcide Antiochus: he will have remained there after its surrender to him (xxxv. 50–1).

Epirotae: they had been *amici* of Rome since the Second Macedonian War, but had played little part in the events of the intervening years. Cf. xxxv. 27. 11 n., and on the present episode Oost, *RPEA*, 59–60.

et Elei: Sabellicus, *ex Pelei* BNV, *ex plebei* L, *et Pelei* φ. The Eleans had been Roman allies in the First Macedonian War, and were technically still such. Cf. Walbank, *Commentary*, ii. 516.

e Peloponneso: Frob. 1. *e Pelopononse* B, *et Peloponensis* φ, *et Peloponensi* ψ.

2. Elei ... illaturos: Pol. xx. 3. 5: οἱ δ' Ἠλεῖοι παρεκάλουν πέμπειν τῇ πόλει βοήθειαν· ἐψηφισμένων γὰρ τῶν Ἀχαιῶν τὸν πόλεμον εὐλαβεῖσθαι τὴν τούτων ἔφοδον. L. alters the order followed by Polybius and reports first the requests of the Epirotes and Eleans, then the responses to each. Cf. Tränkle, 112 n. 37. Tränkle, 183–4, is wrong to take Polybius' words ἐψηφισμένων γὰρ τῶν Ἀχαιῶν τὸν πόλεμον as meaning that the Achaeans had declared war on Elis. The reference is simply to the Achaean declaration of

war against Antiochus and the Aetolians reported in xxxv. 50. 2.
The Eleans were afraid that the Achaeans would use the war as an
excuse for action to incorporate them into the League. Cf. Errington,
115 and further 31. 1–3, 35. 7 n.

non . . . indictum: clearly an addition by L. The Eleans were
in no position to participate in the Achaean decision.

⟨credebant⟩: the transmitted text has no grammar, but it
might be simpler to delete *quos* rather than supplement with a verb.

3. mille . . . missi: Pol. xx. 3. 7 τοῖς δ' Ἠλείοις ἐξαπέστειλε χιλίους
πεζούς, ἡγεμόνα συστήσας Εὐφάνη τὸν Κρῆτα. Euphanes is not
otherwise known.

Epirotarum . . . Romanos: nothing corresponds to this in
Polybius.

partem ullam: 'in any respect'. Cf. Cic. *fam.* xiii. 1. 2, Walker,
Supplementary Annotations, 209.

liberi: free to say what they really felt.

simplicis: 'ingenuous'.

cum eo: 'on the condition that'. Cf. H–S, 259, 640.

4. Pol. xx. 3. 2: οἱ μὲν οὖν Ἠπειρῶται παρεκάλουν αὐτὸν μὴ προεμβι-
βάζειν σφᾶς εἰς τὸν πρὸς Ῥωμαίους πόλεμον, θεωροῦντα διότι
πρόκεινται πάσης τῆς Ἑλλάδος πρὸς τὴν Ἰταλίαν. *primos . . . excepturos*
does not correspond to anything in Polybius.

5. Pol. xx. 3. 3–4: ἀλλ' εἰ μὲν αὐτὸς δύναται προκαθίσας τῆς Ἠπείρου
παρασκευάζειν σφίσι τὴν ἀσφάλειαν, ἔφασαν αὐτὸν δέξασθαι καὶ ταῖς
πόλεσι καὶ τοῖς λιμέσιν· εἰ δὲ μὴ κρίνει τοῦτο πράττειν κατὰ τὸ
παρόν, συγγνώμην ἔχειν ἠξίουν αὐτοῖς δεδιόσι τὸν ἀπὸ Ῥωμαίων
πόλεμον. L. enlivens the narrative with *cupide* and *nudos atque inermes*.

6. exercitus Romanos: the phrase is unusual and one would
expect merely *Romanos* as J. F. Gronovius proposed. But it is hard
to see why *exercitus* should have been added, and I am inclined to
keep the MSS. text. The plural will refer to the forces with Baebius
as well as those of Glabrio.

8. Pol. xx. 3. 6: ὁ δὲ βασιλεὺς τοῖς μὲν Ἠπειρώταις ἀπεκρίθη διότι
πέμψει πρεσβευτὰς τοὺς διαλεχθησομένους αὐτοῖς ὑπὲρ τῶν κοινῇ
συμφερόντων. I see no reason to think that the ambassadors were
not sent, as claimed by Larsen, *Greek Federal States*, 417, Walbank,
Commentary, iii. 65.

perplexae: cf. pp. 6, 8.

ad eos: χ, om. B, perhaps rightly. Cf., e.g., xxxiii. 29. 10.

6. 1–5. *Boeotia.* From Polybius xx. 7. 3–5. Except for the summary in

§ 2, L. omits Polybius' long excursus on the social and political state of Boeotia at this time. Cf. Tränkle, 106 n. 18.

1. causas ... illatum: Pol. xx. 7. 3: οἱ πολλοὶ πρόφασιν μὲν εἶχον τῆς πρὸς Ῥωμαίους ἀλλοτριότητος τὴν ἐπαναίρεσιν τὴν Βραχύλλου καὶ τὴν στρατείαν, ἣν ἐποιήσατο Τίτος ἐπὶ Κορώνειαν διὰ τοὺς ἐπιγινομένους φόνους ἐν ταῖς ὁδοῖς τῶν Ῥωμαίων.

causas ... irae: *causas irae* go together. Cf. p. 14.

quas ante dixi: xxxiii. 27. 5—29.

Brachyllae: Sigonius. *Brachylli* B, *Bracchili* χ. Cf. xxxiii. 27. 9, xxxv. 47. 3 nn.

Coroneae: *Coroneam* Bψφmg, *Coream* φ. ix. 25. 1 is the only instance in L. of *in* + accusative with *bellum inferre*. On all other occasions the dative is used. Since emendation is required, the dative seems the more probable. On Coronea cf. xxxiii. 29. 6 n.

2. re uera: Pol. xx. 7. 4 τῇ δ' ἀληθείᾳ.

diuturnus ... mutatione: a deliberate paradox. The situation is chaotic and can only be maintained so by further change. L. is, of course, reflecting Polybius' biased attitude towards events in Boeotia. See Walbank, *Commentary*, iii. 66 ff.: add D. Hennig, *Chiron* vii (1977), 119 ff., D. Mendels, *Ancient Society*, viii (1977), 161 ff.

3. obuiam ... uenit: Pol. xx. 7. 5: καὶ γὰρ τοῦ βασιλέως συνεγγίζοντος ἐξῇεσαν ἐπὶ τὴν ἀπάντησιν οἱ τῶν Βοιωτῶν ἄρξαντες· συμμίξαντες δὲ καὶ φιλανθρώπως ὁμιλήσαντες ἦγον αὐτὸν εἰς τὰς Θήβας.

ad Delium ... Chalcidem: xxxv. 50–1.

3–4. eandem ... qua: L, Gel. *eadem morationem exorsus quia* B, *eadem oratione exorsus quam* PENV, *eadem oratione exorsus qua* A. The ablative with *exordiri* occurs only at Tac. *A.* vi. 6. 1 (*TLL*, v. 2. 1559. 82).

⟨**est⟩ exorsus:** cf. p. 12. *tamen* precludes the possibility that it is a true participle, with *fallebat* as the main verb.

4. colloquio ... Chalcidem: cf. xxxv. 46. 5 n. In fact the speech on that occasion was made by the Aetolians.

in concilio Achaeorum: xxxv. 48. 8–9.

institui: χ, *constitui* B. For *amicitiam instituere* cf. vii. 31. 2, xxxiv. 31. 19, 32. 3. There is no example of *amicitiam constituere* in L.

5. The decree, though expressed in mild language, was in fact directed against Rome—i.e. the Boeotians accepted Antiochus' request merely to make *amicitia* with him. There is no trace of any participation by the Boeotians in subsequent events (cf. Cloché, *Thèbes de Béotie* [Namur, 1952], 256–7).

praetextu: χ, *praetexto* B. Neither *praetextus* nor *praetextum* occurs before L. or elsewhere in him, and it is impossible to say what he wrote. At *per.* cxviii the MSS. have *praetexto* (*TLL*).

6. 6—7. *Antiochus' council of war*

Cf. App. *Syr.* 13. 53–14. 58, Just. xxxi. 5.

6. principes: probably the *apocleti* (W–M).

diem indictum: *diem indicere* is found also at x. 27. 3 and xxvii. 30. 6, while at 8. 1 Bχ have *dicere*, Mg had *indicere*, and at i. 50. 6 the *Δ* group of MSS. has *indicere*, M *dicere*. Madvig (*Emendationes*, 519 n. 1) wrongly claimed 'indicuntur quae fieri praestarique debent ... tempus rei agendae dicitur ... aut edicitur' and altered *indicere* to *dicere* here and at x. 27. 3, though seemed to be willing to accept it at xxvii. 30. 6. Cf. H. J. Müller, *JPhV* xv (1889), 24–5.

7. Amynander: cf. xxxi. 28. 1 n., xxxv. 47. 5–8.

Hannibal ... adhibitus: cf. xxxv. 42. 6–43. 2.

8. quorum ... temptanda: cf. p. 14.

9. hieme ... media: December 192/January 191. Cf. Walbank, *Commentary*, iii. 74, p. 28.

10. et alii: MSS. *et* should be retained. The first *alii ... alii* relates to the question of timing, the second to the method of approach to the Thessalians.

7. 1. hanc fere: 'virtually all of the discussion was on this issue'. Cf. 8. 1, vi. 40. 2, xxx. 31. 1, *TLL*, vi. 1. 493.

2–21. *The speech of Hannibal.* The presence of a speech by Hannibal in Appian, *Syr.* 14 which, though entirely different in structure, has a number of verbal correspondences with L. (see the detailed notes) suggests that a speech stood in Polybius at this point and was adapted in different ways by L. and Appian. (The speech in Justin xxxi. 5 is quite different, being devoted entirely to arguments in favour of invading Italy.) Cf. Pédech, 270.

The speech falls into two parts: (i) §§ 3–15 the necessity of bringing Philip into the war, or, at the worst, of neutralizing him, (ii) §§ 16–20 the case for invading Italy. Ullmann's analysis (*Technique*, 146–7) is even more inappropriate than usual: indeed Ullmann himself admits that the speech does not easily lend itself to a division into rhetorical *topoi*. His division is: (i) § 2 *prooemium*. (ii) § 3 *propositio*. (iii) §§ 4–15 *tractatio*: (a) §§ 4–6 *utile*; (b) §§ 7–10 *facile*; (*c*) §§ 11–13 *possibile*; (*d*) 14–15 *tutum*. (iv) §§ 16–21 *conclusio*: (*a*) §§ 16–20 *dictio sententiae*; (*b*) § 21 *peroratio*. As explained above, §§ 16–20 are not part of a *conclusio* but the second section of the main argument.

2. cum ... Boeotia: φ, om. *et* Bψ, *de Achaeis deque Boeotia* Mg. For A, B*que*, *et* C cf. § 4, xxxiv. 1. 7 n. The omission of *et* at an early stage of transmission, with Mg's text representing an emendation, is more likely than the transposition of *deque* in F.

For the discussions referred to see xxxv. 46. 2, 47. 2.

3. Cf. App. *Syr.* 14. 58: Φίλιππον δὲ πειρᾶσθαι μὲν προσάγεσθαι μηχανῇ πάσῃ.

4–5. Cf. App. *Syr.* 14. 54: Θεσσαλοὺς μὲν οὐ δυσχερές, εἴτε νῦν εἴτε μετὰ χειμῶνα ἐθέλοις, ὑπάγεσθαι· τὸ γὰρ ἔθνος ἐκ πολλοῦ πεπονηκὸς ἔς τε σὲ νῦν καὶ ἐς Ῥωμαίους αὖ, εἴ τι γίγνοιτο νεώτερον, μεταβαλεῖται.

4. in consilio: in deciding their own policy—i.e. in acceding to the demands of Antiochus. Sage's 'in the council' is nonsense.

5. consuetum imperium: 'the imperial power to which they are accustomed'. For *consuetus* in this sense cf. p. 4.

6. nihil ... sit: 'there would be no free choice available to him in the future'.

7. ego: B, *ergo* χ. Either could be right.

8–9. In Appian, *Syr.* 14. 56 Hannibal says that Amynander and the Aetolians cannot be relied on.

8. constat: W–M (on § 13) strangely regard this as ironical.

9. Amynander ... eo bello: for Amynander's part in the Second Macedonian War cf. xxxi. 28. 1 n.

10. tum ... te ... totam: deliberate alliteration.

ut meam ... taceam: since Hannibal was defeated in the end, he cannot press the point about himself. But of course Pyrrhus too was finally defeated by Rome.

utramque fortunam 'both my good and my bad fortune' is perfectly acceptable, and emendations are quite unjustified.

patrum ... aetate: scarcely true of events 90 years earlier.

erat ... comparatus: Madvig (*Emendationes*, 520), om. *erat* B, *erit* χMg: *comparatus* BNV, *comparatum* φL. *erit* may be correct: 'what will Rome be compared with you'. Cf. Walker, *Supplementary Annotations*, 210 (who, however, wrongly takes *comparatus* to mean 'matched').

12. Thoas: cf. xxxv. 12. 4 n.

12–13. fremere ... aequabat: cf. xxxv. 18. 6 *ferarum modo ...*
uoluere, but that is in fact put in the mouth of Alexander of Acarnania.

soluamus ... erumpere: not ironical, as W–M claim. For the
transitive use of *erumpere* cf. *TLL,* v. 2. 840. 13 ff.

14–15. Cf. App. *Syr.* 14. 58: ἦν δ' ἀπειθῇ, τὸν σὸν υἱὸν αὐτῷ Σέλευκον
ἐπιπέμπειν διὰ Θρᾴκης, ἵνα καὶ ὅδε, περισπώμενος οἰκείοις κακοῖς,
μηδὲν ᾖ τοῖς πολεμίοις χρήσιμος.

14. adiungere ... adiungi: Bχ. *coniungere ... coniungi* Mg. Either
is possible.

15. Seleucus ... Lysimachiae: cf. xxxiii. 40. 6 n., xxxv. 15. 5. It
is uncertain whether Seleucus had been there continuously since
196. W–M's note is misleading.

per Thraciam: sc. *profectus.* Cf. xxxiv. 26. 9 n., Pettersson, 86.

16. de ratione ... ignorasti: cf. App. *Syr.* 14. 56: τῆς δὲ γνώμης
ἔχομαι τῆς αὐτῆς.

castellum ... expugnatum: cf. xxxv. 51. 7 ff.

oram: cf. App. *Syr.* 14. 57: τὰ παράλια τῆς Ἰταλίας.

Hannibalem ... audirent: for the memory of the terror caused
by Hannibal, and his transformation into a 'bogeyman' cf. N. M.
Horsfall, *Philologus* cxvii (1973), 138.

18–19. Cf. App. *Syr.* 14. 57: χρὴ τὸ μὲν ἥμισυ τῶν νεῶν τὰ παράλια τῆς
Ἰταλίας πορθεῖν, τὸ δὲ ἥμισυ ναυλοχεῖν, ἐφεδρεῦον ἐς τὰ συμφερόμενα,
αὐτὸν δὲ σὲ πεζῷ παντὶ προκαθήμενον τῆς Ἑλλάδος, ἀγχοῦ τῆς Ἰταλίας
δόξαν ἐμποιεῖν ἐσβολῆς καί, εἰ δύναιό ποτε, καὶ ἐσβαλεῖν.

19. Bullinum agrum: Byllis in Epirus is an inland town, and it
will be its territory that is involved. On Byllis cf. Tomaschek, *RE,*
iii. 1105–6, on Hannibal's proposal Oost, *RPEA,* 62–3, Hammond,
Epirus, 623.

20. te: χ, om. B, perhaps rightly. Cf. p. 12.

bonis malisque meis: cf. § 10 *utramque fortunam.*

21. optima: χ, om. B, perhaps rightly. Cf. xlv. 29. 3, F. Walter,
PhW lx (1940), 350.

8–12. *Further activities of Antiochus*

8. 1. ferme: cf. 7. 1 n.

nisi quod ... misit: cf. App. *Syr.* 14. 59.

Polyxenidam: cf. xxxv. 50. 7 n.

2. exercitui Pheras: the text as it stands, with the double dative, is clearly impossible. H. J. Müller's deletion of *exercitui* (*JPhV* xv [1889], 24) is attractive, but it is hard to see why it should have been inserted. J. F. Gronovius's *cum exercitu* remains the simplest solution.

Pheras: cf. xxxii. 13. 9 n.

dictus: Bχ, *indictus* Mg, perhaps rightly. Cf. 6. 6 n., H. J. Müller, loc. cit. On the gender see appendix.

3–6. For this episode cf. App. *Syr.* 16. 66–7, Walbank, *Philip V*, 200–1.

3. ubi: Bχ, *ibi* Mg, perhaps rightly.

Philippum Megalopolitanum: cf. xxxv. 47. 5–8.

hominum: χ, om. B, perhaps rightly. Cf. xxxi. 46. 12 n.

4. ipso: Philip of Megalopolis. For his hopes for the throne of Macedon cf. xxxv. 47. 7.

insita ... uanitate: for other comments on innate human characteristics cf. xxviii. 24. 1, 25. 14, xlii. 39. 3, Hellmann, 28.

amplum: 'impressive'.

animo adiecto: cf. p. 4.

5–6. Anger over Antiochus' action can scarcely have been the real, or at least the only reason for Philip's decision to commit himself to Rome: cf. De Sanctis, iv. 1. 153 ff. For the offers allegedly made to Philip by Antiochus in order to secure his support cf. xxxix. 28. 6.

5. tumulus est ... factus: *ecphrasis*: 'there is a mound, made ...' (thus rightly W–M: Sage mistranslates). Philip thus adopted the traditional Macedonian method of burial. For the burial of the dead of Chaeronea in a tumulus cf. N. G. L. Hammond and G. T. Griffith, *A History of Macedonia*, ii (Oxford, 1979), 598.

6. fortunam ... consilio: 'ready to let fortune (i.e. what happened in the conflict) be the guide of his policy'. For proverbial contrasts between *fortuna* and *consilium* cf. Otto, 143 (though here, of course, *consilium* is used metaphorically in the sense of 'advisory body').

habiturus in consilio: B, *in consilio habiturus* χ. Cf. p. 15 n. 3.

M. Baebium: (44). Cf. xxxiv. 45. 3 n., p. 37.

propraetorem: the consular year 191 has now begun (cf. 5. 1–6. 5 n.). There was, it seems, no formal prorogation of his *imperium*. See further 10. 10, 13. 1–9, 22. 8.

9. 1. ab Larisa: it is clear from §§ 4 and 15 that these are representatives of Larisa alone, not of the Thessalian κοινόν. Cf. Deininger, 93 n. 9.

3. Hippolocho: he will be the Thessalian *strategos* of 181/0. Cf. Sundwall, *RE*, viii. 1862. He is not to be identified with the Hippolochus who served under Ptolemy Philopator and then deserted to Antiochus in 217 (Pol. v. 70. 11 ff.).

    Scotusam: cf. xxxiii. 6. 8 n. Mog. and Frob. 2 have *Scotussa(m)* here, at § 13, and at 14. 11: Bχ present, in various guises, *Scotusa* in all three passages. The normal form in coins and inscriptions is Σκότουσσα (Stählin, *RE*, iiiA. 613) and perhaps we should read *Scotussa* on all three occasions. *Scotussa* is clearly the transmitted reading at xxviii. 5. 12, 15, though not at xxviii. 7. 3. B has *Scotusa* at xxxiii. 6. 8, 11.

4. stabiliendae libertatis: cf. v. 12. 8.

5. Pausaniam: the first *strategos* of the Thessalian κοινόν (196/5). Cf. Eus. *Chron.* i. 243 Schöne, Deininger, 92.

6. Chalcidensibus ... dicta: xxxv. 46. 4 ff.

7. etiam atque etiam: cf. xxxv. 6. 4 n.

8. haec ... esset: for the word-order cf. p. 14 and addendum ad loc., for *renuntiata ... legatio* cf. xxxi. 17. 4 n.
    fors ... tulisset: cf. xxxi. 41. 7 n.

9. oppugnare ... adgressus: *adgredior* with the infinitive is perfectly common in L. (*TLL*, i. 1320. 71 ff.). W–M are misleading.

10. positum esse ... sperni ... timeri: a unique instance of *positum esse in* with the infinitive. At Caes. *BG* vii. 32. 6 it is followed by *ne*, at Cic. *Att.* xvi. 16B. 8 by *ut*, and at viii. 25. 11 by *utrum* (*TLL*).

11. propugnantes: a substantival participle. Cf. Adams, *Glotta* li (1973), 131.

12. castigationibus: Mg, *castigatione* χ, *castigationes* B. The plural is perhaps more appropriate in this context.

15. rege ... rex: for the repetition cf. p. 13.

10. 1. intra ... quam: for *quam* = *postquam* cf. K–St, i. 405, H–S, 597–8. On *decimum diem* see appendix.
    Crannonem: Crannon is *c.* 20 km. south-west of Larisa. Cf. Stählin, *RE*, xi. 1580 ff., *HTh*, 111–12.

2. Cierium et Metropolim: cf. xxxii. 13. 11, 15. 3 nn. The second Metropolis referred to by W–M does not exist: cf. Stählin, *HTh*, 27 n. 2.

recepit: cf. xxxiii. 18. 22 n.

Atracem: Mg, *ad regem* Bχ. We should probably read *Atragem* both here and at 13. 4. Cf. xxxii. 15. 8 n., H. J. Müller, *JPhV* xxxiii (1907), 9.

Gyrtonem: identified by Stählin (*HTh*, 91–2: cf. also *RE*, vii. 2101–2) with Barkana (now Gyrtone) near the Peneius about 13 km. north of Larisa.

4. quadrato agmine: cf. xxxv. 3. 2 n.

absentium: χ, *absentem* B. The latter is impossible. One could alter *praesentem* to *praesentium*, but the variation should probably be accepted.

5. Pellinaeum: the normal form of the name is Πέλιννα, though Πελινναῖον is also found. It lay about 12 km. east of Trikkala. Cf. Stählin, *HTh*, 117–19, *RE*, xix. 327 ff.

Menippus: cf. xxxiv. 57. 6 n. He was last heard of at xxxv. 51. 8.

Perrhaebiam ... Malloeam ... Cyretias: cf. xxxi. 41. 5 nn. *Chyretias* is read by Mog. here and cited from Mg at 13. 4.

Tripolitanum: the Tripolis consisted of the towns of Azorus, Pythium, and Doliche in the north of Perrhaebia. Cf. xlii. 53. 6, Stählin, *HTh*, 19 ff., Kirsten, *RE*, viiA. 207 ff., Walbank, *Commentary*, iii. 345–6.

7. uim adhibendam: Bχ, *afferendam uim* Mg. For *uim adferre* cf. iii. 45. 9, 49. 3, iv. 4. 8, xxxv. 35. 1, xxxviii. 20. 8, xlv. 19. 12, for *uim adhibere* v. 43. 1, vii. 39. 13, xxvi. 44. 10, xxvii. 31. 7. But (i) L. would probably have avoided *afferendam ... differendum* (ii) Bχ's word-order is preferable, and this should be allowed to weigh in favour of their reading as a whole.

in plano ... aditu: on the central Thessalian plain cf. xxxi. 41. 7 n.

8. Pheris: *Phaereis* B, *Phereis* χ. *Phereis* should be retained. For the *comparatio compendiaria* cf. 7. 13 with W–M's note, Anderson on ix. 10. 3, K–St, ii. 566–7.

9–13. Cf. the account of Appian, *Syr.* 16. 68–9.

9. Pharsalo: for the Aetolian claim to possession of Pharsalus cf. xxxiii. 13. 9–12, 34. 7, 49. 8 nn.

10. M. Baebius ... congressus: cf. 8. 6. Baebius and Philip agreed that the latter could keep any Thessalian towns captured from the Aetolians. Cf. xxxix. 23. 10–12, 25. 5, Walbank, *Philip V*, 207 n. 2.

Dassaretiis: cf. xxxi. 33. 4 n.

Ap. Claudium: (294). Pulcher. Cf. xxxiii. 29. 8 n.

per Macedoniam: north-west to south-east.

montium ... Gonnos: on Gonni cf. xxxiii. 10. 6 n. Add B. Helly, *Gonnoi* (Amsterdam, 1973). The mountains are the Erimon range to the south of the Peneius (Stählin, *HTh*, 88), not the foothills of Mt. Olympus, as claimed by W–M.

11. uiginti milia: the direct distance from Gonni to Larisa is *c.* 27 km. If L.'s figure is correct, it must, as W–M say, be for a march along the Peneius.

in ... situm: not true. Gonni is about 4 km. from the beginning of the gorge. L. may have misunderstood Polybius. On Tempe cf. xxxii. 15. 9 n.

quam pro: cf. Walsh on xxi. 29. 2.

quam quot: cf. xxxv. 12. 14 n.

12. instare: *stare* Bχ. If *instare* is right, it will mean 'was pressing upon them', not 'was imminent', and would not therefore involve a mistranslation of Polybius, as claimed by Walbank, *Philip V*, 328 n. 10, *Commentary*, iii. 75. But Duker's *obstare* may be right.

rediit: MgL, *redit* BNV (om. φ, reading *ad Demetriadem*), perhaps rightly. Cf. p. 12.

in suos ... fines: cf. p. 15.

11. 1–4. *The marriage of Antiochus.* This extraordinary episode is recounted by Polybius xx. 8 (from Athenaeus: but it seems, despite one close verbal echo in L.—cf. § 2 n.—that Athenaeus was paraphrasing rather than quoting Polybius), Diod. xxix. 2, Plut. *Phil.* 17. 1, *Flam.* 16. 1, App. *Syr.* 16. 69, Dio fr. 62. 1, Zon. ix. 19. 5, Just. xxxi. 6. 3, Flor. i. 24. 9, *uir. ill.* 54. 1. The allegations of debauchery are rightly doubted by e.g. De Sanctis, iv. 1. 157 n. 79, Walbank, *Philip V*, 202 n. 1, *Commentary*, iii. 76, Seibert, 61, Bar-Kochva, 96. Seibert suggests that Antiochus' aim was to tie Chalcis to him more closely. On the status of Antiochus' existing marriage to Laodice cf. Schmitt, *Antiochus*, 10 ff., Walbank, *Commentary*, iii. 75, xxxvii. 44. 6 n.

1. Chalcidem a Demetriade: the omission of *profectus* after *Demetriade* is a misprint.

captus: cf. p. 4.

ipse: cf. xxxi. 3. 5 n.

2. grauioris ... condicioni: a rather compressed expression apparently meaning 'a marriage involving him in fortunes more burdensome than he wished'. Sage's 'a match which promised too great difficulties' is somewhat misleading.

quantas ... liberandam: Pol. xx. 8. 1: δύο τὰ μέγιστα τῶν ἔργων ἀνειληφώς, τήν τε τῶν Ἑλλήνων ἐλευθέρωσιν, ὡς αὐτὸς ἐπηγγέλλετο, καὶ τὸν πρὸς Ῥωμαίους πόλεμον.

bellum ... liberandam: cf. xxxv. 20. 7 n.

in conuiuiis ... uoluptatibus: Pol. xx. 8. 2: οἰνοπότης ὢν καὶ μέθαις χαίρων.

3–4. Cf. Diod. xxix. 2: καὶ οἱ στρατιῶται τὸν χειμῶνα κατατετριφότες ἐν ἀνέσει καὶ τρυφῇ and Plut. *Phil.* 17. 1: τοὺς δὲ Σύρους ἐν ἀταξίᾳ πολλῇ καὶ χωρὶς ἡγεμόνων ἐν ταῖς πόλεσι πλαζομένους καὶ τρυφῶντας.

5. principio ueris: March, 191.

per Phocidem Chaeroneam: i.e. Antiochus did not go directly to Chaeronea, but went through Locris into Phocis and then back eastwards into Boeotia.

6. Alexandrum ... Acarnana: cf. xxxv. 18. 1. The MSS. have *Ac (Ach-)arnanam* here and *Ac(Ach-)arnana* at xxxvii. 45. 17: it seems certain therefore that L. formed the accusative in -*a*.

Stratum: Gel. 'nescioquis deprauauit', *magistratum* Bχ. On Stratus, near the border of Acarnania, and once an Acarnanian town, cf. Zschietzschmann, *RE*, ivA. 331 ff., Walbank, *Commentary*, i. 240.

7. consilio: J. Gronovius, *concilio* Bχ. Cf. xxxv. 34. 2 n.

7–8. L.'s description of these events is scarcely intelligible. The army starts from Chaeronea and meets Antiochus at a point on the road between Naupactus and Stratus via Calydon and Lysimachia. It is hard to see how such a route could take them anywhere near the Malian Gulf. Unless the text is corrupt, we must assume that L. has misunderstood or distorted Polybius. Similarly, in § 8 *ibi* apparently refers to the road to Stratus, but, of course, Mnasilochus' intrigues must take place in Acarnania, not on a road in Aetolia.

On Calydon, at the mouth of the Corinthian Gulf, cf. von Geisau, *RE*, x. 1763 ff., on Lysimachia Bölte, *RE*, xiii. 2552 ff., Walbank, *Commentary*, i. 543–4. The date of its foundation is uncertain.

ad Stratum: to be taken with *fert*, not with *occurrit*.

8–12. 11. On these events cf. Oost, *RPEA*, 60 ff. (note p. 62 on Seleucid symbols on Acarnanian coins).

8. Mnasilochus: perhaps the son of the Echedamus of xxxiii.

16. 5: cf. Deininger, 48–9 n. 7. See further xxxvii. 45. 17, xxxviii. 38. 18.

Clytum: not known apart from these events. The MSS. have *Clitum* here, at 12. 2 χ has *Cliti* with the name omitted in B, and at 12. 5 they have *exaclito*. It may be that he was called Κλεῖτος rather than Κλύτος.

9. Leucadios ... caput: cf. xxxiii. 17. 1 n. For *quod* cf. K–St, i. 30, Ogilvie, 370: but Ogilvie's description of the construction as an 'inelegancy' is scarcely justified. The attraction of the relative (and of *is*) into the neuter is L.'s regular practice with *caput*. Cf. xxiii. 11. 11, xxxii. 30. 6, xxxiii. 1. 1, xxxv. 51. 10, xxxviii. 1. 4.

Atilio: on A. Atilius Serranus (60) cf. xxxiv. 54. 3, xxxv. 20. 10–12, 22. 2, 35. 1, 37. 3 nn.

quaeque: Weissenborn, *quae* Bχ. It seems that Atilius had detached a small part of his fleet under A. Postumius (12. 9) to stand off Cephallenia, while he himself remained at the Piraeus (cf. 20. 7–8. He was last heard of off Laconia—xxxv. 37. 3. There is no reason to place him at Corinth, as is done by Thiel, 285, 289.) But *quae cum Atilio quaeque circa Cephallaniam* is very obscure Latin for 'that part of the fleet which was with Atilius and that part which was off Cephallenia' and it is in any case odd that the Acarnanians should have anticipated the arrival of the main fleet. I suspect that *quae cum Atilio* should be deleted as a gloss.

The detachment under Postumius later, it seems, rejoined Atilius (cf. Thiel, 290).

Cephallaniam: the island was an ally of the Aetolians: cf. Walbank, *Commentary*, i. 454. On its siege in 189 cf. xxxviii. 28. 5 ff. It cannot be determined whether L. spelt it with one or two *l*s. The evidence does suggest that he wrote *-lan-* rather than *-len-*, perhaps following Polybius. Cf. Nissen, *KU*, 137 n.

10. concilio: probably the primary assembly (cf. xxxiii. 16. 3 n.).

Medionem ... Thyrreum: on Medion cf. Walbank, *Commentary*, i. 154, on Thyrreum ibid., 454. The MSS. evidence as a whole suggests that L. spelt the latter *Thyrreum*. Cf. W–M, p. 182.

12. 2. eoque: 'and for that reason'.

accepta: Bχ, *accepta est* Mg. Cf. p. 12.

4. de industria: 'deliberately'. The phrase occurs twenty-nine times in L., but is completely absent from Tacitus.

coniecti: Bχ, *collecti* Mg. The reading is not in doubt, though I can find no precise parallel for *conicere* in this sense. xlv. 15. 5 and Cic. *Phil.* v. 15, adduced by W–M, are not quite the same, and the section in *TLL* (iv. 310. 56 ff.) in which this passage is placed contains nothing exactly parallel.

6. aliis . . . qui: cf. vi. 1. 10, Cic. *parad.* 37, *TLL*, i. 1640. 70 ff.

uulgatae: Madvig (*Emendationes*, 520) argued that Antiochus' *clementia* had not yet spread widely and that the hopes of the Acarnanians were that it would be extended to them. Hence he proposed *uulgandae*. But *spem uulgatae clementiae* means 'the hope for the clemency which had been widely talked about' and the MSS. text should be retained.

7. eodem: i.e. to Thyrreum.

8. perplexo: cf. pp. 6, 8.

9. Cn. Octauius: (16). Cf. xxxi. 3. 2, 11. 18 nn., xxxv. 23. 5. His earlier activities on this mission have not been catalogued.

A. Postumio: probably A. Postumius Albinus (46), the consul of 180. He was curule aedile in 187, praetor in 185, a *legatus* to Macedonia, and perhaps a *iuuir* for the dedication of a temple in 175, censor in 174, a *legatus* to Crete in 171, and perhaps a military *legatus* under Paullus in 168. He was a member of the commission for the settlement of Macedon in 167 and a *xuir sacris faciundis* from 173 until his death. On the present episode cf. Münzer, *RE*, xxii, 926.

legato: in fact Atilius will certainly have been a propraetor (cf. Münzer, loc. cit., Schleussner, 112 n. 42: the fact that his *imperium* had not been formally prorogued and that he was to be succeeded by Livius makes no difference to his status, as Thiel, 279, claims). Perhaps we should read *ab A. Postumio legato, qui ab Atilio Cephallaniae . . .* (Perizonius proposed *legatus* for *legato* but such a predicative use of *legatus* would be very strange.)

Cephallaniae propositus: in fact only of the fleet off Cephallenia. It is most unlikely that Rome had taken possession of the island, only for it to be immediately lost again. Cf. 11. 9 n.

10–11. Acilium . . . faciebat: L. leaves it unclear whether or not Acilius had in fact arrived in Thessaly by this time. For the date of his arrival (probably March–April) see Walbank, *Philip V*, 329. Cf. p. 28.

13. *Events in Thessaly*

On the route followed by the Roman and Macedonian forces cf. Kromayer, ii. 136. I cannot follow Niese's claim (ii. 702 n. 1) that L. describes these events somewhat grudgingly.

13. 1. Repeated from 10. 10. *sub idem tempus* refers to the main clause *principio ueris . . . descenderunt.*

2. in hiberna: for Baebius probably still at Apollonia (W–M) Cf. xxxv. 24. 7.

3. Malloeam Perrhaebiae: cf. 10. 5 n.

Phacium: cf. xxxii. 13. 9 n. Its capture by Antiochus and the Aetolians has not previously been mentioned.

Phaestum: Sigonius. *Phaustum* BPENV, *Phacium* L, *Plaustrum* A. To be identified with Φαῦττός, just north of the Peneius in the extreme east of Hestiaiotis. Cf. Stählin, *HTh*, 115, Kirsten, *RE*, xix. 1904–5. In view of the MSS. evidence, there is no case for reading *Phaestum*, a form found in Ptol. iii. 12. 41, though whether L. wrote *Phaustum* or *Phauttum* I would not care to say.

Atracem: cf. 10. 2 n. At 10. 2 it is explicitly said not to have been in Antiochus' possession. It must be left uncertain whether it had surrendered to him subsequently, or whether it now made a voluntary *deditio* to Baebius.

4. Cyretias: cf. 10. 5 n.

et Eritium: P, *et Erititium* B, *et Eriticium* AL, *et Criticium* E, *etereticium* NV. It seems as if L. wrote *Eriticium*, which is not otherwise known, and Stählin, *HTh*, 28 n. 10 (thinking, of course, that L. wrote *Eritium*) plausibly suggested that the town involved is in fact Ericinium, which is near Chyretiae, while Erit(ic)ium will be one of the places near Gomphi captured from Amynander in § 6. If Stählin is right, the error is probably to be attributed to L. himself, and textual transposition is not to be recommended. If the town was called *Eriticium*, the error would have been all too easy.

recepta: Bχ, *capta* Mg, perhaps rightly, though the repetition of *recipere* in a different sense is no objection to *recepta*. Cf. p. 13.

rursus: with *se coniungit.*

6. Walbank (*Philip V*, 202 n. 4) suggested that some of these towns had been held by Amynander since 196, when he had been allowed to keep places he had captured during the Second Macedonian War (cf. xxxiii. 34. 11 n.). Of the towns here listed only Gomphi is known to have been taken then (xxxii. 14. 2) and none of the other towns mentioned in xxxii. 14. 1–3 is included in the present list. I would regard it as more probable that the other towns mentioned here are recent captures of Amynander.

Aeginium: cf. xxxii. 15. 4 n.

Ericinium: *Ercinium* Bχ. Cf. § 4 n.

Gomphi: cf. xxxi. 41. 6 n.

Silana: not otherwise known.

Tricca: cf. xxxii. 13. 5 n.

Meliboea: *Moelibea* B, *Moelibe* φNV, *Moebibe* L. The Magnesian Meliboea appears as *Moelibea* in the Vienna MS. at xliv. 13. 1 and 46. 3 respectively and perhaps L. wrote *Moeliboea* or *Moelibe* here.

Phaloria: cf. xxxii. 15. 1 n.

7. Pellinaeum: cf. 10. 5 n.

8. Romanis: i.e. to the Romans alone, without Philip of Macedon being present.

9. Limnaeum: placed by Stählin (*HTh*, 83–4, *RE*, xiii. 707–8) just to the north of the River Pamisus, *c.* 5 km. south of Pharcadon. It was probably captured at the same time as Pellinaeum (10. 5).

14. *Arrival and initial actions of M'. Acilius Glabrio*

On these events cf. Appian, *Syr.* 17. 71–3, Zon. ix. 19. 7.

14. 1. forte: cf. xxxii. 39. 4 n.

uiginti: see pp. 37–8.

pedestris ... uenit: through Epirus, as Flamininus in 198. Cf. Hammond, *Epirus*, 623, Cabanes, 281: denied, without argument, by Larsen, *Greek Federal States*, 417, Walbank, *Commentary*, iii. 65.

4. fratrem: P. Klose, *Die völkerrechtliche Ordnung der hellenistischen Staatenwelt in der Zeit von 280–168 v. Chr.* (Munich, 1972), 82 n. 265, thinks that Philip's use of the term refers to a custom of Hellenistic kings of addressing each other as 'brother'. The only evidence for such a custom is Welles, *RC*, no. 71, dating from 109 B.C., and Josephus, *AJ* xiii. 45. 126, and Klose's notion must be regarded as uncertain.

haud sane ... ioco: cf. xxxii. 34. 3 n.

5. deditorum ... oppidorum: i.e. Limnaeum and Pellinaeum, though perhaps others as well. Walbank, *Philip V*, 203, wrongly implies that all the prisoners were in Pellinaeum alone.

quattuor milia: Bekker, om. *milia* B, $\overline{iii}$ A, *tria* P, $\overline{iii}$ m. E, *tria milia* ψ. Appian (*Syr.* 17. 72) says that there were 3,000 Seleucid prisoners and makes no mention of Athamanians. It would be rash to take this as evidence that Polybius specified 3,000 Seleucid and 1,000 Athamanian prisoners. Rather Appian gives support to χ's *tria* against B's *quattuor*.

6. Cierio et Metropoli: for their surrender to Antiochus cf. 10. 2 n.

7. indulgenter: the only occurrence of the word in L. It is not at all certain that in fr. 54 anything but *non triumphabor* is a direct quotation from L. and W–M may be misleading in adducing the passage.

9. Ambraciamque: Ambracia had been an Aetolian possession since *c.* 230: cf. Walbank, *Commentary*, i. 158.

10. uelut: indicating Acilius' belief, not implying that the belief was incorrect. Cf. K–St, i. 791.

renouato: Mg, *reparato* Bχ. Either is possible. For *renouare* in this sense cf. xxi. 21. 8, for *reparare* xliv. 38. 11 (if the MS. reading is accepted).

Crannonem: cf. 10. 1 n.

11. Pharsalus: cf. 10. 9.
Scotusa: cf. 9. 3 n.
Pherae: cf. 9. 5–12.

12. Proernam: between Pharsalus and Thaumaci. Cf. Stählin, *HTh*, 157 ff., Kirsten, *RE*, xxiii. 107–8. Its previous capture by or surrender to Antiochus has not been mentioned. Walbank, *Philip V*, 203 n. 3 suggests that it occurred at the same time as the surrender of Pharsalus.

in sinum Maliacum: i.e. southwards from Pharsalus.
faucibus ... Thaumaci: cf. xxxii. 4. 1–3 nn.
misit: Madvig, *mittere* Mg, *missi* Bχ. I would prefer J. F. Gronovius's *missis*.

15. Hypataeorum: on Hypata cf. Stählin, *HTh*, 221 ff., *RE*, ix. 236 ff., Béquignon, 308 ff. It is, of course, part of the Aetolian League. On Glabrio's route from Thaumaci to Hypata see Béquignon, 280–1.

15–19. *The battle of Thermopylae*

Other sources for the battle are Diod. xxix. 3, Plut. *Cato mai.* 13–14, App. *Syr.* 17–20, Front. *Strat.* ii. 4. 4, *uir. ill.* 47. 3, Flor. i. 24. 11, Oros. iv. 20. 20, Zon. ix. 19. 8–10. Both L. and Appian derive from Polybius, adapting him in different ways. In Plutarch's version Cato himself conceives the plan of going over the mountains, and the manœuvre is intended as a means of turning Antiochus' position, while in L. the aim is merely to attack the Aetolian detachments (17. 1). There can be no serious doubt that Plutarch's version is that of Cato himself. See Pédech, 368–70, Astin, *Cato*, 57 ff.: *contra* Pritchett, i. 74.

On the battle and the topography see Kromayer, ii. 134 ff., Béquignon, 43 ff., *RA* 6, iv (1934), 18–20, A. R. Burn, *Persia and the*

Greeks (London, 1962), 407 ff., C. Hignett, *Xerxes' Invasion of Greece* (Oxford, 1963), 127 ff., Pritchett, i. 71 ff., Bar-Kochva, 158 ff.

15. 2. uana: cf. xxxiv. 24. 1 n.

Hannibalem . . . admirari: cf. Diod. xxix. 3: τὸν δὲ Ἀννίβαν τὴν ἐναντίαν γνώμην ἐσχηκότα τότε ἐθαύμαζε, App. *Syr.* 17. 74 τῆς εὐβουλίας Ἀννίβου τότε ᾔσθετο.

misit: B, *mittit* χ, perhaps rightly. Cf. p. 12.

Lamiam: *iam* Bχ. Duker's correction is inevitable. Cf. xxxii. 4. 3, xxxv. 43. 9 nn.

3. decem milia: cf. xxxv. 43. 6 n.

qui . . . Asia: part of the expected reinforcements, but much less than he had hoped for. Cf. § 5, Diod. loc. cit.: τὰς δὲ ἐκ τῆς Ἀσίας δυνάμεις ὑστερούσας, App. loc. cit.: ἄλλους ἐπ' ἄλλοις ἔπεμπεν ἐπισπέρχειν Πολυξενίδαν ἐς τὴν διάβασιν.

4. conuenissent: clearly the Aetolians, despite the violent change of subject. Bar-Kochva, 17, wrongly takes the Seleucid forces to be the subject.

4–5. The Aetolians are making excuses. There cannot be any doubt that a regular levy had been made, and it was not a case of only volunteers being involved, as W–M suggest. In fact the Aetolians may have had perfectly respectable military reasons for not wanting to commit all their forces to Antiochus at once. Cf. Kromayer, ii. 138 ff., De Sanctis, iv. 1. 160–1.

cum paucis clientibus: L. imports a Roman notion which probably does not correspond to any real feature of Aetolian society.

6–12. *The site of Thermopylae.* There can be no doubt that Polybius gave a description of the site of the battle. Cf. App. *Syr.* 17. 76–7, Pédech, 517, 533: Luce's suggestion (81–2) that the passage is L.'s own addition is absurd. But L. himself clearly had no idea of the realities of the topography and his exposition is muddled. In § 6 L. talks of a *iugum* dividing Greece as the Apennines divide Italy (the comparison is obviously his own). The *iugum* must be the whole mountain range from the Adriatic to the Malian Gulf, but the only respect in which this range divides Greece in the way that the Apennines divide Italy is that it separates the Thessalian plain, eastern Locris, Phocis, and eastern Boeotia from the less mountainous areas near the Adriatic. L. quite inappropriately equates the *iugum* with the pass of Thermopylae, and the division which follows is of those parts of Greece which were accessible without forcing the pass from those which were not.

7. uersa ... est: χ, om. *est* B, perhaps rightly, particularly in view of its position in the sentence. But if *est* is right, it means 'are the areas facing ...', and is not modal, as W–M claim. *uersa* is an odd word to use. These lands do not face north more than any other direction. They lie to the north of Thermopylae.

Perrhaebia ... Thessalia: cf. xxxiii. 32. 5 n.

8. et ... tergo: M. Müller, *sita ab tergo et* Bχ. There is no reason to alter the MSS. reading. Given the general character of this passage, L. may well have described Attica as being 'behind Euboea'. We should punctuate, with Madvig (*Emendationes*, 521 n. 1), *Attica terra, sita ab tergo, et ...*

9. Leucate: *Leucade* Bχ. Leucates is the cape at the southern end of Leucas (Meuli, *RE*, xii. 2259). But L. could as well have spoken of the *iugum* beginning from Leucas island and there is no real reason for changing the MSS. reading, particularly as in the two passages where L. certainly was referring to the cape (xxvi. 26. 1, xliv. 1. 4) the ablative is *Leucata*.

10. Oetam ... Callidromon: Οἴτη is sometimes used, as here, to refer to the whole mountain range west of Thermopylae. Sometimes, as in 22. 5, 30. 3, xxxvii. 5. 5, in its modern sense of the mountains immediately west of the Asopus. Cf. Lenk, *RE*, xvii. 2294 ff. Callidromus is the mountain range between the Asopus and Thermopylae: cf. von Geisau, *RE*, x. 1633–4. For the fort Callidromus cf. 16. 11 n.

ualle: i.e. the foot of the mountain. The term is not really appropriate in the context.

sexaginta passus: according to Herodotus (vii. 176. 2) the width is 50 feet, narrowing to a carriage-width. Kromayer, ii. 147, thinks that the east gate was wider in the second century B.C.

12. Pylae ... Thermopylae: cf. Hdt. vii. 201, Strabo, ix. p. 428C. Polybius uses both forms (ii. 52. 8, x. 41. 5).

pugna: i.e. the present battle.

16. 1. pari: like that of Leonidas in 480. *tum*, of course, refers to Antiochus, not to Leonidas, as Sage's translation 'with a spirit totally unlike theirs at the time' implies.

intra portas: Polybius will have referred to the three 'gates' of Thermopylae. Antiochus' position was at the eastern gate, unlike that of Leonidas, who made his initial stand at the central gate (cf. 17. 11). See Kromayer, ii. 147–9, Pritchett, i. 79. But L. probably had no clear idea of what was meant by πύλαι. From 17. 4 one gets the impression that he believed that there really were gates at Thermopylae (as there had been once, at the Phocian wall—Hdt. vii. 176. 3).

munitionibus ... muro: App. *Syr.* 18. 78: τεῖχος οὖν ἐνταῦθα διπλοῦν ὁ Ἀντίοχος ᾠκοδομήσατο καὶ τὰς μηχανὰς ἐπὶ τὸ τεῖχος ἐπέθηκεν. For remains of this wall see Béquignon, *RA* 6, iv (1934), 18–20, Pritchett, i. 73, 79 ff. Pritchett reports traces of a double wall, but he is wrong to say that this is attested by L. as well as by Appian. *duplici* can refer only to *uallo* (cf. Kromayer, ii. 150 n. 1).

3. Romanum exercitum: cf. xxxvii. 46. 7 n.

Heracleam: Heraclea Trachinia, *c.* 8 km. to the west of Thermopylae. It was founded at the site of Trachis by Sparta in 426. Cf. Thuc. iii. 92–3, Béquignon, 254 ff., Gomme, *Historical Commentary on Thucydides*, ii. 396. It commanded the gorge of the Asopus, and the Aetolian garrison was placed to prevent Glabrio from trying to march through the gorge itself and use the route followed by the Persians in 480. Cf. Kromayer, ii. 142. On the topography of Heraclea see further chs. 22–4.

4. Hypatam: cf. 14. 15 n.

5. prope ... aquarum: between the western and middle gates. Cf. Hdt. vii. 176. 3, with How and Wells's note.

utraeque ... manus: i.e. both the section which had been sent to Heraclea and that which had been supposed to go to Hypata.

7–8. App. *Syr.* 18. 78: ἔς τε τὰς κορυφὰς τῶν ὀρῶν Αἰτωλοὺς ἀνέπεμψε, μή τις λάθοι κατὰ τὴν λεγομένην ἀτραπὸν περιελθών, ᾗ δὴ καὶ Λακεδαιμονίοις τοῖς ἀμφὶ Λεωνίδαν Ξέρξης ἐπέθετο, ἀφυλάκτων τότε τῶν ὀρῶν ὄντων.

7. For the breaching of the pass in 480 cf. Hdt. vii. 213 ff. But that route was not open because of the occupation of Heraclea. Cf. § 3 n.

Philippum ... Romanis: not, of course, at Thermopylae, but at the Aous in 198 (xxxii. 11–12). L. has expressed himself carelessly.

8. uertices circa montium: the attributive use of *circa* is common in L. Cf. *TLL*, iii. 1080. 26 ff.

10. opem ... suis: cf. p. 14.

ut dissipatos: cf. 1. 7 n.

11. App. *Syr.* 18. 79: Αἰτωλοὶ δὲ χιλίους μὲν ἑκατέρῳ τῶνδε τῶν ἄκρων ἐπέστησαν, τοῖς δὲ λοιποῖς ἐστρατοπέδευον ἐφ᾽ ἑαυτῶν περὶ πόλιν Ἡράκλειαν. For the identification of the three forts see above all the discussion of Pritchett, i. 71 ff. Bar-Kochva, 260–1 n. 4, argues that L. is wrong to call them *castella* and that they were in fact 'posts in the open field'. He suggests that L. misunderstood ἄκρα in Polybius. I cannot see the evidence for Bar-Kochva's statement that there were no fortifications in the range before 207 and no conclusions can be drawn from Plutarch's failure to mention them in view of the more fundamental differences between his account and that of L. (cf. 15–19 n.). Frontinus' account (*Str.* ii. 4. 4) is too brief for his omission of the forts to be significant.

17. 1. App. *Syr.* 18. 80: ὁ δὲ Μάνιος, ἐπεὶ κατεῖδε τὴν τῶν πολεμίων παρασκευήν ... δύο τῶν χιλιάρχων, Μᾶρκον Κάτωνα καὶ Λεύκιον Οὐαλέριον, ἐκέλευσε νυκτός, ἐπιλεξαμένους ἑκάτερον, ὁπόσους ἐθέλοι, τὰ ὄρη περιελθεῖν καὶ τοὺς Αἰτωλοὺς ἀπὸ τῶν ἄκρων, ὅπῃ δύναιντο, βιάσασθαι.

insessa ... uidit: Bχ. *uidit occupata ab Aetolis superiora loca* Mg, probably arising from a gloss on *insessa*. For similar glosses replacing the true reading cf. § 5 *seruituti nata* Bχ, *seruitutis digna* Mg, § 7 *sileam* Bχ, *omittam* Mg.

M. Porcium ... legatos: the two consuls of 195. Most sources call them military tribunes (Pol. xx. 10. 10—of Flaccus alone—, Cic. *sen.* 32, Front. *Str.* ii. 4. 4—adding the plausible detail that Cato was elected to the office by the people—Plut. *Cato mai.* 12. 1, App. loc. cit. Only Phlegon of Tralles (*FGH* 257 F36 iii. 1) and Zonaras ix. 19. 9 agree with L. Phlegon quotes Antisthenes 'the Peripatetic' but it is not certain that he is identical with the contemporary historian Antisthenes of Rhodes (cf. Walbank, *Commentary*, ii. 518) and even if he is, the statement could not be held to outweigh the other evidence. L. may have been confused by the fact that Cato was later a *legatus* from Glabrio to Rome (21. 4–8 n.). Cf. Astin, *Cato*, 56 n. 15. I am unconvinced by arguments that the two designations are not mutually exclusive (thus Mommsen, *StR*, ii. 695 n. 1, Walbank, *Commentary*, iii. 78, Schleussner, 103 ff.).

2–16. *Glabrio's speech before battle.* Nothing in Appian corresponds to this, and though it cannot be proved, it is very likely that this purely conventional speech before battle is not based on anything in Polybius. Cf. vol. i, 18, Ullmann, *Technique*, 20, 147–8, Tränkle, 29 ff.: *contra* Harris, 109 n. 1. Ullmann analyses the speech as follows. (i) § 2 *prooemium*. (ii) §§ 3–15 *tractatio*: (a) §§ 3–7 *tutum*; (b) §§ 8–12 *facile*; (c) §§ 13–15 *utile*. (iii) § 16 *conclusio*. As usual the division forces the speech into a preconceived pattern. There is no significant break between §§7 and 8, and the only meaningful division, as W–M saw, is between §§ 3–12, reasons for confidence in the outcome of the battle, and §§ 13–15, the advantages that victory will bring.

2. plerosque ... militaueritis: Glabrio's career (cf. xxxi. 50. 5 n.) makes it unlikely that he had fought in the Second Macedonian War, and it is thus improbable that he could actually recognize many among his audience who had served under Flamininus.

3. inexsuperabilior: *inexsuperabilis* is not found before L., who uses it on twelve occasions. Cf. p. 9.

4. portae: cf. 16. 1 n.

unus ... transitus: a somewhat strange expression, since the pass in fact borders on the Aegean. Once again L. betrays his hazy idea of the topography.

clausis omnibus: 'when the whole terrain is blocked'. W–M are wrong to say that we should expect *ceteris omnibus*. It is not the case that all other *transitus* are blocked: Thermopylae is the only *transitus* (cf. 15. 11).

fuerunt ... impositae: cf. p. 14.

5. Thracesque et Illyrii: cf. xxxiii. 4. 4, 7. 11 n.

ferocissimae: Bχ, *bellicosissimae* Mg. The effect of *bellicosissimus* in § 6 would be spoilt by its use here.

Syri ... nata: cf. xxxv. 49. 8 n. *Asiatici Graeci* probably refers to the Hellenized peoples of Asia Minor rather than to the inhabitants of the old Greek colonies. Cf. in general Petrocheilos, 18 ff., who shows how Cicero's attitude to the Greeks of Asia Minor is far more favourable in *ad Q. fr.* i. 1 than (for obvious reasons) in the *pro Flacco*. Note particularly *pro Flacco* 65 *quis umquam Graecus comoediam scripsit in qua seruus primarum partium non Lydus esset?*

uilissima: B, *leuissima* χ. For the Romans, *levitas* was, it seems, a Greek characteristic (cf. Petrocheilos, 40 ff.), but, as W–M say, *uilissima* is more appropriate for *Syri et Asiatici Graeci* and goes better with *seruituti*.

6. inde: *ille* Bχ. For *iam inde* cf. Packard, ii. 923. It is hard to see why *ille* should have been added, and the old emendation is therefore preferable to deletion (thus Novak: cf. H. J. Müller, *JPhV* xx. [1895], 51).

iuuenta: cf. p. 5.

finitimis ... bellis: kings of Macedon were constantly occupied with wars against their barbarian neighbours. Cf. xxxi. 28. 1 n. on the Dardanians and in general Walbank, *Philip V*, ch. i.

ut ... sileam: Glabrio conveniently forgets Antiochus' exploits during the great eastern expedition of 212–205.

obscuri: but Polybius (xx. 8. 3) apparently said that the girl's father was τῶν ἐπιφάνων.

8. saginatus: 'stuffed full'. *saginare* is used metaphorically at vi. 17. 2 and literally at xxxviii. 17. 7. It also occurs metaphorically at Cic. *Sest.* 78 and *Bell. Afr.* 46. 2 and the only other occurrence of its being used literally of humans is Sen. *Contr.* ix. 2. 27 (*TLL*).

uanissima: cf. xxxiv. 24. 1 n.

ingratissima: Bχ, *leuissima* Mg. Despite the other errors in Mg in this chapter (cf. § 1 n.) *leuissima* may be right. The examples that follow are cases of lack of constancy and reliability, not of ingratitude.

9. A confused summary of 16. 3 ff. L. has not previously said that the Aetolians had themselves asked to guard Heraclea and Hypata. One wonders whether Glabrio would in fact have had precise information about such matters.

uenerunt frequentes: Bχ, *frequentes conuenerunt* Mg, again perhaps rightly. There is no point in emphasizing *uenerunt* and for Mg's *conuenerunt* cf. 15. 4 *quam umquam antea conuenissent.*

pars: cf. iii. 61. 9 with W–M's note ad loc.

10–11. ne ante ... castris: cf. Hdt. vii. 223.

11. quod ... incluserit: a striking ellipse for *quantum interest utrum hoc fecerit an ... incluserit.* xxviii 44. 2, adduced by W–M, is not parallel, as it involves merely the omission of *utrum.*

13. in regiis: *regis* Bχ. *regis* may be correct. Cf. xxxv. 49. 10, xliv. 26. 8. See also 19. 2 n.

14–15. The senate had, of course, no intention of annexing the whole of the Seleucid Empire. But it is not impossible for a Roman general to have spoken thus in the heat of the moment. Cf. Pol. xv. 10. 2, Harris, 116–17.

14. Romano imperio: B, *imperio Romano* χ. The emphatic position of *Romano* is clearly preferable.

15. Very much the language of L.'s own time. There is, in fact, a striking similarity to *RG* 26. 2 *qua includit Oceanus a Gadibus* ... Cf. also Hor. *Od.* i. 12. 55, Tac. *A.* i. 9. 5.

deinde: χ, *inde* B. For *quid deinde* cf. Packard, iv. 152. There is no example of *quid inde* in a temporal sense.

mare rubrum: as in xlii. 52. 14, xlv. 9. 6 L. uses the phrase to refer not to the Arabian Gulf, its normal meaning, or even to the whole area between the gulf and the west coast of India, as in Herodotus and Horace, *Od.* i. 35. 32, but to the sea at the eastern extremity of the οἰκουμένη. I can find no other example of such a usage, and it may be that L. was confused about what was normally meant by *mare rubrum*. Cf. Berger, *RE*, vi. 592 ff.

dignos: for the *prolepsis* cf. Ullmann, *Étude*, 91.

18. 1. arma telaque: om. *-que* Bχ, clearly correctly. Cf. x. 4. 2, xxix. 4. 2, Sall. *Iug.* 51. 1, 76. 1, Preuss, 86–7. See p. 11.

arta fronte: in columns (ἐς λόχους ὀρθίους) according to Appian, *Syr.* 18. 82.

2. leuis ... locauit: App. *Syr.* 18. 83 καὶ ὁ βασιλεὺς τοὺς μὲν ψιλοὺς καὶ πελταστὰς προμάχεσθαι τῆς φάλαγγος ἐκέλευσεν.

Macedonum robur: the Seleucid phalanx is regularly described as 'the Macedonians'. It was originally recruited from the Macedonian settlers in the colonies planted by Alexander and the Successors, but the precise extent of true Macedonians in the army of this period is disputed. For the most recent discussions see Bar-Kochva, 20 ff., with the literature cited at 227 n. 109 (to which add Magie, ii. 973–4, E. Will, *Le Monde grec et l'orient*, ii [Paris, 1975], 461), G. Cohen, *The Seleucid Colonies* (Wiesbaden, 1978), 31–2.

sarisophorus: M. Müller, *sariphorus* Bχ. The Vienna MS. has *hippagogus* at xliv. 28. 7. This is the only evidence for the name being used for the Seleucid phalanx. Cf. Bar-Kochva, 54 and 231 n. 1.

munitiones: cf. 16. 2 n.

3. his ... posuit: App. *Syr.* 18. 83: ἐπὶ δεξιὰ (sic) δ' αὐτῆς τοὺς σφενδονήτας καὶ τοξότας ἐπὶ τῶν ὑπωρειῶν.

3–4. his ... Macedonibus: I can see no precise parallels for these datives. The second can be assimilated to datives with *proximus* and *uicinus*, but as W–M say, the addition of *cornu* makes the first very strange.

4. ab dextro ... posuit: App. *Syr.* 18. 83: τοὺς δ' ἐλέφαντας ἐν ἀριστερᾷ (sic) καὶ τὸ στῖφος, ὃ μετ' αὐτῶν αἰεὶ συνετάσσετο, παρὰ τῇ θαλάσσῃ.

claudunt: 'block the way'. Cf. xxii. 5. 6, 47. 2, xxxvii. 39. 11, *TLL*, iii. 1307. 51 ff.

cum adsueto praesidio: perhaps fifty to each elephant. Cf. Bar-Kochva, 82.

ceteras copias: other light-armed troops, no doubt. The omission of any such reference in Appian should not cast doubt on L.'s notice, as W–M imply.

5–6. In L. the initial Roman assault is met by the phalanx, who are assisted by the light-armed troops stationed on the slopes, but a

further attack causes them to withdraw to their first *uallum*. Appian
(*Syr.* 18. 84) says that at first the Seleucid light-armed troops caused
trouble to the Romans, but an attack by the Romans caused the
light-armed troops to withdraw to the phalanx. L. has failed to
distinguish the phalanx, whose position was probably on the *uallum*,
from the πελτασταί mentioned by Appian (83), who may in fact be
the *argyraspides* (Bar-Kochva, 63), while Appian conflates the actions
of the peltasts with those of the light-armed troops on the hills. See
Kromayer, ii. 153, Witte, 395. Pritchett's account (i. 80) is misleading.

nimbum: 'shower'. See Tränkle, *WS*, 117, p. 3 n. 4.

7. ualli: i.e. the real (front) *uallum*.

8. incepto irrito: cf. xxxv. 39. 7 n.

ni ... apparuisset: cf. 15–19 n. Appian (*Syr.* 18. 86) agrees with
Plutarch (*Cato mai.* 13. 7) against L. in having Cato pursue the
Aetolians towards Antiochus' camp, thus causing additional confusion. They should probably be followed on this detail. Appian
omits L.'s statement that at first Antiochus' troops thought that the
Romans were Aetolians, L. Appian's that they thought Cato's force
was larger than it actually was.

19. 2. regiis: Mg (but reading *castris fuerant regiis*), *regis* Bχ. Cf.
17. 13 n.

4. quam in proelio: i.e. to the enemy. In fact the cavalry seem to
have played virtually no part in the battle.

6–7. App. *Syr.* 19. 89: ὁ δὲ Μάνιος μέχρι μὲν ἐπὶ Σκάρφειαν ἐδίωκεν
αὐτοὺς κτείνων τε καὶ ζωγρῶν, ἀπὸ δὲ τῆς Σκαρφείας ἐπανιὼν διήρπαζε
τὸ στρατόπεδον τοῦ βασιλέως καὶ τοὺς Αἰτωλούς, ἐπιδραμόντας τῷ
Ῥωμαίων χάρακι παρὰ τὴν ἀπουσίαν αὐτῶν, ἐξήλασεν ἐπιφανείς. Appian
places the Aetolian attack on the Roman camp during the pursuit
rather than during the battle itself.

6. Scarphaeam: cf. xxxiii. 3. 6 n.

multis ... interfectis: a rather rambling sentence, *quos ...
interfectis* coming somewhat strangely after *caesis captisque* (on which
phrase cf. xxxv. 29. 3 n.).

7. temptata ... fuerant: cf. p. 14.

9. ut qui ... cursu: App. *Syr.* 20. 91: αὐτὸς δ' ὁ βασιλεὺς ἀπὸ μὲν
τῆς πρώτης τροπῆς μετὰ πεντακοσίων ἱππέων εἰς Ἐλάτειαν διέδραμεν.

11. App. *Syr.* 20. 90: Ἀντιόχου δέ, σὺν τοῖς ληφθεῖσιν, ἀμφὶ τοὺς μυρίους.

decem milibus ... scripsimus: cf. xxxv. 43. 6 n.

quos: χ, *quod* B, perhaps rightly. Cf. xxxv. 1. 2 n.

12. Antiati Valerio: cf. xxxii. 7. 5, xxxiii. 30. 10, xxxiv. 5. 9 nn. For his inflated enemy casualty figures cf. p. 64. Actually Antias' figures represent a higher proportion of survivors, 25 per cent against 5 per cent. One may doubt whether only 500 survived (cf. Bar-Kochva, 16).

inde: = *ex iis:* cf. *TLL*, vii. 1. 1119. 47 ff.

Romanorum ... interfecti sunt: App. *Syr.* 20. 90: ἀπέθανον δ' ἐν τῇ μάχῃ καὶ τῇ διώξει Ῥωμαίων μὲν ἀμφὶ τοὺς διακοσίους.

incursu Aetolorum: § 7.

20. 1–4. *Glabrio in Phocis and Boeotia*

20. 1. consule ... ciuitates: Phocis had become part of the Aetolian League in 196 (xxxiii. 34. 8 n.) and had not therefore 'defected' on its own account.

uelamentis: cf. xxxv. 34. 7 n.

hostiliter diriperentur: cf. ii. 14. 4, xxxvii. 21. 7, *TLL*, vi. 3. 3053–4. In such phrases (cf. *hostiliter depopulari* at xxviii. 24. 4, xxxvii. 17. 3, 18. 3) *hostiliter* serves merely to give emphasis. It is hard to see how such action could be carried out in a non-hostile fashion.

2. per omnis dies: W–M rightly remark that Coronea is not all that far from Thermopylae and suggest that Glabrio in fact called at many of the cities of Phocis and Boeotia on his way. It may be, though, that the phrase is an addition by L. Madvig's deletion of *dies* (*Emendationes*, 521) is a desperate remedy.

⟨**in**⟩: om. Bχ. It is not necessary. Cf. xxvi. 11. 11, xxix. 2. 2.

Coroneum: on Coronea cf. xxxiii. 29. 6 n. On the form of the name and its ethnic cf. Pieske, *RE*, xi. 1425. In § 3 L. writes *Coronensis.* The Vienna MS. has *Coronaeus* at xlii. 44. 4, 46. 9, 67. 12, *Coroneus* at xliii. 4. 11, and *Coronitanus* at xlii. 63. 3. Polybius has Κορωνεῖς at xxvii. 1. 8, but Κορωναῖοι at xxxii. 5. 2.

3. Antiochi: χ, om. B, perhaps rightly.

Mineruae Itoniae: Ἰτωνία is an epithet of Athena, probably deriving from the Thessalian town Iton or Itonos. Her temple at Coronea was very old (cf. Strabo, ix. p. 411C) and Athena Itonia seems to have been the patron goddess of the Boeotian federation. The Pan-Boeotian games were held at the temple (Strabo loc. cit.,

Plut. *Mor.* 774F–775A, Paus. ix. 34. 1). Cf. Adler, *RE*, ix. 2374–6, Roesch, 107, Walbank, *Commentary*, iii. 276.

It is not clear whether the statue was part of a cult of Antiochus at Coronea.

4. ingratum . . . animum: cf. xxxv. 31. 8 n.

beneficiis: χ, *benefactis* B. The latter may be correct: cf. Packard, i. 602.

20. 5–8. *Naval events*

On these events cf. Thiel, 290–2.

5. Isidoro: cf. 33. 7. He is not known apart from these events.

Thronium: cf. xxxii. 36. 3 n.

Alexander Acarnan: cf. xxxv. 18. 1 n.

trepidae: for similar personification of ships cf. xxvii. 31. 3, xxix. 35. 1 (W–M).

Cenaeum: the north-western tip of Euboea. Cf. von Geisau, *RE*, xi. 163–4, Gomme, *Historical Commentary on Thucydides*, ii. 398, P–K, i. 569–70.

6. tres . . . naues: cf. p. 15.

Demetriadem: Thiel, 291–2, discusses the question of why no attempt was made to capture Demetrias and Isidorus' ships at this point.

si forte: for *si forte* of precautions against unlikely events cf. 41. 6, J. Champeaux, *REL* xlv (1967), 367.

7–8. For Appian, *Syr.* 20. 91 the ships were part of Antiochus' main fleet and were captured as it was retreating across the Aegean. For the possible co-operation of Eumenes in this episode cf. *IvP* 62, Hansen, *Attalids*, 79.

A. Atilius: cf. 11. 9 n.

frumenti . . . diuisit: Thiel, 291 n. 404, thinks that this was compensation for supplies provided for the Roman fleet.

21. *Further episodes after Thermopylae: reports to the senate and* ouatio *of M. Fulvius Nobilior*

1. Chalcide: Antiochus' main fleet had apparently remained at Chalcis. Cf. Thiel, 290.

Tenum: Glareanus. The MSS. have *Tenedum*, which is geographical nonsense. The reference must be to Tenos, which lies immediately south-east of Andros.

2. Aristoteles: not otherwise known.

3. post paucosque dies: Mg, *paucosque per dies* Bχ. xxiii. 43. 7 is the only other example of *-que* being separated from a monosyllabic preposition in L., and there are no other examples anywhere with *post*. But since Mg's reading is possible, while Bχ's requires emendation, I would prefer to keep to the former. Cf. H. J. Müller, *JPhV* xxi (1905), 51.

perpacatis: *perpacare* does not appear in Latin before the present passage: it reoccurs at 42. 3 (*TLL*).

ullius . . . urbis: any single city. *ullius* is placed first for emphasis.

L. makes no mention of Plutarch's account (*Flam.* 16) of Flamininus assuaging Glabrio's rage against Chalcis, and the gratitude of the Chalcidians to Flamininus. It is hard to think that the episode was not in Polybius, and it is odd that L. should have chosen to ignore it.

multo . . . laudabilior: for the sentiment cf. Cic. *Marc.* 12.

4–11. Cf. Plut. *Cato mai.* 14. 3–4. The account of two *legati* being sent to announce the victory at Thermopylae is puzzling. Why should Glabrio first send Scipio and then, later, Cato? The account of Cato's journey, with the multiplicity of Greek place-names, suggests Polybian origin, while the details of the *supplicatio*, and the following information concerning the *ouatio* of M. Fulvius Nobilior, are manifestly annalistic. To make the situation more puzzling, the *ouatio* of Fulvius is repeated, with only very slight differences, at 39. 1–2. It is there preceded by an account of the victory of Scipio Nasica in Gaul, and Nissen (*KU*, 182–4) suggested that L. Scipio was in fact sent to Rome by his cousin to report events in Gaul, and that L., or one of his sources, confused the two victories. Tränkle, 63, follows Klotz, *Livius*, 13, in regarding the whole of §§ 5–11 as deriving from an annalistic account. He holds that the story of Cato's mission stems from the *Origines*, coming to L. via an annalist and to Plutarch via Cornelius Nepos.

The confusion suggested by Nissen seems extremely unlikely at any stage. L. can easily repeat information by mere carelessness (cf. xxxii. 26. 1–2, xxxiv. 42. 1 nn.) and such repetitions are not necessarily indications of the use of different sources. As to Tränkle's view, there can be no doubt that Cato described his mission in the *Origines*, and I would be prepared to believe that L. read about it there. But there is no reason why the episode should not also have been described by Polybius, and since L. is quite capable of joining Polybian and non-Polybian material in such a way that the 'join' is not obvious it is rash to conclude that §§ 7 and 8 do not also represent what stood in Polybius. The absence of any reference to L.

Scipio in Plutarch is not significant: the biographer naturally concentrates on the actions of his subject.

Tränkle follows Gelzer's view (*RE*, xxii. 119: cf. Leuze, *Hermes* lviii
[1923], 274) that Lucius was allowed by Glabrio to go home before
the battle in order to stand for the consulship of 190, and was not
sent to report on the battle. *dimissus* by itself could, but need not,
have this sense, but it is clear from § 8 that Scipio reported on the
battle itself and that L. regarded him as having been sent by Glabrio
for this purpose. (It should be observed that *IDelos* 442 B 89–90 does
not prove that Lucius was in Greece in 191, as Tränkle claims: cf.
xxxv. 14. 5–12 n.). See also Luce, 77 ff.

We should therefore accept L.'s narrative, and look for a historical
explanation of the double mission. Nissen started from the mistaken
assumption that Glabrio was a political opponent of the Scipios: he
was in fact an ally (cf. vol. i. 31 n. 5). Perhaps Glabrio first sent
Lucius Scipio, who could be relied on to present a report favourable
to the consul, and then realized that his enemies might claim that
Scipio was biased. He would be better off with somebody whom
no one could believe to be favourably disposed towards the consul
(for Cato's later hostility to Glabrio cf. xxxvii. 57. 9 ff. and nn.).
Cato's haste is easily understood as a desire to be able to present
his own report, and, no doubt, emphasize his part in the victory.
Cf. Scullard, *RP*², 125.

4. quem ... dubio auctore: cf. W–M (add x. 35. 19), K–St,
i. 786–7, Pettersson, 124 n. 1, H–S, 139–40.

5. Creusa ... emporium: on Creusa, or Creusis, see Pieske, *RE*,
xi. 1824–5, Roesch, 219, plates xviii–xix. It is referred to also at
xlii. 56. 5, xliv. 1. 4.

   emporium: cf. xxxv. 10. 12 n.

   Patras: Cato had earlier been responsible for keeping Patrai
loyal to Rome (Plut. *Cato mai.* 12. 4). On Patrai cf. Ernst Meyer,
RE, xviii. 2. 2191 ff. It was one of the original members of the
Achaean League (Pol. ii. 41. 12).

   litora legit: cf. xxxv. 27. 6 n.

   Hydruntum: modern Otranto, on the heel of Italy. Cf. Weiss,
RE, ix. 87. The MSS. all present forms in *-em*, and since this is also
found at Cicero, *Att.* xv. 21. 3, xvi. 5. 3, *fam.* xvi. 9. 2, and the only
evidence for *Hydruntum* is in the *Antonine Itinerary*, there can be little
doubt that L. wrote *Hydruntem*.

   traicit: B, *traiecit* χ. Cf. p. 12.

6. quinto die: Plut. *Cato mai.* 14. 3 πεμπταῖος.

   M. Iunium: (48). Brutus. The *praetor urbanus et peregrinus* (2. 6).
Cf. xxxiv. 1. 4 n.

7. in senatum uocauit: the senators, not Cato. Cf. ii. 55. 10, xxiii. 32. 3.

9. hostiis maioribus: cf. xxxi. 5. 3 n.

10. M. Fuluius . . . praetor: (91). Praetor in 193. Cf. xxxiii. 42. 8, xxxv. 7. 8, 22. 5–8 nn.
   erat profectus: Mg, *profectus est* Bχ. Cf. p. 15.

11. bigati: cf. xxxiv. 10. 4 n.
   numeratum: 'cash'. Probably coined in Rome before the triumph, not Roman coins brought from Spain.
   duodecim milia: Mg, *x∞* B, *xcc* P, *x̄c̄c̄* AE, *x m̄* LN, *decem milia* V. It is impossible to decide between *duodecim* and *decem*.

22–24. *The siege of Heraclea*

Cf. Phlegon of Tralles, *FGH* 257 F36 III. 1, App. *Syr.* 21. 94, Zon. ix. 19. 11–12. On Heraclea cf. 16. 3 n., on the topography Stählin, *HTh*, 207 ff., Béquignon, 243 ff., Pritchett, i. 81–2.

22. 1. regiam uanitatem: the theme of Flamininus' speech to the Achaeans in xxxv. 49.

2. ceteras . . . ciuitates: not all of them, of course.

3. et duces: χ, om. *et* B, perhaps rightly. Cf. p. 11.
   paenitere . . . esse: cf. p. 14 n. 1.

4. est circumuectus: χ, om. *est* B. Cf. p. 12.

5. sita est Heraclea: χ, *Heraclea sita est* B. Cf. p. 15.
   Oetae montis: cf. 15. 10 n.
   imminentem: overhanging the city.

6. urbem: χ. om. B, perhaps rightly.

7. Asopo . . . gymnasium: south-east of the city. For possible remains of the gymnasium (no longer visible) cf. Béquignon, 250, 253.
   L. Valerium: cf. 17. 1 n.
   partem . . . qua: M. Müller (thus, but with *quae*, for *qua*, Madvig), *arcem extra muros quae* Mg, om. Bχ. Mg's reading is perfectly good Latin, but topographical nonsense. The *arx* was not outside the walls, was not thickly populated, and was not occupied until the rest of the town had fallen (24. 6). H. J. Müller's *ab arce, qua extra muros* (*JPhV* xvii [1891], 167) is based on the fact that in the case of the other three detachments L. indicates with *a* or *ex* the direction in which the attack took place (cf. xxxi. 24. 9 n.). But (i) all lines of

attack were in fact towards the *arx* (ii) Müller's proposal departs a long way from the transmitted text (iii) the reading involves the further difficulty of having to understand *urbem* with *oppugnandam*. Madvig's *partem* is a simple change, and the corruption could easily have been caused by *arcem* above. I would not exclude the possibility, however, that L. misunderstood Polybius and wrote what Mg transmits. (M. Müller [iv] also suggested *infra arcem*. Damsté's *arcem* ⟨*et aream*⟩ [*Mnemosyne* n.s. xliii (1915), 451] is impossible on grounds of both topography and Latinity.)

in urbe: Bχ. *urbs* Mg, perhaps rightly (with *quae*, of course, not *qua*).

Ti. Sempronio Longo: (67). The consul of 194. Cf. xxxi. 20. 5 n.

8. e regione ... quae: Weissenborn. *a sinu Maliaco quae* Gel. 'Moguntinus et Spirensis codices' (in fact the reading can have been only in Mg: cf. p. 16). *et regione mella quoque* B, *et regionem mellea quoque* χ. Mg's reading is perfectly good and Madvig (*Emendationes*, 522) was right to follow it. The transmitted reading is clearly *Maliaco* and if *et regione*(*m*) is regarded as part of the tradition, we have to assume a very complicated series of corruptions in late antiquity. I would regard *et regione*(*m*) as an attempt to make sense of the corruption of *sinu Maliaco quae* which had already occurred.

quae ... pars: cf. p. 15.

M. Baebium: (44). Tamphilus. Cf. xxxiv. 45. 3 n.

Melana: Herodotus (vii. 199) describes Trachis as being between the Asopus and the Melas. It is the modern Mavroneria (cf. Béquignon, 64).

Ap. Claudium: (294). Cf. 10. 10 n.

10. proceris arboribus: doubtless poplars, still a feature of the plain of Lamia. Cf. Béquignon, 86, 252.

11. laterem ... caementa ... saxa: tiles, cut (but not squared) stones, and uncut rocks. *caementa* occurs elsewhere in L. only at xxi. 11. 8. Sage wrongly translates 'cement'.

23. 2. laqueis: nooses thrown over the siege-engine to prevent it progressing any further. See Caes. *BG* vii. 22. 2, Vitr. x. 16. 12, Aen. Tact. 32. 4, Veg. iv. 23.

3. fornices: vaulted passages. Cf. xliv. 11. 5, *CIL* i². 2112, ii. 1087, Cic. *har. resp.* 22, Degering, *RE*, vii. 10, *TLL*, vi. 1. 1126. 39 ff.

5. rebus ... res: cf. p. 13.

7. ex spatio: M. Müller (*JPhP* cxxxv [1887], 867), *expectatio* Bψ, *expectatione* φ, *ex ratione* Gel. 'deprauatum erat in *expectatione temporis*'. *ex spatio* makes excellent sense of the paradosis and is surely right.

7. tale: cf. p. 6.

8–9. There are no extant references to hours of the day in Polybius, but such distinctions were certainly made in his time, though they had not been in the Classical period (cf. Rehm, *RE*, viii. 2418), and there is no reason to doubt that the details of L.'s narrative come directly from Polybius.

8. milites omnes: B, *omnes milites* χ. Cf. p. 15.

10. ipsi quoque: *ipsi hoc* φ, *spe hac* B, *spe ac* ψ. *ipsi hoc* represents the transmitted text and it is unnecessary to add *quoque*.

decedebant ... apparebant: the tense indicates that Glabrio followed this procedure for more than the two occasions L. actually describes. But I cannot see that *rursus* at 24. 1 also shows this, as claimed by W–M.

24. 1. quarta uigilia: the last watch of the night. Cf. Kromayer–Veith, 347, Neumann, *RE*, Supp. ix. 1693 ff.

2. ab una: Mg. *una* Bχ. Since Sempronius is to stay where he is, *ab* is not essential, and could be an addition in Mg.

Ti. Sempronium: cf. 22. 7 n.

expectare: Mg. *expectantes* Bχ, possibly correctly. The soldiers 'alert, waiting for the signal' would be a graphic picture, appropriate to the excitement of the narrative. On the other hand, it is Sempronius, not his soldiers, who should be waiting for the signal.

3. moliebantur: cf. p. 5.
in tenebris: with *currunt*.

4. concurrunt: Mg, *occurrunt* Bχ. Either is possible.

5–6. Note the short sentences, typical of L.'s description of the climax of a military action. Cf. p. 10.

5. pars ... erant: cf. 22. 7 n.

6. dilucescebat: the only occurrence of the verb in L. It is found in Cicero, *Cat.* iii. 6, *Phil.* xii, 5, Lucr. v. 176, and Horace, *Epp.* i. 4. 13 (*TLL*, v. 1. 1186).

partim ... scalis: Weissenborn. *partim per erutos partim scalis per* Mg, *partim per semiruta partim scalis* Gel. 'in nostris exemplaribus', *partim scalis* χ, *parti scalis* B. *erutos* makes no sense, and *semirutos* both gives a better antithesis to *scalis integros* and is closer to Mg's reading than Gelenius' *semiruta*.

7. coercitus ... urbibus: cf. 20. 1–4, 21. 3.

fructum ... sentiret: 'experience the fruits of their victory'. For *sentire* of a pleasant experience cf. v. 20. 8, xxvi. 20. 2 (both with *fructum*), xxxiv. 7. 1.

8. a medio: for *ab* = after cf. K–St, i. 494.

8–9. rupem ... possint: for the topography see Pritchett, i. 81–2 with plate 83.

fastigio altitudinis: 'the peak of its height'. Cf. Caes. *BG* vii. 69. 4.

par: *pars* BχMg. Bannier (*TLL*, vi. 1. 321. 26) suggests reading *pari*, as in Caesar, loc. cit.

possint: χ, *possent* BMg, probably rightly. Cf. xxxiv. 29. 7 n.

12. Damocritus ... posuissent: cf. xxxv. 12. 6, 33. 9–10 nn.

25. *Philip's assault on Lamia*

25. 1. Philippus ... congressus: i.e. the decision to embark on the dual siege was made at the meeting between Philip and Glabrio. Philip may have acquired certain towns on the coast road from the Malian Gulf to Demetrias before the meeting; cf. Walbank, *Philip V*, 204–5.

Lamiam: cf. xxxv. 43. 9 n.

uictoriam ... gratularetur: for *gratulari* with the accusative cf. K–St, i. 261.

3. septem ferme milia: the figure is correct (cf. Béquignon, 251–252). B has *ferme milia*, χ *milia ferme*, and Mg had *millium ferme*. It is impossible to choose between *ferme milia* and *milia ferme*: cf. Packard, ii. 586, iii. 265, p. 15.

et quia ... sunt: all completely true.

posita ... tumulo: Gel. 'ex fide archetyporum' (cf. p. 16). *posita in tumulo est* Bχ. Cf. p. 15.

oppido quam: not found before L., and elsewhere in L. only at xxxix. 47. 2. Cf. K–St, i. 14, H–S, 164.

in conspectu sunt: i.e. Heraclea and Lamia can be seen from each other.

4. uineis: cf. xxxiv. 17. 12 n.

Macedones ... occurrebat: cf. Pol. fr. 82 (Walbank, *Commentary*, iii. 77).

paene: Mg, *saepe* Bχ. Either is possible. If *saepe* is right, it would go more naturally with *inpenetrabilis* than with *occurrebat*. *occurrere* can be used absolutely (*TLL*, ix. 2. 392. 83 ff.) but is better taken with *ferro* whether we read *paene* or *saepe*.

inpenetrabilis: Mg, *inpenetralibus* Bχ. Not found before L. (*TLL*, vii. 1. 549).

6. obsidione liberanda: for *liberare* with an accusative of the burden removed cf. vii. 21. 8, xxvi. 8. 5, Cic. *r.p.* ii. 59, Tac. *H.* iv. 37. 2, *TLL*, vii. 2. 1309. 83 ff.

7. For Philip's resentment at Glabrio's order cf. xxxix. 23. 9, 28. 3. It may be that the withdrawal of Philip from Lamia was in fact one of the terms of the truce agreed at 27. 3. Cf. Walbank, *Philip V*, 205 n. 4, *Commentary*, iii. 83.

ab: cf. 24. 8 n.

cum Aetolis: Bχ, *quam Aetolos* Mg. Madvig (*Emendationes*, 523) wanted to delete the phrase entirely on the grounds that the battle of Thermopylae was fought principally with Antiochus, not the Aetolians, and argued that *cum Aetolis* was an attempt to emend the nonsensical *quam Aetolos*. But the point is that Lamia is an Aetolian town and its sacking is a just consequence of the Aetolians having fought against Rome. It is, therefore, the Aetolians' part in the battle that is relevant here. *quam Aetolos* is much more reasonably seen as a corruption of *cum Aetolis*, influenced by *aequius*, than an addition to complete the comparison.

7–8. praemia ... est: Bχ, *praemia habere victoriae, itaque recessum est ab Lamia* Mg. Cf. p. 15.

8. recessum ab Lamia est: cf. Pol. xx. 11. 3 (of the arrival of Nicander: cf. 29. 3 ff.) τοὺς ⟨δὲ⟩ Μακεδόνας ἀφεστῶτας μὲν ἀπὸ τῆς Λαμίας.

ne ... effugerunt: for (*ef*)*fugere ne* ... cf. K–St, ii. 227.

26. *Aetolian embassy to Antiochus*

26. 1. Hypatam: cf. 14. 15 n. A special assembly is involved.

2. qui ... est: *missus est* goes with *Thoas idem*, not with *qui*, which would require the pluperfect. Mg omits *et*, perhaps correctly. The double *et* = *etiam* is a little strange. On Thoas cf. xxxv. 12. 4 n., on his earlier mission xxxv. 32. 2 n.

terrestribus naualibusque: χ, om. *-que* B, correctly. Cf. xxxiii. 38. 10 n., xxxvii. 53. 9, p. 11.

3. pecuniam: cf. 29. 5 n., Walbank, *Commentary*, iii. 83.

6. Antiochus' motive in detaining Thoas is unclear. Perhaps he was afraid that his tendency to exaggerate would lead him to misrepresent to the Aetolians what Antiochus was promising. *et ipsum* does not imply, as W–M say, that Antiochus was glad to keep Thoas, and that this contrasts with Antiochus' recriminations against him at 15. 2. It is more likely that it was precisely Antiochus' distrust of Thoas that led to the latter's detention. For other examples of the detention of ambassadors cf. xxvi. 24. 15 (Aetolians at Rome), Xen. *Hell.* i. 4. 4 ff. (Cyrus and Athenian ambassadors), Pol. xv. 25. 13, xvi. 22. 3 (Philip V and Ptolemy, the son of Sosibius).

exactor: 'to supervise'. Before L. the word is found only in Caes. *BC* iii. 32. 4 (meaning a 'tax-collector'), Sall. *H.* iv fr. 51M (if the text is sound: it there appears to mean 'judge'). It occurs six times in L.

27–29. *Negotiations with the Aetolians*

Part of Polybius' version survives in xx. 9–11. The differences between Polybius and L. are searchingly analysed by Tränkle, 170–8 (with references to earlier literature: add Witte, 360 ff. on 28. 8—29, Merten, 6–7), and the following comments are greatly indebted to his discussion. Tränkle has shown that it is wrong to think that L. was trying to tone down Polybius' picture of Glabrio's brutality. Such toning-down is indeed found on three occasions—at 27. 3, where Glabrio's instruction to the Aetolian ambassadors to hold preliminary discussions with Flaccus is expressed less brusquely than in Polybius, at 28. 6, where he refers only to *catenae*, not to the iron halter to be placed round the neck of each of the Aetolians, and makes such action conditional on the non-performance of his instructions rather than an immediate order, and, at the same place, in L.'s omission of Flaccus' appeal to the consul to have regard for the status of the Aetolians as ambassadors (L. transfers this to another context—28. 8). On the other hand L.'s picture is harsher than that of Polybius at 27. 3, where he fails to mention Glabrio's alleged reason for being unable to deal with the Aetolians immediately, at 28. 5–6 where he omits Polybius' statement that Glabrio was really only trying to make the Aetolians realize the true nature of their predicament, and at 29. 1 in his reference to the *saeuitia* of the Roman demands.

Tränkle argues that the reason for L.'s alterations is that he found Polybius' account inconsistent in two respects. Firstly, how could it be that the Aetolians did not discover from Flaccus the true meaning of *deditio in fidem* before communicating their decision to Glabrio? Secondly, the picture of the cruel and insensitive Glabrio did not harmonize with the view of him elsewhere as a man trying to achieve his aims by negotiation, not force, if at all possible (cf. 14. 13, 20. 2, 4, 21. 3, 34. 1–35. 6, 35. 9–11). The first problem he dealt with by importing the notion of the Aetolians' double-dealing and omitting the statement that they did not understand the nature of *deditio* (27. 8). As to the second—here I depart somewhat from Tränkle's view—the apparently inconsistent alterations to portray Glabrio sometimes as harsher, sometimes as milder than he appears in Polybius will be explained by L.'s desire to produce a consistent narrative. He accepts the basic outline of Polybius' story and he disapproves of Glabrio's conduct. Hence where Polybius appears to put things in a more favourable light, he sharpens the picture. But the centre-piece of Polybius' narrative—the order to put the halter round the necks of the ambassadors—he found incredible and he suppressed it (I would not take seriously the possibility, entertained by Tränkle [175 n. 138], that L. omitted it because he was unable to discover the meaning of σκύλαξ). This suppression entailed the omission of Flaccus' appeal to the consul.

There are, of course, a large number of other alterations, documented in the detailed notes. These, however, do not depart from L.'s normal methods in adapting Polybius. There is certainly no reason to think that anything in L. comes from an annalistic source. (On 27. 7 see Tränkle, 176 n. 114, Walbank, *Commentary*, iii. 79).

The episode is, of course, of great importance for our knowledge of the procedure of *deditio*. What is made clear is that *deditio* meant handing over all power of decision to Rome. A reasonable response could be expected—that was the nature of *fides Romana*—but could not be assumed in advance, and the act of *deditio* precluded formal negotiations about terms. Cf. xxxi. 27. 3 n., with literature there cited, Dahlheim, 33 ff., Walbank, *Commentary*, iii. 79–81. The discussion of Flurl, 26 ff., despite several valuable detailed remarks, is based on his fantastic notion that L. was implicitly rejecting Polybius' equation of *deditio* and *deditio in fidem*, and does not merit detailed discussion.

27. 1–2. Pol. xx. 9. 1: οἱ περὶ τὸν Φαινέαν τὸν τῶν Αἰτωλῶν στρατηγὸν μετὰ τὸ γενέσθαι τὴν Ἡράκλειαν ὑποχείριον τοῖς Ῥωμαίοις, ὁρῶντες τὸν περιεστῶτα καιρὸν τὴν Αἰτωλίαν καὶ λαμβάνοντες πρὸ ὀφθαλμῶν τὰ συμβησόμενα ταῖς ἄλλαις πόλεσιν, ἔκριναν διαπέμπεσθαι πρὸς τὸν Μάνιον ὑπὲρ ἀνοχῶν καὶ διαλύσεως. Unless Polybius' text has been shortened by the excerptor, *paucos . . . legatos* is an addition by L. L. omits the names of the Aetolian ambassadors (Pol. xx. 9. 2: cf. 5. 1 n.).

paucos post dies: Drakenborch, *ad paucos post dies* Bχ, *post paucos dies* Gel. 'lege'. For the combination of *paucos post dies* with *quam* cf. K–St, i. 404–5.

miserant: Bχ, *dimiserant* Mg. *dimittere* of *legati* normally applies to the end of an embassy's reception. iv. 52. 5 is the only example of *dimittere legatos* of the dispatch of an embassy, and it is there determined by the fact that the *legati* are going to a number of different places.

3. quos ... interfatus: Pol. xx. 9. 3: οἱ συμμίξαντες τῷ στρατηγῷ τῶν Ῥωμαίων προέθεντο μὲν καὶ πλείους ποιεῖσθαι λόγους, μεσολαβηθέντες δὲ κατὰ τὴν ἔντευξιν ἐκωλύθησαν.

interfatus: cf. xxxii. 34. 2 n. L. uses it again at 28. 4, and in both places Polybius has μεσολαβεῖν.

cum ... dixisset: Pol. xx. 9. 4: ὁ γὰρ Μάνιος κατὰ μὲν τὸ παρὸν οὐκ ἔφασκεν εὐκαιρεῖν, περισπώμενος ὑπὸ τῆς τῶν ἐκ τῆς Ἡρακλείας λαφύρων οἰκονομίας.

L. omits Glabrio's reason, thus giving the impression, whether deliberately or not, that Glabrio was merely making excuses for not seeing the Aetolian delegation immediately.

praeuertenda: deliberately taking up the language of Damocritus' reply to Flamininus at xxxv. 33. 10. Tränkle's doubts about this (174 n. 136) are not justified.

3–4. redire ... foret: Pol. xx. 9. 5–6: δεχημέρους δὲ ποιησάμενος ἀνοχὰς ἐκπέμψειν ἔφη μετ' αὐτῶν Λεύκιον, πρὸς ὃν ἐκέλευε λέγειν ὑπὲρ ὧν ἂν δέοιντο. γενομένων δὲ τῶν ἀνοχῶν, καὶ τοῦ Λευκίου συνελθόντος εἰς τὴν Ὑπάταν, ἐγένοντο λόγοι καὶ πλείους ὑπὲρ τῶν ἐνεστώτων. L. adapts considerably, making Glabrio order the Aetolians to go to Hypata, and adding that they there discussed with Flaccus how they should approach the consul. *eique ... alia* is less abrupt than Polybius' πρὸς ὃν ... δέοιντο.

3. L. Valerio Flacco: cf. 17. 1 n. The fact that a M. Valerius Laevinus had concluded the original treaty with the Aetolians will have made Flaccus a particularly suitable intermediary, though the precise degree of his relationship to Laevinus is uncertain. Cf. Münzer, *RE*, viiiA. 19, Dahlheim, 33 n. 23.

4. principes: there is nothing corresponding to the word in Polybius, and we cannot therefore be sure whether it was the *apocleti* (cf. xxxv. 34. 2 n.) who conducted the negotiations, as W–M suggest.

5–7. Pol. xx. 9. 7–9: οἱ μὲν οὖν Αἰτωλοὶ συνίσταντο τὴν δικαιολογίαν ἀνέκαθεν προφερόμενοι τὰ προγεγονότα σφίσι φιλάνθρωπα πρὸς τοὺς Ῥωμαίους· ὁ δὲ Λεύκιος ἐπιτεμὼν αὐτῶν τὴν ὁρμὴν οὐκ ἔφη τοῖς παροῦσι καιροῖς ἁρμόζειν τοῦτο τὸ γένος τῆς δικαιολογίας· λελυμένων γὰρ τῶν ἐξ ἀρχῆς φιλανθρώπων δι' ἐκείνους, καὶ τῆς ἐνεστώσης ἔχθρας δι'

Αἰτωλοὺς γεγενημένης, οὐδὲν ἔτι συμβάλλεσθαι τὰ τότε φιλάνθρωπα πρὸς τοὺς νῦν καιρούς. διόπερ ἀφεμένους τοῦ δικαιολογεῖσθαι συνεβούλευε τρέπεσθαι πρὸς τὸν ἀξιωματικὸν λόγον καὶ δεῖσθαι τοῦ στρατηγοῦ συγγνώμης τυχεῖν ἐπὶ τοῖς ἡμαρτημένοις. Again there is considerable adaptation. On § 7 cf. 27–29 n.

5. antiqua ... meritaque: Polybius has no reference to treaties and in view of their rebuff in 197 (cf. xxxiii. 13. 9–12 n.) it is doubtful whether the Aetolians continued to argue on the basis of treaty rights.

6–7. The language takes up that of 22. 1 and anticipates that of xxxvii. 1. 2, 49. 1–3. Cf. Flurl, 38 ff. For the sentiment see also xxviii. 34. 6 (again in the context of a *deditio*).

7. se ... adfuturum: Gel. 'scribo'. om. *se, profuturum* Bχ. A simpler change would be to read *agere* for *agentibus*.

8. Pol. xx. 9. 10–11: οἱ δ' Αἰτωλοὶ καὶ πλείω λόγον ποιησάμενοι περὶ τῶν ὑποπιπτόντων ἔκριναν ἐπιτρέπειν τὰ ὅλα Μανίῳ, δόντες αὑτοὺς εἰς τὴν Ῥωμαίων πίστιν, οὐκ εἰδότες τίνα δύναμιν ἔχει τοῦτο, τῷ δὲ τῆς πίστεως ὀνόματι πλανηθέντες, ὡς ἂν διὰ τοῦτο τελειοτέρου σφίσιν ἐλέους ὑπάρξοντος. L. omits Polybius' comment on the Aetolian misunderstanding of what was involved in *deditio* (cf. 27–9 n.) but *et ... ostendisset* is his own addition, presumably with reference to Aetolian hopes of further aid from Antiochus.

uia ... est: B, *uia ... et* χ, *uia uisa est omnibus ad salutem* Mg. Cf. p. 15.

in fidem se: Mg, *se in fidem.* Mg's order, with *se* in the unemphatic position, is preferable.

28. 1. Pol. xx. 10. 1–2. Πλὴν ταῦτα κρίναντες ἐξέπεμψαν ἅμα τῷ Λευκίῳ τοὺς περὶ Φαινέαν διασαφήσοντας τὰ δεδογμένα τῷ Μανίῳ κατὰ σπουδήν· οἳ καὶ συμμίξαντες τῷ στρατηγῷ καὶ πάλιν ὁμοίως δικαιολογηθέντες ὑπὲρ αὑτῶν, ἐπὶ καταστροφῆς εἶπαν διότι κέκριται τοῖς Αἰτωλοῖς σφᾶς αὑτοὺς ἐγχειρίζειν εἰς τὴν Ῥωμαίων πίστιν. *longam ... compositam* is an elaboration by L.

Phaeneas: cf. xxxii. 32. 11 n.

2. Pol. xx. 10. 3: ὁ δὲ Μάνιος μεταλαβών 'οὐκοῦν οὕτως ἔχει ταῦτα,' φησίν, 'ὦ ἄνδρες Αἰτωλοί;' τῶν δὲ κατανευσάντων. L. invents Phaeneas showing the decree to Glabrio. W–M suggest that he may have been misled by Polybius' reference to τὰ δεδογμένα (xx. 10. 1), but in view of the degree of deviation from Polybius in these chapters, it is best to regard it as a simple addition to give the events more colour. Cf. Walbank, *Commentary,* iii. 81.

etiam ... permittatis: 'consider what it is you are doing by making a surrender of this sort'. A considerable elaboration on the simple question in Polybius. *ita* goes closely with *permittatis*, otherwise it would assort strangely with an indirect question introduced by *ut*. L.'s choice of *ita* was probably influenced by οὕτως in Polybius. On *etiam atque etiam* cf. xxxv. 6. 4 n. *uidere ut* with the indicative is common in Plautus and perhaps L. was giving a deliberately colloquial flavour to Glabrio's reply. (*uidere etiam atque etiam ut* occurs at *Aul.* 614, but the *ut* there is final.)

3. Pol. xx. 10. 4–5: 'τοιγαροῦν πρῶτον μὲν δεήσει μηδένα διαβαίνειν ὑμῶν εἰς τὴν Ἀσίαν, μήτε κατ' ἰδίαν μήτε μετὰ κοινοῦ δόγματος, δεύτερον Δικαίαρχον ἔκδοτον δοῦναι καὶ Μενέστρατον τὸν Ἠπειρώτην,' ὃς ἐτύγχανε τότε παραβεβοηθηκὼς εἰς Ναύπακτον, σὺν δὲ τούτοις Ἀμύνανδρον τὸν βασιλέα καὶ τῶν Ἀθαμάνων τοὺς ἅμα τούτῳ συναποχωρήσαντας πρὸς αὐτούς. L. omits the condition that no Aetolian is to go to Asia and makes two wrong additions. He makes Menestas responsible for the revolt of Naupactus. It was, of course, part of the Aetolian League, and there was no question of it 'revolting' by itself. And he wrongly says that it was on the advice of the Athamanians that the Aetolians had 'defected', when in fact exactly the reverse was the case (xxxv. 47. 5–8). Cf. Tränkle, 172–3 n. 133.

Dicaearchum: cf. xxxv. 12. 6 n.

Menestam Epirotam: called Menestratos in the MSS. of Polybius here, but at xxi. 31. 13 = L. xxxviii. 10. 6 both Polybius and L. call him Menestas, and there can be no doubt that this is his name. He is not known apart from these passages. He is to be regarded as a privateer, and his activities did not involve the Epirote state. Cf. Oost, *RPEA*, 127 n. 153, Hammond, *Epirus*, 624, Cabanes, 282.

4. Pol. xx. 10. 6: ὁ δὲ Φαινέας μεσολαβήσας 'ἀλλ' οὔτε δίκαιον', ἔφησεν, 'οὔθ' Ἑλληνικόν ἐστιν, ὦ στρατηγέ, τὸ παρακαλούμενον.' Further elaboration by L. *prope dicentem interfatus* is not a toning-down of μεσολαβήσας, as claimed by Hellmann, 92–3. L. means that Phaeneas interrupted Glabrio's flow of speech, but not when he was actually in the middle of a sentence. Cf. Flurl, 57 n. 1.

interfatus Romanum: B, *interfatus Romanorum* χ. Indication of the subject is essential at this stage and *Phaeneas* (dett.) must be inserted. At § 8 the transmitted reading (Bψ) is *exposuissent* and I wonder if *Phaeneas* has been displaced to that sentence.

tradidimus: Mg, *tradimus* Bχ. Either is possible.

habeo te: Frob. 2, *te habeo* edd. uett., om. *te* Bχ, perhaps rightly. Cf. xxxiv. 31. 5 n.

5–6. ad ea ... iubebo: Pol. xx. 10. 7: ὁ δὲ Μάνιος οὐχ οὕτως ὀργισθεὶς ὡς βουλόμενος εἰς ἔννοιαν αὐτοὺς ἀγαγεῖν τῆς περιστάσεως καὶ καταπλήξασθαι τοῖς ὅλοις, 'ἔτι γὰρ ὑμεῖς ἑλληνοκοπεῖτε' φησὶ 'καὶ περὶ τοῦ πρέποντος καὶ καθήκοντος ποιεῖσθε λόγον, δεδωκότες ἑαυτοὺς εἰς τὴν πίστιν; οὓς ἐγὼ δήσας εἰς τὴν ἅλυσιν ἀπάξω πάντας, ἂν τοῦτ' ἐμοὶ δόξῃ.' L. omits Polybius' description of Glabrio's motivation, thus increasing the impression of the consul's harshness: on the other hand the addition of *ni* ... *impero* makes the threat conditional on non-performance by the Aetolians, not a demonstration of the absoluteness of *deditio*. Cf. 27–9 n.

The suggestion in *ante armis uictos* that the victories at Thermopylae and Heraclea themselves gave Rome arbitrary power over the Aetolians is another misleading addition by L. I do not see an allusion here to claims that the Aetolians were not really Greeks, as argued by Tränkle, 175.

5. inhibeam: cf. p. 5.

6. fit ... iubebo: for the combination of a present in the protasis with a future in the apodosis cf. Madvig, *Emendationes*, 523–4, K–St, i. 146, H–S, 549.

adferri ... iussit: Pol. xx. 10. 8: ταῦτα λέγων φέρειν ἅλυσιν ἐκέλευσε καὶ σκύλακα σιδηροῦν ἑκάστῳ περιθεῖναι περὶ τὸν τράχηλον. For L.'s omissions cf. 27–9 n. He adds *circumsistere lictores* from his knowledge of Roman practice. Cf. Tränkle, 175 and n. 139.

tum ... senserunt: an anticipation of Polybius' statement concerning the *apocleti* at xx. 10. 13.

7. Pol. xx. 10. 10–12: ἤρξατο λέγειν ὁ Φαινέας· ἔφη γὰρ αὐτὸν καὶ τοὺς ἀποκλήτους ποιήσειν τὰ προσταττόμενα, προσδεῖσθαι δὲ καὶ τῶν πολλῶν, εἰ μέλλει κυρωθῆναι τὰ παραγγελλόμενα. τοῦ δὲ Μανίου φήσαντος αὐτὸν ὀρθῶς λέγειν, ἠξίου πάλιν ἀνοχὰς αὐτοῖς δοθῆναι δεχημέρους. Polybius says that the *apocleti* would agree to Glabrio's demands, L. that those present at Heraclea would do so. L. thus does not predict the result of the meeting of the *apocleti* described in §§ 8–9.

concilio: (A^z, *consilio* Bχ). See Walbank, *Commentary*, iii. 82.

8–9. Pol. xx. 10. 12–14: συγχωρηθέντος δὲ καὶ τούτου, τότε μὲν ἐπὶ τούτοις ἐχωρίσθησαν· παραγενόμενοι δ' εἰς τὴν Ὑπάταν διεσάφουν τοῖς ἀποκλήτοις τὰ γεγονότα καὶ τοὺς ῥηθέντας λόγους. ὧν ἀκούσαντες τότε πρῶτον ἔννοιαν ἔλαβον Αἰτωλοὶ τῆς αὐτῶν ἀγνοίας καὶ τῆς ἐπιφερομένης αὐτοῖς ἀνάγκης. διὸ γράφειν ἔδοξεν εἰς τὰς πόλεις καὶ συγκαλεῖν τοὺς Αἰτωλοὺς χάριν τοῦ βουλεύσασθαι περὶ τῶν προσταττομένων.

8. apocletos: cf. xxxv. 34. 2 n.

29. 1–2. This is very distant from Polybius xx. 10. 15–16, where the fury of the Aetolians prevents a meeting of the League assembly from taking place at all. And while Polybius merely talks of the impossible nature of the Roman demands in general, L. gives the specific example of Amynander (who was, in fact, in Aetolian territory: cf. 14. 9 n., Tränkle, 173 n. 134).

1. animi exasperati: B, *exasperati animi* χ. The latter is perhaps preferable, both as the less expected order and because it avoids the temptation to take *animi* with *indignitate*. In earlier and contemporary writers *exasperare* occurs only in Ovid, *Amores* ii. 11. 27. L. uses it on eight occasions, the earliest in book xxviii (*TLL*, v. 2. 1186). Cf. pp. 9 15.

3–4. Pol. xx. 10. 16–11. 2: ἅμα δὲ καὶ τοῦ Νικάνδρου κατὰ τὸν καιρὸν τοῦτον καταπλεύσαντος ἐκ τῆς Ἀσίας εἰς τὰ Φάλαρα τοῦ κόλπου τοῦ Μηλιέως, ὅθεν καὶ τὴν ὁρμὴν ἐποιήσατο, καὶ διασαφοῦντος ⟨τὴν⟩ τοῦ βασιλέως εἰς αὐτὸν προθυμίαν καὶ τὰς εἰς τὸ μέλλον ἐπαγγελίας, ἔτι μᾶλλον ὠλιγώρησαν, τοῦ μηδὲν γενέσθαι πέρας ὑπὲρ τῆς εἰρήνης. ὅθεν ἅμα τῷ διελθεῖν τὰς ἐν ταῖς ἀνοχαῖς ἡμέρας κατάμονος αὖθις ὁ πόλεμος ἐγεγόνει τοῖς Αἰτωλοῖς. περὶ δὲ τῆς συμβάσης τῷ Νικάνδρῳ περιπετείας οὐκ ἄξιον παρασιωπῆσαι. παρεγενήθη μὲν γὰρ ἐκ τῆς Ἐφέσου δωδεκαταῖος εἰς τὰ Φάλαρα πάλιν, ἀφ' ἧς ὡρμήθ' ἡμέρας. L. adds the statement that Nicander's report constituted an exaggeration of Antiochus' promises.

3. Nicander: cf. xxxv. 12. 6 n. Polybius does not mention that this was not Philip's first contact with him. Cf. K. S. Sacks, *JHS* xcv (1975), 95 and n. 14 for the possibility that Nicander himself was Polybius' source for this episode.

uana: cf. xxxiv. 24. 1 n.

4. duodecumo is die: it is clear from Polybius xx. 11. 2 that the twelve days are the return journey from Phalara and back again, not just the journey back from Ephesus, as W–M hold. Their argument appears to be that since Nicander set out a few days before the first Aetolian embassy to Glabrio, a return journey of twelve days would have meant that he reached Phalara during the first ten-days truce rather than the second. But there is no need to assume that the first truce had expired when the second was granted.

Phalara: cf. xxxv. 43. 9 n.

5. Pol. xx. 11. 3–5: καταλαβὼν δὲ τοὺς Ῥωμαίους ἔτι περὶ τὴν Ἡράκλειαν, τοὺς ⟨δὲ⟩ Μακεδόνας ἀφεστῶτας μὲν ἀπὸ τῆς Λαμίας, οὐ μακρὰν δὲ στρατοπεδεύοντας τῆς πόλεως, τὰ μὲν χρήματ' εἰς τὴν Λαμίαν διεκόμισε παραδόξως, αὐτὸς δὲ τῆς νυκτὸς ἐπεβάλετο κατὰ τὸν μεταξὺ τόπον τῶν στρατοπέδων διαπεσεῖν εἰς τὴν ʽΥπάταν. ἐμπεσὼν δʼ εἰς τοὺς προκοίτους τῶν Μακεδόνων ἀνήγετο πρὸς τὸν Φίλιππον ἔτι τῆς συνουσίας ἀκμαζούσης. *cum expeditis* is an addition by L., but he omits Polybius' comment that it was surprising that Nicander was able to take the money to Lamia.

Romanaque: Bχ, *Romanorumque* Mg. Correction to the genitive is more likely than corruption to the accusative.

6–7. A free paraphrase of Polybius xx. 11. 5–7: προσδο⟨κῶν⟩ πείσεσ-θαί τι δεινὸν πεσὼν ὑπὸ τοῦ Φιλίππου τὸν θυμὸν ἢ παραδοθήσεσθαι τοῖς ʽΡωμαίοις. τοῦ δὲ πράγματος ἀγγελθέντος τῷ βασιλεῖ, ταχέως ἐκέλευσε τοὺς ἐπὶ τούτων ὄντας θεραπεῦσαι τὸν Νίκανδρον καὶ τὴν λοιπὴν ἐπιμέλειαν αὐτοῦ ποιήσασθαι φιλάνθρωπον. μετὰ δέ τινα χρόνον αὐτὸς ἐξαναστὰς συνέμιξε τῷ Νικάνδρῳ. (ἐξαναστάς does not mean that Philip went into another room, as Luce, 207, imagines.)

6. hospitis, non hostis: cf. Ogilvie, 225.

iussit: Bχ, *iussum* Mg. *iussit* is clearly right. *eum* would not be expected in a participial construction and *atque* far more naturally joins the contrasted *iussit* and *uetuit* than *iussum* and *retentum*.

8. Pol. xx. 11. 7: καὶ πολλὰ καταμεμψάμενος τὴν κοινὴν τῶν Αἰτωλῶν ἄγνοιαν, ἐξ ἀρχῆς μέν, ὅτι ʽΡωμαίους ἐπαγάγοιεν τοῖς ῞Ελλησι, μετὰ δὲ ταῦτα πάλιν Ἀντίοχον. For the sentiment cf. Sall. *H.* i. fr. 77. 1, Skard, 36–7.

9–10. sed ... debere: Pol. xx. 11. 7–8: ὅμως ἔτι καὶ νῦν παρεκάλει λήθην ποιησαμένους τῶν προγεγονότων ἀντέχεσθαι τῆς πρὸς αὐτὸν εὐνοίας καὶ μὴ θελῆσαι συνεπεμβαίνειν τοῖς κατʼ ἀλλήλων καιροῖς. ταῦτα μὲν οὖν παρῄνει τοῖς προεστῶσι τῶν Αἰτωλῶν ἀναγγέλλειν· In Polybius, Philip urges the Aetolians to forget the past, in L. he promises to do this himself. W–M go too far in saying that Philip was seeking an alliance with the Aetolians. On Philip's motives in speaking to Nicander as he did cf. Walbank, *Philip V*, 206.

9. praeteritorum ... possint: cf. xxx. 30. 7, Otto, 286, Flurl, 78 n. 1 (a).

10–11. et Nicandrum ... superuenit: Pol. xx. 11. 8: αὐτὸν δὲ τὸν Νίκανδρον παρακαλέσας μνημονεύειν τῆς εἰς αὐτὸν γεγενημένης εὐεργεσίας ἐξέπεμπε μετὰ προπομπῆς ἱκανῆς, παραγγείλας τοῖς ἐπὶ τούτῳ τεταγμένοις ἀσφαλῶς εἰς τὴν ʽΥπάταν αὐτὸν ἀποκαταστῆσαι. L. omits Polybius' reference to Nicander's subsequent loyalty to the Macedonian royal house.

30. *Glabrio begins the siege of Naupactus*

30. 1. uendita: not with *militi*. The procedure differs from that at
xxxv. 1. 12, where all the booty is sold and the proceeds distributed
to the soldiers. Cf. Walbank, *Commentary*, ii. 217. It is uncertain
whether the population of Heraclea was enslaved (cf. Volkmann,
26).

2. Ap. Claudio: (294). Cf. 10. 10 n.
    Oetam: cf. 15. 10 n.

3. Herculique . . . crematum: for the site, on the south-east side
of Mt. Oeta, see Nilsson, *ARW* xxi (1922), 310 ff., *JHS* xliii (1923),
144 ff., Walbank, *Commentary*, iii. 84. Nilsson claimed that the
archaeological evidence of a fire-cult demolished the view held by
many scholars (cf. e.g. Gruppe, *RE*, Supp. iii. 941 ff.) that the story
of Heracles' self-destruction by fire was an oriental legend. But there
is no reason why the myth should not be an aetiological explanation
as well as of eastern provenance.

4–5. Cf. App. *Syr.* 21. 95–6.

4. Coracem: Pol. xx. 11. 11 (from Steph. Byz.): Κόραξ, ὄρος μεταξὺ
Καλλιπόλεως καὶ Ναυπάκτου. On the topographical problems see
Walbank, *Commentary*, iii. 84–5.
    uentum est: B, *est uentum* χ. Cf. p. 15.
    homines uexati: troubled by the terrain. One might imagine
that L. meant that they were attacked by the Aetolians, but that is
excluded by the following sentence. For *uexare* of difficulties caused
by the terrain cf. xliv. 5. 10, 43. 4.

6. tum . . . descendit: the meaning, presumably, is that as well as
getting them over the mountains and despite their being *uexati*, he
led them down to begin the siege of Naupactus. For *quoque* 'what is
more' cf. xxiii. 21. 6, xxvi. 38. 7, xxxvii. 31. 2 n.

31–32. *Events in the Peloponnese*

On these events cf. Aymard, *PR*, 338 ff., Roebuck, 91 ff., Errington,
122 ff., Meyer, *RE*, Supp. xv. 274–5, Walbank, *Commentary*, iii. 193.

31. 1. Messene: still technically an ally of Rome (cf. xxxiv. 32.
16 n.), unless Rome regarded her pro-Seleucid actions as a breach
of the *foedus* (cf. Roebuck, 91 n. 113). No specific action on the part
of the Messenians is known (cf. Errington, 123).

3. praesidio regio: sent by Antiochus during the winter of 192/1:
cf. 5. 3 n.
    se: χ, om. B. Cf. xxxiv. 31. 5 n., p. 12.

4. trepidi rerum: cf. v. 11. 4, Virg. *A.* xii. 589, Tränkle, *WS*, 113.

5. Chalcidem: for his actions here after Thermopylae cf. 21. 3 n. I cannot see why W–M should even contemplate the possibility that it is not the Euboean Chalcis that is involved.

   auctorem libertatis: of Greek freedom in general, unless it is to be taken predicatively. Flamininus had done nothing specific for the Messenians, and the clauses in their favour in the treaty with Nabis (xxxiv. 35. 6) hardly add up to *libertas*.

6. a Megalopoli: i.e. when he reached Megalopolis.

   Diophanem: *strategos* in 192/1, not 191/0, as stated by W–M. On his career see Deininger, *RE*, Supp. xi. 534–8, Walbank, *Commentary*, iii. 93. He and Flamininus had earlier attempted to invade Sparta, but had been thwarted by Philopoemen. Cf. Plut. *Phil.* 16. 1–3, Paus. viii. 51. 1, Aymard, *PR*, 330 ff., Errington, 118, Walbank, *Commentary*, iii. 85.

   iuberet: Flamininus was probably claiming to act by virtue of the Messenians' *deditio* (cf. Walbank, *Commentary*, iii. 193). But the brusqueness of his order to Diophanes is one of the clearest examples of the way he envisaged Rome's, and his own, relationship with the Greek states.

7. Andaniam: for the site cf. Walbank, *Commentary*, i. 623.

9. Polybius xxii. 10. 6 refers to a διάγραμμα of Flamininus concerning the Messenian exiles. It may be that his instructions to Messenia were conveyed entirely in writing, without a personal visit. Cf. Aymard, *PR*, 345–6 n. 11. For arguments to show that Deinocrates was one of the exiles cf. Errington, 124 ff. As Errington says, the terms cannot at all have been what the Messenians who made the *deditio* were hoping for. For the possibility that some parts of Messenian territory joined the League as independent cities cf. Aymard, *PR*, 347, Roebuck, 94 n. 124, Meyer, *RE*, Supp. xv. 275.

   si qua . . . uenirent: the reference is to possible disputes over the details of Messenian membership of the Achaean League and does not indicate a claim to permanent rights over Messene, either for Rome or for Flamininus personally. Cf. Aymard, *PR*, 346–7 n. 14.

   caueri: Bχ, *cauere* Mg. The latter is possible (cf. vii. 41. 2) but corruption from the passive is rather more likely than the reverse.

10—32. Zacynthus had been independent until captured by Philip in 217 (Pol. v. 102. 10). It was taken, except for the acropolis, by M. Valerius Laevinus in 211 (xxvi. 24. 15) but Philip soon recaptured it, perhaps in 207 (Walbank, *Philip V*, 98). The expedition referred to in § 11 is that of 207 (cf. xxxi. 1. 8 n., Walbank, *Com-*

mentary, ii. 278). This passage is the only evidence for Amynander's part in Philip's success on that occasion. I see no reason to believe that Rome permanently annexed the island, as Harris, 94, implies.

10. concilium: a *syncletos*. Cf. Larsen, *Representative Government*, 173.

12. Philippum Megalopolitanum: cf. 8. 3, 14. 3–5, xxxv. 47. 5–8.
quo ... coniunxit: cf. 28. 3 n.
Hieroclen Agrigentinum: not otherwise known.

32. 1. Amynandrumque ... pulsum: 14. 7–9.
pecunia pactus: for similar purchases cf. the sale of Aegina to Attalus by the Aetolians (xxxi. 14. 10–11 n.) and of Caunus to Rhodes by Ptolemaic generals (xxxiii. 20. 11–12 n.). *pecunia* (Bψ, *pecuniam* ϕ) is the transmitted reading. For the ablative cf. W–M on ix. 43. 6. It is used of the price received also at xxiv. 49. 7, xxxviii. 24. 4.
tradidit: *tradit* Bχ. The historic present would not be appropriate in this context.

2. non enim ... pugnasse: the same attitude as that taken towards Philip at 25. 7 (Aymard, *PR*, 342).

3. purgare interdum: *interdum purgare* χ, *purgare* B. There is no reason to depart from χ's order.

4. quidam Achaeorum: for their identity cf. Errington, 128 ff., arguing that they included Philopoemen.
increpitabant: Mg, *increpabant* Bχ. *increpitare* is found at i. 7. 2 and Caes. *BG* ii. 15. 5, 30. 3. Corruption to the more usual form is far more likely than the reverse.

5–8. Plutarch (*Flam.* 17. 4: cf. *Mor.* 197B–C) also reports the tortoise simile in the context of general comments about Flamininus' lack of lasting bitterness. The image, like that of Flamininus' story of his Chalcidian host (xxxv. 49. 6–7), is doubtless typical of the informal style of discourse used by Flamininus towards the Greeks to such effect. There is no evidence that the simile had been used before, nor any for W–M's statement that the tortoise on (sc. Aeginetan) coins symbolized the Peloponnese.

Later Rome did allow the League to acquire territory outside the Peloponnese (Aymard, *PR*, 349 n. 2).

5. si cederes: 'if you gave way'. For the imperfect subjunctive cf. K–St, ii. 206, for the second personal singular xxxiv. 50. 7 n.
omissa: Bχ. *omissa igitur* Mg, perhaps correctly.

sinerent: P, *sineret* BAE, *sinere* ψ. *sineret* is probably correct: for the singular after *senatus populusque Romanus* cf. 21. 4, xxi. 40. 4, xxxi. 5. 4.

6. exserit: PˣL², *exiret* Bχ. The reading is not in doubt, though *exserere* occurs for certain only once before the Augustan period (Caes. *BG* vii. 50. 2). At Cic. *Phil.* xi. 13 its meaning would be unique, and the reading has been questioned (cf. *TLL*, v. 2. 1859. 20 ff.).

9. The words do not imply a second vote, or further debate, in the assembly. Cf. Aymard, *Assemblées*, 395 n. 1.

33. Activities of Philip

Cf. Plut. *Flam.* 15. 5–6, Walbank, *Philip V*, 207.

33. 1. percunctatus si: cf. xxxiv. 3. 5 n. For *percunctari si* cf. xxxiii. 35. 3.

2. turbatio: not found before L., and in L. only here and at xxiv. 28. 1 (*TLL*). Cf. p. 9.

3. destituti ... spe: L. is particularly fond of *a spe destitui*, which in earlier or contemporary writers occurs only in Ovid, *Her.* iii. 143, and rarely after him. (*TLL*, v. 1. 763. 37 ff.) Cf. p. 9.
  spe ... spem: cf. p. 13.

4. incondita: *inconditus* referring to persons is found before L. only in Sall. *H.* iii. fr. 23. Cf. *TLL*, vii. 1. 1001. 34 ff.

5. qui: *quia* Bχ, perhaps rightly. With *qui* one expects *ostenderent* (cf. xxxiv. 28. 2, xxxvii. 6. 2, xlii. 38. 10, xliv. 4. 11). In either case *praemissis* is dative.
  impetrabilis: cf. pp. 4, 8. *impetrabilis ueniae* is pleonastic, merely emphasizing *spem ... ueniae*.

6. Eurylochus: cf. xxxv. 31. 6 n.
  Lysimachiam: cf. xxxii. 33. 15 n., xxxiii. 38. 10–13, 40. 6, xxxiv. 58. 5, xxxv. 15. 5.

7. erant ... Isidorus: cf. 20. 5–6 nn.
  inde ... recipit: Both L. (xxxix. 23. 11, 28. 4) and Plutarch (*Flam.* 15. 6) refer to actions in Athamania at this time, but Philip had taken possession of that land before the battle of Thermopylae (14. 7–9) and no more than border activities can have been involved. Cf. Walbank, *Philip V*, 207 n. 3.

Dolopiam: cf. xxxiii. 34. 6 n. Its defection, like that of the states of Perrhaebia referred to below, is not specifically recorded.

Aperantia: to the south-west of Dolopia. πόλις Θεσσαλίας at Pol. xx. 11. 12 is a mistake by Stephanus of Byzantium, since Aperantia is neither a city nor in Thessaly. For its location and history cf. Walbank, *Commentary*, iii. 85.

34–35. 6. *Flamininus at Naupactus*

Cf. Plut. *Flam.* 15. 6–9, Zon. ix. 19. 14. Dio fr. 62. 1a may belong here. Plutarch's account differs in details from that of L., but it is rash to attempt to decide which is closer to Polybius. Flamininus' aim is the preservation of a balance of power in Greece: cf. § 4 *nullam . . . euerti*, *Latomus* xxxi (1972), 33–4.

34. 1. ab Achaico concilio: from Corinth (31. 9).

2. iam . . . erat: W–M's claim that this is inconsistent with Glabrio's agreement to withdraw is mistaken. The Aetolians were ready to negotiate and Glabrio was influenced by the arguments of Flamininus.

For the repetition of *iam* cf. p. 13. At iv. 28. 1 and xxiv. 32. 4–5, adduced by W–M, the second *iam* is nowhere near so close to the first.

nomen . . . uenturum: cf. ix. 45. 17 *nomenque Aequorum prope ad internecionem deletum.*

nomen ibi: B. *ibi nomen* χ, perhaps rightly. Cf. p. 15.

3. obtrectasse . . . suae: referring especially to the beginning of Flamininus' quarrel with the Aetolians in 197. Cf. xxxiii. 11 n., Sacks, *JHS* xcv (1975), 98 ff.

cum . . . deterreret: in 192 (xxxv. 33). Cf. particularly xxxv. 33. 11 *tantus furor.*

accidebant: Madvig, *acciderat* Bχ. The simplest change is to *acciderant* (edd. uett.).

obambulare: cf. p. 5.

5. consonante: cf. p. 4.

6. moueretur: for the subjunctive with *quamquam* cf. K–St, ii. 442.
fefellit: *fallit* Bχ. There is no reason for alteration.

7. peruideas: xxxiii. 5. 11 is the only other occurrence of *peruidere* in L.

8. quin expromis: cf. xxxiv. 59. 1 n.
prope . . . tui: the consuls of 190 Varr. entered office on 18

November 191 (Jul.). (Cf. p. 25.) Flamininus seems to have had an obsession with the ends of years of office (cf. vol. i, 24 ff., xxxiv. 33. 14 n.)—though, of course, we cannot be sure that he expressed himself in precisely this way.

9. Athamaniam ... Dolopiam: cf. 14. 7 ff., 33. 7 nn.

et ... habere: this clause stands after *crescere* in the MSS. (Bχ have *tot* for *duas* [Mg]). It makes no sense in this position (Pettersson's defence [131–2] is absurd) and Madvig was probably right to place it after *adiunxisse*. But I would not exclude Bekker's deletion of the clause. It represents the ideas, and in *duas urbes* and *tot gentes* the language, of what precedes, and may well originate from a paraphrase.

35. 1. The point, apparently, is that Glabrio wanted any decision to withdraw to be made by Flamininus rather than himself.

irrito incepto: cf. 18. 8 n.

3. Phaeneas: he may still be *strategos* (*pace* W–M), as 34. 8 cannot be pressed to indicate a date later than the Aetolian *strategos*' entry into office. The *strategos* was elected by the assembly in September (cf. xxxi. 29. 1 n., Walbank, *Commentary*, i. 154).

prouolutis ad pedes: cf. vi. 3. 4, xxxiv. 11. 5.

irae ... temperem: cf. p. 6.

4. ego ... datus: Flamininus appears to have genuinely convinced himself that this was the case.

ingratis: cf. xxxv. 31. 8 n.

5. tanti: N, *tantum* BLVφ. I should prefer Drakenborch's *in tantum*. *tantum tempus* never occurs in L., while *tantum temporis* is found at xl. 15. 13, xlv. 2. 4.

deprecator defensorque: Mg, *defensor deprecatorque* Bχ. Cf. p. 15.

6. in diem certam: see appendix.

obsidio est: Mg. om. *est* Bχ, perhaps rightly. Cf. p. 12.

35. 7–10. *Embassies from Elis, Sparta, and Epirus*

For the activities of Glabrio at Delphi, not mentioned by L., see *Syll.*[3] 607–10, *SEG* xxii. 465, Walbank, *Philip V*, 289, J.-P. Michaud, *BCH* Supp. iv (1977), 125–36.

7. Achaicum ... Aegium: a *synodos*. Cf. xxxi. 25. 2 n., Larsen, *Representative Government*, 173. On Aegium cf. xxxv. 26. 6 n.

de Eleis: 31. 3.

de exulibus Lacedaemoniorum: the exiles are those expelled
by the Spartan 'tyrants'. They had come to Flamininus' camp in
195, but no provision for their return had been made in the peace
settlement with Nabis (cf. xxxiv. 26. 12–14 nn., 36. 2). For the
earlier attempt by Diophanes and Flamininus to invade Sparta cf.
31. 6 n.

suae ... Achaei: for the reasons, in fact those of Philopoemen,
cf. Plut. *Phil.* 17. 6, Errington, 130–1. At about the same time Sparta
sent an embassy to Rome asking for the return of the Laconian coast
towns, and were asked why they had not restored the 'old exiles'.
Cf. Pol. xxi. i, Errington, 286–7, Walbank, *Commentary,* iii. 3, 88–9.

exulum causam: Madvig's brilliant emendation (*Emendationes,*
526–7) for the transmitted *eam* (Bψ Gel. 'exemplaria'), *ea* ϕ). As he
showed, *eam* could not be used to refer to one of two cases and though
(*contra* Madvig) *hanc* or *illam* might be possible in reference to the
Spartans, it would need to be at the beginning of the clause.

Elei ... concilio: for their motives, coinciding with Achaean
interests, cf. Errington, 131.

8. Epirotarum: for their earlier attitude to Antiochus cf. 5. 3–8 nn.
non sincera fide: cf. 5. 3 *non simplicis animi.*

9. pacatorum: 'peoples at peace with Rome', not 'defeated foes',
as Sage translates. Cf. xliii. 17. 8, Sall. *Iug.* 32. 3.

35. 11—40. *Events in Rome and Italy*

35. 11–14. *Embassies from Epirus and Philip*

Polybius' account of the reception of the Macedonian embassy
survives in xxi. 3. 1–3 and he will have also related the arrival of the
Epirote embassy. The request to sacrifice and dedicate a gift on the
Capitol is not in Polybius, while L. omits Polybius' statement that
the senate promised to remit Philip's tribute if he remained loyal in
the present crisis (cf. § 13 n.). But though this passage is immediately
followed by material in chs. 36–40 which is is manifestly of annalistic
origin, it is wrong to say (as W–M and Nissen, *KU,* 185, do) that L.
is here using only annalistic sources. We have to do with a typical
transition passage (cf. p. 2). L. has read both Polybius and the
annalists, and what we have is a combination of the two.

11. responsum ... possent: doubtless a typical ambiguous *s.c.*
(cf. *Studies in Ancient Society,* 65). Cabanes (282–3) argues unconvincingly that the senate made it clear that Epirus was not free
to pursue an independent foreign policy. In 189 the Epirotes fought
against the Aetolians (xxxviii. 3. 9 ff., Pol. xxi. 26, Niese, ii. 717).

12. et Philippi ... de uictoria: Pol. xxi. 3. 1–2: κατὰ τοὺς αὐτοὺς καιροὺς ἡ σύγκλητος ἐχρημάτισε τοῖς παρὰ Φιλίππου πρεσβευταῖς· ἧκον γὰρ παρ' αὐτοῦ πρέσβεις ἀπολογιζόμενοι τὴν εὔνοιαν καὶ προθυμίαν, ἣν παρέσχηται Ῥωμαίοις ὁ βασιλεὺς ἐν τῷ πρὸς Ἀντίοχον πολέμῳ.

sacrificare ... senatu: for similar dispensations for dedications by foreigners cf. xxviii. 39. 18, xliii. 6. 6, xliv. 14. 4, xlv. 13. 17, Mommsen, *RF*, i. 347. For gifts of crowns to Rome cf. Walbank, *Commentary*, iii. 422, to individual commanders xxxvii. 46. 4 n.

13. non responsum ... datus est: Pol. xxi. 3. 3: ὧν διακούσασα τὸν μὲν υἱὸν Δημήτριον ἀπέλυσε τῆς ὁμηρείας παραχρῆμα · ὁμοίως δὲ καὶ τῶν φόρων ἐπηγγείλατο παραλύσειν, διαφυλάξαντος αὐτοῦ τὴν πίστιν ἐν τοῖς ἐνεστῶσι καιροῖς. Cf. xxxiv. 57. 1, xxxv. 31. 5, xxxvii. 7. 16 n.

36. 1–2. *Games of Scipio Nasica*

36. 1. praetor ... uouisset: xxxv. 1. 8: in fact as a promagistrate in 193 (cf. addenda on xxxv. 1. 5).

nouum atque iniquum: as W–M say, it is the demand for public funds, not the making of the vow itself, that the senate regards as unprecedented. The passage contradicts Polybius' statement (vi. 12. 8) that a consul in Rome could use public funds on his own authority. Cf. Walbank, *Commentary*, i. 678.

2. inconsulto senatu: φL, *sine consultu senatus* B, *sine consultos senatus* N, *in e consultos senatus* V. *inconsulto* clearly has no authority, and would be the only example of *inconsultus* in a participial sense before the younger Pliny (*TLL*, vii. 1. 1014. 30 ff.). Perhaps L. wrote *sine senatus consulto*. Alternatively the words could be regarded as originating from a gloss on *ex unius sententia*.

36. 3–7. *Dedications of temples*

3–4. This notice, taken together with 3. 14 and 37. 1, causes a major chronological problem, not, as far as I can see, noticed by previous writers, and drawn to my attention by Professor Jocelyn. The date of the dedication of the temple of Magna Mater was 10 April (*I.I.* xiii. 2. 438). At 37. 1 the text printed by all editors states that at the time *haec*—i.e. the events described in ch. 36—*agebantur*, Acilius had left Rome *ad bellum* but Scipio Nasica was still in the city. Yet at 3. 14 Acilius leaves Rome *a.d. quintum Non. Maias* and hence should still be in Rome at the time of the dedication of the temple. The statement that Glabrio was not in Rome might appear to be given support by the fact that it was the praetor M. Iunius Brutus who performed the dedication. The dedication of a temple of a goddess brought from Asia with the help of Pergamum could be seen as emphasizing Rome's Trojan origin and therefore a peculiarly suitable task for a consul about to set out to wage war with a man who claimed rule over Asia. But an even stronger claim could be made for the other consul, as the man chosen by the senate to receive the Magna Mater at the time of her arrival in 204 (§ 3 n.). Indeed, if both consuls were in Rome, it could be that Brutus was chosen as a compromise between their conflicting claims. (It was the praetors who subsequently superintended the rites of the Magna Mater [DH ii. 19. 4], and if they had been doing so since 204, the *praetor urbanus* would have been a logical choice.)

There are five possible solutions:

(*a*) To reject the dedication date—the actual date will be 1 December 192 (cf. p. 25) and that might not seem a good occasion for the performance of plays in an open-air theatre. But such dates are just the sort of thing that would be recorded, and since it falls at the end of the *Megalesia* (cf. xxxiv. 54. 3 n.) the grounds for accepting it are very strong, and the difficulty of the winter performances is not sufficient to outweigh them.

(*b*) To reject or emend the date in 3. 14. No easy emendation is to hand, it is hard to see why so precise a date should be invented, and it harmonizes with other chronological indications for the campaign of 191 (cf. p. 28).

(*c*) To hold that the statement in 37. 1 originally applied only to the dedication of the temple of Iuventas, for which no dedication date is known, and was mistakenly applied to all the events described in ch. 36.

(*d*) To reject the statement in 37. 1. It could be seen as caused by puzzlement that Glabrio had not made the dedication himself.

(*e*) To emend 37. 1. First of all, it is clear that the usual text has no authority. Bψ have *iam haec*, Mg *haec iam* and φ *quo haec*. Without *quo*, *principio eius anni* goes with *agebantur* and the separation of *haec* from *agebantur* by the ablative absolute is impossible (it is not all that much easier with *quo*). At first sight *agebantur* is suspicious: one would expect *acta sunt* in a formal expression of this sort. At xxviii. 17. 1, however, we find *aestatis eius principio qua haec agebantur* (cf. xxii. 19. 1) and this not only vindicates *agebantur*, but suggests that Colonna's *quo* is in fact correct. All problems would be solved by reading *principio eius anni quo haec agebantur, iam profecto* . . .

For the bringing of the Magna Mater to Rome, and the earlier *ludi Megalenses* cf. xxxiv. 3. 8, 54. 3 nn. For the site of the temple on the Palatine see Nash, ii. 27–31.

3. is P. Cornelius . . . detulerat: xxix. 14. 10 ff. In fact this was in 204, not 205, as L. states. There is, however, no real conflict of dates. The original decision to bring the Magna Mater to Rome was taken in 205 (xxix. 10. 4 ff.) and that is the date L. has in mind.

postea: B, *post* χ, perhaps rightly. Cf. xxv. 2. 6.

P. Licinio: (69). Crassus. Cf. xxxi. 9. 7 n.

M. Liuius ... consulibus: 204. On M. Livius Salinator (33) cf. xxxi. 12. 8 n., on C. Claudius Nero (246) xxxi. 2. 3 n., on M. Cornelius Cethegus (92) xxxiii. 42. 5 n., on P. Sempronius Tuditanus (96) xxxi. 2. 3 n.

4–5. quos ... dedicauit: L. appears to be saying that according to Antias 191 was the first occasion on which plays were produced at *ludi* and that the first *Megalesia* were held on the dedication of the temple. Since, however, Antias recorded the provision of separate seats for senators at the theatre in 194 (cf. xxxiv. 44. 5 n.) we must conclude either that Antias merely said that the first plays at the *Megalesia* were performed in 191 rather than 194 (cf. xxxiv. 54. 3 n., Tränkle, 67 n. 46) or that Antias was inconsistent on the matter. Accius placed the first plays in Rome in 197 (cf. Cic. *Brut.* 73, xxxi. 12. 10 n.) on the occasion of the dedication of the temple of Iuventas, and it may be that Antias made some reference to Accius' view. The true date of the dedication of the temple of Iuventas cannot be determined: the fact that a Cornelius was consul in both 197 and 191 could have led to an error in either direction. (The ease of such mistakes is shown by the fact that Latte, *RRG*, 256 n. 2, gives Accius' date as 193, when, as in 197, both a Cornelius and a Minucius were consuls.)

4. Antias Valerius: Bχ, *Valerius Antias* Mg. For the inversion cf. xxxiii. 30. 10, xxxiv. 5. 9 n. In the case of Antias it occurs eight times in L. and is probably what L. wrote here. Cf. p. 15.

5. Iuuentatis aedem: the site of the temple is not known. Earlier Iuventas had a statue in the cella of Minerva in the Capitoline temple. Cf. Latte, loc. cit., Ogilvie, 750.

6. quo die ... cecidit: the battle of the Metaurus in 207 (xxvii. 43–51).

7. eo: Gel. 'lege'. om. Bχ. It is hardly necessary.

37. *Prodigies: departure of Nasica for the north*

Cf. xxxi. 12. 5–10 n.

37. 1. Cf. 36. 3–4 n.

2. boues ... aedificii: for a similar prodigy cf. xxi. 62. 3, Krauss, 121, with speculations about the reason for the prodigy being regarded with such horror. The two passages provide important evidence for the existence of tenement houses with upper storeys at this date. See A. Boethius and J. B. Ward-Perkins, *Etruscan and Roman Architecture* (Harmondsworth, 1970), 113.

Carinis: a residential district in the southern part of the Esquiline. Cf. P–A, 100. Pompey lived there (Vell. ii. 77. 1).

3. Tarracinae: cf. 3. 6 n. For other prodigies there see xxiv. 44. 8, xxvii. 4. 13, xxviii. 11. 2, xxix. 14. 3, xl. 45. 3, Obs. 12, 14, 24, 28, Phlegon, *FGH* 257F13, Wülker, 100.

Amiterni: cf. xxxv. 21. 4 n.

lapidibus pluuisse: cf. xxxiv. 45. 8 n.

Menturnis: cf. 3. 6 n. The MSS. have *Men-* here, but *Min-* at 3. 6. Cf. Philipp, *RE* xv. 1935. For other prodigies at Minturnae cf. xxvii. 37. 2–3, xliii. 13. 3, Obs. 27a, Wülker, 98, J. Johnson, *Excavations at Minturnae*, ii (Philadelphia, 1933), 130.

aedem Iouis: for the site cf. Johnson, op. cit., i (Philadelphia, 1935), 16–17, *RE*, Supp. vii. 468. Johnson argues from coin evidence (= Crawford, *Roman Republican Coin Hoards* [London, 1969], no. 98) that the temple was destroyed by this lightning.

de caelo ... ictas: cf. xxxii. 1. 10 n.

Volturni: cf. xxxii. 29. 3, xxxiv. 45. 1–5 nn.

4. libros Sibyllinos: cf. xxxi. 12. 9 n.

renuntiauerunt: B, *renuntiarunt* φVL, *renuntiare* N. Cf. 3. 6 n.

ieiunium ... seruandum: this is the first occurrence of such a rite. For discussion see Le Bonniec, 446–51, who stresses that it is hard to see what prodigies specially demanded the new rite, and suggests that it was a concession to plebeian sentiment, as a counterweight to the honours for the Magna Mater which were seen as the particular preserve of the *nobilitas*. The fast later became annual and was celebrated on 4 October (*I.I.* xiii. 2. 517), but so late a date is clearly impossible for the present occasion. Le Bonniec seems right in distinguishing the *ieiunium*, probably a complete fast, from the abstinence from bread and wine which was part of the *castus Cereris* (cf. Le Bonniec, 404 ff.). Schlag, 153, holds that the decision to hold the *ieiunium* was intended to delay Nasica's departure for his province.

5. nouemdiale sacrum: cf. xxxiv. 45. 8 n.

coronati: cf. xxxiv. 55. 4 n.

quibus ... decemuiri: contrast the freedom given to the praetor at 21. 9.

6. Cn. Domitium: (18). Ahenobarbus, the consul of 192. Cf. xxxiii. 42. 10 n.

dimisso exercitu: according to 1. 9 Nasica could keep either of the two consular armies which had served in the north in 192 and send the other back to Rome. Presumably, then, Domitius' army was *dimissus* in Gaul, but was to remain on call in Rome. There is no real conflict with 1. 9 and W–M's statement that the two passages come from different sources is unjustified. Cf. Zimmerer, 35 (though she wants to take *Romam* with *dimisso*). *Contra* Mezzar–Zerbi, *RSC* vii (1959), 164–5.

induxit: χ, *duxit* B. Either is possible. For *inducere* cf. xxxiv. 14. 6 n.

38–40. *Wars in the north: debate on triumph for Nasica*

38. 1. lege sacrata: cf. iv. 26. 3, vii. 41. 4, ix. 39. 5, x. 38. 3, Ogilvie, 575.

nocte improuiso: cf. iii. 23. 1, xliv. 35. 11, Preuss, 59. See xxxv. 21. 9 n. (*nocte clam*) and p. 11.

Q.... proconsulis: (65). Thermus. Cf. xxxii. 27. 8 n. Both he and L. Flamininus had been in Liguria in 192: cf. xxxv. 20. 6, 21. 7–11, 22. 3, 40. 2–4 n.

3. eruptionem: a word especially used in descriptions of military engagements, first in Sisenna. It never occurs in verse. Cf. *TLL*, v. 2. 846–7.

4. quattuor milia: χ, *quattuor* B. Mg had *quattuor milia nonaginta*, but such a precise figure would be absurd after *supra*.

5–7. On this final defeat of the Boii see Schlag, 50–1, p. 34. It is also referred to by Oros. iv. 20. 21, Zon. ix. 19. 6.

6. duodetriginta: Oros. l.c. puts the dead at 20,000, but it is most unlikely that he was using any source other than L.

7. For similar criticisms of Antias cf. p. 64.

ubi: 'in which matter'.

intemperantior: *intemperatior* Bχ. *intemperatus* occurs at Cicero *am.* 75 and in the oldest MSS. at *Vat.* 1, but *intemperans* is clearly the transmitted reading elsewhere in L. and should probably be read here.

39. 1–2. The *ouatio* of Fulvius, which breaks into the otherwise continuous narrative concerning Nasica, is repeated from 21. 10–11. The only essential difference is that in the first passage the amount of uncoined silver is 10,000 pounds, here it is 12,000 (Mg has *duodecim milia*, B *decem ∞ ∞*, V *decem Ꝯ Ꝯ*, N *decem* followed by a space AE *x̄*, P *x*: the evidence of BV shows that *duodecim* is indeed the transmitted reading). For the reasons for the duplication cf. 21. 4–11 n.

2. transtulit: cf. xxxiv. 52. 4 n.

  bigati: cf. xxxiv. 10. 4 n.

  centum triginta: this passage and 40. 12 apart, amounts of coined silver are always of individual coins (cf. Packard, i. 606) and a number under a thousand is incredible. *milia* should be added on both occasions. See H. J. Müller, *Hermes* xviii (1883), 319–20.

3. colonias: in fact only Bononia was founded in this region (cf. xxxvii. 47. 2, 57. 7–8 nn.). Strabo's statement (v, p. 213, 216C) that the Boii were completely removed from their lands is exaggerated. Cf. Harris, 211.

4. adesse ... triumphi: it seems that Nasica not only assumed that he would be granted a triumph, but decided on its date as well.

5. ipse ... uocato: the Latin does not in itself indicate, as W–M say, that Nasica himself summoned the senate, though it is quite likely that he did.

6. P. Sempronius Blaesus: (31). Only five Sempronii Blaesi are known, Gaius, the consul of 253 and 244, Gaius, quaestor in 217 and tribune in 211, the present tribune (not known apart from this episode), and Gaius, plebeian aedile in 187 and praetor in 184.

  There is no obstacle to regarding Blaesus as an opponent of the Scipios. The only branch of the Sempronii who can be regarded as friends of the Scipios before the 170s (cf. *JRS* liv [1964], 76, *Latomus* xxvii [1968], 155) are the Sempronii Longi (cf. xxxi. 20. 5 n.).

  bella ... iuncta: in fact serious attempts to subdue the Ligurians of the north-west Apennines did not begin until after the defeat of the Boii. Cf. Toynbee, ii. 261–2 n. 2.

7. ibi annum: Bχ, *annum ibi* Mg. Cf. xxvii. 9. 4.

8. etiam: for *etiam* = *adhuc* cf. viii. 16. 6, *TLL*, v. 2. 927 ff. Emendation is unjustified.

9. ius iudiciumque: for the alliterative phrase cf. Wölfflin, *Ausgewählte Schriften*, 263, Lambert, 28.

10. in magistratu non triumphauerunt: in the third century almost all triumphs were held either by consuls in office or by promagistrates holding *imperium* directly prorogued from their consulship. Cf. J. S. Richardson, *JRS* lxv (1975), 50 ff.

  triumphauerunt: cf. xxxiv. 20. 2 n.

40. 3. biduo post: two days after the battle, not the following day.
Cf. Nisbet, *in Pisonem*, 67.

4. uerum enimuero: cf. xxxi. 30. 4 n.
  quot cum: *quod cum tot* Bχ. It is hard to think of any alternative
to *quot cum*, but *tantum numerum . . . quot cum milibus* is a very strange
expression.
  certe Boiorum: 'of the Boii at any rate'.

5. plus . . . caesam: reflecting the figures of Valerius Antias given
in 38. 6. But L. allows his rhetoric to carry him away, and it would
be rash to conclude that Nasica's speech stood in Antias in anything
like the form in which it appears in L.

7. detractatione: 'objection'. Probably to be read in a fragment of
Cicero (B22 Schoell) and then six times in L. (*TLL*, v. 1. 834).

8. illo . . . senatus: cf. 36. 3 n.

9. titulo . . . imaginem: literally, with reference to the inscriptions
underneath the *imago*.
  addatur: the tense is determined by the fact that Nasica had not
yet got his triumph.
  honestam honoratamque: conferring *honos* and having had
honos conferred on it. See the passages adduced by W–M.

10. tribunum . . . intercessionem: for a similar situation cf.
xxxi. 20. 6 n.
  compulit: in the sense that Blaesus felt that he was left with no
alternative. There was neither physical nor constitutional com-
pulsion. For similar uses of ἀνάγκη and ἀναγκάζειν in Greek cf.
G. E. M. de Ste. Croix, *The Origins of the Peloponnesian War* (London,
1972), 61.

12. in Gallicis . . . factis: 'in the form of Gallic vases'. Cf. xxxviii.
14. 5, Tränkle, 107 n. 23. P. Jacobsthal (*AJA* xlvii [1943], 306–12)
wrongly denied that the usage was possible and proposed transposing
in Gallicis . . . factis to follow *bigatorum nummorum*, taking them to be
the containers for the coined silver. Archaeological evidence for
Gallic pottery in Northern Italy at this period does not exist.
(Jacobsthal, op. cit., 310).
  infabre: found elsewhere in this sense only in Horace, *Sat.* ii.
3. 22. At Pacuvius, *trag.* fr. 271 it means *foede*. Cf. *TLL*, vii. 1. 1335.
  bigatorum: cf. xxxiv. 10. 4 n.
  ducenta . . . quattuor: cf. 39. 2 n.

14. exauctoratos: cf. xxxii. 1. 5 n.

41–45. 8. *Events at sea and in Asia*

Cf. App. *Syr.* 21. 97–99, 22. 101–7, Just. xxxi. 6. 7–9 (conflating the battle of Corycus with that of Side [xxxvii. 22–4]).

41. 1. tamquam ... transituris: cf. xxxiv. 36. 5 n.
  amicorum: the φίλοι. Cf. xxxi. 28. 5, xxxv. 15. 7 nn.

3. propius ... traicere: as W–M say, an odd construction, apparently a conflation of *propiorem esse Graeciam Asiae quam Graeciae Italiam* and *facilius esse ex Graecia in Asiam quam ex Italia in Graeciam traicere*. Perhaps the construction is colloquial: in English we sometimes say 'it is nearer to go this way'.

3. [enim]: Bχ, del. dett. Such an affirmative use of *enim* would be unique in Classical prose.

  iam ... esse: probably in reference to Atilius' presence at Gytheum in 192 (xxxv. 37. 2). No part of the Roman fleet would actually have stayed near Malea for any length of time, given the dangerous nature of the waters in that region. L. has probably misunderstood Polybius. On Malea cf. xxxi. 44. 1 n., where the information given about MSS. readings here and at 42. 5 is incorrect. The MSS. have *Maleum* at both places, and should probably be followed.

4. nouumque imperatorem: C. Livius Salinator.

6. itaque ipse ... firmaret: cf. App. *Syr.* 21. 98–9: ἔς τε Χερρόνησον διαπλεύσας πάλιν αὐτὴν ὠχύρου καὶ Σηστὸν καὶ Ἄβυδον ἐκρατύνετο, δι' ὧν ἔδει τὴν φάλαγγα τὴν Ῥωμαίων ἐς τὴν Ἀσίαν ὁδεῦσαί τε καὶ περᾶσαι. Λυσιμάχειαν δὲ ταμιεῖον τῷδε τῷ πολέμῳ ποιούμενος ὅπλα καὶ σῖτον πολὺν ἐς αὐτὴν συνέφερεν, ἡγούμενος αὐτίκα οἱ Ῥωμαίους πεζῷ τε πολλῷ καὶ ναυσὶν ἐπιθήσεσθαι. L. will have omitted some of the details in Polybius. Cf. Witte, 373.
  si forte: cf. 20. 6 n.
  Polyxenidam: cf. App. *Syr.* 21. 97: ναυαρχοῦντος αὐτῷ Πολυξενίδου Ῥοδίου φυγάδος. Cf. xxxv. 50. 7 n.

7. speculatorias: cf. xxxv. 26. 9 n.

42–45. 8. On these events cf. Rodgers, 398 ff., Thiel, 293 ff. Thiel's notion that it was Livius' own idea to cross to Asia is improbable. He will have been given some instructions by the senate. On the similarities between L.'s accounts of three of the four naval battles in the war (cf. xxxvii. 23–4, 29–30) see Walsh, *RhM* xcvii (1954), 100 ff., *Livy*, 232–3. On L.'s use of terminology drawn from military registers in describing naval battles see W. K. Lacey, *CQ* n.s. vii (1957), 118.

42. 1. praefectus: in fact, of course, a praetor in office. Cf. 12. 9 n.
quinquaginta: cf. 2. 14 n.

2. sex Punicas naues: cf. App. *Syr.* 22. 101: καὶ παρὰ Καρχηδονίων αὐτῷ τισι δοθείσαις. See 4. 9 n.
Reginis: cf. xxxi. 29. 10–11 n.
Locrisque: cf. xxxi. 12. 1 n. For the conjunction of ethnic and city cf. J. L. Catterall, *TAPhA* lxix (1938), 295–6.
lustrata classe: on the *lustratio classis* cf. Latte, *RRG*, 119, Ogilvie, *JRS* li (1961), 35.
Lacinium: to the south of Croton. Cf. Philipp, *RE*, xii. 345–6, Walbank, *Commentary*, i. 364–5. Livius will have sailed along the coast from Locri to the Lacinian promontory.

3–4. percunctatus ... regem esse: at first sight one might think that L. is referring to Glabrio and Antiochus before the battle of Thermopylae. But this is excluded by the chronology and the possibility of a misunderstanding of Polybius is excluded by *necdum ... perpacata erant*, which cannot possibly mean 'the battle of Thermopylae had not yet taken place'. As W–M say, therefore, *regem* must indicate Philip, and the reference is to the sieges of Heraclea and Lamia. Cf. p. 28.

3. perpacata: cf. 21. 3 n.

4. classem ... stare: it had returned to Piraeus after intercepting the supply ships off Andros (20. 8).

5. Samen Zacynthumque: Same is Cephallenia: cf. 11. 9, xxxii. 15. 3 nn. The attack on Zacynthus will precede the sale of the island to the Achaeans by Hierocles of Agrigentum (32. 1). Cf. Aymard, *PR*, 340.
petit: χ, *petiit* B. Cf. p. 12.

6. Scyllaeum: cf. xxxi. 44. 1 n.

7. quinque et uiginti: cf. xxxv. 37. 3 n.
est profectus: χ, *profectus est* B. Cf. p. 15.

8. multis ... minoribus: at 43. 12–13 L. says that Eumenes arrived *cum quattuor et viginti nauibus tectis, apertis pluribus paulo* and gives the total number of allied *apertae* as *ferme quinquaginta*. Appian (*Syr.* 20. 101) says that Eumenes contributed 50 ships, of which half were κατάφρακτοι. We may therefore assume that Eumenes had 26 *apertae* and reckon Livius' *apertae* as 22 or 23 (McDonald and Walbank, *JRS* lix [1969], 32–3 n. 15, give 20, Thiel [269] 24).

rostratae: 'combat galleys'. Cf. McDonald and Walbank, op. cit., 32 n. 14.

Delum: for Livius' dedications at Delos cf. *IDelos* 439 A78, 442 B86, 1429 A30.

43. 1. consul ... Naupactum: cf. 30. 6, 34–35. 6. Cf. p. 28.

et est: χ, *est* B. For *et est* in similar explanations cf. xxv. 11. 9, xxxii. 15. 6, xxxviii. 29. 6.

uentosissima ... diuisas: cf. the passages quoted by Nisbet and Hubbard, i. 188.

3. poterat: Bχ, *potuit* Mg. Cf. xxiii. 28. 3, xxxvii. 22. 5.

5. auxiliorum: better taken as 'auxiliary forces'—i.e. assistance from land forces—than, with W–M and McDonald and Walbank (op. cit., 32), as 'advantages', explained in what follows. For except for the last sentence of § 7 all that follows explains the supposed Seleucid superiority *celeritate nauium*, and *multum ... essent* is in no sense explicative of *uarietate auxiliorum*, which is, in fact, not explained at all.

6. nam ... immobiles esse: an unreasonable claim. See Thiel, 296 n. 428.

inscite: *inscitus* occurs in Plautus, Terence, and Cicero's philosophical works. This is its only occurrence in L., and the only time the adverb is used of artefacts. Cf. *TLL*, vii. 1. 1842–3.

8. centum: Appian (*Syr.* 22. 103) says 200, which makes far better sense, since Polyxenidas, facing a fleet of 155 ships, welcomes the chance of a battle (44. 1). See Kromayer, ii. 157 n. 4, Thiel, 273–5. McDonald and Walbank (op. cit., 32–3 n. 15) argue for 100 on the grounds that if Antiochus had 130 *apertae* it is odd that they play no part in the subsequent battles and that *non ferme impares* (43. 5) makes no sense if Polyxenidas outnumbered the Romans by 2 to 1. But, as Thiel (274) says, Polyxenidas may have realized that they were of no assistance at Corycus and made no use of them thereafter, and Polybius may have referred to the numbers of *naues tectae* and been misunderstood by L. McDonald and Walbank's explanation of Polyxenidas' subsequent enthusiasm for battle as being due to confidence in his own seamanship fails to convince.

Since the corruption is so easy, I should prefer to follow Sigonius in reading *cc* here rather than assume a mistake by L. himself.

ceterae ... formae: the *tectae* are quadriremes and quinqueremes of smaller build, not triremes, as argued by Thiel, 274 n. 345. Cf. McDonald and Walbank, op. cit., 33.

Phocaeam: the date of its occupation by Antiochus is not certain: it may have occurred during the expedition of 197. Cf. Hier. in Dan. xi. 18 (*FGH* 260F47), Schmitt, *Antiochos*, 283. See further § 11 n., 45. 7, xxxvii. 9. 1–4, 11. 15, 31. 8—32 nn.

9. cum audisset ... classem: doubted by Thiel, 301 n. 434.

Magnesiam ... Sipylum: modern Manisa, inland to the east of Phocaea. On the site cf. Magie, i. 122–3, ii. 976. It had belonged to Antiochus since *c.* 216–213. Cf. Schmitt, loc. cit.

10. Cissuntem: not otherwise known, and its identity with the Κασύστης of Strabo xiv. p. 644C cannot be regarded as certain. Erythrae is on the north side of the Çeşme peninsula (on the site cf. Bean, *Aegean Turkey*, 153 ff.), but § 13 guarantees that Cissus is on the south coast. Cf. § 13 n., Hansen, *Attalids*, 80 n. 32. For the reasons for Polyxenidas' move cf. Thiel, 300.

tamquam ... expectatura: cf. xxxiv. 36. 5 n.

11. tenuerunt: 'continued'. *tenere* does not occur before Virgil and L. in this intransitive sense (K–St, i. 93). Cf. p. 9.

Phanas: modern Kato-Fana, a sheltered bay in south-west Chios (*in Aegaeum mare uersum* is somewhat misleading). A temple of Apollo lay nearby. Phanae is also the name of Cape Masticho, the southernmost promontory of Chios, to the east of Kato-Fana. Cf. xliv. 28. 7, xlv. 10. 1, Thuc. viii. 24. 3, K. Kourouniotes, *AD* i (1915), 72 ff., ii (1916), 190 ff., Herbst–Schmidt, *RE*, xix. 1758–9, J. Boardman, *AntJ* xxxix (1959), 170 ff.

Chiorum: Chios, an independent state allied to Rhodes, had early relations with Rome, as witnessed by an inscription (published by Th. Ch. Sarikakis, Χιακὰ Χρονικά, 1975, 14 ff.) and probably to be dated not later than 225 (this is the view of Professor W. G. Forrest: Sarikakis and others [cf. R. Mellor, Θεὰ 'Ρώμη (Göttingen, 1975), 60] date it shortly after the war with Antiochus) recording the existence of a resident community of 'Ρωμαῖοι (a term which can mean no more than 'Italians': cf. J. Hatzfeld, *BCH* xxxvi [1912], 102 ff., *Les Trafiquants Italiens dans l'Orient hellénique* [Paris, 1919], 243 ff.) and the dedication by a Chian to 'Ρώμη, containing the story of the birth of Romulus and Remus. In the present war it served as Rome's principal naval supply base. Cf. xxxvii. 14. 2 n., 27. 1 ff., 31. 5–7. For Roman relations with Chios cf. Sarikakis, *EEThess* xiv (1975), 351 ff.

Phocaeam traiciunt: thus, apparently, slipping past Polyxenidas. See Thiel, 301. L. does not make it clear that Phocaea received the Romans, making a *deditio* to Livius, and abandoned Antiochus. Cf. xxxvii. 32. 9, App. *Syr.* 25. 121.

12. Elaeam: cf. xxxv. 13. 6 n.

post inde: the only example in L. of such a collocation. When *inde* and *post* occur together (cf. *TLL*, vii. 1. 1110. 42 ff., 1121. 72 ff.) *inde* is usually temporal, but here it must have a spatial meaning.

quattuor ... pluribus paulo: cf. 42. 8 n.

Phocaeam: Duker, *a Phocea* Bχ (*a focea* ψ). I think it possible that it has been transposed from the *Eumenes ... profectus* clause. *rediit* indicates that he had already met Livius.

13. As Thiel, 303–4, rightly argues, *primo ... terram* must refer to the journey westwards from Phocaea, but *deinde ... traicere* to the part after the fleet has turned eastwards round Cape Argennum. The journey through the straits of Chios is omitted altogether. Thiel is surely right to hold that L. has abbreviated Polybius. He goes on, however, to argue that *Corycum ... Cissuntem est* indicates that Cissus is west of Corycus. Hence since once Livius had seen Polyxenidas' fleet, he could not have conceived of such a plan, Polybius must have described the aim of reaching Corycus as being the plan before the fleet rounded Cape Argennum. But all this is quite uncertain. We cannot be sure what Greek word or phrase L. was translating by *super* and we must admit that we do not know the relative positions of Cissus and Corycus. Nor is it certain that Polyxenidas' fleet was visible as soon as Livius rounded the Cape. Corycus is the southernmost promontory of the Çeşme peninsula (mod. Koraka). The exact location of the harbour cannot be determined. Cf. Bürchner, *RE*, xi. 1451.

quinque: dett., *l* Bχ. The emendation is determined by the earlier information. Livius had 81 *constratae* (41. 8) and Eumenes 24 (§ 12).

cogebantur ... ire: to prevent the ships being dashed against the sides of each other. For the formation cf. Casson, 280 n. 38.

paulum: χ. *paululum* B, perhaps rightly (cf. xxxv. 5. 11 n.).

44. 1. explicare: 'deploy'. Cf. Thiel, 305.

2. inclinat: 'lowered'. For *inclinare* used literally cf. *TLL*, vii. 1. 941 ff.

armamenta componens: 'stowing their tackle' (Sage). Cf. Casson, 236 n. 53.

3. For explanation of the manœuvre see Thiel, 305–6.

dolonibus: on the *dolo* see Thiel, 305–6, Casson, 237–8, 264–5.

4. ut . . . primum: cf. p. 15.

tumultuari: for the impersonal passive cf. xxi. 16. 4, xxv. 21. 2, Caes. *BG* vii. 61. 3.

5. iam omnibus . . . erant: 'were visible to all the Seleucid ships', not 'were visible with all their own ships', as W–M think.

6–9. Cf. App. *Syr.* 22. 104–6. According to Appian both Punic ships were captured.

6. detergunt: Gel., *defringunt* Bχ. For *detergere* in similar contexts cf. xxviii. 30. 11, xxxvii. 24. 2, 30. 10. *defringere* does not occur in L.

7. quae: *cum* Bχ, *quae compari* Frob. 2. Hirt. *BG* viii. 19. 2, Curt. vi. 1. 7 are the only other occurrences of the phrase. *aequo Marte* occurs in the same sense at xxvii. 12. 10, Virg. *A.* vii. 540, Curt. iv. 15. 29, Luc. iii. 585. *compari Marte* is unparalleled and *quae* remains the simplest change (*TLL*).

8. demittere remos: cf. Thuc. ii. 91. 4.

remos in aquam: B, *in aquam remos* χ. Cf. p. 15.

9. ferreas manus: grapnels, not landing bridges. See Thiel, 307.

regia mancipia: cf. 17. 5 n. Not, of course, an indication of their real social status (cf. K.–W. Welwei, *Unfreie im antiken Kriegsdienst*, ii (Wiesbaden, 1977), 136 n. 82.

11. [extremus]: Mg, om. Bχ. It could have arisen from a marginal note referring back to § 4, but *extremus commisso certamine aduenerat* is perfectly good Latin, and an omission in F is just as likely.

45. 1. Both L. and Appian (*Syr.* 22. 104–7) concentrate on the initial incidents and pass rapidly over the main part of the battle. Presumably Polybius did the same.

fuga coepit: *fugam fecit* Bχ. The latter is nonsense and the old emendation, or something very like it, is inevitable.

sublatis dolonibus: cf. 44. 3 n., Casson, 238 n. 63.

3. abstiterunt: for *absistere* used absolutely, before L. found only in Virg. *A.* i. 192, cf. *TLL*, i. 172. 22 ff. Emendation is quite unnecessary. Cf. p. 9.

tredecim captis: mainly by boarding parties, no doubt. Cf. Thiel, 307.

4. Ephesi: his starting-point (42. 6).

5. unde: i.e. at Cissus.

regia classis: B, *classis regia* χ. Cf. p. 15.

medio ... in cursu: according to Appian (ibid.) the Romans had put into Chios when the Rhodians joined them.

quinque et uiginti: χ, *qui q̄ et xxx* B. Appian, *Syr.* 22. 107 has 27. **Pausistrato:** cf. xxxiii. 18. 2 n.

6. confessionem ... expresserunt: i.e. by Polyxenidas' failure to sail out from Ephesus to meet them. For *confessionem exprimere* cf. xxxvii. 13. 7, 31. 5, and, in other contexts, xxvi. 16. 13, xxxvii. 1. 3, xlii. 47. 8.

7. Phoenicuntem: the Phoenicus of Thuc. viii. 34 must be north of Erythrae, and we must either assume that Livius did not go directly from Ephesus to Chios, or that there was another Phoenicus further south. See Keil, *RE*, xx. 384–5.

portum Erythraeae terrae: Frob. 2. *portu rithreo* B, *portu erithreo* φL, *portu eritreo* NV. There is no need for *terrae*. Cf. xxxvii. 12. 10, xliv. 28. 12.

ipsam urbem: Chios town, in the centre of the east coast of the island.

8. Canas: for the site, a little south of the modern Dikili, cf. C. Schuchhardt, *Altertümer von Pergamon* i (Berlin, 1912), 118.

45. 9. *Events in Rome—election of consuls and praetors*

9. creati sunt: Mg, om. *sunt* Bχ. L. regularly omits *sunt* with *creati consules, praetores*, etc. (cf. Packard, i. 997–8), though in the other occurrences of *comitia, quibus creati* (xxxi. 49. 12, xxxiv. 54. 1, xl. 59. 4) *sunt* is unanimously attested. It is hard to make a decision. Cf. p. 12.

L. Cornelius Scipio: (337). Cf. xxxiv. 54. 2 n.

C. Laelius: (2). Cf. xxxiii. 24. 2 n.

Africanum ... cunctis: not an anticipation of the events related in xxxvii. 1, as W–M claim. Lucius' election was certainly due, in part at least, to the expectation that he would have his brother's assistance in fighting Antiochus.

praetores: it is remarkable that L. gives the *cognomen* in only one case, though he knew the *cognomina* of both Aemilius and Iunius (xxxvii. 2. 1). The case is unique (at xlii. 9. 8 there are only two *cognomina* in the list of the praetors for 172, but there is no reason to think that L. knew of *cognomina* for the other four, or indeed that they had *cognomina*).

M. Tuccius: (5). Cf. xxxv. 41. 9 n.

L. Aurunculeius: (4). Otherwise known only as one of the commissioners to administer the peace with Antiochus (xxxvii. 55. 7).

Cn. Fuluius: (12). Not known apart from his praetorship. The absence of a *cognomen* makes speculation about his affiliations fruitless.

L. Aemilius: (127). Regillus. Known only for his activities as naval commander in 190 (xxxvii. 14–32, 58. 3–4).

P. Iunius: (54). Brutus. Cf. xxxiv. 1. 4 n.

C. Atinius Labeo: (9). Cf. xxxiv. 46. 12 n.

BOOK XXXVII

190 B.C.

1–4. 5. *Events in Rome*

1. 1–6. *Embassy from the Aetolians*

The Aetolian embassy is recounted by Polybius xxi. 2. 3–6. That passage corresponds only to §§ 5–6 of L.'s account, but it is clear that there has been considerable abbreviation by the excerptor of Polybius, and it is not necessary to think that §§ 2–4 do not derive from Polybius. (Diodorus xxix. 4 also contains material not to be found in Polybius: cf. p. 2 n.2.)

§§ 1–2 of the excerpt of Polybius describe the voting of a *supplicatio* for the naval victory of Livius (xxxvi. 43 ff.). L. has omitted this, presumably because he had recounted the battle in book xxxvi and wanted to begin the new book with the reception of the Aetolian embassy, not with something that belonged to the previous book. When he concluded his account in book xxxvi he did not have the details of the present passage of Polybius in his mind. Cf. Nissen, *KU*, 188, Walbank, *Commentary*, iii. 90–1 : *contra* Tränkle, 27–8 n. 10.

1. 1. religiones: not the prodigies, which are reported later (3. 1 ff.), but the taking of auspices and so forth. This was done before each meeting of the senate (Varro *ap.* Gell. xiv. 7. 9), but the procedure was perhaps more elaborate at the first session of the consular year. It was, it seems, unusual to begin the year with a debate on a specific subject: usually there was a general debate *de re publica* (cf. xxxi. 5. 4 n.).

institerunt: B, *institere* χ, *insistere* Mg. The evidence suggests that *institere* is the transmitted reading.

breuem ... diem: cf. xxxvi. 35. 6. For *breuis, longa,* etc. with *dies* to mean a 'day (not) far off' cf. xxxviii. 52. 1, xli. 10. 12, Cic. *Verr.* i. 6, *Att.* xiii. 3. 1, *Bell. Alex.* 71. 1.

ab T. Quinctio: as he had helped them to get a truce from Glabrio (xxxvi. 35. 5). Cf. *Latomus* xxxi (1972), 50.

2–3. Cf. xxxvi. 27. 6–7 n.

2. pensantes: *pensare,* found before L. only in Sallust, *H.* iii. fr. 48. 19, is used by L. on nine occasions (*TLL*).

3. confessionem ... exprimentium: 'seeking to elicit ...': i.e. their questions were really rhetorical ones. For *confessionem exprimere* cf. xxxvi. 45. 6 n.

4. insociabili: reflecting Polybius' views of the Aetolians. Cf. xxxiv. 22. 4, xxxv. 49. 2 nn. *insociabilis* does not occur before L., who uses it here and at xxvii. 39. 8. It is then found once in Curtius (in the sense of 'not to be divided') and three times in Tacitus (once in the latter sense). Cf. *TLL,* vii. 1. 1928, p. 9.

5. Pol. xxi. 2. 4: γενομένων δὲ πλειόνων παρ' ἀμφοῖν λόγων, ἔδοξε τῷ συνεδρίῳ δύο προτείνειν γνώμας τοῖς Αἰτωλοῖς, ἢ διδόναι τὴν ἐπιτροπὴν περὶ πάντων τῶν καθ' αὑτοὺς ἢ χίλια τάλαντα παραχρῆμα δοῦναι καὶ τὸν αὐτὸν ἐχθρὸν καὶ φίλον νομίζειν Ῥωμαίοις.

liberum ... permitterent: i.e. the strict interpretation of *deditio,* as insisted on by Glabrio when the Aetolians agreed to a *deditio* in 191 (xxxvi. 28).

eosdemque ... haberent: a full offensive–defensive alliance (cf. xxxv. 50. 2 n.). This is what they were eventually forced to accept (xxxviii. 8. 10, 11. 3).

6. exprimere ... cupientibus: Pol. xxi. 2. 5: τῶν δ' Αἰτωλῶν ἀξιούντων διασαφῆσαι ῥητῶς ἐπὶ τίσι δεῖ διδόναι τὴν ἐπιτροπήν, The Aetolians are still under the impression that they can make a limited *deditio.*

nihil est: Polybius (loc. cit.) says οὐ προσδέχεται τὴν διαστολὴν ἡ σύγκλητος. διαστολήν is probably to be taken here as 'distinction' rather than 'detailed account' and Polybius is saying that the senate refused to admit of any distinction between what was included in the *deditio* and what was not. L.'s phrase suggests an ambiguous reply.

1. 7—2. *Provinces and armies*

1. 9–10. L.'s version of these events differs from that given in Cic. *Phil.* xi. 17. In L.'s account Laelius wants the command against Antiochus: this is highly improbable, for Laelius' attachment to the Scipios is beyond question. In Cicero Lucius draws the war against Antiochus by lot, the senate wants to give the command to Laelius but is deflected from this course by a speech from Africanus. This makes much better sense. The senate seems to have had, potentially at least, an anti-Scipionic majority at the time and it might have been thought that if Laelius could have been persuaded to accept, Africanus' guns would have been partially spiked. Cicero (*Mur.* 32) says that it was the senate that asked Africanus to go as a *legatus* to Lucius. This is unlikely and probably a mere slip by Cicero.

Val. Max. v. 5. 1 is consistent with either version. One may notice that L. does not subscribe to the view (Cic. *Phil.*, Val. Max. ll. cc., App. *Syr.* 21. 100) that Lucius was regarded as lacking in ability. Klotz (*Livius*, 94–5) unconvincingly holds that the imputation stood in Polybius and was removed by L. For a powerful defence of Lucius Scipio's ability see Balsdon, *Historia* xxi (1972), 224 ff.

The conflict between L. and Cicero was noted by Petrarch in the margin of P.

The above largely reproduces what I wrote in *Latomus* xxxi (1972), 51, where further references will be found. Add Scullard, *SA*, 202–3, Dorey, *Klio* xxxix (1961), 196–7.

9. res ... relata: i.e. for the senate to assign consular provinces itself. For such cases see Ogilvie, 395.

⟨ei⟩: Duker. om. Bχ. The addition is not essential.

10. uicto ... uictore: the verbal contrast occurs also in Just. xxxi. 7. 2.

2. 1. On the praetors cf. xxxvi. 45. 9 n.

Tuscos: presumably to guard against any further trouble from the Ligurians.

2. exercitum ... erant: on Glabrio's army cf. p. 37.

addita: Bχ. *additi* Mg, perhaps rightly: cf. K–St, i. 26.

3. Just as in 205 Scipio was assigned Sicily, with permission to cross to Africa (xxviii. 45. 8). *Graecia*, not *Asia*, was decreed as Lucius' province partly because the senate thought that it would be necessary to deal with the Aetolians before crossing to Asia, partly, perhaps, because they reckoned with the possibility that Antiochus would again invade Greece.

5. Q. Minucius: (65). Thermus. Cf. xxxii. 27. 8 n. For his activities in Liguria in 191 cf. xxxvi. 38. 1–4.

P. Cornelio: Nasica, the consul of 191. For the land involved cf. xxxvi. 39. 3 n.

proconsuli: there is no specific reference to prorogation of his command. This is the only occasion where B exhibits a case of *proconsul* or *propraetor* other than the ablative. Cf. p. 17.

traducere: Bχ, *deducere* Mg. *deducere* is clearly influenced by *deducenti* (-*dae*) below, and is in any case the wrong word for moving an army to another province.

5–6. deducenti duae: Madvig (*Emendationes*, 528), *deducendae* Bχ. With the MSS. reading, and a stop after *iussus*, L. would be saying that the *urbanae legiones* were to be moved from the land which Nasica had taken away from the Boii. This is near to nonsense: the *legiones urbanae* had not been in Gaul, and if they had been they would no longer be *urbanae*. Madvig's emendation makes excellent sense of the paradosis and for that reason is preferable to the simple *deducenti* (H. J. Müller). On the *legiones urbanae* cf. xxxvi. 1. 9, 37. 6 nn. They had not in fact been levied in 191, as they had originally belonged to the consuls of 192. But L. is writing loosely, and it is unnecessary to assume that he is using a source other than the one followed at xxxvi. 1. 9 (thus W–M, Mezzar-Zerbi, *RSC* vii [1959], 164–5).

6. et equites: B, om. *et* χ. Asyndeton is possible, but it is not B's habit to make additions to what he found in F and this makes it likely that *et* is correct.

7–8. A. Cornelio ... remaneret: see p. 38. On A. Cornelius Mammula (258) cf. xxxv. 24. 6 n.

7. si ita consuli uideretur: i.e. Lucius Scipio. The caveat is added because the disposition of troops in Greece is subject to the *maius imperium* of the consul.

legiones: i.e. the ones he had in Bruttium. Cf. xxxvi. 2. 7 n.

8. si ... mallet: it is odd for such a decision to be left to the individual concerned. But the senate may have felt that a direct instruction to serve under his successor would be an affront to Glabrio's *dignitas*.

a M. Aemilio: *ab L. Aemilio*: Bχ. On M. Aemilius Lepidus (68) cf. xxxi. 2. 3 n., xxxvi. 2. 10–12. If the texts on which Packard is based accurately reflect MSS. readings L. rarely uses *ab* before *m*.

The absence of any reference to L. Valerius Tappo (cf. xxxvi. 2. 11 n.) is of no significance and not an indication of a different source (cf. Kahrstedt, 29 n. 1).

10. uiginti ... iussus: cf. xxxvi. 2. 15. In the event eighteen of these were probably left at Cephallenia and Regillus reached the Piraeus with only two (14. 1). See Thiel, 262–3.

11. duas ... obtinentibus: i.e. C. Flaminius in Citerior (he had been there since 193), L. Aemilius Paullus in Ulterior, and L. Oppius Salinator in Sardinia.

12. aeque ac proximo: Madvig, *eo* Bχ, *eaeque proximae* Mg. The same had indeed been ordered in 191 (xxxvi. 2. 12–13 n.) but it is quite possible that L. wrote simply *eo anno* and that Mg's reading is the result of a marginal note relating the passage to xxxvi. 2. 12–13.

3. 1–6. *Prodigies*

Cf. xxxi. 12. 5–10 n. The passage is epitomized by Obsequens 1 (on the text cf. P. L. Schmidt, *Hermes* xcvi [1968], 726–7).

3. 1. The alliteration is remarkable, but probably not deliberate. Cf. Goodyear, 339 n. 1.

per pontifices: cf. xxxiv. 45. 7 n.

2. Iunonis Lucinae templum: on the temple, on the Mons Cispius, cf. P–A, 288–9, on Iuno Lucina, the goddess of childbirth, Latte, *RRG*, 95–6, 105–6.

ualuaeque: 'folding doors'. Cf. Schuppe, *RE*, viiiA. 293 ff.

Puteolis: cf. xxxii. 7. 3 n. For other prodigies at Puteoli cf. xli. 9. 5, Obs. 25, Wülker, 99.

3. Nursiae ... ortum: Nursia, mod. Norcia, in the Sabine country, lies in a hollow, completely surrounded by mountains. It was known in antiquity for its cool weather (Virg. *A.* vii. 715–16, Sil. viii. 417, Pliny, *NH* xviii. 130) and odd climatic occurrences are not surprising. But in fact sudden appearances of thunderclouds and thunderstorms (though I am not convinced by Tränkle's claim [*WS*, 117] that *nimbum* here means 'rain') on clear, hot days are quite common in Italy, and it is rather surprising that the phenomenon should have been treated as a prodigy.

Nursia appears in Festus' list (p. 262L) of *praefecturae*, but it is uncertain at what date it achieved full citizenship. Cf. L. R. Taylor, *Voting Districts of the Roman Republic* (Rome, 1960), 65–6. For other prodigies at Nursia cf. Obs. 40, 46, 48, Wülker, 98.

terra ... pluuisse: cf. xxxiv. 45. 7 n.

Tusculani: on Tusculum, above modern Frascati, see Ogilvie, 198–9. It had possessed citizenship since *c.* 381 (vi. 26. 8, Taylor, op. cit., 79–80).

Reatini: Reate, mod. Rieti, in the Sabine country. It too appears in Festus' list of *praefecturae*. Cf. Taylor, op. cit., 65–6.

mulam ... peperisse: for a similar prodigy, also at Reate, cf. xxvi. 23. 5. The Sabines were famous for the breeding of donkeys. Cf. R. Syme, *Sallust* (Berkeley–Los Angeles, 1964), 8–9.

4. Latinaeque ... fuerat: cf. xxxii. 1. 9 n.

Laurentibus: the inhabitants of Lavinium. There is no separate place called Laurentum. Cf. Ogilvie, 39. On the importance of Lavinium for the cult of the Roman state see, *inter alios*, A. Alföldi, *Early Rome and the Latins* (Ann Arbor, 1963), 246 ff.

carnis: χ, *carinis* B. The passage is quoted by Priscian (*Inst.* vi. 17 = *GL* ii. 208) as the archaic nominative of *caro*; the only other instance adduced by Priscian is a passage of Livius Andronicus and Madvig (*Emendationes*, 529) argued that L. could not have used the archaic form and in fact wrote *pars carnis*, *pars* having dropped out of the text before the time of Priscian. Such an early corruption cannot be excluded, but since at xxxii. 1. 9 L. simply says that the meat had not been given, it is rather unlikely that he should have used the more pedantic form of expression here. He was dealing with an ancient rite, and I would be willing to accept that he therefore adopted an archaic form. Cf. pp. 4, 8.

5. quibus ... ediderunt: cf. xxxvi. 37. 5 n.

6. decem ... adhibiti: it is best to take these words simply as a statement of what happened on this occasion, and not attempt to deduce general rules about sacrificial procedure from them. Thus W–M claim that in the *graecus ritus*, which was used following instructions from the *decemuiri*, children of freedmen could participate. They adduce xxii. 1. 18, but that indicates nothing of the kind. And the present passage is the only evidence for Marquardt's statement (*StV*, iii. 221), followed by W–M, that only children both of whose parents were alive could take part.

lactentibus: cf. xxii. 1. 15. Normally the victims at such sacrifices were *maiores*. Cf. Wissowa, *RuK*², 415. Bχ have *lactentibus*, Mg *lactantibus*: there is no difference in meaning between the two forms. Cf. *TLL*, vii. 2. 848.

3. 7. *Dedication by Africanus*

aduersus ... escenditur: this is the only evidence for the arch of Scipio. It is clear from what L. says that it was at the top of the Cliuus Capitolinus. Cf. P–A, 212. For other arches erected in this period cf. xxxiii. 27. 4–5, Harris, 261.

signis septem auratis: the attempt by G. Spano (*MAL* 8, iii [1951], 173–205) to show that the seven statues represented the seven planets, and thus anticipated the *septizonium*, is quite speculative. It is hardly likely that the statues included the one of Lucius Scipio in a *chlamys* and Greek slippers, mentioned by Cicero, *Rab. Post.* 27: cf. Scullard, *SA*, 203.

labra: 'basins'. For the decoration of arches with fountains cf. Spano, op. cit., 175–7.

3. 8. *Arrival of Aetolian prisoners*

8. eosdem: χ, *eos* B. Either is possible; cf. Packard, ii. 842–3.

principes: those handed over to the Romans after the capture of Heraclea (xxxvi. 24. 12: Damocritus is mentioned there but his brother is not otherwise known).

Lautumias: cf. xxxii. 26. 17 n.

3. 9–11. *Embassy from Egypt*

9. ab Ptolomaeo et Cleopatra: there was no official joint rule of Epiphanes and Cleopatra, and documents are dated by Epiphanes alone. But the pair were known as θεοί ἐπιφανεῖς or ἐπιφανεῖς καὶ εὐχάριστοι and they often make dedications jointly. Cf. Stähelin, *RE*, xi. 739. It is perfectly possible for a message of congratulations to be sent in their joint names and doubt about its authenticity is out of place (cf. xxxvi. 4. 1–4 n.). As Antiochus' daughter Cleopatra must have had mixed feelings (cf. xxxiii. 40. 3, xxxv. 13. 4 nn.).

4. 1–5. *Departure of L. Scipio and L. Aemilius Regillus*

4. 1. pro contione edixit: *edicere pro contione* is used seven times by L., but not by any other author (*TLL*, iv. 732. 63 ff., cf. p. 9). All L. means is that Scipio made his announcement at a *contio*, not that all those he had conscripted were themselves at the *contio* (those in Bruttium [cf. 2. 7 n.] could clearly not be there). We do not know the details of the machinery by which such instructions were conveyed to the troops concerned.

ut milites ... ut hi omnes: cf. xxxvi. 1. 7 n.

idibus Quinctilibus: 18 March 190 (Jul.). Cf. pp. 25, 29.

2. Sex. Digitium: (2). Cf. xxxiv. 42. 4 n.

L. Apustium: (2, 5). Cf. xxxi. 4. 7 n.

C. Fabricium Luscinum: (10). Cf. xxxiii. 42. 7 n.

qui ... contraherent: transport ships, not to form part of the main Roman fleet. Thiel (313 n. 476) notes that both Digitius and Apustius had previous naval experience. If we identify Apustius with the Apustius of 16. 12, it seems that though appointed to this post by Scipio, he later joined the fleet.

3. The loyalty of Scipio's African veterans is remarkable. These are genuine volunteers and W–M's reference to xxxi. 8. 6, xxxii. 3. 3 is misleading. For Scipionic veterans joining Flamininus in 198 see vol. i, 32. On volunteers in the Roman army cf. Harris, 46.

4. per . . . consul: since Scipio left on a specific day, L. must mean that the eclipse took place on a day near the day of Scipio's departure. The sources clearly did not give a precise date for the latter event.

ludis Apollinaribus: they were first performed in 212 (xxv. 12. 8 ff.), repeated in 211 and subsequent years (xxvi. 23. 3), and established on a fixed date in 208 (xxvii. 23. 5 ff., where *Nonas* must be a mistake for, or corruption of *Idus*). They later became an eight-day festival beginning on 6 July. If the text here is correct, they must have started by at least 11 July, and lasted at least three days. See Degrassi, *I.I.* xiii. 2. 477 ff. and references there cited.

a.d. quintum . . . subisset: see pp. 17 ff.

5. triginta . . . faceret: perhaps never built. See Thiel, 264–6, xxxv. 20. 12, 24. 8 nn.

4. 6—7. *Events in Greece*

6. Achaeis: they will have acted thus only after the expiry of the truce with Glabrio. Cf. Aymard, *PR*, 373 and n. 2.

7. Coracem: cf. xxxvi. 30. 4 n.

8. inopinatam: A^z, *opinatam* Bχ. Zingerle (*SAW* cxxviii [1893], 5, 7) argues for *necopinatam*, but *res necopinata* occurs only in the first decade, *res inopinata* thereafter. Cf. Packard, ii. 1225, iii. 458. On L.'s use of *necopinatus* and *inopinatus* see xxxiv. 28. 10 n.

Lamiam: cf. xxxv. 43. 9 n. Philip had been ordered to desist from the siege of Lamia in 191 (xxxvi. 25. 8 n.).

9. eo . . . incautos posse: cf. Vell. ii. 118. 2, Woodman, 196.

10. Elatia: cf. xxxii. 18. 9 n. Doubtless Glabrio made Elatia his winter quarters, as Flamininus had: cf. xxxiv. 25. 1 n. For his activities at Delphi cf. xxxvi. 35. 7–10 n.

Spercheum: to the south of Lamia.

corona: cf. xxxiv. 38. 3 n.

5. 2. tunc: Mg, *quidem* Bχ. *quidem* would be otiose: *tunc* goes closely with *cibo . . . corporibus*, in strong contrast to Glabrio's threats concerning the next day.

3. eodem . . . pridie: i.e. *prima luce*.

pluribus: Bχ, *multis* Mg. *pluribus* has more force. The previous attack had been in only a limited number of places.

iam . . . iam . . . iam: cf. xxxiv. 6. 11 n.

partim . . . praeda: on the procedure cf. xxxvi. 30. 1 n. The fate of the inhabitants is uncertain (cf. Volkmann, 24).

4. iri: Bχ, *ire* Mg. L. regularly uses the impersonal passive (cf. *TLL*, v. 2. 641–2) and corruption to the active is far more likely than vice versa.

aestiua: the time available for the summer's campaign.

non impetratam . . . senatu: *non impetratam* is placed first for emphasis.

Amphissam: *Amplisam* B, *Amphisam* χ. The name is spelt with one *s* at 6. 2 (the first occasion), 7. 7 (twice), and 7. 11; the corruption on the second occasion at 6. 2 (*amplissimam* BV, *amphissimam* N, *amplissimum* L, *amplissimum agmen* φ), however, suggests that F there had *Amphissam*. The standard Greek spelling is Ἄμφισσα (Klaffenbach, *IG* ix². 1. 3. 110, puts Ἄμφισα in brackets but I can see no examples of this spelling) and it is safest to assume that L. wrote *Amphissa* throughout.

On Amphissa, *c.* 12 km. north-west of Delphi, cf. Hirschfeld, *RE*, i. 1955–6, P. Lerat, *Les Locriens de l'Ouest* (Paris, 1952), i. 15 ff., 78, 174 ff., Walbank, *Commentary*, iii. 94.

Oetam: cf. xxxvi. 15. 10 n. In fact only the initial part of the march was over Mt. Oeta.

deductus: B, *ductus* χ. *deductus* makes excellent sense (the army is led down from the mountains to Amphissa) and since B's general tendency is to omit, not to add to what stood in F, it should be accepted.

5. comminisci: *eminisci* χ, om. spat. rel. B. In republican and Augustan Latin *eminisci* occurs only in *Rhet. ad Her.*, Varro, and Nepos. *comminisci* is found in four other passages of L. (xxii. 16. 6, xxvi. 27. 8, xxix. 37. 4, xl. 8. 19) and is almost certainly the correct reading here.

6. The asyndeton helps to highlight the rapidity of the action.

machinas: B, *machinationes* ψAE, *machinati omnes* P. χ could have been influenced by *machinationis* above, but it is equally possible that B is guilty of abbreviation. For *machinatio = machina* cf. xxiv. 19. 8, xxv. 11. 10, xxvii. 15. 5, xxxiv. 34. 4, *TLL*, viii. 16.

6. 1. per Epirum ac Thessaliam: cf. xxxvi. 14. 1 n., Cabanes, 283.

2. tredecim: Sigonius, *tribus* Bχ. *tredecim* gives the total of 3,000 *ciues Romani* and 5,000 *socii* at 2. 2–3, and the 5,000 volunteers of 4. 3. Although 3,000 is clearly impossible, an inconsistency between annalistic and Polybian sections cannot be excluded, and Sigonius's emendation cannot be regarded as certain.

quingentis: 300 in 2. 2–3: perhaps the rest are volunteers.

iam . . . uenerat: *iam enim in sinu Maliaco uenerat* B, *iam in sinu Maliaco uenerat* χ. There is no example of a pregnant construction with *uenire* and emendation is inevitable. Corruption of *erat* to *uenerat* (Weissenborn) is less likely than *sinum* being changed to *sinu* (i.e. *sinu* for *sinū*) and the epithet being altered to agree with *sinu*.

Hypatam: cf. xxxvi. 14. 15 n. The message is presumably addressed to, and the reply comes from the local magistrates of Hypata. In fact, though, the Aetolian leaders are all at Hypata at the time, as emerges from the subsequent narrative.

Amphissa . . . Amphissam: cf. 5. 4 n.

3. moenibus nudata: B, *nudata moenibus* χ. Cf. p. 15.

arcem: on the citadel of Amphissa cf. A. Bon, *BCH* lxi (1937), 164 ff., Lerat, op. cit. (5. 4 n.), 174 ff., Walbank, *Commentary*, ii. 94.

6. 4–7. 7. For this section the account of Polybius survives at xxi. 4–5. (The episode is also reported by Appian, *Syr.* 23. 109 and Zonaras ix. 20. 1.) At the beginning of the narrative there is a discrepancy between L. and Polybius. In Polybius the Athenians approach Africanus who encourages them to seek peace. In L. they see both Africanus and Lucius. It is hard to see how the excerptor could have abbreviated Polybius in this way and it must be either that L. has conflated Polybius with an annalist or that he has been misled by Polybius' words ἐντειλάμενος ἅμα μὲν ἀσπάσασθαι τοὺς περὶ τὸν Λεύκιον καὶ Πόπλιον (xxi. 4. 2) and made them into a specific meeting with the consul. In itself, however, L.'s account is quite coherent. W–M say that *eo . . . agmen* (6. 4) is inconsistent in that *eo* implies that Lucius was at the camp when the Athenians arrived, *praegressum* that he had not arrived. But all L. means is that Publius had arrived at the camp site before the consul. See in general Witte, 366–8. Flurl's discussion (83–106) is again completely unconvincing (cf. xxxvi. 27–29 n.).

4. consul: Mg, om. Bχ. Omission of *consul* is impossible after *sub aduentum . . . concessere* in 6. 3. *Romani . . . posuerunt* would eliminate

the difficulty discussed in the preceding note, but is far too violent
a change to be seriously considered.

sex milia: BL, *in sex milia* φNV, *ab sex milibus* Mg. It is impossible
to decide between *sex milia* and *ab sex milibus*: for the latter cf. K–St,
i. 427. Polybius (xxi. 4. 9, in connection with the Aetolian embassy)
gives the distance as 60 stades from Amphissa, which is more than
six Roman miles, and Tränkle, 113 n. 39, therefore proposes *septem*
here (thus also Weissenborn). I should prefer to attribute the slight
inaccuracy to L.

Athenienses: cf. xxxv. 32. 7 n. L. does not mention the name of
Echedemus (Pol. xxi. 4. 1) until 7. 4. Cf. xxxvi. 5. 1 n.

5. Pol. xxi. 4. 3–6: ὧν παραγενομένων ἀσμένως ἀποδεξάμενος ὁ Πόπλιος
ἐφιλανθρώπει τοὺς ἄνδρας, θεωρῶν ὅτι παρέξονται χρείαν αὐτῷ πρὸς τὰς
προκειμένας ἐπιβολάς. ὁ γὰρ προειρημένος ἀνὴρ ἐβούλετο θέσθαι μὲν
καλῶς τὰ κατὰ τοὺς Αἰτωλούς· εἰ δὲ μὴ συνυπακούοιεν, πάντως διειλήφει
παραλιπὼν ταῦτα διαβαίνειν εἰς τὴν Ἀσίαν, σαφῶς γινώσκων διότι
τὸ τέλος ἐστὶ τοῦ πολέμου καὶ τῆς ὅλης ἐπιβολῆς οὐκ ἐν τῷ χειρώσασθαι
τὸ τῶν Αἰτωλῶν ἔθνος, ἀλλ' ἐν τῷ νικήσαντας τὸν Ἀντίοχον κρατῆσαι
τῆς Ἀσίας. διόπερ ἅμα τῷ μνησθῆναι τοὺς Ἀθηναίους ὑπὲρ τῆς διαλύσεως,
ἑτοίμως προσδεξάμενος τοὺς λόγους ἐκέλευσε παραπλησίως πειράζειν
αὐτοὺς καὶ τῶν Αἰτωλῶν. L. abbreviates considerably and omits
Polybius' statement that Scipio was willing to abandon the Aetolian
war even without the agreement of the Aetolians.

6–7. Pol. xxi. 4. 7–14: οἱ δὲ περὶ τὸν Ἐχέδημον, προδιαπεμψάμενοι καὶ
μετὰ ταῦτα πορευθέντες εἰς τὴν Ὑπάταν αὐτοί, διελέγοντο περὶ τῆς
διαλύσεως τοῖς ἄρχουσι τῶν Αἰτωλῶν. ἑτοίμως δὲ κἀκείνων συνυπακου-
όντων κατεστάθησαν οἱ συμμίξοντες τοῖς Ῥωμαίοις· οἳ καὶ παραγενόμενοι
πρὸς τοὺς περὶ τὸν Πόπλιον, καταλαβόντες αὐτοὺς στρατοπεδεύοντας
ἐν ἑξήκοντα σταδίοις ἀπὸ τῆς Ἀμφίσσης, πολλοὺς διετίθεντο λόγους,
ἀναμιμνήσκοντες τῶν γεγονότων σφίσι φιλανθρώπων πρὸς Ῥωμαίους.
ἔτι δὲ πρᾳότερον καὶ φιλανθρωπότερον ὁμιλήσαντος τοῦ Ποπλίου καὶ
προφερομένου τάς τε κατὰ τὴν Ἰβηρίαν καὶ τὴν Λιβύην πράξεις καὶ
διασαφοῦντος τίνα τρόπον κέχρηται τοῖς κατ' ἐκείνους τοὺς τόπους αὐτῷ
πιστεύσασιν καὶ τέλος οἰομένου δεῖν ἐγχειρίζειν σφᾶς αὐτῷ καὶ πιστεύειν,
τὰς μὲν ἀρχὰς ἅπαντες οἱ παρόντες εὐέλπιδες ἐγενήθησαν, ὡς αὐτίκα
μάλα τελεσιουργηθησομένης τῆς διαλύσεως· ἐπεὶ δέ, πυθομένων τῶν
Αἰτωλῶν ἐπὶ τίσι δεῖ ποιεῖσθαι τὴν εἰρήνην, ὁ Λεύκιος διεσάφησεν διότι
δυεῖν προκειμένων αὐτοῖς αἵρεσις ὑπάρχει—δεῖν γὰρ ἢ τὴν ἐπιτροπὴν
διδόναι περὶ πάντων τῶν καθ' αὐτοὺς ἢ χίλια τάλαντα παραχρῆμα καὶ
τὸν αὐτὸν ἐχθρὸν αἱρεῖσθαι καὶ φίλον Ῥωμαίοις—ἐδυσχρήστησαν μὲν
οἱ παρόντες τῶν Αἰτωλῶν ὡς ἔνι μάλιστα διὰ τὸ μὴ γίνεσθαι τὴν ἀπόφασιν
ἀκόλουθον τῇ προγενομένῃ λαλιᾷ, πλὴν ἐπανοίσειν ἔφασαν ὑπὲρ τῶν
ἐπιταττομένων τοῖς Αἰτωλοῖς. Again considerable abbreviation and

adaptation. In particular, notice how L. makes it explicit that the
terms offered by Lucius were the same as those laid down by the
senate at 1. 5.

commemorantis ... reliquisse: for the sentiment cf. 34. 4.
L.'s succinctness makes the point far more sharply than Polybius.
Cf. Burck, *Wege zu Livius*, 135, Flurl, 87 ff., Tränkle, 140.

idem ... rettulit: 'repeated the earlier reply'. *referre* is widely
used of speech by L., and is particularly appropriate here to
emphasize the identity of the two replies. Cf. its use at xlii. 11. 4,
xlv. 10. 7 to indicate the rehearsal of past events. Emendation is out
of the question.

7. 1. Pol. xxi. 5. 1–4: οὗτοι μὲν οὖν ἐπανῄεσαν βουλευσόμενοι περὶ τῶν
προειρημένων· οἱ ⟨δὲ⟩ περὶ τὸν Ἐχέδημον συμμίξαντες τοῖς ἀποκλήτοις
ἐβουλεύοντο περὶ τῶν προειρημένων. ἦν δὲ τῶν ἐπιταττομένων τὸ μὲν ἀδύνατον διὰ τὸ πλῆθος τῶν χρημάτων, τὸ δὲ φοβερὸν διὰ τὸ πρότερον αὐτοὺς
ἀπατηθῆναι, καθ' ὃν καιρὸν ἐπινεύσαντες ὑπὲρ τῆς ἐπιτροπῆς παρὰ μικρὸν
εἰς τὴν ἄλυσιν ἐνέπεσον. διόπερ ἀπορούμενοι καὶ δυσχρηστούμενοι περὶ
ταῦτα ... L. omits the fact that the Athenians joined in this discussion, and *ne in corpora sua saeuiretur* does not make explicit the
connection with the attempted *deditio* to Glabrio, as is done by
Polybius (cf. Flurl, 98).

2. Pol. xxi. 5. 4: πάλιν ἐξέπεμπον τοὺς αὐτοὺς δεησομένους ἢ τῶν
χρημάτων ἀφελεῖν, ἵνα δύνωνται τελεῖν, ἢ τῆς ἐπιτροπῆς ἐκτὸς ποιῆσαι
τοὺς πολιτικοὺς ἄνδρας καὶ τὰς γυναῖκας. L. has understood Polybius
correctly. τοὺς πολιτικοὺς ἄνδρας means 'citizens', not 'politicians':
see Walbank, *Commentary*, iii. 95.

redire: Mg (*metuebant redire ne in corpora sua saeuiretur*), *uenire* Bχ.
redire is clearly required by the sense.

permissionem: as W–M observe, this is a unique usage and
must be a calque on ἐπιτροπή. Cf. p. 10 n. 1.

3. Pol. xxi. 4. 5–6: οἳ καὶ συμμίξαντες τοῖς περὶ τὸν Πόπλιον διεσάφουν
τὰ δεδογμένα. τοῦ δὲ Λευκίου φήσαντος ἐπὶ τούτοις ἔχειν παρὰ τῆς
συγκλήτου τὴν ἐξουσίαν, ἐφ' οἷς ἀρτίως εἶπεν, οὗτοι μὲν αὖθις ἐπανῆλθον.
L. is much more succinct and pointed.

nihil ... consul: a combination of *non impetratum ut quidquid
mutaret* and *nihil eorum impetratum*.

4–5. Pol. xxi. 5. 7–9: οἱ δὲ περὶ τὸν Ἐχέδημον ἐπακολουθήσαντες
εἰς τὴν Ὑπάταν συνεβούλευσαν τοῖς Αἰτωλοῖς, ἐπεὶ τὰ τῆς διαλύσεως
ἐμποδίζοιτο κατὰ τὸ παρόν, ἀνοχὰς αἰτησαμένους καὶ τῶν ἐνεστώτων
κακῶν ὑπέρθεσιν ποιησαμένους πρεσβεύειν πρὸς τὴν σύγκλητον, κἂν
μὲν ἐπιτυγχάνωσι περὶ τῶν ἀξιουμένων· εἰ δὲ μή, τοῖς καιροῖς ἐφεδρεύειν.

χείρω μὲν γὰρ ἀδύνατον γενέσθαι τῶν ὑποκειμένων τὰ περὶ σφᾶς, βελτίω
γε μὴν οὐκ ἀδύνατον διὰ πολλὰς αἰτίας. L. elaborates with *complor-
antis . . . gentis* (cf. Tränkle, 111). He mentions the length of the truce
here, Polybius only when it is granted.

4. Echedemus: Mg, preserving the correct form, as is clear from
Polybius; *Echidemus* Bχ. He comes from a notable Athenian family.
Cf. P. MacKendrick, *The Athenian Aristocracy, 399 to 31 B.C.* (Cam-
bridge, Mass., 1969), 37, 44, Walbank, *Commentary*, iii. 94–5.

6. Pol. xxi. 5. 10–12: φανέντων δὲ καλῶς λέγειν τῶν περὶ τὸν Ἐχέδημον, ἔδοξε πρεσβεύειν τοῖς Αἰτωλοῖς ὑπὲρ τῶν ἀνοχῶν. ἀφικόμενοι δὲ
πρὸς τὸν Λεύκιον ἐδέοντο συγχωρηθῆναι σφίσι κατὰ τὸ παρὸν ἑξαμήνους
ἀνοχάς, ἵνα πρεσβεύσωσι πρὸς τὴν σύγκλητον. ὁ δὲ Πόπλιος, πάλαι πρὸς
τὰς κατὰ τὴν Ἀσίαν πράξεις παρωρμημένος, ταχέως ἔπεισε τὸν ἀδελφὸν
ὑπακοῦσαι τοῖς ἀξιουμένοις. L. does not repeat Africanus' desire to
get to Asia as soon as possible (cf. 6.5).

idem: *item* Bχ. The correction is inevitable: *item* is not used for
iterum by L., and even if it were possible, the omission of *legati* would
be intolerable. The notion that they were the same ambassadors is
L.'s own, though he is quite likely to be correct.

7. et . . . decessit: Pol. xxi. 5. 13: γραφεισῶν δὲ τῶν ὁμολογιῶν, ὁ
μὲν Μάνιος, λύσας τὴν πολιορκίαν καὶ παραδοὺς ἅπαν τὸ στράτευμα καὶ
τὰς χορηγίας τοῖς περὶ τὸν Λεύκιον, εὐθέως ἀπηλλάττετο μετὰ τῶν
χιλιάρχων εἰς τὴν Ῥώμην.

7. 8–16. *The mission of Gracchus and the journey through Macedon and Thrace*

The journey is also described by Appian, *Mac.* 9. 5, *Syr.* 23. 100.
See Walbank, *Philip V*, 210–11. For the possibility that the letter of
Scipio to Philip referred to by Polybius x. 9. 3 was sent on this
occasion cf. Walbank, *Commentary*, ii. 204 who argues plausibly that
it is rather to be seen as a result of the good relations between the
two men established on this occasion.

8. iter . . . insistis: cf. p. 5.

9. in uoluntate Philippi: despite the concessions made to him in
the previous year (cf. xxxvi. 35. 11–14 n.) Scipio was still uncertain
of Philip's loyalty.

imperio nostro: Polybius would not have expressed himself in
this way.

fidus: Bχ, *fidelis* Mg. There is no essential difference in meaning
between *fidus* and *fidelis*, and it is quite uncertain which L. used
here. He uses *fidelis* more frequently than *fidus*, but *fidus* is common

enough for it to be impossible to argue that corruption to the more usual word is more likely than the reverse.

destituit: *destituat* Bχ. Despite *est* above, *destituet* would be more natural here. Loyalty is a continuing state, desertion an instant action.

10. nihil . . . agentem: the proposal of Nitsche (reported by W–M) to delete these words as a gloss on *opprimet* is absurd.

11. Ti. Sempronius Gracchus: (53). The first appearance of the father of the Gracchi. He was tribune in 187 (cf. *Latomus* xxvii [1968], 155 n. 1), an ambassador to Greece and Macedon in 185, a *iiiuir* for the foundation of Saturnia in 183, curule aedile in 182, praetor in 180, with command prorogued in 179–178, consul in 177, with command prorogued in 176–175, censor in 169, and an ambassador to the East in 165 and 162. In 163 he held a second consulship and was an augur from (probably) 204 onwards.

The high praise in *longe tum acerrimus iuuenum* may well come from Polybius. As the son-in-law of Africanus (not, of course, at this time: for the date of the marriage cf. *JRS* liv [1964], 76 n. 113, *Latomus* xxvii [1968], 155 n. 5) he is likely to have been praised by Polybius, and there is no need to see in the phrase a reflection of the later propaganda which emphasized the virtues of the elder Gracchus in contrast to the vices of his sons (cf. Münzer, *RE*, iiA. 1409).

The choice of Gracchus for this task, despite its importance, cannot be used as an indication of his political position at this time: cf. *Latomus* xxvii (1968), 155 n. 1.

incredibili: vii. 33. 4 is the only other passage in L. where *incredibilis* has the sense of 'extraordinary'. Elsewhere it means literally 'unbelievable'.

Pellam: the capital of Macedon. For a description see R. Lane Fox, *Alexander the Great* (London, 1973), 30–1, with references at the foot of p. 505.

12. in multum uini: deep drinking was a characteristic of Macedonians, not least their kings. Given their habits, Gracchus' deductions were not entirely justified.

13. paratos benigne: 'liberally provided'. Cf. ix. 32. 2.

15. regio apparatu: 'magnificence worthy of a king'. Cf. Cic. *r.p.* vi. 10. W–M's reference to Polybius fr. 181 (B-W) is misleading. It is far from clear that it belongs here (who would Γάιον be?).

et accepit: Mg., om. *et* Bχ. *regio apparatu* goes with both *accepit* and *prosecutus est* and *et . . . et* is therefore necessary.

multa . . . auersum: Scipio had in fact been attacked both for his luxurious habits and for behaving like a king in Spain (cf. xxix. 19. 4, Plut. *Cato mai.* 3. 5 [cf. xxxiv. 4. 1 n.], Scullard, *RP²*, 84). Polybius may well have been seeking here to defend him against such charges. It is entirely probable that he and Philip should have got on well in personal terms.

commendabilia: *commendabilis* does not occur before L., who uses it also at xlii. 5. 5. Cf. p. 9.

16. At xxxviii. 41. 12 L. reports a story from Claudius Quadrigarius relating to this march and W–M and Nissen (*KU*, 210) draw the strange conclusion that at this point L. had not read Claudius' account. Probably Claudius himself mentioned the episode only in connection with the return journey. Cf. Luce, 148–9 n. 17, 202–3.

L. does not mention the fact that the Scipios announced the senate's now firm remission cf. the balance of Philip's war indemnity (App. *Syr.* 23. 110). Cf. 25. 12, xxxiv. 57. 1, xxxv. 31. 5, xxxvi. 35. 11–14 nn., Walbank, *Philip V*, 210.

8–45. *Events in Asia*

8–17. *Naval events*

8. 1. naualem ... pugnam: xxxvi. 43 ff. On Corycus cf. xxxvi. 43. 13 n.

hiemem: the winter of 191/0. L. is following Polybius' account for Ol. 147. 2.

2. et: *ut* Bχ. The anaphora of *ut* would be inappropriate in so straightforward a sentence.

3. itaque ... accersendas naues: cf. App. *Syr.* 22. 108: Ἀντίοχος δὲ περὶ τῆσδε τῆς ναυμαχίας πυθόμενος Ἀννίβαν ἔστελλεν ἐπὶ Συρίας εἰς νεῶν ἄλλων ἔκ τε Φοινίκης καὶ Κιλικίας παρασκευήν.

res gesta: B, *gesta res* χ. For the latter order cf. xxi. 49. 13, xxvii. 20. 3, 27. 13, xxx. 40. 3, xxxv. 7. 8, xl. 43. 4. It is perhaps more likely that it should have been altered to the normal order than vice versa.

4. Gallograeciam: for L.'s account of the migration of the Galatians into Asia see xxxviii. 16. They remained independent, organized on a tribal basis. This is not the place for a detailed discussion. Cf. xxxiii. 21. 3 n., Magie, i. 6 ff., ii. 731 ff., and for Galatians in Antiochus' army 18. 7, 38. 3, 40. 5, 40. 10 ff., Magie, i. 21 n. b, Bar-Kochva, 51.

bellicosiores: than at the time Polybius was writing.

5. Seleucum: cf. xxxiii. 18. 22 n., 40. 6 n., xxxv. 15. 5, xxxvi. 7. 15 n. He will, therefore, have left Lysimachia.

Phocaea Erythrisque: on Phocaea cf. xxxvi. 43. 8, 11 nn.
Erythrae, it seems, had earlier been in Antiochus' possession (cf.
xxxvi. 43. 10) but must have defected from him after the battle of
Corycus. It continued to support Rome (cf. 11. 14, 12. 10) and
remained free after the settlement of Apamea: see Schmitt, *Antiochos*,
282–3, Walbank, *Commentary*, iii. 106.

6. classis … hibernabat: cf. xxxvi. 45. 8 n.

duobus: *uiginti* BχMg. Eumenes was never in a position to put
anything like 20,000 soldiers in the field. The actual figure must
remain in doubt. At Magnesia there were 3,000 Pergamene and
Achaean infantry (39. 9). If the Achaeans are the contingent under
Diophanes (cf. n. ad loc.) the remainder will number 2,000.

equitibus: Bχ, *equitibusque* Mg. Asyndeton is the regular construction. At xxxviii. 12. 8 editors print Mg's *equitibusque quingentis*,
but since Bχ there omit *quingentis* as well as *-que*, that reading too is
open to question.

7. Thyatiram: Mg, *hyratiram* BφLV, *iratiram* N. The Greek name is τὰ
Θυάτειρα, and at 21. 5 *Thyatira* is clearly the transmitted reading.
But here and at 37. 6, 38. 1, 44. 4 the evidence suggests that L.
regarded the name as a feminine singular. He was not necessarily
consistent, but the balance of probability is that the survival of the
neuter plural at 21. 5 is a coincidence, and that we should read
Thyatiram there. Thyatira (mod. Akhisar) was a Lydian town on the
river Lycus. Cf. Keil, *RE*, viA. 657–9, Magie, i. 123, ii. 977. It was
Pergamene at the end of the third century but may have been
captured by Antiochus in 198: see Schmitt, *Antiochos*, 265, 273–4 n. 3.

9. 1–4. *Civil strife in Phocaea.* In this case the natural class tendencies
manifest themselves, the rich supporting Rome, the masses (and
their leaders) Antiochus. See *Studies in Ancient Society*, 57. Polybius
(xxi. 6. 1–6) reports the beginning of the conflict and gives details,
omitted by L., of an embassy from the magistrates asking Seleucus
to leave Phocaea alone. The embassy is composed, however, of both
pro- and anti-Romans. Seleucus pays attention to the latter and
moves towards Phocaea. Walbank, *Commentary*, iii. 5, suggests that
this embassy in fact belongs to the time of the betrayal of Phocaea
reported at 11. 15.

2. Pol. xxi. 6. 1: οἱ δὲ Φωκαιεῖς, τὰ μὲν ὑπὸ τῶν ἀπολειφθέντων
Ῥωμαίων ἐν ταῖς ναυσὶν ἐπισταθμευόμενοι, τὰ δὲ τὰς ἐπιταγὰς δυσχερῶς
φέροντες, ἐστασίαζον.

tributum: consisting of goods, not money payments.

3. tum: i.e. when the garrison and fleet left.

4. optimates: xxxii. 38. 9 is the only other passage where L. uses *optimates* of the upper classes in a Greek state.

5. Pausistratum: cf. xxxvi. 45. 5 n.

6–11. Cf. App. *Syr.* 23. 112–13.

6. Canis: cf. xxxvi. 45. 8 n.

⟨**suis**⟩: Madvig's supplement is necessary. If L. had written *quinqueremibus* uel. sim. there would be no problem, but since quadriremes are also ships 'thirty ships and seven quadriremes of Eumenes' is impossible.

quem ... opinabatur: it is unclear whether Livius' belief was based on previous information or purely on his own speculations. For criticism of his action see Thiel, 317 ff. Appian's statement (*Syr.* 23. 112) that he actually knew of the Scipios' journey is impossible (cf. p. 29).

7. portum ... Achaeorum: due north of Troy. On the site and ancient references to it see Kirsten, *RE*, xxii. 404, Cook, *Troad*, 185 n. 2.

Elaeunte: cf. xxxi. 16. 5 n.

Dardano: *c.* 16 km. south of Abydus. Cf. Bürchner, *RE*, iv. 2163–4, Cook, *Troad*, 57 ff.

et Rhoeteo: *et Rhoetio* BϕL, *ethroetio* NV. The name in Greek is either 'Ροίτειον or 'Ροίτιον and the evidence suggests that on this occasion L. wrote *Rhoetio* (cf. 37. 1 n.). On the site, north-east of Troy, cf. Bürchner, *RE*, iA. 1007, Cook, *Troad*, 87 ff. Despite its *deditio* now, it was later given to Ilium (xxxviii. 39. 10).

8. Sestum oppugnandam: *Seston oppugnandam* Mg, *Sestum oppugnandum* Bχ. It cannot be excluded that L. used the Greek form, particularly as Mg alone preserves the correct gender. According to Appian, *Syr.* 21. 98, Antiochus had garrisoned Sestus in 191: one must assume that the garrison had been subsequently withdrawn. Cf. Thiel, 318 n. 492.

9. Pol. xxi. 6. 7: ἐξελθόντες μὲν Γάλλοι δύο μετὰ τύπων καὶ προστηθιδίων ἐδέοντο μηδὲν ἀνήκεστον βουλεύεσθαι περὶ τῆς πόλεως. L. increases the number of priests for dramatic effect.

fanatici Galli: for *fanaticus* in its literal sense of relating to the cult of such deities as Cybele cf. xxxviii. 18. 9, xxxix. 13. 12, 15. 9, *TLL*, vi. 1. 270.

sollemni habitu: for details see Walbank, *Commentary*, iii. 96.

On the cult of the Magna Mater in Greek states cf. Nilsson, *Geschichte der griechischen Religion* (2nd edn., Munich, 1961), ii, 126, H. Graillot, *La Culte de Cybèle* (Paris, 1912), 495 ff. On the Galli see Graillot, ch. 8: they were believed to be so named from the river Gallus. They are not Galatians, though L. may well have thought they were. It was not until after 189 that Galatians took over the priesthood at Pessinus (cf. Ruge, *RE*, xix. 1106–7).

10–11. *The battle of Panhormus.* The episode is also narrated by Appian, *Syr.* 24. 114–20. The scepticism of V. Costanzi, *RFIC* xxxvi (1908), 392 ff. about the authenticity of the narrative and his supposition that Polybius was misled by Rhodian historians are unjustified.

10. 2. certamine animi: for the phrase cf. ii. 59. 1, iv. 56. 9, vi. 24. 10, xxxii. 20. 3, xl. 17. 3. J. F. Gronovius's alteration to *unum* because of *animo* following is quite unjustified (cf. p. 13) and Nitsche's proposal (followed by Damsté, *Mnemosyne* n.s. xliii [1915], 454) to delete *animi* is absurd.

4. ea: χ, *haec* B, perhaps rightly.

mirabundus: on L.'s use of verbal adjectives in -*bundus* cf. R. Pianezzola, *Gli aggettivi verbali in -bundus* (Florence, 1965), 159 ff.; (166 ff. on *mirabundus*). *mirabundus* does not occur before L. (*TLL*, viii. 1053). Cf. p. 9.

5. internuntius: xxxiii. 28. 11 is the only other occurrence of the word in L. Mg inserts *aperit* after *internuntius*. The omission of a verb of saying is common enough in L., and though it could be argued that a scribe adding a verb would use *ait* or *dixit*, this argument is outweighed by the fact that there is no example in L. of *aperire* followed by an accusative and infinitive (it is followed by an indirect question at ii. 12. 7) and I would see *aperit* as a corruption of an inserted *ait*.

eius: Bχ, om. Mg. Such an addition in F is very unlikely.

6. crederet . . . aspernaretur: cf. xxi. 34. 4 *nec temere credendum nec aspernandos.*

effecit: χ, *efficit* B, perhaps rightly. Cf. p. 12.

Panhormum Samiae terrae: clearly to be identified with the deep bay on the east side of which stands the modern town of Samos (or Vathi). Cf. L. Bürchner, *Philologus* lxv (1906), 481 ff., De Sanctis, iv. 1. 184 n. 16, Schmitt, *RE*, xviii. 2. 656.

7. ultro citroque ... cursare: cf. Cic. *Rosc. Am.* 60 *cursare ultro et citro. cursare* does not occur elsewhere in L., but the phrase is perfectly natural Latin and there is no need to see a direct imitation of Cicero.

sua manu: App. *Syr.* 24. 116 ἐπιστολὴν αὐτόγραφον.

facturum: φ, *facturum esse* Bψ. Carbach's quotation from Mg stops after *facturum* and Mg's reading is therefore uncertain. *esse* is clearly the reading of F and should be retained.

8. Pausistratus felt that if the letters came into Antiochus' possession, the latter would not believe that Polyxenidas' promises had not been genuine.

auctoratum: this is the first instance of *auctoratus* in reference to persons other than gladiators (*TLL*, ii. 1234).

9. socios naualis: since L. normally includes the rowers in the *socii nauales* (cf. xxxiv. 6. 12 n.) the phrase should be taken as an intensification—'not rowers, not indeed any part of the crew'. Cf. Milan, *CS* x (1973), 198.

10. si ... cogeret: i.e. if Polyxenidas could not refrain from moving into battle without his deception being made manifest.

11. Halicarnassum: after its defence by Rhodes in 197 (xxxiii. 20. 12) it remained under Rhodian influence, even if still *de iure* an ally of Ptolemy.

ad urbem: mod. Pithagoreio, in the south of the island.

⟨ipse ... mansit⟩: the transmitted text is nonsense, since sending ships to Halicarnassus and Samos town could not possibly enable Pausistratus to be ready for a signal. But of course all supplements are purely conjectural, and mere indication of a lacuna would be the more prudent course.

12. Magnesiam: on the Maeander. Cf. Magie, i. 78–9, ii. 894–5, Bean, *Aegean Turkey*, 246 ff. It had come into Antiochus' control some time after 196 (cf. Schmitt, *Antiochos*, 281–2).

11. 1. forte: for *forte* introducing a new episode cf. J. Champeaux, *REL* xlv (1967), 375.

Samum: not necessarily Samos town, as W–M say. The soldier has come to the island from Polyxenidas' fleet off Ephesus.

3. [ad Sipylum] missum: *missum ad Sipylum* Mg. In fact, of course, it is Magnesia-on-the-Maeander that is in question: cf. 10. 12 n. It is unlikely that L. would have specified (wrongly) which Maeander was involved, not having done so in the previous passage, and the differing position of *ad Sipylum* in Bχ and Mg lends weight to the view that we have to do with a marginal or interlinear gloss inserted in the text at different points in F and Mg (cf. xxxiv. 6. 15. n.).

detegi: Weissenborn, *tegi* BEPVL, *regi* ANL². *detegi* is supposed to mean 'dismantled', marking a contrast with *naualia reficit* in 10. 12 but it constitutes a unique usage in that sense (cf. *TLL*, v. 1. 792. 82, accepting the emendation and describing it as 'per hypallagen'). The problem is that we have no real idea of the nature of the naval base at Ephesus. Permanent bases would be roofed (cf. Casson, 363 ff.) and there would be no question of covering, uncovering, or dismantling. But even if the base was not of this sort, it is hard to see why Polyxenidas should be dismantling it at this point. I think *tegi* can stand. We are, perhaps, to imagine temporary docks which could not be covered when the ships were in them but are covered as a protection against the weather while the fleet is away.

(One might consider reading *detegi* and taking it to mean 'uncovered'. The *naualia* would not be so much docks as a base with supplies, spares, etc. I would not exclude the possibility that L. has misunderstood Polybius.)

4. conspici: I do not understand W–M's comment that L. is referring to avoiding being seen in general, and not simply by Pausistratus. It is the latter whom L. has in mind all the time.

5. Pygela: to the south-west of Ephesus, and perhaps now in the latter's possession. Cf. Strabo xiv, p. 639C, Magie, ii. 886 n. 84.

6. Cf. App. *Syr.* 24. 117–18: ὁ δὲ Πολυξενίδας, ἐπεὶ κατεῖδεν αὐτὸν ἐνηδρευμένον, αὐτίκα τὴν παρασκευὴν συνῆγε καὶ Νίκανδρον τὸν πειρατὴν σὺν ὀλίγοις ἐς τὴν Σάμον περιέπεμπε, κατὰ τὴν γῆν ὄπισθεν τοῦ Παυσιμάχου θορυβοποιεῖν. ἐκ δὲ μέσων νυκτῶν αὐτὸς ἐπέπλει καὶ περὶ τὴν ἑωθινὴν φυλακὴν ἐπέπιπτεν ἔτι κοιμωμένῳ.

Nicandro: not known apart from this incident. For other pirates apparently assisting Antiochus cf. 13. 12, 27. 4 n., Thiel, 319 n. 497.

quinque: Bχ, *cum quinque* Mg. L. alternates with no apparent rationale between the inclusion and the omission of *cum* in such contexts and there is no way of deciding what he wrote here.

Palinurum: unknown, but obviously somewhere on Samos. (The author of the *RE* article on the famous Italian Palinurus includes the present passage among the evidence for it!)

7. Cf. App. *Syr.* 24. 118: ὃ δὲ ἐν αἰφνιδίῳ κακῷ καὶ ἀδοκήτῳ τοὺς στρατιώτας ἐκέλευε, τὰς ναῦς ἐκλιπόντας, ἀπὸ τῆς γῆς ἀμύνεσθαι τοὺς πολεμίους. Polybius fr. 142 probably belongs here: cf. Walbank, *Commentary*, iii. 5, 97.

uetus miles: 'an experienced soldier'. Cf. Cic. *Tusc.* ii. 38.

8. telis: ed. Asc., *ex* Bχ. *tela ancipitia* occurs in a similar context at
xxx. 33. 3 but the emendation can by no means be regarded as
certain.

id inceptum ... iubet: App. *Syr.* 24. 119: προσπεσόντος δ'
ὄπισθεν αὐτῷ τοῦ Νικάνδρου, νομίσας καὶ τὴν γῆν προειλῆφθαι οὐχ ὑπὸ
τῶν ἑωραμένων μόνων, ἀλλ', ὡς ἐν νυκτί, πολὺ πλειόνων, πάλιν ἐς τὰς
ναῦς ἐνέβαινε ...

Nicander ... uisus: 'the sight of Nicander'. For the construction, particularly common in L. and Tacitus, cf. 12. 7, 24. 3, K–St,
i. 766 ff. For a very striking example see v. 39. 4.

9. mari terraque: Bφ, *terra marique* ψ, trivializing to the usual
order. In fact this is the only example of the inverse order in L.,
and is, of course, quite deliberate. The phrase here is not just the
usual 'by land and sea' but indicates that the Rhodians were not
only surrounded by sea, as they expected, but also, as they now
discovered, by land. (Cf. 52. 3 n.)

12. Appian (*Syr.* 24. 120) gives twenty as the total number of
captured ships. Cf. Thiel, 270 n. 330, 321.

moliuntur: 'getting themselves away'. Cf. p. 5.

13. The Rhodian fire pans are described by Polybius xxi. 7. 1–4,
Appian, *Syr.* 24. 114, 120. The Rhodians also used them at the battle
of Myonnesus (cf. 30. 3). They were an invention of Pausistratus.
For details cf. F. Graefe, *Hermes* lvii (1922), 433 ff., Thiel, 320,
Walbank, *Commentary*, iii. 97 ff.

duabus Cois: Gel. 'uetus lectio', *Cois duabus* Mg (Carb.), *duabus
copiis* Bχ. Carbach's report of Mg is probably mistaken, since, given
the agreement of Bχ, Gelenius cannot be quoting Sp. Earlier an ally
of the Ptolemies, Cos was now an independent state friendly with
Rhodes. Cf. 16. 2, 22. 2, S. M. Sherwin-White, *Ancient Cos*
(Göttingen, 1978), 131 ff.

terrore flammae micantis: a vivid expression, but not
obviously poetic, as W–M claim.

contis: for *contus* in nautical contexts cf. *TLL*, iv. 809. 59 ff.

14. Erythraeae: cf. 8. 5 n.

15. Appian, *Syr.* 25. 121 wrongly includes Samos. Cf. Thiel,
322 n. 511. (Appian's statement is strangely accepted by Bernhardt,
64.)

Seleucus ... Phocaeam: cf. 9. 1–4 n.

Cyme: it is uncertain whether Antiochus had possessed it at an
earlier date. It was free after 188, so presumably returned to Rome
again before the battle of Magnesia: cf. Schmitt, *Antiochos*, 283. On

the site cf. Bean, *Aegean Turkey*, 103 ff., J. Bouzek, *Soziale Probleme im Hellenismus und im Römischen Reich* (Prague, 1973), 265 ff., S. Mitchell and A. W. McNicoll, *AR* xxv (1978–9), 64. For a new inscription from Cyme, possibly of third-century date, honouring a Tarentine, cf. G. Petzland and H. W. Pleket, *Chiron* ix (1979), 73 ff.

12. 1. haec in Aeolide: i.e. the events described in 11. 15. The battle of Panhormus, of course, was not in Aeolis.

    Abydus: cf. 9. 11.

2. Philota: not otherwise known. It is a common Macedonian name.

3. emissa: ed. Ald., *omissa* Bχ. *omittere de manibus* is the reading of the Vienna MS. at xliv. 8. 3 and should probably be retained here. For *emittere de manibus* cf. xxi. 48. 6, Lucr. iv. 504.

4. App. *Syr*. 25. 121: δείσας δ' ὁ Λίβιος περὶ τῶν σφετέρων νεῶν, ἃς ἐν τῇ Αἰολίδι καταλελοίπει, κατὰ σπουδὴν ἐς αὐτὰς ἐπανῄει. καὶ Εὐμένης πρὸς αὐτὸν ἠπείγετο.

    inflatus: Bχ, *elatus* Mg. Both are perfectly possible (cf. Packard, ii. 63, 1202). *inflatus* is perhaps a little more likely to be corrupted to *elatus* than vice versa, but there is very little in it.

    Canas ... Canis: cf. xxxvi. 45. 8 n.

    Elaeam: cf. xxxv. 13. 6 n.

5. Mitylenaeas: Lesbos had presumably remained independent, allied to Pergamum, throughout the 190s.

6. maxime hominum: i.e. most of the booty was human. Sage's translation wrongly implies that it was the human booty that was put into the ships particularly quickly.

7. audita clades: cf. 11. 8 n.

9. decem ... decem: Appian, *Syr*. 25. 121 gives twenty as the total. Thiel (321) holds that they included the seven that escaped from Panhormus (11. 13).

    quem ... credebant: cf. Pol. xxi. 7. 5–7: Παμφιλίδας ὁ τῶν Ῥοδίων ναύαρχος ἐδόκει πρὸς πάντας τοὺς καιροὺς εὐαρμοστότερος εἶναι τοῦ Παυσιστράτου διὰ τὸ βαθύτερος τῇ φύσει καὶ στασιμώτερος μᾶλλον ἢ τολμηρότερος ὑπάρχειν. ἀγαθοὶ γὰρ οἱ πολλοὶ τῶν ἀνθρώπων οὐκ ἐκ τῶν κατὰ λόγον, ἀλλ' ἐκ τῶν συμβαινόντων ποιεῖσθαι τὰς διαλήψεις. ἄρτι γὰρ δι' αὐτὸ τοῦτο προκεχειρισμένοι τὸν Παυσίστρατον, διὰ τὸ πρᾶξιν ἔχειν τινὰ καὶ τόλμαν, παραχρῆμα μετέπιπτον εἰς τἀναντία ταῖς γνώμαις διὰ τὴν περιπέτειαν. The mention of Pamphilidas is a mistake of the *Suda* (cf. H. van Gelder, *Geschichte der alten Rhodier* [The Hague, 1900], 136 n. 3, Thiel, 323 n. 517, Tränkle, 34 n. 41, Walbank, *Commentary*, iii. 99). Kirchner's argument (*RE*, xviii. 2. 329) that Pamphilidas was the commander of the first squadron is misguided.

Bχ have *Eudemus* here but *Eudamus* at all other occurrences of the name. He is known also from *Syll.*³ 673 (Walbank, *Commentary*, ii. 511, iii. 99).

10. [Pelorum]: Bχ. The word is meaningless but it is hard to see it as a gloss: a reference to Cape Pelorum in Sicily would be of no relevance. Corycus (cf. xxxvi. 43. 13 n.) is very close to Teus and the emendation *Teiorum* (Milan edn., 1505) is attractive.

11. miserunt: BχMg. A wide range of emendations has been proposed (to those listed by W–M add P. Damsté, *Mnemosyne* n.s. xliii [1915], 455 *se commiserunt*, C. Brakman, *Mnemosyne* n.s. lv [1927], 61 *enisi sunt*), none of them compelling. The question is really whether *mittere* used absolutely could be a technical nautical term, as was considered possible by Madvig (*Emendationes*, 529: though in the end he chose to emend) and Weissenborn. There is no clear parallel (xxix. 7. 2, mentioned by Weissenborn, has *naues* as the object of *mittere*).

12. aquilone ... septentrionem: north-east veering to north. I do not see the conflict between Pliny, *NH* ii. 119 and Seneca, *NQ* v. 16 alleged by W–M.

13. For defence of the accuracy of L.'s narrative here see Thiel, 324–6.

13. 1. Myonnesum: for the site, on the west side of the Doganbey peninsula, see Keil, *RE*, xvi. 1080–1, Bean, *Aegean Turkey*, 146–9.

Macrin: *Macri* BψAE, *matri* P. At 28. 5 BNV have *acri*, φ has *maiori*, L *maori*, while at 29. 5 Bχ have *Macrin*; it seems likely that L. used the Greek form on all three occasions. It is Doganbey Adasi, just south of the promontory.

praeteruehentis: *praeteruehentis* B, *praeteruehenitis* AE (-*nitis* A), *praeteruehementis* ψP. The evidence clearly indicates that the genitive is the transmitted text, and there is no case for Weissenborn's suggestion of *praeteruehenti classi*.

2. increbrescente uento: for *uentus increbrescere* cf. Cic. *fam.* vii. 20. 3, Caes. *BC* iii. 26. 2, Hor. *Sat.* ii. 5. 93, Sen. *epp.* 77. 2, *TLL*, vii. 1. 1036. 83–4.

uoluente fluctus: cf. Virg. *A.* i. 86, vii. 718, Hor. *Od.* ii. 9. 22 (De Regibus), pp. 4 n. 3, 9.

3. Aethaliam: P, *Aethaleam* BAEψ. For the identification see Thiel, 324 n. 524. Aethalia is said to be the name for both Chios (Pliny, *NH* v. 136) and Elba (Philipp, *RE*, ix. 1090). How L. spelt the name is uncertain (at § 5 the MSS. have *Aetoliam*).

4. pars exigua: cf. xxxiv. 56. 5 n.

portum ... Samiae: at § 6 the Roman fleet arrives at Samos, producing an apparent conflict with this passage. Either, then, the present harbour is a Samian possession on the mainland (though almost certainly not understood by L. as such) or *Samum* at § 6 is Samos town (cf. Thiel, 324 n. 524). I see no way of deciding between the two alternatives.

nocte tota: when *totus* is used in phrases indicating time how long the ablative is regular. Cf. 31. 2 n., H–S, 41.

decurrit: Mg, *currit* Bχ. Everything points to *decurrit* being the correct reading. The omission of the prefix is far more likely than its insertion and for *decurrere* of a fleet running for harbour see *TLL*, v. 1. 228. 54 ff. *currere* of ships, moreover, appears to be a poetic usage (*TLL*, iv. 1515. 18 ff.).

5. Corycum: 12. 10.

7. quam ... appareret: so as to give the impression to the enemy that their previous inaction had been planned, not caused by fear. L.'s phraseology leaves it unclear whether Livius in fact knew that the Rhodians were arriving.

confessionem exprimerent: cf. xxxvi. 45. 6 n.

8–9. postquam ... redegit: App. *Syr.* 25. 122: οὐδενὸς δ' αὐτοῖς ἀντεπιπλέοντος τὸ μὲν ἥμισυ τῶν νεῶν εἰς ἐπίδειξιν ἔστησαν ἐν μέσῃ τῇ θαλάσσῃ μέχρι πολλοῦ, ταῖς δ' ὑπολοίποις ἐς τὴν πολεμίαν καταχθέντες ἐπόρθουν, μέχρι Νίκανδρος αὐτοῖς ἐκ τῆς μεσογαίας ἐπιπεσὼν τήν τε λείαν ἀφείλετο καὶ ἐς τὰς ναῦς κατεδίωξεν. Nicander is a simple mistake for Andronicus, who is not otherwise known.

9. [iam] ingentem ... iam moenibus: Mg, *iam ingentem ... moenibus* Bχ. *iam* is otiose before *ingentem* but has point before *moenibus*. The evidence suggests that it was omitted, then inserted in two places in Mg and the wrong place in F.

10. eliciendum: B, *eliciundum* χMg. The latter is clearly the transmitted form and should be accepted. Cf. xxxiv. 4. 7 n.

inde: Mg, *unde* Bχ, perhaps rightly.

11. et terra: χ, om. B, perhaps rightly. Cf. p. 11.

Epicrate Rhodio: Perizonius, *Epicrate Rhodiorum* Bχ. Epicrates had been in charge of a Rhodian fleet in the Second Macedonian

War, part of whose purpose was to deal with pirates. See *Syll.*[3] 582, xxxi. 22. 8 n.

Cephallaniae: cf. xxxvi. 11. 9 n.

12. Hybristas: χ, *Hibristas* B. A Hybristas was Aetolian *strategos* in 165/4 (*IG* ix. 1². 1, p. lii). It is not surprising that Aetolians and pirates should have been willing to possess such names. Cf. the Aetolian Λάϊστας (*IG* ix. 1². 1, p. xxxiii. 87, drawn to my attention by Dr. A. H. Jackson). One may wonder, though, whether they were given them at birth.

14. 1. L. Aemilio Regillo: cf. xxxvi. 45. 9 n.

2. qui: Regillus, somewhat harshly. For such occurrences cf. K–St, ii. 286–7.

duas ... quinqueremes: cf. 2. 10 n. It was because he had left eighteen ships off Cephallenia that Regillus was able to divert Epicrates from the task given to him by Livius.

Epicratem ... nauibus: Epicrates with his four ships—i.e. the four of 13. 11.

apertae: Damsté (*Mnemosyne* n.s. xliii [1915], 456) may have been right to think that a number has been omitted.

3. ⟨Chium⟩: it is clear that L. must have said in this sentence that Regillus went to Chios (on the strangeness of the route cf. Thiel, 327). It is from Chios that he goes to Samos in § 4 and *eodem* in the following sentence here can refer only to Chios. But I am not at all sure that *Chium* alone is the right supplement. The ablative *Aegaeo mari* is puzzling (one may compare xxi. 56. 9, xxxv. 48. 3, but *traicere* there is in the passive). I suspect that the corruption is deeper. On Chios cf. xxxvi. 43. 11 n.

Timasicrates: not otherwise known.

intempesta: *in tempestate* Bχ. L. must have written *nocte intempesta*, a phrase he also uses at xxxviii. 5. 8, xl. 9. 7. For its meaning see Nisbet, *in Pisonem*, 164. (*TLL*, vii. 1. 2110. 64 seem to regard *in tempestate* as a serious possibility.)

praesidii ... ait: there is no implication that this was not the truth, as De Regibus claims.

regiae naves: probably privateers: cf. Thiel, 327.

4. sacrificio ... facto: the *lustratio classis* by the new commander. See xxxvi. 42. 4 n. *ut adsolet* is often used in sacral contexts—of a *lustratio* at i. 28. 2. See Ogilvie, 664.

4–6. For a defence of Livius' plan see Thiel, 329 ff. Polybius fr. 154 belongs here (cf. Tränkle, 30 n. 25, Walbank, *Commentary*, iii. 5, 99).

6. molimenti: cf. 15. 2 n., v. 22. 6. Before L. the word is found only at Sisenna fr. 72, Caes. *BG* i. 34. 3. Cf. *TLL*, viii. 1357.

quod . . . sit: on the gradual silting up of the harbour of Ephesus (now, of course, complete) see Bürchner, *RE*, v. 2778–80, Bean, *Aegean Turkey*, 163 ff.

15. 1–4. Eumenes' response to Livius' proposal is expressed in a highly rhetorical fashion. Note the balancing of the two alternatives with their consequences in §§ 1–2 and the double tricolon in § 3. L. will, one imagines, have elaborated on Polybius here.

1. frenassent: there is no real parallel for this metaphor. Cf. *TLL*, vi. 1. 1288. 56.

claustra: as W–M say, *claustra* here means the narrow entry to the harbour, while in 14. 6 it refers to the means of blocking up that entry. The repetition, like that of *molimentum* in § 2, is clearly deliberate. Cf. p. 13.

2. siue . . . sin: for this rare usage cf. Cic. *Tusc.* i. 97–8, *acad.* i. 7, K–St, ii. 436 n. 3.

extracturi: Mg, *detracturi* Bχ. *detrahere* is clearly the wrong word for removing a sunken object.

sit, quid: om. *sit* Bχ, *quid* φ, *quod* ψ, *quit* B. Since *sit* is omitted in χ, it is not possible to see *quit* as a conflation of *sit quid* in F and in this rhetorical passage the omission of *sit* is quite possible. Cf. p. 12.

attinere: Bχ, *attineret* Mg, not realizing that rhetorical questions in *oratio obliqua* are expressed in the infinitive.

3. tutissimo portu: best taken as an independent phrase, rather than with *fruentis*.

6. Thiel, 331, points out that the logic of Epicrates' plan entailed the permanent stationing of part of the allied fleet at Patara.

Patara . . . adiungenda: J. F. Gronovius, *Patara . . . adiungendam* B, *Parayam* P, *Pataxam* AL², *Patayam* E, *parata* NV, *paratam* L, *. . . adiungendam* φ, *adiungendas* ψ. Πάταρα is the normal form in Greek and the MSS. evidence both here and at other occurrences of the name suggests that this is what L. wrote. On the site of Patara see Radke, *RE*, xviii. 2. 2556 ff., Magie, i. 520, Bean, *Lycian Turkey*, 82 ff. For Antiochus' conquests in Lycia in 197 cf. xxxiii. 20. 13 n.

8. in Cilicia compararetur: cf. 8. 3 n. L. makes no mention of Cilicia there.

16. 1. Zmyrnaeis: Smyrna continued to resist Antiochus, and there is no reason to think that it was ever captured by him. Cf. xxxiii. 38. 3 n., Schmitt, *Antiochos*, 283.

2. Miletus ... Cous: Mg, *Miletus Myndus* Bχ. Though the omission in F would be well explained by the scribe jumping from *Myndus* to *Cnidus*, there is nothing particularly strange in the simple omission of the final three names, and the positive evidence of Mg should be accepted, not altered to ... *Cous Cnidus* (thus W–M, following Heusinger).

Of the five states Myndus and Halicarnassus had been saved from Antiochus by the Rhodians in 197 (xxxiii. 20. 11–12 n.). On Cos cf. 11. 13 n. Cnidus (cf. xxxi. 27. 6 n.) had remained an independent ally of Rhodes (Schmitt, *Antiochos*, 280). It contributed one ship to the Rhodian fleet at the battle of Side (22. 2) but appears to have been given to Rhodes in 188 (Fraser and Bean, *RPI*, 93 and n. 3). Miletus may have been captured by Antiochus in 197 but have recently revolted from him (Schmitt, op. cit., 281).

3. approbantibus cunctis: for this phrase, often used in official or semi-official contexts by L., cf. 52. 6, Adams, *BICS* xx (1973), 130.

4. circumagente ... mare: cf. Lucian, Πλοῖον 8 (De Regibus).
   fluctibus dubiis: cf. p. 4.
   tenerent terram: 'keep close to the land' (cf. W–M).

6. Phoenicunta: this Phoenicus (to be distinguished from the one near Erythrae [cf. xxxvi. 45. 7 n.] and the mountain near Olympus in Eastern Lycia) must be identified with the bay of Kalamaki, though L.'s indication of distance is too short. Cf. Ruge, *RE*, xx. 384.

8. difficilia ad: cf. xxxiv. 34. 8 n.
   Issaeos: cf. xxxi. 45. 10 n. It is uncertain whether the Issaeans were in their own *lembi*, or merely serving as marines on Roman ships: see Thiel, 272 n. 336.
   Zmyrnaeorum: cf. § 1 n.

9. hi, dum: B, *ii dum* Mg, *hii dum* φ, *idum* ψ. As usual in such cases MSS. authority is useless (particularly with B and Mg split) and on this occasion both *hi* and *ii* make perfectly good sense.
   leuibus excursionibus: om. *excursionibus* Bχ, *leuibus et excursionibus* Mg. *leuis excursio* does not appear elsewhere and though *leue proelium* and *leue certamen* do, *leuis excursio* is an odd phrase. The *et* in Mg perhaps suggest that those who have made a further supplement are on the right lines, though since Mg omits *et* before *aduersus*, its presence here may simply be the result of transposition.

10. ex urbe: B, *ab urbe* χ. *ex* 'out of the city' gives the better sense.

11. etiam naualis: Mg, *naualis etiam* Bχ. sed ... *etiam* is the normal order and should be followed here.

naualis socios ... turbam: Mg, *naualis socios naualium remigum turbam* Bχ. *naualis socios* normally means crews in general (cf. 10. 9 n.) and should include the rowers. Mg's reading is, therefore, perfectly acceptable. For other instances of rowers being armed cf. xxiii. 40. 2, xxvi. 17. 2, Cato, *ORF*³, fr. 66, Milan, *CS* x (1973), 206–7.

12. L. Apustius: (2, 5): cf. 4. 2 n.

13. Telmessicum: Telmessus is north-west of Patara: cf. Magie, i. 516–17, ii. 1371, Ruge, *RE*, vA. 410 ff., Bean, *Lycian Turkey*, 38 ff., Walbank, *Commentary*, iii. 170. On its history see 56. 4 n.

omisso ⟨consilio⟩: ed. Asc., om. B, *omissa* ψ, *omisso* φ. Other supplements have included *conatu* (Mog.) and *omissa spe* (Frob. 2, Drakenborch). The last might appear to be given some support by ψ's *omissa*, but it is perhaps more likely that a masculine or neuter noun was omitted and the participle altered to agree with *Patara* (thus χ, *Pataram* B: cf. 15. 6 n.) than that *spe* was omitted, since there would then be no obvious reason for altering *omissa* to *omisso*.

14. qui ... erant: an important synchronism, typical of Polybius (cf. Pol. xxxix. 8. 6, Pédech, 467). See p. 29 n. 2.

in Italiam traiceret: he must have had authority from Regillus to do so. 17. 1 is not to be taken as an indication that Regillus previously had no idea that Livius would return to Italy.

17. 1. irrito incepto: this, as W–M point out, is inconsistent with 15. 9 *ad inferendum hostibus terrorem*, which indicates that Regillus did not intend to launch a full-scale attack on Ephesus. For the phrase cf. xxxv. 39. 7 n.

3. Bargylietico sinu escensionem: *Bargylletico sinu escensionem* Gel. 'lege', *Barcylia et icosō descensionem* B, *Barcylliam et icosom descensionem* φV, *Barcillia et icoso in descensionem* N, *Barcilliam et icoso in descensionem* L. Polybius will have referred, as at xvi. 12. 1, to Βαργυλιητικὸς κόλπος and it may be assumed that L. wrote *Bargylietico*. (The bay lies between Iasus and Bargylia: the text of Polybius is lacunose, and Polybius probably said that it was sometimes called the bay of Bargylia, sometimes the bay of Iasus.) On *escensio* cf. xxxi. 24. 9 n.

On Bargylia and Iasus cf. xxxii. 33. 6–7 n. and addendum thereto: add Mastrocinque, *PP* xxxi (1976), 311 ff. For Iasus' capture by Antiochus in 197 see xxxiii. 30. 3 n.

hostiliter: cf. xxxvi. 20. 1 n.

5. ii: Frob. 2, *ibi* Mg, om. Bχ. The pronoun is not essential, but *ibi* is better seen as a corruption of *ii* than as a corruption caused

by the similarity of (*Ro*)*manis ibi* to the following (*uic*)*inam sibi*, as
argued by Pettersson, 47. Cf. p. 12.

uicinam: Rhodes and Iasus are not all that close to each other.

cognatam: presumably, as W–M say, as both of Dorian stock.
Iasus claimed to have been founded from Argos (Pol. xvi. 12. 2).

perire sinerent: Mg, *perisse liceret* Bχ. There is no other instance
of *sinere* with the perfect infinitive (for which cf. K–St, i. 133 ff.) and
it is therefore better to retain Mg's text as a whole.

6. sint: Frob. 2, *sunt* Bχ, perhaps rightly. Cf. xxxiv. 20. 2 n.

effugerent: Bχ, *effugere uellent* Mg. Madvig (*Emendationes*, 529 n. 1)
followed Mg, but altered *uellent* to *uelint* because of *maneant* and *sint*
above (in fact L. often alternates between historic and primary
tenses in *oratio obliqua* [cf. xxxiv. 26. 7 n.]: it would be hard to avoid
the imperfect in *perire sinerent*). *uellent*, however, is weak. *mentem esse
ut* is to be taken as introducing a final clause ('their purpose is
to . . .') not a consecutive clause ('their state of mind is such that
they wish'). Cf. Cic. *fam.* xii. 14. 1.

7. abstineretur: Mg, *absisteretur* Bχ. *absistere* would be appropriate
to desisting from a siege already started, *abstinere* to not starting it
in the first place. Unfortunately it is not clear whether Regillus had
actually embarked on the siege of Iasus before the exiles' pleas, and
both readings are therefore equally possible.

8. oram legerent: cf. xxxv. 27. 6 n.

Loryma: probably not to be distinguished from places referred to
as Laryma and Larymna, it stood at the very end of the Rhodian
Chersonese and formed part of the Rhodian state: see Fraser and
Bean, *RPI*, 59–61.

9. in principiis: the meaning must be 'in the officers' quarters'
not just 'at the officers' meetings', as W–M suggest.

tribunos militum: cf. Thiel, 277.

ab suo bello: Bχ. Mg adds *ad regiam classem*. This should be seen
as a gloss, meant to explain *suo bello*—the war against Antiochus—
and attempts to base emendations on it are misguided.

10. [utrum]num: Weissenborn: *utrumnam* Bχ, *posset ne*, omitting
posset at the end of the sentence, Mg. Mg's reading looks like an
attempt to emend *utrumnam*. Whether we should read *num* or *an*
(M. Müller, vi) is uncertain. H. J. Müller (*JPhV* xvii [1891], 168)
suggests that *utrumnam* was imported into the text in late antiquity
by someone acquainted with its use in indirect questions in the
Vulgate.

naues reduxit: B, *reduxit naues* χ. Cf. p. 15.

18–21. 5. *Siege of Pergamum*

See Polybius xxi. 10, Appian, *Syr.* 26, Hansen, *Attalids*, 83 ff.

18. 1. Seleucus: cf. 8. 5 n.

3. Elaeam: cf. xxxv. 13. 6 n.

oppugnandam: Bχ, *oppugnandum* Mg. Decision is impossible. If L. wrote *oppugnandam* it would be easier to take it with *arcem*, rather than assume, as W–M suggest, that L. regarded the nominative as *Pergamus* feminine.

4. Attalus: cf. xxxv. 23. 10 n.

leuisque: χ, *et leuis* B. As both *equitum* and *leuis armaturae* go with *excursionibus*, and the latter is joined to what precedes by *et*, *-que* makes for greater clarity.

6. ferme tempore: *tempore ferme* Bχ. *eosdem dies ferme* is attested at xxxiii. 18. 22 and Cicero, *Brutus* 95 has *isdem temporibus ferme*. L.'s standard order is *eodem fer(m)e tempore* (Packard, ii. 94) but what he wrote here must remain uncertain.

Apamea: cf. xxxv. 15. 1 n.

Sardibus: the administrative capital of Asia Minor, and Antiochus' main headquarters for the present war. See Magie, i. 121–2.

caput: cf. xxxiii. 41. 7 n., p. 10 n. 1. On its location at this time see Hansen, *Attalids*, 84 n. 36, arguing that had it been, as now, near Elaea, Eumenes could not have escaped the Seleucid troops on his arrival at Elaea (§ 8).

7. in Gallorum ... erat: cf. p. 15.

Gallorum: cf. 8. 4 n., Bar-Kochva, 49.

paucis ... misit: M. Müller, *paucos admixtos ... milites emisit* Bχ. At first sight it seems obvious that *admixtos* must be changed to *admixtis* and *milites* deleted. Some proper name must have fallen out but any supplement, of course, is purely speculative and mere indication of a lacuna is preferable. (C. Brakman, *Mnemosyne* n.s. lv [1927], 61, suggests *regiis*. They are not identical with the 4,000 of 20. 7, as assumed by Damsté, *Mnemosyne* n.s. xliii [1915], 456–7, proposing *equitibus*.) It is possible, however, that there is far deeper corruption in the sentence as a whole. There is nothing obviously wrong with *emisit*, however, and no reason to change it to *misit*.

8. Polybius fr. 228 belongs here: cf. Walbank, *Commentary*, iii. 5, 101.

nuntiata sunt: B, *sunt nuntiata* χ. Cf. p. 15.

sentirent: cf. xxxii. 17. 8 n.

mouerentur: for *moueri* to refer to movements of troops cf. iv. 33. 6, xxviii. 5. 7, Sall. *Iug.* 53. 1, *TLL*, viii. 1539. 9 ff.

9. ibi: χ, *ubi* B, perhaps rightly.

10. audiuit … esse: Pol. xxi. 8. 3: ὁμοίως δὲ καὶ τοῖς περὶ τὸν Ἀντίοχον καὶ Σέλευκον ταῦτα (i.e. the truce with the Aetolians and the Scipios' journey to the Hellespont) διεσαφεῖτο παρὰ τῶν Αἰτωλῶν. L. does not mention the similar message from the Scipios to Regillus reported by Polybius xxi. 10. 1–2.

11–12. Pol. xxi. 10. 1–3: Ἀντίοχος ὁ βασιλεὺς εἰς τὸν Πέργαμον ἐμβαλών, πυθόμενος δὲ τὴν παρουσίαν Εὐμένους τοῦ βασιλέως καὶ θεωρῶν οὐ μόνον τὰς ναυτικάς, ἀλλὰ καὶ τὰς πεζικὰς δυνάμεις ἐπ᾽ αὐτὸν παραγινομένας, ἐβουλεύετο λόγους ποιήσασθαι περὶ διαλύσεως ὁμοῦ πρός τε Ῥωμαίους καὶ τὸν Εὐμένη καὶ τοὺς Ῥοδίους. ἐξάρας οὖν ἅπαντι τῷ στρατεύματι παρῆν πρὸς τὴν Ἐλαίαν καὶ λαβὼν λόφον τινὰ καταντικρὺ τῆς πόλεως τὸ μὲν πεζικὸν ἐπὶ τούτου κατέστησε, τοὺς δ᾽ ἱππεῖς παρ᾽ αὐτὴν τὴν πόλιν παρενέβαλε, πλείους ὄντας ἑξακισχιλίων. αὐτὸς δὲ μεταξὺ τούτων γενόμενος διεπέμπετο πρὸς τοὺς περὶ τὸν Λεύκιον εἰς τὴν πόλιν ὑπὲρ διαλύσεων. θεωρῶν … παραγινομένας, though the words of the excerptor (see Walbank, *Commentary*, iii. 101) correspond to *priusquam … urgeretur* and the latter is not an addition by L., as W–M say.

11. pace: Mg, *pace esse* Bχ. *uenisse* and *esse* perhaps appeared as variants in the archetype. *uenisse* has more point.

12. cum equitatu … descendit: a simplification of Polybius, who says that Antiochus placed his cavalry near Elaea, and himself took up position between the cavalry and the hill on which he had placed the infantry. The sense of what L. wrote is improved by placing a comma after *relictis*.

uelle … agere: perhaps Antiochus was hoping to gain time by negotiations and a truce, rather than seriously expecting an acceptable peace. Cf. De Sanctis, iv. 1. 186, Thiel, 336.

19. In this chapter L. remains remarkably close to Polybius.

1. Pol. xxi. 10. 4–5: ὁ δὲ στρατηγὸς ὁ τῶν Ῥωμαίων συναγαγὼν τούς τε Ῥοδίους καὶ τὸν Εὐμένην ἠξίου λέγειν περὶ τῶν ἐνεστώτων τὸ φαινόμενον. οἱ μὲν οὖν περὶ τὸν Εὔδαμον καὶ Παμφιλίδαν οὐκ ἀλλότριοι τῆς διαλύσεως ἦσαν· ὁ δὲ βασιλεὺς οὔτ᾽ εὐσχήμονα τὴν διάλυσιν οὔτε δυνατὴν ἔφησε κατὰ τὸ παρὸν εἶναι.

a Pergamo accito: L.'s own explanation. With Antiochus wanting to negotiate, Eumenes will have been given a safe conduct and there will have been no need for the secret manœuvres of 18. 8.

adhibitis et Rhodiis: Bχ, *adhibitisque Rhodiis* Mg. *adhibitis et Rhodiis* perhaps gives too much emphasis: there is no need to stress that the Rhodians too were brought into the council. H. J. Müller's *et adhibitis Rhodiis* does unnecessary violence to the MSS. evidence.

Rhodiis ... Rhodii: L. omits their names. Cf. xxxvi. 5. 1 n.

haud aspernari: for Rhodian motives cf. Thiel, 336 n. 566.

honestum ... esse: the word-order is the equivalent in *oratio obliqua* of the order in *oratio recta* where the subject and *inquit* are divided by the first word or phrase spoken. Cf. e.g. viii. 33. 7, xl. 7. 5.

2–3. Pol. xxi. 10. 6–8: 'εὐσχήμονα γάρ' ἔφη 'πῶς οἷόν τε γίνεσθαι τὴν ἔκβασιν, ἐὰν τειχήρεις ὄντες ποιώμεθα τὰς διαλύσεις;' καὶ μὴν οὐδὲ δυνατὴν ἔφησε κατὰ τὸ παρόν· 'πῶς γὰρ ἐνδέχεται, μὴ προσδεξαμένους ὕπατον, ἄνευ τῆς ἐκείνου γνώμης βεβαιῶσαι τὰς ὁμολογηθείσας συνθήκας; χωρίς τε τούτων, ἐὰν ὅλως γένηταί τι σημεῖον ὁμολογίας πρὸς Ἀντίοχον, οὔτε τὰς ναυτικὰς δυνάμεις δυνατὸν ἐπανελθεῖν δήπουθεν εἰς τὴν ἰδίαν οὔτε τὰς πεζικάς, ἐὰν μὴ πρότερον ὅ τε δῆμος ἥ τε σύγκλητος ἐπικυρώσῃ τὰ δοχθέντα.' L. makes the possibility of withdrawal into a rhetorical question and doubles the reference to the need for the approval of the senate and people (cf. Pianezzola, 46).

2. aut ... aut: distinguishing the two questions, despite the position of the first *aut.* See 24. 2 n., Pettersson, 8.

moenibus: χ, om. B. It could conceivably be a gloss, though cf. x. 45. 10, xxv. 40. 8, xxxv. 12. 7.

4–5. Pol. xxi. 10. 9–10: 'λείπεται δὴ καραδοκοῦντας τὴν ἐκείνων ἀπόφασιν παραχειμάζειν ἐνθάδε καὶ πράττειν μὲν μηδέν, ἐκδαπανᾶν δὲ τὰς τῶν ἰδίων συμμάχων χορηγίας καὶ παρασκευάς· ἔπειτ', ἂν μὴ σφίσι παρῇ τῇ συγκλήτῳ διαλύεσθαι, καινοποιεῖν πάλιν ἀπ' ἀρχῆς τὸν πόλεμον, παρέντας τοὺς ἐνεστῶτας καιρούς, ἐν οἷς δυνάμεθα θεῶν βουλομένων πέρας ἐπιθεῖναι τοῖς ὅλοις.' Note *restat* for λείπεται.

5. instauremus nouum: for the pleonasm cf. Cic. *Rosc. Am.* 153, Sil. xiii. 878, *TLL*, vii. 1. 1976.

impetu rerum: I can find no parallels for this expression though cf. *motu rerum* at xxv. 3. 8.

perfecisse: a true perfect (W–M).

6. Pol. xxi. 10. 11: ὁ δὲ Λεύκιος ἀποδεξάμενος τὴν συμβουλίαν, ἀπεκρίθη τοῖς περὶ τὸν Ἀντίοχον ὅτι πρὸ τοῦ τὸν ἀνθύπατον ἐλθεῖν οὐκ ἐνδέχεται γενέσθαι τὰς διαλύσεις. ἀνθύπατον may be a corruption of ὕπατον: cf. Walbank, *Commentary*, iii. 102.

7–8. Pol. xxi. 10. 12–14: ὧν ἀκούσαντες οἱ περὶ τὸν Ἀντίοχον παραυτίκα μὲν ἐδήουν τὴν τῶν Ἐλαϊτῶν χώραν· ἑξῆς δὲ τούτοις Σέλευκος μὲν ἐπὶ τούτων ἔμεινε τῶν τόπων, Ἀντίοχος δὲ κατὰ τὸ συνεχὲς ἐπιπορευόμενος

ἐνέβαλεν εἰς τὸ Θήβης καλούμενον πεδίον, καὶ παραβεβληκὼς εἰς χώραν
εὐδαίμονα καὶ γέμουσαν ἀγαθῶν ἐπλήρου τὴν στρατιὰν παντοδαπῆς λείας.
This text contains no mention of Adramytteum or of Homer. It is
unlikely that such details would have been added by L. and we
should therefore assume abridgement of Polybius by the excerptor
(cf. Walbank, loc. cit.).

7. Elaeensium: *Elensium* B, *Eleensium* χMg. The agreement of χ
and Mg renders improbable Heraeus's suggestion that L. wrote
Elaensium. (He also proposed *Phocaensium* at 21. 7 and 32. 11: cf.
nn. ad locc.)

Adramytteum: on the site see Hirschfeld, *RE*, i. 404, Magie,
i. 83, ii. 905 n. 124.

Thebes ... nobilitatum: cf. Magie, ii. 806 n. 39, Walbank,
Commentary, ii. 502. Homer refers only to Thebe, not the plain, but
it is absurd to emend to *nobilitate* on that basis, and not even necessary to explain it by enallage of the epithet, as do W–M. Polybius
may have made the error, or L. translated him carelessly. Cf.
Walbank, *Commentary*, iii. 102.

8. eodem Adramytteum: for the repetition in apposition cf. xxi.
17. 9, xli. 17. 8 (2. 12, adduced by W–M, is different). There is no
case at all for deleting *Adramytteum*.

20. 1. For the Achaean decision to send these troops see Polybius
xxi. 3b, Walbank, *Commentary*, iii. 92.

forte: cf. xxxii. 39. 4 n.

Diophane: cf. xxxvi. 31. 6 n. On Philopoemen's motives for
sending him cf. Errington, 136.

2. et ipse ... discipulus: cf. Pol. xxi. 9, considerably abbreviated
by L. Cf. Witte, 374–5, Tränkle, 80 n. 43.

3. collis ... urbs: on the site of Pergamum see Hansen, *Attalids*, 2.

libera ... populatio: L. presumably means that the Seleucid
forces could ravage behind their own lines without fear of anyone
attacking them from the city.

4. As Madvig (*Emendationes*, 529) explained, the contempt arose
because no one sallied out of the city after the Pergamene forces
had shut themselves up, not just because they had so shut themselves up.

infrenatos: cf. p. 5.

5–6. pars ... contemplatus: cf. App. *Syr.* 26. 125: ἀπὸ τοῦ τείχους
ἰδὼν τοὺς Σελευκείους παίζοντάς τε καὶ μεθύοντας ἐκ καταφρονήσεως.

5. iuuenales: cf. p. 5.

6. portam: Bχ, *iussa* Mg. One could not rule out the possibility that L. wrote *iussa* . . . *iubet* (cf. p. 13) but as *ad iussa praesto esse* is not paralleled elsewhere while *ad portas praesto fuere* occurs at v. 45. 1 (cf. Cic. *diu.* i. 57 *praesto ad portam fuisse*) it is easier to think that Mg wrote *iussa* under the influence of *iubet* than that F corrupted *iussa* to *portam*—in any case not an easy corruption to explain.

adit: Bχ, *adiit* Mg. Either is possible. Cf. p. 12.

7. aegre . . . Attalo: Appian (*Syr.* 26. 126) states that the Per-gamenes refused to join Diophanes in his venture. Hansen (*Attalids*, 84 n. 37) argues that Diophanes would not have to seek Attalus' permission as to what he should do with his own troops, and that Attalus would have wanted to attack with all his forces. Appian, unsupported by L., may well be wrong about the request for Pergamene troops to join in the sally, but it is wrong to argue to what Attalus actually did from what it would have been sensible for him to do. On the other point, the Achaeans had been sent to aid Pergamum and their over-all strategy was surely subject to Eumenes'—and in his absence Attalus'—veto.

sescentos: B, *sexcentos* χ, *ducentos* Mg. In view of the 4:1 propor-tion in infantry it is very unlikely that the Seleucid cavalry would have numbered only 200.

consedit: *considet* BφNV, *consideret* L. There is no reason for altering *considet*. Cf. § 6 n., p. 12.

8. nec ipsi: Mg, *nec* Bχ. 'Neither did they themselves'. Cf. xxxiv. 32. 9 n.

10. quam potuit: M. Müller. *quam posset* Bχ, *quantum potuit* Mg. *quantum posse* occurs only with verbs and is presumably influenced by *quantum . . . possent* above, while Bχ's *posset* is similarly influenced by *possent*. Weissenborn's *potest* makes it harder to explain Mg's *potuit*.

effusissimis habenis: cf. *Pan. Mess.* 92. W–M's statement that *effusus* as an adjective is not found in prose before L. is incorrect: cf. *TLL*, v. 2. 227. 4 ff.

11. cum . . . fecerunt: with *equi*. It is the addition of *trepidationem* . . . *fecerunt*, not that of *cum . . . abrupissent* (as W–M say) that is harsh.

21. 1. regiae: since Pergamum is the enemy, the word is not all that apt (De Regibus). L. regularly uses *regius* of Antiochus' troops.

posuerunt castra: as W–M say, an odd expression with *stationes* as subject. *stationes* are outposts in front of a camp and can hardly set up camp themselves. L. clearly means just 'took up position'.

2. iam futurum: 'about to happen at that very moment'. Cf. v. 39. 6 (again, as it happens, followed by *occasus solis*).

expectauere: χ, *expectare* B, *expectauerant* Mg. The pluperfect may well be right.

haud procul: for *procul* of time cf. Cic. *r.p.* i. 1, Sall. *Iug.* 85. 48.

signis collatis: 'brought together'. Usually, of course, *signa conferre* means 'join battle', but it makes perfectly good sense here (cf. W–M) and emendation is unnecessary.

4. haec ... coegit: as W–M say, the return of the allied fleet must also have been a factor. Polybius doubtless concentrated his account on the exploits of the Achaeans and exaggerated their importance. Cf. Hansen, *Attalids*, 84.

Adramytteum: cf. 19. 7 n.

Peraeam: Frob. 2. *Pheream* Bχ. L. must have misunderstood Polybius here. Peraea is not a place, but refers to the mainland possessions of Mitylene as a whole. On their extent see Bürchner, *RE*, xi. 1453, 1542, Ruge, *RE*, xix. 584–5.

5. Cotton ... Corylenus ... Aphrodisias ... Prinne: none of these four places is otherwise known, and the form of the last uncertain (*Prinne* BAPLV, *Prime* E, *Princie et* N, *Crene* Gel. 'uetus lectio').

Thyatiram: cf. 8. 7 n.

21. 6—32. *Naval events (contd.)*

7. Bacchium: presumably the same as *Bacchina* mentioned by Pliny, *NH* v. 138.

Phocaeensium: *Phocensium* BχMg. Cf. 19. 7 n.

quibus ... signisque: in 191. Cf. xxxvi. 43. 11 n.

hostiliter: cf. xxxvi. 20. 1 n.

8. A cumbersome sentence.

uideretur ... posse: B, *uiderent ... posse* ψ, *uiderent ... non posse* φ. *non* is clearly an addition by Colonna, who did not realize that L. was saying that though the allies could begin the siege without siege-works, the arrival of Antiochus' garrison forced them to desist.

9. nihil aliud quam: cf. xxxiv. 46. 7 n.

22. 1. praeparare: *praeparari* Bχ. The implication is clearly that Eumenes is to make the necessary preparations and the MSS. reading has been influenced by the preceding passage and, perhaps, by 18. 10.

2. M. ... praetoris: (129). Not otherwise known.

22. 2—24. *The battle of Side.* See Thiel, 338 ff.
    Coa ... Cnidia: cf. 11. 13, 16. 2 nn.

3. biduo ante: 'two days before'. Cf. xxxvi. 40. 3 n.
    Eudamus: cf. 12. 9 n.
    Pamphilida: cf. 12. 9 n., Walbank, *Commentary*, iii. 101–2.
    Daedala: an outlying part of the incorporated Peraea, on the borders of Lycia. See Fraser and Bean, *RPI*, 54 ff., W. Huss, *Untersuchungen zur Aussenpolitik Ptolemaios' IV* (Munich, 1976), 194.
    exire: from Rhodes.

4. sex: φ, *tres* BLMg, *res* NV. Presumably an emendation by Colonna to fit the figures of 23. 4. Retention of *tres* here would not solve the problem of the omission of the quinqueremes there and *sex* should be accepted.

5. Megisten: in fact an island off the Lycian coast: cf. Strabo, xiv. 666C. It too formed part of the incorporated Peraea. See Fraser and Bean, *RPI*, 54.
    Phaselidem: on the western side of the Pamphylian gulf. See Bean, *Turkey's Southern Shore*, 151 ff., *Lycian Turkey*, 150 ff.

23. 1. prominet ... petentibus: Phaselis does not project particularly far into the sea, nor would it, rather than any other part of the Lycian coast, be the first place visible to ships sailing westwards from Cilicia.
    prominet in altum is repeated at § 6 and 27. 7, and occurs also at xxxviii. 59. 5. For *prominere* of inland mountains cf. xxvii. 48. 7, xxviii. 33. 4.
    petentibus: for the dative cf. xxxii. 4. 3.
    ut in obuio: B Gel. 'non ut obuii', *uti obuii* χ. If Gelenius was quoting a manuscript reading, it will follow that *ut in obuio* is the transmitted text, and it is hardly possible to doubt that it is what L. wrote, even if it is the only example in Latin of *in obuio* (*TLL*, ix. 2. 322. 35–6).

2. prouiderunt: cf. W–M's note on i. 1. 1 (though in fact the transmitted reading in that passage is *fuerant*), K–St, i. 129 ff., Naylor, 203–4.
    ingruere: cf. p. 5.

3. Pamphylium ... Eurymedontem: cf. xxxiii. 41. 6 n.
    ab Aspendiis ad Sidam: Mg (Carb.), *ab Aspendiis ad Sidam iam* Gel. 'in manuscriptis legitur', *ad Aspendiis iam* Bχ. Though *iam* is readily explicable as a corruption of *ad Sidam*, Gelenius's report must

be of Mg, not of Sp (cf. p. 16) and we should therefore perhaps read *ad Sidam iam.*

On Side cf. xxxv. 13. 5 n. Aspendus lies a little inland, on the west bank of the Eurymedon. Cf. Bean, *Turkey's Southern Shore*, 67 ff. Hannibal had not actually reached Side: cf. Thiel, 340 n. 576.

4. etesiarum ... fauoniis: on Etesians see Rehm, *RE*, vi. 713 ff. The prevailing winds in the area between June and September are in fact north-westerly (*Mediterranean Pilot*, v [5th edn., London, 1961], 29). Leuze (*Hermes* lviii [1923], 282 n. 1) wrongly says that they are northerly or north-easterly.

Rhodiorum ... fuere: Eudamus had thirteen ships together with one Cnidian and one Coan quinquereme (22. 2), and was later given six *apertae* (22. 4). Pamphilidas had seventeen ships (22. 3). That makes a total of 38. Here only 36 are mentioned, the two non-Rhodian quinqueremes presumably being omitted. We must assume that all the triremes and two of the quadriremes were *apertae*. Cf. Thiel, 340 n. 574.

4–5. fuere ... erant: for the *uariatio* cf. 30. 2.

hepteres ... hexeres: the Latinized forms are found, in the case of *hepteris*, here and at 24. 3, 24. 9, and 30. 2, and in the case of *hexeris* here and at 30. 2, xxix. 9. 8, Val. Max. i. 8. ext. 11. Cf. *TLL*, vi. 3. 2613, 2681.

maioris formae: after the defeat at Corycus Antiochus had abandoned the use of the smaller built quadriremes and quin-queremes. Cf. xxxvi. 43. 8 n., McDonald and Walbank, *JRS* lix (1969), 33–4.

habebat ... erant: for *habebat* cf. 30. 2. There is no case for alteration (cf. W–M, 259).

6. tamquam ... pugnatura: cf. xxxiv. 36. 5 n.

mouit et: χ, om. *et* B, perhaps rightly. Cf. p. 11.

7. Hannibal ... praeerat: see Thiel, 341 n. 578.

8. prima: on L.'s use of *primus* in naval contexts cf. W. K. Lacey, *CQ* n.s. vii (1957), 118 ff.

Chariclitus: not known apart from these events.

9 ff. On the details of the engagement see Thiel, 341 ff.

9. derigere: for the absolute use cf. Tac. *H.* iv. 58. 5, *TLL*, v. 1. 1250. 38 ff.

11. relicti: most of Weissenborn's parallels (W–M, 259) are not exact, but xxx. 12. 30 has a gerundive in a similar construction and is enough to let the transmitted reading stand.

24. 1. maritimae rei: B, *rei maritimae* χ. The former occurs at xxxiv. 29. 2, xxxix. 1. 3, while there are no examples of *rei maritimae*.

2. nam ... dedere: i.e. some ships took up position on Eudamus' right, on the seaward side of him, leaving room for others to come on to his landward side. Cf. Thiel, 341–2.

aut ... lacerabat: in fact, as W–M say, this applies only to *si qua ... rostro*. Cf. 19. 2 n., Pettersson, 8.

libero ... dabat: the διέκπλους. Cf. Thiel, 343.

discursu: before the Augustan period *discursus* is found only in Hirt. *BG* viii. 29. 2 (*TLL*, v. 1. 1369).

impetum dabat: cf. Ogilvie, 287.

3. exterruit: i.e. the fleet of Antiochus. Cf. p. 4.

hepteris: cf. 23. 4–5 n.

demersa: not completely, as is clear from § 9. Cf. Thiel, 343 n. 582.

iam: φ, om. Bψ. It clearly has no authority and should be deleted.

4–5. Nepos, *Hann.* 8. 4 makes Hannibal victorious on his wing, while the rest of the Seleucid fleet is overwhelmed *multitudine aduersariorum sui*.

4. in dextro cornu: the Seleucid right. Emendation is quite un-necessary (cf. Thiel, 343 n. 583).

6. reficerent uires: χ, *reficerentur* B, *reficerentur uires* Mg. Since *uires* stood in Mg, there can be no case for reading *reficerentur*. Probably *reficerent* was corrupted in late antiquity and χ's reading represents a successful emendation.

remulco trahentis: cf. xxv. 30. 7, xxxii. 16. 4.

uiginti paulo amplius: for the construction cf. xxxiv. 1. 3 n. *paulo amplius* occurs also at xxix. 2. 17, xxxviii. 4. 4, xlv. 10. 4.

turri: for towers on ships cf. Casson, 122 n. 92.

spectaculum: cf. xxxv. 11. 8 n.

capessite oculis: *capessere* is used several times by L. (cf. *capessunt fugam* in § 5) but *capessere oculis* is a usage unparalleled in Latin. Cf. *TLL*, iii. 310. 39, p. 9.

7. [ac] prope: BψMg, om. *ac* φ. It is quite possible that *contemplati* is to be taken as an indicative with an ellipse of *sunt*. Cf. Pettersson, 95–7, p. 12.

9. hepterem: cf. 23. 4–5 n.

11. ictus: χ, *uictus* BMg. *uictus* is clearly the transmitted reading, and since *proelio uincere* occurs nine times in L. (Packard, iii. 1156, 1158), while there is no parallel for *proelio ictus*, it should be retained.

ne tum . . . Lyciam: not even when the Rhodians had returned to Rhodes. The transmitted reading is quite unimpeachable (for emendations see Zingerle ad loc.).

12. Megisten: cf. 22. 5 n.

25. 2. profectio . . . Sardibus: for Antiochus' return to Sardis cf. 21. 5. According to Polybius xxi. 11. 1 the embassy to Prusias was dispatched when Antiochus was still at Sardis (as L. himself implies at 26. 1).

⟨**metusque inde**⟩ **. . . prohibuerunt:** either something has dropped out, or we should read *prohibuit* (dett.). The latter is the simpler solution.

ne . . . urbes: by a combined naval and land attack, presumably. For the states of Ionia and Aeolis not under Antiochus' control at this time see Schmitt, *Antiochos*, 281 ff.

3. miserunt: the Rhodians. Cf. p. 12.

4–14. *Negotiations with Prusias.* See Polybius xxi. 11, Appian, *Syr.* 23. 111.

4–7. Cf. Pol. xxi. 11. 1–2. L. has converted what Polybius represents as the thoughts of Prusias into statements by Antiochus, and enlarged them into a general attack on Roman imperialism. Cf. Hoch, 99, Tränkle, 105, Walbank, *Commentary*, iii. 103.

4. ciuitatium . . . praesidia: it is not clear which cities are involved.

quae circa . . . erant: i.e. around Sardis. For *se* and *suus* of the subject of the main clause cf. Riemann, 146, K–St, i. 607. Madvig's deletion of *se* is quite unjustified. For the repetition cf. p. 13.

Prusiam: cf. xxxii. 34. 6 n.

legatos miserat: B, *miserat legatos* χ. Cf. p. 15.

increpabat: for actions as the object of *increpare* cf. *TLL*, vii. 1. 1054. 14 ff.

5. L. has generalized from Polybius' statement that it was Roman policy to downgrade all kings to a claim that Rome was aiming at world-wide dominion. Such thoughts are also found in Sallust, but, as in L., in the mouth of Rome's enemies (*Iug.* 81. 1, *H.* iv, fr. 69. 5).

[**orbis**] **terrarum:** Bχ. Madvig (*Emendationes*, 529 n. 1) proposed *in orbe terrarum* on the grounds that Antiochus is complaining that there will be no empires anywhere in the world except that of Rome, not that Rome wants to remove all world-wide empires. But, as W–M saw, *usquam* goes closely with ⟨*orbis*⟩ *terrarum* (cf. xxxix. 54. 8, xl. 12. 5). I see no reason, however, for following Weissenborn in deleting *orbis* as a gloss.

6. proximus ab: as W–M suspected, this is the only example of *proximus a* in L.

incendium peruasurum: cf. Cic. *II Verr.* 3. 66 *quantum incendium ... peruaserit.*

7. quando: for causal *quando* cf. xxxiii. 2. 9 n.

8–10. Pol. xxi. 11. 3–8. L. has given more point to Scipio's claims by emphasizing the cases which were due to Africanus himself. Polybius refers to τῆς ἰδίας προαιρέσεως (xxi. 11. 5) but lists the Spanish examples and Massinissa as instances of Roman policy as a whole.

9. regulos ... reliquisse: Pol. xxi. 11. 7: ὧν κατὰ μὲν τὴν Ἰβηρίαν Ἀνδοβάλην καὶ Κολίχαντα προεφέροντο L. omits the names, partly because of his general tendency to do so when adapting Polybius (cf. xxxvi. 5. 1 n.), but perhaps also because he realized that the examples were not all that well chosen. Andobales, after a series of revolts, had been killed (on his career cf. Münzer, *RE*, ix. 1325–7) and Culchas had defected in 197 (cf. xxxiii. 21. 7 n.).

For *acceptos ... reliquisse* cf. Suet. *Aug.* 28. 3 (Damsté, *Mnemosyne* n.s. xliii [1915], 459).

Masinissam ... imposuisse: cf. xxxi. 11. 4–18 n. For *non modo ... sed* cf. K–St, ii. 60. Damsté's addition of *et* (loc. cit.) is quite unnecessary.

11–12. Philippum ... eum: Pol. xxi. 11. 9: ὁμοίως κατὰ τὴν Ἑλλάδα Φίλιππον καὶ Νάβιν, ὧν Φίλιππον μὲν καταπολεμήσαντες καὶ συγκλείσαντες εἰς ὅμηρα καὶ φόρους, βραχεῖαν αὐτοῦ νῦν λαβόντες ἀπόδειξιν εὐνοίας ἀποκαθεστακέναι μὲν αὐτῷ τὸν υἱὸν καὶ τοὺς ἅμα τούτῳ συνομηρεύοντας νεανίσκους, ἀπολελυκέναι δὲ τῶν φόρων, πολλὰς δὲ τῶν πόλεων ἀποδεδωκέναι τῶν ἁλουσῶν κατὰ πόλεμον·

12. anno priore ... remissum: in fact it was only a promise in 191; the actual remission dates from the current year: cf. 7. 16 n.

filium ... redditum: xxxvi. 35. 13 n.

quasdam ... eum: cf. xxxvi. 10. 10 n., 13–14, 25. 1 n., 33, Walbank, *Commentary*, iii. 104.

in eadem ... absumpsisset: Pol. xxi. 11. 10: Νάβιν δὲ δυνηθέντες ἄρδην ἐπανελέσθαι, τοῦτο μὲν οὐ ποιῆσαι, φείσασθαι δ' αὐτοῦ, καίπερ ὄντος τυράννου, λαβόντες πίστεις τὰς εἰθισμένας. L. adapts in the light of the events which he described in book xxxv. L. omits the content of Polybius xxi. 11. 11, which imply that the Scipios were seeking more than neutrality from Prusias. Cf. Hopp, 40 n. 29.

13. maxime ... uenit: Pol. xxi. 11. 12: ὡς δὲ καὶ παρεγενήθησαν
πρὸς αὐτὸν πρέσβεις οἱ περὶ τὸν Γάιον Λίβιον, τελέως ἀπέστη τῶν κατὰ
τὸν Ἀντίοχον ἐλπίδων, συμμίξας τοῖς προειρημένοις ἀνδράσιν. It is
unclear whether the statement that Livius had come from Rome
was omitted by the excerptor of Polybius, is L.'s own deduction, or
stood in a Latin source. For Livius' return to Italy cf. 16. 14.

14. Again it is unclear whether this is an addition by L. or represents
material omitted by the excerptor.

26. 1–2. Pol. xxi. 11. 13: Ἀντίοχος δὲ ταύτης ἀποπεσὼν τῆς ἐλπίδος
παρῆν εἰς Ἔφεσον καὶ συλλογιζόμενος ὅτι μόνως ἂν οὕτω δύναιτο
κωλῦσαι τὴν τῶν πεζικῶν στρατοπέδων διάβασιν καὶ καθόλου τὸν πόλεμον
ἀπὸ τῆς Ἀσίας ἀποτρίβεσθαι ... βεβαίως κρατοίη τῆς θαλάττης,
προέθετο ναυμαχεῖν καὶ κρίνειν τὰ πράγματα διὰ τῶν κατὰ θάλατταν
κινδύνων. Polybius presumably referred to the fleet in the section
immediately following what we now have in xxi. 11. Notice that
decidit follows ἀποπεσών closely.

quae ... fuerat: Antiochus' fleet had returned to Ephesus after
the events that followed the battle of Panhormus (13. 6)—i.e.
probably in April. We are now in August/September: cf. p. 29.

2. quia: explaining the decision to risk a naval battle, not that to
visit the fleet.

3. momentum ... spei: 'incentive for hope'. *spei* is to be taken as
a genitive. Cf. iii. 12. 6, Sil. viii. 251. For the word-order cf. p. 14.
   magnam partem: twenty-four ships (24. 12, 25. 3).
   Eumenem ... profectum: 22. 1.

4. animos: for the plural cf. 37. 9, xxxi. 18. 3–4 n.

5. temptandam ... fortunam: cf. x. 43. 7: for *fortunam belli
experiri* cf. xxxi. 31. 16 n.
   Notium ... passuum: the actual distance is about 17 km, and
duo may be corrupt. Notium was known in this period as Colophon-
on-the-sea and formed a dual city with Old Colophon. Jerome (*in
Dan.* xi. 18 = *FGH* 260F47) says that Antiochus captured Colophon
in 197, but this is uncertain. Notium is clearly independent at this
time. See Magie, i. 79–80, ii. 898 n. 110, Schmitt, *Antiochos*, 282,
Bean, *Aegean Turkey*, 185 ff. For the Scipios' letter to Colophon cf.
SEG i. 440.

6. ipsam urbem: in fact Notium, as is clear from the following
narrative, but L. seems to have thought that he was talking about
Old Colophon, as he again does at 28. 4.

7. et hos: Madvig (*Emendationes*, 530), *quos* Bχ. Madvig argued that there was nothing to follow *et ipsam urbem*. But L. thinks that Polybius is talking about Old Colophon (see above), and *et ipsam urbem* means 'Colophon itself as well': *quos* can therefore stand.

8. ad mare: B, *et ad mare* χ, perhaps rightly. Cf. p. 11.

　　uineas: cf. xxxiv. 17. 12 n.

　　testudinibus: the 'ram tortoise' or *testudo arietica*, a device for carrying the ram and protecting its operators. For details of its construction see Vitruvius x. 13. 2, 6.

9. Samum ... Aemilium: cf. 22. 1.

10. bis ... prouocatum: 13. 7 ff., 15. 9. But the first occasion was under the command of Livius, not of Regillus.

11. incertam: *finis* feminine occurs six times in the MSS. of L. Cf. *TLL*, vi. 787. 47 ff.

12. qui et tenuerat: a supplement is necessary. Since the restraining took place at Samos on both occasions it makes no sense to say 'Eudamus who had also restrained him at Samos'. *ante* (F. W. Otto, *Diuinationes Liuianae e codicum maxime uestigiis petitae* [Karlsruhe, 1829], 77) seems right. The previous occasion, not explicitly mentioned by L., will have been at the time of the decision to send Eumenes to the Hellespont (22. 1).

　　instare et [dicere]: Bχ, om. *dicere* M. Müller. Madvig (*Emendationes*, 530) rightly argued that an indirect question, even a rhetorical one, would not be expressed in the infinitive immediately after *dicere*. L. often omits verbs of saying (cf. p. 12) and it is better to assume that a scribe added *dicere* than to change *esse* to *esset* or to follow Madvig's *ut duceret*. But there is no case for deleting *et* as well. As M. Müller (vii–viii) pointed out, *et*, without a verb of saying, often introduces an indirect question. Cf. in particular xxxviii. 22. 5.

13. uictam iam semel: at Corycus.

　　⟨hosti⟩: om. Bχ. It is by no means a necessary supplement.

27–30. *The battle of Myonnesus.* See Thiel, 349 ff. The battle is also described by Appian, *Syr.* 27. Ennius, *Ann.* frs. 384–8V may come from his account of the battle.

27. 1. L. passes abruptly from the council to the actions of the fleet, without explicitly stating the decisions reached: cf. Thiel, 349 n. 602, For the possibility that some ships were nevertheless sent to the Hellespont cf. Thiel, 349. The decisions probably included agreeing to Notium's request for help (Thiel, 350).

　　Chium: cf. xxxvi. 43. 11 n.

2. obiecta: *quae obiecta* Mg. Either could be right.

3. Teios: we now know that Teus had been under Seleucid control since *c.* 203. See the inscription published by P. Herrmann, *Anadolu* ix (1965), 29 ff., with J. and L. Robert, *REG* lxxxii (1969), 502 ff. In 193 Rome had granted Teus *asylia* (*Syll.*³ 601: cf. xxxiv. 57. 6 n.) but that of course would not protect it on the present occasion. On the site of Teus see Bean, *Aegean Turkey*, 136 ff.

ex medio cursu: as W–M observed, a strange phrase, for they are still at Samos town. L. has probably been carried away by his desire to emphasize the suddenness of the change of plan.

4. Myonnesum: cf. 13. 1 n.

institit: χ, *instituit* B, perhaps rightly.

piraticos: perhaps identical with the pirates of Nicander (11. 6): cf. Thiel, 351 n. 610.

celoces: 'cutters', Greek κέλητες. It appears as a masculine both here and at xxi. 17. 3, and the testimony of the MSS. at both passages should be accepted, even though it is feminine elsewhere in Latin. L. may have been influenced by the masculine form in Greek. Cf. *TLL*, iii. 771.

5. postquam ... uerterunt: Pol. xxi. 12: οἱ δὲ πειραταὶ θεασάμενοι τὸν ἐπίπλουν τῶν Ῥωμαϊκῶν πλοίων, ἐκ μεταβολῆς ἐποιοῦντο τὴν ἀναχώρησιν.

fabrefactis: cf. xxxiv. 52. 5 n. W–M's statement that the verb is normally used of works in metal is misleading. L. alone of Classical writers uses *fabrefacere*, twice in the case of metal (xxvi. 21. 8, xxxiv. 52. 6), and in the present passage.

6. perfugerunt: χ, *profugerunt* B. *perfugerunt* ('they reached Myonnesus in their flight') is the sense required here.

7. An *ecphrasis* of the position of Myonnesus.

inter Teum Samumque: a perfectly reasonable description and Glareanus's proposal to change *Samum* to *Lebedum* is unnecessary.

metae: 'a cone'.

superpendentia: as a compound not found elsewhere in Classical Latin (*TLL*) and perhaps to be taken separately here. Kreyssig's *superimpendentia* (found only in Catullus 64. 286) is quite unjustified.

9. portu ... Geraesticum: the northern harbour. See Bean, *Aegean Turkey*, 140 ff.

emisit milites: B, *milites emisit* χ. Cf. p. 15.

28. 1. infulis et uelamentis: cf. xxv. 25. 6, xxxv. 34. 7 n.

2. purgantibus ... hostilis: the genitive is regularly used with verbs of accusing, condemning, etc., and is extended to other analogous verbs in early Latin, and again in L. and later writers. This, though, is the only instance of *purgare* in this sense with the genitive (Horace, *Sat.* ii. 3. 27 has *morbi purgatum*). Cf. K–St, i. 463–464. (*TLL*).

commeatu: *omni commeatu* Bχ. Though there is no other instance of *omnis commeatus* in the sense of 'all kinds of supplies' (Nepos, *Milt.* 7. 2 *omni commeatu priuauit* is, of course, not parallel), it is a perfectly natural phrase and the transmitted reading should be retained.

4. Colophone: cf. 26. 6 n.

5. Macrin: cf. 13. 1 n.

nautici: used by L. for 'sailors' also at xxviii. 7. 7, xxix. 25. 5, xxx. 25. 11, xxxix. 26. 4, xli. 3. 1, but not before him (*TLL*). Cf. p. 9.

6. primo: the events that forestalled Polyxenidas' hopes are narrated in §§ 9 ff. The sequence of thought, which worried W–M, is clear enough.

quem ... expugnasset: at the battle of Panhormus.

7. uix ... exire: an exaggeration. Cf. Bean, *Aegean Turkey*, 139.

8. [inde]: Bχ (*inde nocte occupare inde* NV), om. Frob. 2. It scarcely makes sense here and is probably repeated from *inde naues*. It is not necessary to assume a variant in the archetype, as M. Müller (viii) argues.

sicut ... fecerat: 11. 6.

9. eum ... est: the southern harbour. Cf. Bean, loc. cit.

29. 1. uinum maxime: 'particularly the wine'. Cf. 27. 2.

3. tribunos: cf. 17. 9 n.

4. The construction of the period well portrays the state of confusion.

incertisque clamoribus: cf. Ogilvie, 593.

5. partibus diuisis: 'dividing the tasks between them' (sc. Regillus and Eudamus).

primus: cf. 23. 8 n.

7 ff. On the details of the engagement see Thiel, 353 ff.

7. Corycum: cf. xxxvi. 43. 13 n.

9. Cf. App. *Syr.* 27. 133: ὧν ὁ στρατηγὸς Εὔδωρος ἐτέτακτο μὲν ἐπὶ τοῦ λαιοῦ κέρως, ἰδὼν δὲ ἐπὶ θάτερα Πολυξενίδαν πολὺ προύχοντα Ῥωμαίων ἔδεισέ τε, μὴ κυκλωθεῖεν, καὶ περιπλεύσας ὀξέως ἅτε κούφαις ναυσὶ καὶ ἐρέταις ἐμπείροις θαλάσσης τὰς ναῦς τὰς πυρφόρους τῷ Πολυξενίδᾳ πρώτας ἐπῆγε, λαμπομένας τῷ πυρὶ πάντοθεν.

quod: a pronoun, with *non posse . . . cornu* in apposition, not, as W–M suggest as an alternative, *quod ubi* = 'but when' (cf. K–St, ii. 322).

30. 1–2. On the fleet numbers at Myonnesus see Thiel, 349 with n. 602, 354 n. 617. Appian (*Syr.* 27. 132) gives 25 Rhodian ships and an allied total of 83.

totis classibus simul: Frob. 2, *totis simul classibus* Bχ (cf. p. 15). L. would appear to be referring both to the fact that in the initial stage of this battle the Rhodians alone had been engaged, and to the fact that in none of the previous battles (Corycus, Panhormus, Side) had both the Roman and the Rhodian fleets been present.

maximae . . . hepteres: cf. 23. 4–5 nn.

praestabant: Madvig, *Rhodios praestabant* BχMg. As Madvig saw (*Emendationes*, 531), L. is giving the two different spheres in which the Romans and the Rhodians respectively excelled, and a statement that the Romans surpassed the Rhodians is quite inappropriate. Since it is the relative merits of the Romans and Rhodians in both respects that is in question, reference to the Seleucid forces is equally uncalled for, and *Rhodios* should therefore be regarded as a gloss, not as a corruption of *regios*.

3. quae . . . fuerat: cf. 11. 13 n.

5. qua concurrerat . . . obruebatur: Mg, *quae concurrerant . . . obruebantur* Bχ. Either is possible.

6. in bello: really going with *solet* (De Regibus).

7. sociorum: sc. *naualium*, not true allies. Cf. xxxiv. 6. 12 n.

terrebantur: Bχ, *terrebatur* Mg. Either is possible.

sublatis . . . dolonibus: cf. xxxvi. 45. 1 n.

quadringinta . . . decem tres: Appian (*Syr.* 27. 136) wrongly gives the total losses as 29. Regillus later claimed that all 42 were captured (xl. 52. 6: cf. 46. 2 n.).

9–10. Appian (*Syr.* 27. 134–6) makes this into the major episode of the battle, and one which allowed the allied fleet to gain the victory. *hoc maxime modo* at § 10 perhaps indicates L.'s awareness that he may not have understood Polybius properly at this point, though his description is not as obscure as it seemed to Thiel (357 n. 626). The anchor of the Rhodian ship became entangled with the prow of the Sidonian ship. The Rhodians backed water and the anchor rope was dragged along and became entangled with the oars, finally sweeping away one side of oars entirely.

10. inhiberent: a technical term for rowing astern. Cf. Cicero, *Att.* xiii. 21. 3 (Cicero had only just learnt the true meaning of the word), *TLL*, vii. 1. 1592. 23 ff.

tractum ancorale: *ancorale* 'anchor cable' does not occur before L. (*TLL*, ii. 31). On anchor cables see Casson, 250–1, J. S. Morrison and R. T. Williams, *Greek Oared Ships, 900–322 BC.* (Cambridge, 1968), 301.

detersit: for *remos detergere* cf. 24. 2, xxxvi. 44. 6 n., where, however, the meaning is rather 'break off' than 'sweep away' as here.

31. 1–4. Appian (*Syr.* 28) gives a long and critical account of Antiochus' change of heart and similar sentiments occur, though more briefly, in Diodorus xxix. 5. It seems that Polybius, in accordance with his fondness for criticizing military decisions (cf. xxxi. 38 n.) dealt with the matter at length and that L. abbreviated to a considerable extent (cf. 44. 7 n.). For more favourable evaluations of Antiochus' action see Kromayer, ii. 160 ff., De Sanctis, iv. 1. 192, Thiel, 357 ff.

2. tueri solum Lysimachiam: for the position of *solum* cf. p. 14.

tota hieme: Bχ, *per totam hiemem* Mg. The latter is almost certainly an emendation by Mg, puzzled by the ablative (cf. 13. 4 n.).

et . . . quoque: 'and, what is more'. No others are being reduced to *inopia*. Cf. xxxvi. 30. 6 n.

3. Colophonis obsidione: cf. 26. 5 n.

4. Ariarathen: Ariarathes IV. His mother was Stratonice, daughter of Antiochus II and he himself married Antiochis, the daughter of Antiochus III. Cf. Magie, i. 201 ff., ii. 1096 n. 7. In 188 he became an *amicus* of Rome (xxxviii. 37. 5–6, 39. 6, Pol. xxi. 41. 4–7, 45, Walbank, *Commentary*, iii. 164). See also Seibert, 56–7, 64–5, 113–14.

5. Regillus Aemilius: for the inversion cf. xxxiv. 5. 9 n.

confessionem . . . expressisset: cf. xxxvi. 45. 6 n.

Chium . . . intenderat: 27. 1–2.

6. quassatas: cf. p. 6.

L. Aemilium Scaurum: (138). Probably a *legatus*. G. Bloch (*Mélanges d'histoire ancienne* [Paris, 1909], 4) denied that he was a *legatus* on the grounds that at this time only consulars held the post of military *legatus*. That is not the case, though it is true that most attested *legati* are of at least praetorian standing. He is the first recorded Aemilius Scaurus, but Bloch is probably right to think that he had senatorial ancestors with a different *cognomen*. (He is omitted from the index to *MRR*.) Cf. xxxv. 5. 1 n.

Rhodios ... decoratos: perhaps including the captured ships. Cf. Thiel, 359 n. 634.

7. ad traiciendas ... iere: Bχ. This makes no sense, and *iere* is better explained as a gloss than emended to *ire* with Madvig (*Emendationes*, 531). *praeuertere ad* is found in later writers (cf. W–M) while I can find no example of *praeuertere* with the infinitive (*TLL*).

8–10. L.'s description of the site of Phocaea is clearly taken from Polybius, and it is not at all unlikely that he has misunderstood his source. For discussion see Bean, *Aegean Turkey*, 122 ff., McDonald, *Ancient Macedonia*, ii (Thessaloniki, 1977), 196–7. Lampter is probably the narrow piece of land between the north and south harbours, and the *lingua* the rest of the promontory dividing the two harbours. L.'s error is to imply that the city abutted on to the *cuneus* at the joining point of the two harbours, when it is in fact in the middle of the south harbour and to exaggerate the length of the *lingua*. For a plan of Phocaea see Bean, op. cit., fig. 21. But his fig. 22 (L.'s description) should be amended to:

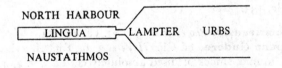

Bean holds that Lampter was in fact the peninsula on which the modern town stands. It seems more probable, however, that L. was right in making it the area where the promontory begins, whose shape could well be regarded as resembling a beacon. For Phocaea's capture by Seleucus cf. 11. 15.

9. mille ... passus: the figure is inconsistent with that given for the circumference of the city walls, though it is in fact the distance from the modern town to the beginning of the promontory. Cf. McDonald, loc. cit., Bean, op. cit., 123.

10. quia ... capit: a necessary explanation of *Naustathmon*. It could not possibly be a gloss, as claimed by Crévier and Ruhnken.

32. 4. stragem ruinarum: for the language cf. xxxiii. 17. 13, xlii. 63. 4. The phrase is taken up by *ruinis strata* in § 7.

5. restitere: NV, *resistere* BφL. The infinitive is the transmitted reading and should be retained (cf. p. 12).

6. desperatione ac rabie: cf. ii. 47. 6, xxxi. 17. 5.

7. munienda: 'strengthening'.

obmolienda: *obmoliri* occurs four times in Latin—here and at xxxiii. 5. 8 and twice in Quintus Curtius. This is the only place where it means 'block by moving material' rather than 'move blocking material'. Cf. *TLL*, ix. 2. 118. 53 ff., p. 9.

8. Q. Antonius: (33). Not otherwise known.

9. qua ... uenissent: for the occasion of the *deditio* cf. xxxvi. 43. 11 n. *in fidem* counts as a word-complex and since L. wants to emphasize *Liuii*, in contrast to the present occasion, he writes *C. Liuii in fidem* not *in C. Liuii fidem*. *in fidem* very rarely has a word between *in* and *fidem*: cf. *TLL*, vi. 1. 664 ff.

Flurl (219) vainly tries to see a distinction in this passage between *in fidem uenire* and *se tradere*.

10. A rather remarkable period.

11–14. Note that L. makes no attempt to conceal this episode, despite the bad light it casts on Roman soldiers. Cf. xxxviii. 24. 2–11, Tränkle, 133.

11. Phocaeensis: *Phocensis* Bχ (*-es* χ). Cf. 19. 7 n.
    impune eludere: cf. Cic. *II Verr.* 3. 9, Tac. *A.* xvi. 28. 1. For *eludere* 'to make mock of' used absolutely cf. *TLL*, v. 2. 432. 48 ff.

12. captas ... urbes: the point is not that a Roman commander could not order the sacking of a city which had made a *deditio*. In Roman eyes *deditio* meant handing over complete power to Rome to act as she thought fit (cf. xxxvi. 27–29 n.). But it was understood that it was not Roman practice to treat with extreme harshness those who had made a *deditio* (cf. ii. 17. 6). The distinction made at Tacitus, *H.* iii. 19. 2 (adduced by W–M) is entirely different. See Dahlheim, 7–8, Volkmann, 87, and for other cases of massacres in cities that had surrendered Harris, 52 n. 3.
    in iis tamen: for the brachylogy (*tamen = etsi captae sint, tamen*) cf. Cic. *Sest.* 63 (W–M).

13. fides constitit: cf. ii. 13. 9, xlii. 24. 4, *TLL*, iv. 530. 79 ff.

14. urbem ... restituit: not as compensation for the looting, as W–M say.

hiems ... appetebat: the end of October: cf. *Historia* xxvi (1977), 248, p. 29.

33–36. *Prelude to the battle of Magnesia*

33. 1. Aeniorum Maronitarumque: cf. xxxi. 16. 4–5 n. It appears from 60. 7 they had Seleucid garrisons which were not expelled at this time. The garrisons will have been installed during Antiochus' Thracian expeditions of 195–194 (cf. xxxiv. 33. 12 n.).

2. refertaque ... commeatibus: cf. App. *Syr.* 28. 139: ὅσος ἦν ἐν αὐτῇ σῖτος σεσωρευμένος πολὺς ἢ ὅπλα ἢ χρήματα ἢ μηχαναί.

proposuerant sibi: Bψφmg, *proposuerant ibi* φ. *sibi proponere* is perfectly good Latin, common in Cicero, and little weight should be attached to the fact, which worried Novak (cf. *JPhV* xxvii [1901], 28), that it is not found elsewhere in L.

3. impedimenta ... ut: Bχ, *ut impedimenta* Mg. A clear case of alteration to the more usual word-order.

5. transitum cernentibus: *transire cernentibus tum* Bχ. For the reason for the corruption see M. Müller, viii, Schmidt, *ZöG* xliii (1892), 979–80.

6–7. Pol. xxi. 13. 10–14: αἴτιον δ᾽ ἦν καὶ τοῦ μένειν τὸ στρατόπεδον ἐπὶ τῆς πρώτης παρεμβολῆς καὶ τοῦ κεχωρίσθαι τὸν Πόπλιον ἀπὸ τῶν δυνάμεων τὸ σάλιον εἶναι τὸν προειρημένον ἄνδρα. τοῦτο δ᾽ ἔστιν, καθάπερ ἡμῖν ἐν τοῖς περὶ τῆς πολιτείας εἴρηται, τῶν τριῶν ἓν σύστημα, δι᾽ ὧν συμβαίνει τὰς ἐπιφανεστάτας θυσίας ἐν τῇ Ῥώμῃ συντελεῖσθαι τοῖς θεοῖς ... τριακονθήμερον μὴ μεταβαίνειν κατὰ τὸν καιρὸν τῆς θυσίας, ἐν ᾗ ⟨ποτ᾽⟩ ἂν χώρᾳ καταληφθῶσιν οἱ σάλιοι οὗτοι. ὃ καὶ τότε συνέβη γενέσθαι Ποπλίῳ· τῆς γὰρ δυνάμεως μελλούσης περαιοῦσθαι κατέλαβεν αὐτὸν οὗτος ὁ χρόνος, ὥστε μὴ δύνασθαι μεταβαλεῖν τὴν χώραν. διὸ συνέβη τόν τε Σκιπίωνα χωρισθῆναι τῶν στρατοπέδων καὶ μεῖναι κατὰ τὴν Εὐρώπην, τὰς δὲ δυνάμεις περαιωθείσας μένειν ἐπὶ τῶν ὑποκειμένων καὶ μὴ δύνασθαι πράττειν τῶν ἑξῆς μηθέν, προσαναδεχομένας τὸν προειρημένον ἄνδρα. The Salii, priests of Mars legendarily created by Numa, but possibly of even older origin (cf. Ogilvie, 98–9) performed ritual dances with the sacred shields (*ancilia*) in March. It is clear from Polybius that the army was only delayed because it had to wait for Scipio. It was only the Salii themselves whose movements were affected, and there was no general ban on campaigning in March (cf. Balsdon, *CR* n.s. xvi [1966], 146–7). But L. appears to have misunderstood Polybius: *causaque et is* suggests that the army would have had to wait anyway, and that Scipio caused still further delay.

The Roman March 189, corresponded to 25 October–24 November 190 (Jul.) (cf. p. 25). W–M ad loc. (though they get it right on 37. 5), Marquardt, *StV*, iii. 437 n. 1, Rappaport, *RE*, iA. 1883, and Balsdon, loc. cit. forget the dislocation of the calendar and hence posit a second period of restriction, in October at the time of the *armilustrium*. In fact there is no evidence for such a second forbidden period or for sacred dances in October (Festus, pp. 144–6L, quoted by De Sanctis, iv. 1. 392, makes no reference to the Salii). Nor is there any reason to hold with Matzat, *Römische Zeitrechnung für die Jahre 219 bis 1 v. Chr.* (Berlin, 1889), 204 n. 2, followed by De Sanctis, loc. cit. and Walbank, *Commentary*, iii. 105, on the basis of Festus, p. 346L, that the period in question ran from *a.d. vi Kal. Mart.* to *a.d. ix Kal. Apr.* The sacred dances began on 1 March (*I.I.* xiii. 2. 417) and it is reasonable to regard the whole of March as the forbidden period.

Ap. Claudius Pulcher (*cos.* 143) and C. Claudius Pulcher (*pr.* 56) are the only other known republican Salii. Cf. G. J. Szemler, *The Priests of the Roman Republic* (Brussels, 1972), 176–7 (with unnecessary scepticism about the latter).

34–36. *Peace negotiations.* Other sources: Pol. xxi. 13–15, Diod. xxix. 7–8, App. *Syr.* 29, Just. xxxi. 7. 4 ff., Dio fr. 62. 2, Zon. ix. 20. 4, *uir. ill.* 54. 3.

34. Polybius reports Antiochus' decision to dispatch Heraclides, with a summary of the terms he was offering, before mentioning the delay caused by Africanus' religious obligations. He then narrates the arrival of Heraclides and the actual negotiations. L. naturally avoids this somewhat unnecessary repetition. Cf. Tränkle, 90 n. 82, 116–17.

34. 1. forte: cf. xxxii. 39. 4 n.

Byzantius Heraclides: Olshausen, no. 137. He is known only from this episode and is not to be identified with the father of the Heraclides who was a minister of Antiochus Epiphanes, as claimed by Otto, *RE*, viii. 464–5. Cf. Olshausen, loc. cit., Walbank, *Commentary*, iii. 105. For another Heraclides of Byzantium cf. D. L. Stockton, *Historia* viii (1959), 75 ff.

2. Pol. xxi. 13. 8: τὰς μὲν ἀρχὰς ἥσθη, νομίζων αὐτῷ συνεργὸν εἶναι πρὸς τὴν ἔντευξιν τὸ μένειν ἐπὶ τῶν ὑποκειμένων καὶ πρὸς μηδὲν ὡρμηκέναι τῶν ἑξῆς τοὺς ὑπεναντίους.

3–4. statuit ... fuisset: Pol. xxi. 13. 9: πυθόμενος δὲ τὸν Πόπλιον ἔτι μένειν ἐν τῷ πέραν ἐδυσχρήστησε διὰ τὸ τὴν πλείστην ῥοπὴν κεῖσθαι τῶν πραγμάτων ἐν τῇ 'κείνου προαιρέσει cf. xxi. 13. 6: ἰδίᾳ δὲ πρὸς τὸν Πόπλιον ἑτέρας. It is not stated in Polybius that Heraclides was instructed to approach Publius first, and it is not easy to see how it could have been omitted by the excerptor (cf. § 4 n.). In fact he does not do so. The general comments on Scipio's policy also appear to be L.'s own addition.

4. gentibus: 'foreign peoples'. Cf. xxxix. 36. 4, *TLL*, vi. 2. 1851. 57 ff.

   qui uictor: 'what sort of a victor'. Cf. xxiii. 15. 12. On the usage of *qui* and *quis* see H–S, 540–1. Cf. Scipio's own claims in 25. 8 ff.

4–6. etiam quod ... deductum esse: Polybius does not mention Scipio's son until he reports Heraclides' private interview with Scipio (xxi. 15. 2–3: πρῶτον μὲν χωρὶς λύτρων ὁ βασιλεὺς αὐτῷ τὸν υἱὸν ἀποδώσει· συνέβαινε γὰρ ἐν ἀρχαῖς τοῦ πολέμου τὸν υἱὸν τὸν τοῦ Σκιπίωνος γεγονέναι τοῖς περὶ Ἀντίοχον ὑποχείριον·). There is equally no mention of the occasion on which he was captured, but the fact that something similar to L.'s first version appears in Appian and Diodorus suggests that it in fact stood in Polybius, and the details were omitted by the excerptor. A third version appears in Val. Max. iii. 5. 1 and Pliny, *NH* xxxv. 22, where the young Scipio seems to be captured in the battle of Magnesia, while in Dio fr. 62. 2 he is captured by Seleucus while crossing from Greece (sc., presumably, to Asia). L.'s second version perhaps comes from an annalist, but 48. 1 does not by any means prove that it stood in Antias, and it cannot be excluded that both versions stood in Polybius.

   Scipio had two sons, Lucius, praetor in 174 (325) and Publius, the adoptive father of Aemilianus, who was an augur from 180 (331). Publius was a physical weakling (cf. Münzer, *RE*, iv. 1437–8) and it is rather improbable that he undertook any military service. Lucius, then, would be the one captured.

   See Nissen, *KU*, 14, 194–5, Mommsen, *RF*, ii. 515–18, Münzer, *RE*, iv. 1431–3, Tränkle, 33, 60, Walbank, *Commentary*, iii. 107–8.

5. a Chalcide Oreum: perhaps he was with the garrison when Chalcis surrendered to Antiochus. This is stated to consist only of Achaean and Pergamene troops (xxxv. 50. 6) but it would not be surprising if one or two Roman officers were present. Or perhaps he was part of the force attacked at the *castellum* on the Euripus (xxxv. 51. 9). Mommsen (*RF*, ii. 516), followed by Thiel (286) argued from Appian's statement (*Syr.* 29. 146) that Scipio was captured on his way from Chalcis to Demetrias that both Oreus and Demetrias were mentioned by Polybius and that the incident belongs to the time when Villius was going from Chalcis to Demetrias (xxxv. 39) and that Scipio was intercepted by Antiochus' fleet crossing to Pteleum (xxxv. 43. 4). It is, however, very hard to think that there was a chronological overlap between Polybius' accounts of Greek events of 193/2 and 192/1 and even if that were possible, it is most unlikely that Antiochus would have taken such action before open hostilities had commenced. Appian's statement is best regarded as a mere mistake.

6. est: Bχ, *sit* Madvig. Cf. xxxiv. 20. 2 n.

Fregellana: Fregellae, on the Liris just north of its junction with the Trerus, was founded as a Latin colony in 328 (viii. 22. 2, Salmon, *Samnium*, 212).

in eo ... equo: J. F. Gronovius, *in eo tumultu delapso equo* φ, *in eo tumultu delapsu equo* ψ, *delapsum equo* B, *in eo delapsum tumultu ex equo* Mg. There is no other instance of L. using *labi* or *delabi* with *equo(-is)* alone and Mg's *ex equo* should be retained. Between Gronovius's reading and Zingerle's *delapsum in eo tumultu ex equo* (*SAW* cxxviii, 5, 10) it is impossible to decide.

7. ita ad: Bχ. *et ad* H. J. Müller, unnecessarily. For *ita* continuing the narrative cf. *TLL*, vii. 2. 522. 26 ff.

maneret ... esset: for the imperfect subjunctives cf. K–St, ii. 396 ff., H–S, 662.

priuatim: as there was between the Marcii Philippi and the Antigonids (xlii. 38. 8–9).

8–35. 1. Pol. xxi. 14. 1: ὁ δ' Ἡρακλείδης, μετά τινας ἡμέρας παραγενομένου τοῦ Ποπλίου, κληθεὶς πρὸς τὸ συνέδριον εἰς ἔντευξιν διελέγετο περὶ ὧν εἶχε τὰς ἐντολάς.

35. 2–3. is ... dicerent: nothing corresponding to this stands in Polybius. L. deliberately sharpens Polybius' picture of Heraclides' failure to see the true situation. See the excellent remarks of Tränkle, 123–4.

2. ultro citroque nequiquam: B, *nequicquam ultro citroque* χ. *ultro citroque* goes closely with *legationibus*, and B's order is therefore preferable.

eam ... fiduciam ... quod: a striking brachylogy for *id causam esse fiduciae quod*.

Zmyrnam ... Troadem: cf. xxxv. 42. 2 n.

3. Lysimachia ... dicerent: not, of course, Antiochus' real reason for his abandonment of Lysimachia. Cf. 31. 1–2.

eas ... uelint: Pol. xxi. 14. 2: φάσκων τῆς τε τῶν Λαμψακηνῶν καὶ Σμυρναίων, ἔτι δὲ τῆς τῶν Ἀλεξανδρέων πόλεως ἐκχωρεῖν τὸν Ἀντίοχον, ὁμοίως δὲ καὶ τῶν κατὰ τὴν Αἰολίδα καὶ τὴν Ἰωνίαν, ὅσαι τυγχάνουσιν ᾑρημέναι τὰ Ῥωμαίων. At Pol. xxi. 13. 4 Antiochus' offe is of those cities which Rome claims as having taken her side, here those which she has actually captured. L. follows the former version (for the places involved see Walbank, *Commentary*, iii. 106).

quod ... fuerint: Bχ, *quas suarum partium ediderant* Mg. *ediderant* is an odd corruption, and Madvig (*Emendationes*, 531–2) emended to *ediderint*—i.e. 'such states as Rome named as being on her side'. But this assorts oddly as a parenthesis with *uindicare ... uelint* and in view of some other remarkable corruptions in Mg it is better to retain the quite unobjectionable text of the extant MSS.

4. Pol. xxi. 14. 3: πρὸς δὲ τούτοις τὴν ἡμίσειαν ἀναδέχεσθαι τῆς γεγενημένης αὐτοῖς δαπάνης εἰς τὸν ἐνεστῶτα πόλεμον.

5. Pol. xxi. 14. 4–5: πολλὰ δὲ καὶ ἕτερα πρὸς ταύτην τὴν ὑπόθεσιν διελέχθη, παρακαλῶν τοὺς Ῥωμαίους μήτε τὴν τύχην λίαν ἐξελέγχειν ἀνθρώπους ὑπάρχοντας, μήτε τὸ μέγεθος τῆς αὐτῶν ἐξουσίας ἀόριστον ποιεῖν, ἀλλὰ περιγράφειν, μάλιστα μὲν τοῖς τῆς Εὐρώπης ὅροις· καὶ γὰρ ταύτην μεγάλην ὑπάρχειν καὶ παράδοξον διὰ τὸ μηδένα καθῖχθαι τῶν προγεγονότων αὐτῆς. For the theme cf. Walbank, *Commentary*, i. 155.

memores rerum humanarum: cf. Sall. *Iug.* 38. 9, Koestermann, 368.

6. Nothing corresponds to this in Polybius.

potuisse ... posse: emphasizing the distinction between having acquired empire in the past, and keeping it in the present.

7. quod si ... passurum: Pol. xxi. 14. 6: εἰ δὲ πάντως καὶ τῆς Ἀσίας βούλονταί τινα προσεπιδράττεσθαι, διορίσαι ταῦτα· πρὸς πᾶν γὰρ τὸ δυνατὸν προσελεύσεσθαι τὸν βασιλέα. L. adds the need to avoid ambiguous boundaries—perhaps with Africa (cf. xxxiv. 62. 4 n.), rather than subsequent difficulties in Asia, in mind. L. also adds the rhetoric of *uinci ... passurum*, creating the contrast, as Tränkle (124) well says, of the greed of Rome with the moderation of Antiochus.

7–10. ea ... cedat: Pol. xxi. 14. 7–8: ῥηθέντων δὲ τούτων, ἔδοξε τῷ συνεδρίῳ τὸν στρατηγὸν ἀποκριθῆναι διότι τῆς μὲν δαπάνης οὐ τὴν ἡμίσειαν, ἀλλὰ πᾶσαν δίκαιόν ἐστιν Ἀντίοχον ἀποδοῦναι· φῦναι γὰρ τὸν πόλεμον ἐξ ἀρχῆς οὐ δι' αὐτούς, ἀλλὰ δι' ἐκεῖνον· τῶν δὲ πόλεων μὴ τὰς κατὰ τὴν Αἰολίδα καὶ τὴν Ἰωνίαν μόνον ἐλευθεροῦν, ἀλλὰ πάσης τῆς ἐπὶ τάδε τοῦ

Ταύρου δυναστείας ἐκχωρεῖν. ea . . . uisa and sed sicut . . . urbes are L.'s
own additions. Cf. Tränkle, 109.

10. For the Taurus line in the eventual treaty see McDonald, *JRS*
lvii (1967), 1 ff. (the issues raised are not appropriately dealt with
in relation to the present passage).

36. 1. Pol. xxi. 14. 9: ὁ μὲν οὖν πρεσβευτὴς ταῦτ᾽ ἀκούσας παρὰ τοῦ
συνεδρίου, διὰ τὸ πολὺ τῶν ἀξιουμένων τὰς ἐπιταγὰς ὑπεραίρειν οὐδένα
λόγον ποιησάμενος, τῆς μὲν κοινῆς ἐντεύξεως ἀπέστη, τὸν δὲ Πόπλιον
ἐθεράπευσε φιλοτίμως and xxi. 13. 6, quoted at 35. 3–4 n.

    legatus postquam: χ, *postquam legatus* B. Cf. p. 15.

    censebat: for *postquam* with the imperfect, very common in L.,
cf. K–St, ii. 356.

2. Pol. xxi. 15. 2 (quoted at 34. 4–6 n.), xxi. 15. 4: δεύτερον δὲ διότι
καὶ κατὰ τὸ παρὸν ἕτοιμός ἐστιν ὁ βασιλεὺς ὅσον ἂν ἀποδείξῃ διδόναι
πλῆθος χρημάτων καὶ μετὰ ταῦτα κοινὴν ποιεῖν τὴν ἐκ τῆς βασιλείας
χορηγίαν, ἐὰν συνεργήσῃ ταῖς ὑπὸ τοῦ βασιλέως προτεινομέναις διαλύσεσιν.
L. has misunderstood Polybius. Antiochus was offering Scipio
the usufruct of the income of his kingdom (cf. the grants made
to various Greeks by Persian kings in the fifth century [De Ste.
Croix, *The Origins of the Peloponnesian War* (London, 1972), 38–9]
and for such gifts by Seleucid kings Bikerman, *Institutions*, 181), not a
share in the kingdom. See Tränkle, 181 n. 13.

    pollicitus: cf. p. 12.

3–8. On L.'s conversion of Polybius' indirect speech into direct
speech cf. Lambert, 61–2.

3. Pol. xxi. 15. 6: περὶ δὲ τῶν ἄλλων ἀγνοεῖν αὐτὸν ἔφη καὶ παραπαίειν
ὁλοσχερῶς τοῦ σφετέρου συμφέροντος οὐ μόνον κατὰ τὴν πρὸς αὐτὸν
ἔντευξιν, ἀλλὰ ⟨καὶ⟩ κατὰ τὴν πρὸς τὸ συνέδριον. L. adapts considerably.

4. Pol. xxi. 15. 7–8: εἰ μὲν γὰρ ἔτι Λυσιμαχείας καὶ τῆς εἰς τὴν Χερρόνησον εἰσόδου κύριος ὑπάρχων ταῦτα προύτεινε, ταχέως ἂν αὐτὸν
ἐπιτυχεῖν. ὁμοίως, εἰ καὶ τούτων ἐκχωρήσας παραγεγόνει πρὸς τὸν
Ἑλλήσποντον μετὰ τῆς δυνάμεως καὶ δῆλος ὢν ὅτι κωλύσει τὴν διάβασιν
ἡμῶν ἐπρέσβευε περὶ τῶν αὐτῶν τούτων, ἦν ἂν οὕτως αὐτὸν ἐφικέσθαι
τῶν ἀξιουμένων. Cf. App. *Syr.* 29. 148 ἰδίᾳ . . . ἐφύλασσε.

    tamquam: Mg, om. Bχ. It is not necessary, but there is no
obvious reason why it should have been added in Mg.

5. Pol. xxi. 15. 9: ὅτε δ᾽ ἐάσας ἐπιβῆναι τῆς Ἀσίας τὰς ἡμετέρας δυνάμεις
καὶ προσδεξάμενος οὐ μόνον τὸν χαλινόν, ἀλλὰ καὶ τὸν ἀναβάτην παραγί-
νεται πρεσβεύων περὶ διαλύσεως ἴσων, εἰκότως αὐτὸν ἀποτυγχάνειν καὶ
διεψεῦσθαι τῶν ἐλπίδων. Cf. App. *Syr.* 29. 148 νῦν δε . . . ὀλίγοις.

By changing ἀναβάτην to *iugo* L. ruins the point of the story first
told by Stesichorus (orally, it seems, not in a poem). Cf. Ar. *Rhet.*
1393 b10 ff. (Page, *Poetae Melici Graeci*, no. 281). Cf. Bowra, *Greek
Lyric Poetry*² (Oxford, 1961), 119, Pianezzola, 38–9, Walbank, *Commentary*, iii. 108. I do not understand why Tränkle (117 n. 46) denies
that Polybius' version has anything to do with Stesichorus' fable.

6–7. Pol. xxi. 15. 11: ἀντὶ δὲ τῆς κατὰ τὸν υἱὸν ἐπαγγελίας ὑπισχνεῖτο
δώσειν αὐτῷ συμβουλίαν ἀξίαν τῆς προτεινομένης χάριτος. Cf. App. *Syr.*
29. 149. Again L. elaborates.

6. aliis: the other gifts offered by Heraclides.

8. Pol. xxi. 15. 11: παρεκάλει γὰρ αὐτὸν εἰς πᾶν συγκαταβαίνειν, μάχεσθαι
δὲ κατὰ μηδένα τρόπον Ῥωμαίοις.
possim: Bχ. *possum* dett., perhaps rightly.

9. Pol. xxi. 15. 13: Ἀντίοχος ⟨δὲ⟩ νομίσας οὐδὲν ἂν βαρύτερον αὐτῷ
γενέσθαι πρόσταγμα τῶν νῦν ἐπιταττομένων, εἰ λειφθείη μαχόμενος, τῆς
μὲν περὶ τὰς διαλύσεις ἀσχολίας ἀπέστη, τὰ δὲ πρὸς ἀγῶνα πάντα καὶ
πανταχόθεν ἡτοίμαζεν.
tutam: because he would have no worse terms imposed on him
if defeated in battle. Hence he had nothing to lose and a lot to gain.
The point is made rather more clearly by Polybius.

37–44. *The battle of Magnesia*

See Diodorus xxix. 8. 2, Front. *Strat.* iv. 7. 30, Appian, *Syr.* 30–37,
Just. xxxi. 8. 6–7, Flor. i. 24. 15 ff., Veg. *de re mil.* iii. 24, *uir. ill.* 53,
Zon. ix. 20. 5–8, Kromayer, ii. 163 ff., Bar-Kochva, 163 ff.

37. 1. Dardanum ... Rhoeteum: cf. 9. 7 nn.
utraque ciuitate ... effusa: *utramque ciuitatem ... effusam* χ. B
has *utramque ciuitatem,* but I am unable to determine whether it has
effusa or *effusam.* There is a dot over the *a* but not the usual line
indicating *-m.* The accusatives should be retained. For *ciuitas* used
of both the place and the people cf. 16. 2.

2–3. Ilium ... arcis: cf. xxxv. 43. 3 n.

3. Iliensibus ... origine sua: by this time the legend of Rome's
Trojan ancestors was well established. It had first been used for
political purposes by Pyrrhus who claimed that he was a new
Achilles fighting the descendants of the Trojans (Paus. i. 12. 1). In
263 Segesta proclaimed her connection with Aeneas in taking
Rome's side against Carthage (cf. Kienast, *Hermes* xciii [1965],
480 ff.). If we may believe the story in Suetonius (*Claud.* 25. 3) the

senate offered Seleucus II *amicitia* and *societas* if *consanguineos Ilienses ab omni munere immunes praestitisset* and in 196 the Lampsacenes referred to their συγγενεῖα with Rome in their appeal for assistance against Antiochus (*Syll.*³ 591: cf. xxxiii. 38. 3 n., p. 402). See in general Petrocheilos, 137, Walbank, *Commentary*, iii. 182–3.

sextis castris: for *castra* to mean a day's march cf. Walsh on xxi. 31. 4. It occurs once in Caesar (*BG* vii. 36. 1) and fourteen times in L. See *TLL*, iii. 563. 24 ff. De Sanctis (iv. 1. 196 n. 132) holds that a daily average of 34½ km. would have been excessive and that six days was in fact the time from Assus, not from Ilium.

caput Caici amnis: cf. 18. 6 n.

4. Elaeam: cf. xxxv. 13. 6 n.

Lecton promunturium: the extreme south-west tip of the Troad peninsula. Cf. Cook, *Troad*, 227 ff. Magie, i. 83, ii. 905 mentions the difficulty of rounding it.

principiis rerum: 'the beginning of the action'. Cf. xxi. 39. 1. In previous writers *principia rerum* has a philosophical meaning. Cf. p. 9.

5. hiems opprimeret: for the date cf. 33. 6–7 n., p. 29.

6. Cf. Diod. xxix. 8. 2: ὁ Ἀντίοχος πρὸς τὰ παράλογα τῆς τύχης ἔκρινε συμφέρειν ἀποδοῦναι τῷ Σκιπίωνι τὸν υἱόν, καὶ τοῦτον ἀπέστειλε κοσμήσας πολυτελέσι κατασκευαῖς.

Thyatiram: cf. 8. 7 n.

8. App. *Syr.* 31. 151: ὁ δὲ τοῖς ἄγουσι συνεβούλευε μὴ μάχεσθαι τὸν Ἀντίοχον, ἕως αὐτὸς ἐπανέλθοι. The meaning of Scipio's advice is obscure. There cannot be any intention of implying that the battle will be fought any less fiercely for Africanus' presence. Nor would Polybius have reported anything which formed part of the accusations levelled against Scipio in the following years (though if the words of Scipio had become widely known, they would certainly have provided ammunition for such accusations). Cf. Scullard, *SA*, 205–6, Balsdon, *Historia* xxi (1972), 228.

aliam gratiam: B, *gratiam aliam* χ. *aliam* needs emphasis and B's order is therefore preferable.

9. sexaginta ... equitum: Bχ. Mg had *sexaginta duo*. Appian (*Syr.* 32. 161) gives a total of 70,000. The individual contingents listed in ch. 40, however, amount to only 45,200 infantry. Most of the discrepancy can be accounted for by following Bar-Kochva, 8–9, in regarding the *argyraspides*, for whom no figure is given at 40. 7 as numbering 10,000. For the rest Bar-Kochva reasonably suggests that 3,000 were guarding the camp and a further 3,000 were attached to the elephants. In order to make the discrepancy as small as possible, it is desirable to read *sexaginta*, though there is no other reason for preferring this to Mg's reading. The cavalry contingents listed in ch. 40 amount to 11,700. The number of Tarentini (40. 13) is not given and this can easily account for the difference. See also Kromayer, ii. 209 ff.

animos . . . faciebant: cf. xxxi. 18. 3–4 n.

ad incertos . . . subsidia: cf. Cic. *Cat.* ii. 9 *industriae subsidia* and Caes. *BG* iv. 31. 2 *ad omnes casus subsidia comparabat.* L. appears to combine both constructions in one. One would naturally take *industriae* in the Cicero passage as a dative, and I wonder if we should read *omni* here.

recepit se et . . . circa: *recepit et* B, *recepit se* χ, *recepisse* φmg; *circaque* Bχ. If we read both *et* and *circaque*, *transgressus* will be a main verb, with ellipse of *est*. Omission of *et*, and subordination of *transgressus* to *recepit* is impossible, since Antiochus crosses the Phrygius a considerable time after his departure from Thyatira. In this case it seems best to omit -*que* with most editors, rather than to add the passage to the list of L.'s ellipses of *esse* (cf. p. 12). Goodyear (348) rightly says that to take *transgressus* as a main verb (thus Pettersson, 97) would throw far too much emphasis on to Antiochus' crossing of the river. (For A *et* B C*que* joining clauses cf. xxxii. 31. 3.)

Phrygium amnem: mod. Kum, flowing into the Hermus east of Magnesia. Strabo (xiii. p. 626C) says that it was previously called the Hyllus, and this name occurs in Homer, *Il.* xx. 392 and Herodotus i. 80. 1. It is called the Phrygius in Appian's account of the battle (*Syr.* 30. 151) and in *Syll.*³ 606 (cf. 39. 9 n.). See Kromayer, ii. 167, Magie, ii. 783–4 n. 8. For the place at which Antiochus crossed the river see Kromayer, ii. 169.

Magnesiam . . . est: to distinguish it from Magnesia-on-the-Maeander. Cf. xxxvi. 43. 9 n. On *ab Sipylo* at 44. 4 cf. n. ad loc.

10. cubita: as a unit of measure *cubitum* occurs once in Cicero (*Att.* xiii. 12. 3), in Vitruvius, and three times in L., all in the account of the battle of Magnesia (40. 12, 41. 6). Cf. *TLL*, iv. 1275. 72 ff.

11. interiore labro: sc. of the ditch.

38. 1. Scipio is proceeding south from the mouth of the Caicus (cf. 37. 1–5).

Hyrcanum campum: the Hyrcanian plain is probably the whole area between Thyatira and Magnesia, in the valleys of the Phrygius and the Hermus. See Kromayer, ii. 166 and n. 4. Hyrcanis, a military settlement, lay to the east of the Phrygius (cf. J. and L.

Robert, *Hellenica* vi [1948], 16–26, Launey, i. 340, Magie, ii. 972 n. 3).

Hyrcanum: *Hyrcanium* Bχ, which should be retained. Cf. Strabo xiii. 629C, Steph. Byz. s.u. Ὑρκανία (Drakenborch).

2. citra: χ, *circa* B. Corruption to *circa* is more likely than the reverse, and since it is clear that the Romans took up position first of all west of the Phrygius (cf. Kromayer, ii. 171) *citra* should be accepted.

3. Gallograeci: cf. 8. 4 n.
  Dahae: cf. xxxv. 48. 5 n.
  sagittarii equites: cf. xxxv. 48. 3 *sagittis ex equo utentes.*

4. conati circa: a comma should be placed after *conati*, since *circa ripam amnis* goes with *interfecti sunt*, not with *recipere se conati.*
  aliquot: for the limiting apposition cf. xxxiv. 56. 5 n.

5. silentium: cf. xxxii. 20. 1 n.
  tertio ... castra: Appian (*Syr.* 30. 152, 154) makes both this move and that described in § 9 the responsibility of Cn. Domitius (i.e. Ahenobarbus, the consul of 192), whom Africanus left as a σύμβουλος to his brother (*Syr.* 150) during his own absence. There is a similar implication in Plutarch, *Mor.* 197D–E. He is mentioned at 39. 5, but L. has no indication that the consul himself was not making the strategic decisions. The story belongs to the tradition that consistently belittled the abilities of Lucius (cf. 1. 9–10 n.) and should be rejected. See Balsdon, *Historia* xxi (1972), 229 ff.
  tertio post die: a clear case of inclusive counting.

6. metantibus ... occupatis: it is perhaps an unreal question to ask whether L. regarded these participles as datives or ablatives.
  terrore ac tumultu: deliberate alliteration. The phrase occurs nine times in L., otherwise only in Lucretius v. 1336 (in asyndeton). Cf. Wölfflin, *Ausgewählte Schriften*, 277.

8. campi: Bχ, *campum* Mg. L. often uses *medium* with the genitive. Cf. K–St, i. 433.

9. extremi: the rear of the Seleucid troops. Cf. Kromayer, ii. 172.

39. Note the amount of ellipse in this chapter—*in consilium uocare*, the indirect question depending on *consilium*, perhaps the omission of *fore*, *conclamatum ... duceret.*

1–2. Kromayer (ii. 173) wrongly thinks that Lucius does not want to fight, and that he is asking the *consilium* to decide between keeping the soldiers *sub pellibus* or retreating *in hiberna*. In fact Lucius is indicating that these are the alternatives to fighting immediately, clearly the course he favours himself.

1. in consilium aduocauit: cf. ix. 2. 15. The phrase is similar to *in senatum uocare* (cf. xxxvi. 21. 7 n.).

2. sub pellibus: cf. Ogilvie, 633.
fore: χ, om. B, perhaps rightly. Cf. p. 12.

4. pecorum trucidandus: cf. the passages collected by Woodman, 202.

5. Cn. Domitius: cf. 38. 5 n.
iter: scarcely a journey, given the relatively short distance between the two camps (38. 5).
hostium uallum: B, *uallum hostium* χ, perhaps rightly. There is no need for *hostium* to be emphasized.
omnia certa: 'complete and firm information'. Cf. ix. 36. 2.
admoueri castra: B, *castra admoueri* χ. Cf. p. 15.

6–13. Cf. App. *Syr.* 31. 156–60.

7. duae socium: Bχ. Crévier may have been right to insert *alae*. *legio* is not properly applied to allied troops, and *alae* (cf. xxxi. 21. 7 n.) could easily have been omitted after *duae*.
quina ... quadringenos: cf. xxxiii. 1. 2 n.

8. hastatorum ... principum ... triarii: cf. Walbank, *Commentary*, i. 702.
postremos claudebant: *agmen, aciem* etc. *claudere* is a common expression in L., and he sometimes adds *postremum* or *extremum* (40. 9, xxx. 32. 11). But of people who can be neither the *triarii* themselves nor the *principes* the expression is most odd. Perhaps we should read *postremam aciem*.

9. uelut iustam aciem: as being the main part of the Roman army. As W–M say, the troops that follow are equally part of the *acies*.
Achaeorum: perhaps the force under Diophanes (cf. Aymard, *PR*, 375). For a dedication recording their part in the battle cf. *Syll.*[3] 606.
aequata fronte: exactly in line with the legions and allied *alae*.
opposuit: 'placed as protection'. Cf. 40. 6, *TLL*, ix. 2. 771. 13 ff.
Romanus: not excluding Italian cavalry.

10. Trallis: cf. xxxi. 35. 1 n. They were perhaps sent by Philip.

Others, presumably mercenaries, served in the Seleucid army (40. 13). They are, of course, light-armed troops, not cavalry.

Cretensis: mercenaries. Cf. Launey, i. 266.

11. laeuum ... claudebant: with the river behind them—i.e. the part of the Phrygius which ran north–south. See Bar-Kochva, 165.

egere uidebatur: *uidebatur egere* Mg, *uerebatur* Bχ. Mg's reading is perfectly acceptable and neither transposition nor emendation is necessary.

quattuor ... oppositae: Appian's statement (*Syr.* 31. 158) that 'Domitius' (cf. 38. 5 n.) had four troops of cavalry round him can hardly refer to the same matter, as W–M suggest. For Appian Domitius is on the right wing.

12. et: 'and in addition'. Cf. *TLL*, v. 2. 892. 53 ff.

uoluntate ... erant: mercenaries, presumably. The phrase applies only to the Thracians. The Macedonians will have been sent by Philip.

castris relicti sunt: Bχ, *relicti sunt castris* Mg. The latter is a highly unusual word-order, and one might suspect that it was altered in F or its predecessor to a more normal order. But Mg's order reads very strangely in this purely factual description and is best regarded as a simple transpositional error.

13. praeterquam ... ne ... quidem: cf. iii. 34. 8, but the present construction, with combination of a general and a specific statement, is harsher.

magnitudine ... praestant: the common view of the ancient writers. For a defence of its validity against modern attacks see Scullard, *Elephant*, 60 ff. On the source of the Roman elephants cf. xxxi. 36. 4 n.

40. 1. uaria ... gentibus: a normal feature of the Seleucid army. Cf. 2 Macc. 8:9, Bar-Kochva, 48.

decem ... diuisa: cf. App. *Syr.* 32. 162: διελὼν ἀνὰ χιλίους καὶ ἑξακοσίους εἰς δέκα μέρη.

more ... appellabantur: cf. xxxvi. 18. 2 n.

2. partes ... distinguebat: Appian (*Syr.* 32. 162) says that there were 22 elephants between each section, an unlikely figure. Perhaps there were 22 altogether, as suggested by Bar-Kochva, 167 and 263 n. 18.

distinguebat: sc. Antiochus. Emendation is unnecessary. Cf. p. 12.

a fronte ... patebat: i.e. 32 lines of 50 men in each of 10 divisions, producing the total of 16,000. Cf. App. *Syr.* 32. 162:

καὶ τούτων ἑκάστου μέρους ἦσαν ἐπὶ μὲν τοῦ μετώπου πεντήκοντα
ἄνδρες, ἐς δὲ τὸ βάθος δύο καὶ τριάκοντα. 32 lines is double the usual
depth. Cf. Kromayer, ii. 181 n. 5 and on phalanx depths in Greek
armies Pritchett, *The Greek State at War* (Berkeley–Los Angeles–
London, 1974), i. ch. xi.

introrsus: used in other passages where a line is shortened and
deepened. Cf. xxxii. 17. 8 n.

patebat: 'extended'.

4. frontalia: the word occurs otherwise only in Pliny, *NH* xxxvii.
194 (of horses), Amm. xxiii. 4. 12 (of the front part of an artillery
machine), and (in the singular, in relation to a building) *CIL* iii.
7960. Cf. *TLL*, vi. 1. 1365. 48 ff., p. 9.

turres ... armati: cf. App. *Syr.* 32. 162: ἡ δ' ὄψις ἦν τῆς μὲν
φάλαγγος οἷα τείχους, τῶν δ' ἐλεφάντων οἷον πύργων. There can be little
doubt that it is L. who represents Polybius more accurately here.
Kromayer, ii. 181 n. 6 oddly claims that L. and Appian are saying
the same thing.

Towers on fighting elephants are first attested in the time of
Pyrrhus and then became regular. See P. Goukowsky, *BCH* xcvi
(1972), 488 ff., Scullard, *Elephant*, 104–5, 240 ff.

5. Gallograecorum: cf. 8. 4 n.

pedites: W–M say all that is necessary on Sigonius's emendation
to *equites*, based on Appian, *Syr.* 32. 163: ἱππεῖς δ' ἑκατέρωθεν αὐτοῦ
παρατετάχατο Γαλάται τε κατάφρακτοι. Cf. the similar mistake by
Appian in the passage corresponding to § 7.

cataphractos: cf. xxxv. 48. 3 n. Brakman's suggestion (*Mnemosyne* n.s. lv [1927], 61) that since L. has already explained the word
there the comment here should be deleted as a gloss is absurd.

agema: App. *Syr.* 32. 163: καὶ τὸ λεγόμενον ἄγημα τῶν Μακεδόνων·
εἰσὶ δὲ καὶ οἵδε ἱππεῖς ἐπίλεκτοι, καὶ παρ' αὐτὸ ἄγημα λέγεται. The
two main cavalry squadrons of the Seleucid army are the *agema*
and the *regia ala* (§ 11). See Bar-Kochva, 67 ff., who suggests that
the men involved came from the military settlements in the areas
indicated (cf. § 11 n.).

6. continens ... in subsidiis: behind them. Cf. Bar-Kochva, 169.

7. paulum: Bχ, *paululum* Mg, inappropriately in a straightforward
narrative of this sort (cf. xxxv. 5. 11 n.).

regia cohors ... argyraspides: Appian (*Syr.* 32. 164) wrongly
describes them as cavalry. They are the royal infantry guard. See
Kromayer, ii. 210 n. 1, Bar-Kochva, 56 ff. (arguing that they were
Macedonian military settlers), Lock, *Historia* xxvi (1977), 373–8.

8. Dahae ... ducenti: cf. 38. 3 n. Appian (*Syr.* 32. 164) makes them only 200. L. should be followed (cf. Kromayer, ii. 211, Bar-Kochva, 263 n. 19).

tum leuis armatura: L. lists light-armed infantry first on the right wing (§§ 8–9) and then on the left (§§ 13–14). Appian (*Syr.* 32. 166–7) lists them all together after he has described the end of the line. Bar-Kochva (166–7) argues from this that they were in fact skirmishers placed in front of the phalanx. He claims that if L. were right, the light-armed troops on the Seleucid right would have had to face the *ala* of the *socii* on the Roman left, and that Antiochus could not have exposed light-armed troops to heavy-armed opponents: those on the left, moreover, would have so far outflanked the Roman right as to be useless. But even on Bar-Kochva's view, with the phalanx facing the right-hand legion and *ala*, it is the *argyraspides* who face the left *ala* (see his map 14). In fact there is no reason why the phalanx should not face both legions and in that case the light-armed troops on the Seleucid left are not as far away from the Roman right as Bar-Kochva claims. There certainly were front-line skirmishers (42. 3, App. *Syr.* 35. 178) but I cannot accept Bar-Kochva's rejection of so major a part of L.'s detailed exposition.

Cretenses ... Tralles: cf. 39. 10 nn.

Mysi: Mysia, to the east of Pergamum, had been captured by Attalus in 218. Some of it passed to Prusias in the early years of the second century, some had been occupied by Antiochus in 198. See Schmitt, *Antiochos*, 266, 273. The area held by Antiochus, however, is unlikely to have been large enough to produce 2,500 archers and they are to be regarded either as independent allies (Bar-Kochva, 51) or mercenaries (Magie, ii. 974). On the status of Mysians still appearing in the Seleucid army after the battle of Magnesia see Walbank, *Commentary*, iii. 449–50. See further 56. 2 n.

9. Cyrtii: see Walbank, *Commentary*, i. 582. They are Seleucid subjects. Cf. Bar-Kochva, 48, 51.

Elymaei: cf. xxxv. 48. 5 n.

10. Ariarathe: cf. 31. 4 n.

regi: χ, *regii* B, *rege* Gel. 'uetus scriptura'. In this position the dative is clearly correct.

11. regia ala ... equorumque: App. *Syr.* 32. 164: καὶ ἦν ἐκάλουν ἵππον ἑταιρικήν, ὡπλισμένη κούφως. Bar-Kochva, 68 ff., shows that ἴλη βασιλική, ἑταῖροι, and ἵππος ἑταιρική all refer to the same unit. He argues that these Syrians, Lydians, and Phrygians were in fact settlers of Graeco–Macedonian descent, not indigenous peoples (cf. § 5 n.).

12. falcatae quadrigae: described in more detail in 41. 5–9. See nn. ad loc.

cameli . . . possent: App. *Syr.* 32. 167: Ἄραβες, οἳ καμήλους ὀξυτάτας ἐπικαθήμενοι τοξεύουσί τε εὐμαρῶς ἀφ' ὑψηλοῦ καὶ μαχαίραις, ὅτε πλησιάζοιεν, ἐπιμήκεσι καὶ στεναῖς χρῶνται.

13. alia . . . erat: i.e. of light-armed troops. Cf. § 8 n.

primi Tarentini: L. does not give numbers for the *argyraspides* (cf. 37. 9 n.) and though numbers appear in what immediately follows, there is no need to posit a lacuna here. On the Tarentini cf. xxxv. 28. 8 n.

Neocretes: cf. Walbank, *Commentary*, i. 540.

Cares et Cilices: subjects from the areas of Antiochus' recent conquests. Cf. Bar-Kochva, 51.

14. Pisidae . . . Pamphylii: cf. xxxv. 13. 5 n.

sedecim: ψφmg, *quindecim* φ, *vii* B. Cf. § 6.

41–4. On the differences between L. and Appian in these chapters cf. Witte, 388–93, who is, however, too critical of L. and too ready to regard Appian as faithfully following Polybius.

41. 1. App. *Syr.* 33. 170: ἐφειστήκει δὲ τοῖς μὲν δεξιοῖς ἱππεῦσιν Ἀντίοχος αὐτός, τοῖς δ' ἐπὶ θάτερα Σέλευκος, ὁ υἱὸς Ἀντιόχου, τῇ δὲ φάλαγγι Φίλιππος ὁ ἐλεφαντάρχης καὶ τοῖς προμάχοις Μύνδις τε καὶ Ζεῦξις.

Antipatrum fratris filium: Antipater had served at Raphia (Pol. v. 79. 12, 82. 9) and Panion (Pol. xvi. 18. 7). At v. 79. 12 Polybius calls him ὁ βασιλέως ἀδελφιδοῦς, at xxi. 16. 4 just ἀδελφιδοῦς, and *fratris filium* is L.'s interpretation (cf. xxxii. 36. 10 n.). But in fact it seems clear that he was a cousin, not a nephew of Antiochus. He will have been the nephew of Seleucus II and the title remained with him. See 45. 5 n., Holleaux, *Études*, iii. 195–8, Schmitt, *Antiochos*, 29, Walbank, *Commentary*, i. 609.

Minnioni: cf. xxxv. 15. 7 n.

Zeuxidi: Zeuxis is one of the foremost of Antiochus' generals and courtiers. He first appears in 222 (Pol. v. 45. 4). He had been *strategos* in Lydia since at least 205 (cf. 45. 5, Bengtson, ii. 109 ff., Musti, *SCO* xv (1966), 109–10, Olshausen, no. 144, *RE*, xA. 381 ff., Walbank, *Commentary*, ii. 503, iii. 109. For his part in the battle see 42. 7–43. 5 n., for his part in the subsequent peace negotiations 45. 5 ff.

Philippo: doubtless the same as the Philip who served as ἐλεφαντάρχης at Raphia (Pol. v. 82. 8). Cf. Treves, *RE*, xix. 2336 (Philippos [21]), Walbank, *Commentary*, i. 611.

2–4. App. *Syr.* 33. 171: ἀχλυώδους δὲ καὶ ζοφερᾶς τῆς ἡμέρας γενομένης ἥ τε ὄψις ἔσβεστο τῆς ἐπιδείξεως, καὶ τὰ τοξεύματα πάντα ἀμβλύτερα ἦν ὡς ἐν ἀέρι ὑγρῷ καὶ σκοτεινῷ.

2. leuata ... omnia: Bχ have *in nubes caliginem dedit,* Mg *in nubibus dedit caliginem. in nubes* is clearly right, going with *leuata.* The mist rises to form low clouds, it does not rarefy in the clouds. This produces a fog and moisture in the atmosphere. The problems lie in the second part of the sentence. The MSS. read *umor inde ab austro uelut perfudit omnia.* This is impossible. *uelut* cannot go with *perfudit* (as Walker, *Supplementary Annotations,* 218 and, originally [1863 edn., xii], Madvig thought), for *perfudit* is meant literally and stands in no need of qualification. Nor can it be taken postpositively with *austro,* as is apparently done by Sage ('as if borne on a southerly wind'). Attempts at emendation have fallen into two groups, supplying a word after *uelut (pluuia, pluuialis, imber,* even *nix*) or emending *uelut* to a participle (*secutus, inuectus, illatus, orsus*). I think, however, that Professor Nisbet has seen the right solution, a simple transposition to *uelut austro.* The moisture is like that borne on a southerly wind. (*imber* or *pluuia* in Front. *Strat.* iv. 7. 30, Flor. i. 24. 17, *uir. ill.* 53. I do not prove that L. used some such word, as W–M argue: they could all derive simply from *umor.*)

3. nihil admodum: Bχ, *admodum nihil* Mg. Cf. Packard, iii. 483.

3–4. umor ... emollierat: it is hard to see how the conditions could have affected the two armies in the way that L. describes (particularly as Eumenes too had light-armed troops), or that Polybius could have said that they did so. There is no similar comment in Appian (which in itself proves nothing). It is hard to see why L. should have added a comment of this nature and we must assume that he misunderstood Polybius. Cf. Bar-Kochva, 264 n. 29.

    toto ... armatu: 'almost all the troops being heavily armed'.

    hebetabat: *hebetare* is not found before Virgil and L. (also at viii. 10. 3, xxx. 35. 8). Cf. *TLL,* vi. 3. 2584 ff., p. 9.

4. cornua ... conspicere: *cornua (cornu* B) *circumspicere* Bχ. Madvig (*Emendationes,* 532) rightly argued that there was nothing to stop the centre turning their eyes in the direction of the wings, but the mist made it impossible actually to see them.

    amenta: 'thongs'. The word does not occur elsewhere in L.

6–7. A far from perspicuous passage, though scarcely unintelligible, as Sage claims. Interpretation is aided by descriptions of such chariots used by Darius III at the battle of Gaugamela—the only other occasion when they were intended to play a significant part

in a major battle, with equally disastrous results (cf. F. E. Adcock,
The Greek and Macedonian Art of War (Berkeley–Los Angeles, 1957],
47. For these descriptions see Diodorus xvii. 53. 1–2, Quintus Curtius
iv. 9. 4–5, and for other references to these chariots in Seleucid
armies Bar-Kochva, 83–4. For another reference in L. to scythed
chariots see fr. 2.

There are three elements:

(*a*) Spikes attached to the yoke at the point where it joined the
pole. They were presumably two in number, if the comparison with
horns of an animal is to have any sense. The MSS. describethese as
being ten cubits long. W–M print Drakenborch's emendation *duo*.
Ten cubits would certainly be a prodigious length for a spear-like
object projecting above the horses, and it is far from clear what
value such a spike would have. Diodorus describes a projection with
a cutting edge, and that could be ten cubits long. Spears would
make sense only if they projected forward and the *uelut cornua* simile
applied to a charging bull. It may be that L. has again misunderstood Polybius.

(*b*) Two scythes attached to the end of the yoke, one horizontal, one
pointing towards the ground. As W–M say, this implies that the
yoke joined all four horses, rather than only the central pair, as was
normal. Cf. Schneider, *RE*, xxiv. 681–6, who, however, restricts
himself to artistic and numismatic evidence.

(*c*) Two further scythes attached to the wheels, again one horizontal,
one pointing downwards.

8. ut ante dictum est: 40. 12.

9–42. 1. Cf. App. *Syr.* 33. 172–4.

9. quam anceps ... et: Fügner, *pugnae quam anceps esset et* B,
pugnae et quam anceps esset χ. Editors have followed Fügner's transposition, influenced by the position of *et* in B (cf. M. Müller, ix).
For *genus pugnae* one may compare xxxi. 35. 3, but *pugnae et auxilii
genus* is an odd phrase and I wonder if *pugnae et* is the remains of a
gloss.

⟨**cum aliquot turmis**⟩**:** clearly something has been omitted,
but precisely what must remain conjectural. Appian (*Syr.* 33. 172)
makes no mention of cavalry in this context and though omissions
in Appian's account are a very unsure basis for textual argument it
could be that *equitum* is part of a gloss, arising from a mistaken belief
that the Cretans mentioned at 39. 10 were cavalry.

et ex: Bekker, om. *et* Bχ. Perhaps we should read just *et*.

10. Vegetius' version (*de re mil.* iii. 24) that the Romans frightened
the horses by scattering *tribuli* can hardly have any authority.

11. et leuis ... Cretensis: they are all *leuis armatura* though comparison with § 9 indicates that *leuis armatura* refers, oddly, only to the *iaculatores*.

12. inani ludibrio: 'an ineffectual side-show'. L.'s division between these preliminaries and the battle proper is misleadingly schematic. Kromayer (ii. 190) rightly argues that Eumenes began his cavalry charge (42. 2 n.) immediately the chariots had been removed, and it was this that caused the panic described in 42. 1.

42. 1. uana ... uerae: cf. xxxiv. 12. 4 n.

subsidiaria: the light-armed troops of 40. 13–14.

proxima: Bχ, *proxime* Mg. Cf. viii. 32. 12, xxix. 7. 6. *proxime* in such contexts does not occur in L.

cataphractos equites: 40. 11. Cf. App. *Syr.* 33. 173: καὶ μετὰ ταύτας ἡ κατάφρακτος ἵππος. It is unclear what happened to the *regia ala*.

2. Appian (*Syr.* 34. 175–6) makes the attack go against the infantry on the left of the phalanx. These were, however, next to the cataphracts and there is no substantial disagreement. Appian's explicit statement that Eumenes was responsible for the attack should be accepted. See Kromayer, ii. 189–90 n. 3.

dissipatis subsidiis: the troops just mentioned, not further *subsidia*.

pars ... fusi sunt: *impetum pars eorum sustinuerunt, alii fusi sunt* Bχ. It is unlikely that *alii* would be glossed by *pars eorum* and the best explanation of the paradosis is that *pars eorum* and *sustinuerunt* were transposed and *alii* inserted to make sense.

oppressi [sunt]: the passages quoted by W–M for the repetition of *sunt* (57. 8, xxxv. 1. 12 n., xxxviii. 44. 3) are not parallel and editors have been right to reject the second *sunt*.

3. totum ... laeuum cornu: i.e. those to the left of the phalanx (40. 10).

auxiliaribus: 40. 10–11.

quos ... phalangitas: it is odd that L. feels it necessary to repeat the explanation he gave at 40. 1.

4–5. L. deals with the attack on the phalanx very briefly. For details cf. Appian, *Syr.* 35. 178–83. The cavalry also played a considerable part in this attack. See Kromayer, ii. 191.

4. ibi simul: Bχ, *ubi semel* Mg. For *simul = simulac* cf. K–St, ii. 359–60. *simulac*, in fact, occurs only twice in L. *ubi semel*, however, is equally possible (cf. xxii. 2. 7, xxxii. 20. 6).

354

intercursu suorum: light-armed troops being received between the ranks of the phalanx, as described by Appian, *Syr.* 35. 178. Cf. Bar-Kochva, 171. (Kromayer, ii. 191–2 holds that L. and Appian are describing different episodes.)

sarisas: L. also explains the word at xxxviii. 7. 12 and, perhaps, ix. 19. 7 (cf. Ogilvie, *TCS* xxiii [1973], 163).

5. interpositi . . . elephanti: cf. 40. 2.

neruos incidere: to hamstring them. Cf. Scullard, *Elephant*, 181.

6. media acies: the phalanx. I cannot understand W–M's note.

accepere: the Romans. Cf. p. 12.

7–43. 5. Cf. Appian, *Syr.* 34. 177, 36. 184–6. On this part of the battle see Kromayer, ii. 193–5. For an incident in the attack involving Zeuxis, not mentioned by L., see Zonaras, ix. 20. 8, Bar-Kochva, 171.

Bar-Kochva, 170, claims that L.'s account is 'little short of amazing' on the grounds that Antiochus would not have used 4,000 troops (3,000 cataphracts and the *agema*, if the latter is what is meant by *auxiliis* in § 7) to attack 120 Roman cavalry and that if the *cataphracts* had made such a diagonal attack they would have left the phalanx exposed. He therefore uses Justin's statement (xxxi. 8. 6) that a Roman legion was routed to argue that the cataphracts and *agema* made a frontal attack on the left-hand Roman legion. This is quite unjustified. In part it depends on his view of the relative position of the phalanx *vis-à-vis* the legions (cf. 40. 8 n.): on my view the *cataphracts* would have been facing the left-hand *ala*. But in any case L. does not say that the cataphracts and *auxilia* attacked 120 cavalry. These cavalry had left a gap between the river and the left-hand *ala* and Antiochus was thus able to launch a successful attack on that *ala*. That Justin should have confused an *ala* with a legion is perfectly intelligible, and there is no reason at all for rejecting L.'s detailed account.

7. nulla subsidia: 39. 11.

auxiliis: see above.

43. 1. M. Aemilius . . . factus est: the son of M. Aemilius Lepidus (68), consul in 187 and 175 (cf. xxxi. 2. 3 n.), who became *pontifex maximus* in 180. The present comment cannot come from Polybius xxii. 3. 2, as claimed by W–M; that passage is concerned with a completely different matter. The present passage is acutely used by Rich, 129, as an argument that the consul of 187 cannot have been born later than 227 if he is to have a son old enough to be a *tribunus militum* in 190, and hence that he was not as young as is

usually supposed at the time of his interview with Philip V at
Abydus in 200 (cf. xxxi. 18. 3–4 n.). It is possible, however, that
the statement that the military tribune was the son of the consul of
187 is a mistake. (The possibility that *M. Lepidi filius* is a gloss and
that Lepidus himself is the military tribune is excluded by the fact
that Lepidus was a candidate for the consulship of 189 [47. 6].)

2. ⟨is⟩: om. Bχ. Pettersson (48) defended the asyndeton but with
praererat castris preceding, it is quite different from 45. 5, where it
is not necessary to add *hi* before *prius Eumene conuento*. Cf. p. 12.

    occurrit ... iubebat: cf. xxxiv. 17. 4 n.

3. perniciem suam: Bχ, *suam perniciem* Mg. There is no point in
emphasizing that it is their own *pernicies* and Bχ's order is therefore
preferable.

4. hic ... uicit: cf. Pliny, *Epp.* vi. 16 (Brakman, *Mnemosyne* n.s.
lv [1927], 62).

    primo constiterunt: a delay in the action, and the situation is
reversed. See Ogilvie, 260.

5. Attalus: according to Appian (*Syr.* 36. 185–6) Antiochus returns
from the Roman camp ὡς ἐπὶ νίκῃ and defeats Attalus' cavalry. Cf.
Kromayer, ii. 194–5 n. 4.

7. et robur ... impedierant: i.e. the fact that the bravest soldiers
were in the phalanx and the heaviness of their armour meant that
few took flight. The conjunction of ideas is rather odd.

9. erat sua ... ruerent et incursu: Heusinger. *erat et sua ...
ruerent incursu* Bχ. *et sua* scarcely makes sense and it seems likely that
et has been displaced from the following line. Cf. Madvig, *Emendationes*, 532–3.

10. primorum: Bχ, *priorum* Mg. As W–M say, the reference is to
those put to flight at the beginning of the battle (42. 1 ff.).

44. 1–2. Cf. Appian, *Syr.* 36. 188–9. Klotz (*RhM* lxxxiii [1934],
251–4) argued that the figures derive, via Polybius, from the official
report by the Roman commander. He points out that Appian
regards the Roman dead as τῶν ἐξ ἄστεος—i.e. *ciues Romani* and this
well explains the very small number, since the main brunt of the
attack by the Seleucid right was borne by the *socii* (cf. 42. 7–43. 5 n.).
The official report will have concerned itself only with citizen dead
and exaggerated Antiochus' losses. Klotz's argument is ingenious,
but it is equally possible that exaggerated figures reached Polybius
from non-official sources and that Appian's language is merely
some form of misunderstanding.

1. tria milia: χ, om. *milia* B, *quattuor milia* Mg. It must remain uncertain whether L. wrote *tria* or *quattuor*.

mille . . . capti: Appian includes the captives in the 50,000 while Justin (xxxi. 8. 8) makes the figure 11,000.

2. quinque et uiginti: Appian says 15 cavalry. L.'s figure probably includes infantry as well. Cf. G. Barbieri, *PhW* lv (1935), 703–4; *contra* Klotz, op. cit., 253.

3. postero: Bχ, *postera* Mg. See appendix. For leaving the spoiling of the corpses until the following day De Regibus compares xxii. 51. 5 (Cannae).

4. Thyatira: cf. 8. 7 n.

Magnesia ab Sipylo: cf. xxxvi. 43. 9 n. Madvig (*Emendationes*, 533 n. 1) and W–M demonstrate that L. uses *ab* here because it is a question of ambassadors coming from Magnesia.

5. App. *Syr.* 36. 186: καὶ μέχρι μέσων νυκτῶν ἐς Σάρδεις παρῆλθε.

concessit: Bχ, *contendit* Mg. *concessit* is more appropriate for the description of a flight (cf. the passages adduced by M. Müller, ix).

6. App. *Syr.* 36. 187: παρῆλθε δὲ καὶ ἀπὸ Σάρδεων ἐς Κελαινάς, ἣν Ἀπάμειαν καλοῦσιν, οἷ τὸν υἱὸν ἐπυνθάνετο συμφεύγειν.

Apameam: cf. xxxv. 15. 1 n.

progressos: B, *praegressos* χMg. The latter is the transmitted reading and should be accepted.

coniuge ac filia: not necessarily his Chalcidian wife (xxxvi. 11. 1–4 n.) as is assumed by W–M. Antiochus may have been still, or again, married to Laodice (cf. Schmitt, *Antiochos*, 10 ff., Walbank, *Commentary*, iii. 75), in which case the daughter could be the one earlier offered in marriage to Eumenes (53. 13, Schmitt, *Antiochos*, 25–6).

7. Xenoni: doubtless to be identified with the Xenon active against Molon in 222 (Pol. v. 42. 5, 43. 7). W–M strangely also identify him with the Xenon of xxxviii. 1. 10: the latter is an officer of Philip. Cf. Schmitt, *RE*, ixA. 1537.

urbis: Sardis.

Timone . . . praeposito: not otherwise known. He succeeds Zeuxis (45. 5: cf. 41. 1 n.) and is to be regarded as the *strategos*, not the satrap, of Lydia (Bengtson, ii. 112 ff.). Bengtson argues that the *strategos* of Lydia had over-all military control in Asia Minor, and that Timon's appointment indicates that Antiochus was making plans for possible further, if limited, military resistance to Rome.

Appian (*Syr.* 37) has a long section consisting of criticisms of Antiochus' strategy put into the mouth of his φίλοι. There can be little doubt that the passage is Polybian in origin and that L. omitted it: cf. 31. 1–4 n.

quibus ... missi sunt: cf. Pol. xxi. 16. 1: μετὰ τὴν νίκην οἱ Ῥωμαῖοι τὴν αὑτῶν πρὸς Ἀντίοχον παρειληφότες καὶ τὰς Σάρδεις καὶ τὰς ἀκροπόλεις.

45. 1. Trallibus: east of Ephesus at modern Aydin. On the site cf. Ruge, *RE*, viA. 2093–2128, Magie, i. 129–30, Bean, *Turkey beyond the Maeander*, 208–11, Walbank, *Commentary*, iii. 172.

Magnesia ... est: cf. 10. 12 n. At § 19 L. says *ad Maeandrum*, these being the only two places where he gives the name in full.

2. Polyxenidas: last mentioned after the battle of Myonnesus (30. 7). For the reality of the motivation here given see Thiel, 362 n. 647.

Patara: cf. 15. 6 n.

Rhodiarum ... Megisten: cf. 22. 5 n., 24. 12.

3. Asiae ciuitates: vague, after the mention of specific cities. Polybius presumably said that a considerable number of unnamed towns surrendered.

45. 4–21. *Peace negotiations*

See Pol. xxi. 16–17, Diod. xxix. 10, App. *Syr.* 38, Just. xxxi. 8. 8, Eutr. iv. 4. 3, Zon. ix. 20. 9. Comparison with Polybius reveals a considerable number of additions by L. At § 7 the notion of Antiochus' atoning for his error is also found in Diodorus and we should reckon with the possibility that this and other additions come from a source other than Polybius who was also used by Diodorus and Appian (see §§ 14–15 n.). Cf. p. 2 n. 2. It is still worth reading Mommsen's discussion (*RF*, ii. 519 ff.) of the differences between Polybius and L., and see in general Tränkle, 126 ff. (Tränkle unfortunately eschews a detailed discussion of the passage).

4–5. Pol. xxi. 16. 1–4: ἧκε Μουσαῖος ἐπικηρυκευόμενος παρ' Ἀντιόχου. τῶν δὲ περὶ τὸν Πόπλιον φιλανθρώπως προσδεξαμένων αὐτόν, ἔφη βούλεσθαι τὸν Ἀντίοχον ἐξαποσταλῆναι πρεσβευτὰς τοὺς διαλεχθησομένους ὑπὲρ τῶν ὅλων. διόπερ ἀσφάλειαν ἠξίου δοθῆναι τοῖς παραγινομένοις. τῶν δὲ συγχωρησάντων οὗτος μὲν ἐπανῆλθεν, μετὰ δέ τινας ἡμέρας ἧκον πρέσβεις παρὰ τοῦ βασιλέως Ἀντιόχου Ζεῦξις ὁ πρότερον ὑπάρχων Λυδίας σατράπης καὶ Ἀντίπατρος ἀδελφιδοῦς. L. abbreviates the preliminaries and, as often, omits the proper name (cf. xxxvi. 5. 1 n.: on Musaeus see Olshausen, no. 141). L. uses only one verb of coming and going, compared with three in Polybius. Cf. Tränkle, 90 n. 81, with other examples of the same stylistic technique in L.

5. Zeuxis ... fuerat: cf. 41. 1 n.

Antipater ... filius: cf. 41. 1 n. In this passage it is clear from
Polybius that ἀδελφιδοῦς is simply a title, and that L. translated it
as *fratris filius*. The insertion of *regis* (Weissenborn) is one of the most
demonstrably false conjectures that could be imagined.

6. Pol. xxi. 16. 5–6: οὗτοι δὲ πρῶτον μὲν ἔσπευδον ἐντυχεῖν Εὐμένει τῷ
βασιλεῖ, διευλαβούμενοι μὴ διὰ τὴν προγεγενημένην παρατριβὴν φιλοτι-
μότερος ᾖ πρὸς τὸ βλάπτειν αὐτούς. εὑρόντες δὲ παρὰ τὴν προσδοκίαν
μέτριον αὐτὸν καὶ πρᾷον, εὐθέως ἐγίνοντο περὶ τὴν κοινὴν ἔντευξιν.
L. adds that Publius was approached first.

prius: Bχ, *is prius* Mg, *hi prius* Frob. 2. Polybius' οὗτοι proves
nothing as far as L. is concerned and Bχ's text is perfectly acceptable (cf. Pettersson, 48).

placatiore: the comparative of *placatus* occurs at ii. 60. 3 and
Cicero, *Att.* xi. 21. 3 (*TLL*).

7–9. Pol. xxi. 16. 7–9: κληθέντες δ' εἰς τὸ συνέδριον πολλὰ καὶ ἕτερα
διελέχθησαν, παρακαλοῦντες πρᾴως χρήσασθαι καὶ μεγαλοψύχως τοῖς
εὐτυχήμασι, φάσκοντες οὐχ οὕτως Ἀντιόχῳ τοῦτο συμφέρειν ὡς αὐτοῖς
Ῥωμαίοις, ἐπείπερ ἡ τύχη παρέδωκεν αὐτοῖς τὴν τῆς οἰκουμένης ἀρχὴν
καὶ δυναστείαν· τὸ δὲ συνέχον ἠρώτων τί δεῖ ποιήσαντας τυχεῖν τῆς
εἰρήνης καὶ τῆς φιλίας τῆς πρὸς Ῥωμαίους. L. makes Zeuxis the
speaker, reverses the order of the main statements, and elaborates
on Polybius in other ways (cf. Tränkle, 126 ff.). He omits, however,
the thought contained in φάσκοντες ... Ῥωμαίους. On the idea of
Antiochus' atoning for his errors cf. 4–21 n.

dicamus ... ⟨ueni⟩mus: M. Müller. *dicamus habemus* Mg,
dicamus Bχ. The transmitted text is clearly impossible since *ut
quaeramus* cannot depend on *habemus*. I prefer Madvig's *quam a
uobis quaerimus* to either H. J. Müller's *quam adsumus ut* (which is
very weak) or *habentes uenimus*.

piaculo expiare: as if he had sinned against the gods, connecting with the ideas of § 9.

8. maximo ... ignouistis: on the theme cf. xxxiii. 12. 7 n.

quae ... fecit: Polybius makes the same point in the Rhodians'
speech at xxi. 23. 4 (= 54. 15): cf. Tränkle, 131 n. 81. But I doubt
if he was deliberately dating the beginning of Rome's complete
domination of the *oikoumene* from the battle of Magnesia (for such
an idea cf. Aemilius Sura *ap.* Vell. i. 6. 6). Such phrases are often
used to describe the result of great victories. Cf. xxix. 17. 6, xxx.
32. 2, xxxvi. 17. 14–15 n., Momigliano, *JRS* xxxii (1942), 53 ff.,
Weinstock, *MDAI(A)* lxxvii (1962), 313, Fraenkel, *Horace*, 451
n. 4.

9. This is really extraordinary language, recalling some of the religious language of L.'s own time (cf. Nisbet and Hubbard, i. 35): but laying aside hostility towards all men is not at all like Augustan concepts of peace, which meant that there was no one else left to fight. On *generi humano* cf. xxxv. 33. 6 n.

10–12. Pol. xxi. 16. 10–17. 1: οἱ δ' ἐν τῷ συνεδρίῳ πρότερον ἤδη συνηδρευκότες καὶ βεβουλευμένοι περὶ τούτων, τότ' ἐκέλευον διασαφεῖν τὰ δεδογμένα τὸν Πόπλιον. ὁ δὲ προειρημένος ἀνὴρ οὔτε νικήσαντας ἔφη Ῥωμαίους οὐδέποτε γενέσθαι βαρυτέρους, . . . Though there is evidently a lacuna in our texts of Polybius, L. has probably again elaborated considerably.

11–12. Romani . . . gerimusque: for the sentiment Walker, *Supplementary Annotations*, 219, compared Horace, *Epp.* i. 18. 111–12.

12. animos . . . mentis: the *mens* is the reasoning part of the soul, the *animus* the part that conceives ambitions for further conquests etc. (Plato's θυμοειδές).

   neque . . . extulerunt: cf. App. *Syr.* 38. 196: οὐχ ὑβρίζομεν ταῖς εὐπραξίαις. See Polybius xxvii. 8. 8 for a particularly clear statement of Roman refusal to abate their demands following a defeat.

13. Pol. xxi. 17. 2: διὸ καὶ νῦν αὐτοῖς τὴν αὐτὴν ἀπόκρισιν δοθήσεσθαι παρὰ Ῥωμαίων, ἣν καὶ πρότερον ἔλαβον, ὅτε πρὸ τῆς μάχης παρεγενήθησαν ἐπὶ τὸν Ἑλλήσποντον. Again a great deal of elaboration by L. (cf. Walsh, *RhM* xcvii [1954], 110–11). *postquam . . . esset* is placed first for emphasis, although it limits *quas . . . condiciones*. But there is nothing illogical in L.'s mode of expression, as claimed by Bornecque, 186.

   communis Mars: for the notion cf. xxviii. 19. 11, 41. 14, xlii. 14. 4, Cic. *fam.* vi. 4. 1, *de or.* iii. 167, *II Verr.* 5. 132, *Sest.* 12, *Phil.* x. 20, Ovid, *am.* i. 9. 29, ii. 9. 47 (*TLL*).

14–15. Pol. xxi. 17. 3–6: δεῖν γὰρ αὐτοὺς ἔκ τε τῆς Εὐρώπης ἐκχωρεῖν καὶ ⟨τῆς Ἀσίας⟩ τῆς ἐπὶ τάδε τοῦ Ταύρου πάσης. πρὸς δὲ τούτοις Εὐβοϊκὰ τάλαντ' ἐπιδοῦναι μύρια καὶ πεντακισχίλια Ῥωμαίοις ἀντὶ τῆς εἰς τὸν πόλεμον δαπάνης. τούτων δὲ πεντακόσια μὲν παραχρῆμα, δισχίλια δὲ καὶ πεντακόσια πάλιν, ἐπειδὰν ὁ δῆμος κυρώσῃ τὰς διαλύσεις, τὰ δὲ λοιπὰ τελεῖν ἐν ἔτεσι δώδεκα, διδόντα καθ' ἕκαστον ἔτος χίλια τάλαντα. ἀποδοῦναι δὲ καὶ Εὐμένει τετρακόσια τάλαντα ⟨τὰ⟩ προσοφειλόμενα καὶ τὸν ἐλλείποντα σῖτον κατὰ τὰς πρὸς τὸν πατέρα συνθήκας. Asia may be an addition by L.: cf. Walbank, *Commentary*, iii. 110. On the details of the peace terms L. follows Polybius closely. Appian (*Syr.* 38. 197–9) and Diodorus (xxix. 10) add some details from the final settlement (xxxviii. 38. 8 = Pol. xxi. 43. 12–13), though it is possible

that these were in fact stipulated at this point and merely omitted
by Polybius. Cf. 55. 3 n., Mommsen, *RF*, ii. 521. 2, De Sanctis,
iv. 1. 205–6 n. 143.

14. Taurum montem: cf. 35. 10 n.
   talentum Euboicorum: cf. Walbank, *Commentary*, i. 27, corrected at ii. 630, iii. 161.
   senatus populusque Romanus: L., aware of the proper procedure, adds *senatus*.
   ⟨**milia**⟩: Gruter. om. Bχ. W–M print Wesenberg's *duodecim milia*
but Polybius has χίλια and the omission of merely *mille* or *milia* is
easier to explain.

15. It is clear from Polybius that it is both the money and the corn
that were outstanding to Eumenes under the terms of the treaty with
Attalus and that the money is not for reparations for the war as a
whole. L. hints at this in *reddi* but fails to make it clear that the
money is also covered by the treaty. Cf. Mommsen, *RF*, ii. 520. The
treaty was probably concluded after Antiochus' invasion of Pergamum in 198: see Schmitt, *Antiochos*, 276, 296, Walbank, *Commentary*, iii. 110.

16–17. Pol. xxi. 17. 7–8: σὺν δὲ τούτοις Ἀννίβαν ἐκδοῦναι τὸν Καρχηδόν-
ιον καὶ Θόαντα τὸν Αἰτωλὸν καὶ Μνασίλοχον Ἀκαρνᾶνα καὶ Φίλωνα καὶ
Εὐβουλίδαν τοὺς Χαλκιδέας. πίστιν δὲ τούτων ὁμήρους εἴκοσι δοῦναι
παραχρῆμα τὸν Ἀντίοχον τοὺς παραγραφέντας. L. elaborates and reverses the order of the demands for hostages and named persons.
Mommsen (*RF*, ii. 520) argued that §§ 7 and 8 have been transposed
in the text of Polybius, since σὺν δὲ τούτοις must refer to the hostages.
But it surely means 'in addition to these terms'.

17. Thoantem: cf. xxxv. 12. 4 n.
   concitorem: *concitor* occurs four times in L. (xxiii. 41. 2, xxix. 3. 3,
xlv. 10. 10), and otherwise only in Tacitus, Justin, and Ammianus.
Cf. *TLL*, iv. 69, p. 9. L. uses *concitator* only at xxv. 4. 10. On his
use of *concio* and *concito* see Adams, *Antichthon* viii (1974), 58–9.
   Philonem et Eubulidam: they are not otherwise known, but
are presumably the leading anti-Romans in Chalcis after the exile
of Euthymides (xxxv. 37. 4). They will have fled to Antiochus after
the recapture of Chalcis in 191: see Deininger, 85–6.

18. L.'s own addition.
   sciat ... praecipitari: cf. Suet. *Iul.* 29. 1 *difficilius se principem
ciuitatis a primo ordine in secundum quam ex secundo in nouissimum detrudi.*
Could L. have had this remark of Caesar in mind?

19. cum iis ... placuit: Pol. xxi. 17. 9: ταῦτα μὲν οὖν ὁ Πόπλιος
ἀπεφήναθ᾽ ὑπὲρ παντὸς τοῦ συνεδρίου. συγκαταθεμένων δὲ τῶν
περὶ τὸν Ἀντίπατρον καὶ Ζεῦξιν, ἔδοξε πᾶσιν ἐξαποστεῖλαι πρεσβευτὰς
εἰς τὴν Ῥώμην τοὺς παρακαλέσοντας τὴν σύγκλητον καὶ τὸν δῆμον
ἐπικυρῶσαι τὰς συνθήκας. L.'s statement that the ambassadors had
been instructed to accept any terms is scarcely likely to be correct,
and is clearly wrong if Bengtson is correct in his interpretation of the
appointment of Timon in place of Zeuxis (44. 7 n.). For a similar
exaggeration cf. xxxiii. 24. 6 n.

consul ... diuisit: Pol. xxi. 17. 10: καὶ τότε μὲν ἐπὶ τούτοις
ἐχωρίσθησαν, ταῖς δ᾽ ἑξῆς ἡμέραις οἱ Ῥωμαῖοι διεῖλον τὰς δυνάμεις ...
We must assume a lacuna in the text of Polybius.

20–21. Pol. xxi. 17. 11–12: μετὰ δέ τινας ἡμέρας παραγενομένων ⟨τῶν⟩
ὁμήρων εἰς τὴν Ἔφεσον, εὐθέως ἐγίνοντο περὶ τὸ πλεῖν εἰς τὴν Ῥώμην
ὅ τ᾽ Εὐμένης οἵ τε παρ᾽ Ἀντιόχου πρεσβευταί, παραπλησίως δὲ καὶ παρὰ
Ῥοδίων καὶ παρὰ Σμυρναίων καὶ σχεδὸν τῶν ἐπὶ τάδε τοῦ Ταύρου
πάντων τῶν κατοικούντων ἐθνῶν καὶ πολιτευμάτων ἐπρέσβευον εἰς τὴν
Ῥώμην. L. does not mention the Rhodian and Smyrnan delegations, despite their later prominence in the narrative.

46–47. *Events in Rome*

46. 1–6. *Return of Minucius and Glabrio*

46. 1. Q. Minucius ex Liguribus: Q. Minucius Thermus (65),
consul in 193 (cf. xxxii. 27. 8 n.). He had been in Liguria since then
(xxxiv. 55. 6, 56. 3–7, xxxv. 3. 1–6, 6. 1–4, 11, 20. 6, 21. 7–11,
xxxvi. 38. 1–4). His claim to a triumph was attacked by Cato (*ORF*[3],
frs. 58–63). Cato's hostility is to be connected with the fact that
Thermus is a supporter of the Scipios (cf. xxxi. 4. 4 n.) and the
episode forms a prelude to the major series of attacks on the Scipios
and their friends in the coming years (cf. McDonald, *JRS* xxviii
[1938], 161, Scullard, *RP*[2], 133–4: *contra* Astin, *Cato*, 69 ff.).

2–6. An extract from the *tabula triumphalis* of Glabrio is quoted (as
a Saturnian) by Caesius Bassus (*GL* vi. 265) *fundit fugat prosternit
maximas legiones*. He also quotes from that of Aemilius Regillus (cf.
58. 3) *duello magno dirimendo regibus subigendis*. L. himself quotes (as
prose) the *tabulae* dedicated in temples by Regillus (xl. 52. 5–6) and
Ti. Sempronius Gracchus (xli. 28. 8 ff.), the opening of the former
being identical with the line quoted by Bassus. Cf. Harris, 261.

3. tetrachmum: Bekker, *tetracmum* BNVP, *tetractnum* A, *detracmum*
E, *tetracinum* L. For the genitive plural in -*um* cf. 59. 4, xxxix. 7. 1.
The former passage has *Atticorum*, the latter again *Atticum*. At 58. 4,

however, *tetrachma Attica* occurs in apposition to *milia*. Cf. Neue-Wagener, i. 171.

cistophori: it should probably be taken as a nominative, in apposition to the numeral, as at 58. 4 and perhaps xxxix. 7. 1, rather than a genitive with *argenti* understood, as W–M suggest. Cistophori, however, did not exist at this period and like the comments on the relation of the tetradrachm and the *denarius* at xxxiv. 52. 4, the statement must be regarded as an analistic anachronism. Cf. xxxiv. 52. 4 n., Thomsen, *Early Roman Coinage*, ii. 146–8.

4. suppellectilem: the first syllable is short in verse and we must therefore write *supellex*.

coronas ... ciuitatium: cf. xxxviii. 37. 4, xxxix. 7. 1, F. Millar, *The Emperor in the Roman World* (London, 1977), 141, xxxvi. 35. 12 n.

sex et triginta: there were originally 43 (3. 8). Clearly some had died, and W–M's alternative explanation of a different source is quite unnecessary (cf. p. 3).

duxit: B, *ducit* χ. The historic present is not appropriate in a triumph report.

5. Damocritus: cf. xxxv. 12. 6 n. For his capture see xxxvi. 24. 12.

6. milites ... defuerunt: because Glabrio's army had passed directly to Lucius Scipio. On occasions a triumph was refused on the grounds that the army had not been brought home. Cf. J. S. Richardson, *JRS* lxv (1975), 61.

46. 7–8. *News from Spain*

7. huius ... laetitiam: cf. p. 14.

Bastetanis: *Vastetanis* Bχ. They must be the Bastetani mentioned by other writers, but what L. wrote is uncertain. They lived in south-west Spain, to the east of Gades. Cf. p. 36, Hübner, *RE*, iii. 113, Schulten, *FHA*, iii. 199–200, Walbank, *Commentary*, i. 362.

L. Aemilii: (114). Paullus. Cf. xxxvi. 2. 6. For his subsequent victory in Spain cf. 57. 5–6, 58. 5. Plutarch (*Paull.* 4. 3) converts this defeat into a victory, Orosius iv. 20. 23 says that Paullus' army was destroyed by the Lusitanians. (Schlag [39] strangely assigns the victory to 191.)

proconsulis: cf. vol. i, 5, *MRR*, supp. 3–4.

Lyconem: cf. xxxv. 7. 7 n.

Romano exercitu: Bχ, *exercitu Romano* Mg. At first sight the latter seems preferable, for there is no point in emphasizing that it is the Roman army. But *Romanus exercitus* occurs elsewhere without emphasis on *Romanus* (cf. e.g. xxv. 25. 4, xxxvi. 16. 3, xliii. 23. 5) and it is perhaps more likely that it was altered in Mg to the more usual word-order.

8. in modum: Mg, *ad modum* Bχ. *quem ad modum* apart, *ad modum* is not used by L. and does not appear in prose before Quintilian. *in modum* with the genitive is common in L. (Packard, ii. 1097–8). *TLL*, viii. 1271–2 misleadingly omits L.'s usage of *in modum*.

46. 9–47. 2. *Supplementation of Placentia and Cremona: foundation of Bononia*

For supplementation of colonies cf. xxxi. 49. 6 n. The present case is an especially large supplement: cf. Salmon, *Colonization*, 171 n. 48. There is no need to think that *taedio accolarum Gallorum* refers only to the period before the victory of 191 (xxxvi. 38. 5) as W–M argue. The inhabitants may still not have enjoyed having Gauls for neighbours.

9. L. Aurunculeius: the *praetor urbanus*. Cf. xxxvi. 45. 9 n.

10. aliis … aliis … reliquisse: I can see no parallel for this change of construction.

  M. Atilius Serranus: (68). Praetor in 174, with command prorogued in 173.

  L. Valerius P. f. Flaccus: (173). The consul of 195. Cf. xxxi. 4. 5 n., where this appointment is omitted.

  L. Valerius C. f. Tappo: (350). Cf. xxxiv. 1. 2 n. Notice that the consular is not listed first. G. V. Sumner, *AJPh* xcvi (1975), 321 ff. wrongly uses the order of names at xxxi. 4. 3 as an argument for doubting the commonly accepted identifications. See 57. 7 n.

47. 1. rediit: *redit* Bχ, probably rightly. Cf. p. 12.

2. nouae … duae: in the event only one, at Bononia, was founded, probably because insufficient settlers could be found.

47. 3–5. *News from Asia*

3. eodem tempore: the battle of Myonnesus took place in September 190, and there is no difficulty about news of it reaching Rome before the end of the consular year. But the army did not cross the Hellespont until the Roman month of March (cf. 33. 6–7 n.) and it is hard to see how news of this could have reached Rome before the elections, even if they did take place on the last day of the consular year (cf. §§ 6–7 n.). Balsdon (*Historia* xxi [1972], 227) strangely thought that Scipio had 'dawdled' behind the rest of the army.

4. supplicatio: a combination of a *supplicatio* as a thank-offering and one as a prayer for the future: cf. xxxi. 8. 2, 22. 1 nn.

5. maioribus hostiis: cf. xxxi. 5. 3 n.

47. 6–8. *Elections*

6–7. *Consular elections.* There were three candidates for the patrician place, but M. Fulvius Nobilior seems to have had no (or at least no serious) opposition for the plebeian place, and he was elected immediately. The three patrician candidates divided the vote, and none obtained an over-all majority of the *centuriae*. Hence the bottom candidate, M. Valerius Messalla, retired and the contest was now between Cn. Manlius Vulso and M. Aemilius Lepidus. Under Fulvius' presidency, it seems, Manlius was elected. The passage is the prime example of the fact that if no one candidate secured an over-all majority of the voting units, a second election had to be held. Although L. does not say so here, it is clear from later passages that Fulvius in fact worked for the defeat of Lepidus (cf. xxxviii. 35. 1, 43. 1). For their subsequent enmity see xxxviii. 42. 9 ff., xxxix. 4–5, *Latomus* xxvii (1968), 149 n. 3.

If Fulvius presided over the election of his colleague, it follows that the elections took place on *pr. Id. Mart.*, the very last day of the consular year. This is somewhat odd, and it is possible that L. is wrong in saying that Fulvius presided over the election. I see no justification for the view of Mommsen (*StR*, i³. 217 n. 4), followed by Rilinger, *Der Einfluss des Wahlleiters bei den römischen Konsulwahlen von 366 bis 50 v. Chr.* (Munich, 1976), 18 n. 42, that Fulvius was elected under the presidency of an interrex. The MSS. in fact read *duxit collegam,* but this cannot possibly mean 'he took as his colleague' and the normal emendation to *dixit* must be right. But *dixit* merely means that Fulvius announced Manlius as the winner, not that he 'co-opted' him without an election, as Scullard, *RP²*, 135 n. 4, D. C. Earl, *Tiberius Gracchus, a Study in Politics* (Brussels, 1963), 13, believe. Cf. vii. 24. 11, U. Hall, *Athenaeum* n.s. l (1972), 11 n. 18.

6. quod ... reliquisset: cf. xxxi. 48. 2 n. His command in Sicily had not been prorogued for 190 (cf. 2. 8). Either his successor had arrived late (W–M) or perhaps he had in fact been assigned command over the part of Sicily held by L. Valerius Tappo in 191 (cf. xxxvi. 2. 11 n., *MRR*, i. 357).

7. M. Fuluius Nobilior: (91). Cf. xxxiii. 42. 8 n.

Cn. Manlius ⟨Vulso⟩: (91). Cf. xxxiii. 25. 1 n. It is unlikely that L. would have omitted the *cognomen* here.

M. Valerius Messalla: (252). Cf. xxxiv. 54. 2 n.

deiecto: cf. iii. 35. 9, iv. 44. 5, xxxviii. 35. 1, xxxix. 41. 1, xl. 46. 14, E. Dutoit, *Hommages Herrmann* (Brussels, 1960), 335.

iacuit: i.e. did not compete in the second election, not, as W–M imply, obtained only a few votes in it. For *iacere* of lack of electoral success cf. Cic. *Mur.* 45, *off.* iii. 79, Asc. p. 82. 17C.

8. duo ... Pictor: on Q. Fabius Labeo (91) cf. xxxiii. 42. 2 n. Q. Fabius Pictor (127) is known only as praetor in 189 and *flamen Quirinalis*. H. B. Mattingly's suggestion (*LCM* i [1976], 4) that this Pictor is the first Roman historian, and that he wrote in Latin, can be rejected out of hand.

flamen Quirinalis: one of the three major *flamines*, together with the *Dialis* and the *Martialis*. Cf. Samter, *RE*, vi. 2484 ff., Weinstock, 306.

M. Sempronius Tuditanus: (95). Cf. xxxv. 7. 5 n.

Sp. Postumius Albinus: (44). The consul of 186, he had perhaps been curule aedile in 191. He was an augur from 184 until his death in 180.

L. Plautius Hypsaeus: (19). Known only from this praetorship and its prorogation in 188.

L. Baebius Dives: (25). Probably to be identified with the *legatus* of 203 (*MRR*, i. 315 n. 8, Walbank, *Commentary*, ii. 442).

189 B.C.

48–59. *Events in Rome*

48. *A story in Valerius Antias*

On the relation of Antias' report to the different versions of the capture of Africanus' son cf. 34. 4 n. It should be stressed that Antias was only reporting a *rumor* at Rome, not vouching for its accuracy and it cannot be excluded that such rumours were circulating both in Aetolia and at Rome (cf. Gabba, *Athenaeum* n.s. liii [1975], 10). L.'s words at the end of the chapter are a suspension of judgement on the existence of the rumour, not, of course, on the facts.

The story is remarkably similar to that of the death of Crassus in 53, but that should be regarded as a coincidence, not used as an additional argument for dating Antias in the Ciceronian period. (On that matter see Ogilvie, 12–13: *contra* J. D. Cloud, *LCM* ii [1977], 205–13, 225–7.)

48. 1. M. Fuluio ... consulibus: the standard way of beginning the narrative of a fresh year. It is perfectly natural here, and not

inconsistent with the statement that the election of Manlius took
place on Fulvius' first day in office (as W–M say in commenting on
postero die at 47. 7).

    celebrem: cf. pp. 4, 8.

2–3. et ipsos . . . et ducibus . . . eaque expugnata et deletas:
one wonders whether this rather artless polysyndeton is a deliberate
reflection of the style of Antias. (Cf. p. 10.)

4. ob haec . . . facere: in fact, of course, there is only a truce with
the Aetolians and no orders exist to be disobeyed.

5. A. Terentium Varronem: (80). For his true role cf. 49. 8. He
was praetor in 184 with command prorogued in 183–2, a *legatus*
to Illyria in 172, and a member of the commission to administer the
settlement after the Third Macedonian War. He was perhaps the
son of the consul of 216 (Münzer, *RE*, vA. 678).

6. M. Claudium Lepidum: (204). Almost certainly a non-person.
The name could be explained only as an Aemilius Lepidus adopted
by a Claudius (? a Marcellus). That would be a very strange adop-
tion at this time, and since there is no other trace of such a person,
he is best consigned to limbo.

    A. Cornelio propraetore: (258). Mammula. Cf. p. 38, xxxv.
24. 6 n.

6. subtexit: Bχ. *adiecit* Mg, a clear gloss. Cf. pp. 6, 8.

    legatos Aetolos: cf. 49. 1. On *Aetolos* cf. xxxv. 46. 3 n.

49. *Aetolian embassy*

The close agreement between L. and Diodorus xxix. 9 would appear
to show that Polybius is the source of at least §§ 1–7. Nissen (*KU*,
198), however, argued that § 8 is annalistic, as it is inconsistent with
a later passage of Polybius. That is, however, explicable (cf. n. ad
loc.). Nor is anything proved by the mention of Varro. His presence
in Antias' story (48. 5) could be based on the part he actually played
in the reception of the Aetolian envoys (for *tria nomina* in Polybian
passages of L. cf. 14. 1, xxxvi. 17. 1). On the other hand we cannot
exclude the possibility that both L. and Diodorus used a source
other than L. (cf. p. 2 n. 2) and the whole question is best left open.
(Walbank, *Philip V*, 212 labels the passage (P), but at 332 it has
become (A): Tränkle, 27–8 n. 10 denies Polybian origin.)

    On the language of §§ 1–3 cf. xxxvi. 27. 6–7 n., on the date of the
episode § 6 n.

49. 2. Philippo: a misprint for Philippi.

4. permitterentne ... essent: cf. 1. 5 nn.
   templo: probably the temple of Bellona. Cf. xxx. 21. 12, 40. 1, xxxiii. 24. 5, xlii. 36. 2, P–A, 83.

5. perdomandosque ... esse: Bχ. The emphatic position of *feroces* is preferable, but Mg's asyndeton could be right (cf. p. 11).

6. Dolopiae ... Athamaniae: the events described in xxxviii. 1–3. 8. They took place in December 190–January 189 (cf. Walbank, *Philip V*, 332), and cannot have been known in Rome at the very beginning of the consular year (cf. p. 25). Either the episode is misplaced or the charge was not in fact made. But in any case the Aetolians had been kept waiting a long time for an audience. For another instance of Aetolian ambassadors being detained in Rome cf. xxvi. 24. 15, for Achaean ambassadors—though after the senate had received them—Polybius xxiii. 9. 14.

7. quintum decimum: cf. appendix.

8. When the Aetolians send a further embassy (xxxviii. 3. 7, Pol. xxi. 25. 11) no request is sought for the consul's permission, and no hostile action taken by the senate. But it may be that Fulvius' permission was in fact obtained, or the senate may just have ignored its previous decision. There is no need to doubt the fact of the present decision, or to hold that it cannot have stood in Polybius.

50. *Provinces and armies*

50. 1–2. placuit; qui Asiam ... exercitus ei: om. *placuit* B, om. *placuit qui Asiam* χ (*qui Asiam* P³, Aᶻ, Emg). B has ȧ before *qui* but it would be hazardous to see this as evidence for an *et* before *qui* and use it as an argument for transposing *ei* to precede *qui* (a transposition made by Madvig, *Emendationes*, 533 n. 1). In the deliberately annalistic style of this passage, the position of *ei* is far from impossible.
   For the political significance of the immediate supersession of the Scipios cf. *Latomus* xxvii (1968), 149 n. 3.

3. octo: Mg, *sex* BPELV (om. *Romanorum ... peditum* AN). Either is possible: on the ratio of allied to Roman cavalry in this period cf. Brunt, 683.
   ut bellum: Mg, om. *ut* Bχ, perhaps correctly.

4. exercitus ... Aetolia: under A. Cornelius Mammula (2. 7–8). See p. 38.
   in supplementum: Bχ. L. uses both *in supplementum* and *sup-*

plementum in apposition to the troops involved (Packard, iv. 847). There is no reason why he should not have alternated between the two idioms here and W–M's deletion of *et* is quite unjustified.

5. The notice should probably be rejected, since the 18 ships left at Cephallenia (2. 10 n.) were sufficient for Fulvius' purposes. Cf. De Sanctis, iv. 1. 211 n. 154, Thiel, 263.

naues ... erant: 4. 5.
Cephallaniam: cf. xxxvi. 11. 9 n.

6. ut ... ut: cf. xxxvi. 1. 7 n.
ueniret: Bχ, *rediret* Mg. Either is possible.

7. placere creari: perhaps the phrase should be seen as evidence that though censors were normally elected every five years, it was the custom for the senate to vote to hold a censorial election.

8. urbanam ... peregrinos: cf. xxxi. 6. 2 n.

9. legio ... Siculis: cf. 2. 8, xxxv. 23. 6 n., xxxvi. 2. 12 n.

11. W–M's note is totally wrong. The Baebius of xxxv. 20. 8 is a different person and the man involved at 2. 11 is C. Flaminius.

Hispaniam: the addition of *ulteriorem* (Wesenberg) has a lot to be said for it.

Latini nominis: without implying that non-Latin *socii* are excluded. Cf. xxii. 7. 5, xxx. 43. 13, xxxix. 20. 1, Wegner, 103.

12. ducenti ... nominis: Mg, om. Bχ (the reports in W–M and Zingerle are totally wrong). There are no Roman cavalry (cf. § 3 n.).
singulas legiones: those already there (cf. p. 38).

13. magistratibus ... prorogatum ... prorogatum et: I find it hard to believe that L. wrote this. I would prefer to delete *prioris anni magistratibus* as a gloss, rather than the second *prorogatum*, with W–M.

C. Laelio: in Northern Italy (1. 10).
P. Iunio: cf. 2. 1, 9.
M. Tuccio ... Apulia: cf. 2. 1, 6.

51. 1–6. *Dispute between the* pontifex maximus *and the* flamen Quirinalis

(i) *Procedure.* Similar disputes, with similar results, are recorded in 180 (xl. 42. 8 ff.), 159 (*per.* xlvii), 131 (Cic. *Phil.* xi. 18), and at an unknown date (Fest. pp. 462–4L). In two of them we also have reference to *prouocatio.* This is not the place for a discussion of the whole issue of what is meant by *prouocatio,* and, in any case, it would be rash to argue from these cases of fines imposed by a *pontifex maximus* to capital cases, the chief field for the operation of *prouocatio*. In the present instance, like that in 180, it seems that the order not to go abroad, and the fine, were imposed by the *pontifex maximus* in virtue of his own authority over the *flamines*. The person fined called on the tribunes and the case was eventually decided by the *comitia* (probably the tribal assembly: cf. xl. 42. 10 *tribus*, though for *tribus* used of the voting units in the *comitia centuriata* cf. Staveley, *AJPh* lxxiv [1953], 16 ff.). Whether the appeal was made directly to the people by Fabius by virtue of an individual's right of *prouocatio*, or by the tribunes laying the matter before the assembly cannot be determined.

For discussion see Bleicken, *Hermes* lxxxv (1957), 446 ff., *ZRG* lxxvi (1959), 341 ff., Kunkel, *ABAW* n.f. lvi, 23, J.-C. Richard, *Latomus* xxvii (1968), 786 ff., A. H. M. Jones, *The Criminal Courts of the Roman Republic and Principate* (Oxford, 1972), 10, A. W. Lintott, *ANRW*, i. 2. 244–5.

(ii) *Political importance*. Crassus is a supporter of the Scipios (xxxi. 9. 7 n.) and it is plausible to regard the Fabii as Fulvians at this time: the completely undeserved triumph of Labeo (60. 6 n.) makes sense on that hypothesis, though adherence to Cato cannot be excluded. Crassus' action should therefore be added to the other instances of his using his position as *pontifex maximus* against his political opponents. Cf. p. 23.

51. 1. pontificem maximum: *maximum pontificem* Bχ. The latter order is attested also at xxvii. 6. 17 and should be retained here.

Pictorem: *praetorem* Bχ. The apposition is not impossible in itself and L. does not give the *cognomen* for the *pontifex maximus* but the contrast in §§ 2–3 *consulem . . . praetorem* would be spoilt by *praetorem* here and the assumed corruption is very easy.

patrum memoria: 'as their ancestors remembered', not 'as the senators remembered'. Cf. xxxi. 12. 10 n.

L. Metellum: (72). L. Caecilius Metellus, consul in 251, with command prorogued in 250, *magister equitum* in 249, consul again in 247, dictator in 224, and *pontifex maximus* from 243 until his death in 221.

Postumium Albinum: (30). A. Postumius Albinus, consul in 242 and censor in 234. For his dispute with Metellus cf. *per.* xix, Tac. *A.* iii. 71. 3, Val. Max. i. 1. 2. It is uncertain whether or not this case, like its successors, also led to a comitial vote and a compromise. Cf. Bleicken, op. cit., 50, Richard, op. cit., 787. The MSS. omit Postumius' *praenomen* but L. would surely have given it on such an occasion.

2. C. Lutatio: (4). Catulus, consul in 242, when he won the victory of the Aegates Isles which brought the First Punic War to an end.

2–3. illum ... hunc: for this inversion of the normal connotation of *hic ... ille* cf. *TLL*, vi. 3. 2715. 40 ff., H–S, 182.

  ad sacra: the restrictions on the *flamines Quirinalis* and *Martialis* were gradually relaxed in the course of time. Cf. Samter, *RE*, vi. 2486, 2490, Serv. *ad. Aen.* viii. 552.

3–4. L. evokes the excitement of the conflict with the sixfold repetition of *et* in one sentence (the effect is quite different from that at 48. 23: cf. n. ad loc.). It is not clear whether he intends the items to be in chronological order, and whether there are thus two occasions when the matter is put before the people. The probability is that he does not, and that either L. is merely summarizing the episode n the opening phrase, or the first *ad populum* refers only to a *contio*.

4. imperia: there is no evidence for the *pontifex maximus* possessing *imperium* as such and Kunkel (op. cit., 22 n. 49) argued that *imperia* refers to consuls and praetors intervening on different sides. But the *pontifex maximus* had authority over the *flamines* and L. could well have described this as *imperium*. Cf. Bleicken, op. cit., 451 n. 2.

  inhibita: cf. p. 5.

  pignera: pledges for payment of the fine if it were ratified: cf. xliii. 16. 5.

  multae dictae: prima facie this should be taken as a rhetorical plural, not, with W–M, as referring to mutual fines imposed by Fabius and Crassus on each other. But at § 5 Bχ read *multae ex iussu populi remissae*, which has been rejected by editors in favour of Mg's *multa iussu populi ei remissa*. But it is possible that the plural is right (though *ex iussu* cannot stand, and it is certainly plausible to see it as a transposed corruption of Mg's *ei*), in which case W–M's interpretation of this passage would be correct. (They read the singular at § 5 and strangely take it to mean that the fine imposed on Crassus was remitted.) Cf. Bleicken, op. cit., 452.

  tribuni appellati: I cannot follow Bleicken's argument (op. cit., 463 n. 2) that the tribunes could not have been responsible for the eventual compromise, as they had no concern with sacral matters. The whole episode, as Bleicken himself shows, is a conflict between sacral and political forces.

5. ut ... iussus: the text is perfectly acceptable and there is no case for alteration to *et ... esse* (Frob. 2). For the formal phrase *dicto audiens* (+ dative) see G. W. Williams, *Hermes* lxxxvi (1958), 97 n. 1, Ogilvie, 636, Packard, i. 1239.

51. 8—56. *Senatorial decisions on the settlement in Asia*

See Pol. xxi. 18–24, Diod. xxix. 11, App. *Syr.* 39. At the end of this
section (cf. 55. 4–56. 6 n.) it is clear that L. has supplemented
Polybius from an annalistic source and at the beginning he has
blended together Polybian and annalistic material (cf. p. 2).
Nissen (*KU*, 198) placed a dividing line after 52. 6, but that section
is as close to Polybius as much else that is clearly of Polybian origin.
The details in § 2 are clearly non-Polybian, the contents of § 3 cannot have stood in Polybius (cf. n. ad loc.), and what follows has all
the appearance of being another version of Eumenes' assumed
reluctance to speak, repeated in the Polybian account in 52. 6–10.
Given this situation, we must reckon with the possibility that L.'s
deviations from Polybius in the rest of the account come directly
from his annalistic source and are not his own inventions.

51. 9. tantum . . . quam: cf. vi. 9. 9, vii. 15. 10, xxvi. 1. 3, xxxviii.
34. 9, K–St, ii. 459.

ab: 'after': cf. xxxvi. 24. 8 n.

a uetere fama: Rubens, *auerterunt fama* BNV, *auerterunt famam*
φL. For explanation of the corruption cf. W. Heraeus, *Quaestiones
criticae et palaeographicae de uetustissimis codicibus Liuianis* (Berlin, 1885),
80.

rectorem: for *rector* in this sense cf. Adams, *Glotta* li (1973), 131.

10. nihil . . . metu: a combination of *nihil aut de consule mittendo aut
de minuendis eius copiis mutandum* (cf. xxiii. 28. 1) and *nec tamen de
consule mittendo mutandum nec minuendas eius copias*. It is more difficult
than the cases in which L. places a disjunctive particle inside one
of the disjoined clauses (cf. 19. 2 n.) and it would be simple to
delete the first *aut*. But in view of other changes of construction
(cf. 7. 3, 46. 10, xxxv. 20. 7, xxxvi. 11. 2, xxxvii. 7. 3 nn.) I would
prefer to retain the transmitted text.

ne . . . bellandum: perhaps more an anticipation of what actually happened than a real motive. The senate may not have been
certain that peace would be concluded with Antiochus. T. Lieb-
mann-Frankfort, *La Frontière orientale dans la politique extérieure de la
République romaine* (Brussels, 1969), 55 ff. argues unconvincingly that
the senate had already decided to suppress the Galatians.

52. 1. Pol. xxi. 18. 1: ἤδη τῆς θερείας ἐνισταμένης μετὰ τὴν νίκην τῶν
Ῥωμαίων τὴν πρὸς Ἀντίοχον παρῆν ὅ τε βασιλεὺς Εὐμένης οἵ τε παρ'
Ἀντιόχου πρέσβεις οἵ τε παρὰ τῶν Ῥοδίων. L. omits Polybius' mention
of the delegations from the cities of Asia (xxi. 18. 1–2).

haud multo post: in fact in early summer (Pol., loc. cit., Walbank, *Commentary*, iii. 111).

M. Aurelius Cotta: not otherwise known.

2. in triduum: cf. xxxi. 22. 1 n.

3. quod ... uindicassent: in fact the Romans played no direct part in the relief of Pergamum, though the arrival of their fleet contributed to Antiochus' decision to withdraw (cf. 21. 4 n.). There is no possibility of an omission by the excerptor of Polybius (cf. xxi. 18. 4: ἐπειδὴ δ' ὁ τῆς ἐντεύξεως καιρὸς ἦλθεν, εἰσεκαλέσαντο πρῶτον τὸν βασιλέα καὶ λέγειν ἠξίουν μετὰ παρρησίας ὧν βούλεται τυχεῖν παρὰ τῆς συγκλήτου) and it must be assigned to an annalistic source.

fratrem: despite other references to Eumenes' brothers in the plural (he had three: cf. xxxiii. 21. 4 n.) emendation to *fratres* is unwise, particularly as the passage is of annalistic origin.

terra marique: B, *mari terraque* χ. Unlike 11. 9 (cf. n. ad loc.) there is no point here in departing from the normal word-order.

5. sua ... suis ... se: *sua* and *se* refer to Eumenes, *suis* to the Romans.

cognoscere: Frob. 2, *cognosci* Bχ. *imperatoribus suis* excludes the possibility (suggested by Weissenborn) of deleting *eos*.

6. Pol. xxi. 18. 4, quoted above, xxi. 18. 7: διότι πρόκειται τῇ συγκλήτῳ πᾶν αὐτῷ χαρίζεσθαι τὸ δυνατόν.

approbantibus cunctis: cf. 16. 3 n.

propensius: the adverb occurs elsewhere only in Lentulus *ap.* Cic. *fam.* xii. 15. 3 (*TLL*).

cumulatius: *cumulate* 'abundantly' occurs 29 times in Cicero, only here in L., and nowhere else in republican or Augustan Latin. Cf. *TLL*, iv. 1384–5.

7–8. Pol. xxi. 18. 5–6: εἰ καὶ παρ' ἑτέρων τυχεῖν τινος ἐβούλετο φιλανθ-ρώπου, 'Ρωμαίοις ἂν ἐχρήσατο συμβούλοις πρὸς τὸ μήτ' ἐπιθυμεῖν μηδενὸς παρὰ τὸ δέον μήτ' ἀξιοῦν μηδ' ἐν πέρα τοῦ καθήκοντος· ὁπότε δ' αὐτῶν πάρεστι δεόμενος 'Ρωμαίων, ἄριστον εἶναι νομίζει τὸ διδόναι τὴν ἐπιτροπὴν ἐκείνοις καὶ περὶ αὐτοῦ καὶ περὶ τῶν ἀδελφῶν.

7. posset: Bχ. *possit* Mg, perhaps rightly. Cf. xxxiv. 26. 7 n.

8. uerum enim uero: cf. xxxi. 30. 4 n.

9. Pol. xxi. 18. 7–8: τῶν δὲ πρεσβυτέρων τινὸς ἀναστάντος καὶ κελεύοντος μὴ κατορρωδεῖν, ἀλλὰ λέγειν τὸ φαινόμενον ... ἔμεινεν ἐπὶ τῆς αὐτῆς γνώμης, χρόνου δ' ἐγγινομένου ὁ μὲν βασιλεὺς ἐξεχώρησεν. There is clearly abbreviation by the excerptor of Polybius (denied by Tränkle, 111) but even so L. has probably adapted considerably.

facilitate: 'courteousness'.
ex templo: B, *templo* χ. Cf. xxxv. 4. 4 n.

10. Pol. xxi. 18. 8–9: ἡ δὲ ἐντὸς ἐβουλεύετο τί δεῖ ποιεῖν. ἔδοξεν οὖν τὸν Εὐμένη παρακαλεῖν αὐτὸν ὑποδεικνύναι θαρροῦντα περὶ ὧν πάρεστιν· καὶ γὰρ εἰδέναι τὰ διαφέροντα τοῖς ἰδίοις πράγμασιν ἐκεῖνον ἀκριβέστερον τὰ κατὰ τὴν Ἀσίαν. It cannot be excluded that something corresponding to *ut . . . uenerit* also stood in Polybius.
accommodata: 'suited to'. Cf. xxxviii. 59. 1.
longe: for *longe* with the comparative cf. xxiv. 28. 5, xxxix. 31. 7, xl. 6. 7, Sall. *H.* iii. fr. 48. 9, *Bell. Alex.* 46. 4, *Bell. Hisp.* 7. 5, Virg. *A.* ix. 556, K–St, i. 403, ii. 463 n. 6, *TLL*, vii. 2. 1648. 64 ff. (wrongly including Cic. *red. Quir.* 9).
cogendum . . . expromere: stronger than in Polybius.

53–54. L. follows in essentials the order of the speeches in Polybius and Ullmann (*Technique*, 150 ff.) rightly refrains from analysis on his normal rhetorical principles (though he implausibly suggests that 54. 17–28, to which nothing corresponds in Polybius, should be divided §§ 17–22 *dignum*; §§ 23–5 *rectum*; §§ 26–7 *iustum*; § 28 *conclusio*).

The speeches in Polybius may well not represent what was actually said by Eumenes and the Rhodians, though they are not necessarily so far away from it as Bikerman, *REG* l (1937), 232–4, thought. Cf. Will, *HP*, ii. 190, Hopp, 48 n. 74, Walbank, *Commentary*, iii. 112.

53. 1. reductus . . . iussus: Pol. xxi. 18. 10: δοξάντων δὲ τούτων εἰσεκλήθη, καὶ τῶν πρεσβυτέρων τινὸς ἀποδείξαντος τὰ δεδογμένα λέγειν ἠναγκάσθη περὶ τῶν προκειμένων. L. adds a *praetore*, perhaps from his annalistic source.

1–3. perseuerassem . . . debere: Pol. xxi. 19. 1–5, 7: ἔφασκεν οὖν ἄλλο μὲν οὐδὲν ἂν εἰπεῖν περὶ τῶν καθ᾽ αὑτόν, ἀλλὰ μεῖναι . . . τελέως διδοὺς ἐκείνοις τὴν ἐξουσίαν · ἕνα δὲ τόπον ἀγωνιᾶν τὸν κατὰ τοὺς Ῥοδίους· διὸ καὶ προῆχθαι νῦν εἰς τὸ λέγειν ὑπὲρ τῶν ἐνεστώτων. ἐκείνους γὰρ παρεῖναι μὲν οὐδὲν ἧττον ὑπὲρ τῆς σφετέρας πατρίδος συμφερόντως σπουδάζοντας ἤπερ αὐτοὺς ὑπὲρ τῆς ἰδίας ἀρχῆς φιλοτιμεῖσθαι κατὰ τὸ παρόν· τοὺς δὲ λόγους αὐτῶν τὴν ἐναντίαν ἔμφασιν ἔχειν τῇ προθέσει τῇ κατὰ τὴν ἀλήθειαν. τοῦτο δ᾽ εἶναι ῥᾴδιον καταμαθεῖν. ἐρεῖν μὲν γὰρ αὐτούς, ἐπειδὰν εἰσπορευθῶσιν, διότι πάρεισιν οὔτε παρ᾽ ὑμῶν αἰτούμενοι τὸ παράπαν οὐδὲν οὔθ᾽ ἡμᾶς βλάπτειν θέλοντες κατ᾽ οὐδένα τρόπον, πρεσβεύονται δὲ περὶ τῆς ἐλευθερίας τῶν τὴν Ἀσίαν κατοικούντων Ἑλλήνων. . . .
ἡ μὲν οὖν διὰ τῶν λόγων φαντασία τοιαύτη τις αὐτῶν ἔσται· τὰ δὲ κατὰ τὴν ἀλήθειαν τὴν ἐναντίαν ἔχοντα τούτοις εὑρεθήσεται διάθεσιν.

L. is briefer, but *quod ea . . . me sit* does not correspond to anything in Polybius.

2. quod ea: Mg, A , *quod* Bψ, *quidem qui* A, PE. I would prefer to keep *quod,* clearly the reading of F. *ea* has no reference.

3–4. quo impetrato . . . habituri sint: Pol. xxi. 19. 8–10: τῶν γὰρ πόλεων ἐλευθερωθεισῶν, ὡς αὐτοὶ παρακαλοῦσιν, τὴν μὲν τούτων συμβήσεται δύναμιν αὐξηθῆναι πολλαπλασίως, τὴν δ' ἡμετέραν τρόπον τινὰ καταλυθῆναι. τὸ γὰρ τῆς ἐλευθερίας ὄνομα καὶ τῆς αὐτονομίας ἡμῖν μὲν ἄρδην ἀποσπάσει πάντας οὐ μόνον τοὺς νῦν ἐλευθερωθησομένους, ἀλλὰ καὶ τοὺς πρότερον ἡμῖν ὑποταττομένους, ἐπειδὰν ὑμεῖς ἐπὶ ταύτης ὄντες φανεροὶ γένησθε τῆς προαιρέσεως, τούτοις δὲ προσθήσει πάντας. τὰ γὰρ πράγματα φύσιν ἔχει τοιαύτην· δόξαντες γὰρ ἠλευθερῶσθαι διὰ τούτους ὀνόματι μὲν ἔσονται σύμμαχοι τούτων, τῇ δ' ἀληθείᾳ πᾶν ποιήσουσι τὸ κελευόμενον ἑτοίμως, τῇ μεγίστῃ χάριτι γεγονότες ὑπόχρεοι.

3. ueteres stipendiarias: on the Attalid tributaries cf. 55. 6, 55. 4–56. 6 n.

5. Pol. xxi. 19. 6: τοῦτο δ' οὐχ οὕτως αὐτοῖς εἶναι κεχαρισμένον φήσουσιν ὡς ὑμῖν καθῆκον τοῖς γεγονόσιν ἔργοις ἀκόλουθον. L. alters the position of the sentiment.

affectabunt: in the sense of 'strive for' *affectare* occurs first in Sallust, once in Nepos, and frequently in L. Cf. *TLL*, i. 1181. 43 ff.

6. Pol. xxi. 19. 11–12: διόπερ, ὦ ἄνδρες, ἀξιοῦμεν ὑμᾶς τοῦτον τὸν τόπον ὑπιδέσθαι, μὴ λάθητε τοὺς μὲν παρὰ τὸ δέον αὔξοντες, τοὺς δ' ἐλαττοῦντες τῶν φίλων ἀλόγως, ἅμα δὲ τούτοις τοὺς μὲν πολεμίους γεγονότας εὐεργετοῦντες, τοὺς δ' ἀληθινοὺς φίλους παρορῶντες καὶ κατολιγωροῦντες τούτων.

inaequaliter: not found before L., who uses it also at xxviii. 20. 3. Cf. *TLL*, vii. 1. 811. 61 ff., p. 9.

qui . . . uestri: illogical, because Eumenes has just argued that the states which are freed will become *de facto* subjects of Rhodes. It is the difference of treatment, not of ultimate position, that is emphasized by Polybius.

et (amici): ed. Ald., *aut* Bχ. The disjunctive is quite inappropriate in this formulaic phrase.

7. quod ad . . . possum: Pol. xxi. 20. 1: ἐγὼ δὲ περὶ μὲν τῶν ἄλλων, ὅτου δέοι, παντὸς ⟨ἂν⟩ παραχωρήσαιμι τοῖς πέλας ἀφιλονίκως, περὶ δὲ τῆς ὑμετέρας φιλίας καὶ τῆς εἰς ὑμᾶς εὐνοίας ἁπλῶς οὐδέποτ' ἂν οὐδενὶ τῶν ὄντων ἐκχωρήσαιμι κατὰ δύναμιν. L. elaborates considerably. *honoris . . . habebitur* has nothing corresponding to it in Polybius.

uestrae: Bχ, *nostrae* Mg. *uestrae* is guaranteed by τῆς ὑμετέρας φιλίας in Polybius.

7–8. hanc ego . . . perduxit: Pol. xxi. 20. 2–3: δοκῶ δὲ καὶ τὸν πατέρα τὸν ἡμέτερον, εἴπερ ἔζη, τὴν αὐτὴν ἂν προέσθαι φωνὴν ἐμοί. καὶ γὰρ ἐκεῖνος, πρῶτος μετασχὼν τῆς ὑμετέρας φιλίας καὶ συμμαχίας, σχεδὸν πάντων [κατὰ] τὴν Ἀσίαν καὶ τὴν Ἑλλάδα νεμομένων, εὐγενέστατα διεφύλαξε ταύτην ἕως τῆς τελευταίας ἡμέρας. L. changes Eumenes' statement that Attalus would have taken the same view into one that he inherited his attitude from Attalus.

7. primus . . . uestram: by omitting σχέδον L. has converted an exaggeration into a falsehood. The Aetolians had a full *foedus* with Rome before Attalus participated in the First Macedonian War, and Rhodes and the Ptolemies had long been *amici* (cf. xxxi. 2. 1–2, 4 nn.).

8. uitae finem: B, *finem uitae* χ. B's word-order, determined by the position of *extremam* and L.'s desire to enclose the genitive, is clearly right (cf. Adams, *IF* lxxxi [1976], 80).

9. Pol. xxi. 20. 3–4: οὐ μόνον κατὰ τὴν προαίρεσιν, ἀλλὰ καὶ κατὰ τὰς πράξεις. πάντων γὰρ ὑμῖν ἐκοινώνησε τῶν κατὰ τὴν Ἑλλάδα πολέμων καὶ πλείστας μὲν εἰς τούτους καὶ πεζικὰς καὶ ναυτικὰς δυνάμεις παρέσχετο τῶν ἄλλων συμμάχων, πλείστην δὲ συνεβάλετο χορηγίαν καὶ μεγίστους ὑπέμεινε κινδύνους. L. does not mention the Attalid forces and the dangers Eumenes underwent.

nec . . . uobis: Bχ, *nec dumtaxat animum . . . in uos* Mg. Both postposition and anteposition are possible with *dumtaxat* (*TLL*, v. 1. 2236 ff.). For *fidelis* with the dative cf. xxi. 61. 5, xliv. 18. 4. *fidelis in* + accusative occurs only at Sall. *Cat.* 9. 2 in republican and Augustan Latin.

omnibus . . . Graecia: cf. Walbank, *Commentary*, iii. 113.

terrestribus naualibus: cf. xxxvi. 26. 2 n.

posset: B. *possit* χ, perhaps rightly ('could not be equalled'), despite § 15 *ut nemo . . . posset*.

10. Pol. xxi. 20. 5: τέλος δ' εἰπεῖν, κατέστρεψε τὸν βίον ἐν αὐτοῖς τοῖς ἔργοις κατὰ τὸν Φιλιππικὸν πόλεμον, παρακαλῶν Βοιωτοὺς εἰς τὴν ὑμετέραν φιλίαν καὶ συμμαχίαν. For the events cf. xxxiii. 2. 2–3, 21. 1. He in fact died at Pergamum.

intermortuus: the only occurrence of the participle in L. Cf. Cic. *Att.* i. 14. 4, *Mur.* 16, *Pis.* 16, *Mil.* 12, *TLL*, vii. 1. 2230. 9 ff. *intermori* occurs at xxxiv. 49. 3 (cf. p. 5).

exspirauit: cf. p. 4.

11. Pol. xxi. 20. 6: ἐγὼ δὲ διαδεξάμενος τὴν ἀρχὴν τὴν μὲν προαίρεσιν τὴν τοῦ πατρὸς διεφύλαξα—ταύτην γὰρ οὐχ οἷόν τ' ἦν ὑπερθέσθαι. L. elaborates.

inexsuperabilia: cf. xxxvi. 17. 3 n.

12. Pol. xxi. 20. 6–7: τοῖς δὲ πράγμασιν ὑπερεθέμην. οἱ γὰρ καιροὶ τὴν ἐκ πυρὸς βάσανον ἐμοὶ μᾶλλον ἢ 'κείνῳ προσῆγον.

impensis officiorum: 'expenditure arising from my obligations'. Sage's 'expenditure of effort' is wrong.

13. Pol. xxi. 20. 8: 'Αντιόχου γὰρ σπουδάζοντος ἡμῖν θυγατέρα δοῦναι καὶ συνοικειωθῆναι τοῖς ὅλοις, διδόντος ⟨δὲ⟩ παραχρῆμα μὲν τὰς πρότερον ἀπηλλοτριωμένας ἀφ' ἡμῶν πόλεις, μετὰ δὲ ταῦτα πᾶν ὑπισχνουμένου ποιήσειν, εἰ μετάσχοιμεν τοῦ πρὸς ὑμᾶς πολέμου ... For the episode see also Appian, *Syr.* 5. 18–20. The date cannot be precisely determined.

filiam: the name of the girl is not known. She is not Laodice, as W–M say. See Schmitt, *Antiochos*, 25–6.

restituebat ... nobis: probably the coastal states captured in 197: cf. xxxiii. 38. 2 n., Schmitt, *Antiochos*, 275 n. 2, Walbank, *Commentary*, iii. 113.

amplificandi regni: Mg, *ampliandi regna* Bχ. Other than in the technical judicial sense *ampliare* is found only in *Bell. Hisp.* 42. 2, Horace, *Sat.* i. 4. 32 before the Trajanic period, while *amplificare* is common in L. (The epitomist writes *ampliatum regnum* in summarizing the senate's decision on this occasion, and uses *ampliare* on two other occasions also.) Cf. *TLL*, i. 2002. 8 ff.

14. Nothing corresponds to this in Polybius, who merely says (xxi. 20. 9) τοσοῦτον ἀπέσχομεν τοῦ προσδέξασθαί τι τούτων. Cf. Tränkle, 124.

uetustissima: exaggerated.

15. Pol. xxi. 20. 9: ὡς πλείσταις μὲν καὶ πεζικαῖς καὶ ναυτικαῖς δυνάμεσιν τῶν ἄλλων συμμάχων ἠγωνίσμεθα μεθ' ὑμῶν πρὸς Ἀντίοχον, πλείστας δὲ χορηγίας συμβεβλήμεθα πρὸς τὰς ὑμετέρας χρείας ἐν τοῖς ἀναγκαιοτάτοις καιροῖς, εἰς πάντας δὲ τοὺς κινδύνους δεδώκαμεν αὐτοὺς ἀπροφασίστως μετά γε τῶν ὑμετέρων ἡγεμόνων.

naualibus ... omnibus: L. has forgotten that Eumenes was not present at the battle of Myonnesus.

16. Pol. xxi. 20. 10: τὸ δὲ τελευταῖον ὑπεμείναμεν συγκλεισθέντες εἰς αὐτὸν τὸν Πέργαμον πολιορκεῖσθαι καὶ κινδυνεύειν ἅμα περὶ τοῦ βίου καὶ τῆς ἀρχῆς διὰ τὴν πρὸς τὸν ὑμέτερον δῆμον εὔνοιαν.

17–19. liberatus ... uoluit: an elaboration by L., taking up again the ideas in Polybius xxi. 20. 9.

17. liberatus ... occurri: in fact Antiochus and Seleucus had left Pergamum before Eumenes set out for the Hellespont. See 21. 4–22. 1, 26. 13.

relictis meis rebus: J. F. Gronovius wanted to delete *meis* because of *mei* preceding. It is far from clear what *relictis rebus* would mean.

18. posteaquam: attested four times in L. (ix. 46. 11, xxiii. 29. 17, xxvi. 31. 7).

19–20. non sum … comparare: L.'s way of introducing Eumenes' comparison of himself with other kings well treated by the senate. Cf. Tränkle, 124–5.

19. in acie … steti: cf. Ogilvie, 485.

21–22. Pol. xxi. 21. 2: εἰ Μασαννάσαν μὲν τὸν οὐ μόνον ὑπάρξαντα πολέμιον ὑμῖν, ἀλλὰ καὶ τὸ τελευταῖον καταφυγόντα πρὸς ὑμᾶς μετά τινων ἱππέων, τοῦτον, ὅτι καθ' ἕνα πόλεμον τὸν πρὸς Καρχηδονίους ἐτήρησε τὴν πίστιν, βασιλέα τῶν πλείστων μερῶν τῆς Λιβύης πεποιήκατε … L. elaborates but omits Polybius xxi. 21. 3 on Pleuratus (cf. Tränkle, 125 n. 64). On Massinissa cf. xxxi. 11. 4–18 n. He is used as an *exemplum* by the Scipios to Prusias at 25. 9–10.

21. extorris, expulsus: cf. ii. 6. 2 *extorrem, egentem.*

22. quia: *qui* Bψ, *quod* φ. A causal clause is clearly required (and cf. ὅτι in Polybius) and since *qui* is the transmitted reading, it is virtually certain that L. wrote *quia.*

Africae reges: apart from Massinissa, the only one known to have contacts with the Romans at this time is Vermina (cf. xxxi. 11. 13–18), though they probably knew something of Mauretania.

23–24. Pol. xxi. 21. 4: ἡμᾶς δὲ τοὺς διὰ προγόνων τὰ μέγιστα καὶ κάλλιστα τῶν ἔργων ὑμῖν συγκατειργασμένους παρ' οὐδὲν ποιήσεσθε. L. elaborates as a final build-up to Eumenes' statements of his requests.

25. quid … est: Pol. xxi. 21. 5–6: τί οὖν ἐστιν ὃ παρακαλῶ, καὶ τίνος φημὶ δεῖν ἡμᾶς τυγχάνειν παρ' ὑμῶν; ἐρῶ μετὰ παρρησίας, ἐπείπερ ἡμᾶς ἐξεκαλέσασθε πρὸς τὸ λέγειν ὑμῖν τὸ φαινόμενον. Polybius' makes the senate's demand that Eumenes speak into a reason for his παρρησία, while L. portrays him as still reluctant to express himself.
utique: 'in any case'.

25–26. si uos … spero: Pol. xxi. 21. 7–8: εἰ μὲν αὐτοὶ κρίνετέ τινας τόπους διακατέχειν τῆς Ἀσίας τῶν ὄντων μὲν ἐπὶ τάδε τοῦ Ταύρου, ταττομένων δὲ πρότερον ὑπ' Ἀντίοχον, τοῦτο καὶ μάλιστα βουλοίμεθ' ἂν ἰδεῖν γενόμενον· καὶ γὰρ ἀσφαλέστατα βασιλεύσειν ὑμῖν γειτνιῶντες ὑπολαμβάνομεν καὶ μάλιστα μετέχοντες τῆς ὑμετέρας ἐξουσίας.

25. emostis Antiochum: Mg, *Antiochum emostis* Bχ. Cf. p. 15.
accolas: cf. pp. 3, 7.

27. Pol. xxi. 21. 9: εἰ δὲ τοῦτο μὴ κρίνετε ποιεῖν, ἀλλ' ἐκχωρεῖν τῆς
Ἀσίας ὁλοσχερῶς, οὐδενί φαμεν δικαιότερον εἶναι παραχωρεῖν ὑμᾶς τῶν
ἐκ τοῦ πολέμου γεγονότων ἄθλων ἤπερ ἡμῖν.
bello: χ, *in bello* B. *parere* is always used with the ablative alone.

28. Pol. xxi. 21. 10–11: νὴ Δί', ἀλλὰ κάλλιόν ἐστι τοὺς δουλεύοντας
ἐλευθεροῦν. εἴγε μὴ μετ' Ἀντιόχου πολεμεῖν ὑμῖν ἐτόλμησαν. ἐπεὶ δὲ
τοῦθ' ὑπέμειναν, πολλῷ κάλλιον τὸ τοῖς ἀληθινοῖς φίλοις τὰς ἁρμοζούσας
χάριτας ἀποδιδόναι μᾶλλον ἢ τοὺς πολεμίους γεγονότας εὐεργετεῖν.
si ... fecerunt: Eumenes is thinking more of states that stayed
loyal to Antiochus than of those which deserted him in the course of
the war.

54. On L.'s adaptation of Polybius in this chapter cf. Hoch, 12 ff.

54. 1. Pol. xxi. 22. 1: ὁ μὲν οὖν Εὐμένης ἱκανῶς εἰπὼν ἀπηλλάγη, τὸ δὲ
συνέδριον αὐτόν τε τὸν βασιλέα καὶ τὰ ῥηθέντα φιλοφρόνως ἀπεδέχετο
καὶ πᾶν τὸ δυνατὸν προθύμως εἶχεν αὐτῷ χαρίζεσθαι. *munifice* is far away
from προθύμως.

2. Pol. xxi. 22. 2–4: μετὰ δὲ τοῦτον ἐβούλοντο μὲν εἰσάγειν Ῥοδίους.
ἀφυστεροῦντος δέ τινος τῶν πρεσβευτῶν εἰσεκαλέσαντο τοὺς Σμυρναίους.
οὗτοι δὲ πολλοὺς μὲν ἀπολογισμοὺς εἰσήνεγκαν περὶ τῆς αὐτῶν εὐνοίας
καὶ προθυμίας, ἣν παρέσχηνται Ῥωμαίοις κατὰ τὸν ἐνεστῶτα πόλεμον·
οὔσης δὲ τῆς περὶ αὐτῶν δόξης ὁμολογουμένης, διότι γεγόνασι πάντων
ἐκτενέστατοι τῶν ἐπὶ τῆς Ἀσίας αὐτονομουμένων, οὐκ ἀναγκαῖον ἡγούμεθ'
εἶναι τοὺς κατὰ μέρος ἐκτίθεσθαι λόγους. L. abbreviates and converts
a long speech by the delegation from Smyrna into a short one.
On Smyrna cf. 16. 1, 35. 2, xxxiii. 38. 3 n., xxxv. 42. 1. The name
is spelt *S-* in the MSS. here (cf. xxxiii. 38. 3 n.).
collaudatis ... maluissent may be a misunderstanding of Polybius'
τῆς περὶ αὐτῶν δόξης ὁμολογουμένης: cf. Walbank, *Commentary*, iii. 114.
aderat: Ruperti, *aderant* Bχ. According to Polybius there is only
one Rhodian missing, but in view of the other changes in the passage,
it would perhaps be better to retain the transmitted reading.

3. Pol. xxi. 22. 5: ἐπὶ δὲ τούτοις εἰσῆλθον οἱ Ῥόδιοι καὶ βραχέα
προενεγκάμενοι περὶ τῶν κατ' ἰδίαν σφίσι πεπραγμένων εἰς Ῥωμαίους,
ταχέως εἰς τὸν περὶ τῆς πατρίδος ἐπανῆλθον λόγον. I am not certain
that Tränkle (181 n. 13) is right to hold that L. wrongly took
κατ' ἰδίαν = *priuatim* as meaning *singula quaeque*. Holleaux (*Rome*,
44 n. 1) used this passage to argue that the *initia amicitiae* with
Rhodes were no older than the Second Macedonian War (cf. xxxi.

2. 1–2 n.). Quite apart from the fact that nothing corresponding to this stands in Polybius, the conclusion is unjustified. It may be true that the closest collaboration did not come until the time of the Second Macedonian War, but there is nothing in L.'s words to suggest that *amicitia* itself was not established 100 years earlier.

4–5. Pol. xxi. 22. 6: ἐν ᾧ μέγιστον αὐτοῖς ἔφασαν γεγονέναι σύμπτωμα κατὰ τὴν πρεσβείαν, πρὸς ὃν οἰκειότατα διάκεινται βασιλέα καὶ κοινῇ καὶ κατ' ἰδίαν, πρὸς τοῦτον αὐτοῖς ἀντιπεπτωκέναι τὴν φύσιν τῶν πραγμάτων.

4. actione: 'our case'. Usually used in reference to a real trial (*TLL*, i. 441 ff.).

5. publicum ... hospitium: cf. Ogilvie, 690. In fact there was very little love lost between the Attalids and Rhodes, and the Second Macedonian War is the first occasion on which they are known to have co-operated. Cf. McShane, 96 ff.

6. Pol. xxi. 22. 7–8: τῇ μὲν γὰρ αὐτῶν πατρίδι δοκεῖν τοῦτο κάλλιστον εἶναι καὶ μάλιστα πρέπον Ῥωμαίοις, τὸ τοὺς ἐπὶ τῆς Ἀσίας Ἕλληνας ἐλευθερωθῆναι ⟨καὶ⟩ τυχεῖν τῆς αὐτονομίας τῆς ἅπασιν ἀνθρώποις προσφιλεστάτης, Εὐμένει δὲ καὶ τοῖς ἀδελφοῖς ἥκιστα τοῦτο συμφέρειν· φύσει γὰρ πᾶσαν μοναρχίαν τὸ μὲν ἴσον ἐχθαίρειν, ζητεῖν δὲ πάντας, εἰ δὲ μή γ' ὡς πλείστους, ὑπηκόους εἶναι σφίσι καὶ πειθαρχεῖν. L. abbreviates.

serua omnia: *seruus* as an adjective, previously used only with *homo*, is common in L. Cf. p. 9.

7. Pol. xxi. 22. 9: ἀλλὰ καίπερ τοιούτων ὄντων τῶν πραγμάτων, ὅμως ἔφασαν πεπεῖσθαι διότι καθίξονται τῆς προθέσεως, οὐ τῷ πλεῖον Εὐμένους δύνασθαι παρὰ Ῥωμαίοις, ἀλλὰ τῷ δικαιότερα φαίνεσθαι λέγοντες καὶ συμφορώτερα πᾶσιν ὁμολογουμένως. A considerable elaboration. Cf. A. Bauer, *Stromateis* (Graz, 1909), 64.

sese: χ, *se* BMg. B has a continuation sign after *se* at the end of the line, and may, therefore, have intended to write *sese*.

perplexam: cf. p. 6.

8–9. Pol. xxi. 22. 10–11: εἰ μὲν γὰρ μὴ δυνατὸν ἦν ἄλλως Εὐμένει χάριν ἀποδοῦναι Ῥωμαίους, εἰ μὴ παραδοῖεν αὐτῷ τὰς αὐτονομουμένας πόλεις, ἀπορεῖν εἰκὸς ἦν περὶ τῶν ἐνεστώτων· ἢ γὰρ φίλον ἀληθινὸν ἔδει παριδεῖν, ἢ τοῦ καλοῦ καὶ καθήκοντος αὐτοῖς ὀλιγωρῆσαι καὶ τὸ τέλος τῶν ἰδίων πράξεων ἀμαυρῶσαι καὶ καταβαλεῖν.

8. in seruitutem traderetis ei: B, om. *in seruitutem* χ, *ei in seruitutem traderetis* Mg. The position of *ei* in Bχ is odd and Mg's order may be correct.

9. inhonoratum: the word is found twice in Cicero (*Tusc.* iii. 57, 81) and not otherwise before L. and Ovid (*TLL*, vii. 1. 1598–9).

10. Pol. xxi. 22. 12–13: εἰ δ' ἀμφοτέρων τούτων ἱκανῶς ἔξεστιν προνοηθῆναι, τίς ἂν ἔτι περὶ τούτου διαπορήσειεν; καὶ μὴν ὥσπερ ἐν δείπνῳ πολυτελεῖ, πάντ' ἔνεστιν ἱκανὰ πᾶσιν καὶ πλείω τῶν ἱκανῶν. L. alters the simile. For *fortuna* as equivalent to the gods cf. vi. 9. 1 ff., xxx. 30. 5, Kajanto, 26, 84 ff.

11. Pol. xxi. 22. 14: καὶ γὰρ Λυκαονίαν καὶ Φρυγίαν τὴν ἐφ' Ἑλλησπόντου καὶ τὴν Πισιδικήν, πρὸς δὲ ταύταις Χερρόνησον καὶ τὰ προσοροῦντα ταύτῃ τῆς Εὐρώπης ἔξεστιν ὑμῖν οἷς ἂν βούλησθε...

Lycaonia: on the extent of Lycaonia, lying between Pisidia, Cappadocia, and Phrygia, see Magie, i. 455, ii. 1312 n. 15, Walbank, *Commentary*, iii. 115.

Phrygia ... omnis: Tränkle (184) thinks that L. misunderstood Polybius, not realizing that 'Pisidian Phrygia' was another name for Greater Phrygia (Harris, 143 n. 2, apparently takes the same view). But ἡ Πισιδική means 'Pisidia' in Polybius v. 57. 7, 72. 9 and the excerptor has probably omitted Polybius' reference to Greater Phrygia. See Magie, ii. 1314, Walbank, *Commentary*, iii. 115.

B. Levick, *Roman Colonies in Southern Asia Minor* (Oxford, 1967), 19 n. 1, strangely uses this passage as evidence for the cession of Pisidia to Eumenes. For the actual extent of Eumenes' subsequent possessions in Pisidia cf. Magie, ii. 761 ff.

12. Pol. xxi. 22. 15: προστεθέντα πρὸς τὴν Εὐμένους βασιλείαν δεκαπλασίαν αὐτὴν δύναται ποιεῖν τῆς νῦν ὑπαρχούσης· πάντων δὲ τούτων ἢ τῶν πλείστων αὐτῇ προσμερισθέντων, οὐδεμιᾶς ἂν γένοιτο τῶν ἄλλων δυναστειῶν καταδεεστέρα.

regi: Koch's ingenious emendation to *regio* is unnecessary: cf. xxxviii. 39. 14.

13–16. L. expresses far more briefly the sentiments contained in Polybius xxi. 23. 1–10.

13. ditare: cf. p. 4.

aduersus Antiochum: χ, om. *aduersus* B. One would need a parallel to justify such an ellipse.

belli: Bχ, *bello* Wesenberg. For the genitive cf. iii. 67. 9, xxxiv. 59. 1.

14. et probabilis est causa: Bχ, *est et probabilis causa* Mg, perhaps rightly.

15. cum ... sit: cf. 45. 8 n.

16. quod ... intuetur: cf. xxxvi. 17. 15.

17–25. An elaboration by L. on the theme of Rome's championship of the Greeks (though cf. Pol. xxi. 23. 10: τοιγαροῦν σεμνότατον τῶν ὑμετέρων ἔργων ἡ τῶν Ἑλλήνων ἐλευθέρωσις. τούτῳ νῦν ἐὰν μὲν προσθῆτε τἀκόλουθον, τελειωθήσεται τὰ τῆς ὑμετέρας δόξης. ἐὰν δὲ παρίδητε, καὶ ⟨τὰ⟩ πρὶν ἐλαττωθήσεται φανερῶς.) On the reasons for L.'s departing so far from Polybius see Tränkle, 125–6. His abbreviation of Polybius xxi. 23. 1–10 (cf. 13–16 n.) renders implausible Walsh's view (*AJPh* xcvii [1954], 104) that his aim was to equalize the length of the speeches of Eumenes and the Rhodians.

17. patrocinium ... clientelam: the slogan-words of Rome's attitude towards the Greeks. Cf. Badian, *FC*, ch. iii.

18. solo [modo] antiquo: Bχ, del. *modo* Crévier. It is easiest to think that *modo* was an attempt to gloss *solo* by someone who did not realize that it was the ablative of *solum*.

nec ... mores: cf. § 21 *si ... gentes*: for the theme of environment shaping character cf. ix. 13. 7, xlv. 30. 7. Cic. *agr.* ii. 95, *r.p.* ii. 7 ff., Luce, 280 ff. On the effect of climate on character cf. Hippocrates, *Airs, Waters, Places*, 12 ff. For the sentiment cf. Horace, *Epp.* i. 11. 27, Brakman, *Mnemosyne* n.s. lv (1927), 55.

19. et conditoribus: Bχ, om. Priscian, *Inst.* xvii. 165 (*GL* iii. 191). The words could be a gloss but (i) Priscian earlier trivializes *ac* to *et*; (ii) they are not essential for the point Priscian is making; (iii) the word-order, at first sight strange, is probably determined by the fact that *cum parentibus et conditoribus suis quaeque ciuitas* would leave *quaeque* unnaturally late in the colon, while *suis* is postponed to make the separation of *conditoribus* from *parentibus* less abrupt.

20. adistis ... plerique: it is quite improper to use this as a genuine piece of evidence for Romans visiting Greece at this time, as is done by J. Griffin, *JRS* lxvi (1976), 91.

21. Massiliensis: cf. xxxiv. 9. 1 n.
    insita: L. is very fond of *insitus* (Packard, ii. 1239) and Novak's proposal to delete it is absurd. For *natura insita* cf. Tacitus, *H.* i. 55. 1.
    ingenio: cf. p. 5.
    audimus: χ, *audiuimus* B, perhaps rightly. Cf. xxv. 6. 8.
    umbilicum ... colerent: cf. xxxv. 18. 4 n.

22. A different view is expressed by Manlius Vulso at xxxviii. 17. 12. There is, of course, no inconsistency, as both occur in speeches without L. committing himself to what is said. On Massilia's reputation see Ogilvie and Richmond, *Cornelii Taciti de uita Agricolae* (Oxford, 1967), 143, Momigliano, *Alien Wisdom* (Cambridge, 1975), 50 ff.,

Petrocheilos, 65–6 n. 2. See in particular Cicero, *Flacc.* 63 *cuius ego ciuitatis disciplinam atque grauitatem non solum Graeciae, sed haud scio an cunctis gentibus anteponendam iure dicam.*

integrumque a contagione: Luce, 280 n. 110, points to similar medical metaphors at *praef.* 9, xxxviii. 17. 18, xxxix. 9. 1.

23. mons Taurus: cf. 35. 10 n.

cardinem: 'limit'. The only other occurrence in Classical Latin of *cardo* in this sense (and that not certain) is Pliny, *NH* vi. 45 (*TLL,* iii. 445. 35 ff.). xl. 18. 8, xli. 1. 3 are rather different.

longinquum: too far away to bother about.

debet uideri: B, *uideri debet* χ. Cf. p. 15.

ius . . . perueniat: a favourite theme of L. Cf. Tränkle, 126 and add to his references ix. 20. 10.

24. barbari . . . habeant: reflecting the Aristotelian view that some people are born for slavery. Cf. xxxv. 49. 8 n.

25. imperium amplectebantur: scarcely applicable to the Asiatic Greeks.

26. at enim: deliberately counterpointing Eumenes' objection at 53. 28 (Tränkle, 126).

Tarentini: cf. xxxi. 29. 10–11 n.

27. negare . . . negastis: a double chiasmus (Ullmann, *Étude,* 96).

28. Pol. xxi. 23. 11–13: '*ἡμεῖς μὲν οὖν, ὦ ἄνδρες, καὶ τῆς προαιρέσεως γεγονότες αἱρετισταὶ καὶ τῶν μεγίστων ἀγώνων καὶ κινδύνων ἀληθινῶς ὑμῖν μετεσχηκότες, καὶ νῦν οὐκ ἐγκαταλείπομεν ⟨τὴν⟩ τῶν φίλων τάξιν, ἀλλ' ἅ γε νομίζομεν ὑμῖν καὶ πρέπειν καὶ συμφέρειν, οὐκ ὠκνήσαμεν ὑπομνῆσαι μετὰ παρρησίας, οὐδενὸς στοχασάμενοι τῶν ἄλλων οὐδὲ περὶ πλείονος οὐδὲν ποιησάμενοι τοῦ καθήκοντος αὐτοῖς.' οἱ μὲν οὖν 'Ρόδιοι ταῦτ' εἰπόντες πᾶσιν ἐδόκουν μετρίως καὶ καλῶς διειλέχθαι περὶ τῶν προκειμένων.* L. adapts in a way that conforms to what precedes.

⟨**et in hoc**⟩: om. Bχ. An alternative would be to delete *et* before *in.*

ora: i.e. the area where the Greeks live. The singular is a little odd in reference to both the mainland and Asia Minor.

forti fidelique: for this alliterative conjunction, occurring also at xxi. 44. 2, xxii. 60. 20, xxiii. 46. 6, xlv. 14. 2, cf. Wölfflin, *Ausgewählte Schriften,* 232–3, 260.

uestro . . . relinquimus: taking up 52. 4–5, as W–M note. A sort of ring composition.

55. 1. post . . . sunt: Pol. xxi. 24. 1: *ἐπὶ δὲ τούτοις εἰσήγαγον τοὺς*

παρ' Ἀντιόχου πρεσβευτὰς Ἀντίπατρον καὶ Ζεῦξιν. L. typically omits
the names of the ambassadors (cf. xxxvi. 5. 1 n.).

1–2. ii ... auctoritate sua: Pol. xxi. 24. 2: ὧν μετ' ἀξιώσεως καὶ
παρακλήσεως ποιησαμένων τοὺς λόγους ... Further elaboration by
L. for dramatic effect and to emphasize Roman *clementia* (cf. xxxiii.
12. 7~ Pol. xviii. 37. 3, Hoch, 38).

2. obtestati sunt: om. *sunt* Bχ, perhaps rightly. Cf. p. 12.

3. Pol. xxi. 24. 2–3: εὐδόκησαν ταῖς γεγενημέναις ὁμολογίαις πρὸς
τοὺς περὶ τὸν Σκιπίωνα κατὰ τὴν Ἀσίαν, καὶ μετά τινας ἡμέρας τοῦ
δήμου συνεπικυρώσαντος ἔτεμον ὅρκια περὶ τούτων πρὸς τοὺς περὶ τὸν
Ἀντίπατρον.

eam pacem: comparison of the preliminary peace (45. 14 ff.~
Pol. xxi. 17. 3 ff.) and the final settlement at Apamea (xxxviii. 38~
Pol. xxi. 43) shows differences concerning the numbers of ships,
the enrolment of mercenaries, and the surrender of elephants, as
well as a closer definition of the land and sea limits imposed on
Antiochus (cf. McDonald, *JRS* lvii [1967], 1 ff., McDonald and
Walbank, *JRS* lxix [1969], 30 ff.). It is not certain that Polybius'
version of the preliminary peace is complete (cf. 45. 14–15 n.) but
in any case it is wrong to think that the senate altered the spirit of
the Scipios' peace, as argued by Scullard, *SA*, 206. Appian (*Syr.*
39. 201) describes the additions as βραχέα ἄττα, though, of course,
he had included some of them in his account of the preliminary
agreement (45. 14–15 n.).

in Capitolio: not in Polybius, but Appian (*Syr.* 39. 203) refers
to the records of the peace being deposited on the Capitol. The
detail may well have stood in L.'s annalistic source. On the relationship between the ratification and oath-swearing in Rome and that
at Apamea (xxxviii. 39. 1~Pol. xxi. 44. 1) see Walbank, *Commentary*,
iii. 116–17.

Antipatro ... fratris filio: cf. 41. 1 n.

4–56. 6. The details of the senate's decisions provide the most important passage where information in L., deriving from an annalistic
source, is superior to that of Polybius on an eastern matter. (The
attempt of Tränkle, 36 ff., to return to Nissen's view [*KU*, 200] that
the sections in L. not corresponding to anything in Polybius were
omitted by the excerptor of Polybius is unconvincing: he ignores the
historical conflict between the two statements of the senate's decisions.) In 55. 5–6 L. follows Polybius xxi. 24. 7–8 and then adds
details of the settlement from an annalistic source. The general
statements of Polybius, both here and at xxi. 46. 2–3, are vague and

misleading (46. 4 ff. is closer to L. here, but there are still important differences and the passages cannot be regarded as equivalent). Polybius obscures the fact that it is not the cities' previous relationship to Pergamum or Antiochus that decided their fate, but their status *vis-à-vis* Rome at the time of the battle of Magnesia. There were states that had in the past been subject to Antiochus, but were now freed, and in at least one case, that of Teus (cf. 27. 3 n.), a state that had paid tribute to Attalus was free after 188: for tribute cf. *Anadolu* ix (1965), 35 l. 34, for its status after 188, Magie, ii. 958–9, Walbank, *Commentary*, iii. 167–8.

For the possibility that Claudius Quadrigarius' translation of Acilius (cf. xxxv. 14. 5–12 n.) is the source of L.'s information cf. McDonald, *JRS* lvii (1967), 2. On the whole matter, and for details of the status of various states after 188, see Bikerman, *REG* l (1937), 217 ff., Magie, ii. 758 ff., 950–1, 958–61, Bredehorn, 230 ff., R. Bernhardt, *Imperium und Eleutheria* (Hamburg, 1971), 53 ff., Walbank, *Commentary*, iii. 117–18, 167–74.

4. Pol. xxi. 24. 4–5: μετὰ δὲ ταῦτα καὶ τοὺς ἄλλους εἰσῆγον, ὅσοι παρῆσαν ἀπὸ τῆς Ἀσίας πρεσβεύοντες· ὧν ἐπὶ βραχὺ μὲν διήκουσαν, ἅπασιν δὲ τὴν αὐτὴν ἔδωκαν ἀπόκρισιν. αὕτη δ' ἦν ὅτι δέκα πρεσβεύοντας ἐξαποστελοῦσι τοὺς ὑπὲρ ἁπάντων τῶν ἀμφισβητουμένων ταῖς πόλεσι διαγνωσομένους.

5–6. Pol. xxi. 24. 7–8: περὶ δὲ τῶν ὅλων αὐτοὶ διέλαβον ὅτι δεῖ τῶν ἐπὶ τάδε τοῦ Ταύρου κατοικούντων, ὅσοι μὲν ὑπ' Ἀντίοχον ἐτάττοντο, τούτους Εὐμένει δοθῆναι πλὴν Λυκίαν καὶ Καρίας τὰ μέχρι τοῦ Μαιάνδρου ποταμοῦ, ταῦτα δὲ Ῥοδίων ὑπάρχειν, τῶν ⟨δὲ⟩ πόλεων τῶν Ἑλληνίδων ὅσαι μὲν Ἀττάλῳ φόρον ὑπετέλουν, ταύτας τὸν αὐτὸν Εὐμένει τελεῖν, ὅσαι δ' Ἀντιόχῳ, μόνον ταύταις ἀφεῖσθαι τὸν φόρον. Polybius places notice of the appointment of the ten *legati* before his statement of their instructions (xxi. 24. 6), L. afterwards, as a result of his annalistic addition (cf. Bikerman, *REG* l [1937], 223).

5. Rhodiorum essent: χ, *essent Rhodiorum* B. Cf. p. 15.

6. ceterae ciuitates: misleading. It is not states other than those inside Antiochus' kingdom, but the Greek city states (called Ἑλληνίδων here by Polybius, but αὐτονόμων at xxi. 46. 2) that are involved.

uectigal Eumeni: B, *Eumeni uectigal* χ. Cf. p. 15.

7. decem legatos ... decreuerunt: the fact that they did not reach Asia until 188 is no argument against their having been appointed now, as W–M claim.

Q. Minucium Rufum: (22, 55). Cf. xxxi. 4. 4 n.

L. Furium Purpurionem: (86). Cf. xxxi. 4. 4 n.
Q. Minucium Thermum: (65). Cf. xxxii. 27. 8 n.
Ap. Claudium Neronem: (245). Cf. xxxii. 35. 6–7 n.
Cn. Cornelium Merulam: (268). He is not otherwise known
and Duker's emendation of *Merulam* to *Merendam*—i.e. the praetor
of 194 (xxxiv. 42. 4 n.) has a lot to be said for it. Cf. *MRR*, i. 365 n. 8.
M. Iunium Brutum: (48). Cf. xxxiv. 1. 4 n.
L. Aurunculeium: (4). Cf. xxxvi. 45. 9 n.
L. Aemilium Paullum: (114). He could well have returned
from Spain (cf. 57. 5–6 n.) before the appointment of the commission (cf. *MRR*, i. 364 n. 5), but even if he had not there is no
reason why he could not have been appointed in his absence.
P. Cornelium Lentulum: (214). Cf. xxxiii. 35. 1–2 n.
P. Aelium Tuberonem: (152). Aedile in 202, praetor in 201, he
held a second praetorship in 177 (cf. xxxiv. 53. 2 n.) and was a *iiiuir*
for the foundation of Luna in the same year. It is a very strange
career.

56. 1. Cf. Pol. xxi. 24. 6–7, introducing the provisions rendered by
L. at 55. 5–6: οἷς περὶ μὲν τῶν κατὰ μέρος ἔδωκαν τὴν ἐπιτροπήν, περὶ
δὲ τῶν ὅλων αὐτοὶ διέλαβον.

2. Lycaoniam ... utramque: cf. 54. 11 nn.
   Mysiam ... Milyas: M. Müller, *Misias (Mysias) regias siluas* Bχ,
Mysiam regias siluas Mg. Editors have emended to insert a reference
to the land taken from Attalus by Prusias, and to Milyas, on the
basis of xxxviii. 39. 15 *Mysiam quam Prusia rex ademerat ei ... et
Lycaoniam et Milyada*, an accurate translation of Polybius xxi. 46. 10
(assuming a small corruption in Polybius). But as we have seen
(55. 4–56. 6 n.), that passage cannot be regarded as directly equivalent to the present one and McDonald's proposal to read *Mysiae
regias siluas* (*JRS* lvii [1967], 2 n. 8) makes excellent sense (though I
cannot follow McDonald's argument that reference to Milyas—on
the extent of which see Magie, ii. 761–2—would be inappropriate
at this point). The reference will be to the area captured by Antiochus in 198—at this stage no provision is made for the rest of
Mysia, which is in the hands of Prusias (cf. 40. 8 n.).
   Lydiam ... oppida: Mg, *Lydiae Ioniaeque extra oppida* Bχ. The
cities to be freed are in Ionia, not Lydia, and this tells against
Madvig's *Lydiae Ioniaeque oppida extra ea*.

2. quo die: in § 4 L. says *ante bellum*, in § 6 *pridie*. The provision
must have been the same in all cases and I imagine that the day
before the battle is correct. The battle took place in the early

morning (41. 2) and *pridie* would exclude those cities that surrendered immediately after the battle. For a similar provision in the
s.c. de agro Pergameno cf. *OGIS* 435. 15, Hopp, 139. States that were
free after 188 despite this provision include Cyme (cf. 11. 15, xxxviii.
39. 8, Pol. xxi. 46. 4) and Magnesia-on-the-Maeander (cf. 45. 1,
Tac. *A.* iii. 62. 1).

pugnatum est: cf. xxxiv. 20. 2 n.

3. Magnesiam ad Sipylum: cf. xxxvi. 43. 9 n. It surrendered
after the battle (44. 4).

Hydrela ... Hydrelitanum: the area will be the north-eastern
part of Caria: see Magie, ii. 762. The *ager Hydrelitanus* will be named
after the town Hydrela (cf. Strabo xiv, p. 650C, Steph. Byz. *s.u.*),
but Caria Hydrela must refer to a well irrigated region. There may
be some misunderstanding: cf. Bürchner, *RE*, ix. 77–8.

castella ... amnem: Bχ. Mg had *trans Maeandrum* which would
mean 'south of the Maeander' and this is the area given to Rhodes.
For *ad* meaning 'up to' cf. *TLL*, i. 514 ff. There is no need to insert
usque.

4. et oppida: Mg, om. Bχ. It is necessary since it is only cities that
are freed.

4–5. The identity and affiliations of Ptolemy of Telmessus have
given rise to an enormous literature, of which see particularly
Holleaux, *Études*, iii. 365 ff., Segre, *Clara Rhodos*, ix (1938), 181 ff.,
Magie, ii. 762–4, A. G. Roos, *Mnemosyne* 4, iii (1950), 54 ff., Volkmann, *RE*, xxiii. 1596–7, Walbank, *Commentary*, iii. 173–4, Huss,
Untersuchungen zur Aussenpolitik Ptolemaios IV (Munich, 1976), 192–3,
203–4 n. 195, M. Wörrle, *Chiron* viii (1978), 201 ff., ix (1979), 83 ff.
What follows is a summary of what seems to me the most plausible
interpretation of the evidence.

Ptolemy, the son of Lysimachus and Arsinoe II, gained possession of lands in the vicinity of Telmessus from Ptolemy Philadelphus,
and eventually exercised control over Telmessus itself (Segre, op. cit.,
183 ff., *OGIS* 55). The lands remained in his family, passing first to
his son Lysimachus (Segre, *Atti di IV congresso internazionale di papiro-
logia* [Milan, 1936], 359 ff.) and then to the latter's son Ptolemy.
The area was occupied by Antiochus in 197 (cf. xxxiii. 20. 13 n.).
Segre argued that an inscription of Eumenes, dated to 189/8, and
referring to land sold by Ptolemy to οἱ κατοικοῦντες ἐν Καρδάκων
κώμῃ showed that Antiochus had left Ptolemy in possession of his
lands and that in 193 the latter had sold part of them to the Cardaces, military settlers planted there by Antiochus. The rest of the
lands were occupied by Antiochus in 190. It seems possible, though,

that Ptolemy was expelled from his lands in 197 and that the sale to the Cardaces comes after 189.

It is possible that the Πτολεμαῖος ὁ Λυ[σιμάχο]υ who made a dedication at Delos in 189 (*IDelos* 442 B94–5) is Ptolemy of Telmessus, though it cannot be excluded that he is dead by this time and that the lands passed to his descendants. Whether the Ptolemy son of Lysimachus of *OGIS* 224 (= Welles, *RC*, no. 36) is also our Ptolemy is more doubtful. If he is, he is shown to have been related to Antiochus and this makes it surprising that the senate should have given him or his family special treatment (see below).

On the site of Telmessus see 16. 13 n.

4. praeter ... fuisset: Magie's argument (ii. 763, accepted by Walbank, *Commentary*, iii. 173, Wörrle, *Chiron* viii [1978], 222, ix [1979], 86) that *praeter* means 'in addition' not 'except' and that the lands of Ptolemy were in fact given to Eumenes is most implausible. In § 5 Magie takes *excepta* to mean 'received by' and sees the sentence as a resumé of the lands given to Eumenes and Rhodes. This removes the difficulty of the transmitted reading in § 5 (see below) but a summary at that point would be quite out of place.

haec: L. here switches into *oratio recta*. It is not really an anacoluthon, as W–M label it.

quae ... scripta: the phrase is unique in L. and perhaps reflects the language of the *s.c.* itself. Cf. Bredehorn, 232, who draws attention to *suprad scriptum est* in the *s.c. de Bacchanalibus*.

5. hic ... exceptus: *haec ... excepta* Bχ. Since Telmessus and the *castra Telmessium* were in fact given to Eumenes, and Magie's explanation (see above) is unacceptable, emendation to *hic ... exceptus* is inevitable.

6. trans Maeandrum: i.e. south of it.

qui ... uergunt: i.e. the eastern parts of Caria. It comes rather oddly here, since the *agri* of western Caria are not excluded and the free *oppida* all belong to western Caria.

pridie: cf. § 2 n.

7–10. On Soli cf. xxxiii. 20. 4 n. It was, in fact, probably a Rhodian colony, founded *c*. 700. Cf. Magie, ii. 1148–9, J. D. Bing, *JNES* xxx (1971), 103, Walbank, *Commentary*, iii. 118.

7. Pol. xxi. 24. 10–12: ἤδη δὲ τούτων διῳκημένων, προσῆλθον αὖθις οἱ Ῥόδιοι πρὸς τὴν σύγκλητον, ἀξιοῦντες περὶ Σόλων τῶν Κιλικίων· διὰ γὰρ τὴν συγγένειαν ἔφασαν καθήκειν αὐτοῖς προνοεῖσθαι τῆς πόλεως ταύτης. εἶναι γὰρ Ἀργείων ἀποίκους Σολεῖς, καθάπερ καὶ Ῥοδίους· ἐξ ὧν ἀδελφικὴν οὖσαν ἀπεδείκνυον τὴν συγγένειαν πρὸς ἀλλήλους. ὧν

ἕνεκα δίκαιον ἔφασαν εἶναι τυχεῖν αὐτοὺς τῆς ἐλευθερίας ὑπὸ ʿΡωμαίων
διὰ τῆς ʿΡοδίων χάριτος.

egissent ... egerunt: cf. p. 13.

Argis: for the legend of the foundation of Rhodes from Argos cf.
H. van Gelder, *Geschichte der alten Rhodier* (The Hague, 1900), 32, 63,
Walbank, *Commentary*, iii. 118.

extraordinarium ... regia: considerably stronger language
than in Polybius.

8. Pol. xxi. 24. 13–14: ἡ δὲ σύγκλητος διακούσασα περὶ τούτων εἰσεκα-
λέσατο τοὺς παρ᾽ Ἀντιόχου πρεσβευτάς, καὶ τὸ μὲν πρῶτον ἐπέταττε
πάσης Κιλικίας ἐκχωρεῖν τὸν Ἀντίοχον· οὐ προσδεχομένων δὲ τῶν περὶ
τὸν Ἀντίπατρον διὰ τὸ παρὰ τὰς συνθήκας εἶναι, πάλιν ὑπὲρ αὐτῶν
Σόλων ἐποιοῦντο τὸν λόγον. φιλοτίμως δὲ πρὸς τοῦτο διερειδομένων
τῶν πρεσβευτῶν ... L. omits the senate's demand for the cession of
all Cilicia, perhaps in embarrassment at the senate's bad faith in
trying to go back on what had already been agreed.

foedera: as at xxxviii. 40. 1 the reference must be to individual
articles of the treaty. I can find no other example of such a usage and
imagine that L. was influenced by the plural συνθήκας in Polybius.
Cf. p. 10 n. 1.

9. Pol. xxi. 24. 14: τούτους μὲν ἀπέλυσαν, τοὺς δὲ ʿΡοδίους εἰσκαλεσάμ-
ενοι διεσάφουν τὰ συναντώμενα παρὰ τῶν περὶ τὸν Ἀντίπατρον καὶ
προσεπέλεγον ὅτι πᾶν ὑπομενοῦσιν, εἰ πάντως τοῦτο κέκριται ʿΡοδίοις.

10. Pol. xxi. 24. 15: τῶν δὲ πρεσβευτῶν εὐδοκουμένων τῇ φιλοτιμίᾳ τῆς
συγκλήτου καὶ φασκόντων οὐδὲν ἔτι πέρα ζητεῖν, ταῦτα μὲν ἐπὶ τῶν
ὑποκειμένων ἔμεινεν. L. elaborates.

57. 1–6. *Events in Liguria and Spain*

1–2. Cf. Orosius iv. 20. 24. On Baebius (25) cf. 47. 8 n. W–M suggest that he went to Spain by sea, like Cato in 195, and was attacked
when landing in Liguria. It cannot, however, be regarded as certain
that it was normal to go to Spain by sea at this time. Cf. G. Clemente,
I Romani nella gallia meridionale (Bologna, 1974), 15, J. M. Blazquez,
Economia de la Hispania Romana (Bilbao, 1978), 243. For the possibility that it was the Ingauni who attacked Baebius cf. Toynbee,
ii. 279 n. 3.

3. P. Iunius Brutus: cf. 50. 13, xxxiv. 1. 4 nn.

4. Sp. Postumio praetore: cf. 47. 8 n.

5–6. On Paullus' defeat in 190 cf. 46. 7 n. This victory in fact took place before the end of the consular year 190/89, for Paullus was acclaimed *imperator* before *a.d. xii Kal. Feb.* (= 16 September 190 [Jul.]). See *ILLRP* 514, *MRR* supp. 3, E. Meyer, *ANRW*, i. 2. 982 ff. (who, however, strangely claims that the inscription is inconsistent with L.'s narrative and provides evidence in favour of that of Plutarch [cf. 46. 7 n.]). I am quite unconvinced by the argument of R. Develin, *Latomus* xxxvi (1977), 110–13, that at this date *imperator* merely denotes a holder of *imperium* and that the inscription does not therefore provide evidence for the date of Paullus' victory, and by that of A. Deman, *Latomus* xxxv (1976), 805–7, that the inscription can belong to the consular year 189/8.

57. 7–8. *Foundation of Bononia*

For the authorization of the colony cf. 47. 2 n.

7. ante diem ... Ianuarias: 'birthdays' of colonies are also known for Brundisium and Placentia. For the significance of the date cf. Salmon, *Colonization*, 26.

L. Valerius Flaccus ... L. Valerius Tappo: cf. 46. 10 n. On this occasion the consular is listed first.

8. septuagena ... quinquagena: the allotments are larger than at other Latin colonies (cf. xxxv. 9. 8 n.), perhaps because of the difficulty of finding colonists. Cf. Brunt, 191, Bleicken, *Chiron* iv (1974), 397 n. 91, suggesting that there was dispute whether Bononia should be a citizen or Latin colony, as was the case over Aquileia— which also had particularly large allotments (cf. xxxix. 55. 5, xl. 34. 2). For traces of the centuriation cf. Rubbiani, op. cit. (xxxiv. 22. 1 n.), 78 ff.

ager ... expulerant: cf. xxxiv. 45. 2 n.

57. 9–58. 2. *Censorial elections*

On the political importance of the elections and the trial of Glabrio cf. *Latomus* xxxi (1972), 52, McDonald, *JRS* xxviii (1938), 162: *contra* Astin, *Cato*, 69 ff.

10. There are three patrician candidates, the consuls of 198, 195, and 191 competing for one place, and three plebeians, the consuls of 196, 195, and 191, competing for the other.
Antiochum ... deuicerat: cf. p. 15.

11. congiaria distribuerat: M. Müller, *congiaria habuerat* BMg, *concilia habuerat* χ. No sense can be made of the transmitted readings and we are clearly dealing with a very old corruption. *congiaria* is not likely to be corrupt and Madvig's *e copia regia habuerat* (*Emendationes*, 536–7 n. 1) imports an alien notion: L. himself is not committed to accepting as a fact that Glabrio was distributing loot obtained from Antiochus. Zingerle's *dederat* is perhaps the simplest solution.

magnam partem ... populi: i.e. the *prima classis* and the *equitum centuriae*, whose votes mattered.

12. nobiles: though Cato, as L. later remarks (§ 15), was also a *nouus*.

P. Sempronius ... Rutilus: (49, 81). Neither is otherwise known. For a Sempronius Rutilus in the late republic cf. Caesar, *BG* vii. 90. 4.

⟨tribuni plebis⟩: om. Bχ. It is unlikely that L. would not have specified their office in such a context.

ei ... dixerunt: a direct tribunican accusation before the assembly, not a case of *prouocatio*. On the procedure cf. Kunkel, *ABAW* n.f. lvi (1962), 21–3, A. H. M. Jones, *The Criminal Courts of the Roman Republic and Principate* (Oxford, 1972), ch. i, who, however, regards all such cases as examples of *prouocatio*.

quod ... rettulisset: this cannot have been the real charge, for it is clear that the general had complete discretion over disposal of booty as he saw fit. He might incur odium if he pocketed an excessive amount for himself but could not be prosecuted for such action. Cato's accusations were, then, a side-issue. Perhaps the real accusation was embezzling funds voted from the *aerarium*. See Vogel, *RE*, xxii. 1211–12, I. Shatzman, *Historia* xxi (1972),191–2; *contra* F. Bona, *SDHI* xxvi (1960), 157 n. 131.

13. M. Cato: for Cato as a military tribune under Glabrio cf. xxxvi. 17. 1 n., for a fragment of a speech of Cato against Glabrio *ORF*³, fr. 66.

perpetuo tenore uitae: for praise of Cato's way of life cf. xxxii. 27. 3, xxxiv. 18. 3–5 nn. On *tenor* cf. xxxv. 16. 8 n.

14. castris captis ... praedam regiam: B, *captis castris ... regiam praedam* χ. Cf. p. 15.

15. intestabili: (Bψ, *inextimabili* φ, *inaestimabili* Mg.) *intestabilis* here has a good deal of its literal sense of 'not worthy of being regarded as a *testis*' rather than simply 'loathsome'.

incesseret: in the sense of *reprehendere*, with a neuter object, *incessere* occurs only here in L. and not again before Statius, Quintilian, and the younger Pliny. Cf. *TLL*, vii. 1. 890. 57 ff., p. 9.

58. 1. centum milia: 100,000 asses.

bis ... tertio: the three *contiones* preceding the final session at which the vote was taken. Cf. Jones, op. cit. (57. 12 n.), 6 ff.

ea: Bχ, *ea re* Mg. But *ea* is the *multa* (cf. xl. 42. 9) and *re* should be seen as an emendation in Mg.

de petitione: Bχ, del. *de* Novak. *desistere* with the ablative alone is the normal usage, but *desistere de petitione* occurs at Cicero, *Planc.* 52 and *de negotio desistere* at *Bell. Afr.* 45. 4. Despite *negotio destiterunt* below, the transmitted text should be retained.

58. 3—59. *Triumphs of Regillus and L. Scipio,*
supplicatio *for Paullus*

The two triumphs are briefly recorded in Polybius xxi. 24. 16–17. On the *tabula triumphalis* of Regillus cf. 46. 2–6 n. Pliny, *NH* xxxv. 22 records that Scipio set up a picture of his victory on the Capitol.

3. praefectum: Polyxenidas.
aede Apollinis: cf. xxxiv. 43. 2 n.

3. triumphus naualis: the first naval triumph was by C. Duilius in 260. It is not known in what ways, if any, it differed from the normal triumph. Cf. Ehlers, *RE*, viiA. 497.

4. Kal. Februariis: confirmed by the *Fasti Triumphales*. The date is 16 September 189.

translatae: cf. xxxiv. 52. 4 n.

nequaquam [tanta] pro: Madvig (*Emendationes*, 537 n. 1) plausibly argued that *tanta* was a gloss on *pro* (sc. *tanta quanta conueniret speciei*). But it is possible to understand the correlative, as with *non tam* at xxxviii. 21. 10: cf. Cicero, *Brut.* 58, *fin.* i. 1, H–S, 591.

cistophori: cf. 46. 3 n.

5. Paullus is credited with a triumph as praetor by Velleius Paterculus (i. 9. 3) and with three triumphs altogether in an *elogium* (*I.I.* xiii. 3. 71). But there is no trace of such a triumph in the other *elogium* (*I.I.* xiii. 3. 81) or in the *Fasti*. The version probably arose from a confusion with Paullus' three imperatorial acclamations (cf. 57. 5–6 n.) and it is to this that *ter* on coins of the Aemilii refers. See *MRR*, i. 362, M. G. Morgan, *Klio* lv (1973), 228–9, Degrassi on *ILLRP*, 392, Crawford, *RRC*, i. 441, E. Meyer, *ANRW*, i. 2. 983.

6. Asiaticum: in fact he called himself Asiagenus or Asiagenes and Asiaticus first appears in the Augustan period. Cf. Münzer, *RE*, iv. 1475, *TLL*, ii. 785–6.

7. in contione: this could well have taken place in the Campus Martius outside the *pomerium* and there is no need to hold, with

W–M, that L. has antedated a speech which in fact came after the triumph. For *contiones* in the Campus Martius see Taylor, *RVA*, 56 ff.

erant qui: the political opponents of the Scipios.

interpretarentur: for *interpretari* with the accusative and infinitive cf. *TLL*, vii. 1. 2260. 56 ff.

praefloratam: Mg, *defloratam* Bχ. *deflorare* does not occur in Classical Latin. *praeflorare*, perhaps a neologism of L. (cf. p. 9) is found also at Pliny, *Pan.* 58. 4. See Francis, *YCS* xxiii (1973), 36 n. 78. F. Walter's justification of *defloratam* (*PhW* lx [1940], 350) on the grounds that *deflorescere* occurs at vi. 23. 4, xxxviii. 53. 9 is quite unconvincing.

8. L. commits himself to the contrary view. Tacitus would have put both views into the mouths of other people.

Asia ... Asiae: cf. p. 13.

ultimis orientibus finibus: Weissenborn, *ultimi Orientis in* B, *ultimis Orientis* φ, *ultimis orientis in* VL, *ultimis orientis momentium* (for *omnium*) N. '*ab ultimis orientis*: partibus non additur in uetere scriptura' Gel. *ultimis* is clearly the transmitted reading, and if *in* is also part of such a reading there is a lot to be said for Zingerle's *terminis* as the whole phrase occurs at xxxv. 48. 8. L. writes *ultima Hispaniae* at xxvii. 20. 5, and *ultima Celtiberiae* at xl. 47. 1 but these expressions with *ultima* in the accusative cannot be regarded as justifying *ultimis orientis* here.

59. 2. mense ... Martias: demonstrating that the year 189/8 was intercalary. See Derow, *Phoenix* xxvii (1973), 347. The date is 5 November 189.

3. oppidorum simulacra: cf. Ehlers, *RE*, viiA. 503, Harris, 29 n. 2.

4. cistophori: cf. 46. 3 n.

nummos aureos ... milia: om. *milia* BPN, $\overline{CXL}$ L, $\overline{C}$ XL AEV. Despite the high figure in comparison with the number of Philippics (on which cf. xxxiv. 52. 7 n.) in other triumphs, there is no real case for emending to * *milia centum quadraginta* with Madvig, *Emendationes*, 538.

5. mille ... uiginti tria: BVL, om. *mille* spat. rel. N, om. *tria* φ. Pliny, *NH* xxxiii. 148 gives this figure as *MCCCCL* and the following one as *MD*. They should be regarded as different versions, and Pliny should certainly not be used for emending L. (or vice versa, for that matter).

purpurati: B, *et purpurati* χ, possibly rightly. On *purpurati* cf. xxxi. 35. 1 n. The figure is the total for all three categories.

6. militibus: as W–M observe, Scipio's army was still in Asia, and in that respect Scipio's triumph was the same as Glabrio's (cf. 46. 6). In his enthusiasm for describing the lavishness of the triumph, L. appears to have forgotten this fact. It provides another argument against the total authenticity of the triumph notices (cf. 46. 3 n.).

denarii: as W–M note, this is the first occasion on which donatives are recorded in *denarii*. For the date of the introduction of the *denarius* see Crawford, *RRC*, i. 28 ff.

⟨**iam**⟩ ... **duplex:** Heusinger, M. Müller. Madvig (*Emendationes*, 538) argued that L. would have had to say that Scipio had already given double corn and pay if he had given the same amount on both occasions, and proposed changing one or other *duplex* to *triplex*. Most subsequent editors have inserted *iam*. Neither is necessary: in this sort of plain narrative L. can easily have simply stated that he gave double after the battle, without feeling the need for any other kind of connection or explanation.

Lucius had used the first instalment of Antiochus' indemnity to pay his troops (Pol. xxiii. 14. 7) and it was this, in particular, that gave rise to the charges against him in 187. Cf. Scullard, *RP²*, 142.

60. *Fabius Labeo in Crete and Thrace*

The chapter is of Polybian origin (Nissen, *KU*, 200–1, doubted, apparently, by Tränkle, 27 n. 10). L. probably ended the book with this brief account of Fabius' activities so as to devote book xxxviii, as far as 189 B.C. was concerned, entirely to the actions of the consuls. One may note, though, that books xxxiii, xxxiv, and xxxvi also conclude with isolated (though by no means so short) Polybian sections.

It seems clear enough, as L. indicates, that Fabius was looking for something to do, doubtless as a counterpoise to Scipionic prestige. Rome had no *locus standi* for interfering in Crete. We are, however, at the beginning of the period where Rome poses as arbiter of all matters in the Hellenistic world, and Fabius' action is a foretaste of what is to come. I am unconvinced by the suggestion that Labeo's actions were connected with Roman knowledge that Hannibal had fled to Gortyn after the battle of Magnesia (Nepos, *Hann*. 9, Just. xxxii. 4. 3: cf. Walbank, *Commentary*, iii. 163). See in general Thiel, 363 ff.

2. insisteret: *insistere* with the dative, meaning 'devote oneself to' does not occur before the Augustan period. Cf. *TLL*, vii. 1. 1925. 69 ff., p. 9.

otiosam: *otiosus* in the sense of providing *otium* occurs four times in L., of a *prouincia* again at xxiii. 27. 12, xl. 35. 1, and of *statiua* at xxiii. 35. 6.

3. Cydoniatae ... Gortynios Gnosiosque: on Cydonia see Walbank, *Commentary*, i. 510. Cnossus and Gortyn had earlier been in conflict with each other. See Errington, 35 ff.

captiuorum: cf. Flamininus' action in Greece in 194 (xxxiv. 50. 3–7), Ducrey, 249 n. 1, Toynbee, ii. 31. For Crete as a repository of slaves, especially those captured by pirates, cf. Thiel, 364–5, Ducrey, 183.

4. ciuitates: all the states, not just the combatants. W–M's note is irrelevant.

quaeque: with *in suis* ... *conquisitos*: cf. Madvig, *Kleine philologischen Schriften* (Leipzig, 1875), 371–2.

reducerent: it is hard to see how the Cretans could be asked to 'bring back' those enslaved, and in view of *reddiderunt* and *reddita* below Nitsche's *redderent* seems right.

6. L.'s words indicate only that the number of returned slaves stood only in Antias. They are not meant to cast doubt on the triumph, and it does not follow that Polybius had no reference to a triumph. L. later refers to the triumph (xxxviii. 47. 5) and it appears in the *Fasti* as *Asia de rege Antiocho*, justified, no doubt, by his expulsion of the garrisons from Aenus and Maronea (§ 7) and his actions off the Asiatic coast in 188 (xxxviii. 39. 2). Fabius' 'achievements' are commemorated on the coins of his grandson (Crawford, *RRC*, i. 294). The triumph will have been supported by the Scipios' opponents in order to diminish Scipionic glory. The reference at xxxviii. 47. 5 is put in the mouth of Scipionic opponents of the 'Fulvians'. It may be noticed that while Fabius made dedications at Delos (*IDelos* 442 B103), he does not appear in the Cretan inscription honouring the Scipios and Aemilius Regillus (*IC* ii. 3. 5: cf. M. Guarducci, *RFIC* vii [1929], 60–85).

quattuor milia: *ad quattuor milia* ψ, *ad quattuor* Bφ. The omission of *ad* in the Teubner is probably a misprint.

timuerint: Bekker, *timuerunt* Bχ, perhaps rightly. Cf. xxxiv. 20. 2 n.

7. Fabius redit: Bχ, *rediit Fabius* Mg. Cf. pp. 12, 15.

Aeno et Maronia: on their position cf. xxxi. 16. 4–5 n. They had been freed from Philip in 196 (xxxiii. 35. 2, Pol. xviii. 48. 2) and will have been captured by Antiochus during one of his Thracian expeditions (cf. p. 27 n. 1, xxxv. 23. 10 n.). The senatorial decree had dealt only with Asiatic towns. For Philip's later occupation of Aenus and Maronea see Walbank, *Philip V*, 223 ff.

APPENDIX

THE GENDER OF *DIES* IN LIVY XXXIV–XXXVII

When Fraenkel wrote his famous article[1] establishing that in early
Latin and Classical prose *dies* masculine refers to a specific day while
dies feminine indicates the beginning or end of a space of time, he
had to admit that L. did not always observe these rules.[2] Books
xxxiv–xxxvii provide a number of interesting examples of L.'s practice. Of xxxiv. 35. 3 *et qua die scriptae condiciones pacis editae Nabidi
forent, ea dies ut indutiarum principium esset, et ut ex ea die intra decimum
diem* . . . Fraenkel observed[3] that while Cicero would have written
ex ea die he would have used the masculine on the two preceding
occasions. L. would have had more justification for writing *intra
decimam diem*, though in fact Cicero used the masculine when a
precise date was indicated.[4] L. similarly uses the masculine with an
ordinal at xxxvi. 10. 1 and xxxvii. 49. 7. The masculine at xxxvi. 6. 6
and the feminines at xxxv. 7. 3 and xxxvi. 35. 6 accord with the
rules, but at xxxvi. 8. 2 *dies ad conueniendum exercitui Pheras est indictus*
we should expect the feminine.[5] At xxxvii. 44. 3 Bχ have *postero die*,
Mg had *postera die*. The masculine is correct and is L.'s regular
usage.[6] *postera die* is attested unanimously at ii. 49. 2 and is the
reading of M at x. 25. 9. Fraenkel[7] argued for *postero* at all three
places. On balance he was probably right but in view of L.'s practice as a whole it can by no means be excluded that he wrote *postera*
on all three occasions.

---

[1] *Glotta* viii (1917), 24 ff. = *Kleine Beiträge zur klassischen Philologie* (Rome, 1964),
i. 27 ff. All references are to the latter.
[2] 56–7. Fraenkel (62) nevertheless proposed emending transmitted feminines at
ii. 49. 2 (see below), iii. 20. 4, 46. 8, v. 42. 2, xl. 9. 10, xlix. 4. 6. Ogilvie now keeps
the feminine at iii. 20. 4, 48. 6: see *JRS* lxvii (1977), 241.
[3] 56–7 n. 4.
[4] Fraenkel, 32.
[5] Cf. Caes. *BG* i. 6. 4, v. 57. 2, Fraenkel, 32 n. 1, 33 n. 1.
[6] Packard, ii. 1008–10.
[7] 62.

ADDENDA AND CORRIGENDA

BOOKS XXXI–XXXIII

I do not list here the many passages in books xxxi–xxxiii discussed by Tränkle, *Livius und Polybios*, and Luce, *Livy, the Composition of his History*. Their indexes will provide guidance to those interested in particular passages. For notes in the present volume referring to passages in books xxxi–xxxiii see index 3A.

pp. 1 ff. See Luce, ch. v.

p. 11. R. A. Laroche, *Historia* xxvi (1977), 358 ff. argues for mystical significance in the number of dead reported by Antias.

p. 15 n. 3. On L.'s attitude to Sallust cf. H. Aili, *The Prose Rhythms of Sallust and Livy* (Stockholm, 1979), 122 ff.

pp. 22 ff. See A. M. Eckstein, *Phoenix* xxx (1976), 119 ff.

p. 28 n. 2. Add *SEG* xxii. 465 (drawn to my attention by Mr. G. Shirinian).

pp. 36 ff. On the outbreak of the Second Macedonian War see R. Werner, *ANRW*, i. 1. 539 ff., L. Raditsa, ibid., 564 ff., Rich, 73 ff., 107 ff., 128 ff., Harris, 212 ff.

p. 36 n. 5. On the date of the death of Philopator see Walbank, *Polybius*, 111 n. 75.

p. 37 n. 4. The order Lade–Pergamum–Chios is supported by R. M. Berthold, *Historia* xxiv (1975), 150 ff., Harris, 213 n. 2.

p. 37 n. 8. Cf. W. E. Thompson, *TAPhA* cii (1971), 615–20. On Philip's attack on Cos see S. M. Sherwin-White, *Ancient Cos* (Göttingen, 1978), 131 ff.

p. 39, l. 10. Read 'agreement not to obstruct' (pointed out by A. M. Ward, *CW* lxviii [1975], 456).

Book xxxi. See the Budé edition of A. Hus, with my review in *CR* n.s. xxix (1979), 152–3.

p. 49. **xxxi. 1. 1–5.** On the structure of L.'s work see G. Wille, *Der Aufbau des Livianischen Geschichtswerks* (Amsterdam, 1973), with my review in *JRS* lxv (1975), 224–5, A. Hus, *RPh* 3, xlvii (1973), 225 ff., P. Jal, ibid., xlix (1975), 278 ff., Walsh, *Livy* (*Greece and Rome*, New Surveys in the Classics, Oxford, 1974), 8 ff., Luce, ch. i.

p. 51 l. 3. Add a reference to Aristotle, *EN* 1098 b7.

xxxi. 1. 7 claritate . . . imperii: add references to L. Castiglioni, *RIL* 2, lxi (1928), 625 ff., Momigliano, *Athenaeum* n.s. xii (1934), 45 ff., G. W. Bowersock, *Augustus and the Greek World* (Oxford, 1965), 109 ff., Luce, *TAPhA* xcvi (1965), 218 ff.

p. 58. **xxxi. 2. 5. subitariis:** for *subitarius* in a military metaphor see Plautus, *Mil.* 225 (drawn to my attention by Dr. D. M. Bain).

p. 61. **xxxi. 3. 3. propraetor:** see now *BRL* lxii (1980), 323. ff.

p. 68. **xxxi. 5. 4. de re publica . . . consulerent:** add references to Ogilvie, 468–9, Walsh on xxi. 6. 3, W. K. Lacey, *JRS* lxiv (1974), 176.

p. 69. **xxxi. 6.** On the war-vote cf. L. Raditsa, *Helikon* ix–x (1969–1970), 671–2.

xxxi. 6. 1. sorti: cf. O. Skutsch, *BICS* xxiii (1976), 76.

p. 70. **xxxi. 6. 1. Philippo . . . Macedonibusque:** *contra* see Errington, *JHS* xciv (1974), 36.

p. 71. **xxxi. 6. 5–6. damno dedecorique:** cf. Ogilvie, 554.

p. 85. **xxxi. 11. 11.** Cf. E. Rawson, *JRS* lxv (1975), 155.

p. 88. **xxxi. 12. 5–10.** Add references to J. J. Delgado, *Helmantica* xii (1961), 27–46, 441–6, xiv (1963), 381–419, E. Ruoff-Väänänen, *Arctos* vii (1972), 139 ff., Walsh on xxi. 46. 1.

p. 89. **xxxi. 12. 6. Sospitae Iunonis:** after '*de n.d.* i. 82' add Pease ad loc., viii. 14. 2, Cic. *Mur.* 90, Kienast, *Hermes* xciii (1965), 482, J. R. Fears, *Historia* xxiv (1975), 595 ff.

p. 93. **xxxi. 13. 6. sibimet . . . esse:** on the construction cf. Walsh on xxi. 27. 3.

pp. 97 ff. **xxxi. 14. 11–16. 8.** On L.'s adaptation of Polybius in this section cf. A. Hus, *Mélanges Boyancé* (Rome, 1974), 419 ff.

p. 99. **xxxi. 15. 7. et Rhodiorum . . . dederant:** on ἰσοπολιτεία cf. W. Gawantka, *Isopolitie* (Munich, 1975).

xxxi. 15. 8. Ceam: for a decree of Carthaea referring to an alliance concluded with Rhodes at this time cf. C. Dunant and J. Thomopoulos, *BCH* lxxviii (1954), 338 ff.

p. 101. **xxxi. 16. 4–5. cum magno labore:** cf. Burck, *Gnomon* xlvii (1975), 258.

Callimedis: he is in fact probably identical with the man referred to in *PTebt.* 8. 12: cf. Fraser, *JEA* xxxix (1953), 91–2 n. 5, R. S. Bagnall, *JEA* lxi (1975), 177 ff.

p. 107. **xxxi. 18. 6–7. repente:** cf. Walsh on xxi. 9. 2.

p. 108. **xxxi. 19. 5–6.** The authenticity of the notice is rejected by Kahrstedt (Meltzer–Kahrstedt, iii. 579).

pp. 112–14. **xxxi. 21. 12.** Cf. Burck, op. cit., 256. On Veiovis see A. Alföldi, *Chiron* ii (1972), 215 ff., E. Gjerstad, *ORom.* ix (1973), 35 ff.

p. 115. **xxxi. 22. 4. cum autumno . . . exacto:** see now *Historia* xxvi (1977), 248–50.

p. 118. **xxxi. 24. 2.** Cf. Burck, op. cit., 258.

p. 121. **xxxi. 25. 2. circumdatum:** cf. K. Wellesley, *Cornelius Tacitus, the Histories book iii* (Sydney, 1972), 113.

p. 122. **xxxi. 25. 2.** On the Achaean assemblies add Larsen, *CPh* lxvii (1972), 178–85, Walbank, *Commentary*, iii. 406 ff.

p. 124. **xxxi. 26. 3. praedantes:** cf. Adams, *Glotta* li (1973), 131.

p. 126. **xxxi. 27. 5. Codrionem:** for xliv. 40. 1 read xlii. 40. 1.

p. 131. **xxxi. 29. 7. et Messanam et Syracusas:** cf. R. T. Pritchard, *Historia* xxiv (1975), 33–48.

pp. 133–4. **xxxi. 30. 2.** Cf. Walbank, *Polybius*, 90–1. Mention should be made of Diodorus xxx. 18. 2 who refers to quasi-laws of war, which do forbid specific actions. Cf. de Ste. Croix, *The Origins of the Peloponnesian War* (London, 1972), 20.

pp. 125, 134. **xxxi. 26. 9, 30. 6.** Cf. Frederiksen, op. cit. (p. 24 n. 5) 346.

p. 136. **xxxi. 31. 6.** Cf. Burck, op. cit., 258.

p. 137. **xxxi. 31. 11.** for *inde . . . deinde* cf. xxxv. 38. 8.

pp. 139 ff. **xxxi. 33 ff.** For the campaign of 199 see Hammond, *A History of Macedonia*, i (Oxford, 1972), 60 ff.

p. 140. **xxxi. 34. 4–5. nam qui . . . cernebant:** cf. Harris, 52.

p. 141. **xxxi. 35. 1. Cretenses:** to addendum on p. 344 add Daux, *RD* 4, xlix (1971), 373 ff.

p. 142. **xxxi. 35. 5. gladiis rem gerebant:** cf. Ogilvie, 307.

   xxxi. 35. 6. concursator: cf. Walsh on xxxi. 35. 2.

   xxxi. 36. 4. Cf. Seibert, *Gymnasium* lxxx (1973), 348 ff., Scullard, *Elephant*, ch. vii.

p. 143. **xxxi. 37. 7. uersa . . . erant:** for the theme cf. K. Stiewe, *WJA* n.f. ii (1976), 158.

p. 145. **xxxi. 39. 11.** On the ρομφαία cf. Lehmann, *Beiträge zur alten Geschichte und deren Nachleben*, i (Berlin, 1969), 403 n. 48.

   xxxi. 40. 1. Celetrum: cf. Hammond, op. cit., 116.

   xxxi. 40. 4. Pelion: cf. Hammond, op. cit., 100, Cabanes, 320 n. 232, J. and L. Robert, *REG* lxxxvi (1973), 112, no. 267.

p. 148. **xxxi. 41. 10. inopinantibus:** cf. Goodyear, 207.
xxxi. 41. 14. Cf. Burck, op. cit., 258.

p. 149. **xxxi. 41. 2. tale:** cf. Burck, loc. cit.

p. 151. **xxxi. 44. 4. maiorum eius:** cf. P. Roussel, *BCH* liv (1930), 270–1.

p. 156. **xxxi. 46. 12. militibus ... uidebatur:** Burck, op. cit., 257 suggests *relictis quod satis ⟨uirium⟩ uidebatur.*

p. 161. **xxxi. 49. 4. consul:** for other instances of *consul* meaning proconsul cf. R. E. Smith, *Service in the post-Marian Roman Army* (Manchester, 1958), 12.

p. 162. **xxxi. 49. 9.** Cf. Burck, op. cit., 258.

p. 166. **Book xxxii.** For a highly implausible view of the structure of this book see T. A. Suits, *Philologus* cxviii (1974), 257 ff.

p. 170. **xxxii. 2. 3.** Cf. M. J. Moscovich, *Historia* xxiii (1974), 417 ff.

pp. 170–1. **xxxii. 2. 5. Gaditanis ... conuenisset:** cf. R. Bernhardt, *Historia* xxiv (1975), 419.

p. 172. **xxxii. 3.** Cf. Burck, op. cit., 253 n. 1.

p. 175. **xxxii. 5. 4–5.** On Aliphera cf. J. Roy, *Talanta* iv (1972), 39 ff.

p. 176. **xxxii. 5. 9. in Chaoniam ... misit:** on Antigonea cf. J. and L. Robert, *REG* lxxxvi (1973), 110, no. 259.

xxxii. 5. 11. inter montes: add a reference to xxxii. 38. 9.

p. 186. **xxxii. 10. 2. Pausanias praetor:** cf. J. Tréheux, *REG* lxxxviii (1975), 156 ff.

p. 187. **xxxiii. 11.** Add references to Pol. xxvii. 15. 2, Diod. xxx. 5, and cf. O. Skutsch, *LCM* iii (1978), 261–2. In the last line of the note read 52 n. 38.

p. 190. **xxxii. 13. 9. Palaepharsalus:** cf. C. B. R. Pelling, *Historia* xxii (1973), 250 n. 18.

p. 195. **xxxii. 16. 10 ff.** For an inscription claimed (unjustifiably) to provide evidence for games in honour of Lucius Flamininus at Eretria see *Ergon* 1976, 20–1, H. W. Catling, *AR* xxiv (1977/8), 17.

p. 198. **xxxii. 17. 17. trepidationemque insanam:** Burck, op. cit., 258 suggests *iniectam* or *subitam.*

p. 199. **xxxii. 17. 6. Phanoteam:** Klaffenbach's interpretation is rejected by J. and L. Robert, *REG* lxxxv (1972), 405 no. 199.

p. 207. **xxxii. 21. 17. sociorum ... erant:** for the alliteration cf. Walsh on xxi. 25. 3.

p. 209. **xxxii. 21. 28. unde:** cf. Shackleton Bailey, *Propertiana* (Cambridge, 1956), 74–5, Burck, op. cit., 257.

p. 210. **xxxii. 21. 36. mare:** cf. Burck, op. cit., 258.

p. 211. **xxxii. 23. 11. Argiui ... credunt:** cf. C. F. Edson, *HSPh* xlv (1934), 213 ff., O. Müller, *Antigonos Monophthalmos und 'das Jahr der Könige'* (Bonn, 1973), 115.

p. 213. **xxxii. 24. 12.** Cf. Burck, op. cit., 256.

p. 218. **xxxii. 26. 18.** Kahrstedt (Meltzer–Kahrstedt, iii. 590) denies the truth of the notice.

pp. 229–31. **xxxii. 32. 9–16.** Cf. H. A. Gärtner, *Beobachtungen zu Bauelementen in der antiken Historiographie* (*Historia*, Einzelschriften, 25), 24 ff.

p. 224. **xxxii. 29. 1. priusquam ... placuit:** on the alliteration cf. Goodyear, 339 n. 1.

p. 229. **xxxii. 32. 10.** Cf. Burck, op. cit., 256.

p. 244. **xxxii. 38. 9. rogationes ... unam ... alteram:** cf. addendum to xxxii. 5. 11 n.

p. 248. **xxxiii. 1. 1. quod caput ... Boeotiae:** D. Hennig, *Chiron* vii (1977), 126 n. 20 denies that the assembly normally met at Onchestus in this period.

p. 249. **xxxiii. 1. 3.** Cf. Walbank, *JHS* xcvii (1977), 209.

p. 252. **xxxiii. 4. 1. ⟨i⟩terum a:** cf. Burck, op. cit., 257.

p. 271. **xxxiii. 12. 10–11.:** *contra* cf. Harris, 141 n. 7.

p. 283. **xxxiii. 18. 22.** Cf. Walbank, *Commentary*, iii. 457–8.

p. 284. **xxxiii. 19. 3.** For excavations at Stobi cf. J. Wiseman and D. Mano-Zissi, *AJA* lxxv (1971), 395 ff., lxxvi (1972), 407 ff., lxxvii (1973), 391 ff.

xxxiii. 19. 5. On Hellenistic Thessalonica cf. M. Vickers, *JHS* xcii (1972), 156 ff.

xxxiii. 19. 6—20. Cf. A. Mastrocinque, *PP* xxxi (1976), 307 ff.

p. 286. **xxxiii. 20. 2. mole ... belli:** cf. Ogilvie, 278, Woodman, 102.

p. 287. **xxxiii. 20. 4. Anemurio:** cf. E. Alföldi-Rosenbaum, *Anamu Nekropolü, The Necropolis of Anemurium* (Ankara, 1971), S. Mitchell and A. W. McNicoll, *AR* xxv (1978–9), 89.

p. 288. **xxxiii. 20. 11–12. Cauniis:** cf. Walbank, *Commentary*, iii. 426, 457.

p. 297. **xxxiii. 25. 7. in Capitolio:** cf. E. S. Staveley, *Greek and Roman Voting and Elections* (London, 1972), 151 and n. 281.

p. 302. **xxxiii. 28. 8. sibi conscius:** cf. Sall. *Iug.* 40. 2, Koestermann, 163.

p. 305. **xxxiii. 30. 3. Iaso:** to the addendum on p. 347 add Y. Garlan, *ZPE* xiii (1974), 197–8, J. and L. Robert, *REG* lxxxvii (1974), 288 n. 544, Mastrocinque, *PP* xxxi (1976), 311 ff.

p. 315. **xxxiii. 34. 11.** Cf. Hammond, *A History of Macedonia*, i. 96 n. 4.

p. 319. **xxxiii. 37. 9. agrum Comensem:** cf. G. Luraschi, *Athenaeum* n.s. liii (1975), 338 ff.

pp. 320 ff. **xxxiii. 38–41.** Cf. Mastrocinque, *PP* xxxi (1976), 318 ff.

p. 321. **xxxiii. 38. 3.** Badian, *Entretiens Fondation Hardt* xvii, 178–9, plausibly suggests that Ennius, *Ann.* fr. 358–9V refer to the appeal of Lampsacus. For *Syll.*[3] 591 see *Die Inschriften von Lampsacus* (ed. P. Frisch, Bonn, 1978), no. 4.

p. 322. **xxxiii. 38. 10. Lysimachiam:** for fragments of a treaty between Lysimachia and Antiochus see Z. Tasiklioğlu and P. Frisch, *ZPE* xvii (1975), 101 ff.

p. 327. **xxxiii. 42. 7. ad capita ... fluminis:** for a similar calque on *caput* = ῥίζα cf. Cato, *Agr.* 133. 2.

p. 328. **xxxiii. 42. 1.** On the *Leges Licinia et Aebutia* cf. Badian, *ANRW*, i. 1. 705 n. 113.

p. 329. **xxxiii. 42. 3.** On the alliteration cf. Goodyear, 339 n. 1.

p. 331. **xxxiii. 43. 5. P. Porcius ... Pisas:** to the addendum on p. 348 add Wiseman, *Epigraphica* xxxiii (1971), 27 ff.

p. 367. Under *ILLRP* add 188, **168.**

* * *

The above items were collected between October 1972 and November 1979. The following came to my notice after the latter date.

p. 28 n. 1. On the staters of Flamininus and the honours paid to him cf. Crawford, *RRC*, i. 544.

p. 49. **xxxi. 1. 1–5.** Add T. Crosby, *LCM* iii (1978), 113 ff.

p. 91. **xxxi. 12. 9. P. Licinius Tegula:** for the possibility that Licinius Imbrex and Licinius Tegula got their *cognomina* from the manufacture of tiles in Southern Etruria see A. Andren, *NSA*, 8, xxiii (1969), 71, C. and Ö. Wikander, *ORom* xii (1979), 9–10.

p. 115. **xxxi. 22. 1. supplicatio:** on the *supplicatio* as a thank-offering see G. Freyburger, *Latomus* xxxvi (1977), 283 ff.

p. 128. **xxxi. 28. 5. ex amicorum numero:** on the φίλοι see Chr. Habicht, *Vierteljahrschrift für Sozial- und Wirtschaftsgeschichte* xlv (1958), 1–16.

p. 130. **xxxi. 29. 4. qui cum . . . fecistis:** Appian's date for the Aetolian embassy is defended by P. S. Derow, *JRS* lxix (1979), 7–8.

p. 203. **xxxii. 19. 6, 33. 2.** For L.'s use of *simplex, simplicitas, simpliciter* cf. A. M. Ferrero, *AAT* cx (1976), 53–69.

p. 266. **xxxiii. 10. 7–10.** R. A. Laroche, *C & M* xxxi (1970), 120–3, suggests that the figures of Polybius, Claudius, and Antias are due to misinterpretations of abacus calculations.

p. 303. **xxxiii. 29. 8.** Cf. xlii. 23. 6.

BOOKS XXXIV–XXXVII

p. xii. Add Bernhardt   R. Bernhardt, *Imperium und Eleutheria* (Hamburg, 1971).

p. xvii. *ORF.*[3] There is now a fourth edition (Pavia, 1976).

Add Rodgers   W. L. Rodgers, *Greek and Roman Naval Warfare* (Annapolis, Md., 1937).

p. 2. To the list of transition passages (para. 2) add xxxv. 25. 1. To the list of probable or possible misunderstandings of Polybius add xxxvii. 11. 3, 26. 6, 28. 4, 31. 8–10, 33. 7, 36. 2, 54. 2, 54. 3.

pp. 4–6. Add the following items. *agedum*: cf. xxxiv. 32. 12 n. It occurs in Flamininus' speech to Nabis (p. 6 line 7). *circumducit* used absolutely: cf. xxxiv. 14. 1 n. It occurs in the account of Cato's battle near Emporiae (p. 9). *in rem esse* occurs also at xxxiv. 18. 3. *spe posse*: cf. xxxiv. 13. 5, 24.7 nn. Its use is probably determined by L.'s desire to avoid a periphrastic construction.

pp. 7–8 n. 4. Add references to *antesignanus* in the speech of Alexander of Acarnania (xxxv. 18. 4) and to *quin* with the present indicative at xxxvi. 34. 8.

p. 8. *inclutus* (p. 4) is probably to be explained in the same way as *fidere, pauere,* and *perplexus,* though it occurs in a passage immediately preceding the account of the meeting of the Achaean League and the context of the claims of Alexander of Acarnania to descent from Alexander the Great would naturally lead to the use of high-flown language.

p. 9. Add the following items. *auctoratus* other than of gladiators xxxvii. 10. 8, *detractator* xxxiv. 15. 9, *dimidium quam* xxxv. 1. 2, *exaequatio* xxxiv. 4. 14, *exigere* = 'export' xxxiv. 9. 9, *fabrefacere* xxxiv. 52. 5, xxxvii. 27. 5, *hepteris, hexeris* xxxvii. 23. 5, 24. 3, 24. 9, 30. 2, *impetu rerum* xxxvii. 19. 5, *in obuio* xxxvii. 23. 1, *inpenetrabilis* xxxvi. 25. 4, *inscitus* of artefacts xxxvi. 43. 6, *interequitare* xxxiv. 15. 4, xxxv. 5. 10, *nudare* = 'lay bare' also at xxxiv. 24. 7, *obequitare* xxxv. 11. 6, *oppido quam* xxxvi. 25. 3, *procella equestris* xxxv. 5. 9 cf. xxxvii. 41. 10, *publicare* used metaphorically xxxiv. 61. 16, *rebellare* xxxiv. 13. 9, *restituti animi* xxxv. 27. 12 (perhaps influenced by an ἀναλαμβάνειν in Polybius), *saginare* used literally of humans xxxvi. 17. 8, *satis iam* not used colloquially xxxiv. 28. 1.

p. 10. For another example of legal language see xxxiv. 62. 14.

p. 11. In the list of textual problems involving asyndeton add xxxvii. 8. 6.

p. 12. In the list of ellipses add xxxv. 27. 13, xxxvii. 10. 7 (*esse*), xxxvii. 10. 5 (verb of saying), xxxiv. 18. 2, 29. 10 (apodosis).

p. 13. In the list of repetitions add xxxiv. 55. 4, xxxvii. 35. 6 (deliberate), xxxv. 27. 6, xxxvii. 53.17 (non-deliberate).

p. 14. xxxvi. 9. 8 is similar to xxxv. 47. 1. For a striking example of the postponement of *cum* (not involving the separation of a participle from a part of *esse*) see xxxiv. 5. 1.

n. 1. In the list of examples of chiastic word-order add xxxv. 29. 2.

p. 15. To the list of passages in para. 2 add the following. xxxiv. 3. 6, 4. 14, 5. 7, 6. 15, 7. 3, 50. 10, 61. 1–2, xxxv. 4. 4, 5. 7, 16. 12, 21. 5, 21. 9, 22. 2, 26. 7, 30. 10, 32. 7, 33. 10, 34. 9, 35. 1, 35. 11, 14. 2, xxxvi. 8. 6, 10. 7, 17. 14, 36. 4, xxxvii. 8. 3, 11. 9, 16. 11, 48. 6, 30. 6, 35. 2, 39. 11, 41. 2, 41. 3, 49. 5, 51. 1, 52. 3.

p. 28. On xxxvi. 4 see xxxvi. 4. 1–4 n.

pp. 33 ff. On the wars in Northern Italy see B. D. Hoyos, *Antichthon* x (1976), 44–55.

p. 35 n. 1. Against the view of Sumner see R. C. Knapp, *Aspects of the Roman Experience in Iberia*, 206–100 B.C. (Valladolid, 1977), 93 n. 20.

p. 43. **xxxiv. 1. 2. L. Valerius:** for Tappo's praetorship see xxxv. 10. 11, 20. 8, 23. 8–9, for its prorogation xxxvi. 2. 11 n., for his office as *iiiuir* xxxvii. 46. 11, 57. 7.

p. 45. **xxxiv. 1. 3. urbe oppidoue:** cf. H. Galsterer, *Herrschaft und Verwaltung im Republikanischen Italien* (Munich, 1976), 134.

p. 59. **xxxiv. 6. 11. Arpos:** cf. P. D. A. Garnsey, *PCPhS* n.s. xxv (1979), 10 and n. 50.

p. 60. **xxxiv. 7. 1. sentient:** cf. xxxvi. 24. 7 n.

pp. 65–6. On my chronology *frumentum in areis Hispani haberent* (9. 12) can be taken to refer to a second harvest. Cf. Tränkle, *Cato*, 22.

p. 68. **xxxiv. 9. 1. Massilienses:** for early relations between Rome and Massilia see C. Ebel, *Transalpine Gaul: the emergence of a Roman province* (Leiden, 1976), 4 ff.: *contra* cf. J. S. Richardson, *JRS* lxix (1979), 157.

p. 71. **xxxiv. 10. 4.** J. S. Richardson, *JRS* lxvi (1976), 149 n. 86, suggests 178 as the date of the Spanish *denarius* coinage.

p. 82. **xxxiv. 18. 3–5.** For another example cf. xliv. 4. 10.

p. 85. **xxxiv. 22. 4—41.** Various matters in this section are discussed by D. Mendels, *Athenaeum* n.s. lvii (1979), 311 ff. Unfortunately he thinks that *tamquam aemulus Lycurgi* at 32. 4 means 'no more than an imitator of Lycurgus'.

p. 88. **xxxiv. 24. 7. nudaret:** cf. xxxv. 32. 2 n.

pp. 91, 96. **xxxiv. 26. 11. iam . . . iam . . . iam; xxxiv. 29. 6. iam . . . iam:** cf. Chausserie-Laprée, 511. But 26. 11, regarded as parallel to 29. 6 by Chausserie-Laprée, does not have the same effect.

p. 110. **xxxiv. 37. 4. solet:** add a reference to xxxi. 34. 3.

p. 114. **xxxiv. 41. 1. die stata:** see appendix and addendum thereto.

pp. 115–16. **xxxiv. 42. 5–6.** See Galsterer, op. cit., 88, 112 n. 12, 162.

p. 117. **xxxiv. 43. 7.** J. S. Ruebel, *CW* lxxi (1977), 167, thinks Scipio did try to obtain the Spanish command.

p. 127. **xxxiv. 51. 1. conuentum . . . ciuitatium:** cf. O. Picard, *Chalcis et la confédération eubéenne* (Athens, 1979), 287 ff.

p. 128. **xxxiv. 52. 5.** At the beginning of the note add 'the MSS. have $\overline{xviii}$. Madvig (*Emendationes*, 506–7) proposed *quadraginta tria* on the basis of Plutarch, *Flam.* 14. 2.'

p. 129. **xxxiv. 52. 6.** On the date of the introduction of the cistophori see F. S. Kleiner and S. P. Noe, *The Early Cistophoric Coinage* (New York, 1977), 10 ff.

p. 132. **xxxiv. 53. 5–6.** xliii. 13. 5 also refers to the temple of *Fortuna primigenia* on the Quirinal.

p. 134. **xxxiv. 54. 3. A. Atilius Serranus:** for references to his praetorship and propraetorship see xxxv. 10. 11, 20. 8–13, 22. 2, 24. 4, 37. 3, xxxvi. 12. 9 n.

L. Scribonius Libo: for his praetorship cf. xxxv. 10. 11, 20. 8, 21. 1.

p. 136. **xxxiv. 56. 6.** W. V. Harris, *Caratteri dell' ellenismo nelle urne etrusche*, ed. M. Martelli and M. Cristani (Florence, 1977), 62 n. 9, thinks that there was no departure from normal practice. See also Galsterer, op. cit., 160.

p. 138. **xxxiv. 57. 6. simpliciter:** see addendum on xxxii. 19. 6, 33. 2 above.

p. 141. **xxxiv. 59. 8. P. Aelium:** (101). Paetus. Cf. xxxi. 2. 5 n.

p. 145. **xxxiv. 62. 16. omnia suspensa:** Professor Jocelyn draws my attention to *suspensa omnia* at xxxv. 6. 2.

p. 152. **xxxv. 6. 2–4.** R. Rilinger, *Der Einfluss des Wahlleiters bei den römischen Konsulwahlen von 366 bis 50 v. Chr.* (Munich, 1976), 40 ff., argues that from 366 the *consul prior* normally held the elections. He does not, however, consider the implications of the present passage and 20. 2.

p. 153. **xxxv. 7. 2–5.** Cf. Galsterer, op. cit., 131–2.

p. 154. **xxxv. 7. 4.** For Tuditanus' praetorship see xxxvii. 47. 8, 50. 8.

pp. 157–8. **xxxv. 9. 7–8.** Cf. Galsterer, op. cit., 53.

p. 160. **xxxv. 10. 12. porticum ... adiecto:** against recent attempts to deny the identification of the remains referred to see Coarelli, *PBSR* xiv (1977), 9.

p. 168. **xxxv. 15. 7. princeps amicorum:** L. Mooren, *Antike Diplomatie*, ed. E. Olshausen (Darmstadt, 1979), 289 n. 118, denies that the phrase is technical here.

p. 173. **xxxv. 19. 2. simpliciter:** see addendum on xxxiv. 57. 6.

p. 174. **xxxv. 20. 2.** See addendum on 6. 2–4.

p. 179. **xxxv. 23. 7.** Oppius is the only *priuatus cum imperio* between 197 and 81: cf. Schleussner, 128.

xxxv. 29. 11. aedes liberae ... lautia: Timpanaro's discussion is now reprinted (with additions) in his *Contributi di filologia e di storia della lingua latina* (Rome, 1978), 516 ff.

p. 183. **xxxv. 26. 5. octaginta ... ueheret:** R. Urban, *Wachstum und Krise des Achäischen Bundes* (*Historia*, Einzelschriften, xxxv), 10, accepts 272 as the date of the capture of the Macedonian ship.

p. 192. **xxxv. 32. 1. concilio:** cf. xxxiii. 12. 1, xxxiv. 17. 11, 26. 4 nn.

p. 196. **xxxv. 34. 8. simplices:** see addendum on xxxiv. 57. 6.

p. 200. **xxxv. 37. 5.** On Chalcis as a commercial centre cf. Picard, op. cit. (addendum on xxxiv. 51. 1), 339 ff.

p. 201. **xxxv. 38. 1. Micythio:** for a different Micythio cf. *IG* xii. 9. 900B. See Picard, op. cit., 289 n. 4.

xxxv. 38. 3. Amarynthidis Dianae: see Picard, op. cit., 219.

p. 205. **xxxv. 41. 9. M. Tuccio:** for the prorogation of his praetorship in 189 see xxxvii. 50. 13.

xxxv. 41. 10. inter lignarios: as Professor Jocelyn points out to me, probably the timber-market rather than the quarter of the carpenters.

p. 216. **xxxv. 50. 8. auxilium missum:** Thiel, 288, thinks that this contingent is not to be identified with the one dispatched at 39. 2: *contra* see Picard, op. cit., 283n. 4.

p. 220. **xxxvi. 2. 5. faxit:** cf. xxxiv. 4. 21 n.

p. 222. **xxxvi. 3. 4–6.** Cf. Galsterer, op. cit., 43 ff.

p. 227. **xxxvi. 5. 3. simplicis:** see addendum on xxxiv. 57. 6.

p. 228. **xxxvi. 6. 3. obuiam . . . uenit:** L. interprets ἄρξαντες to mean 'those who have held office', perhaps correctly. See Walbank, *Commentary*, iii. 74.

p. 231. **xxxvi. 7. 19.** On the site of Byllis see Hammond, *Epirus* 225 ff.

p. 240. **xxxvi. 13. 6. Meliboea:** not otherwise known. Cf. Stählin, *HTh*, 127.

p. 252. **xxxvi. 21. 3. ullius . . . urbis:** cf. Picard, op. cit., 290.

pp. 252–3. **xxxvi. 21. 4–11.** Lucius' mission is rejected by J. S. Ruebel, *CW* lxxi (1977), 170 n. 30.

p. 254. **xxxvi. 21. 9. quibus . . . uideretur:** G. Freyburger, *Latomus* xxxvi (1977), 308, implausibly argues that in deciding the details the praetor consulted the records of the vows made by the general on his departure from Rome.

p. 271. **xxxvi. 33. 7. Perrhaebiae:** cf. xxxi. 41. 5 n.

p. 274. **xxxvi. 36. 3–4.** Plautus' *Pseudolus* was produced at these *Megalesia* (*didasc. Ambr.*).

p. 291. **xxxvii. 1. 9–10.** Cf. Schleussner, 174–5 n. 249.

p. 297. **xxxvii. 5. 6.** Cf. p. 10.

p. 306. **xxxvii. 9. 9.** See D. E. Koutroubas, *EEAth* xxiv (1973–4), 799–807.

xxxvii. 10. 6. Samos was an independent state allied to Rhodes. Cf. xxxiii. 20. 11–12 n.

p. 321. **xxxvii. 19. 8 eodem Adramytteum:** cf. xlii. 47. 9.

p. 323. **xxxvii. 22. 1. Eumenen:** here, at 26. 3, and at xxxviii. 12. 6

the MSS. have *Eumenen,* elsewhere in the fourth decade *Eumenem.* The Vienna MS. of books xli–xlv has *Eumenen* frequently.

p. 339. **xxxvii. 34. 4–6.** P. Botteri, *Index* ii (1971), 198 ff., argues that Africanus had only one son, the adoptive father of Aemilianus.

p. 342. **xxxvii. 36. 4.** On Scipio's remarks here see *Latomus* xxxi (1972), 51 n. 6.

p. 343. **xxxvii. 37–44.** J. P. V. D. Balsdon, *Romans and Aliens* (London, 1979), 82, wrongly takes xxxviii. 41. 13 to refer to an incident during the battle of Magnesia.

p. 353. **xxxvii. 41. 10.** *tribuli,* as Vegetius explains, are iron instruments with three prongs sticking into the ground, one projecting upwards.

p. 366. **xxxvii. 48.** On the date of Antias see T. P. Wiseman, *Clio's Cosmetics* (Leicester, 1979), 117 ff.

p. 369. **xxxvii. 50. 9.** A force of allied troops had been sent to Sicily in 198 (xxxii. 8. 7). It was supplemented in 192 (xxxv. 23. 8) and 190 (2. 8).

p. 373. **xxxvii. 52. 3. fratrem:** a further argument in favour of *fratrem* is that it was Attalus who, for most of the time, was in charge of the defence of Pergamum.

p. 384. **xxxvii. 55. 3. in Capitolio:** cf. Schleussner, 31–2 n. 73.

p. 390. **xxxvii. 57. 8. septuagena . . . quinquagena:** Brunt, 191, also suggests that the colonists were expected to employ Gauls as labourers or lease land to them. Cf. P. D. A. Garnsey, *PCPhS* n.s. xxv (1979), 16.

p. 394. **xxxvii. 59. 5. purpurati:** for *et purpurati* cf. xxxiv. 23. 9 n.

p. 396. Cicero would have written *stato die* at xxxiv. 41. 1.

MAPS

The maps that follow indicate the location of all places mentioned in books xxxiv–xxxvii, with the exception of a few places whose position cannot be determined.

1—Italy

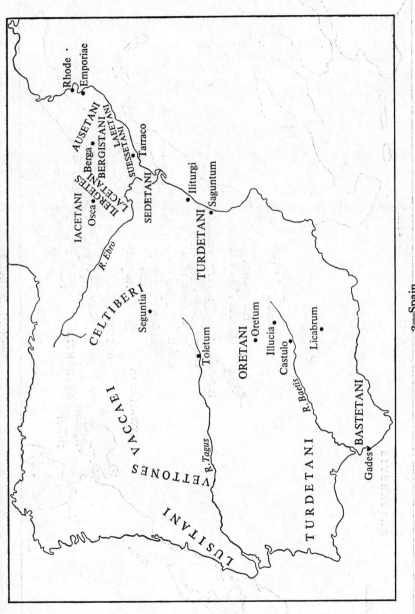

2—Spain

3—Northern Greece

4—Southern Greece

5—Asia Minor

INDEXES

1. GENERAL

Figures followed by a colon or in brackets indicate a date.

1. GENERAL

Cn. Cornelius Scipio (*cos.* 222), 81.

L. Cornelius Scipio (*cos.* 190), 193: praetorship, 134; 192: candidate for consulship of 191, 180; 191: sent to Rome after battle of Thermopylae, 252–3; elected consul for 190, 287; 190: appointed to eastern command, 291–2; army, 38; chronology of campaign, 29; departure from Rome, 295–6; negotiations with Aetolians, 298–301; Africanus' speech to, 7, 301–2; letter to Prusias, 328; negotiations with Antiochus, 337–42; sacrifice at Ilium, 207, 343–4; battle of Magnesia and subsequent peace negotiations, 343–62; 189: triumph, 30, 392–4; belittling of by sources, 291, 346; *cognomen*, 392.

L. Cornelius Scipio (*pr.* 174), 339–40, 366.

P. Cornelius Scipio, son of Africanus, 339.

P. Cornelius Scipio Africanus (*cos.* 205, 194), in Second Punic War, 20, 74, 302–3; 194: consulship, 22, 66, 115; hopes for command in Greece, 105, 116–17; and seats for senators in theatre, 118; and colonies, 119; in Northern Italy, 124; 193: embassy to Africa, 145; and elections for 192, 158–9; alleged meeting with Hannibal, 165–7; 191: and election of L. Scipio to consulship for 190, 287; 190: appointment as *legatus* to L. Scipio, 291; dedication of arch, 294; veterans of join L. Scipio, 296; negotiations with Aetolians, 298–301; speech to L. Scipio, 7, 301–2; letter to Prusias, 328; delayed as *Salius*, 337–8, 364; negotiations before battle of Magnesia, 337–43; absence from battle, 346; peace negotiations following battle, 9, 358–62; relations with Philip V, 301–3.

P. Cornelius Scipio Nasica (*cos.* 191), 28, 34–5, 38, 115, 117, 147, 158, 180, 218, 252, 274–80, 292.

Corcyra, 127.

corona, 111, 296.

Coronea, 228, 250.

Corribilo, 178.

Corupaedium, battle of, 30, 169.

Corycus, 285, 311–12, 332; battle of, 28, 281–7, 303–4, 325, 330, 333.

Corylenus, 323.

Cos, 309, 315, 324, 397.

Cotton, 323.

Crannon, 233, 241.

Craterus, 183.

Cremona, 33, 43, 84, 364.

Crete, Cretans, 30, 103, 108, 182–3, 187, 348, 350–1, 394–5.

Creusa, 253.

Croton, 119.

crowns, as gifts, 274, 363.

Culchas, 328.

Cusibi, 178.

Cydonia, 395.

Cylarabes, Cylarabis, 90.

Cyme, 309–10, 387.

Cynoscephalae, battle of (197), 21, 162, 212.

Cyrtii, 350.

Cyzicus, 167.

Daedala, 324.

Dahae, 211–12, 214, 346, 350.

Damocles, 89–90.

Damocritus of Aetolia, 33 n. 8, 163, 194, 257, 261, 295, 363.

Dardanians, 346.

Dardanus, 305, 343.

Darius III, 352.

Dassaretis, 235.

debt, 23–4, 27, 153–4, 305.

decemvirate, 58.

declamations, 58.

decuma, 221.

deditio, 113, 138–9, 259–64, 290, 300, 336.

Delium, 28, 216–17, 224, 228.

Delos, 165–6, 283, 395.

Delphi, 165, 272.

Demetrias, 8, 28, 87, 103, 125, 191, 195–6, 202–3, 207, 224, 251, 257, 340.

Demetrius, son of Philip V, 130, 138, 274, 328.

denarii, 153, 394.

Dexagoridas, 97.

Dicaearchus, 27, 163, 171, 263.

Sex. Digitius (*pr.* 194), 115, 146, 295.

Diocles, 196.

Diodorus, sources of, 2 n. 2.

Diophanes, 268, 273, 304, 321–3, 347.

Doliche, 234.

dolo, 285, 333.

Dolopia, 28, 271–2, 368.

1. GENERAL

Magna Mater, 28, 49, 134, 274-7.
Magnesia-ad-Sipylum, 284, 307, 345; battle of, 29, 304, 309, 339, 343-59, 385-7, 394.
Magnesia-on-the-Meander, 307, 345, 358, 387.
Magnetes, 190.
Malea, Maleum, cape, 104, 281.
Malian Gulf, 236, 241, 257.
Malis, 207.
Malloea, 234. 239.
Malta, 179.
P. Manlius (*pr.* 195, 182), 74, 79-80, 131.
A. Manlius Vulso (*cos.* 178), 131.
Cn. Manlius Vulso (*cos.* 189), 158, 180, 365, 382.
Mandonius, 72.
manuscripts, 12 n. 2, 15-17, 97, 109, 151, 155.
M. Marcius, Q. Marcius (*tr. mil.* 193), 152.
Cn. Marcius Coriolanus, 56.
Marcii Philippi, 340.
Maronea, 337, 395.
marriage, Roman, 45, 47.
Mars, 22; altar of, 160.
Massilia, 67-9, 75, 382-3.
Massinissa, 19-20, 144-5, 222, 225, 328, 378.
Mauretania, 378.
Medes, 212.
Mediolanium, 122.
Medion, 237.
Megalesia, see *ludi Megalenses.*
Megalopolis, 104, 199, 268.
Megiste, 324, 327.
Melas, river, 255.
Meliboea, 240.
Menelaeum, Menelaus, 95.
Menestas, 263.
Menippus, 27, 33 n. 8, 138-41, 192, 215, 234.
Messene, Messenians, 90, 95, 101, 103, 108-9, 267-8.
Metaurus, river, battle of, 276.
Metropolis, 234, 240.
Micythio, 201, 209, 216.
Miletus, 315.
Milyas, 386.
mines, Spanish, 71, 84.
Minnio, 31, 168, 183, 351.
minores magistratus, 222.
Minturnae, 223, 277.

P. Minucius, Q. Minucius (*tr. mil.* 193), 150-1.
M. Minucius Rufus (*pr.* 197), 131, 145.
Q. Minucius Rufus (*cos.* 197), 385.
Q. Minucius Thermus (*cos.* 193), 28, 34-5, 71-2, 79, 133, 152, 174, 177, 203, 278, 292, 362, 386.
mixed constitution, the, 100.
Mnasilochus, 236.
Molon, 357.
Mons Cispius, 293
— Sacer, 63.
Munda, battle of, 68.
Musaeus, 358.
Mutina, 149.
Mycalessus, 216.
Mycenae, 87, 107, 114.
Myndus, 315.
Myonnesus, 311; battle of, 9, 29, 309, 330-4, 358, 364, 377.

Nabis, 7, 26-7, 85-114, 116, 125, 138, 164, 181-90, 196-8, 200; see also Sparta.
Q. Naevius (*pr.* 184), 131.
Naples, 169.
Nar, river, 121.
Naupactus, 7-8, 28-9, 236, 263, 267.
Nemean games, 114.
Neocretes, 351.
Nicaea, wife of Alexander of Corinth, 183.
Nicaea, conference of, 20.
Nicander of Aetolia, 163, 265-6.
—, pirate, 308, 331.
Noliba, 178.
Notium, 329-30.
nouemdiale sacrum, 121, 157, 277.
Numa, 337.
Numantia, 82-3.
Numidia, Numidians, 20, 144-5, 161; see also Massinissa.
Nursia, 293.

Cn. Octavius (*pr.* 205), 121, 179, 238.
Oenus, river, 94.
Oeta, mt., 243, 254, 267, 297.
Onchestus, 401.
C. Oppius (*tr. pl.* 215), 44.
L. Oppius Salinator (*pr.* 191), 179, 181, 293.
Oretani, Oretum, 36, 154, 178.
Oreus, 127, 339-40.
Oricum, 127-8.

2. LANGUAGE AND STYLE

3. AUTHORS AND PASSAGES

A. LITERARY

References to prose authors, with a few exceptions, are given only to chapters, not to sections. The references to Livy exclude passages in books xxxiv–xxxvii themselves. The figures in bold type indicate the pages of this book.

3. AUTHORS AND PASSAGES

orator 21, **169**.
de oratore i. 48, **99**; 60, **194**; 169,
  ii. 292, iii. 62, **99**; iii. 206, **113**;
  113, **194**; 167, **360**.
Philippics ii. 84, **223**; v. 15, 237; 49,
  202; vi. 5, vii. 26, **45**; viii. 21, **208**;
  x. 20, **360**; xi. 13, **270**; 17, **291**; 18,
  369; xii. 5, **256**; xiii. 37, **5**.
in Pisonem 4–5, **41**; 8, **61**; 16, **376**; 23,
  61; 44, **5**; 45, **223**.
pro Plancio 11, **140**; 31, **192**; 52, **392**.
de prouinciis consularibus 10, **214**.
pro Quinctio 79, **24** n. **6**.
ad Q. fratrem i. 1, **51**, **246**; ii. 3, **116**.
pro Rabirio Postumo 18, **209**; 27, **295**.
de re publica i. 1, **323**; 14, **128**; ii. 7 ff.,
  382; 15, 24, **100**; 40, **128**; 42–3,
  100; 47, **104**; 48, **88**; 50, 58, **100**;
  59, **258**; vi. 10, **302**.
post reditum ad Quirites 9, **374**.
pro Roscio Amerino 19, **223**; 60, **307**;
  96, 98, **223**; 153, **320**.
de senectute 13, **192**; 32, **245**; 38, **56**.
pro Sestio 12, **360**; 38, **99**; 78, **247**.
Tusculanae disputationes i. 97–8, **314**;
  ii. 23, **6**; 24, **91**; 38, **308**; iii. 57, 81,
  381; iv. 53. **43**.
in Vatinium 1, **278**.
in Verrem i. 6, **290**; 21, **223**; ii. 3. 9,
  336; 25, **215**; 66, **328**; 95, **46**; 163,
  221; 4. 129, **128**; 5. 52, **221**; 93,
  223; 132, **360**.
Columella, *RR* i. 3, **53**.
P. Cornelius Lentulus Spinther, *ap.* Cic.
  fam. xii. 15, **373**.
Curtius, iv. 9, **353**; 15, **286**; 16, **198**;
  v. 5, **88**; vi. 1, **286**.

Dio, fr. 62, **235**, **271**, **338–9**; xxxvii. 49,
  137; lv. 8, **60**; 22, lx. 7, **118**.
Diodorus, xvii. 17, **207**; 39, **110**; 53,
  253; xxvii. 1, **99**; xxviii. 13, **106**,
  116, **124**, **126**; 15, **137–8**; xxix. 1,
  206, **215–16**; 2, **235–6**; 3, **241–2**;
  4, **289**; 5, **334**; 7–8, **338–9**, **343–4**;
  10, **358**, **360**; 11, **372**; xxx. 5, **400**;
  18, **399**.
Dionysius of Halicarnassus, *AR* ii. 19,
  275; iii. 22, **175**.

Ennius (ed. Vahlen), *Annales* 317, **94**;
  352, **42**; 358–9, **402**; 368, **78**; 381–
  383, **141**; 384–8, **330**; 503, **66**; 628,
  160.

Eusebius, *Chron.* (ed. Schöne), i, p. 243,
  202, **233**.
Eutropius, iv. 4, **358**.

Fabius Pictor, fr. 20P, **57**.
Festus (ed. Lindsay), pp. 144–6, **338**;
  176, **220**; 258, **179**; 262, **293–4**;
  372–3, 384–5, **76**; 462–4, **369**.
Florus, i. 14, **132**; 23, **114**; 24, **235**, **241**,
  343, **352**.
Frontinus, *Strat.* i *praef.*, **172**; 1, **81**; 5,
  160–1; ii. 4, **241**, **245**; iii. 1, **82**;
  iv. 1, **146**; 7, **82**, **352**.

Gellius, iii. 18, **222**; vi. 19, **188**; x. 25,
  76; xiv. 7, **289**; xx. 1, **53**.
Gratius, *Cyn.* 241, **187**.

ad Herennium iv. 66, **4**.
Herodotus, i. 80, **345**; iii. 46, **100**; vi.
  61, **95**; vii. 43, **207**; 176, **243–4**;
  201, **243**; 213 ff., **244**; 223, **247**;
  viii. 68, **214**; 109, **213**.
Hieronymus, *in Dan.* 11:18, **284**, **329**.
Hippocrates, *Airs, Waters, Places* 12 ff.,
  382.
Hirtius, *BG* viii. 19, **286**; 29, **326**.
Homer, *Iliad* ii. 614, **183**; iv. 274, xvi.
  66, xvii. 243, **213**; xx. 392, **345**.
Horace, *Epistles* i. 4. 13, **256**; 11. 27,
  382; 18. 111–12, **360**; ii. 1. 13,
  206; 223, **56**.
  Odes i. 12. 55, **247**; 35. 29–30, **166**;
  ii. 9. 22, **311**; iii. 24, **50**.
  Satires i. 4. 32, **377**; 5. 36, **60**; ii. 2. 78,
  206; 3. 22, **280**; 27, **332**; 5. 47, **192**;
  93, **311**; 8. 73, **213**.
Hyperides, (ed. Kenyon), fr. 28, **60**.

Isocrates, x. 63, **95**.

Josephus, *AJ* xiii. 45, **240**.
Justin, xiv. 5, **93**; xxxi. 3, **141**, **181**, **189**;
  4, **141**; 5, **229**; 6, **235**, **281**; 7, **291**,
  338; 8, **343**, **357–8**; xxxii. 4, **394**;
  xliii. 3, **68**.
Juvenal, 9. 118, **112**.

Livy, *praef.*, **50**, **383**; i. 7, **269**; 10, **196**;
  13, **56**; 20, **174**; 29, **96**; 31, **121**; 35,
  118; 39, **199**; 50, **229**; 51, **155**; 52,
  153; 56, **171**; 57, **95**; ii. 6, **378**; 7,
  159; 12, **306**; 13, **336**; 14, **250**; 17,
  188, **336**; 19, **149**; 21, **150**; 31–3,

431

B. INSCRIPTIONS

C. PAPYRUS

4. LATIN

Entries in this index refer to notes which deal with the form, meaning, or usage of a word or phrase. References to notes dealing with matters of substance will be found in the General Index. The items discussed in section 2 of the Introduction (see also addenda thereto) are not tabulated here.

ab = after, 257, 372.
—, omitted with persons, 57.
abscidere, 192.
absistere, abstinere, 317.
accersere, 110.
accommodatus, 374.
accuratus, 55, 190.
actio, 380.
ad, with numerals, 177.
ad id, 219.
adequitare, 161.
adfatim, 91, 110.
adgrediri + infinitive, 233.
aedes liberae, 179.
aedicula, 205.
aequare, 48.
aequo, pari Marte, 286.
Aetolus, 209, 367.
affectare, 375.
agmen claudere, cogere, 95, 186, 347.
agmen incautum, 149.
alaris, -ius, 151.
alius atque alius, 180.
alligare, 209.
altercatio, 170.
amicitiam constituere, instituere, 228.
ampliare, amplificare, 377.
anceps, 185.
angulus, 67.
animos facere, inflare, 329, 345.
annona, 208.
antequam, postquam + subjunctive, 72.
antesignanus, 172.
approbantibus cunctis, 315.
aquari, 187.
a spe destitui, 270.
atque, before consonants, 42.
auersus, 76.
aurum et purpura, 49.
aut, position of, 320, 326, 372; see also *-ue*.
autem, in parentheses, 111.

bellum inferre, 228.
— *profligare*, 152.
bene ac feliciter, 218–19.

bene uertat, 105.
biduo ante, 280, 324.
bona pacis, 85.
bruma, brumalis, 213.

caecus, 76, 112.
caementa, 255.
capessere, 326.
caput, 318, 344, 402.
castellanus, 92–3.
castra, = day's march, 344.
— *hiberna*, 65.
— *statiua*, 185.
cauea, 135.
cauere, 125.
certamen, 80.
— *animi*, 306.
celox, 331.
censere, 48, 54, 162.
circa, 244.
citato gradu, 198.
claudere, 248.
claustra, 314.
clupeus, 160.
coepisse, 54.
comminatio, 113.
comminisci, 297.
communis, 82.
compages, 184.
concessere, 357.
concilium, consilium, 81, 90, 192, 194, 197, 236.
concire, concitare, concitor, concitator, 361.
concoquere, 142.
concursator, 399.
confessionem exprimere, 287, 290, 313, 334.
confragosus, 188.
consessor, 315.
consistere, 149.
consternatio, 46.
consul = *proconsul*, 400.
contio, 102–3.
conuallis, 188.
cubitum, 345.
cum . . . tunc, 112.
cumulate, 373.

437

illigare, 209.
immo, 215.
impedimenta, 187.
imperator, 390.
impetum dare, 326.
implorare, 86.
impos, 112.
in praesenti, in praesentia, 108.
in = in the case of, 187.
in principiis, 317.
in subsidiis, 150.
in triduum, 204.
inaequabilis, 187.
inanis, 210.
inclinare, inclinatus, 104, 285.
inconditus, 270.
inconstantia, 100.
inconsultus, 274.
increbrescere, 311.
incredibilis, 302.
increpare, 327.
increpitare, 269.
incruenta uictoria, 152.
incumbere, 151.
inde = *ex iis,* 250.
inde protinus, 192.
inducere, 75–6, 278.
indulgenter, 240–1.
infestus inuisusque, 210.
inhibere, 334.
inhonoratus, 381.
inicere, 182.
iniucundus, 198.
inopinatus, 95, 296.
insultare, 83.
intemperans, intemperatus, 278.
inter duos pontes, 176.
interdicere, 61.
intermortuus, 376.
internuntius, 306.
interponere, 145.
interpretari, 393.
intertrimentum, 62.
intestabilis, 391.
intromissus, 193.
introrsus, 349.
irrito incepto, 203, 249, 316.
is, antecedent to first and second persons, 101.
ita, 340; omitted after *sicut,* 70.
iter flectere, 190.
iure dicundo, 124.

labi, 340.

lactare, -ere, 294.
lanista, 194.
laxamentum, 177.
legio, 347.
leuitas, 246.
liberare, 258.
liberator, 127, 171.
lignarii, 205.
locus et lautia, 179.
longe + comparative, 374.
lumina, 102.
lustrum condere, 156.

Macedonia, 175.
machinatio, 297.
Marte, see *aequo, pari Marte.*
mare rubrum, 247–8.
medium, 346.
-met, 100.
ministerium, 168.
mittere, 311.
modum, ad, in, 364.
moderatio, 85.
molimentum, 314.
mouere, 193–4, 318.
muliercula, 62.
multa nocte, 150.

ne . . . quidem, 206.
nec ipse, 102, 322.
necesse, -um, 55.
necopinatus, 95, 296.
nihil aliud quam, 122, 323.
nimbus, 249, 293.
nisi = *non nisi,* 78.
niti, 159.
nocte intempesta, 313.
non modo (non) . . . sed ne . . . quidem, 112, 209.
non modo . . . sed, 328.
numerum inire, 197.
nunc, 41.
nuncupare, 220.
nuntiare, 223.
nutus, 191.

obterere, 46.
opera, 113.
opponere, 77.
optimates, 305.
orbis terrarum, 163.
otiosus, 395.

pacisci, 269.

titulus, 140.
totus, 312, 334.
transducere, -ferre, -uehere, 128, 279, 392.
transcribere, 153.
tueri, 99.
tumultuari, 286.

uanus, 210.
uariare, 191.
-ue, uel, aut, 107.
uerius, 155.
uersicolor, 44–5.
uerum enim uero, 373.
uetus miles, 308.

uexillarius, 152.
uidere ut, 263.
uim adferre, adhibere, 234.
uindicta, 125.
uir clarissimus, grauissimus, 55.
ultima + genitive, 393.
umbilicus, 172.
uocare ad, in, 102.
uoluere fluctus, 311.
ut, repetition of, 40, 219, 295.
ut adsolet, 313.
ut iam, 103.
ut ne, 81.
ut . . . sic, 53.
utrumnam, 317.

5. GREEK

ἀδελφιδοῦς, 351, 359.
ἄκρα, 245.
ἀναβάτης, 343.
ἀνάγκη, ἀναγκάζειν, 280.
βύρσα, 145.
γέροντες, 143.
διαστολή, 290.
διάγραμμα, 268.
διέκπλους, 326.
ἐλευθερωτής, 127.
ἐπιτροπή, 10, 300.
εὔνοια, εὐνοεῖν, 173.
θεοὶ ἐπιφανεῖς, 295.
ἱκετηρία, 196.

ἰσοπολιτεία, 398.
μεσολαβεῖν, 261.
ὀμφαλός, 172.
ὁπλάρια, 214.
Πισιδική, 181.
πολιτικός, 300.
πύλαι, 243.
ῥίζα, 402.
ῥομφαία, 399.
σκύλαξ, 260.
στρατηγός, στρατηγὸς ὕπατος, 166.
σωτήρ, 126.
φίλοι, see Index 1, *s.u.* amici, Hellenistic.
φρούριον, 217.